www.wadsworth.com

wadsworth.com is the World Wide Web site for Wadsworth and is your direct source to dozens of online resources.

At wadsworth.com you can find out about supplements, demonstration software, and student resources. You can also send email to many of our authors and preview new publications and exciting new technologies.

wadsworth.com
Changing the way the world learns®

TOTAL LITERACY

Reading, Writing, and Learning

THIRD EDITION

MARY BETH SAMPSON
Texas A&M University–Commerce

TIMOTHY V. RASINSKI
Kent State University

MICHAEL SAMPSON
Texas A&M University–Commerce

THOMSON
™
WADSWORTH

Australia • Canada • Mexico • Singapore • Spain
United Kingdom • United States

THOMSON

WADSWORTH

Publisher: Edith Beard Brady
Education Editor: Dan Alpert
Development Editor: Tangelique Williams
Editorial Assistant: Heather Kazakoff
Technology Project Manager: Barry Connolly
Marketing Manager: Dory Schaeffer
Marketing Assistant: Neena Chandra
Advertising Project Manager: Bryan Vann
Project Manager, Editorial Production: Trudy Brown
Print/Media Buyer: Barbara Britton

Permissions Editor: Joohee Lee
Production Service: Jupiter Productions
Text Designer: Lisa Buckley
Copy Editor: Kay Mikel
Proofreader: M. Kate St.Clair
Indexer: Do Mi Stauber
Cover Designer: Stephen Rapley
Cover and Chapter Opening Images: © James Heater/SIS
Compositor: Graphic World, Inc.
Text and Cover Printer: Transcontinental Printing, Louiseville

For more information about our products, contact us at:
Thomson Learning Academic Resource Center
1-800-423-0563

For permission to use material from this text, contact us by:
Phone: 1-800-730-2214
Fax: 1-800-730-2215
Web: http://www.thomsonrights.com

Library of Congress Control Number: 2002111204

Student Edition with InfoTrac College Edition:
ISBN 0-534-60318-1

Student Edition without InfoTrac College Edition:
ISBN 0-534-60319-X

Wadsworth/Thomson Learning
10 Davis Drive
Belmont, CA 94002-3098
USA

Asia
Thomson Learning
5 Shenton Way #01-01
UIC Building
Singapore 068808

Australia
Nelson Thomson Learning
102 Dodds Street
South Melbourne, Victoria 3205
Australia

Canada
Nelson Thomson Learning
1120 Birchmount Road
Toronto, Ontario M1K 5G4
Canada

Europe/Middle East/Africa
Thomson Learning
High Holborn House
50/51 Bedford Row
London WC1R 4LR
United Kingdom

Latin America
Thomson Learning
Seneca, 53
Colonia Polanco
11560 Mexico D.F.
Mexico

Spain
Paraninfo Thomson Learning
Calle/Magallanes, 25
28015 Madrid, Spain

With love to Claryce Allen
and in memory of Roach Van Allen—
our mentors and friends
MBS, MS

To Donald Cushenbery and Jim Akers
TVR

CONTENTS

Preface: Our Voyage Begins   xix
About the Authors   xxiii

Chapter 1   A Total Literacy Program   1

What Is a Total Literacy Classroom?   2

Theories of Language Acquisition   3
Behaviorism   3
Classroom Literature Connections   6
Nativism   6
Cognitive Field   7

The Total Literacy Model   8
Strand 1: Self-Expression   9
Strand 2: Impression   11
Strand 3: Conventions   11

Implementation of the Total Literacy Model   13
Acquisition   14
Perception   15
Prediction   15
Production   16

Standards for the English Language Arts   18

What Are the Language Arts?   19
Listening   19
Speaking   20
Reading   20
Author Study   Bill Martin Jr   20
Writing   21
Viewing   21
Visually Representing   21

What Does a Total Literacy Classroom Look Like?   21

Cooperative Learning   27
How Cooperative Learning Works   28
The Structure of Cooperative Groups   30

Heterogeneous or Homogeneous Grouping?   32

The Multiage Classroom   32

Connecting with Parents   33
   Further Words   35
Summary   36
Total Literacy Anchors   36

Chapter 2   Early Literacy   37

Reading: The Beginnings   38
   Should the Alphabet Be Taught to Children?   38
   How Children Become Aware of Print   40
   Author Study   Eric Carle   42
   Awareness of Sound Is Important Too   44
   Natural Readers   46
Writing: The Beginnings   47
Literacy Learning in School Settings   50
   Sharing   52
   Doing   53
Experiences: The Foundation of Literacy   54
   Responding to the Natural Environment   57
   Classroom Literature Connections   58
   Responding to Sensory Impressions   59
   Further Words   62
Summary   62
Total Literacy Anchors   63

Chapter 3   Talk and Literacy Development   64

Oral Language in the Classroom   65
Oral Sharing Activities   67
   Storytelling   67
   Spontaneous Expression   69
   Poetry   69
   Reader's Theater   72
   Story Theater   76
   Reporting   76
   Author Study   Gloria Houston   78

Dramatization   79

The Teacher and Dramatization   81

Talking and Discussing   83

   Experiences to Talk About   83

   Classroom Literature Connections   84

   Enthusiastic Participation   84

   Enriched Vocabulary   84

   Observing Common Courtesies in Conversation   86

   Connecting Oral Language to Written Language   88

   Further Words   88

Summary   89

Total Literacy Anchors   89

Chapter 4   Listening and Literacy Development   91

A Good Listener   92

   Classroom Literature Connections   94

Factors Affecting Listening and Learning   94

   Physical Environment   94

   Psychological Environment   95

   Emotional Factors   95

   Physical Factors   95

   Language Development   96

   Preformed Opinions   96

   High Intelligence   97

Kinds of Listening   97

   Author Study   Lynne Cherry   98

Propaganda and Listening   101

Developing Listening Abilities   102

Listening and Reading Instruction   103

Reading Aloud and Telling Stories   104

   Reading Aloud   104

   Developing Active Listeners through Storytelling   106

Activities That Enhance Listening Abilities   109

   Further Words   112

Summary 112

Total Literacy Anchors 113

Chapter 5 The Reading Process 114

What Is Reading? 115

The Child's View of the Reading Process 116

The Teacher's View of the Reading Process 118

Literacy Cueing Systems 118

The Role of Phonics and Rimes in a Total Literacy Program 120

Redundancy and the Cueing Systems 126

Reading as Transaction 127

Miscues and Reading Proficiency 128

"Errors" and Language Growth 130

Classroom Literature Connections 132

The Implications of Miscues for Teachers 132

Attention and Automaticity 132

Other Factors That Affect Reading Comprehension 133

Schema Theory and Comprehension 133

Textual Factors 137

Contextual Setting 138

Author Study Brian Pinkney 138

Comprehension Modes 139

Comprehension Instruction and Assessment 141

Further Words 141

Summary 142

Total Literacy Anchors 142

Chapter 6 Basal Readers 144

Elements of a Basal Reading Program: Framework for Teaching Key Skills and Strategies 146

Classroom Literature Connections 146

Textbook 147

Big Books 147

Supplemental Books   149

Workbooks and Worksheets   149

English Language Learner Materials   150

Assessment Materials   152

Parent Materials   152

Technology and Multimedia Materials   152

Teacher's Guide   152

Teaching with a Basal   153

Prereading   153

Guided Reading   155

Postreading Response to Text   156

Skill and Strategy Development and Practice   157

Extension and Enrichment   157

Background to Basals   158

Using Basal Programs   165

Basal Programs as a Foundation for Instruction   166

Author Study   Steven Kellogg   168

Resource, Guide, or Prescription?   170

Further Words   172

Summary   172

Total Literacy Anchors   173

Chapter 7   Reading Comprehension Strategies   174

Teacher-Directed Strategies   175

PRAISE   175

RISE   178

Think-Alouds   179

Author Study   Ted Rand   180

Shared Book Experience   181

Directed Reading–Thinking Activity (DR–TA)   182

Directed Listening–Thinking Activity (DL–TA)   184

Prevoke   186

Brainstorming   187

Link   190

Circle of Questions   191

Conceptual Mapping   192

Story Maps   193

K-W-L   196

Anticipation-Reaction Guide   199

Conferencing about Text   200

Classroom Literature Connections   200

Reciprocal Questioning Technique   201

Cloze Procedure   203

Reader-Directed Strategies   204

SMART   204

REAP   207

Sketch to Stretch   212

Save the Last Word for Me   213

Making Strategies Work for You   214

Further Words   217

Summary   217

Total Literacy Anchors   217

Chapter 8   The Writing Process   219

Understanding Writing   220

Children as Authors   222

Classroom Literature Connections   222

The Process Writing   224

Prewriting   226

Drafting   226

Revision   227

Editing   227

Publication/Celebration/Sharing   228

Collaborative Writing   228

Dictation and the Language Experience Approach   228

The Dictation Process   230

Interactive Writing   231

Understanding Conventions through Collaborative Writing   232

Freeing Students to Write   235

   Journals   235

   Author Study   Becky Chavarría-Cháirez   236

   Individual Stories   238

   Chapter Books   243

   Research Reports   243

   Personal Observations   246

   Aspirations   247

   Imagination   249

   Self-Concept   249

   Response to Experiences   252

   Descriptive   252

   Current Interest   253

   Personal Poetry   253

Teachers as Writers   257

   Further Words   259

Summary   260

Total Literacy Anchors   260

Chapter 9   Writing Patterned Stories and Poetry   261

Predictable Subgenre Stories   263

   The Repetitive Language Pattern   264

   Classroom Literature Connections   264

   The Rhyming Language Pattern   265

   The Interlocking Pattern   266

   The Cumulative Pattern   267

   Author Study   Donald Crews   268

   The Chronological Pattern   268

   The Culturally Familiar Pattern   270

   The Circle Pattern   270

   The Value of Genre Writing   272

Patterned Poetry   272

   Haiku   273

   Senryu   275

   Snapshot   275

   Tanka   276

   Sijo   277

Poetry Patterns That Feature Form Class Words 278

   Couplet 279

   Cinquain 279

   Terquain 281

   Diamante (Diamond Poetry) 281

   Renga 283

   Limerick 283

   Shape Patterns 284

   Further Words 286

Summary 286

Total Literacy Anchors 287

Chapter 10 **Organizing and Managing the Writing Classroom** 288

The Writing Classroom 289

   Interactive in the Writer's Workshop 292

   Minilessons in the Writer's Workshop 295

   Conferencing 297

   Collaborative Committees 302

A Physical Environment for Authors 306

   The Writing Center 306

   Classroom Literature Connections 310

   The Publishing Center 311

   Computers and Writing and Publishing 312

Young Authors' Conference 315

   Author Study Floyd Cooper 316

   Further Words 318

Summary 319

Total Literacy Anchors 319

Chapter 11 **Literacy Conventions: Words, Spelling, Grammar, and Handwriting** 320

Spelling and Word Study 322

   The Beginnings 324

   Stages of Spelling Development 325

The Process-Centered View of Spelling Instruction   328
  Language Experience and Spelling   329
  Spelling Resources for the Process Classroom   330
The Direct Instruction View of Spelling   330
  Selecting Spelling Words   330
  Instructional Strategies   338
  Routines in Direct Spelling Instruction   348
Word Study and Spelling Summary   350
Grammar   351
  Classroom Literature Connections   352
  Refining Grammar   353
  Three Views of Grammar   354
  Exploring Grammar   355
  Author Study   Ruth Heller   356
Refining Punctuation and Capitalization   358
  Punctuation   358
  Capitalization   359
Refining Handwriting   360
  Helping Students Refine Their Handwriting   360
  Evaluating Handwriting   364
Linguistic Guidelines for Refining Communication   367
  Further Words   368
Summary   368
Total Literacy Anchors   369

Chapter 12   Assessing Literacy Learning   371

The Culture of Assessment   373
What Are Standardized Tests?   377
Assessment through Observation   380
  Anecdotal Records   381
  Checklists   382
Assessment through Interaction   382
Assessment through Analysis of Student Work   385
  Work Samplings   387
  Holistic Scoring of Writing   387

Assessment through Student Self-Evaluation   389
   Author Study   Tomie dePaola   390

Assessment through Running Records   392

Assessment through Portfolios   393
   What Is a Portfolio?   393
   What's in a Portfolio?   394
   Classroom Literature Connections   396
   Portfolio Conferences   396
   Maintaining the Student Portfolio   398

Report Cards   400

Evaluating the Total Literacy Classroom   400
   Further Words   410

Summary   411

Total Literacy Anchors   411

Chapter 13   Children's Literature   412

Encouraging Children's Interest in Books   413

Making Connections with Books   414

Books I've Come to Love   418
   Books to Start With   418
   Humorous Books   419
   Poetry   419
   Wordless Picture Books   419
   Author Study   Patricia MacLachlan   420
   Folktales   420
   Books of Artistic Merit   421
   Informational Books   421
   Realistic Fiction   421
   Historical Fiction and Biography   422
   Books Focusing on Social Issues   422
   Storybooks   422
   Picture Books   422
   Cinderella Folktale Variants   423
   Fantasy   423
   Read-Alouds   423

Facilitating Children's Interactions with Books   424

    Literature Circles   425

    Acting Out Stories   426

Keeping Abreast of Children's Books   430

Author Studies   431

    Further Words   437

Summary   437

Total Literacy Anchors   438

Chapter 14   Using Theme Cycles   439

The Value of Thematic Approaches for Real Learning   440

Different Styles of Theme Cycles   443

Sources for Planning Theme Cycles   445

    Classroom Literature Connections   446

A Framework for Planning Theme Cycles   446

    Initiating Activities   448

    Enhancing Activities   448

    Synthesizing Activities   449

Principles for Planning Units   450

    Don't Force Coverage of the Curriculum   450

    Provide Balance within or between Units   450

    Use the Plan as a Guide Only   451

    Identify the Crucial Aspects of the Unit   451

    Do What Comes Naturally   451

    Vary Time for Working on Theme Cycles   452

Theme Cycle Teaching as Action Research   453

Theme Cycles and Parent Participation   454

The Teacher's Role in Theme Cycles   456

    Choosing Language Activities That Exploit Content   456

    Monitoring and Supporting Students' Learning   456

    Focused Learning Episodes   457

Planning a Unit: A General Sequence   457

    Author Study   Jose Aruego   458

    SUCCESS Stories   461

    PRISE Stories   461

    Further Words   464

Summary   465

Total Literacy Anchors   465

Chapter 15   **Content Area Literacy**   466

Children's Literature and Content Area Instruction   467

    Comparing Story/Narrative and Content/Expository Text   469

    Descriptive Text   470

    Author Study   Jerry Pallotta   472

    Sequential Text   473

    Comparison and Contrast Text   477

    Cause/Effect Text   478

    Problem/Solution Text   482

    Becoming Independent Learners   484

Developing Research Skills   489

    Promoting a Searching Attitude   489

    Using a Variety of Resources   492

    Using a Table of Contents and Index   494

    Using Alphabetical Arrangement   495

    Classroom Literature Connections   496

    Using Library Reference Skills   496

Art and Literacy   497

    Encourage Creativity   498

    Evaluate Possible Solutions   498

    Study Design Ideas   498

    Harmonize Design Elements   499

    Incorporate Visual Representations   499

    Accentuate the Feeling Component   499

    Interpret Natural Materials   500

    Use Exaggeration for Effect   500

    Show Movement   500

Math and Literacy   503
  Responding to Numerals and Numbers   503
  Numbers in Stories and Poems   504
  Geometric Shapes Surround Us   504
  Responding to Graphic Aids   506
  Children's Books and Mathematical Concepts   507

Music and Literacy   508

Social Studies and Literacy   510

Science and Literacy   511
  Further Words   514

Summary   514

Total Literacy Anchors   515

Afterword   517
  The End of Our Voyage

Appendix A   520
  Caldecott Medal Winners

Appendix B   522
  Newbery Medal Winners

Appendix C   524
  Coretta Scott King Award Winners

Appendix D   528
  Reader's Theater Scripts

References   535

Name Index   554

Subject Index   559

Photograph Credits   568

PREFACE:
OUR VOYAGE BEGINS

Total Literacy: Reading, Writing, and Learning is not just a book, it's a voyage filled with experiences and images of children learning and teachers teaching. From the first chapter to the last, this comprehensive overview of the total literacy program will move you from the "why" to the "how"—from theory to practice.

We believe all children can learn and that different children learn in different ways; *Total Literacy: Reading, Writing, and Learning* reflects this belief both in the book's new title and in its diverse content. It is imperative that teachers use a multitude of literacy strategies—not just a single way of teaching that is "hot" at the time. Our total literacy model, introduced in the first chapter and carried throughout the book, is built around three major strands of learning—self-expression, impression, and conventions. All three are important and must be in balance if all learners are to have equal access to literacy.

The original version of this textbook was written by Roach Van Allen; Michael and Mary Beth Sampson joined Allen for the next two editions under the new title, *Pathways to Literacy*. With the passing of Roach Van Allen, Timothy Rasinski has joined the authorship team, and this Third Edition of *Total Literacy* has many new features. You'll enjoy the two chapters by our guest authors. Bill Martin Jr, a legend in the world of children's books, wrote Chapter 13 on children's literature. Geoff and Cherry Ward, master teachers from Australia, contributed Chapter 14, an examination of theme cycles. Because basal readers are used in most classrooms in the United States, we have written a new Chapter 6, which features best practices in using basals with primary, intermediate, and middle grade students. We describe how basals are designed to be used—and how you can make them better.

Join us on our "literacy cruise" and discover what we have learned about students, teachers, and learning. We believe literacy learning results from the transaction between children's self-expressions and children's impressions from the world that surrounds them. And best of all, we'll show you, chapter by chapter, how you can develop and implement your own Total Literacy Classroom.

Features

Total Literacy has many ports, or stopping places, where students can pause and learn more within each chapter. We invite the reader to explore our "ports of call":

- In **Classroom Literature Connections** we recommend great books for the classroom, some for primary grades and some for the upper grades. This is a new feature for this edition.

- **Kid's Korner** uses Total Quality Management (TQM) procedures from the business world. We interviewed our customers (elementary school children) and asked them what they thought about their experiences in school. Their candid comments offer great advice to teachers.

- For **Author Study,** we interviewed fifteen children's book authors and illustrators to learn more about them and their books. You'll encounter great authors and illustrators including Eric Carle, Patricia MacLachlan, and Brian Pinkney. Video clips of nine authors are included on the CD-ROM in Meet the Author segments.

- In **Diverse Learners** we deal with many types of diversity—from the child with diabetes to the child with a learning disability to the child from a minority culture to the child with a hearing loss, and more. As the United States becomes more diverse, it is crucial for literacy teachers to understand diversity and its impact on instruction. This is also a new feature for this edition.

- In **Teacher-to-Teacher,** classroom teachers are featured in every chapter as they demonstrate how they implement literacy strategies with their students. More than 100 classrooms are featured in this book.

- **Further Words,** at the close of each chapter, features recommended readings, some of which are included on InfoTrac® College Edition, an online library of thousands of full-text articles (not abstracts) from top scholarly journals and popular publications.

Total Literacy CD-ROM

We are very excited about the new **Total Literacy CD-ROM.** The two CD-ROMs packaged with your textbook feature 100 QuickTime® video clips, categorized into five parts.

- **Author Words:** chapter introductions by your textbook authors
- **America's Finest:** twenty-two of our nation's best classroom teachers provide commentary on literacy strategies as they appear in the textbook

- **Teaching Strategies:** an in-depth examination of seven literacy strategies through thirty-three video clips that demonstrate how they work in the classroom
- **Author Visit:** how to bring a children's author to your school and how to prepare your students for the visit
- **Meet the Author:** video interviews with leading authors and illustrators of children's books

We use these clips as a "visual extension" of what we have written. As you read, CD-ROM icons in the margin of the textbook pages will direct you to the CD, category, and specific video clip that applies to the material you have just read. For example, after you read about Literature Circles, you can pop a CD into your computer and "see" Patty Engle's fourth-graders implementing the strategy.

We believe **Total Literacy CD-ROM** is a major breakthrough in teacher education and a perfect integration of words and images. Seeing is believing!

Acknowledgments

We wish to thank our reviewers for their insightful comments—their ideas made this a better book: Jennifer Altieri, St. Louis University; Sandra Ayers, Columbia College (SC); Kelvin Broad, Northern Arizona University; Anitra Butler, Prince George's Community College; Cassandra El-Amin, Winston Salem State University; Nancy Gibney, University of Detroit, Mercy; David Landis, University of Northern Iowa; Arlene Moliterno, College of Mount St. Vincent; Michael Muise, Wayne State University; Beth Musser, West Liberty State College; Sherrie Pardieck, Bradley University; Mary Robbins, Sam Houston State University; Leonie Rose, Central Michigan University; Gary Smithey, Henderson State University; Bev Stratton, Georgia Southern University; and Robin Trainor, Vassar College.

We are indebted to the classroom teachers featured in the Teacher-to-Teacher vignettes and to the twenty-four teachers, known as America's Finest, who provided video clips for our book. We are also grateful to the sixteen children who provided their insights through our Kid's Korner feature.

Thanks to our assistant, Maureen Preston, for her tireless work in managing this manuscript through copy editing and permissions. Without her we would never have finished this Third Edition.

And we wish to thank a host of colleagues at Wadsworth: Dan Alpert, our editor, who saw the potential for this book and helped us bring it alive; Trudy Brown, our project manager, who held the entire operation together; Tangelique Williams, our developmental editor; Linda Jupiter, our production editor; Lisa Buckley, our designer; Kay Mikel, our copy editor; Bryan Vann, our advertising manager; Dory Schaeffer, our marketing manager; and Barry Connolly, our technology project manager. Thanks also to Josh Sampson, who shot and edited the video clips.

MBS
TVR
MS

ABOUT THE AUTHORS

MARY BETH SAMPSON is an associate professor of elementary and reading education at Texas A&M University—Commerce, where she teaches both graduate students and preservice teachers. She has written professional articles, textbooks, book chapters, newspaper columns, curriculum materials, and children's books. As a consultant, she has interacted with teachers in more than 500 professional development sessions and keynotes across the nation on various aspects of literacy instruction. Her present research interests include preservice preparation and in-service professional development for literacy teachers, the use of children's literature in content classrooms, and teachers' beliefs about literacy instruction. She currently serves as an editor for the College Reading Association Yearbook.

TIMOTHY V. RASINSKI is a professor of education in the Department of Teaching, Leadership, and Curriculum Studies at Kent State University. Rasinski teaches graduate and undergraduate courses in literacy education. His major interests include working with children who find reading difficult, phonics and reading fluency instruction, and teacher development in literacy education. He has published more than 100 articles and 10 books on various aspects of reading education. A past editor of *The Reading Teacher,* the most widely read journal in reading education in the world, Rasinski is currently an editor for the *Journal of Literacy Research.* He has served as president of the College Reading Association and is currently on the board of directors of the International Reading Association.

MICHAEL SAMPSON is a professor of reading education at Texas A&M University—Commerce, where he teaches graduate and undergraduate courses in literacy education. Sampson's experience is rooted in the public schools, where he taught kindergarten through grade 9. After earning his Ph.D. in reading from the University of Arizona in Tucson, he turned his attention to research, teaching, writing, and staff development. His collaboration with Bill Martin Jr has spawned 20 picture books, 16 professional books for teachers, and more than 100 conferences for teachers. He has served as president of the Texas Association for the Improvement of Reading and is currently on their board of directors. Sampson loves theater and is frequently found on the stage when he is not writing, traveling, or teaching.

CHAPTER 1

A Total Literacy Program

As You Read . . .

◆ What is a total literacy classroom?

◆ Which of the theories of language acquisition is most in line with your beliefs about how children learn?

◆ What are the key components of a total literacy model?

◆ Why is it important for teachers to illustrate the interactive nature of the language arts?

◆ What impact should the NCTE/IRA standards have on my teaching?

◆ How does the teacher integrate the six language arts?

◆ How can students participate in cooperative learning?

◆ Should I group students for instruction? If so, how?

◆ Are multiage classrooms effective?

◆ What is the role of the parent?

Together we begin an exciting exploration of literacy. In the pages ahead you will encounter literacy activities that involve children both cognitively and affectively. You will see examples of children's work. You will meet many classroom teachers and their students through the Teacher-to-Teacher features in each chapter. You will discover that literacy is synonymous with learning and that learning is synonymous with thinking. And you will discover many different ways students may become empowered through language and literacy.

What Is a Total Literacy Classroom?

What is language? We define human language as communication. In this broad sense, language is not restricted to oral forms. Rather, language is a Picasso painting, it is a Beethoven composition, it is a figure skater's performance at the Winter Olympics. Yes, language may be "seen" in children's writing or heard in children's voices, but let us always remember that language encompasses much more.

Language is rooted in experiences. The more students know about the world that surrounds them, the more articulate they will be in communicating their ideas about that world. Thus our goal is to build language through experiences. Experi-

The total literacy classroom is a beehive of activity.

Courtesy of Lisa Bartlett

ences with books, experiences with art, experiences with drama, experiences through sharing together—all of these experiences build the language foundations of the student.

How do we build language skills? We must remember that the skills of language reside in the arena of communication. Children best learn language through interacting with the ideas of others. Thus a school environment that fosters language growth is one in which children are active in sharing their personal ideas and active in considering the ideas of others—their classmates, their teachers, the authors and artists they meet through books (Cairney, 2000).

In this chapter, we look at instructional planning and organization. We look at different patterns of grouping—whole class, small groups, and teacher as resource. We consider the benefits of the multiage classroom. We examine ways we can better inform parents about our programs. The chapter closes with this question: What are the pillars of a total literacy program? Of all the things teachers do in the name of literacy, which ones really matter? Hold on tight—we are embarking on an exciting voyage through the total literacy classroom.

Theories of Language Acquisition

So where do we begin as we plan for language arts instruction in a total literacy classroom? We start with one question: How do children learn language? The answer will determine how teachers structure the learning environment and what types of instruction they provide students.

Many explanations of how children learn language have been proposed. These major language acquisition theories stand in sharp contrast to one another. One position holds that language learning is an innate ability; another views language learning as an imitation of adult speech. A third position holds that language learning is a process of human interaction and that teachers must stress the child's own active role in experiencing and acquiring language. (Figure 1.1 contrasts the differences in these language learning theories.) A total literacy classroom, as elaborated in this text, relies heavily on the interactive/communicative explanation, which is known as *cognitive field theory*.

Behaviorism

Behaviorism holds that knowledge is discovered by observing the world and that facts or statements are only true when they correspond with what has been observed. Skinner (1957) views thinking as an internalized product of speaking and

BEHAVIORAL VIEW: Stresses the rewarding of certain behaviors through stimulus-response bonds. The student's personal production of language is of no consequence in behavioristic model.

ENVIRONMENT > > > LEARNER

NATIVISTIC VIEW: Language is innate and the learner is central. Learning is related to the assimilation of internal knowledge. Fails to explain how we get from the child's innate knowledge to overt performance.

ENVIRONMENT < < < LEARNER

COGNITIVE FIELD VIEW: Stresses the process of interaction between learners and their environment. Language is embedded and shaped by the sociocultural environment in which it is generated. Meanings result as children interact with environments.

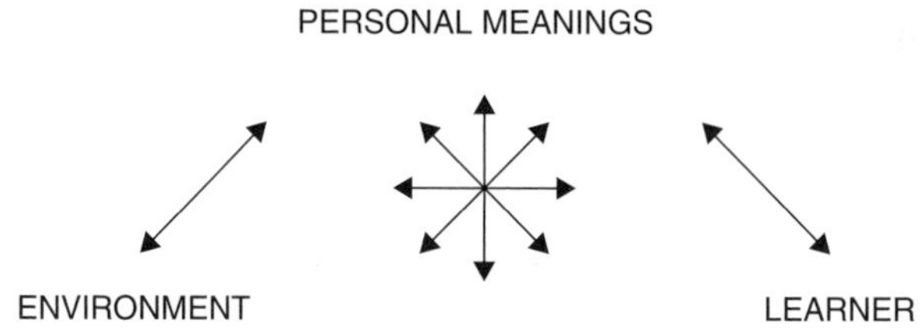

PERSONAL MEANINGS

ENVIRONMENT   LEARNER

FIGURE 1.1
Language acquisition theories

listening. Thus language and thought originate in the environment, and infants are believed to learn all things from their environment. Consequently, learning would be shaped by positive reinforcement of desired behaviors and negative reinforcement of undesirable behaviors (Wardhaugh, 1971). The relationship between a stimulus and a response is the core of behaviorism.

Bloomfield (1933), an early supporter of behaviorism, saw children as passive vessels who only reacted to outside stimuli. He viewed language learning as a process of imitating sounds, words, and phrases that was rewarded by needs fulfillment and praise. The behaviorists who followed Bloomfield examined language patterns in order to identify the components of language. They used rewards to encourage children to demonstrate these components in their speech and actions. The adult role was seen as modeling words and phrases that children would imitate.

Skinner believed the adult would provide reinforcements to children as their approximations to the model became clearer. These responses would become habitual as the children were "conditioned." For example, a 10-month-old infant's

Diverse Learners

A Tapestry of Language and Culture

Our nation was once thought of as a melting pot, a place where the masses of the world could come together and blend into a new people. Immigrants were to put away their past and "melt" together as they became "Americans." But the romanticism of the melting pot theory died hard in reality. People cannot divorce the past, for the past contains their essence as human beings. Culture cannot be left behind or dismissed—when culture is denied, the person is denied. Even with the best efforts of many, "Americans" never became one nation with one culture. Instead, we are one nation with many people, one nation with many cultures, one nation with many strengths. Instead of a melting pot, modern-day America is a beautiful tapestry. And that's good news for children like Hunda, the Korean American child in the story excerpted here (Martin, in press).

I speak American words always when I speak to my father. If he hear me speak in words of my heart, he tell me, "In English! In English!" He does not know American words hurt in my mouth like sharp sticks.

At school when I try first to speak America, everyone laugh ha ha bee bee, and my face hurt with shame and tears in my eyes. I do not speak at school now. I am silent like a busy ant.

"You are now America!" my father tell me. He is lifting baskets of corn and radishes that my uncles take for carry down the outside steps into the room under Yo Grocer. "I learn with all my might to
speak English," he tell me, "I want to better build Yo Grocer. America words belong you to America."

"My uncles not speak America, Father," I say with politeness.

"They are too old to learn America," my father say without politeness. "You, Hunda, are young! You learn to speak America with all your might and Yo Grocer will be with a big sign of bright lights with bigger better room and many more customers coming to buy each day what is fresh for eating."

"Yes, Father," I say. I make a swallow to take the hurt out of my mouth and out of my ears.

Total literacy classrooms value the differences that children bring to the classroom. Many children have failed in school because of the old melting pot theory. Their language and culture were rejected as new language and new ways were imposed on them. They were considered deficient, and many failed because their self-esteem was destroyed and because the techniques used to teach a second language of "standard English" were so different from the way they had learned their first language.

We believe that the solution is to value the culture and language of the learner while at the same time exposing them to alternatives in vocabulary, word choice, and syntax through the sharing of children's literature. By doing this, children will better understand other cultures and will come to the second language the same way they did their first language—through meaningful stories and interactions.

babbling sounds might resemble "dada." The father's excited response would then "shape" the vocalization to resemble and mean "daddy."

The learning of words can be explained through behaviorist theory. However, the analysis and synthesis of sound–symbol relationships do not equal meaning. Language always involves an active interpreter or it is not language. The difference, according to Labov (1982), "between a parrot and human saying, 'I'll meet you downtown,' is that the human is likely to show up" (p. 12).

In addition, Pflaum (1986) questions the theory's application when it comes to the acquisition of sentences. Children often produce sentences that they have never heard before as they apply rules and make hypotheses. Ferreiro and Teberosky (1982) argue that "neither imitation nor selective reinforcement, the key elements of associationistic [behavioristic] learning theory, can account for children's learning of syntax" (p. 11).

Thus the process of learning to communicate is much more complicated than behaviorists claim. They fail to recognize what children bring to the learning environment, and they also lose sight of the child as a hypothesis tester. In truth, through this hypothesis testing, children develop their own rules for analyzing language and form abstract understandings about language that they apply on a daily basis.

Nativism

The move to a more cognitive perspective on language and its acquisition was led by Noam Chomsky (1965). He described language as being present in some po-tential form at birth and stated that language develops innately as children inter-act with their environment. This nativistic perspective declares that children learn language when they encounter it and have need to understand and communicate with others.

Chomsky describes this inductive process through the analogy of an imagi-nary "device" that children have within them. This language acquisition device (LAD) receives information from the environment in the form of language. The language is analyzed and rules are generated. These rules are then applied as ex-pression takes place through language communication. The LAD continues to op-erate as a generating rule system for language as children pass through the levels of maturation. Thus children are able to organize incoming characteristics of lan-guage, including rules, grammar, categories, and other linguistic structures. This internal learning is viewed as developing in a natural manner.

Carol Chomsky (1980) elaborates by stating that although children cannot be taught language in a formal sense, they can acquire it naturally "in the course of ma-turing and developing in an environment where [they] are adequately exposed to it" (p. 228). Consequently, nativism leads to a "hands-off" view of teaching in language arts classrooms. Advocates point out that children will best learn the important com-munication skills through the practice of reading and writing and not through iso-lated studies of skills (Dorn & Soffos, 2001; Morrow & Ashbury, 1999; Smith, 1985).

However, wise teachers can structure learning environments in a manner that ensures children will encounter the language arts in a natural and creative way. Pure nativistic theory fails, however, to take advantage of the opportunity schools have for creating the "teachable moments" that serve as demonstrations to students of how language and literacy work in communication. Cognitive field theory offers perhaps the best model for advancing a natural but structured curriculum.

Cognitive Field

Cognitive field theory recognizes that learning is a process that evolves as children develop new insights and remodel old ones through interactive relationships within a psychological environment or field. In this view, it is believed children acquire knowledge about language as they test hypotheses and restructure their thinking according to new things learned (Canady, 1977; Clay 1998).

Cognitive field theorists refuse to see parts as distinct from whole processes. The outmoded atomistic perspective of listening, speaking, reading, and writing is replaced with a holistic perspective. In this perspective, meaning exists neither in the environment nor in the learner. Instead, it is the result of the learner's interaction with the environment, and the product or meaning created is greater than the sum of the two parts. Language is viewed as open and changing as learners build personal meanings for words and concepts. Words are viewed as being cognitive "placeholders" that have multiple meanings. One child's specific meaning for "fish" might be somewhat different from another's. However, both children share a common meaning for the word because they are members of the same interpretive community.

The research of Harste, Woodward, and Burke (1984b) confirms that children acquire the interpretive rules of language use through "social interaction at very early ages" (p. 56). As children interact through language, they test insights that enable them to construct their own rules of meaning and the grammar of language. This learning is at the subconscious level, and children probably would be unable to articulate the internal rules their language mastery demonstrates. As an adult user of language, you probably are in the same position. You may use "school" grammar, but can you list the rules you somehow use as you build words into phrases and sentences? Garth Boomer (1984) puts it succinctly: "We know more than we can tell" (p. 576).

Cognitive field theory and nativistic theory are similar in many respects. Both hold that individuals are born with the potential to learn language (Page & Pinnell, 1979). The key difference lies in implications for instruction. Nativists support a "hands-off" position. Cognitivists support teaching/learning environments that accelerate the constructive nature of language learning in students. Together, these language acquisition theories are intertwined into a total literacy curriculum, which is elaborated in this book (see Figure 1.1).

As a teacher, you must fine-tune your beliefs about children and how they learn. Theory is crucial because it determines classroom practice. Clarifying your position does not involve learning names of theories or memorizing information from texts. Instead, you need to ask yourself questions about how you think children learn and how students acquire language. Perhaps these theoretical positions will serve as reference points as you examine our assumptions—that children are active, purpose-seeking learners.

The Total Literacy Model

Our instruction of children should be influenced by our knowledge of how children learn. Good teachers do more than just present information to students. They invite children's participation by introducing material in an exciting, enticing manner. Unfortunately, schools have often been places where students enter with great excitement but depart with great boredom. The reason?—students spend twelve or thirteen years in school answering questions they didn't ask. The research we have reviewed thus far suggests that learning best occurs when teachers approach students with a more transactive instructional stance.

Schools in the past have focused on the receptive domain, asking children to "learn" material and information the teachers and texts have presented. We must go beyond the receptive! True, children do benefit greatly when they read great children's books. They learn by listening to others and by studying the world that surrounds them. However, learning is enhanced when children's personal ideas are valued—when they are encouraged to share their own ideas and understandings with others in the school setting.

Our theoretical model, which we call the "total literacy model," is based on the idea that learning occurs in the transaction between impression—children's *receptive* activities—and self-expression—children's *expressive* activities. Our view is that skills, or conventions of literacy, are developed within this transaction of impression and self-expression.

Figure 1.2 pictures this transaction and serves as the theoretical model of this text. We use this model throughout the text to tie literacy learning and instruction together. To visualize this model, think of the strands of a rope, and how much stronger a rope is when the strands are woven together. The three strands of our rope (or model) are self-expression, impression, and conventions.

> **Strand 1** emphasizes acquiring literacy through *self-expression* activities and experiences.
>
> **Strand 2** emphasizes *impression,* the influence of the language and ideas of others on literacy development.
>
> **Strand 3** emphasizes the exploration of those characteristics or *conventions* of language structure that help a person to be literate.

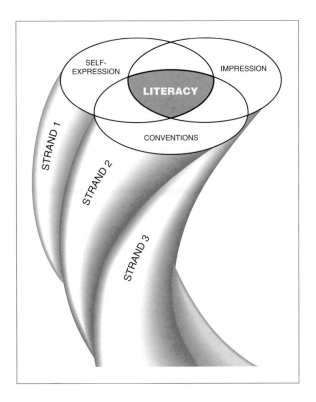

FIGURE 1.2
Total literacy trans-
action model

The model does not suggest that teachers should "teach" these strands in isolation. Instead, it pictures learning as an interaction among these literacy areas. The instructional focus is not on the three strands but on their overlap. Thus literacy lessons are integrated so carefully that the three circles merge into one. Skills are not presented in isolation but in the context of their function.

Strand 1: Self-Expression

Strand 1 emphasizes the natural ways of self-expression—talking, painting, singing, dancing, acting, and writing. All students are unique and have their own language style. The school should preserve this uniqueness while helping students discover alternative forms of expression.

Total literacy teachers recognize that fluency and flexibility in language help pupils make adjustments to life and value their own ideas and feelings. These teachers help students understand and appreciate classmates who are culturally different. Language values relate to all effective teaching/learning situations. Some of these values are described next.

1. *Creative language experiences provide for individual differences.* Students think and reason differently. They have varying abilities, interests, drives, and talents. Students work best when their tasks are appropriate to their

age and abilities and when these tasks are flexible enough to permit individual ways of thinking and working.

2. *Creative language experiences develop imagination.* All young people are endowed with the power of imagination. This resource is available in every classroom at no extra cost. Education sometimes diminishes the power of imagination, however, as other facets of personality are developed. Teachers who implement Strand 1 of the total literacy model are careful not to limit their students' imaginations.

3. *Creative language experiences build self-confidence.* Students must search their own storehouses of experiences and use their own skill, knowledge, and language to solve speech and writing problems. Students need to set personal standards rather than use uniform standards that foster classroom competition.

4. *Creative language experiences provide for emotional expression.* Schools should emphasize ideas and experiences that have emotional importance to children. When students involve their emotions in their subject—whether orally or in writing—others will respond to their output. Masterpieces in writing, art, and music are usually expressions of basic emotions that evoke human responses.

5. *Creative language experiences develop the aesthetic sense.* Students who have been free to express themselves through writing or art can appreciate the written and artistic expression of others. The quality of that expression is not so important. What is important is that students have experience in communicating ideas in various forms.

6. *Creative language experiences deepen appreciation of other people's writing.* Students should have the opportunity to appreciate the work of others in the classroom. A student who has struggled to communicate ideas—orally or in writing—is appreciative of other students who have expressed their ideas in beautiful or diverse ways. Creative language experiences bring balance to educational activities.

7. *Traditional school curricula are convergent in nature.* Students need a balanced classroom experience, one that takes their creative powers into account while they learn the fundamental skills of handwriting, spelling, reading, and the conventions of usage. Total literacy programs provide many such opportunities for divergent thinking. This freedom to create personal communications is a welcome change from the kinds of learning that require students to arrive at the same solution.

Strand 1 skills are developed in total literacy programs as students share their thoughts and ideas with others.

A young writer expresses his ideas through art.

Strand 2: Impression

Strand 2 of the total literacy model emphasizes the influence of the language and ideas of others on the student's personal language and ideas. The focus is on how others use language. Teachers expose students to many forms of communication, helping them choose to change and improve their own language creatively. Six traits characterize the classroom emphasizing Strand 2 activities:

1. *Students acquire new ways of saying things* by repeating ways in which authors write stories and poems.

2. *Teachers provide opportunities for art, creative writing, and drama* to help students interpret ideas they gained from listening and reading.

3. *Students develop organizational abilities*—like those required for comprehending reading—in learning situations that do not require reading and writing abilities, such as painting pictures, constructing, sculpting, and making collages.

4. *Students write, expressing their personal ideas* through personal language and in poetry and predictable story patterns.

5. *Students compare personal ideas with those of other people* who have communicated on the same topic.

6. *Teachers encourage questions*—which are more important than answers—to stimulate students to search many sources for information.

A total literacy curriculum helps students build confidence for communicating in ways that reflect the influence of authors and artists who communicate beautifully and effectively. Students grow in confidence as they see how other language users communicate.

Strand 3: Conventions

Strand 3 of the total literacy model emphasizes that skills, or the conventions of literacy, are learned in the process of reading and writing. It is different from other literacy programs in that students' own stories and poems are used—along with those from other printed sources—to show the relation of personal language to printed language. Six important points underlie Strand 3:

1. The words students use most frequently in speech and writing are the same ones that are most used in the writings of other people (both students and adults). These words tend to be meaningless in themselves, and many of them are nonphonetic (e.g., "the," "are"). These words *must* be learned in context—attempts at isolated phonetic analysis only produce nonsense.

2. Students need to develop an awareness of high-frequency words to facilitate independent reading.

3. Students examine the relation between the sounds of speech and the use of the alphabet to represent those sounds. Understanding of these graphophonic relations occurs as students encounter them over and over again in language. Practice for mastery is provided by the emphasis on writing—rather than reading—in a total literacy classroom.

4. Students acquire language through listening and talking with others, through new experiences, and through the application of new vocabulary to old experiences.

5. Language grows as students learn the names of things, words of movement, and words of description.

6. Listening to and repeating well-written materials extend students' understandings of the many ways authors express their ideas and feelings.

Strand 3 emphasizes the study of the specifics of language that contribute to literacy. These specifics have been identified over many years of research and study. They are elaborated and extended throughout this book.

Implementation of the Total Literacy Model

Implementation of the total literacy model can make literacy learning joyous and successful. The growth is not the result of teaching literacy skills directly in the conventional sense. Rather, it is the result of the interaction of language learnings within the three strands of the total literacy model. Illustrated in a slightly different manner in Figure 1.3, this model suggests that at any point at which the learnings overlap, the result is literacy. The truly literate person relates the strands of the total literacy model so completely that the three strands merge into one. In this model, literacy is holistic. It is always greater than the sum of its parts.

The instructional objective is to plan and implement programs that include some emphasis from each strand daily. Three major ideas interlock in the model:

◆ Each day students communicate in many ways and through many means; they use personal ideas and personal language.

◆ Each day students are influenced by the language and ideas of many people through what they see and hear, and in the process their personal language becomes more and more like the language they are encountering.

◆ Each day students explore those components of language that have most to do with achieving literacy, and in the process of communicating they learn how an alphabetic system of notation works for them as well as for others.

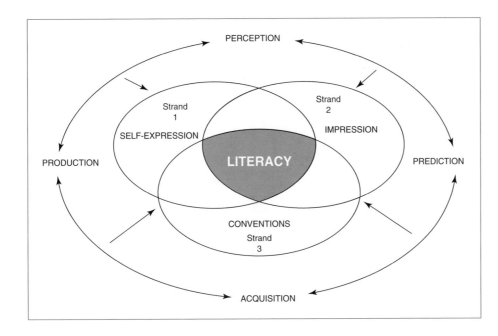

FIGURE 1.3
Curriculum model for a total literacy program

As indicated in the model shown in Figure 1.3, instructional programs are generated in the outer parts of the model. They feature four major classes of activities: acquisition, perception, prediction, and production. These four classes of activities are presented in many formats and instructional experiences. Figure 1.4 pictures the total literacy approach as it is being implemented in the classroom. Note that the experiences (on the outer edge of the model) facilitate the interaction between self-expression and the expressions of others. Successful implementation of these total literacy experiences will accelerate the overlap of the strands and thus contribute to the goal of attaining literacy. Some of these literacy-centered strategies are discussed in this chapter. You will find descriptions of others throughout the book.

Acquisition

How do students acquire new language in school? New language is acquired through transactions with literacy. These transactions include activities that involve singing, chanting, reading, listening to reading, interacting with computer programs, listening to stories and poems, acting out stories and poems, and choral reading.

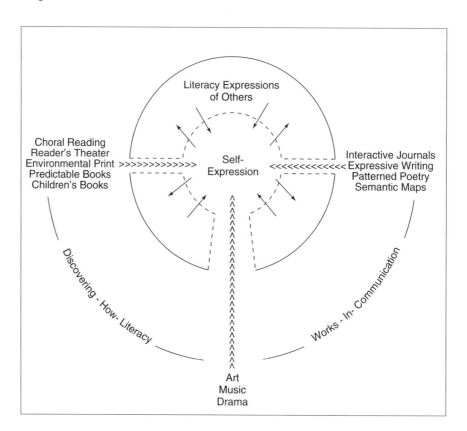

FIGURE 1.4

Implementing the total literacy model

Teachers give priority to acquisition of vocabularies of nouns, verbs, adjectives, and adverbs. Teachers also help students

- Hear language in new and meaningful contexts
- Say things with new words and new language patterns that become permanent through use
- Write with an ever-increasing repertoire of personal language resources
- Sing songs to celebrate language that has rhyme, rhythm, and repetition

Perception

In a total literacy approach, students learn basic skills in the process of communication, not through emphasizing these skills in isolation. A major difference between total literacy approaches and conventional programs is that in total literacy programs the teacher trusts the student's own language to illustrate the characteristics of the language of literature.

Literacy conventions are developed as students communicate. Much of the direct instruction occurs as students edit the works they have written. Skills are reinforced and extended as students read the written works of others. Both the personal language of the student and the language of others illustrate the basic rules and skills of language. Students come to think along with an author and to use their predictive abilities, meaning clues, and visual clues to satisfy their need to communicate with an author.

Prediction

Selections for listening and reading in a total literacy classroom include exposure to materials with repeating patterns and dependable lines. These selections permit students to predict and repeat words, phrases, and whole stanzas without seeing the print. They learn to anticipate language and language patterns that repeat frequently in stories.

Poetry with repeating lines and patterns is important in a total literacy approach. This visual impact of patterns in printed material is helpful in encouraging or releasing students to try to read new materials. They can observe that only a few words are different as they read. Much of the print is repeated. In poetry, the patterns of rhyming words usually give some clue to new words at the end of lines.

Reading in chorus, known as choral reading, is useful in establishing the phonological structure of predictable stories and poems. Once the sound pattern has been established, the words that follow can be predicted with a high degree of certainty. Shy readers lose their hesitation when their voices unite with thirty other voices.

Singing songs and doing chants that repeat language patterns afford children an opportunity to try out new ways of saying things that are typical of personal language. This practice enables students to recognize those patterns in print and to predict the flow of language. Prediction skills are crucial to the reading process. Our goal is for students to incorporate a predicting attitude toward all literacy transactions.

Production

In a total literacy classroom, children create products in the process of self-expression activities. These products include, but are not limited to, individual books, class books, dramatic productions, musical productions, and art displays.

One highlight of the instructional program should be the use of student-authored materials as a cornerstone of the language environment. Such student-authored books reflect familiar vocabulary and current interests. Because the content and language are known to the student authors, these authors can become teachers as they share their books with others. When original manuscripts are read aloud by their authors, the emphasis can be placed on effective interpretation through reading rather than on word recognition skills.

Imagination is encouraged in the process of producing literacy materials. Experiences are expressed through art, media, acting, and talking. Some of the experiences are recorded through independent writing and then reproduced through reading. Students gain a firm grasp of the notion that their ideas, expressed with words, can be written. What is written becomes reading.

As students mature enough to compare and contrast, they realize several things:

- The words they use to write about a topic are much the same as those used by others.
- The sounds they make when they talk are recorded by writing, using an alphabet that is the same for everybody.
- What other people write about comes from real experiences or from imagination.
- Characters must be described so listeners and readers can form mental images even though they have never seen them.
- The settings of stories must be described so listeners and readers can form mental images even though they may have never been there.

Arielle Engle — **Name**

10 — **Age**

writing
acting — **Interests**
drawing

What do you like most about school?

Learning! It helps me be a better student so I can get a good job someday.

What's your favorite subject? Why?

My favorite subject is writing because I like to write stories. I can be funny in them.

What's your favorite book? Why do you like it?

My favorite books are Harry Potter because I think they are cool. I think they are so exciting — I can't put them down.

What advice do you have for teachers?

Play learning games with your kids. We want to have fun learning.

Reprinted with special permission of Patricia Engle and Arielle Engle.

Editing manuscripts to be used in the reading curriculum is a significant part of the production process. Students learn the fine points of reading by editing their writing, just as they learn the fine points of writing by reading well-written materials.

Standards for the English Language Arts

The National Council of Teachers of English (NCTE) and the International Reading Association (IRA) have developed twelve standards for the English Language Arts that include principles that "encourage the development of curriculum and instruction that make productive use of the emerging literacy abilities that children bring to school" (Standards, 2001). These principles should guide administrators and teachers as they develop total literacy programs:

1. Students read a wide range of print and nonprint texts to build an understanding of texts, of themselves, and of the cultures of the United States and the world; to acquire new information; to respond to the needs and demands of society and the workplace; and for personal fulfillment. Among these texts are fiction and nonfiction, classic and contemporary works.

2. Students read a wide range of literature from many periods in many genres to build an understanding of the many dimensions (e.g., philosophical, ethical, aesthetic) of human experience.

3. Students apply a wide range of strategies to comprehend, interpret, evaluate, and appreciate texts. They draw on their prior experience, their interactions with other readers and writers, their knowledge of word meaning and of other texts, their word identification strategies, and their understanding of textual features (e.g., sound–letter correspondence, sentence structure, context, graphics).

4. Students adjust their use of spoken, written, and visual language (e.g., conventions, style, vocabulary) to communicate effectively with a variety of audiences and for different purposes.

5. Students employ a wide range of strategies as they write and use different writing process elements appropriately to communicate with different audiences for a variety of purposes.

6. Students apply knowledge of language structure, language conventions (e.g., spelling and punctuation), media techniques, figurative language, and genre to create, critique, and discuss print and nonprint texts.

7. Students conduct research on issues and interests by generating ideas and questions, and by posing problems. They gather, evaluate, and synthesize data from a variety of sources (e.g., print and nonprint texts, artifacts, people) to communicate their discoveries in ways that suit their purpose and audience.

8. Students use a variety of technological and information resources (e.g., libraries, databases, computer networks, video) to gather and synthesize information and to create and communicate knowledge.

9. Students develop an understanding of and respect for diversity in language use, patterns, and dialects across cultures, ethnic groups, geographic regions, and social roles.

10. Students whose first language is not English make use of their first language to develop competency in the English language arts and to develop understanding of content across the curriculum.

11. Students participate as knowledgeable, reflective, creative, and critical members of a variety of literacy communities.

12. Students use spoken, written, and visual language to accomplish their own purposes (e.g., for learning, enjoyment, persuasion, and the exchange of information).

What Are the Language Arts?

Traditionally, teachers have identified four language arts: listening, speaking, reading, and writing. In the revision and joint passage of their standards, the NCTE and the IRA (Standards, 2001) achieved a broader definition of literacy. These professional organizations added two more language arts areas—viewing and visually representing—and states immediately began to add these two new language arts areas to their programs and assessments.

Total literacy programs have always included viewing and representing. In fact, Roach Van Allen (1976) included "Visually Portraying Experiences" in his Curriculum Rationale for a Language Experience Approach, which has now become our total literacy model. You will find these six areas discussed throughout the book; to get you started thinking about them, here are some of the highlights.

Listening

Listening is the window to our language world. Children learn their first language, their home-rooted language, through the ear by listening. They learn literary level language as parents and teachers read aloud to them as preschoolers. Although many have described listening as a receptive language activity, it is also an expressive activity because children create understandings by applying what they know about the topic in order to comprehend.

Speaking

Talk is a vital language art. Through speech, children become part of a language community and have many opportunities for self-expression. In a total literacy classroom, teachers provide many opportunities for focused talk, including sharing in the Author's Chair, becoming a character in a Reader's Theater performance, or sharing a favorite part of the book they are reading.

Reading

Reading is a student's window to the world. Total literacy teachers strive to develop readers who not only read to learn more about a subject but who choose reading for recreational purposes. Reading is the key to academic success, and it should be the major focus of primary grade teachers. Fluency occurs as children move beyond the skills of reading as they are carried away by the act of reading.

Author Study

②

Meet the Author

Bill Martin Jr

Bill Martin Jr

1. *Which book of yours has given you the greatest pleasure?*
Barn Dance. It appealed to children much younger than I had thought. I enjoyed both the poetry and the subtlety of the fantasy. It starts with dead realism, and the reader is several pages into the story before the fantasy begins and the scarecrow becomes a violinist.

2. *Which book has surprised you most in terms of its public reception?*
Brown Bear, Brown Bear, What Do You See? I never thought of it as being a book that would last or as an important book, even though I was awestruck by Eric Carle's illustrations. *Brown Bear* is not a storybook at all, but children see it as so. Many teachers have told me that they start their year with this book.

3. *What would you like people to remember about your work?*
I want them to remember a line or a combination of words that creates a lasting im-

pression. I want them to visually experience my stories though the graphic work of my wonderful illustrators and to "see" my words through these pictures.

4. *What impact do you hope your work will have on children?*
My work revolves around coming to print through the sentence rather than through the letter. I hope children will realize that they are all readers because they are all language users.

Bill Martin's words delightfully "tune the child's ear to the music of language " He doesn't just write words; he creates lyrics that sing of the joys of life. His compositions include *Brown Bear, Brown Bear, What Do You See?; Adam, Adam, What Do You Hear?; Chicka Chicka Boom Boom; SWISH!; Rock It, Sock It, Number Line; The Little Squeegy Bug; Little Granny Quarterback;* and *Trick or Treat.*

Writing

Writing is one of the key avenues to self-expression. Through writing, students can preserve their thoughts across time and distance. By editing what they write, students can refine their voice and raise their communications to a literary level.

Children's authors provided powerful models of writing that have a profound influence on children's personal writings in total literacy classrooms. Consequently, we will focus on professional authors and on methods of bringing your students under the influence of these masters.

Viewing

Viewing is an important language art because in modern times reading comes from many different sources. We read print on brochures, advertisements, the bottom of the television screen, and in "instant messages" we receive on the Internet. We receive the communications of others in ways that go beyond print—representations through drama, paintings, song, dance, and more. We must be able to "comprehend" these messages in a way similar to printed communications, but we must also look for even more. Seventh-grade student Abby says it this way: "Visuals help me see things in a new way" (Whitin, 1996, p. xi). In the next chapter we will learn more about viewing and what Spencer (1970) calls "primary reading."

Visually Representing

We live in a visual world in the twenty-first century, and we now better understand how communication was viewed centuries ago in Europe when feelings and expressions were represented through paintings and sculpture—not just through writing. With the use of new technology, students have many different platforms for visually representing experiences and ideas. They can use software such as Illustrator to "paint" electronically or Quark® or Microsoft® Publisher to create eye-catching newsletters. When children represent visually through art, they capture degrees of sophistication that go far beyond their literacy level (Steele, 1998). Creative self-expression occurs through many different media in a total literacy classroom.

What Does a Total Literacy Classroom Look Like?

After examining how children grow intellectually, we conclude that the cognitive field theory offers the most realistic picture of how and why children learn. We have introduced you to our total literacy model, which balances self-expression, impression, and conventions. We have examined the NCTE and IRA standards for the language arts, and we have discussed the six areas of the language arts. But now, you ask, how does a teacher make this work in the classroom?

One tool is the *instructional schedule,* which provides time for the teacher and students to explore and learn together. Students' communication skills are developed through numerous activities, experiences, and strategies. To increase the chances of success for more students, every teacher must know and use many ways of involving children in the language arts. You can take a look into three total literacy classrooms—featuring grades 1, 3, and 5—in the Teacher-to-Teacher features that follow. First, let's look at how the instructional schedule works in the classroom of Tom Wrightman, a third-grade teacher in Bend, Oregon.

Teacher-to-Teacher

Tom Wrightman believes the most important function of the teacher is to establish a sense of community in the classroom. Therefore, Tom sets his classroom up in such a way that children are constantly interacting (see Figure 1.5).

Tom starts the day with music. Language arts is the total morning focus. From singing together, children move on to poetry. They write in free form modes as well as patterned poetry modes (discussed in Chapter 9). Tom's language core, which begins at 9:15 A.M., incorporates a potpourri of total literacy strategies. Children work on individual activities, read silently, listen to tapes in the listening center, and meet in small focus groups. After recess, children continue the language core. Monday and Tuesday are devoted to literature patterns (see Chapter 9) and class books that support the current theme cycle (see Chapter 14). Wednesday's encounter is with literature (see Chapter 13); Thursday and Friday are devoted to writer's workshop (see Chapters 8 and 10). At the end of the day, children record what they've learned into their Learning Logs; they then finish the day by reading chapter books.

Math is a special focus in Tom's classroom. Children solve problems with manipulatives and examine multiple solutions as math is presented as a natural attribute of life. Children's books are used to present math concepts and patterns as Tom brings math and language arts together.

Throughout the day, science, health, and social studies content is integrated into the language core. Tom believes children learn content through meaningful holistic activities. His students demonstrate that they learn language arts skills the same way.

Tom is a successful teacher because of the trust he has in the abilities of his children. He creates an environment where literature, art, music, math, and storytelling are daily activities that encourage literacy and learning.

SAMPLE DAILY SCHEDULE

8:00–8:45   **ARRIVAL (Morning Business, Personal Projects)**
The goal is personal contact during this time
(soft music)

8:45–9:00   **SINGING and PLAYING WITH POETRY**

9:00–9:15   **SHARING STORIES (Daily News)**
Reading books—Author Studies, theme-related (SSR)

9:15–10:15   **LANGUAGE CORE**
Individual Literacy Activities, Math Words, Assigned Readings,
Listening Center, Independent SSR, Focus Groups: small/large-phonics
in context

10:15–10:30   **RECESS**

10:30–11:15   **LANGUAGE CORE continued**
Monday and Tuesday—Literature Patterns, Class Books related to
theme of study during this time
Wednesday—Literature-related activities
Thursday and Friday—Writing Workshop

11:15–12:00   **LUNCH/RECESS**

12:00–12:45   **MATH**   *12:00–12:15 Problem of the day (soft music)*
12:15–12:45 Small/whole group activities

12:45–1:15   **MUSIC/P.E.**

1:15–2:15   **SCIENCE/HEALTH/SOCIAL STUDIES CORE**

2:15–2:30   **RECESS**

2:30–2:45   **LEARNING LOG (soft music)**
Summary of the day's events for LEARNING LOG

2:45–3:00   **CHAPTER BOOKS (children come to rug when finished)**

3:00–3:15   **CLOSING BUSINESS and SINGING**

It should be noted that Science, Health, and Social Studies are also integrated topics throughout the Language Core in the morning.

FIGURE 1.5
Tom Wrightman's third-grade classroom schedule

Now we move to the classroom of Randy Methven, a first-grade teacher in Long Island, New York. We will look at the physical arrangement of his classroom, but more important, we will examine his philosophy of teaching and learning.

Visiting Randy Methven's classroom is like visiting Disney World—the environment is permeated with joy and excitement. One of the first things you notice is the openness, not merely in the physical arrangement but in the spirit of the children (see Figure 1.6). The next thing you notice is printed poems and stories dangling from the ceiling, on posters, even on the windows. Last spring, Bill Martin Jr visited Randy's room and was so impressed with the print-rich classroom that he features Randy and how Randy invites children's interactions in our children's literature chapter (Chapter 13).

Randy believes child-centered classrooms require space for children to work collaboratively. Thus he has arranged his room with groupings of desks and tables that enable group work. He has also rearranged time blocks because he believes teachers need to look at the day as a whole rather than as small segments of time. During the week, you will see Randy interacting with his students in the following modes and strategies: (1) reading together, (2) shared book experience, (3) sustained silent reading, (4) guided reading, (5) individualized reading, (6) language experience, (7) children's writing, (8) content area literacy, (9) evaluation, and (10) sharing. We tell you about these strategies throughout this book.

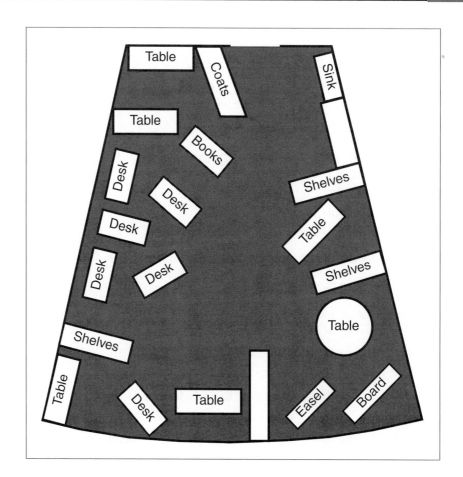

FIGURE 1.6

Physical arrangement of Randy Methven's first-grade classroom

Courtesy of Michael Sampson

Print is everywhere in Randy Methven's classroom—hanging from the ceiling, on the wall, and in books.

Thus far, we have stepped inside a first-grade classroom and a third-grade classroom. Now we move to the intermediate grades and the Texas teaching team of Patty and Alan Engle.

Teacher~to~Teacher

Open the door and step into a world of imagination and discovery. Here you will find energetic and creative fourth- and fifth-graders in this cutting-edge classroom where students are immersed in their learning through hands-on activities and interactive simulations. This is a place where students are guided to become investigators in this technology-enhanced learning environment.

Noticeably absent are state-mandated textbooks, blackboards, seating charts, and desks lined up in neat rows. Instead, students sit casually together at tables in one of two adjoining classrooms. The other room, the student-named CyberMedia Lab, contains a 2,000-plus book library and a bank of computers. This room is filled with area

rugs, overstuffed pillows, a couch, comfy chairs and beanbags, and a stereo with classical music playing in the background.

The students are engaged in fully integrated learning experiences where language arts and reading drive the curriculum. Literacy is best taught in the meaningful context of literature and communication, and for each thematic unit that is explored, students are transformed into that time period. As an example, in the unit "Where Do We Grow from Here?" the classroom is turned into the island of New Atlantis, and students are commissioned as officers in the Federation of Inner Space Habitats (FISH). Their mission,

➤ ➤ ➤

collectively, is to explore, preserve, restore, and wisely use the Ocean Planet's inner space habitats. Not only does each mission specialist have a survival problem to address, but each team also has a mission to accomplish as they set out to build an undersea workstation and submersible. From the "bottom of the ocean" they performed research using a teacher-created WebQuest, an inquiry-based activity in which most or all of the information used by students is drawn from the Internet. Students keep scientific logs to help fulfill their orders from FISH headquarters. These orders include tasks covering language arts, reading, science, and mathematics.

Additionally, in their quest for a new place to grow and the curiosity of how our lives could be different, they read the 1994 Newbery Medal novel, *The Giver,* by Lois Lowry. In this book students examined the idea that people might freely choose to give up their humanity to create a more stable society. Everything is controlled in the community in which the story takes place. There are no wars or fear of pain, and there are no choices, an awareness that came uneasily through the reading, giving students the opportunity to reflect, in their novel response journals, on their own lives.

Students in the Engle's class have experienced life as it was when building the Transcontinental Railroad or when immigrating at turn-of-the-twentieth-century Ellis Island; they have researched their own family history and created a new and useful invention. They have lived through the Dustbowl and Depression Era, related their own lives to those of the children of the Japanese American internment camps, changed their ethnicity and dealt with prejudice, and published an anthology of original poetry.

These themes are further enhanced by the use of technology. Students extend their learning by searching the Internet, corresponding with their KeyPals, completing

curriculum-related assignments through personal email accounts, and by creating individual and group presentations using a variety of multimedia. Not only do students experience their education through these thematic units—which incorporate language arts, reading, social studies, science, and mathematics—but they are creating the desire within themselves to become lifelong learners.

Students are immersed in all aspects of literacy from the first bell of the day to the last, through all content areas. A look at their typical daily schedule demonstrates the intensity of their literacy instruction. Upon entering the room, students answer their daily attendance question, which is generally tied to their current novel. From there they start the day by writing in their daily journals. Prompts are character building but also often tie directly to the curriculum. The next forty-five minutes is spent in Our Time To Enjoy Reading (OTTER), sustained silent reading time. Following OTTER, students group for mathematics, where literature drives the lesson and students are frequently seen writing pattern books using their own mathematical findings. After math, students split into two groups: one teacher focuses on reading, and the other focuses on the simulation in progress. Reading instruction follows a balanced approach, and students are given authentic tasks to complete as well as being asked to write in their response journals after each reading. Simulations encompass a variety of content areas but are usually heavy on language arts and expository reading. After a one-hour block, the student groups switch teachers.

After lunch, students crowd around in the "lounge" at the feet of one of their teachers for daily reading aloud. Immediately following, students spend the bulk of the afternoon engaged in Writer's Workshop. Following a schedule of alternating Personal Research On Basically Everything (PROBE) research, PROBE writing, Writer's Block, and Author's Conference, students scatter throughout the rooms and settle in. During this time, students read and research together, do creative writing, share their own writing, and do peer editing. This is also the time when the teachers focus on small groups for minilessons and remediation. The afternoon comes near an end with interactive centers and, once again, a scheduled rotation. Examples of center topics are Words at Work, Mr. E's Mysteries, Write It Right, Your Own Backyard, and The Language of Mathematics. The day is brought to full circle with the daily Discovery Log, a time for students to reflect on the day's activities and look ahead to tomorrow and beyond.

Cooperative Learning

Teachers in total literacy classrooms recognize that children learn best when they learn together. Learning together is the essence of a movement called cooperative learning that is sweeping American education. *Cooperative learning* is defined as "the instructional use of small groups so that students work together to maximize their own and each other's learning" (Johnson, Johnson, & Holubec, 1993, p. 6). One key word in that definition is "maximize," for research has shown that as students collaborate with each other they improve in content knowledge (Slavin, 1987) and experience increased productivity, self-esteem, and interpersonal skills (Johnson & Johnson, 1998; Johnson et al., 1993). As students have the opportunity to work with other students to achieve a goal, their learning is enhanced as they share understanding and knowledge (Vygotsky, 1978).

America's Finest

Paula Witt, A

Another key component of the definition of cooperative learning is to maximize "their own and each other's learning." Cooperative learning is based on the principle that "when you win, I win" or that "we are all in this together." When this mode of learning is operating in a classroom, all children have the opportunity to use their strengths and be "winners." This is in contrast to the competitive principle of "I win, you lose" found in many traditional classrooms where some children are classified as "high achievers" or "winners" and others as "low achievers" or "losers" (McDanial, 1984; Sharan, 1999).

With this definition in mind, we can see that cooperative learning can be useful in a variety of ways in the total literacy classroom. Cooperative groups can be used in writing, peer editing, implementing comprehension strategies, researching and reporting, and doing thematic studies—in actuality, any activity where active participation, sharing of ideas, and risk taking are desired.

How Cooperative Learning Works

Cooperative groups can vary in size; however, a general rule of thumb is "the smaller, the better" (Johnson et al., 1993). Typically, groups range from two to five students, based on how old the students are, how much familiarity the students have with cooperative group work, and how many students are needed for the particular assignment (Lindgren, 1986). When planning for cooperative groups, it is important to consider the goals of the group, the tasks the group is to complete, the relationships or interdependence between the group members, and the roles or responsibilities of the members within the group (Vacca & Vacca, 1993).

Let's examine some of the considerations and their importance in the implementation of various cooperative learning groups. The goal of the group must be made clear. Let's look at the cooperative learning activity of Jigsaw, which requires each child to become an "expert" in his or her assigned area and then teach the information to the rest of the group (Aronson, 1978; Hotchkiss, 1990). Jigsaw groups are comprised of three to six members, depending on the number of subtopics or themes in a reading selection, topic, or study. Each group member is assigned or chooses one of the subtopics to become an "expert" in. After the group members have had time to read the material, decide on the important areas, and plan how they will "teach" the material to their peers, each member takes a turn teaching "his or her part of the puzzle" to the other group members. For this strategy to be effective, the children must understand that the goal of the group is not only for each group member to learn the information he or she is presenting but also to learn the information presented by the other group members. For the group to succeed, all members must succeed.

The students must understand the steps in the cooperative learning structure. For instance, an activity such as Think-Pair-Share (Kagan, 1990) involves two students who first silently think about their own responses to a question or issue and then share their ideas with each other and discuss the reasons behind them. Formulate-Share-Listen-Create (Johnson, Johnson, & Bartlett, 1990) is a comparable structure that can involve more children. Here are the steps: (1) silently think about your own response to a question or issue; (2) take turns sharing and listening to responses of group members; and (3) work together as a team to formulate a new response that can be shared with the class. Although these may seem like simple procedures, their effectiveness is diminished if students do not follow the procedures of engaging in individual thought time first and then moving into sharing. It is helpful if the teacher models the steps of any cooperative learning procedure with a small group before the entire class tries it. As the children become accustomed to noting the steps to the procedure and adhering to the format, their experiences in cooperative learning will be enhanced.

Courtesy of Michael Sampson

Children work together to learn together.

As we mentioned earlier, the interdependent relationship of the group is critical. The members of the group must understand that the philosophy of the group must be "you win, I win" or "we are all in this together." The teacher may observe the groups to determine if they are engaging in the project or procedure as a group. Individual team-building activities, such as deciding on a group name and exploring interests to determine commonalities, can be conducted. In addition, the group should realize that both individual and group accountability are important.

For instance, when students are involved in a group investigation (Johnson & Johnson, 1998; Sharan & Sharan, 1990), the complexity of the structure requires each group member to contribute to the group. The steps of a group investigation are as follows:

STEP 1   Identify the major topic of study, identify subtopics through brainstorming and group discussion, and identify research/investigation groups for the subtopics.

STEP 2   Research/investigation groups meet and determine job responsibilities for group meetings, decide what parts of the subtopic they plan to investigate, decide how and who will research the various parts (in pairs or individually), determine deadlines, and report decisions to teacher.

STEP 3   Investigate the topic, which includes daily meetings to determine progress and revise assignments.

STEP 4   Organize to prepare for final report, including meeting with the teacher to determine the best way to present the findings to the class, plan individuals' contributions to the final presentation, and devise the final report.

STEP 5   Present the final report to the class, and solicit reactions from the class.

STEP 6   Self-evaluation and group evaluation are conducted by the group members. Individual research reports, group research reports, individual presentation role, and group presentations are evaluated by the teacher.

The Structure of Cooperative Groups

As you can see, success of this cooperative learning structure depends on the participation and commitment of all group members. If one member of the group is not participating or progressing, problem-solving strategies must be used to draw the person into the interaction of the group. Perhaps this is one of the most important components of cooperative learning; children have the opportunity to develop interpersonal skills as well as content skills.

One step that seems to aid in all members participating in the group is to be sure the roles and responsibilities of all group members are defined and to determine that each group member has a responsibility. Here is a list of sample roles and responsibilities:

Reader reads instructions and materials to group

Recorder writes down important information generated by the group

Summarizer verbally organizes the important information generated by the group so the Recorder can write it down

Materials Handler collects and distributes all needed materials for group work

Timekeeper monitors the time and keeps the group on task

Reporter presents group's information to whole group (if desired, this is a role/responsibility that can be shared by all members of the group)

Praiser supplies support and confirmation to group members so they are encouraged and continue to participate

Interactive Listener restates or rephrases what has been said

Spy/Explorer searches for new and additional information from other groups

Inspector makes sure everyone in the group understands the concept and what is going on in the group

Please note this is a sample list. Roles can be combined (such as Reader and Materials Handler) or deleted (such as the Spy/Explorer). Roles should be based on the needs of the group and the particular assignment. However, as we noted previously, it is very important that each group member have a role or responsibility. The most effective way to ensure that a member feels important and maintains interest in the group is for that member to have a well-defined role to fulfill. The Teacher-to-Teacher feature here illustrates cooperative learning in action in two very different classrooms.

Pre-K teacher Paula Witt effectively uses cooperative learning with her 4- and 5-year-olds. When introducing a unit on dinosaurs, she distributes models of dinosaur bones to the children and tells the students they are going to have an opportunity to Think-Pair-Share. The students have engaged in the activity before, so they join in with joy as Paula begins by saying, "You have a chance to be a detective. Look at the bone you have. Think about the dinosaur that had a bone like this. What does this bone tell you about the dinosaur? Can you tell if it moved quickly or slowly? How? Can you tell how big it was? How? Can you tell what type of food the dinosaur ate? How? What other information does this bone give you? How did you figure it out? Which dinosaur do you think it was, and why?

"You will have four minutes to think and five minutes to share. Each person has one minute to share observations and then you can discuss them. The person who has the smallest dinosaur bone will share first."

While Paula sets a timer for four minutes, the children take their bone samples and move quickly to their mats on the floor and sit back to back for their "think" time. When the timer buzzes, the children turn around and face each other, and the child with the smallest dinosaur bone begins to share the information gleaned from the examination with his or her partner. When the timer buzzes, the other child begins to share. When the timer buzzes again, the children begin to discuss their bone samples, contrast and compare, and make new discoveries. At the conclusion of the sharing time, the children have the opportunity to share with the large group. Children volunteer and share many observations because they have already "tried out" their ideas with a peer in a small, non-threatening group situation.

Charles Jones uses marathon writing to bring closure to a unit on weather with his fourth-graders. Children number off to form groups of four. Charles hands each group a different shape of cloud with its name written on it, such as cumulus or cirrus. Charles then instructs the children to think about all they have learned about that particular type of cloud: how it is formed, what type of weather usually occurs when they see that cloud, if it is a common or uncommon cloud and why, why it has that name, and any other information they can think of.

The children are given one minute for "think" time and then are told to get out a sheet of paper. Each child starts writing about his or her group's cloud. When "time" is called, each child passes his or her paper clockwise to the next person in the group. Students are given a short period of time to read what has been written, and then they write again, but this time they try to continue the train of thought started by the first writer so the paper will be coherent. Charles calls time again, and the process is repeated until the fourth and last writer has the paper. Students are instructed to read the paper and bring it to closure during this writing period.

When "time" is called to stop the writing, students return the papers to the original writers. They then share the papers and decide which one they would like to share with the class. Charles finds that this part of the procedure is extremely valuable as children compare and contrast ideas and the presentation of those ideas. He often gives the group an opportunity to revise a paper and include "the best" from all of the selections. As children refine their writing about the subject, their content knowledge is increased.

We believe the keys to the success of the total literacy classroom reside in two factors: (1) teachers are teaching with children's literature, and (2) cooperative learning permeates the entire social and organizational structure of the classroom. Throughout this book you will see examples of children working together and learning together in small groups. Cooperative learning theory is the driving force behind our desire to have children work together in groups. But the reward goes beyond the immediate success of cooperative learning classrooms. The most exciting aspect of cooperative learning is that children are acquiring valuable skills they will use the rest of their lives—the ability to work with others.

Heterogeneous or Homogeneous Grouping?

America's Finest
Tracey Bernal

One of the worst mistakes made by literacy programs in the past was grouping students by ability. Such a school practice—one that usually made reading achievement the *measure of success* in the early grades—highlighted lack of success and usually destroyed the child's self-image as a reader rather than improving his or her reading skills. Instead of homogeneous grouping, we recommend flexible grouping. Flexible groupings emphasize students' success and accept the fact that every child is different and has different strengths and knowledge levels in different areas. Groups should constantly be changing—in membership, in size, in focus—as activities change.

Learning situations must be organized in ways that permit children to view themselves and others as worthy and successful. They must experience working alone, working with other students of similar ability, and working with those whose abilities are significantly different from theirs. They must have repeated opportunities to interact with groups and with the total class. Heterogeneous grouping arrangements are vital to this end. The multiage classroom is perhaps the best means of ensuring this diversity in groups.

The Multiage Classroom

Multiage instruction, or classrooms comprised of children of varying age levels, is not a new concept. The one-room schools that existed through the middle part of the twentieth century were the original multiage classrooms. The one-room school has not returned, but its best feature—multiage groupings—is back. Throughout the United States, school districts are grouping children across age ranges (Bingham et al., 1995; Kasten & Clarke, 1993; Kasten & Lolli, 1998). Why are they doing so? There are numerous benefits; let's consider four:

1. *The multiage classroom is more reflective of society.* Only in schools do we divide people up according to age. In neighborhoods, children don't play together according to what age they are; they join together because of proximity or interests. Throughout life, humans have to communicate and get along with individuals of diverse ages. Why not practice this skill in school?

2. *The multiage classroom is more developmentally appropriate.* It is impossible to narrow a sequence of skills that children are expected to attain to one grade level. The philosophy of the multiage classroom is that children will come to primary school, stay three or four years, then move on to intermediate school. The mad rush to cover the curriculum of the grade is avoided (Chase & Doan, 1996). Parents don't have to answer the tough question, "Should our child repeat first grade?" Instead, there is time to develop, time to explore, time to learn.

3. *The multiage classroom is like a family.* Children make more progress when they are in a friendly, nonthreatening environment. Children become comfortable with their room, their teacher, and their classmates in the multiage classroom. They form deep friendships and really feel "at home" at school.

4. *The multiage classroom enables teachers and children to stay together for three to four years.* Traditional schools lose so much time starting the school year, getting acquainted, and ending the school year. Multiage classrooms avoid these starts and stops; hence, momentum is not lost and learning can continue. Teachers have a better overall view of the children because they can know them better, and they can track their progress over a longer period of time.

Connecting with Parents

Communication between parent and teacher is always important. However, in a total literacy classroom this importance is magnified. The role of the parent as an active participant in the child's learning is greatly enhanced when parents are made aware of the goals of the program and are provided with suggestions concerning ways in which to aid their children in meeting those goals (Nistler & Maiers, 2000). We know that many children do not live with parents but with other caregivers such as relatives or foster families. When we use the term *parents,* please keep in mind that we are referring to any person or persons who have legal guardianship of the child—anyone acting in the role of a "parent" to that child.

Many teachers have found it useful to have parents come to school early in the school year. During this visit, parents may meet the teacher and other parents and receive an overview of the language arts program. This overview is especially important in a program that encourages children to explore language and writing. Differences between a child's edited and unedited work may be explained and the importance of encouraging the child's exploration of language and writing stressed. Through these discussions, teachers can convey important information to the parents about the need for educational support in the home. For example, parents will come to understand that the child will be hesitant to read and write at home if the parent assumes the role of a critic rather than that of an encourager (Erickson, 1989).

Parent conferences throughout the year keep the lines of communication open between parent and teacher. Conferences should be a sharing of information between parent and teacher concerning the child's home and school progress. Such meetings provide a valuable opportunity to discuss the "at home" versus the "at school" child. Many times the child the teacher deals with at school is different from the child the parent sees at home. This is true for all grade levels; therefore, it is important for the parent to be aware of this difference, and it is vital that the teacher know as much as possible about the child at home (Cairney, 1995, 1997; Routman, 1988; Seaborg, 1994).

In addition, a class newsletter is a useful communication tool. The teacher may want to develop a newsletter that gives a brief synopsis of the week's events and a preview of "coming attractions." The teacher of intermediate and middle grades may want to incorporate students' work into the newsletter. This gives students a practical opportunity to use their writing and editing skills and guarantees parental interest in the newsletter. Students can work alone, in pairs, or in groups to write stories concerning activities in the classroom. Book reviews are appropriate. Some students may want to contribute short stories or samples of their art.

In the primary grades, a suggestion for an at-home activity that would correlate with the instructional activities of the class is usually welcome. For instance, a teacher might explain that the ability to match things is an important readiness skill. A parent could aid a child in developing this skill by having the child participate in household activities such as matching socks when folding laundry, arranging groceries that are alike on a shelf, stacking plates and saucers that match, or sorting silverware. The teacher could include suggestions for simple matching games, such as saving labels from groceries that are frequently used and stacking them or matching them with items on the grocery storage shelf in the home. The child could also go on a grocery shopping trip with the parent and match the labels to items on the grocery shelf.

Other ways to maintain contact with parents include telephone calls, email, classroom Web pages, and the more traditional notes sent home to parents. The teacher should be sure these communications do not always contain negative information. Parents especially enjoy hearing from teachers when good things happen.

In addition to the formal feedback the school provides, teachers should be aware that parents are constantly receiving information concerning the literacy program from their children. Students' attitudes toward reading, writing, and other language activities provide one of the most powerful messages the parent receives. Homework and the attitude toward homework convey vivid messages concerning the language arts program. If parents constantly see an uninterested and discouraged child with numerous ditto sheets that involve fill-in-the-blank activities or with numerous definitions to look up, a distinct message is conveyed about the instructional program. However, if the child is involved in assignments that require creative thought and the use of verbal, reading, and writing skills, parents receive a different message. For example, a child might have the assignment to interview his or her parents concerning the television or radio programs they enjoyed as children. The completion of this assignment would require using language arts skills in the context of an enjoyable activity and would make a positive statement about the program.

A classroom in which parents are welcome to visit enhances communication. Although the parents' work or the rules of the school means that teachers may have to plan these visits in advance, the key is that parents know they are welcome in the classroom (Vopat, 1998). Many teachers involve parents in assisting with instructional activities or learning centers. In today's busy classroom, extra help is always welcome. But more important, parents will feel good about their child and the home they have in your classroom.

FURTHER WORDS

 From InfoTrac College Edition

What One Middle School Teacher Learned about Cooperative Learning (brief article), Kathleen Glascott Burriss, *Childhood Education* September 15, 2000 v76 i6 p398

Teaching in Early Childhood: Time to Merge Constructivist Views So Learning through Play Equals Teaching through Play (critical essay), Helen Hedges, *Australian Journal of Early Childhood,* December 2000 v25 i4 p16

Problems in Developing a Constructivist Approach to Teaching: One Teacher's Transition from Teacher Preparation to Teaching (abstract, statistical data included), Leslie Susan Cook, Peter Smagorinsky, Pamela G. Fry, Bonnie Konopak, and Cynthia Moore, *The Elementary School Journal,* May 2002 v102 i5 p389(26)

The Multiage Challenge (multiage classroom), Jill Ostrow, *Instructor (1990),* September 1999 v109 i2 p40(3)

From Professional Journals and Publications

Au, K. H. (1997). Improving Literacy Achievement through a Constructivist Approach: The KEEP Demonstration Classroom Project. *Elementary School Journal, 97,* 203–221.

Cairney, T. H. (2000). The Construction of Literacy and Literacy Learners. *Language Arts, 77,* 496–505.

Cambourne, B. (1995). Toward an Educationally Relevant Theory of Literacy Learning: Twenty Years of Inquiry. *The Reading Teacher, 49,* 182–190.

America's Finest
Ruth Ann Shauf

Summary

In a total literacy curricula, teachers recognize that the language students bring to the school is uniquely their own. This personal speech is a reflection of the vernacular the children have heard used in their homes and communities. Consequently, teachers who endorse a total literacy approach strive to let their students know this personal speech is worthy and welcome as they accept, respect, and build on their literacy communications.

The teacher should be careful to provide some emphasis each day from the total literacy model presented in this chapter. In doing so, the teacher will assure that every student has opportunities for self-expression through Strand 1 activities. The students' personal language will be influenced through Strand 2 activities. Literacy skills will emerge from Strand 3 as students encounter the wonder and beauty of language through holistic activities.

Literacy programs must be built on language strengths students bring to the classroom. Teachers are the key to good programs. They must value the language of students, possess an understanding of how oral and written communications evolve, and view language learning as an integrated process.

Teachers must operate as professionals, balancing state or district requirements with student needs, capitalizing on students' interests, and using their professional judgment wisely as they seek to integrate all of these needs into the curriculum. Such teachers take advantage of every opportunity to release students to discover the beauty of language.

Total Literacy Anchors

- ◆ The teacher understands learning theory and student motivation for learning.
- ◆ The teacher implements the total literacy model to ensure balance between self-expression, impression, and literacy conventions.
- ◆ The teacher structures the learning environment to help ensure success for every learner.
- ◆ The teacher carries topics or themes throughout the day to keep instruction in context.
- ◆ The teacher works with children one on one.
- ◆ The teacher works with small groups of children.
- ◆ The teacher communicates clearly with parents.

CHAPTER 2

Early Literacy

As You Read . . .

- What impact does the exposure of children to print in their environments have on their readiness for literacy instruction?

- Should the alphabet be taught to children?

- What is the relationship between the beginnings of reading and the beginnings of writing?

- What principles from natural literacy learning should be incorporated in the school curriculum?

- How are life experiences the "foundations of thinking"?

- How many life experiences have an impact on literacy instruction?

Ask any parent. The greatest miracle parents have ever witnessed is seeing an infant move from babbles to talk. But how does it happen?

From the first moments of life, infants hear language. Imagine what it must be like being born into our language-rich world and being bombarded with the sounds of language. Infants are immediately immersed in the river of language interaction that flows around them, and family members play a vital role as language models and suppliers of language during this period of language acquisition and discovery.

Within days the infant's role quickly changes from listener to participant as he or she begins to communicate with family members. A miracle of learning soon occurs. An infant's learning of language is fast and sure—virtually every child achieves near mastery of his or her language by age 6 (Read, 1980). This mastery is also evident outside the literacy-dominated culture of the United States. For example, Pflaum (1986) reports that children in nonliterate Papua New Guinea acquire substantial communication skills at an early age.

Language learning is more complicated than it might appear. Language is more than words; language is more than sentences. Children come to know that the same word has many different meanings and that context influences meaning. Thus the need to communicate leads children to refine their language through experimentation. For example, 3-year-old Jonathan was asked to bring the "tape" during a Christmas package-wrapping session. His mother had just played his favorite music on the stereo, and he responded by bringing her the cassette tape. Fortunately, children quickly learn the "tricks" of language that depend on the context of the situation. They discover language is not a constant but a variable.

As children move through the preschool years, they begin to gain control of language as they are exposed to the communication of others (Cambourne, 1995). This internalization of language is then expressed through oral sharing. The process of input (through the communication of others) and output (in the form of self-expression) may be seen as preschoolers "scribble" out messages and develop as writers. They are learning about written language in much the same way they learned about oral language—through experience (McGee & Richgels, 1996).

Reading: The Beginnings

Should the Alphabet Be Taught to Children?

The alphabet is a marvelous tool. Through its 26 letters, writers can convey their thoughts in many ways. Beautiful language may be captured and conveyed across

Kayla _____ Name

6 _____ Age

_____

Playing gam ___Interests

Playing withmy Dog

What do you like most about school?

I like PE bekus we play gams.

What's your favorite subject? Why?

I like sienc bekus you plant seeds.

What's your favorite book? Why do you like it?

Junie b. Jons bekus she is funny.

What advice do you have for teachers?

To let kids Do centers.

time and distance. Funny stories may be shared. Important things to be remembered may be recorded—and thus remembered. The uses of our alphabet are endless.

Parents are eager for their children to learn their ABCs. They teach their children to sing the famous ABC song, and they buy picture books that feature the alphabet to engage little ones. Many kindergarten programs teach the alphabet—one letter per week! Children's television programs feature dinosaurs and kids using the alphabet—episode after episode. But is this necessary? Is it possible that children can learn the alphabet in a natural and engaging manner? We believe the answer is "yes." We'll now turn our attention to the environments children live in and point out ways to help children become more print aware, and show how they can learn the alphabet by using it in their own writing.

We'll begin a discussion on letter sounds and phonemic awareness, but we'll wait until Chapter 5 to elaborate as we begin a more formal study of reading. For emerging readers, we want to keep our focus on environmental print, writing, and fun yet engaging picture books like Bill Martin Jr's *Chicka Chicka Boom Boom* (Martin & Archambault, 1989).

How Children Become Aware of Print

In Chapter 1 we discussed how children learn language, comparing and contrasting three views of language acquisition. We saw that children learn language because of their need to communicate with significant others and that the process of learning language is a natural product of these transactions. The same holds true of reading and writing.

One of the greatest mistakes we have made through the years has occurred in kindergarten and first-grade classrooms through our efforts to get children "ready" to learn to read. In reality, children become readers much earlier than this as they become aware of print in situational contexts. However, many reading programs fail to build on children's early experiences with print as they "teach" reading and reading skills in isolation from the student's language base and knowledge of print (Sampson, 1997).

Research has indicated that children become aware of print at a very early age as they interact with the world about them (Clay, 1975; Doake, 1988; Teale, 1986a). This first exposure occurs as children encounter print "embedded" in their environments (Goodman, 1980; Orellana & Hernandez, 1999; Wells, 1986). Harste, Burke, and Woodward (1982) concluded that children begin their literacy learning process by observing this embedded print and constructing schemata concerning its meaning in context.

Daily activities of young children reinforce their concept of what print is and its value to the significant adults in their lives. When young children go to the store, they are bombarded with printed visual stimuli displaying products they have seen advertised on television. They quickly learn to recognize the printed symbols that

Christopher Welsh — Name

7 — Age

Sports — Interests
read

What do you like most about school?

I like taking A.R. tests.

What's your favorite subject? Why?

Sdense. Becuase you learn stuf that you never new was in life.

What's your favorite book? Why do you like it?

Boxcar Children. It has many mysetrys.

What advice do you have for teachers?

To write notes to them-selves so they dont keep changing during asimints.

Reprinted with special permission of Kimberly Welsh.

signal their favorite restaurants, stores, and landmarks. They learn that certain signs on highways and public buildings control the actions of people. Children assimilate this information and begin to make generalizations concerning print. They realize that print carries a message. Generalizations occur as children quickly learn that generic terms may be substituted for specific trade names. For instance, children may call both Colgate and Crest "toothpaste"; when asked how they know that information, they will point to the printed word (Goodman, 1980).

Children's print awareness is not limited to learning from situational contexts. Children's knowledge of print is also enhanced as they are exposed to print in books, newspapers, magazines, letters, and other printed matter

Author Study

Eric Carle

1. *Which book of yours has given you the greatest pleasure?*

Brown Bear, Brown Bear, What Do You See? It was my first book and my entry into this exciting world and life I have since lived. But best of all, it brought me into contact with my dear friend Bill Martin Jr. I also love *Do You Want to Be My Friend?* because friendships are the most important thing in life.

2. *Which book has surprised you most in terms of its public reception?*

The Very Hungry Caterpillar. I have been amazed at how the book has become such a favorite around the world and how it still sells today after thirty years in the market. It has been translated into more than thirty languages and sold 17 million—plus copies.

3. *What would you like people to remember about your work?*

My hope is that people will remember my books by associating happy times reading together as a family. I hope that those who see it will experience the joy I feel in putting the art together. And I hope that the museum we are building, the Eric Carle Museum of Picture Book Art, will honor all the great children's artists of all time.

4. *What impact do you hope your work will have on children?*

With many of my books, I attempt to bridge the gap between the home and school. To me, home represents, or should represent, warmth, security, toys, holding hands, being held. School is a strange and new place for a child. Will it be a happy place? There are new people, a teacher, classmates—will they be friendly? I want to show children that learning is really both fascinating and fun.

Eric Carle is acclaimed and beloved as the creator of brilliantly illustrated and innovatively designed picture books for very young children. He is known for his more than seventy books, including three bestsellers with Bill Martin Jr.— *Brown Bear, Brown Bear, What Do You See?; Polar Bear, Polar Bear, What Do you Hear?;* and *Panda Bear, Panda Bear, What Do You See?* Many of his books have an added dimension— twinkling lights as in *The Very Lonely Firefly* and the lifelike sound of a cricket's song in *The Very Quiet Cricket.*

Reprinted with special permission of Eric Carle.

(Broad, 2002; Goodman, 1980; McGee & Richgels, 1996; Neuman & Roskos, 1997). These early experiences with books and other printed material directly influence the print awareness of the child (Holdaway, 1979, 1986; Nielsen & Monson, 1996). Thus the more children are read to and the more they see others reading and writing, the more importance print will have in their lives. Environmental print and written discourse both make children aware that print conveys meaning. They also prompt children's awareness of other linguistic constraints that govern their particular language. One of the mainstays of many "reading readiness" programs has been teaching print directionality through exercises in the classroom. However, directionality of print, reading from left to right in English, is a linguistic concept that develops at a young age. In addition, as we survey environmental print, we discover it is often presented vertically and does not always move from left to right. The adaptability of children is apparent because they assimilate this information and recognize it to be the exception rather than the norm (Goodman, 1980). Once again, we find that children know more about language and print than they are usually given credit for.

In addition, children develop the concept that print occurs in groupings of letters that represent verbal responses. The length of the print becomes equated with the length of the utterance (Goodman, 1980). Four-year-old Chrissy received a letter offering her the opportunity to "win" a new boat by visiting a real estate time-share development. When her mother finished reading the letter without including the fine print at the bottom of the page, Chrissy corrected her by saying, "But there's more here, Mom!"

Other generalizations that children develop include knowledge of the form of their particular written language. Harste, Burke, and Woodward's (1982) work with 4-year-olds attending an Indiana preschool illustrates this. When children at the school from three different countries were instructed to "write everything you can write," the results were revealing (see Figure 2.1). In discussing these scribbles, the researchers stated:

> In contrast to the other sample, Dawn's scribbles look undeniably English. When Najeeba finished her writing, she said, "Here, but you can't read it because it is in Arabic." Najeeba then went on to point out that in Arabic one uses "a lot more dots" than in English. Dalia is an Israeli child whose writing bears the predictable look of Hebrew. (p. 107)

When asked to write, young children make markings that reflect the print of their culture. This is an indication that the psycholinguistic processes of reading and writing are sociologically rooted (Harste, Woodward, & Burke, 1984a).

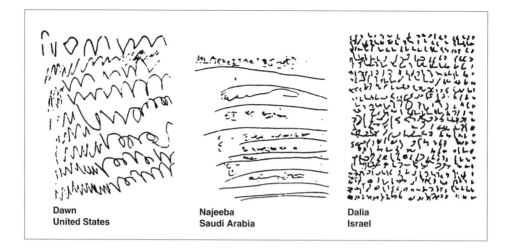

FIGURE 2.1

Writing samples from 4-year-old children

From Comprehension as Setting. In J. C. Harste & R. F. Carey (eds.), *New Perspectives on Comprehension,* 1979. Reprinted with permission.

Dawn
United States

Najeeba
Saudi Arabia

Dalia
Israel

Maria Flores is a first-grade teacher who values the knowledge and experiences that children bring with them to her classroom. Her perspective is that of a cognitive field advocate: she believes the teacher's job is to set up situations where children can use their knowledge about language and print as they learn more about literacy. Maria helps children discover how much they know about reading and language through environmental print such as cereal boxes, soft drink containers, and fast food restaurant sacks. She uses these as a natural link to literacy during the first few weeks of class. She asks the students to bring in words to include on a bulletin board labeled "Words We Can Read."

Children's insights about environmental print provide Maria with valuable clues concerning their knowledge about literacy. She knows her analysis of the student's response to environmental print provides a much richer picture of the child's "readiness" for a given activity than information provided by conventional reading readiness tests. She uses this informal assessment as she plans the instruction a given child will receive and the learning environments she will establish in her classroom.

Awareness of Sound Is Important Too

Clearly, children's developing awareness of print and what print does is an important precursor to learning to read. Sound plays an important role in learning to read as well, and children's development of sound awareness, or what the experts have come to call phonological awareness, plays an important role in children's success in becoming literate (Stahl & Murray, 1998). Phonological awareness refers to the child's awareness of speech sounds. Reading does involve the conversion of written symbols into speech sounds, and the ability to convert written symbols into speech sounds requires some degree of proficiency in hearing distinctions in sounds, blending sounds, segmenting sounds, and otherwise manipulating the sounds made during speech. Hallie Yopp (1995) found that kindergarteners' level of phonological awareness was significantly related to their overall reading development through the middle grades.

Most children develop the phonological awareness necessary for literacy learning through everyday interactions with parents and others at home and preschool. Conversing with others, listening to stories, rhymes, alphabet books, poems, and other forms of written language read to them, and playing with sounds on their own help children develop the sensitivity to sounds that prepares them for making the connection between speech and print that is an important part of learning to read. As children hear nursery rhymes and other rhyming poetry, they develop a sensitivity to the notion of words that are similar through their rhyming patterns. Through other forms of poetry and language, children become sensitive to alliteration and consonant sounds and how words can be changed through the addition and subtraction of sounds (Yopp & Yopp, 2000).

Just as children become sensitive to the print they see around them, so too their sensitivity and perception of sounds is molded by the sounds they hear around them and the sounds they make in response to what they hear and what they need. The sound environment is as important as the print environment when it comes to shaping potential readers.

Not all children, however, appear to develop sufficient proficiency in phonological awareness. This may be due to a developmental shortcoming inherited at birth, a lack of opportunities to play with sounds with parents, or from a history of ear infections during the early childhood years that may distort a child's hearing.

Fortunately, sound awareness can be taught and learned. For those children who appear to be at risk in the development of phonological awareness, it is important that we provide a school environment that stimulates sound awareness and guided opportunities for children to engage in sound perception, analysis, and production. Rhyming poetry, chants, song lyrics, alphabet books, and other language forms that play with sounds provide teachers and children with wonderful opportunities to study sounds in ways that are engaging and entertaining. When those poems, chants, and lyrics are read from books, big books, charts, or from the chalkboard, the teacher (or parent) can provide children with opportunities to develop awareness of print and print conventions as well as phonological awareness. This seems to us to be a most natural way to develop some of the key competencies that will ensure children's success in literacy learning.

Courtesy of Melanie Schauwecker

Young children love to make and read big books.

Natural Readers

Children who become readers without direct instruction before entering school typically come from homes where literacy is a part of daily life routines. In such homes, adults model interaction with all types of reading materials, and print is used frequently and in meaningful situations (Heath, 1983b; Morrow, 1992; Senechal, LeFevre, Thomas, & Daley, 1998; Teale, 1986a, 1986b). The children were read to regularly, and discussions of the books occurred during and after the reading. Writing materials were present, and children saw adults writing frequently for real-life communicative needs and were included in this communication. In addition, the children had easy access to paper and pencil and their communicative efforts were recognized and praised.

Teale (1986a) offers several suggestions from his observations and reviews of research that may help to create home environments that foster literacy development:

- ◆ Provide a wide variety of reading and writing materials that are readily available to the child; in addition to children's books, include magazines, various types of writing instruments (pens, markers, pencils, crayons, chalk), and paper.
- ◆ Have parents and other family members (such as siblings and grandparents) who themselves engage in a variety of reading and writing

THE FAMILY CIRCUS®   By Bil Keane

Reprinted with special permission of Cowles Syndicate. Inc.

activities model for the child the activities and the pleasure and satisfaction found in these experiences.

◆ Read to the child on a regular basis.

◆ Encourage the child's reading and writing activities, both in interaction with the parent and as independent activities by the child.

◆ Have responsive parents answer the child's questions about language, books, reading, and writing. (p. 23)

Literacy should not be pushed on preschoolers. Reading and writing should be enjoyable and natural. Contrived "instruction" can destroy the joy of literacy and rob children of a love of reading. However, it is to a child's advantage to be a reader when beginning school. Taylor (1986) states that it's the early experiences children have with literacy in the home that enable them to overcome the "impossible ambiguity of the decontextualized reading exercises" of first-grade classrooms. Therefore, teachers should encourage parents to share books with children and to promote their natural literacy inquiries.

Writing: The Beginnings

At a very young age, children begin to experiment with writing. They represent meaning through scribbles (Harste, Woodward, & Burke, 1984b; Vygotsky, 1978) and demonstrate their growing awareness of the functions of print through these written communications. The first scribbles produced by a toddler may seem

Paula Witt's pre-schoolers explore environmental print through a letter-matching activity.

meaningless to an adult, but they represent the child's experimentation with the concept that written marks convey meaning in a permanent and concrete way. In a massive study of children's early literacy encounters, Harste, Woodward, and Burke (1984b) discovered that all children "wrote" with the "intent to mean."

Children also realize at an early age that the marks that convey meaning have certain unique characteristics. Remember Dawn, Najeeba, and Dalia's uninterrupted writing samples shown in Figure 2.1? They demonstrate that the cultural form of print is internalized at an early age without formal instruction (Harste et al., 1982).

If children were left to their own devices, some educators believe writing would precede reading (Chomsky, 1971). Others claim that reading is the first accomplishment. In reality, both reading and writing are developmental; hence, they are learned simultaneously through children's explorations with environmental print and scribbles. In cases where reading precedes writing, the development is likely a reflection of parents' and teachers' emphasis on reading and the lack of opportunities for young children to write. It is difficult to determine how this emphasis affects the natural development of reading and writing.

Recent studies have further explored the interactive development of reading and writing as children's concepts concerning print are developed. The case studies of Baghban (1984), Bissex (1980), Kamler (1984), and Rhodes (1979), and the observational research of Heath (1983a), Taylor (1983), and Senechal, LeFevre, Thomas, and Daley (1998) illustrate the concurrent development of literacy awareness in reading and writing. In an important longitudinal study, Wells (1986) determined that children's early communications were always directed toward communicating meaning and that children expect others to have this same meaning-oriented stance.

Such research has reinforced the concept that a child's perception of the world includes a strong realization that print is a vital, valuable, and useful part of the environment. Children strive to make sense of print and to find ways of making it a tool of communication. Our goal in school settings should be to provide opportunities in the curriculum for children to continue their discovery of how print functions in communication (Novick, 1999).

When investigating the representation of written language, children move from scribbling to making marks that begin to look like writing. During this developmental process, children often rely on concrete representations to facilitate the transfer of meaning to the written page. This reliance is illustrated in research studies (Ferreiro & Teberosky, 1982; Morrow, 1992). Four-year-old Joshua's note to his father illustrates this principle (Figure 2.2): He wanted to say "I love you" five

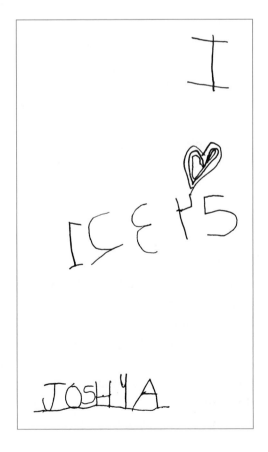

FIGURE 2.2
A 4-year-old writes "I love you" five times

FIGURE 2.3
"Signature" of a young child

times, and he represented this oral language with symbols very effectively, as shown in his "letter." This literacy experience illustrates the interplay that children are constantly involved in as they strive to make sense of the relation between print and the concept or concepts it represents.

In the process of developing ways to communicate messages through print, children often incorporate art experiences in their writing. This inclusion of art reinforces the concept that concrete representation is a part of the process of manipulating writing in a way that makes it meaningful and useful to the child. Figure 2.3 shows what happened when Jonathan (age 4 years 1 month) signed his name on a thank-you note to a friend; he wrote it with the comment, "Now she will know it is me."

Children's scribbles are not random; they usually represent meaning the child is recording on paper. Figure 2.4 shows the story Eric (age 3 years 5 months) wrote for his father as a Christmas present; it was given with the instructions that "I'll read this to you when you are ready." Eric had internalized that print, even the scribbled variety, conveys a message.

Clearly, children are interested in "writing" from an early age, and if given the opportunity, they will explore ways to convey messages in print.

Literacy Learning in School Settings

America's Finest
Kimberly Welsh

In schools, students learn best what they want to learn. The teacher's task is to work in ways that create in each student the desire to know and the desire to act on that knowledge. Teaching with this orientation is the art of improving students' sensitivity to their human and physical environment so they can see more, hear more, feel more—discover the extraordinary in the ordinary—and then communicate their thoughts with clarity, enthusiasm, versatility, and exactness.

Most students do not learn something before they have developed an interest in it through personal experience. Some degree of meaning must be

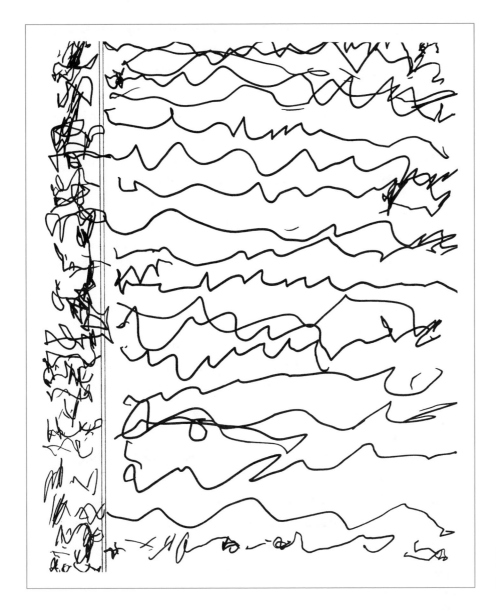

FIGURE 2.4
Writing sample
from a 3-year-old

present before new meanings can be added, especially those meanings that are technical or come from printed materials. We, therefore, take advantage of natural curiosity that is present and operating all the time. Total literacy teachers must remember that each student has a natural language—divergent as it may be—and that new language learning must be related to that natural language.

Because of the wide range of natural language abilities expressed in an assortment of dialects, it is impossible to propose a standard program for the development of basic literacy at any grade level. Rather, it is the responsibility of the teacher to be familiar with the wide range of classroom possibilities. No matter what skills and abilities are emphasized or what experiences are introduced, teachers should help each student to develop competence in several areas:

◆ Communicate effectively with others in many ways.

◆ Succeed in those tasks involving speaking and writing in daily living.

◆ Compare and contrast personal ideas and language with those of others.

◆ Add pleasure to life through such activities as reading, writing, storytelling, choral speaking, pantomime, singing, dancing, and painting.

The best classroom environments for literacy learning in school settings are the ones modeled after principles of natural learning. In studying how children learn before schooling, Holdaway (1986) established the principles of sharing and doing as being critical in school literacy programs. Let's look at each of these principles in more detail.

Sharing

Sharing involves the teacher displaying the desired skills (reading, writing, and publishing) to the children. Holdaway (1986) writes that observing the skilled behavior in the teacher, with "absorbing curiosity and desire," leads the learner into participation.

TEACHER ROLES

1. Demonstrating authentic skill—sharing personally loved literature and engaging in reactions to it.

2. Inducing and rewarding participation.

3. Sharing skill—reading and writing with the children—showing how it's done. (p. 67)

STUDENT ROLES

1. Observing and emulating—enjoying teacher's literacy.

2. Engaging in response to text with teacher and peers.

3. Participating as a skill user.

4. Identifying personally with the skill. (p. 67)

These activities usually take the form of reading and writing to and with the students. Teachers choose from a rich range of literature the books that both they and the children deeply enjoy. Using enlarged print enhances the communal impact of the literature and provides the opportunity for participation without threat of embarrassment. The teacher also writes and "publishes" for and with the children. Song, chant, dance, and mime contribute to the wholeness and vigor of the experiences.

Doing

Doing involves "hands-on" experience. Students have the desire to master the skill or act, and want to practice it in realistic ways. The practice is usually chosen, controlled, and paced by the learner.

The confidence that results from this role playing, and the feeling of belonging in a print culture, result in a desire to perform. Such natural performance takes two forms: (1) attempts to use the skill in "real" or purposeful ways to the limit of current competence or beyond; and (2) attempts to share, to gain approval, and to "show off," especially to the model or bonded people being emulated (Holdaway, 1986, p. 67).

TEACHER ROLES

1. Providing support, encouragement, and suggestions.
2. Acting as an appreciative audience.
3. Observing, recording, and responding to individual needs (diagnosing).
4. Managing the environment.

STUDENT ROLES

1. Role playing as reader, writer, meaning maker, publisher, and so on (includes word processing).
2. Accepting self-regulation as reader and as writer; self-correcting.
3. Exploring meanings through related arts.

Courtesy of The International Institute of Literacy Learning

A preschooler enjoys a good book.

4. Learning skills through instruction and practice.

5. Reading and writing for friendly audiences: teachers, peer(s), or class (includes drama, mime, puppetry, book illustration, and murals). (p. 67)

Experiences: The Foundations of Literacy

Walt Whitman (1900) had it right in his classic poem "There Was a Child Went Forth . . ." In poetic refrain, Whitman comments that "the first thing the child looked upon, he became."

> THERE was a child went forth every day;
> And the first object he look'd upon, that object he became;
> And that object became part of him for the day, or a certain part of the day, or for many years, or stretching cycles of years . . .

In truth, the experiences children have in life make them what they are. The way people respond to them, the books that are read to them, the circus or sporting events they attend—all become part of the child. As humans, what we experience creates the base for interpretations and extension of our own ideas and the ideas of others.

Piagetian theory is based on life experiences as the very foundation of thinking (Piaget, 1959). This theory says that spontaneous curiosity can be deadened or hindered in certain environments in which children grow—at home and especially at school. In addition, spontaneous curiosity must be nourished if children are to reach an operational level of thinking when involved in the school curriculum. In *Piaget for Teachers,* Hans G. Furth (1970) summarizes much of what Piaget has to say on this topic:

> Assuming that many children who come to school are intellectually impoverished but still have enough internal motivation to grow intellectually—as is shown by the fact that their intellects will continue to grow with or without school—what "in effect" is the school offering the child? This is the message that he [or she] gets: "Forget your intellect for a while" come and learn to read and write; in five to seven years' time, if you are successful, your reading will catch up with the capacity of your intellect, which you are developing in spite of what we offer you." Mark well these twin conditions: learn reading and forget your intellect. These things go hand in hand. (p. 4)

Some clarification of the dilemma suggested by Furth is available for teachers through a definition of primary reading abilities as the term is used at the Claremont College Reading Conference. Spencer (1970) explains that letters and words are maps for ideas but not ideas in themselves. These symbols must be

Legal Requirements for Linguistically Diverse Learners

Local education institutions are legally bound to provide equal education opportunities for every student. This includes students whose first language is not English.

Linguistic diversity and bilingualism are not new developments in our society. During the colonial period, official documents were often published in English, French, and German. After the Revolutionary War, however, public sentiment moved toward the necessity of assimilating all immigrants into American culture, and by the end of the 1800s language limitations were placed on the schools. Consequently, bilingual education was practically nonexistent by the 1930s (Vaughan, Bos, & Schumm, 2000).

A move to support equal access and bilingual education gained momentum in 1964 with passage of the Civil Rights Act, which prohibits discrimination based on one's language, and in 1968 when the Bilingual Education Act (Title VII of the Elementary and Secondary Education Act) endorsed bilingual programs in schools. Additional support was given to linguistically diverse students when the Supreme Court ruled in *Lau v. Nichols* (1974) that just providing the same textbooks, facilities, teachers, and curriculum for students who did not understand English did not constitute equal treatment. This litigation was brought to the courts on behalf of 1,800 Chinese-speaking students in San Francisco, a reminder that U.S. schools enroll students representing almost all worldwide language communities, ethnicities, national origins, and social classes.

The move to support the acquisition of English has resulted in development of two classifications of programs: English as a second language (ESL) or English to speakers of other languages (ESOL), and bilingual education. ESL and ESOL instruction focuses on teaching English as a second language with little emphasis given to maintaining and extending the student's first language; therefore, teachers may have non-English-speaking students from numerous language groups in one classroom. The ESL or ESOL teacher is not required to be fluent in the first language of the students but focuses on strategies and techniques to support the students' acquisition of English.

Students may leave their general education classrooms to go to an ESL or ESOL classroom for a specified time, or the teacher may come to the general education classroom and collaborate with the classroom teacher to integrate ESL or ESOL and content-area instruction.

In contrast, students typically spend the entire day in a bilingual classroom. Bilingual programs are usually classified as either *transitional* or *maintenance*. The classifications are self-explanatory: The goal of the transitional program is to help students transition from their first language to English; the focus of the maintenance program is to maintain and extend students' expertise and knowledge of the first language and culture while learning the second language and culture (Chamot, 1998).

Even though legislation and court decisions have supported equal access and instructional support for second language learners, some actions in the last few years have caused concern that the pendulum may be swinging to limit these instructional opportunities. In 1998, the California legislature passed the English for the Children Initiative, which limits the number of years English language learners (ELL) may participate in programs and does not advocate programs that maintain and extend the student's first language.

➤ ➤ ➤

Regardless of whether your school has a bilingual or ESL program, it is probable that you will have students in your classroom who are in the process of learning English as a second language or dialect. Should you find yourself in this situation, researchers have discovered some ways to smooth the way:

- Construct a comfortable instructional environment that communicates to students that you value their culture and language and lets students know that assistance is available.

- Believe all students are capable of achieving academic success and demonstrate this belief by having high expectations.

- Implement strategies that provide opportunities for students to use higher order thinking skills that result in divergent responses that are supported by discussion—not one "right answer."

- Structure opportunities for students to use English in "risk-free" situations that provide an opportunity for rehearsal and group support, such as choral reading and Reader's Theater.

- Never force second language learners to speak if they are uncomfortable.

- Use flexible, cooperative groupings that provide opportunities for support. At times that may mean that learners with the same first language collaborate, and in other situations the groups may include learners with different first languages.

- Modify assignments when necessary.

Most important, remember that culturally and linguistically diverse students bring a wealth of information and experiences to your instructional environment. The learning experience of all students will be enriched by their presence.

linked to meanings that have origins in direct experiences. These concrete experiences must precede or accompany the reading of symbols. Spencer terms this environmental reading "primary reading" and states that it is foundational to successful "secondary reading," or the reading of printed materials:

> We must provide for and make use of primary reading both as a way of behavior and as a source of meaning and of judgments of significance. Word symbols are impotent to supply these. Consequently, a program for reading development which is concerned only with skills of word recognition and the analysis of word patterns is inadequate. (p. 16)

Children feel a sense of accomplishment in being able to "read" in their environment and from their experiences. They come to understand through repeated emphasis that most of their life experiences require the reading of primary sources and that some of them require the reading of secondary sources, or printed materials (Spencer, 1970).

Primary sources are among the nonalphabetic reading that children encounter normally and naturally. These sources include numerals in many forms and in many places, such as clocks, dials, and price tags. They include reading maps and graphs and also reading meaning into photographs, computer images, and paintings. All children need to experience primary reading as a part of a total literacy program, but it is essential that children who are slow to read the language represented by alphabetic symbols have repeated opportunities to experience directly the things they will be asked to read about. These experiences or activities must be a recognized part of the school program.

Teachers must feel that primary reading sources are major sources for language acquisition. They must experience over and over the fact that language grown from primary sources is useful in lessons and activities requiring the reproduction of language represented by the alphabet. It is folly to pretend to study science and social studies with students who have not had experiences verbalizing their personal responses to their natural environment, to their sensory impressions, to numerals and numbers, and to some of the graphic aids that are helpful to them in solving problems.

Responding to the Natural Environment

All children who enter school have had experiences reading signals such as these in their natural environment:

WEATHER

Is it hot or cold?

Is it wet or dry?

Is it windy or calm?

A young scientist studies animal life.

Courtesy of Michael Sampson

Young Readers

I Pledge Allegiance . . . , by **Bill Martin Jr. and Michael Sampson.**
Kindergartners and first-graders who can "say" the pledge of allegiance will be excited that they can "read" this patriotic book.
Boston: Candlewick, 2002.

Max Cleans Up, by **Rosemary Wells.**
Messy Max has to clean his room, and he does it his way—despite "help" from his sister Ruby.
New York: Viking, 2000.

Star of the Circus, by **Michael Sampson and Mary Beth Sampson.**
Preschoolers love to sing "I'm the star of the circus, I'm the star of the circus" as animal after animal perform their circus tricks. The interlocking pattern makes it an easy and successful read for all children, and Jose Aruego's art is captivating.
New York: Henry Holt, 1997.

The Emperor's Egg, by **Martin Jenkins.**
Father Penguin braves an Antarctic winter so his little one can come to life.
Boston: Candlewick, 1999.

PLANTS

> Are they large or small?
>
> Are they green or brown?
>
> Are they for shade or for food?

ANIMALS

> Do they have fur or feathers?
>
> Are they domestic or wild?
>
> Do they hop, run, or fly?
>
> Do they communicate with people?

WATER

> Is it running or still?
>
> Is it dirty or clean?
>
> Is it liquid or frozen?

AIR

> Is it clear or polluted?
>
> Is it moving or still?
>
> Is it warm or cold?

EARTH

> Is it wet or dry?
>
> Is it rocky or sandy?
>
> Is it farmed or forested?

Student experiences in life should be related to the literacy program. These experiences increase interest in reading and writing; students begin to learn more about the topic or share their experience with others through writing. However, students in many schools have been made to feel that reading is simply a subject to be studied, not a dynamic process that brings pleasure and meaning to life.

Students are usually willing to do the things necessary to learn the skills associated with reading and do not complain when they are denied primary reading experiences. In contrast, in a total literacy curriculum, reading is focused on the experiences students encounter in nature and in their environment rather than in decontextualized skill work.

Students who view their world and respond to it through language or writing must be able to read nature's signals and must possess the necessary vocabulary to translate their experiences into their writing and reading experiences. Students encounter references to nature in literary selections so frequently that a knowledge of nature from experience is required for a high level of comprehension. Fortunately, the things of nature are available to all. Travel may be required for extended experiences, but the most basic local experiences need only to be recognized as a major source for language acquisition.

Responding to Sensory Impressions

Sensory impressions provide information from experience that we use to recall and apply meaning when we read. Basic to the whole idea of a total literacy approach is the notion that reading is accelerated by the continuous experience of communicating in many ways what we see, hear, touch, taste, and smell. Sound–symbol relations are strengthened by verbalizing sensory impressions apart from the printed symbols used to record those impressions.

Sight

Color, size, and shape are among the impressions gained through sight, and these sensory impressions are critical to communication in the arts and sciences. Thousands of words have been generated in order to make fine distinctions and to record accurate observations about them. Most of us make these verbal distinctions hundreds of times each day, yet some children come to school with little oral vocabulary in these areas of description. Nonalphabetic reading must precede relating the sounds of words to the alphabetic recording of those words. (See the Teacher-to-Teacher box on p. 60.)

Sound

A wealth of print material is available to help children experience the sounds of language. Stories, patterned stories, rhyming poetry and nursery rhymes, tongue twisters and other alliterative verse, jump rope chants, and lyrics to familiar children's songs are just a few of the wonderful texts to read to and with children. When children have the opportunity to view and track a written version of the story or poem or other text, they will have the added opportunity to experience the written version of the oral language and develop basic print concepts related to reading.

After reading and rereading the text to the children, read it chorally with the children, acting out the text with bodies, hands, or finger. Finding other ways to read and perform the text helps the teacher draw children's attention to specific phonological features of the text. These may include identifying words that rhyme or that have the same beginning consonant sounds, words or sounds that are repeated, words that have one or two beats (syllables), or the way the mouth is posi-

Teacher~to~Teacher

Maria Hernandez has a collection of photographs and paintings on the same or similar subjects. She includes animals, people, houses, mountains, trees, automobiles, and landscapes. Some are very realistic. Others are abstract or give only a faint impression of realism. Some are full color, and others are black and white. Some may be answers to questions in the mind of the viewer; some may seem to ask questions of the viewer.

The pictures are used to stimulate discussion about how each of us views the world in unique ways. According to the way we see things, we respond with words that tell the color, size, shape, and relation of objects or ideas. To communicate impressions, many sense words are required. Maria listens and records words used by the children. The lists go into the Writing/Publishing Center for use during creative writing and into the Game Center as resources for making word games that give practice in sight recognition and spelling.

Color, size, and shape concepts are fruitful in developing figurative language. Many of the words and ideas are so common that new and uncommon ideas can be initiated through comparisons such as these:

◆ As green as new grass

◆ Cardinal red

◆ Small as a tiny ant

◆ An X-shaped design

◆ Pointed like a pyramid

Jeannie Smith provides practice in the concept of size by helping children to arrange objects such as books, rocks, and blocks according to size. Children choose one set of objects and arrange them from the smallest to the largest. As they talk, they gain practice in seeing the size of things in relation to the size of others. Some of her arrangements call for the use of words such as "small," "large," "short," "tall," "long," "wide," and "narrow."

tioned to make particular sounds. Interesting and favorite words can be listed on chart paper to be remembered and read again at other times.

Teacher~to~Teacher

Some songs and poems can be altered by adding or substituting words or sounds in the text. Heather Merillen, a kindergarten teacher, likes to change the nonsense sounds that often find their way into children's song lyrics. For example, the familiar refrain for the song "Camptown Races" went from "doo dah, doo dah" to "boo bah, boo bah" to "loo lah, loo lah" and "goo gah, goo gah" on successive days. Similarly, Heather often takes children's dictation of list poems that have a

sound or taste association. When she asked her class to make a list poem of things they like to eat, all of which had to began with the /b/, the class composed the following poem:

Burgers
Bubble gum
Baloney and cheese.
Bratwurst
Bananas
Give me some please!

Smell

Sensory impressions relating to smell are not as critical in building language meaning for reading as are some of the other senses, but they are a part of life experiences and include a vocabulary that is repeated over and over.

The vocabulary of smell is available in many places and for all children. Flowers and food have odors that may be familiar to many children, but the children may not have words to communicate what they smell.

Teacher-to-Teacher

Gina Guccini includes a vocabulary of smell words in her efforts to introduce children in her second grade to the vocabularies of sensory experiences. She does several things to provide real experiences with smell:

1. Makes a collection of spice cards by brushing glue on cards and sprinkling some spice on them so children can pass the cards around and talk about the odors.

2. Prepares foods, such as applesauce, chile con carne, and gingerbread so children can smell and taste things with and without the spice.

3. Makes available toilet articles, such as toothpaste, cold cream, soap, cologne, perfume, shaving cream, and after-shave lotion for children to smell and name the odors.

4. Dramatizes different smell words with facial expressions.

5. Cooks things such as popcorn that change odor in the process of cooking so children can smell them before and after cooking.

Taste

Sensory impressions from tasting experiences occur daily, but they do not assure the acquisition of a vocabulary of words of taste that might be encountered in reading. These words can be acquired through classroom activities, and through children's literature.

Touch

Our fingers can tell us as much about our surroundings as our eyes do. There is magic in the sense of touch that can release vocabulary useful in responding to sensory impressions throughout life. Vocabulary relating to the sense of touch is found throughout the books and stories children read. Without this vocabulary, students are at a disadvantage in responding to the meanings intended by authors. Teachers may unleash these words by leading children in brainstorming such topics as "What does the fur of our rabbit feel like?" or "What is the difference in the way the skins of an orange and banana feel?"

From InfoTrac College Edition

Four Canadian Kindergarten Teachers' Reports about the Implementation of an Emergent Reading Program, Lise Saint-Laurent and Jocelyne Giasson, *The Elementary School Journal* November 1999 v100 i2 p111

Children's Emergent Literacy (book reviews), Richard Sinatra. *Educational Leadership* May 1995 v52 n8 p86(1)

Read My Story (increasing literacy of preschool children), Marjorie V. Fields and Beth DeGayner, *Childhood Education* Spring 2000 v76 i3 p130

Supporting Early Literacy Development (help young children gain literacy), Rebecca Novick, *Childhood Education* Winter 1999 v76 i2 p70

Children's Literature for Developing Good Readers and Writers in Kindergarten (good book for young readers), Seung-Yoeun Yoo, *Education* Fall 1997 v118 n1 p123(7)

Writing in an Integrated Curriculum: Prekindergarten English Language Learners as Symbol Makers, Celia Genishi, Susan E. Stires, and Donna Yung-Chan, *The Elementary School Journal* March 2001 v101 i4 p 399

From Professional Journals and Publications

Bloodgood, J. R. (1999). What's in a Name? The Role of Name Writing in Children's Literacy Acquisition. *Reading Research Quarterly, 34,* 342–367.

Holdaway, D. (1986). The Structure of Natural Learning as a Basis for Literacy Instruction. In M. R. Sampson (Ed.), *The Pursuit of Literacy.* Dubuque, IA: Kendall/Hunt.

Yopp, H. K., & Yopp, R. H. (2000). Supporting Phonemic Awareness Development in the Classroom. *The Reading Teacher, 54,* 130–143.

Summary

A miracle occurs during the early years of life as children begin to make sense of the world about them. They respond to the love and language of others from birth. They learn language because they have a need to communicate with others.

Writing and reading rapidly become important to children as they seek to extend their knowledge and influence. Total literacy teachers are aware of how children learn before they come to school and incorporate these principles of early learning in the classroom.

Literacy instruction should be centered on the life experiences the children have had and on present experiences that can be used to facilitate literacy growth. The classroom teachers featured in this chapter are good examples of caring, enlightened teachers who demonstrate holistic and natural literacy instruction in their interactions with students. Their classrooms are pictures of the internalization of language arts.

Total Literacy Anchors

- ◆ The student explores books daily.
- ◆ The student explores our alphabetic system.
- ◆ The student writes and draws to communicate thoughts and experiences.

- ◆ The teacher creates an instructional environment that demonstrates and nurtures the relationship between thinking, talking, writing, and reading.
- ◆ The teacher values and extends the home-rooted language students bring to the classroom.
- ◆ The teacher reads aloud daily to students to develop a love of books and enhance language.

CHAPTER 3

Talk AND Literacy Development

As You Read . . .

- ◆ How can teachers demonstrate acceptance of different language patterns?

- ◆ Why is it important for students to have opportunities for oral sharing in the classroom?

- ◆ What is the relation between students' self-concept and the amount of self-expression they demonstrate?

- ◆ Why is dramatization of experiences important in total literacy classrooms?

Author Words

Timothy Rasinski

Oral language is the forgotten language art. Perhaps this is because it is so easy for teachers and researchers to focus on reading and writing and, likewise, so easy to examine the results of writing programs or literature studies. And perhaps it's because children become oral language users so easily.

Oral Language in the Classroom

Do we want to focus on something as specific as oral language? The answer is a resounding "yes." However, in a total literacy classroom we must remember that literacy skills and oral language skills should enjoy a reciprocal relationship. They reinforce each other. Teachers using a total literacy approach do not decide whether reading is more important than speaking or vice versa—they plan for both. They are aware that growth in oral communication is likely to represent growth in reading as well. Research has indicated that the *quality* of oral language production is related significantly to a young child's growth in reading experiences and abilities (Sampson, 1986). Children whose oral language production reflects a high level of mastery of the basic elements of phonological structure, syntactical structure, and morphological structure are the same children who read with minimum instruction. Conversely, children who do not possess a rich language base have difficulty becoming effective readers. The message is clear: We must include time in the curriculum for oral sharing of ideas.

The oral language that children bring to school is a personal possession that, more than anything else, represents *who they are*. To deny the use of natural, home-rooted language is to deny children the right to function as the persons they really are. To degrade this home-rooted language degrades the child. To cast negative reflections on it is to cast negative reflections on the student and the family. Thus we must remember to honor a child's efforts through the language he or she brings to the classroom.

Oral sharing is a process of opening up communication between teacher, students, friends, and classmates. In the process, children reveal interests and aspirations, fears and doubts. At the same time they share influences that come from reading, observing, and imagining, and reflect home-rooted language with attendant strengths and weaknesses. Often children try out new ways of saying things. In this way the process furnishes anecdotal material to the teacher for follow-up instruction and provides evidence of children's growth in the quality of their language.

Oral sharing of ideas is the most basic process in communication available in classroom settings. It may be the most basic language experience in the development of reading and writing abilities. It balances literacy skills with oral language skills, both of which are essential in communication. Many children have immature or divergent speech. One solution is to provide opportunities for language growth through oral sharing. Here are some examples of language challenges and solutions through oral sharing.

CHALLENGE	SOLUTION
1. Some children have unusual pronunciations for words that occur frequently in reading.	Unison reading and choral reading can emphasize phonological structure that is characteristic of reading materials but not characteristic of the oral production of the child. Chants and games that repeat language patterns give practice in pronouncing words. Recording reading and talking on tape provides immediate feedback for evaluation.
2. Some children use syntactical structures that will never be available for replication in reading textbooks.	Sing songs and play games that repeat sentence patterns standard in reading instructional materials. Chat with the child during dictation; offer alternatives rather than corrections. Select sentences to repeat during *reading* to the children. Ask children to read in natural language patterns what they have written and dictated.
3. Some children elaborate with descriptive words that reflect a literacy quality not characteristic of reading instructional materials.	To avoid causing boredom during the acquisition of basic reading skills, add descriptive language to the printed portion of the material—a color word or a size word to each sentence where appropriate, a phrase telling why or where. Make use of the full language power of the learner by substituting orally new nouns and verbs that make meanings more specific or language more creative. Encourage dictation and writing that use the quality of language characteristic of spontaneous expression.
4. Some children are slow in their progress in reading,	Remove the glory of being able to read every word correctly. Reduce emphasis on

yet they are confident in language use.	reading from textbooks with limited examples of sentence patterns. Relate writing more to speech production than to replication of reading books. Introduce poetry patterns, such as those of the haiku and cinquain, to provide opportunities for artful writing with a limited number of words. Read books of literary merit with repeating patterns that can be followed orally and that might serve as models for artful writing. Use dramatic play to keep language power functioning and alive during periods of learning specific skills.
5. Some children pronounce only portions of words that reflect tense and number.	Pronounce word endings that have meaning in language when reading with children. Model the whole word. Make games with root words that have meanings changed by adding sounds represented by *-s, -es, -ing, -ed, -er, -est.* Write dictation on the chalkboard. Erase all endings that have language meanings. Read the passage in unison. Restore the endings and discuss the improved meaning.

2

America's Finest

Jane Moore

Oral Sharing Activities

A total literacy curriculum stresses six major classifications of oral language activities: (1) storytelling, (2) spontaneous expression, (3) poetry, (4) Reader's Theater, (5) Story Theater, and (6) reporting.

Storytelling

Telling and retelling stories are essential oral experiences in a language process approach. When a child is able—from real experience or from imagination—to select characters, a setting, and a plot that contains a climax and an ending, that child has demonstrated the abilities required to comprehend stories written by other authors. Until such abilities are developed, reading is likely to remain word calling. There is no substitute for storytelling in the development of the intellectual base for *reading comprehension.*

We believe we should view children as a tapestry rather than a melting pot. Nowhere is this need more paramount than when we consider the dialects and language patterns of the children in our classrooms.

First, let's define dialect. Dialects are the variety of linguistic speech patterns found in a language population. Dialects vary in terms of pronunciation, grammar, and vocabulary. Dialects may involve both regional varieties, such as the dialect spoken in Maine, and social variety, such as African American vernacular English (Gollnick & Chinn, 1990).

African American vernacular English is spoken primarily by African Americans in poor urban neighborhoods. Teachers should not assume that this dialect is common to all African Americans in these neighborhoods, nor that it is somehow substandard or defective. It is different—but not deficient. African American vernacular English is characterized by a consistent phonological system and grammatical structure different from standard English. Unfortunately, it does not enjoy the prestige of standard English. Once again, what we term *standard* simply means the variety of language in the United States heard on televised national newscasts, used in educational settings, and written in business and national publications; it is generally used by educated speakers and writers, regardless of race.

Dialects and Literacy Learning

Everyone speaks some sort of dialect. We really can't say that regional speech from one section of the country is more standard or acceptable than from another region. Certainly you can "hear" the difference from region to region—you may be able to identify a speaker from the West, New England, the Midwest, or the South. But who is to say which region's speech is superior? The truth lies in the purposes for language—to communicate. Language that communicates is effective language. In a total literacy classroom, our goal is *not* to eradicate children's home-rooted language. Rather, our goal is to add to the language children bring to the classroom, increasing their choice and flexibility in the ways they express themselves.

Understanding, speaking, reading, and writing standard English enhance children's likelihood for success. To score well on standardized tests, make a good impression on a job interview, speak publicly to a multicultural audience, fill out government documents, or travel to other countries often depends on our ability to manipulate standard English. But a key correlate to learning is self-esteem and self-concept, so total literacy teachers realize the importance of honoring language differences in their classrooms even as they share alternatives to word choice and pronunciation.

The telling of stories, real and imaginary, is as important as listening to them. This creative experience develops audience contact that few language activities can do. It encourages voice inflections, sound effects, physical movements, and language embellishments that lend variety to the usual "reporting voice."

Storytelling about experiences develops such language abilities as expressing ideas in thought units, using colorful and descriptive language, developing ideas in sequence, and choosing good action words. All of these are essential communicating abilities of good readers and writers.

Spontaneous Expression

Spontaneous expression is a priceless treasure in any learning situation. It may be the only avenue open in some classrooms for the establishment of rapport that is strong enough to support interaction. Without interaction, it is doubtful that language learning will move forward. The child who is slow to start reading and writing must be made to feel secure in the learning environment. The acceptance of spontaneous expression is a sure way to establish security. Talking in the classroom helps children open up. The fluent child who would probably be bored with preselected reading materials can have free rein of personal language power in spontaneous expression.

Poetry

Poetry is a language genre meant to be expressed through oral interpretation and is a superb vehicle for sharing orally with students (Graves, 1992; Heard, 1989). Through regular sharing of poetry, students learn to love this form of language that

Courtesy of Michael Sampson

Alan Engle shares poetry with his fifth-grade students.

has been called the "neglected genre" of the language arts curriculum (Denman, 1988). Later on students will be more willing and able to express their own thoughts in poetic form. Indeed, the daily sharing of poetry has an affective power that can inspire children to want to read (Durham, 1997). Moreover, through expressive interpretation of poems, teachers model expressive, meaning, and fluent interpretations of text for students, the kinds of expressive interpretations that will foster their own comprehension when reading.

Poetry for children has become so abundant that there is no reason poetry cannot be shared every day of the school year—"a poem for every moment, feeling, and experience" (Durham, 1997, p. 78). There are silly poems, serious poems, funny poems, poems to match moods and feelings, poems to match holidays and times of year, poems to match the weather, poems that connect with different subject areas, and poems that are written in a variety of forms. Here are some of our favorite poets for children:

Arnold Adoff

Brod Bagert

John Ciardi

Nicki Giovanni

Lee Bennett Hopkins

Paul Janeczko

Bruce Lansky

Miriam Cohen Livingston

Eve Merriam

Jeff Moss

Walter Dean Myers

Mary O'Neill

Jack Prelutsky

Shel Silverstein

Judith Viorst

Promoting a love of poetry truly promotes a love of language and a respect for varied ways of interpreting the world. Figure 3.1 lists some collections of poetry that children enjoy.

There are a variety of ways to share poetry in the classroom (Cullinan, Scala, & Schroder, 1995; Dunn 1999; Martin & Sampson, 2002). Teachers' expressive and interpretative reading of poetry is a good start, and this can be expanded to group experiences such as choral reading, echo reading, and antiphonal reading (different groups of children reading different lines). As children become more familiar

Arbuthnot, M., and Root, S. (1968). *Time for Poetry* (3rd ed.). Glenview, IL: Scott, Foresman and Company.

Ashford, A. (1978). *If I Found a Wistful Unicorn*. Atlanta, GA: Peachtree.

Bagert, B. (1995). *Elephant Games and Other Playful Poems to Perform*. Honesdale, PA: Boyds Mills Press.

Bagert, B. (1997). *The Gooch Machine: Poems for Children to Perform*. Honesdale, PA: Boyds Mills Press.

Blishen, E. (1984). *Oxford Book of Poetry for Children*. New York: Peter Bedrick Books.

Booth, D., and Moore, D. (1988). *Poems Please! Sharing Poetry with Children*. Markham, Ontario, Canada: Pembroke Publishers.

Brown, M. (1974). *Margaret Wise Brown's Wonderful Storybook*. New York: Western Publishing Company.

Daniel, M. (1986). *A Child's Treasury of Poems*. New York: Dial Books for Young Readers.

de Regniers, B., Moore, E., White, M., and Carr, J. (1988). *Sing a Song of Popcorn*. New York: Scholastic.

dePaola, T. (1985). *Tomie dePaola's Mother Goose*. New York: G. P. Putnam's Sons.

Fisher, A. (1991). *Always Wondering*. New York: HarperCollins.

Greenfield, E. (1978). *Honey, I Love*. New York: Thomas Y. Crowell.

Hopkins, L. (1987). *Dinosaurs*. San Diego: Harcourt Brace Jovanovich.

Hughes, L., Rampersad, A. (Ed.), and Roessel, D. (Ed.) (1997). *The Collected Poems of Langston Hughes*. New York: Alfred A. Knopf.

Kennedy, D. (1992). *Talking Like the Rain*. Canada: Little, Brown.

Larrick, N. (1983). *When the Dark Comes Dancing: A Bedtime Poetry Book*. New York: Philomel Books.

Lee, D. (1974). *Alligator Pie*. Toronto, Ontario, Canada: Macmillan of Canada.

Martin, B., and Sampson, M. (2002). *Bill Martin's Big Book of Poetry*. New York: North South Books.

Prelutsky, J. (1984). *The New Kid on the Block*. New York: Greenwillow.

Prelutsky, J. (1986). *Ride a Purple Pelican*. New York: Greenwillow.

Silverstein, S. (1974). *Where the Sidewalk Ends*. New York: Harper and Row.

Silverstein, S. (1981). *A Light in the Attic*. New York: HarperCollins.

Silverstein, S. (1996). *Falling Up*. New York: HarperCollins.

FIGURE 3.1
Recommended poetry books

with poetry, some may claim ownership over some of their favorites, practice them, and learn to recite them from memory (Perfect, 1999). Although requiring children to memorize selected poems may not reflect best practice, allowing children to memorize the poems they wish to learn to such a degree of mastery is a wonderful way to help them create personal ownership over the text and the process of interpreting a text—both major aspects of becoming a literate person.

Reader's Theater

Reader's Theater (often spelled *Readers Theatre*) is one of the best ways to introduce students to the dramatic presentation of literature. The work read can be anything from a four-line poem to an adaptation of a novel. The production involves no sets, costumes, or physical actions. The readers simply sit or stand (usually sit) with scripts in their hands and expressively read their parts with minimal gestures and usually even without eye contact. The audience experiences Reader's Theater in very much the same way it would a radio or other audio presentation of a work of literature—the experience comes almost exclusively through the ears.

For younger readers, simple poems may be the best choices for Reader's Theater presentations. Depending on the poem, each line might be assigned to a different reader, or the parts can be divided in many different ways. The lines can be assigned according to any appropriate division: male/female, high-voice/low-voice, loud-voice/soft-voice, solo/chorus, and any other combination the individual poem might suggest.

As the readers become more accustomed to Reader's Theater and their reading capacities increase, they can perform more complex poems and narrative works. As well as performing ready-made adaptations of short stories and plays and works written specifically for group reading, the students themselves can adapt other works of their own choosing and even write their own original Reader's Theater scripts.

In adapting works for Reader's Theater, keep in mind that actions may be expressed in words. Frequently a narrator is used to communicate complex actions, but new dialogue may be written to communicate brief actions expressed in other ways in the original. If the written description in a short story has the characters suddenly in the dark, and one has a flashlight, you could add lines such as "What happened to the lights?" and "Shine that flashlight over here so I can see what I'm doing" to let the audience know what is happening.

The main virtue of Reader's Theater is that it requires audience members to use their own imagination to create the scene, costumes, setting, props, and actions of the work. Stephen, an 8-year-old boy raised on television, illustrates this virtue. He started listening to Saturday morning PBS radio dramas with his father and was immediately hooked. When asked if he preferred the radio or TV shows, he said, "Radio." When asked why, he said simply, "The pictures are better."

Reader's Theater can provide an easy, enjoyable way for all readers to experience the potential power of the written word. Stimulated by both the words read and the vocal expressions of the reader, even students who are reluctant readers come to realize the potential life and excitement the written word can provide. A sampling of Reader's Theater scripts can be found in Appendix D.

Odyssey of the Mind (OM) is an international program that exists as a partnership between schools and parents. The competition includes drama, and these kid-authored scripts use a variation of Reader's Theater that includes simple scenery. An OM script (*Elvis: The Legend*) is shared in this Teacher-to-Teacher feature.

Jonathan and Adrianne had fallen in love with acting as a result of being in Mr. Engle's class. One morning they noticed an announcement on the A. C. Williams Elementary School bulletin board. Odyssey of the Mind (OM) drama teams were forming, and it looked exciting. The children attended a meeting at school that night and joined Mary Beth, Christina, Ryan, and Ashley on a team. Their assignment? Write and perform an eight-minute play about an American legend or an American folktale.

As the children brainstormed about their topic, significant national attention was being

Courtesy of Michael Sampson

Jonathan assumes the role of Elvis Presley.

➤ ➤ ➤

directed at the U.S. Postal Service's decision to issue a commemorative stamp for Elvis Presley. The team became intrigued about the attention the stamp was receiving and decided that Elvis must be an American legend. So they wrote their play with Graceland as the setting and with three children who would have a chance encounter with the "king of rock 'n' roll." Here's the script they developed by applying Mr. Engle's Three Step writing process:

Elvis: The Legend

Cast

Boy:	Ryan
Chrissy:	Mary Beth
Tour Guide:	Adrianne
Girl 2:	Ashley
Girl 3:	Christina
Elvis:	Jonathan

Scene 1: Graceland

TOUR GUIDE: Welcome to Graceland, the home of Elvis Presley. Elvis lives on here. You'll see him through the awards that he won and the hundreds of pictures that document his life. However, the Elvis of today is bigger than life. He's become an American legend, a character as famous as the American folk heroes Paul Bunyan and Johnny Appleseed. True, Elvis is bigger in death than he was in life, but the king of rock and roll left a legacy that changed American culture and music. Just how popular is Elvis? The Elvis stamp was the most popular of all time; five million were printed and sold!

(Walks over, opens a curtain, unveils the stamp. The stamp is the character Elvis, frozen in stillness.)

TOUR GUIDE: More than one million votes were cast for this stamp design; here is the way it looks.

(Pulls cover back over stamp.)

TOUR GUIDE: Let's move on to see more: Elvis's first golden record.

(Tour guide moves on, but two girls and a boy lag behind.)

CHRISSY: I must see that stamp one more time!

GIRL 2: Chrissy, no! We'll get in trouble.

CHRISSY: Come on, what are you, scaaared?

(Girls walk over and pull cover off. Elvis is still in a frozen pose.)

CHRISSY: Oh, he's sooooooooooo cute!

ELVIS: *(Comes alive, and says, in Elvis dialect)* Well, thanks a lot, darlin.

GIRLS: *(SCREAM!!!)*

BOY: Elvis! But you're dead!

ELVIS: Reports of my death are greatly exaggerated.

CHRISSY: How do we know you're really Elvis?

BOY: Yeah, how do we?

ELVIS: Well, this old guitar might be old—but I'll bet it will still play. This should prove that I am who I say I am!

ELVIS: *(Strums and sings, with great soul and movement)*, "You Ain't Nothing But a Hound Dog."

CHRISSY: More, more!

ELVIS: *(Starts singing "Don't Be Cruel.")*

GIRLS: *(Dancing and clapping and going crazy)*

GIRLS: You are Elvis!!!

ELVIS: Yep, I'm still me. But I don't get around as much as the tabloids say I do. There are a lot of people impersonating me. *(Elvis turns to Boy.)* What brings you to Graceland?

BOY: Well, my parents are here on vacation. They made me come! *(Sticks finger in mouth as if gagging himself.)*

CHRISSY: I learned in my history class that you invented rock 'n' roll music and were a great songwriter. I am supposed to write my own song for my music merit badge in Girl Scouts. I thought being here might help me get some ideas.

ELVIS: *(Moves and puts hand on shoulder)* Well, I hope it does, darlin.

BOY: Say, since Elvis is here, why don't you get him to help you?

CHRISSY: Oh, please will you help me? Please, please!

ELVIS: Oh, you don't need my help. You can do it.

CHRISSY: But I'm no songwriter.

ELVIS: I think, therefore, I am.

GIRL 2: What do you mean?

ELVIS: Just what I said, you've got to believe in yourself. What do you want to sing about?

CHRISSY: Oh, about love I guess.

(Elvis strums his guitar as he sings "Love Me Tender." Meanwhile, the girls are really excited. Boy is bored, until the girls start fainting. Boy runs from one girl to the next, catching them as they fall toward the floor. Finally, he starts dancing with one of the girls. When song ends, the girls express their amazement by clapping.)

TOUR GUIDE: *(Reappears from offstage and says in an agitated voice)* Elvis! Now you know you are not supposed to be out. *(She grabs him by the arm and leads him back into the stamp.)*

CHRISSY: Wait, Elvis! But what about my song?

ELVIS: You've got it in you, just do it.

BOY: Like Nike!

TOUR GUIDE: Elvis has left the stage!

(Chrissy picks up the guitar and tries to sing—but halts.)

CHRISSY: At first . . . *(pause)* At first I thought. . . . Oh, there's no hope.

(Voice of Elvis booms from backstage: Just listen to the music inside you and let it out.)

CHRISSY: Hey, wait a minute, that's it. *(The song comes to her and she begins playing and singing.)* At first I thought there was no hope, but then you came along, and at that moment, I knew that I was all wrong. Cause Elvis, you are the one, and Elvis, with you, anything can be done. Cause Elvis, you are the one!

BOY: You sound just like Elvis!　　　　　　　　　　➤ ➤ ➤

GIRL 2: *(Faints.)*

CHRISSY: Yes! Yes! *(Jumps up and down)*

(All of the cast, including Elvis, joins together and holds hands. They sing Chrissy's song together. All take a bow.)

THE END

The children rehearsed for six weeks. During this time, they built a backdrop for the play that depicted a wall at Graceland, complete with a picture of Elvis and two of his gold records. The highlight of the odyssey was an outstanding performance of the script at a regional competition. Oral language development? Yes, indeed. Drama is an excellent activity for language development.

Story Theater

Story Theater encourages students to pull the plot and characters right off the pages of books and bring them to life in the classroom. Stories are more "in the reader than in the book" (Martin, 2001), so Story Theater is a picture of what students are comprehending. Children act out the story while a narrator or narrators are reading it. It may be performed before an audience after practice, but most sessions are impromptu.

Story Theater gives life to a story and enables students to live what they've read. History can come alive with Story Theater. Imagine the difference between reading about slavery and acting out a story that tells about the lives of slaves. Extensions of Story Theater are possible. You might try following a Story Theater performance by asking the class to write a letter home or make a diary entry from the point of view of one of the characters they have just portrayed. The Teacher-to-Teacher feature on p. 77 looks at how a primary teacher makes use of Story Theater in his classroom.

Reporting

What students observe and hear can be recorded, refined, and reported. As student's share via reporting, they must describe their observations to others. Categories of description include color, size, shape, texture, sound, taste, smell, and feeling. The language of contrast and comparison enhances and clarifies meanings. Children may assume different roles when reporting the same experience—from the viewpoint of a scientist, an artist, a teacher, an architect, a musician, or from any other viewpoint possible because of an interest or an experience.

As children mature in reading abilities and interests, much of oral reporting may be related to self-selected and self-assigned reading. Such reporting can be un-

Rick Kilcup, a primary teacher from Bellevue, Washington, makes frequent use of Story Theater. Before children are asked to perform, he gives them practice in a non-threatening atmosphere. By starting out with games and warm-ups that have the whole class "up and doing," and progressing to activities that give small groups a chance to perform before their peers, he builds in students a feeling of confidence about performing. Here are some warm-ups to get you started:

Picking cherries   Have children stretch up high, to the sides, behind them. This gets the blood flowing!

Statues   Give children a statue to become, such as the world's strongest person or a person catching a huge fish.

Rubber band   Tell students that their bodies are rubber bands, and that they stretch them by spreading their hands. Be sure to snap them a time or two, and shoot them too!

Rick finds that the imagination and the ideas of the children carry him quickly beyond these openers. Children rapidly get into the swing of things and join right in.

Rick has discovered that poetry works well for Story Theater too. Paper bag masks add a nice touch to the enactment of this poem written by Rick Kilcup. He adds to the poem by asking students to think of the sounds they can make as they bring the rusty, creaky old robot to life. His children love to act it out.

America's Finest
Richard Kilcup

The Rusty Robot

*There once was a robot, all rusty and stiff, as jerky
    as jerky could be,*
*Who would lurch and glurch and wobble around, it
    was a strange sight to see!*
*It would clank to the right and clunk to the left,
    endangering everyone near.*
*Becoming a nuisance, a bother, a danger, a down-
    right pain in the ear!*
*Oh the noises which came from this rambling wreck
    were enough to make sleeping dogs howl!*
*Those clanks, groans, and squeaks sounded oh so
    absurd like loose nuts and bolts on the prowl!*
*It would rattle about, waving arms in the air, tossing
    wild tin legs to each side.*
*We'd all screech and yell and holler for help, then
    find a good safe place to hide!*
*So time passed as we lived in deep fear of this beast,
    as we ran from its frightening sound.*
*'Til the day that it happened, oh wonderful day,
    when its battery began to wear down!*
*Then it haltered and faltered and jerked to a stop,
    falling down to the ground . . . kerplunk!*
*Now there's peace once again in the old neighborhood,
    Since we threw him out in the junk!*

Reprinted with special permission of Rick Kilcup.

scheduled as well as scheduled. In addition to reporting bare facts from print, children should be expected to add to them by asking these questions:

◆ What else might the author have said if he or she could be here?

◆ What was hinted but not said?

◆ What would I have said or done under the same conditions?

Other topics appropriate for personalizing and illustrating their influence on the reader can be woven into a report.

An important aspect of sharing and reporting is the ability to communicate accurately and with organization that the listener can follow. In the beginning stages, these abilities can be developed and strengthened through questions the teacher might ask: "Did you really see or hear what you reported? Do you think the other children understood your explanation? Did the people in the class listen while you gave your report?" Good reporting can also be stimulated by these exercises:

- Hold brief oral evaluations at the end of the day.
- Summarize what happened in committee work.
- Describe how a construction project was carried out.
- Cooperatively plan the major activities of the day.

Older children begin to learn to organize their ideas and thoughts by outlining or by listing major points of emphasis. They recognize that the purpose of reporting to the class is to supply information needed by the group as a whole, and so they try to give their reports, either oral or written, in a manner both clear and interesting to the audience. Skill in reporting increases as the teacher guides

Author Study

Gloria Houston

1. *Which book of yours has given you the greatest pleasure?*

Mountain Valor. This Civil War book was the greatest joy of my writing career. My editor was satisfied with the book, but I couldn't let go—I just had to keep writing, revising, and playing with the language. I've never enjoyed working with characters so much. In fact, it has a character who is an 80-year-old woman who is no doubt who I'll be and what I'll be like when I reach 80 myself.

2. *Which book has surprised you most in terms of its public reception?*

My Great Aunt Arizona. I thought adults would like this book, but I have been blown away by the response of children—even young primaries. The book traces Arizona's life from her birth through her old age, and I don't think children get much of that. Most children's stories deal with an incident or a day or a few days. *Arizona* gives them the scope of a life. And they seem to have responded to that.

3. *What would you like people to remember about your books?*

First, I want to be remembered for my teaching more than my writing. But as for my writing, I want people to recognize the fact that I respected children and tried to give them rich characters to enjoy.

4. *What impact do you hope your work will have on children?*

I want to provide strong female role models for little girls. I did that for boys also in *Littlejim,* but I especially want to give girls characters they can identify with.

With an ear to the language of the Appalachian Mountains where she grew up, Gloria Houston weaves rich tapestries of language into stories of families, friends, and love. Her books include *My Great Aunt Arizona, The Year of the Perfect Christmas Tree, Mountain Valor, Bright Freedom's Song,* and *Littlejim.*

Reprinted with special permission of Gloria Houston.

the children (1) to recognize and define problems, (2) to gather materials and evaluate their importance according to the problem, and (3) to take brief notes and organize them in a logical sequence for presentation.

Abilities developed through sharing and reporting emphasize the value of individual contributions and the importance of freedom of thought. These experiences characterize the real difference between a society that develops individuals who assume responsibility for contributing to the thought of its citizens, and a society that seeks to teach its youth by rote what governmental or religious officials deem important.

Dramatization

Dramatic play or dramatization is a natural activity of children in the classroom, on the playground, and at home. The classroom version of dramatic play, however, is a far cry from yesterday's school plays. The most noticeable difference is the spontaneity of today's students engaged in creating their own scripts, as we saw earlier in the Elvis Presley play. These students had an idea and cleverly expressed it in script form to dramatize it.

For the majority of students, it is important to express most of their deepest feelings through vicarious experiences. In dramatic play, students consciously pretend they are someone else. They extend their feelings, explore some of their emerging thoughts, seek relief from some of their frustrations, and become animals, people from another planet, persons earning a living, parents, teachers, and other characters who give them an opportunity to experiment with experiences and ideas before an audience.

To express the difference between being generous and selfish, brave and fearful, happy and sad, successful and failing, a child can become a character in a play and show real feelings. One experience in expressing such concepts may lead to confidence in other forms of self-expression and to continued interest in dramatizing an idea. As students play a great variety of roles, new interests are aroused and new problems are faced. These new aspects require the use of more materials and additional information to express clearly the basic ideas or situations. When used as a base for reading, these experiences in drama provide a backdrop for identifying and understanding characters that can never be understood from real-life experiences alone.

Both assertive and shy students benefit from the opportunity to express themselves in dramatic productions. In addition to being an aid to speech production and refinement, realistic dramatic training improves listening, reading, visual, and writing skills. It calls on the same basic mental abilities required for listening with comprehension; it exercises the same skills used for organizing that are gained from silent reading; and it develops fluency and flexibility as an attribute requisite to creative writing. Dramatic experiences can keep learners in touch with language that is full and beautiful during the process of learning specific literacy skills. It can furnish teachers with valuable clues for planning direct instructional activities for the future.

Sociodrama, another creative technique of pretending, is spontaneous dramatic action in which children identify themselves with some personality described in some particular life situation. The acting is called role playing. Sociodramas are not written or memorized because their primary purpose is to open up new levels of awareness of how people feel or behave in a given situation. A simple form of sociodrama is to describe a true-to-life happening, stopping at the climax before the problems are resolved. Students can then choose various roles and create their own feelings about the problem or the situation while pretending to be someone else.

Pretending-to-be requires the use of voice inflections and vocabulary not typical of home-rooted speech. It offers repeated opportunities for children to practice using language they have never used before. It extends oral language experience toward the language found in many reading materials.

As a thinking reader and writer, every student will encounter a great variety of situations in responding to ideas. To have acted a part builds a base of experiences that help make reading and writing into thinking processes. Pretending is basic to literacy.

From their earliest days of listening to reading, students can indicate a level of understanding by simply acting out characters. This ability and interest can be continued and used in total literacy programs to the advantage of students and teachers.

Teacher-to-Teacher

Reggie Dixon reads something of his own choosing to the class almost every day. He uses short selections that he can read with enthusiasm. Then he leads a discussion centered around the main point or the writing style of the author. He demonstrates a feeling of ease and good personal involvement in this activity, which takes from five to seven minutes. He searches for materials well written in African American dialects, in regional dialects, and in language characteristic of ethnic groups represented in the class. Also, he collects recordings of stories and songs illustrating many English dialects from the United States, Australia, Great Britain, Wales, and other places where English is the official language. His goal is to involve every student in discussion, regardless of the quality of the home-rooted language he or she brings into the classroom. Reggie feels he is there to listen, to diagnose, and to offer alternatives. He cannot diagnose apart from hearing natural language.

The Teacher
and Dramatization

The experience of dramatization as well as the dramatization of experience is an integral part of a total literacy classroom. It is important that children participate in activities that enable them to be someone (or something) other than themselves. It is through such experiences in communication that some psychologists believe self is enhanced (Carlton & Moore, 1971). If this theory is true, then teachers must seize the opportunity to create learning environments that permit and promote dramatization. When drama is an integral part of a total literacy program, students have repeated opportunities to become someone else and to discover language unlike their own.

Teachers are wise to keep in mind these five essentials to optimize use of dramatization to promote language growth for reading and writing:

1. *A friendly relationship in which rapport is established between the teacher and the class.* Mutual respect is fostered when the teacher is able to enter into problem-solving situations as a learner. Experiences must be shared, desires must be revealed, ideals must be shared, and stands on moral judgment must be revealed but not offered as the right ones. There is no need for children to enter into personal problem solving when the result is always judged as right or wrong. The process of entering into possible solutions is the goal. In such situations, language production is real and natural. Teachers can gain clues from the performances that will guide them in future encounters, but they cannot gain the privilege of passing final judgment.

2. *An attitude of accepting children's language as it is.* In dramatization there is no need to monitor the correctness of language. A major goal for the teacher is to create opportunities to hear raw natural language coming from a "free spirit." No program of language instruction can be individualized until the chief planner knows individual potential and problems. Such information does not come from pencil-and-paper diagnostic tests or from listening to oral replication of someone else's language through reading. It comes only when the individual is free to be him- or herself or to act as someone else.

3. *An understanding of the essential ingredients through which dramatization functions.* Dramatization, like other art forms, is dependent on contrast and comparison. There can be no drama without contrasts in stillness and motion, silence and sound, and darkness and light. A classroom does not need the equipment of a theater to provide actors with the resources necessary for

a dramatic production. A Dramatization Center does need to have items for producing a variety of sounds not made by human voices. A flashlight or a lantern made of cardboard is all the equipment necessary for a shift from darkness to light when children are acting. Flicking an electric light switch might be enough. Motion is inherent in children's activities, but it may be refined with suggestions and practice in using hands, feet, facial expressions, and body motions to interpret a wide range of feelings.

4. *A willingness to participate in the experience of dramatization.* Children deserve to work *with* the teacher rather than *for* the teacher. Natural situations arise as new techniques and materials are introduced during dramatization. Beyond this, teachers must take character parts when stories are read for dramatization. In many classrooms, it is essential that sometimes the teacher assume the role of a person who speaks with incorrect grammar and with a regional dialect. In some situations, the teacher should be a character whose behavior is intolerable. Children who dramatize other character roles with the teacher come to understand the teacher as another human being.

5. *An awareness of language concepts that can be emphasized and extended through dramatization.* Dramatization objectives include experiencing the joy of being involved with others in human experiences, increasing the understanding of self, becoming self-directed, discovering and selecting values to live by, developing unique human potentialities, developing interest in reading, and developing an appreciation for well-written literature.

The major purpose of dramatization in a total literacy curriculum is to extend language power in a variety of situations. Teachers are not satisfied to listen as one child after another replicates the language of someone else and calls it reading. They are not satisfied to let one child—who raises a hand and begs for a chance to give an answer—answer for the whole class. Teachers in a language-centered curriculum must do several things:

◆ Hear children express themselves orally in an environment of free language use.

◆ Hear each child adjust his or her own language to fit a variety of characters.

◆ Observe expressions of feeling toward known and unknown situations.

◆ Mediate language growth toward the occasional use of literary language.

◆ Orchestrate groups of children into productions reflecting the influence of artist-authors and producers—phrases, sentences, rhymes, songs, and rhythms that fit naturally into spontaneous drama.

Talking and Discussing

The fundamental responsibility of public education is to prepare students for active and worthwhile participation in the democratic way of life. Oral communication is a skill that will contribute to one's ability to earn a living and to participate in the privileges and responsibilities of citizenry.

Conversation brings us more pleasure than dancing, golfing, going to the movies, or eating a favorite dessert. It not only brings pleasure in itself but also keeps alive memories of past pleasures. We would enjoy few activities if we were denied the satisfaction of talking about them. To this end, teachers in a total literacy program have selected some broad oral language goals to be developed:

◆ Experiences to talk about

◆ Enthusiastic participation

◆ Enriched vocabulary

◆ Observe common courtesies in conversation

◆ Connecting oral language with written language

Let's look at each of these goals individually.

Experiences to Talk About

Any classroom with normal children living in our language-rich environment affords many opportunities or topics for discussion. From kindergarten on, children come to realize that ideas for conversation come through listening to other people talk, wide reading, and experiences that school life affords.

Courtesy of Michael Sampson

Fourth-grade students talk about the play they have just seen.

Teachers should use the experiences of children in periods of planned discussion and in periods of free conversation. Children consider all their content subjects as sources of information for conversation and discussion. A field-trip excursion or viewing a DVD for a class in social studies or science usually initiates talk among children, and the teacher takes advantage of such an experience to stress the abilities required for adequate conversation about the subject. In doing this, the teacher has put discussion in its proper place in the curriculum. Assigned topics do not inspire students to talk as much about the things they know and want to share with others as do topics that grow out of everyday school life.

Enthusiastic Participation

Because enthusiasm is usually evidenced by naturalness, children will use their natural language when they are enthusiastic. Thus the goal of enthusiastic participation in oral language can be met in several ways:

- When children whose home-rooted language is characterized by nonstandard speech speak naturally in discussion.
- When children whose first language is a distinct dialect use it in conversation.
- When children whose home language is not English use combinations of two languages when participating.

In classrooms where the children and the teacher live together and love each other enough to speak freely of their deepest feelings, alternative ways of saying things must be accepted. Discussions take place about alternatives in speech rather than about correctness. The teacher does not pose as the one final authority but participates in illustrating one or more ways of saying things.

Significant changes in oral language occur by choice—not by following lessons (Lindfors, 1987). Choice implies alternatives. Through enthusiastic participation in discussions and conversations, alternatives are illustrated in a meaningful way (Miyata, 2001). A look at those that have been useful in the class may be a means of opening up choices for children who need to make significant changes in personal language if they are to enter into the mainstream of education and American life.

Enriched Vocabulary

Our choice of words and the way we use them mark us for what we are. Persons with limited vocabularies find depth of self-expression difficult; those with a broad vocabulary are able to express their feelings and ideas with clarity and power. Teachers do not expect perfection in the use of words that are difficult and strange to children, but they strive to develop strong rapport so children are not afraid to use words they have never used before.

Simplicity and clarity are the keys to better language and are practiced by teachers in what they say and in the books they give children to read. Children are taught the basic principles of semantics rather than a list of meaningless words. They are led to realize that words do not represent things but thoughts. The eyes, ears, and hearts of children become sensitive to the breadth and beauty of language.

Many people are led to believe the large vocabulary is the one full of "big" and unusual words, but children should be encouraged to avoid affectations of speech when there are direct and meaningful ways of communicating. Outlandish phrases, unusual syntax, and vogue words should be evaluated against a backdrop of alternatives. Some children may use them because they lack other means of expressing themselves.

Children with limited vocabularies do not possess the personal language power that permits them to excel in school tasks, especially in tasks of reading language as it is produced in written form. They must have many opportunities to try on a wardrobe of new words in a pleasant, easy environment. The acquisition of language may be a need greater than being able to recognize and analyze a few words from a simple reading text.

Perhaps one of the best ways of developing vocabulary is through literature. Children's literature has been found to be a rich source of wonderful words to explore and use. Indeed, M. R. Sampson (2002) reports that the vocabulary found in trade books for children has a vocabulary load that is more sophisticated than nearly every form of oral speech.

One way to use vocabulary in trade books to build children's speaking vocabulary is simply to ask children to become attentive to the interesting words they hear as they read or are read to by the teacher. Rasinski and Padak (2000) describe a scenario in which teachers ask children to listen for interesting words occasionally as the teacher reads to them. After the read aloud session and the opportunity for children to respond to the story that they had just heard, the teacher asks the children to call out interesting words they may have heard in the story. Nearly any authentic story is a treasure of wonderful words (of course, word choice is one of the criteria for evaluating writing, so it's no wonder we find great words in published children's stories). The words are identified, defined, discussed, and finally listed on the board or chart paper. Then, throughout the next several days, the children (and the teacher) are challenged to use those words in their own speech in the classroom, playground, lunchroom, and at home. When one of the wonderful words is used, the teacher or one of the students brings it to the class's attention. This can be done by ringing a small bell or chime on the teacher's desk. Most children are up to a challenge like this, and before long those wonderful words become a part of their oral (and written) vocabularies.

Older Readers

Presenting Reader's Theater: Plays and Poems to Read Aloud, **by Caroline Feller Bauer.**
Wonderful collection of short plays and poems that are well suited for classroom Reader's Theater.
New York: H. W. Wilson, 2002.

Tales, Then and Now: More Folktales as Literary Fictions for Young Adults, **by Gail de Vos and Anna E. Altmann.**
Contains great ideas for exploring contemporary reworkings of classic folktales and fairy tales that appeal to upper elementary and teen readers.
Englewood, CO: Teachers Idea Press, 2001.

Tales, Rumors, and Gossip: Exploring Contemporary Folk Literature with Young Adults, **by Gail de Vos.**
These stories and urban legends will capture the imagination of your middle school students.
Englewood, CO: Teachers Idea Press, 1996.

Dancing in Cadillac Light, **by Kimberly Willis Holt.**
Great book for dialect study as Holt captures the Texas dialect and keeps it front and center throughout her sassy first-person defense of Grandpap, whom everyone thinks has taken leave of his senses.
New York: Putnam, 2001.

Observing Common Courtesies in Conversation

All students need to come to understand the desirability and importance of observing common courtesies in conversation and discussion. The rude, abrupt, and discourteous person is soon eliminated from a group and left alone, wondering why he or she has no friends. Acquiring the knowledge and ability to practice common courtesies in talking with others is a valuable social skill.

Many desirable abilities and attitudes can be named in connection with this topic; here are some of the most useful skills to learn:

- How and when to interrupt the person talking
- How to disagree with the speaker's statement
- Not to be too demonstrative
- Not to monopolize the conversation
- To avoid unpleasant topics
- Not to whisper in the presence of others
- To include all members of the group in one's remarks
- To express likes and dislikes moderately
- Not to be too personal
- To be considerate of people entering the group after conversation has begun
- Not to hurt the feelings of others
- Not to repeat needlessly
- To greet and to take leave of a host graciously

Keep in mind that children from different cultures may have different ways of expressing common courtesies, as Laura Howard discovered. You can learn more about her experience in the Teacher-to-Teacher feature.

Teacher-to-Teacher

Laura Howard was teaching a group of preschool Native American children in Arizona. She realized that she was not hearing words of courtesy such as *thank you, please,* and *excuse me.* Even with urging, her efforts seemed fruitless. She felt the children should learn to use these words before they began their more formal school program, so she enlisted the help of her Native American aide, a college student who spoke the tribe's language. Lucia, the aide, confided that there are no words to say "thank you" in the Indian language. "We say it with our eyes," she explained.

Immediately Laura realized she had been receiving gestures of gratitude every time a child's eyes sparkled at the pleasure of new toys, the attractive classroom, and the good food. She knew she was participating in a culture that extended courtesies in ways different from her own. She wanted to preserve their culture while at the same time introducing courtesies from her own culture that

Hugo Santana — Name

ten — Age

Soccer
Reading — Interests
ride My Bike

What do you like most about school?

What I like about school is learning and reading, Math and technology.

What's your favorite subject? Why?

My favorite subject is technology because when you need research you get to use the computer.

What's your favorite book? Why do you like it?

My favorite book is My Teacher is an Alien, and I like it because it would be cool to have a teacher as an Alien.

What advice do you have for teachers?

My advice for a teacher is that they need to make things more challenging

would be new to the children. She became gracious and loving when the children said thank-you with their eyes. She imitated them and learned the pleasure of their gestures. She shared her way too, because she knew that as the children grew older they would need to use the expressions of both cultures. She built for herself a basic generalization out of the experience: There is no one right way to communicate common courtesies.

Connecting Oral Language to Written Language

Creating a bridge from oral language to written language is one of the best ways to introduce children to reading and writing. We recommend the Language Experience Approach (LEA) for constructing this bridge. In LEA children have a common experience—perhaps an exploration of stone and rocks in the school yard—talk about the experience in a group setting, and finally dictate a brief account of their experience to the teacher who then writes the children's language on chart paper. This written text becomes the material for reading and writing instruction. Comprehension is already assured as the text is simply an account of an experience of the authors. The students own the text and thus are more likely to want to learn to read it. Done on a regular basis, LEA is a viable and effective way for children to emerge into literacy—writing and reading words in print. Roach Van Allen (1999) captures the LEA process in this sequence of logical progression of ideas:

- ◆ What I can think about, I can talk about.
- ◆ What I can say, I can write (or someone can write for me).
- ◆ What I can write, I can read.
- ◆ I can read what others write for me to read. (p. 41)

LEA is a tangible way for helping students see that talk is a reflection of experience and thought, writing is a reflection of our talk, and reading is a way to unlock writing and discover the thoughts and experiences of the author. The experiences and conversations children have every day provide wonderful fodder for turning oral language growth into the genesis of reading and writing.

FURTHER WORDS

 From InfoTrac College Edition

The Role of the Speech-Language Pathologist in Facilitating Emergent Literacy Skills (brief article), Barbara J. Ehren, *ASHA Leader* February 15, 2000 v5 i3 p28

Scaffolding Oral Language Development through Poetry for Students Learning English, Nancy L. Hadaway, Sylvia M. Vardell, and Terrell A. Young, *The Reading Teacher* May 2001 v54 i8 p796

Oral Language and the Black Dialect Speaker. (What's New In . . .) (brief article), Jesse Perry, *The Clearing House* November–December 2001 v75 i2 p60(2)

Oral Language and Literacy Learning in Context: The Role of Social Relationships, A. D. Pellegrini, Lee Galda, Maria Bartini, and David Charak, *Merrill-Palmer Quarterly* January 1998 v44 i1 p38

From Professional Journals and Publications

Apol, L., & Harris, J. (1999). Joyful Noises: Creating Poems for Voices and Ears. *Language Arts, 76,* 314–322.

Gold, D. (1997). Ashley Bryan's World. *American Visions,* 12, 31.

Rowe, D. W. (1998). The Literate Potentials of Book-Related Dramatic Play. *Reading Research Quarterly, 33,* 10–35.

Summary

In this chapter we examined classroom activities that engage students in self-expression through many media. The language children bring to school is a reflection of the language used in their home and community. Total literacy programs can expand children's language by engaging students in meaningful activities that involve speaking and listening. These activities offer students meaningful experiences with rich and beautiful language during the process of learning specific literacy skills.

Total Literacy Anchors

ORAL LANGUAGE TECHNIQUES

- ◆ The student grows in ability to pronounce commonly used words correctly.
- ◆ The student tries to speak clearly and distinctly so others will hear and understand.
- ◆ The student extends and refines vocabulary.
- ◆ The student relates events in proper sequence.
- ◆ The student uses voice effectively to portray the story.
- ◆ The student selects stories appropriate for the audience.
- ◆ The student develops an easy, natural way for telling a story.
- ◆ The student develops skill in interpreting the mood and character of a story.

SHARING AND REPORTING

- ◆ The student shares ideas and experiences with the class and others.
- ◆ The student presents simple reports to class on observations, trips, reading, and other experiences.
- ◆ The student strives for accuracy in reporting.
- ◆ The student shows increasing skill in making announcements and explanations.
- ◆ The student increases skill in organizing and summarizing ideas to report.
- ◆ The student selects interesting and worthwhile material to report.
- ◆ The student uses notes and simple outlines for oral presentations.
- ◆ The student uses appropriate illustrative material to convey ideas more effectively.
- ◆ The student cultivates clarity of speech, pleasing voice, and good posture.
- ◆ The student realizes the need for presenting accurate information, giving sources.

DRAMATIC PLAY

- ◆ The student participates freely and willingly in dramatic play.
- ◆ The student is spontaneous and natural in oral expression.

- The student uses language appropriate to the character being portrayed.
- The student uses hands, feet, facial expressions, and body to interpret characters.
- The student uses conversation with another person to further the action of the play.

DRAMATIZATION AND READING

- The student shares favorite poems and stories by acting them out.
- The student shows originality in the interpretation of stories, poems, music, and dramatization.
- The student helps to plan and participate in class TV and radio programs.
- The student uses incidents in stories for dramatization.
- The student plans and participates in puppet shows.
- The student creates original plays with plot, characters, and setting.
- The student repeats words and phrases of characters in stories when dramatizing them.

CONVERSATION

- The student talks informally and easily with classmates, teachers, and other adults.
- The student increases skill in choosing interesting topics of conversation.
- The student develops confidence in asking and answering questions and in replying to remarks of teachers and others.
- The student develops understanding of some of the qualities of a good conversationalist.

DISCUSSION

- The student participates willingly in planned discussions to learn from others as well as to make contributions.
- The student takes turns in discussions.
- The student increases skill in participating in group discussions.
- The student practices social courtesies when participating in discussions.
- The student is not overly sensitive to criticism.
- The student reacts thoughtfully to the ideas of others.

LANGUAGE COURTESIES

- The student practices desirable social courtesies as a speaker and as a listener.
- The student develops sensitivity to others.
- The student makes introductions properly and graciously and responds to introductions in a similar manner.

CHAPTER 4

Listening AND Literacy Development

As You Read . . .

◆ Why is it important for students to be good listeners?

◆ How are listening and literacy development related?

◆ How can listening abilities be cultivated in instructional settings?

◆ What is the importance of reading aloud to students?

◆ How can storytelling influence language growth and listening abilities?

Author Words

Timothy Rasinski

Listening is perhaps the most important language art because both oral language and written language have their foundation in the things we hear. In an aesthetic sense, hearing brings us great pleasure as we listen to musical compositions and concerts. In an efferent sense, we listen for information that will help us cope with life, such as directions to a restaurant. But is there too much to hear? Do we simply "tune out" much of what we hear? We certainly are immersed in a sea of sound. Moffett and Wagner (1983) hypothesized that "the perpetual sound issuing from electronic media and urban bustle numb many children to the point of simply tuning out sound" (p. 79). That means it is more important than ever for schools to provide students with specific training in the skills of listening. But should listening be directly taught through efferent modes? Yes, sometimes. But there is little doubt that the most effective way to move children to listen is to captivate students through aesthetic listening experiences and then move to efferent information (Martin, 2001). We'll discuss efferent and aesthetic considerations further in Chapter 5.

A Good Listener

So much of what we learn from our environment, in school and out, comes from listening. Lundsteen (1976) provides a vivid metaphor that emphasizes how heavily biased toward listening our verbal intake and output are. She writes, "It might be said that we listen to a book a day; speak a book a week; read a book a month; and write a book a year" (p. 75).

Listening expertise is important in the classroom. In 1928, Paul Rankin conducted a study and determined that 68 percent of the typical school day was spent in experiences classified as "communication." An analysis of these experiences revealed that 45 percent of the time was spent listening, 30 percent speaking, 16 percent reading, and 9 percent writing. Studies conducted by modern day researchers have confirmed similar breakdowns of classroom activity (Chaney & Burk, 1998; Hunsaker, 1989).

Most of us think listening is something we do automatically—it needs no training. Unfortunately, this is not so. Even though most adults acquire around 80 percent of what they know through listening, they have listening efficiency levels of approximately 25 percent (Hunsaker, 1990). Listening is a participation skill and can best be learned in group and collaborative activities (Brent & Anderson, 1993; Galda, Cullinan, & Strickland, 1993). To expect children to listen effectively just because instructions are clearly given is to expect the impossible for many of

Children listen attentively to a student "TV broadcast."

Young Readers

Books that focus on sounds and listening.

***Listen Buddy*, by Helen Lester.**
Buddy rabbit is always daydreaming rather than paying attention, which results in hilarious disastrous situations that lead him to realize the value of listening.
New York: Scott Foresman, 1997.

***The Other Way to Listen*, by Byrd Baylor.**
Shares the joys of slowing down and listening to the natural world around us.
New York: Scribners, 1978.

***The Listening Walk*, by Paul Showers.**
A young girl takes a "listening walk" with her father and dog and discovers a wealth of "ordinary" sounds.
New York: HarperCollins, 1991.

***Listen to the City*, by Rachel Isadora.**
A listening celebration of New York City with speech bubbles and onomatopoetic words.
New York: Putnam, 2000.

***Sounds All Around*, by Wendy Pfeffer.**
Find out how people and animals use different sounds to communicate.
New York: HarperCollins (paperback edition), 1999.

***Voices in the Park*, by Anthony Browne.**
An afternoon visit to the park by two different families reveals that "listening" is more than just hearing what is said—it involves visual cues.
New York: DK Publishing, 1998.

them. In expanding on work by Carol Chomsky (1969), Patricia Van Metre (1972) found that both bilingual and monolingual children who were poor readers at the end of third grade were confused consistently when listening to syntactic structures that included *ask/tell* constructions, *promise/tell* constructions, *easy-to-see/hard-to-see* constructions, and many constructions that include pronouns.

Teachers use these kinds of constructions all the time. Many children who have been in school for three and four years, however, have not mastered their meanings so they can function with information gained through listening. Listening to language is more than listening to words. Pitch, tone, and volume are added to the syntactic characteristics of language during discussions and conversations. Children who have not been exposed to a wide range of speech will be lost when looking at cold silent print that must be brought back to life through the reading process.

Factors Affecting Listening and Learning

Many factors affect listening, especially listening abilities that relate to classroom settings. These factors are best addressed within a total literacy program that supports the development of a positive classroom community. Using language in socially meaningful interactions within a supportive environment has a positive effect on children's cognitive and emotional development (Vygotsky, 1978, 1981, 1986). Vygotsky (1981) states, "Social relationships or relationships among people genetically underlie all high functions and their relationships" (p. 163). This sense of community is important to encourage students to engage in communication that enhances listening skills such as discussing books they are reading or soliciting feedback about their writing (Webb & Palinscar, 1996; Zebroski, 1994). Mutual trust is promoted as the teacher is an active member of the classroom community and participates in reading, expressing opinions, and writing on topics along with the students. In addition, the teacher must be aware of the impact of the physical environment, emotional factors, physical factors, language development, preformed opinions, and students with high intelligence.

Physical Environment

Remember the model classrooms of Methven, Wrightman, and Engle described in Chapter 1? All of these classrooms shared a common element—seating and furniture arrangement was flexible, which made shifts possible to facilitate face-to-face contact between speakers and listeners in large group and small group discussions. The environment also afforded opportunities for external listening opportunities, or hearing the language of individuals outside the classroom, through CD-ROMs, QuickTime video, DVDs, Internet links, two-way interactive video, cassette tapes, videos, radio, and television.

Psychological Environment

As important as the physical arrangement is, the psychological arrangement is more important. The classroom must be a home—a safe haven for the students where new language or ways of saying things can be tried and heard by others.

Flexible grouping is used for literacy experiences. The classroom community and listening opportunities are enhanced as children have opportunities for whole class, small group, and individual activities. The small group composition changes based on the focus of the group, such as a theme, topic, or book.

Divergent thinking is encouraged to promote risk-taking and participation. Alternatives replace correctness as goals during discussions for problem solving and critical thinking.

Emotional Factors

Students need to feel secure when they share; they need to know that their thoughts will not be ridiculed or criticized. Thus listeners must be considerate of others and not interrupt when other students are sharing.

Listening also includes hearing your inner voice. A quiet place is provided in the learning environment to allow children to retreat into private thoughts with no questions asked. Daydreaming provides a time when a thought might emerge that can be captured for a poem or a story.

Physical Factors

Who likes to sit forever like a statue and listen to others talk? Teachers don't—nor do students. Opportunity for movement among centers or learning areas enhances the potential for success for children who find it difficult to sit and listen for extended periods of time. Teachers should be aware of the physical needs of students and provide frequent opportunities for movement (Witt, 2002).

Hearing loss or limited attention span may be confused with lack of ability unless listening experiences are used as clues. Thus teachers should be aware of the possibility of hearing loss in students who appear disinterested in engaging in classroom activities. The school nurse can make referrals for hearing tests.

A Good Day for Listening, **by Mary Ellen King.**
The story of two brothers, Theodore and Benjamin: one is too busy to listen—the other one listens and reaps many benefits.
Ridgefield, CT: Morehouse, 1997.

The Jazz Fly, **by Matthew Gollub.**
Shares how the Jazz Fly incorporates the animal sounds he has encountered during the day in his band's performance and receives an enthusiastic response from the audience. Book comes with a CD.
Santa Rosa, CA: Tortuga, 2000.

Older Readers

Books for the teacher to read aloud to the entire class

A Blue-Eyed Daisy, **by Cynthia Rylant.**
A young girl from the hills of West Virginia comes to terms with life, dealing with the drinking habits of her father and her first romance.
New York: Simon & Schuster, 1985.

Chocolate Fever, **by Robert K. Smith.**
Henry Green discovers that you can get too much of a good thing. This classic book delivers a firm message for moderation of all things good.
New York: Dell, 1978.

Joey Pigza Loses Control, **by Jack Gantos.**
Joey spends the summer with his estranged father and has to decide whether living with his dad is worth giving up his hard-won battle over his attention deficit disorder.
New York: Harper, 2002.

**CLASSROOM
LITERATURE
CONNECTIONS**
CONTINUED

A Single Shard, **by Linda Sue Park.**
This Newbery Medal winner is set in twelfth-century Korea. The story follows Tree Ear's transformation from apprentice to artist and demonstrates his perseverance. During his pilgrimage to Songdo, robbers shatter the art and he has only a single shard to show.
New York: Clarion, 2001.

Language Development

Language-minority children often find listening challenging if English is the dominant language in the classroom. In addition, children who lack experiences with books or topics addressed in the classroom may become frustrated during listening activities. These children must have multiple opportunities for supportive experiences with both listening and speaking to enhance listening and to permit reading skills to develop. Impaired speech that prohibits the reproduction of sounds selected for instruction can be a limiting factor in listening to the language of others.

Preformed Opinions

Students who hear what they want to hear rather than what was actually said behave quite differently in listening and reading situations from children who are open to new ideas. Teachers should not be surprised that students hold strong opinions that have been shaped by their family. However, inability to integrate new ideas into previous opinions and decisions limits listening and comprehension

Diverse Learners

Children Who Communicate via Sign Language

When Jessica was only an infant, her parents became concerned about her hearing. They took her to an audiologist, and testing revealed that Jessica had a profound hearing loss. As a result, she was having difficulty learning language because her hearing was so poor. Only minimum help was available to her through hearing aids. When she entered school, she was placed at a disadvantage because verbal communication is the most frequently used medium to disseminate information.

Fortunately, Jessica attended a school that had programs in place to reach diverse learners like her. Computer programs and telecommunication devices were used, and Jessica's intelligence was respected. Her teachers found ways to accentuate Jessica's strengths. She was an excellent artist and was the first choice by fellow students in her classroom to illustrate their manuscripts.

She quickly learned sign language, and her classmates learned sign language too. They wanted to communicate with her. The librarian provided books about sign language, including *Amelia Lends a Hand* by Marissa Moss (2002). The book included eight pages of perforated sign language cards that the kids immediately began to use. This was very meaningful to Jessica because it demonstrated the acceptance her classmates and teachers had toward her. However, fluency was a problem because the signing skills of her classmates were poorly developed.

Jessica's sign language teacher believed auditorally impaired children need to spend time together, and she worked hard to facilitate opportunities for these children to sign with one another. An entire culture developed among the children, giving them a peer group through which they could laugh, play, and learn together.

abilities. Students will become more open to the ideas and opinions of others when classrooms provide ample time for discussion and listening to the ideas of others.

High Intelligence

Boredom caused by uniform expectations from teachers and by materials that repeat the same content year after year can create serious listening problems in children of high intelligence. Requiring children of high intelligence to read and listen to reading in "round-robin" ability groups promotes regressive tendencies in attitude and school performance (Opitz & Rasinski, 1999). Environments with diverse learning opportunities accommodate high intelligence in a natural and normal way.

These environmental and experiential factors require the teacher's thoughtful attention. Effective teachers who develop supportive learning communities have classrooms where one finds instructional components such as flexible arrangements, continuous change of groups, diversified materials, and individualized instruction for specific skills and abilities. A wide variety of experiences is required for the multiplicity of abilities in listening and reading. Particular activities planned for one group or for one individual can stimulate interest in others. Experiences planned for one child may extend to others who may not have appeared to be ready for them. Each child's needs, when dealt with honestly and with trust, can positively affect the other children as they all set their own personal goals for improving their abilities in listening.

Kinds of Listening

Listening is not just one element. Listening is a transactive process that involves many facets, including receiving, focusing, attending, discriminating, assigning meaning, monitoring, and remembering (Lundsteen, 1989). Our goal is to develop empathetic listening—listening with the intent to understand (Covey, 1990; Walker & Brokaw, 1998). The teacher must be aware of many kinds of listening if children's abilities are to mature to the level of empathetic listening. Here are some of the types of listening that may be observed and included in classroom instruction:

Simple Listening   Hearing sounds without interpreting any particular meaning of the sound: for example, a car going by, the ring of the telephone, birds singing, water running, or wind blowing.

Discriminative Listening   Listening to hear and identify the likenesses and differences in sounds: for example, high–low sounds on a musical scale, soft–loud sounds at the same pitch, long–short sounds of the same tone, words that have the same beginning sound, words that have rhyming endings, words that have the same sound in internal syllables, and words that are the same.

Interpretive Listening   This includes interpreting character's feelings, drawing conclusions, and making inferences.

Listening for Information   This includes repeating words that tell the names of things when listening to reading, repeating facts heard when listening to stories, understanding oral directives well enough to carry them out independently, and recalling incidents from hearing discussions and from listening to reading.

Listening to Organize Ideas   These skills include the ability to hear and repeat happenings in the order they were heard, the ability to summarize several points in a discussion, and the ability to arrange points from several discussions into a new organization.

Listening for Main Ideas   This involves understanding the important point of a story or discussion and discriminating between major points and illustrations to support and elaborate the points.

Author Study

Lynne Cherry

1. *Which book of yours has given you the greatest pleasure?*
The Great Kapok Tree and *The Armadillo from Amarillo*. They are very different books, but I really loved doing them both. *Kapok* was such an easy book to write—I wrote it on the train going from Washington, D.C., to Connecticut. And I had such fun researching *Armadillo* because I had to spend so much time in Texas, which, I discovered, is a really beautiful state.

2. *Which book has surprised you most in terms of its public reception?*
A River Ran Wild. I had thought this book about the Nashua River would be of limited geographical interest. But people discovered that it tells the story of many rivers. Life really does imitate art—people who read the book started cleaning up the rivers in the places where they lived. It was really very gratifying to me to see this happening.

3. *What would you like people to remember about your work?*
I want people to remember the underlying reason for my books having been written at all—as motivators for children to get involved in cleaning up the environment where they live.

4. *What impact do you hope your work will have on children?*
I want children to realize that they have the ability to change the world around them.

Lynne Cherry's knowledge of and love for nature are evident in her beautifully detailed illustrations. Her books include *The Great Kapok Tree, Who's Sick Today?, A River Ran Wild, The Armadillo from Amarillo, Snail's Spell, The Shaman's Apprentice, The Life of a Wood Thrush,* and *When I'm Sleepy.*

Reprinted with special permission of Lynne Cherry.

2
America's Finest
Kay Williams

Listening for Varied Points of View To do this effectively, children must develop a sensitivity to the language of agreement and disagreement, interpret tones of voice that express controversy, sarcasm, irritation, reasonableness, and perplexity, and watch for basic differences in ideas when listening to discussions.

Critical Listening This includes listening to analyze the purpose of the one speaking by recognizing bias, exaggerated statements, and false connotations, listening for conflicting ideas by the same speaker, evaluating materials, and being aware of propaganda techniques, half-truths, and name-calling.

Creative Listening In this kind of listening, children must learn to visualize characters, settings, moods, and situations while listening, sketch images received through the ear on paper as the teacher reads, evaluate information presented in an oral format such as stories, informational texts, films, tapes, and DVDs in terms of personal feelings, relate ideas heard in various venues such as in political speeches and plays, and incorporate several ideas heard on various occasions into a new whole.

Listening involves processing and interpreting information; read the Teacher-to-Teacher feature to see how one teacher helps her students realize that the same words may have multiple meanings.

Teacher-to-Teacher

Judith Edgar watches for words, phrases, and sentences that undergo obvious changes of meaning when the pitch, tone, inflection, or volume of voice is changed. She will say something and then ask the children to interpret it in many ways. She writes some responses on the chalkboard to highlight changed emphasis and meaning.

Mother is here.

Mother is here?

MOTHER is here!

Mother is here!

Mother is HERE!

Do you think I'll believe that?

Do YOU think I'll believe that?

Do YOU THINK I'LL BELIEVE that?

Do you think I'LL believe that?

Do you think I'll believe THAT?

As Judith works with discussion groups, she helps them develop sensitivity to the language along with the ability to grasp simple meanings.

Other kinds of listening may be more available out of school than in school. Listening for relaxation and enjoyment can be a part of school programs and should be encouraged by suggestions for listening to various media as a homework experience. Multimedia such as audiotapes, videotapes, CD-ROM, DVD, and film provide venues for listening (and sometimes viewing) multiple types of communication. Experiencing various types of multimedia frequently lead students to broaden their listening interests and abilities. Teachers often use high-quality videos, CD-ROMs, or cassette tapes of children's books to enrich a literature study. Various multimedia can be used effectively to extend information concerning a particular content area or focus unit. Some teachers occasionally include assignments such as viewing particular television programs or videotapes for a particular purpose—or pure pleasure. Such assignments give children a set time for listening to various media other than the recreational time they or their family normally chooses. In the Teacher-to-Teacher feature, Paula Witt illustrates one way to creatively use videotapes.

Teacher-to-Teacher

Paula Witt is a Pre-K teacher who knows the power of using media to touch the lives of her students. Prior to the beginning of school, Paula has her son videotape her in her classroom. First she introduces herself and then gives an enthusiastic and welcoming tour of the room as she shares the sequence of a day in Pre-K. She includes information that addresses various aspects of the Pre-K day, including what the children will do and where they will go when they arrive. She tells them where they will gather and provides a sample lesson for large group experiences; she introduces each center, tells where it is located, and what the children will have the opportunity to do if they choose that center. The tape concludes with Paula sitting surrounded by books in the Reading Tub, a old-fashioned bathtub with legs, cushioned with colorful pillows, welcoming each child to join her for a year of excitement with books and learning. She also discusses the importance of the home and recognizes parents as their child's first teacher and asks to form a partnership with them. She notes that this partnership is important for their child to have the most successful and positive year possible, and she stresses the importance of parents sharing books with their children. She closes by extending an open invitation to her classroom and reading a favorite book.

Paula makes multiple copies of the video so that she has one for each child in her classroom. She distributes a copy to each family that attends "Meet the Teacher Night" held prior to the beginning of school and asks them to watch it with their child before the first day of school. She asks them to send it back to school with their child on the first day. Paula then makes a home visit to any families that did not attend "Meet the Teacher Night" and leaves a tape with the same request.

On the first day of school, the students arrive knowing what to expect. They view the video again at the beginning of the day as a whole class and talk about what they are looking forward to doing and what they have questions about. At the conclusion of the day, they again view the video and talk about what they have done, what they enjoyed, what they learned, what they have questions about—and what they are looking forward to tomorrow.

Paula notes that since she has started using the videotape as a listening/viewing experience prior to the first day of school, the first day experiences of her Pre-K students have been much more positive. "The students come to school with a concept of what to expect—the video has provided both the language and visual representation of the day. When I discuss centers, they are familiar with them—and most of the students have made decisions concerning what they want to do. Terms such as 'circle time' have meaning for them. I even hear parents referring to various centers or items in the room when they drop children off. And best of all—since I have started using the videos, I have not had any children crying on that first day!"

She adds that she has always had a 100 percent return rate on the videos and that some families ask to check them out again on holidays to show family members what their child's classroom is like. She has only had one family who did not have a VCR in the home, and that family had a "block party" and viewed the video with friends.

Paula's use of the videotape to provide information about the "school experience" employs a mode of communication families and children are comfortable with. Through listening, viewing, and discussion, the children's knowledge and comfort level are enhanced. They come to school with access to some of the school "vocabulary" and positive expectations concerning the day.

Propaganda and Listening

We live in an information age. Advertisements are everywhere—from the blimps floating above the Super Bowl to the banners that pop up as we browse Web pages. Many "pitches" come to consumers through the ear—such as radio and TV ads and telephone solicitations. Students must develop a critical ear and come to understand propaganda techniques for what they are. Here's how one teacher deals with the issues.

Teacher-to-Teacher

Juan Artiz wants his fourth-grade students to grow in their ability to listen critically. He believes one way to assist them in developing critical listening skills is to provide them with opportunities to recognize propaganda. First, he shares the following propaganda techniques:

Bandwagon   Relies on the concept that to be "part of the group" one must buy what "everyone else is" or do what "everyone else is doing."

Blatant Generality   General terms such as "justice," "brightest," "newest," "best buy," or "ground-breaking" are used in a complimentary way to invoke a positive emotional response.

Name-Calling   Use general terms such as "cheater," "unscrupulous," or "expensive" in a derogatory fashion to cause a negative emotional response.

Testimonial   People who are well known and respected discuss the reasons they are supporting an idea or product.

Card-Stacking   Positive facts or attributes of a person, product, or idea are shared. Negative aspects are not mentioned.

➤ ➤ ➤

Join the Elite   The speaker assures listeners that they "deserve" to participate in or buy whatever is being publicized. Flattery is used to assure members of the audience that they have the necessary qualities such as intelligence, money, or good judgment to join the elite group of individuals who enjoy the product/idea.

Rewards   The promise of "free" rewards such as toys in cereal or rebates for purchasing a product. This technique is also sometimes used by political candidates, who promise "rewards" if they are elected, such as "better education for all" or "increased economic opportunity," yet neglect to explain how the programs will be funded.

Then Juan shares television commercials he has videotaped with his students. He first allows the students to experience the video solely by listening in order to identify any propaganda techniques they hear the speakers utilizing. After the students have had an opportunity to list and discuss the propaganda techniques they heard, they have the opportunity to both hear and see the same videotape. Students then determine whether the addition of the visual message to the auditory message causes them to confirm, reject, or extend their original identifications of propaganda use. Students have the opportunity to discuss their individual decisions concerning the propaganda techniques used and to share why they made individual decisions. Students often ask for the audio portion of the tape to be replayed as disagreement occurs concerning what was said. Through this experience, Juan's students begin to realize how easy it is to hear only a portion of the message and that people often hear the same statements in different ways and internalize different meanings.

Developing Listening Abilities

Listening is a major aspect of communication and, as such, is an ability that should be cultivated in an instructional setting. Listening requires that the sound signals be produced by someone other than the listener, but effective listening is more than a simple intake aspect of communication. Effective listening is an ability close to that of comprehending text. In both, one must internalize the message in a way that is personally meaningful. The chief difference is that when "listening" to the language of others during silent reading the listener must have enough ego strength to "hear without sound." Subvocalization may take place and be helpful in some cases, but the transfer from listening to the sound of language to silent reading is a development in communication that requires many literary transactions.

Listening is an active skill that can best be learned in situations in which every student has opportunities for class participation. Participation is a more challenging experience than merely being quiet while someone else talks: for example, the teacher giving directions. Throughout the day, the teacher can use group discussions as a means of planning, problem solving, arriving at decisions, and evaluating group and individual enterprises. Each student must thoughtfully listen to the other students in order to share ideas and effectively cooperate in achieving the goal of the discussion. A meeting of minds is difficult to achieve on a mature level, and children need many opportunities to sense the satisfaction that comes when they make an honest effort to interact with others. This interactive ability is basic to silent reading and must be developed to the point that the reader is communicating with the author.

Here are some practices total literacy teachers use to provide opportunities to enhance the listening abilities of their students:

1. Ensure that children have opportunities to respond to plans and instructions in meaningful ways. Work toward independence rather than dependence on assignments.

2. Use a portion of each school day for interactive planning. Help students discuss the outcomes of plans formulated in group discussions.

3. Read with students each day on an individual or small group basis. Help them hear how the story goes by taking turns with you in reading orally. Participate in terms of the needs of students. Struggling readers benefit when they listen to models of fluent reading while they are learning how to recognize printed language. Those who struggle to recognize words seldom "hear" what the author has to say.

4. Read to students and let them participate from time to time by telling what they think the author would add if she or he were with them. Help them understand in this way that the printed part is an imperfect representation of what the author had to say. Provide opportunities for them to "think" with an author. Help them recognize that exact oral verbalization of the printed words is not the primary measure of good reading.

5. Listen to music selections without lyrics. View DVDs or films without words. Discuss the ideas and feelings students get during these experiences. Follow up with discussions of what the children heard and saw when no words were spoken. Relate this type of experience to one of silent reading when the reader has communication clues other than sounds of words as the major resource.

Listening and Reading Instruction

The experience of most parents and teachers attests to the value of reading to children. The expanding market for children's literature reflects the concern of parents that children need exposure to language and ideas that are not indigenous to the family and community where the child lives. Research has documented that children who are read to in the home typically are more successful in school than those who have not had read-aloud experiences (Durkin, 1996; Teale, 1984; Wells, 1986). Interest in television programs designed specifically to engage children in language acquisition has highlighted a need for rich listening and viewing experiences prior to and during the time when children are discovering the relationship of oral language to print.

Modeling reading with "read-along" and "echo" techniques has been employed by most adults when they read to young children for years. In recent years, research has validated such practices. Trelease (1995) reports that both language and vocabulary skills are significantly improved when children listen to good books being read. Listening to and reading the language of others is inseparable in effective classrooms. Both experience and research relating listening to language with success in reading suggests that when we improve certain specific skills in listening those same skills improve in reading (Sampson, Briggs, & Coker, 1984). Conversely, research indicates that when children are exposed to material that is not of high literary quality—such as textbooks—they often experience vocabulary regression (Nason, 1983). We must raise serious questions concerning classroom practices that require students to listen to inaccurate and boring models during the learning process.

Reading Aloud and Telling Stories

Reading aloud and telling stories to students are basic strategies for developing the listening capacity of students. We must share the language of many authors with children if they are to be expected to read and write language that goes beyond their home-rooted variety (Beck & McKeown, 2001; Biemiller, 1999). It is difficult to communicate with an author when reading silently if the student is faced with language he or she has never heard. Listening to the language of authors is a basic language experience teachers can implement as they read aloud to students.

Reading Aloud

Reading aloud to students is a critical component of their literacy development. It enhances the listening vocabulary. No part of literacy education is more important because students must recognize words by ear before they can recognize them by sight. They must understand the language of other people by listening to it before they can comprehend that language in print.

Although kindergarteners who have not been read to at home may not initially demonstrate extensive interest or skill in listening to read-alouds, they are the

Children chime in when teachers read books they love.

students who receive the most benefit from this experience that intertwines listening and reading (Dickinson & Smith, 1994; Elley, 1989; Feitelson, Goldstein, Iraqi, & Share, 1993). Numerous studies confirm that children whose teachers read aloud to them daily from quality literature demonstrate more growth in vocabulary, comprehension, and decoding skills than those who do not have this important listening experience (Cohen, 1968; Dickinson & Smith, 1994; Robbins & Ehri, 1994; Sénéchal, Thomas, & Monker, 1995).

Strategies such as the Directed Listening–Thinking Activity (DL–TA) are valuable to enhance listening and comprehension skills during read-alouds. The activity engages students as active listeners by getting them to make predictions as the teacher reads. (DL–TA is discussed more fully in Chapter 7.)

Teacher-to-Teacher

David Canzoneri sets aside fifteen minutes a day for reading aloud. He tries to choose stories and poems that can be read in the time allotted because he feels the total effect of a story or poem is important, especially for children who are not able to read whole stories or books independently. David feels his attitude toward reading aloud will be reflected in the attitude of the students. He wants them to know he really enjoys stories and poems and that reading them is important to him. David demonstrates he is willing to forgo other classroom activities in order to have time to communicate with an author who could not be present. He wants his students to think of him as a reader rather than as a reading teacher. David wants reading to be a communicating experience first of all, and he provides lessons for those who want to improve their abilities.

David uses children's literature to increase students' love for the sounds of nature. He shares *The Other Way to Listen,* by Byrd Baylor and Peter Parnall, a beautiful story about an

➤ ➤ ➤

old man who was so in tune with nature that he could literally hear rocks murmuring, hills singing, and wildflower seeds bursting open. His students then write their own verses about nature's sounds—sounds they have heard or sounds they wish they could hear.

Dorothy Fielder believes listening to good models of reading by the teacher who works with children on reading skills is so important that she follows a checklist of procedures to assure a good situation for reading aloud to her students. Here is her method:

1. Dorothy rehearses the story or poem on a tape recorder if it is new to her. She listens to improve the tone and rhythm of reading.

2. She and the children put all other work away.

3. Special places are planned for the children to gather to listen. Some special places are a rug so children can sit on the floor, the lawn under a tree in warm weather, and a stage behind the curtain when special lighting effects are needed. She believes a good story deserves a good arrangement. Children need to sit near the reader to see the illustrations and hear the subtle qualities of voice that portray mood and characters. Dorothy Felder often chooses stories that provide opportunities for her to use a variety of voice inflections such as small voices, loud voices, gruff voices, angry voices, or whispering voices.

4. Selections that sparkle and have a touch of the dramatic are chosen. She knows the children are attuned to multimedia.

5. She is prepared to repeat favorites over and over.

6. She selects some books with pictures only, no text, and invites children to say their own story as she shows the pictures. She encourages them to select a setting and names for characters before they begin to develop the sequence of events suggested by the pictures.

7. As she reads along, she engages in discussion and poses questions—not too many but enough to whet interest. She tends to ask predictive questions ("What do you think will happen next?" "What makes you think that?" "What causes you to say that?") and to make "I wonder" statements. This tactic enables the listeners to compare their own ideas with those of the author as the story unfolds. Dorothy avoids asking questions that might cause children to feel that they gave the wrong answer. Her proactive approach ensures that reading aloud to her students will result in a positive experience supporting the language growth of every child.

Developing Active Listeners through Storytelling

Many students are poor listeners because they have become accustomed to classrooms where listening is not required for success. They learn to cope with long lectures by daydreaming, and they learn about the content they will be tested on by reading—not listening. When a teacher switches roles from lecturing to storytelling, that changes. Storytelling by the teacher encourages students to listen and to watch for these things:

♦ Language that is embellished with descriptive terms that is not characteristic of ordinary conversation.

- Sound effects and physical movements that highlight meanings.
- Voice inflections and emphasis that most students do not use when reading what someone else has written.
- Ideas expressed in thought units rather than word by word.
- Ideas that are developed in a sequence that reaches a climax and has an ending.

Stories told from memory are usually more dramatic than those read aloud because of the freedom afforded the storyteller. It is still important to preserve the way certain authors use words and phrases. When the beauty and uniqueness of the original language need to be retained, a combination of telling and reading can be employed.

Variety should be the guide in selecting stories for telling and reading. Every teacher's repertoire should include nonfiction, fiction, legends, fairy tales, and every other kind of story from all over the world. Make selections to please and entertain, to stimulate curiosity, to inform, to illustrate the power of the spoken and the written word, and to reveal beauty and truth.

Students must hear stories and poems from many authors if we expect them to understand the language of hundreds of authors found in books. They seldom understand what they see in print if they have not heard similar language and sentence constructions prior to independent reading.

Teacher-to-Teacher

Jane Moore, a Reading Recovery teacher, believes storytelling makes literature come alive, and it enhances the listening abilities of her students. She notices that children listen with rapt attention as their fellow classmates tell stories. Jane encourages every child to select a favorite book and develop it into a storytelling session. She suggests they follow these steps in preparation for sharing the story:

STEP 1 Select a story you like.

STEP 2 Read it aloud.

STEP 3 Know your three-sentence challenge of the story:

In the beginning . . .
In the middle . . .
At the end . . .

STEP 4 Retell the story.

STEP 5 Visualize the story by making a silent movie in your head.

STEP 6 Practice! Practice! Practice!

As Jane's students prepare to be storytellers, they learn to "listen" to their own voice as they rehearse their stories. Is this truly listening? Yes—because once we have learned to "hear" our own voice, we are much better prepared to listen to the voices of others.

Evan Chapin _Name_

I am 9 years old _Age_

reading sport
and Leaning. _Interests_

What do you like most about school?

what I lik most about School is being able to play with my friends. School is the most fun thang on earth.

What's your favorite subject? Why?

My favorite subjects are writing and reading, because in writing you can wight about what ever you wont to. The reason I like reading is that a book can take you anyhere

What's your favorite book? Why do you like it?

My favorte book is swish! beaquse It is a really exciting and It's just a good book

What advice do you have for teachers?

My advice for teachers is to use technolagy dont give homework, and let stodits no you love them

Activities That Enhance Listening Abilities

Every classroom experience that includes oral language can naturally and normally be a good listening experience. However, listening abilities should be promoted and not left to chance. It is important to make a variety of activities such as these available from day to day as specific assignments or for self-selection:

◆ Students who work with games need to listen for specific instructions in order to participate. The instructions can be on video- or audiotape, read by an aide, or read by one of the group members. Listening to the instructions and the rules for games requires a level of attention to specifics that is not characteristic of most listening, but it is comparable to the requirements of some school experiences.

◆ Students who work in discussion-centered classrooms may respond in personal ways to what they hear and see. They can extend ideas to their own experiences with a "That reminds me of the time I . . ." kind of response. They do not need to listen at all times just to be able to repeat what they hear. That ability is important, but it is not more important than responding in personal ways.

Courtesy of Michael Sampson

Dramatic play provides an excellent opportunity to develop listening skills.

- Reading instruction activities should include reading to students on as regular a basis as listening to children read. Students need the experience of hearing good models of oral reading in individual and small group conferences as much as they need to hear reading for pleasure in a large group setting. "You read a sentence, then I'll read a sentence" or "You read a paragraph, then I'll read a paragraph" establishes a rapport for discussing some of the finer points of reading. This level of rapport seldom develops when teachers serve as judges of children's reading abilities.

- Plan so that oral reading by students to a group is prepared reading. Struggling readers do not benefit from listening to other readers struggle with text. When a teacher needs to listen to unrehearsed individual oral reading for ongoing assessment, this should be a private affair with only the teacher listening.

- Drama is an activity where children can act out stories and situations they have heard or read. It is both a listening and a comprehension experience that gives learners the opportunity to organize, sequence, and interpret characters from literature that are outside their life experiences. Through listening they pick up the feelings, moods, language patterns, and thought processes of characters.

- Choral reading is an excellent activity for the refinement of listening. Students listen to each other to evaluate the total effect of their presentation. They make certain they can interpret the selections in a meaningful and dramatic way.

- Provide opportunities for children to listen for and explore rhyming words. During singing or reading rhymes, chants, or songs, encourage children to identify rhyming words. Record their responses by taking group dictation. Continue the exploration by encouraging students to "chunk" the identified words into categories. Continue to take group dictation, and rewrite the words in the categories. Then encourage children to brainstorm additional rhyming words and extend the various categories.

- Students need a time and a place to read their own stories, poems, reports, and essays to an audience. When there is only one copy of a text, everyone in the audience has to listen. Listening in an audience has purpose because there is little chance that some have read ahead and already know what they are to hear. The teacher becomes a member of the listening audience. This places a responsibility on the reader that is never felt in reading groups in which every student has a book opened to the same reading selection. Struggling readers experience success when they have opportunities to rehearse and then read their original manuscripts.

Devalin Drennan encourages the children in his class to prepare programs for the pleasure of others—songs, skits, plays, debates, travelogues, art shows, fashion shows, and musical recordings with live commentary. The programs themselves are important, but so is the opportunity they afford to discuss and practice listening courtesies that are appropriate throughout life.

Rachel Patterson uses oral sharing time as a basis for discussing and practicing listening abilities. Rather than repeating over and over "Let's be quiet and listen while (*child's name*) talks," she asks the children to brainstorm what a good listener "looks like" and "sounds like." She uses a "T-chart" (Figure 4.1) to record the children's responses and discuss facial expressions that show pleasure or bore-

dom, body posture that indicates participation or "cop out," and quiet attention to the person sharing or quiet attention to some other appropriate activity. The be-quiet-and-listen routine, which she tried for too long, does not satisfy her present goals of developing a classroom community that supports sharing and develops effective listeners through participation in discussions and conversations.

A student's ability to profit from school experiences and to participate in a social life will depend as much on listening ability as on reading and writing abilities. No direct measure of progress may be possible or even necessary, but the teacher can always help by focusing children's attention on the need for careful, thoughtful listening as a basic ingredient in learning.

Looks Like:	Sounds Like:
Body is turned toward person speaking – Mandy	Is quiet when it is someone else's turn to talk – Josh
Has both eyes looking at the person talking – Marti	Takes turns asking questions or saying things – Shandrieka
Makes nice faces, might nod or smile – Juan	Might say things like, "Your story made me think of . . ." or " I thought it was interesting when . . ." Matthew
May lean forward a little bit – Kami	Talks about things that have something to do with what the speaker was talking about – Kai Sai

FIGURE 4.1

T-chart of what a good listener looks like and sounds like

- Singing games and listening to singing and other music increases auditory discrimination. The experience also builds confidence in producing language with rhythm and rhyme. Students at all levels of achievement can participate in listening to music and in singing.

- Share various rhythm band instruments with the children and encourage children to use them to add sound effects as you read aloud or for an oral reading prepared by an individual, pair, small group, or whole group of students. They are increasing both auditory discrimination and comprehension skills as they experiment and make decisions concerning what instrument or combination of instruments make sounds that best "fit" various words, settings, scenes, or the tone of the story. In addition, provide opportunities for students to brainstorm words to describe the different sounds they are producing such as "muffled," "clanging," "smooth, " "high," "low," or "harsh."

FURTHER WORDS

 From InfoTrac College Edition

Now Hear This: Without Listening, There Is No Communication, John R. Ward, *Communication World* July 1990 v7 n7 p20(3)

Propaganda, *The Columbia Encyclopedia* Edition 6, 2000 p31441

Teaching and Learning Creatively: Using Children's Narratives, Ana Maria Lo Cicero, Yolanda De La Cruz, and Karen C. Fuson. *Teaching Children Mathematics* May 1999 v5 i9 p544(4)

A Story Every Day (importance of reading aloud to children; includes bibliography), Jamie Swedberg, *MPLS–St. Paul Magazine* May 1999 v27 i5 p108

From Professional Journals and Publications

Chaney, A. L. and Burk, T. L. (1998). *Teaching Oral Communication in Grades K–8*. Upper Saddle River, NJ: Prentice-Hall.

Lundsteen, S. W. (1990). Learning to Listen and Learning to Read. In S. Hynds and D. L. Rubin (Eds.), *Perspectives on Talk and Learning*. Urbana, IL: National Council of Teachers of English.

Sampson, M. R., Briggs, L. D., and Coker, D. R. (1984). Assessing the Listening Comprehension of Children. *Reading Improvement, 21,* 59–63.

Thompson, F. T., Grandgenett, D. J., and Grandgenett, N. F. (1999). Helping Disadvantaged Learners Build Effective Listening Skills. *Education, 120,* 30.

Summary

Listening, like all learning experiences, benefits from collaborative teacher–student planning. There is more to it than the teacher commanding "Now listen up!" dozens of times a day. There must be some aspiration for improving listening ability, some time for planning specific activities, and time for evaluating progress. Together, students and teachers can develop standards of listening to serve as a basis for relating listening to learning.

Total Literacy Anchors

DEVELOPING LISTENING HABITS

- The student makes use of past experiences and information in conversation.
- The student uses imagination in the formulation of original stories.
- The student follows simple instructions after hearing them.
- The student accepts the worth of others' remarks.
- The student speaks in turn.
- The student realizes that different people speak in different ways and for different purposes.
- The student catches added meaning by noting gestures and intonations.
- The student thinks ahead while listening, anticipating what is coming next.

LISTENING TO GET INFORMATION

- The student understands, remembers, and responds to directions of increasing complexity.
- The student gets answers to questions from what is heard.
- The student relays messages accurately.
- The student takes notes from interviews and discussions.
- The student follows reading models heard in instructional conferences.
- The student organizes a sequence and assumes the role of a character to dramatize a story.

LISTENING TO EXCHANGE IDEAS AND FORM JUDGMENTS

- The student participates in group discussions.
- The student reads his or her own compositions to an audience.
- The student grasps the central idea from listening to others read.
- The student recognizes subordinate ideas in stories heard.
- The student distinguishes between fact and opinion, fact and fantasy.
- The student realizes that one's feelings affect one's reaction to what is heard.
- The student seeks clarification of vague and ambiguous ideas.

LISTENING TO ENJOY AND APPRECIATE

- The student becomes aware of beauty in the rhythm and sound of language.
- The student appreciates poetry, stories, music, and dramatization enough to choose listening and reading in learning centers.
- The student develops an understanding of the role and responsibilities of the listener in different situations—face to face, audience to speaker, speaker to audience, radio, television, recordings, and school programs.
- The student realizes how readers and storytellers achieve various effects.
- The student realizes the power of language to communicate.

CHAPTER 5

The Reading Process

As You Read . . .

- ◆ How is reading a transaction?

- ◆ How do readers use literacy cueing systems in the reading transaction?

- ◆ When are miscues a sign of comprehension?

- ◆ What is the importance of schema theory to the classroom teacher?

In this chapter on the reading process, we explore what reading is and how it happens. You will come away with an appreciation for the complexity of the reading process. But you will also discover that children have all the necessary tools within themselves to become good readers.

Reading is an important avenue to exploring and comprehending life. We explore life through listening; we explore life through talking; we explore life through writing. Reading is simply another aspect of our exploration. Without the pillars of language and writing, we could not be readers. Teachers in a total literacy classroom ensure that a multitude of strategies are available to every student so no child will be left behind in his or her pursuit of literacy. This chapter explores what happens when readers read, and what teachers need to know about the reading process. Chapter 6 focuses on curriculum materials called *basal readers* that many schools use to teach reading. Chapter 7 focuses on the numerous comprehension strategies that are built on our total literacy view.

Author Words
Michael Sampson

What Is Reading?

Reading is a transaction that occurs between human beings and their environment. Sometimes reading is appreciating a painting or anticipating the feelings of another person. At other times reading is the more traditional interaction with a book.

America's Finest
Jane White

Reprinted with special permission of Cowles Syndicate, Inc.

Most people take a simplistic and erroneous view that reading is decoding, or constructing meaning from language as represented by graphic symbols. This simplistic definition does not take into account that reading is actually a partnership between a writer and a reader—and that reading is a "give and take" between the two. Thus the literacy transaction is much more involved than simply encoding language.

Reading is communication. Before children can comprehend written language, they must be able to comprehend the feedback the environment provides. They must be able to "read" the faces of people and their emotions. They must be able to comprehend the sounds, actions, smells, and changes of the world that surrounds them. According to Piagetian theory (Piaget, 1959), these life experiences are the very foundation of thinking and comprehending. Peter Spencer (1970) terms this kind of environmental reading "primary reading" and states that it is "fundamental to the giving of meaning and significance to the reading of symbols" (p. 16). These experiences enable children to bring cold silent print to life when they are asked to read from the decontextualized reading exercises that are so common in the early grades. Most children feel a sense of accomplishment in being able to "read" their environment and their experiences. Once confidence is established, children are ready for school-type reading activities, or what Spencer (1970) terms reading from "secondary sources."

Primary reading should continue as a part of the school program and should form the foundation of instructional activities. It is essential that those children who are slow to read the language represented by alphabetic symbols have repeated opportunities to be affirmed through primary reading experiences. Such activities must be important enough in day-to-day operations for children to feel a sense of reading achievement when they are participating. Teachers must demonstrate to the children that they feel such primary reading is an important part of the school curriculum (Smith, 1985).

The Child's View of the Reading Process

Children spend the first years of life experimenting with and manipulating language and print. As we discussed in Chapter 2, it is in these early years that children come to understand the nature of communication. When children arrive at school, most already possess vibrant oral language, a strong sense of the syntactic and semantic structures of language, and a rich oral tradition of stories and rhymes (Sampson, Briggs, & Sampson, 1986).

Some children will enter school already reading, and others will be well on their way to becoming readers. Wise teachers will capitalize on the strengths young children have as language users as they begin formal reading instruction. In addition, teachers will realize that learning to read and learning to become better readers are things children do throughout the school day—not just during the period set aside for "reading."

What do children think reading is? In far too many cases, children view reading as a subject in school or as "sounding out words" (Harste et al., 1982). They fathom reading as being a mysterious activity in which words appear magically to the reader. They don't understand that reading is related to talking—that reading is simply language that has been preserved with a symbol system.

Becoming a good reader is made easy when teachers help children understand the links between reading and other communication forms. Of vital importance is the responsibility of the teacher to help young children conceptualize and internalize that reading is "talk written down." Roach Van Allen (1985, 1999) explains the language experience approach as follows:

"I can think about all the experiences I've had in life." Children live in an exciting world. Their minds are filled with past experiences and memories, as well as a world of daydreams and imagination.

"I can talk about what I think about." And talk they do! Children love to talk about their life—ask any kindergarten teacher. Children have no problem translating their thoughts to oral language.

"What I can talk about or think about, I can communicate to others in many forms." Children become storytellers through writing, or scribbling, as preschoolers. They love to mark paper up with their stories, and are quick to "read" to you the meanings behind their scribbles. They also communicate in other formats—painting, dramatizing, or signing. Teachers can also record children's language—through brainstorming for ideas or through taking dictation.

"I can read what I write by myself and what others write for me to read." Children can read what they have written—be it scribble or stories written with invented spellings. And because others write using the same symbol system, the child can read their writing too.

Children need to know that reading or writing is talk written down. It is very important for children to make this connection between oral and written representations of language. Children need to see the connection or link between their oral language and the written language of others.

The Teacher's View of the Reading Process

We have presented our rationale of how we feel children should view the reading/writing process. Now we turn our attention to you, the teacher, as we consider the question, "What is reading?" Although we present our views of the reading process, our intent is to show you that the view you hold of the reading process affects what children do as readers in your classroom. You need to think through your feelings about reading. As you do, you will become a better teacher as you trust in your own intuitive feelings about the children you instruct. You'll come to trust more in the transactions children have with reading and writing processes as they engage in meaningful literacy activities, and you will rely less on packaged materials.

Literacy Cueing Systems

Reading printed material such as books, newspapers, and even billboards involves the construction of meaning by the reader. Readers arrive at meaning by using their background knowledge or scriptural information about the topic and by using three basic cueing systems: (1) cue systems within words (graphophones), (2) cue systems within the structure or flow of language (syntax), and (3) cue systems

Kim Henderson leads her students in explorations of onsets and rimes.

within the person reading the message (semantics) (DeFord, 1985; Goodman, 1985; Goodman, Smith, Meredith, & Goodman, 1988; Smith, 1982). Although some educators have added a fourth cueing system (pragmatics), which involves the social and cultural context of language (Tompkins, 2003), we believe the semantic system encompasses situational and cultural context. In fact, the environment in which they are found influences all of these cue systems and the circumstances of the reading act.

An understanding of these three literacy language systems—graphophonic, syntactic, and semantic—enables the teacher to understand how readers process text as they reconstruct an author's ideas.

Graphophonic Cues

The *graphophonic system* consists of the relations that exist between the graphemes a reader encounters in print and the phonemes or sound of the spoken language. Children internalize these relations naturally as they are exposed to language and reading. Illustrating this process is the example of Michael and Mary Beth Sampson's 3-year-old son Jonathan. When author Jim Trelease from New England visited Jonathan's Texas home, he asked what the dog in the backyard was named.

Jonathan replied, "Prince." However, because Texans and New Englanders differ in phoneme pronunciation, Jim Trelease thought Jonathan had said "Fritz." Jim walked into the backyard and called "Here, Fritz, here, Fritz!" "No!" a concerned Jonathan replied, "His name is not Fritz, it's *Prince. Prr- Prr- Prince!*" Jonathan had never received any type of phonics instruction or emphasis on the graphophonic system, yet he was learning language orally and auditorily and was making fine discriminations between speech sounds at age 3.

For Jonathan's fourth birthday he received a copy of Donald Crews's award-winning book *Freight Train* (1978). His interest started with the story being shared. Soon he was chiming in with the reader. Finally, his learning of the relations between phonemes and graphemes was demonstrated as he read the book to his little brother. His added emphasis on the initial phonemes "Fr" and "Tr" was obvious as he read "*freight train!*"

Jonathan provides a good example of the message communicated throughout this book: Learning moves from whole to part, not part to whole. Graphophonic cues are useful to readers, and they are internalized by children as they come to understand the English language. Proficient readers rarely rely on graphophonic information alone, however. Consequently, our emphasis should be on demonstrating to children the joy and importance of reading—not isolating the study of word parts.

Syntactic Cues

The *syntactic system* consists of the interrelations among words and among sentences based on the grammar or language rules of the speaker or writer. Syntactic knowledge is implicit—the language user may not be able to verbalize grammatical rules, but mastery of the rules is demonstrated regularly in his or her language use. This cue is very useful in reading. It enables readers to know what part of speech might be used next in a sentence and enables them to finish a sentence someone else has started. All of this is done at the subconscious level—the words just seem to "pop" into one's mind.

Syntactic cues are valuable because they enable children to monitor their reading. When a miscue disrupts the normal flow of language, an "alarm" goes off in the reader's mind and she or he backtracks to find the source of confusion (Goodman et al., 1988).

Although syntax involves the placement of words in sentences according to grammatical rules, words may still be in the correct grammatical position and yet cause confusion to the reader. Syntactic cues are disrupted when the language flow is artificial or contrived. Researchers have found that children who read material with simple syntax do not read that material as well as they read more complex material that features a natural language flow (DeFord, 1981; Sampson et al., 1986).

Semantic Cues

The *semantic system* is the most basic and valuable of the three cueing systems and involves the relation among language and experience that establishes meaning for a reader. This process occurs as the reader interacts with the ideas presented from the text to construct meaning according to the reader's knowledge. Understanding occurs as prior experiences are brought into play in response to graphic input.

The semantic cueing system enables readers to monitor their reading by demanding that the text make sense. When the text does not elicit understanding, a short circuit occurs and the reader retraces the message or print in an attempt to find out *why* the text did *not* make sense (Cambourne, 1995; Goodman & Goodman, 1978).

The Role of Phonics and Rimes in a Total Literacy Program

Helping students master the graphophonic system may be accomplished through phonics instruction. Essentially, in phonics instruction students learn the sound representations for letters and groups of letters or letter patterns. The Report of the National Reading Panel (2000) asserts that systematic and explicit phonics teaching is a critical element of successful literacy programs for students in

JenAnne Shumway — Name

11 yrs. old (eleven) — Age

Family, friends, soccer,
animals, computers, Christ — Interests
horses, working with food

What do you like most about school?

I like school the most because the teachers are funny. I love being around both my friends and teachers.

What's your favorite subject? Why?

My favorite subject is Reading. I read until my head hurts! I like it because you are allowed to use your imaganation. Not like on movies, but your mind will run wild!

What's your favorite book? Why do you like it?

My favorite book is the Harry Potter series. I like Harry Potter because it's action packed. I'm into magic, just not dark magic.

What advice do you have for teachers?

Teachers should give us social time with our friends. More time for reading, and throw away those nasty text books! Math should be more fun! Like with hamburgers and Hershey® Bars!

Diverse Learners

America's Finest

Jeanette Sgambellone

W hat can classroom teachers do to help ESL (English as Second Language) students new to the school or those that need help with content-related vocabulary? Jeannette Sgambellone, an ESL teacher from Ohio, provides these activities to help both the teacher and the student.

The First Few Days

When a new student arrives, there are often many challenges for both student and teacher. Here are some quick tips to help make the transition go more smoothly.

- Assign a buddy. Have a student who will make sure the new student is where he/she needs to be.

- Have the whole class find pictures of lunch menu items and create a visual menu for the new student.

- Tour the school. Make sure the new student knows where important rooms are located.

- Make a book of the school. Show where each room is and who the new student may encounter in that particular room.

Welcoming the New ESL Child

Have students read the book onto a tape and keep it out for reference.

- Try to learn how to say "hello" or "welcome" in the new student's first language.

Backpacks

Create a backpack with bilingual books and activities. These backpacks can be given out on a weekly basis so you do not need to have one for every student. One per language would be a great start! Here are some items to include in a backpack:

Bilingual books

Crayons

Drawing paper

Picture cards

Journal

Puppets

Activity card

Model for the students how to do the activities in the backpack, and encourage them to take it home and teach their par-

---

grades kindergarten through 6 and for children experiencing difficulty learning to read. We agree with the contention that explicit and systematic phonics instruction is important for successful literacy acquisition. But there are alternatives to workbook-like activities and repetitive drills that focus on specific phonic generalizations.

Phonics instruction can and should be fun and engaging for all students. Students can learn the most common sounds of the consonants, consonant blends, and digraphs or onsets (the sounds of consonants and consonant combinations found in the beginning of words or syllables, before the vowel) through movement activities such as pumping or painting for the letter *P*, waving for the letter *W*, and pretending to skate for the consonant blend *SK*. Students can learn alliterative chants to help them with the same sounds. For

ents. Here are some ideas for using the materials in the backpack:

- The activity card lists all of the possible activities to help them remember.
- Bilingual books can be purchased through different catalogs.
- Drawing paper can be used to illustrate their favorite part of the story.
- Picture cards make fun matching games and great review of words.
- Puppets are fun to retell the story or act out their favorite part.
- Journals can be used for the students to respond to a question or write about how they enjoyed the book.

Content Area Dictionaries

Use content area dictionaries to introduce and/or reinforce content vocabulary. The dictionary that is used in my classroom is set up in themes. This dictionary has many components with it; here are a few of them:

- Word cards that can be duplicated for using as a matching game, or flash cards.

- Readings that incorporate all of the new vocabulary words.
- Musical beats that also incorporate all of the vocabulary words.

These dictionaries make it easy to introduce different content area themes.

Vocabulary Cartoons

Using vocabulary cartoons is also a great way to introduce students to new vocabulary. These can be copied and sent home with students so that the whole family can learn and enjoy. The vocabulary cartoons also give words that sound like the new vocabulary word to help students with pronunciation.

These simple activities will help make new students welcome and give them success in their new second language—English. But even more important, they will help ESL students feel that they have found a new home and new friends.

Reprinted with special permission of Jeannette Sgambellone.

example, children can learn the sound of the letter *P* by chanting this silly sentence while looking at the letter *P* printed on the chalkboard:

Peter and Paul pick pink peas in Papa's garden.

And the sound for the letter *S* can be learned through a chant such as this:

Silly Susan likes to sit on the sunny side of school.

Beyond the sounds associated with consonants in the onset position, literacy researcher Marilyn Jager Adams suggests that students learn phonics through the study of rimes or word families. Rimes are the portion of syllables that include the vowel and any letters after the vowel. In the one syllable word "book," for example, the *ook* is the rime, and in the word "fun" the *un* is the rime. It is more efficient to process letters in combinations such as these rimes than in a letter-by-letter fashion. Rimes are more consistent in sound than phonic rules that have many exceptions. Moreover, this focus on letter combinations seems to represent the manner in which proficient readers sound out words. Finally, rimes are much more consistent in the sound they represent than are many of the phonics rules taught to children that have many exceptions.

In traditional approaches to phonics, children are taught patterns through the repetitious reading of words with a particular pattern or by completing a collection of worksheets that provide drill and practice on such patterns. Although rimes are certainly worth teaching to children, we feel that they can be taught directly, explicitly, and enjoyably through more engaging approaches rather than through the silly sentences just explored. Rimes are at the heart of rhyming poetry. Why not have children read and examine poetry that contains whatever rimes you may want to teach? When teaching the very common word family *ill,* we often present children with the nursery rhyme "Jack and Jill." When learning the common rime *ay,* we ask children to read this rhyme:

> *Rain, rain, go away.*
>
> *Come again another day.*
>
> *Little Johnny wants to play.*

If we can't find a rhyming poem that matches the word family we wish to teach, we write our own. For example, after introducing students to the *ank* and *ad* rimes, the children read, reread, and thoroughly enjoyed the poem Tim wrote entitled "Hank's Prank":

> *Happy Hank played a prank*
>
> *On his mom and dad.*
>
> *They didn't like it*
>
> *He got spanked.*
>
> *Now Happy Hank is sad.*

After reading the poem several times—reading and listening while the teacher reads it, reading it chorally as part of a group, reading it with a partner, and reading it individually—the teacher guides the children in identifying the key rimes as well as other interesting words and word parts.

Eventually children can be asked to write and recite their own rhyming poems featuring the word family of the day. Through this authentic, creative, and engaging process of enjoying poetry and creating poems, children learn words and phonics, and even more important, they learn to appreciate poetry and the well-chosen words that make up the poems they read.

Phonics is an important element to the successful acquisition of total literacy, but it need not be taught in isolated and mundane ways. Creative, informed, and artful teachers find ways to integrate phonics with other literacy elements and invite children to participate actively.

In summary, teaching phonics outside of reading and authentic literacy experiences will frustrate both good and struggling readers. Reading springs to life when children are given access to all three literacy cueing systems.

Teacher~to~Teacher

Kimberly Welch is a master second-grade teacher whose students excel in literacy. When her school mandated phonics instruction, she asked her principal to come into her classroom so she could demonstrate that phonics was already a part of her total literacy program. She began by sharing with him that the word *total* is self-defining—her students receive exposure and instruction in phonics as well as all other elements of the literacy process through the three cueing systems. He replied, "Show me your phonics."

Kimberly picked up the book *Trick or Treat* (Martin & Sampson, 2002) from her bookshelf and began to read to her students:

"Mommy, I'm ready to go!"

"My, don't you look scary," mommy says. "You can go trick-or-treating—but only in our apartment building. I'll go with you! And remember—you only knock on doors of people we know. And try not to scare them!"

Up to the second floor, knock on Knicker Knocker's door. "Trick or Treat?" "Treat," says Knicker Knocker as he fills my bag with Candy Bars.

Kimberly paused and asked "Boys and girls, what do you notice about the words Knicker and Knocker?" "They begin the

same," chimed the children. Kimberly continued reading:

Up to the third floor, knock on Slipper Slopper's door.

"Trick or Treat?" "Treat," says Slipper Slopper as she fills my bag with Peanut Cups.

Up to the fourth floor, knock on Wiggle Waggle's door.

"Trick or Treat?" "Treat," says Wiggle Waggle as he fills my bag with Strawberry Drops.

Kimberly continued to read and the students grew more and more excited:

Up to the ninth floor, knock on Teeter Totter's door.

"Trick or Treat?" "Treat," says Teeter Totter as she fills my bag with Jelly Beans.

Up to the tenth floor, knock on Magic Merlin's door.

"Trick or Treat?" There is no answer. "Trick or Treat?" Still no answer. "Trick or Treat?"

"T R I C K !!!" The door flies open and Merlin waves his magic wand at me. "Now everything is wackbards!" Merlin laughs as he slams his door on me.

Down to the ninth floor, knock on Totter Teeter's door. "Trick or Treat," I say. "Trick," says Totter Teeter as he fills my bag with Belly Jeans.

➤ ➤ ➤

"Belly Jeans!" shouted the children—"what's that?" Kimberly answered, "What do you think?" After a minute of silence, one child shouted out "It's Jelly Beans backwards!" "Yes, but are both words totally backwards?" asked Kimberly? "No, just the first sound—the sounds are switched!" declared a freckle-faced boy.

Kimberly continued to read as the action moved downward, floor by floor, as Peanut Cups turned into Ceanut Pups and Candy Bars became Bandy Cars.

After the story ended, Kimberly talked with her principal. Did he understand? She knew he had when he told her what a great phonics lesson he had seen—that he loved the way she taught onsets.

Kimberly was relieved that she could continue to teach initial consonants and consonant combinations, or onsets, in the context of language and books. And the children? They simply enjoyed the story, not knowing that they had just been delivered from a foot-high stack of phonics worksheets.

Redundancy and the Cueing Systems

As readers process print, they may use all three of the language cueing systems in their search for meaning. However, because our language is redundant, more information is provided than is necessary for comprehension to occur. We define *redundancy* as the characteristic of language (1) that restricts the order in which language symbols occur and (2) that provides several clues concerning the same piece of information. The graphophonic system provides redundancy through a narrowing of the elements of sounds. For example, only certain sounds can follow the /b/ in boat. In addition, the unseen rules of spelling help the reader. The reader internalizes these rules through interaction with language and uses them in making predictions while reading.

The syntactic system also provides redundancy. Pearson and Johnson (1985) provide this example of how redundancy operates:

1. The boy thanked the girl.

2. The girl was thanked by the boy.

3. Girl was the by thanked boy the.

4. Thanked girl boy was by the the.

Our knowledge of syntax is demonstrated when we recognize that numbers (1) and (2) are acceptable English sentences; (3) and (4) are not. Our knowledge of syntax is evident when we recognize that sentences (1) and (2) hold the same meaning.

Syntax can also help us answer questions when reading. It is this understanding of sentence structure that enables us to read (5) and then answer questions (6), (7), and (8) (Pearson & Johnson, 1985).

5. The argle zoolked the bordiddy in the ershent because the bordiddy larped the argle.

6. Who zoolked the bordiddy?

7. Why did the argle zoolk the bordiddy in the ershent?

8. What did the bordiddy do to the argle?

The redundancy of our language enables us to answer many such questions. However, it is not clear if our ability to answer questions like (6) and (8) indicate comprehension. Could it be that students often only appear to be comprehending—that, in fact, they are simply getting by using the syntactic system of language to provide the answers to questions?

The semantic system enables us to know what meaning of a word is intended by an author when the word is a homograph and has different possible meanings. For example, does the word "light" mean "the opposite of dark" or "pale or whitish in color"? Or does it mean to "start a fire"? Content alone can answer the question.

In addition, semantic cues enable readers to predict what will come next in the story. These predictions are sometimes possible because of cultural experiences (hearing the story of "The Three Little Pigs" for the fifty-eighth time) and life experiences (the story is about a camping trip and the reader is an experienced camper).

These three cueing systems or sources of information offer, to a degree, overlapping information. Redundancy lessens the need for careful attention to every tiny detail in the print setting—it represents information the reader does not need because he or she already knows what the author is saying and where the author is attempting to lead. Or, as Smith (1982) says, "the more redundancy there is, the less visual information the skilled reader requires" (pp. 18–19).

Reading as Transaction

Reading is a transaction. As readers read, they use semantic cues to simultaneously move from mental predictions to surface features of text, monitoring understanding and moving forward as meanings are confirmed.

Comprehension is influenced by each reader's experiences and belief system. Experiences build cognitive schemata. A *schema* is an organized "block" of experience and knowledge, usually accompanied by feelings or attitudes (Rumelhart, 1980). People comprehend differently partially because they have varied experiences and schemata. No two people have identical thoughts, experiences, or feelings. Therefore, a writer cannot communicate a message; meaning does not reside in the written word or text. Instead, meaning arises during a transaction between the text and a reader.

The concept of transaction was introduced by Dewey and Bentley in 1949. Rosenblatt (1978) elaborates on it by describing the product of the interaction of reader and text as a "poem." This poem, or literary work, is created in the mind of

Conferencing about reading.

the reader. The work created is influenced by the background knowledge and feelings (schemata) activated by the reader, which are selected according to the social or situational context of the reading event. This transaction is depicted in Figure 5.1. In this figure, the sociolinguistic context represents the language schemata activated by the reader. Schemata are influenced by the context or situation in which the reading takes place.

Different "poems" may be created based on the richness of the schemata that are activated. Sampson and White (1983) found that reading in school environments results in different schemata activation than does reading in nonschool situations, which validates the influence of the sociolinguistic and situational context during reading.

The discussion of miscues, which follows, illustrates in greater depth certain sociolinguistic aspects of these transactions.

Miscues and Reading Proficiency

We now turn our attention to oral reading and to the lessons children can teach us about the reading process. Thus far we have stated that reading involves a transaction with print and that readers use the three cueing systems simultaneously and

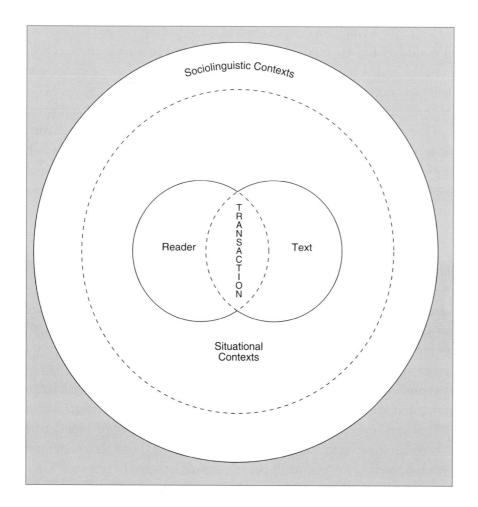

FIGURE 5.1

The literacy transaction

Reprinted with permission of Jerome Harste and the International Reading Association.

interactively in their search for meaning. During this process, effective readers use the strategies of sampling, predicting, confirming, and correcting as they construct their personal representation of the author's message. Goodman (1985) sees effective reading as a search for meaning that involves selectively using the fewest most productive cues to confirm what the reader expects to find. As readers search for meaning, they personalize the author's message by sometimes changing the surface representation of text to reflect their own language patterns and word choice. For years educators corrected all such "mistakes" because they believed these "mistakes" indicated an inability of the reader to respond to an unknown word, a lack of proper word-attack skills, or carelessness. These miscues in the reading process can be illustrated by this example with Jason, a first-grader: Jason read, "The cat was in the home." The text read, "The cat was in the house." As he started to read the next sentence, his teacher stopped him. "Jason, read that last sentence again, carefully. Be sure to look at the last word."

The teacher's emphasis on the "mistake" indicated a great deal to Jason about *what* reading is. He was exposed to the concepts that reading is an exact process and that the goal of reading is saying the words correctly. Receiving meaning from the print was not emphasized.

Correcting the oral reader's "errors" has long been recognized as an important part of the reading teacher's role. However, the indiscriminate practice of correcting all textual deviations, or miscues, by having the pupil stop and reread may have a negative effect on the child's view of reading (Bloome & King Dail, 1997; Phinney, 1989). If this is true, what should the teacher do when a child "reads" something different from what the author wrote? Let's examine that issue further.

"Errors" and Language Growth

Children know that language conveys meaning (Clay, 1998, 2001; Goodman et al., 1988; Holdaway, 1979). Their early years are spent experimenting with and manipulating language as they seek to bring meaning and order to their world. This manipulation involves forming new ways of saying things, molding existing language into new constructs, and experimenting with language patterns. This learning process, on many occasions, results in the children making "errors." However, these communications should be recognized as signs of growth, and such language manipulation should be applauded. When a young child experiments with language and says "mouses" instead of "mice" and "goed" instead of "went," parents usually realize these "errors" are a sign of immaturity and that the child, through growth and practice, will eventually become a proficient user of language. Thus the child receives positive feedback from understanding parents and continues to grow in the language-learning process.

Unfortunately, when the child moves into the educational environment, this reinforcement does not always continue. One need only to observe reading instruction practices to realize that, all too often, "correctness" becomes the overriding goal. Any manipulation of the text by the reader is regarded as an "error" and is corrected. The divergent risk-taking language techniques the child used very successfully in preschool oral language learning may not be rewarded in the contrived school situation. But these miscues should be looked on as "windows on the reading process," for they allow the teacher to "infer what the reader is thinking" (Goodman, 1976, p. 71). An analysis of these miscues can provide valuable information concerning the strategies readers use to discover meaning.

Remember Jason? When he read "The cat was in the home" instead of "The cat was in the house" and continued reading, he showed an awareness of the semantic and syntactic flow of the sentence. His emphasis seemed to be on meaning.

The same emphasis is indicated if a child reads "The cat were in the house," when the child is using a dialectal pattern he or she normally uses in spoken language. In this reading, the child has transformed the text into a meaningful form.

If another child read the passage as "The cat was in the horse" and continued reading, the child's emphasis would seem to be on decoding individual words rather than the meaning of the complete passage. In this instance, the oral reading distorted the meaning.

Bettelheim and Zelan (1982) carried this concept a step further by suggesting that at times miscues can indicate a reader's sophistication and expertise with text. Often, the miscues make equal or more sense than the original text.

Weber (1970) studied the miscues first-graders made when reading and found that substitutions constituted 86 percent of the miscues. The substitute words, however, maintained the meaning of the text. Furthermore, Weber found that nearly all of the beginning readers' substitutions made the text "more colloquial and less stilted, or more sensible" (p. 132). The children's search for meaning was very obvious.

When looking at children's miscues, one soon realizes that all "mistakes" are not created equal. Teachers tend, however, to solve the problem of miscues by using a single approach—having the child stop and reread (Goodman & Burke, 1972). Miscues that maintain or improve meaning give us different information about the child's proficiency in reading than do miscues that cause the semantic and syntactic flow to be disrupted or destroyed. These latter miscues should be viewed differently.

Teachers must realize what concepts about reading are being formed as "errors" are being corrected. When teachers indiscriminately correct all miscues, children assume that reading orally must involve reproducing "exactly what is on the printed page" (Goodman & Burke, 1972, p. 4). This view of reading forces children to become passive reproducers of the author's words, and the concept portrayed to children concerning "what reading is" becomes distorted. The individual words assume prime importance, and meaning is subordinated. Unfortunately, this emphasis on the "correct" word places undue importance on the graphophonic cues at the expense of semantic and syntactic cues, and comprehension suffers.

If we look at accomplished readers, we find that they read in chunks of meaning rather than letter by letter or word by word. Proficient readers become involved in the text and begin to predict words and anticipate thoughts. As stated by Smith (1973), "Fluent readers do not read words, they read meanings . . . [and] make maximum use of a minimum of visual information" (p. 188).

The Implications of Miscues for Teachers

As you have seen, reading cannot be viewed as a one-way street of correctly pronouncing words. Rosenblatt (1978, 1983, 1993) stated that the reader's textual interaction should be active rather than passive in order to cue thinking and derive meaning. Like other communicative processes, reading is not exact, for a reader is "not a blank tape registering a ready-made message" (Rosenblatt, 1978, p. 10). The reader brings a wealth of ideas, emotions, experiences, and expectations to the printed page. This has an effect on the reader–text interaction.

Miscues can tell us a great deal about what children think reading is, what they know, and what they need to learn (Bloome, Landis, & Villemare, 1998). A teacher must be linguistically aware of the information that is available through the analysis of miscues and must not perceive the child who makes miscues as being deficient but rather as an emerging learner.

As stated by Donaldson (1978), "The learner, if . . . an active discoverer, will make mistakes" (p. 110). To be a dynamic learner, the child must be an active risk taker and realize that reading is much more than word-by-word processing. The child must interact with the text through predicting and confirming, with the end result being meaning. In this "risky" process, miscues will occur, but miscues happen in the reading process as an effect of the interaction between reader and text. The teacher's role is to provide reading instruction that helps the child realize that "saying the correct word" is not the reason for reading. Rather, for each individual student, the "why" of reading must involve thinking, which leads to comprehension.

Miscue analysis is invaluable because it helps teachers "understand that words are not the same just because they look the same. Words have different meanings and different syntactic patterns in different contexts even within the same story" (Goodman & Anders, 1999, p. 193). This confirms our notion, introduced earlier in the literacy cueing systems discussion, that situational context plays a major role in readers' use of the semantic cueing system and that syntax is influenced by the reader's semantic stance.

Attention and Automaticity

Another theory of reading suggests that all readers have a finite or limited amount of attention available to them during reading (LaBerge & Samuels, 1974). This attention can be devoted either to the process of decoding words or to the process of comprehension. If too much attention is required to decode words, then less attention is available for comprehending the text.

One goal of reading instruction is to make the decoding process as automatic or attention free as possible. In this way, a maximum amount of readers' attention is available to be applied to comprehension. While reading this book, for example, chances are that most of your decoding is automatic—that is, you are able to recognize or decode the words you come to with little or no effort. The words in this text are sight words that you recognize without effort, attention, or cognitive energy on your part. Thus you can focus your attention on the process of comprehending the text.

How is it that your decoding ability has become largely an attention-free process? This has occurred through lots of reading on your part. The more you read, the more able you are to quickly, efficiently, and effortlessly decode the words you encounter. As teachers, we need to help students develop their decoding ability beyond mere accuracy, to a level of automaticity (Samuels, 1994), or attention-free decoding. This is done by encouraging students to read so that they have plenty of opportunities to see and recognize words.

In addition, practiced or repeated readings help develop students' automatic decoding. This doesn't mean that we ask students to read texts several times without purpose. Rather, we need to think of authentic ways for students to want to practice certain texts. Reading performance texts is a good way to get students to want to practice. Reader's Theater scripts and poetry, for example, are meant to be read aloud and performed by an expressive reader. Giving students regular opportunities to practice, interpret, and perform these kinds of texts is a superb way to develop automaticity in their decoding and, as a consequence, better overall comprehension of what they read (Opitz & Rasinski, 1999).

Other Factors That Affect Reading Comprehension

Teachers are increasingly aware that comprehension is a process students experience rather than a product consisting of numerous memorized comprehension skills. We now know that comprehension resides in the reader, not in the text being read, and that knowledge is constructed by individual learners within the social context (Whitmore & Goodman, 1996). Let's examine some factors that affect reading comprehension.

Schema Theory and Comprehension

Comprehension occurs when readers relate new information to existing knowledge (Anderson & Pearson, 1984). This existing information store is known as the reader's *schema*, an important concept in helping us understand the process of reading comprehension.

As human beings, we have a schema for each of the things we experience in life. This schema includes single events, situations we have encountered, things we

Older Readers

Summer Reading Is Killing Me, **by Jon Scieszka.**
During a summer vacation, three boys find themselves trapped inside their summer reading list, involved in a battle between good and evil characters from well-known children's books. They battle Long John Silver and the Wild Things and are helped out by Laura Ingalls and Anne of Green Gables.
New York: Viking, 1998.

The Library, **by Sarah Stewart.**
Elizabeth Brown loves to read more than anything else, but when her collection of books grows and grows, she decides to share her books by turning her home into a library.
New York: Farrar, Straus & Giroux, 1999.

Tomas and the Library Lady, **by Pat Mora.**
Based on the true story of the Mexican American author and educator Tomás Rivera, a child of migrant workers, this inspirational story suggests what libraries—and education—can make possible.
New York: Random House, 1997.

The Library Card, **by Jerry Spinelli.**
These four stories feature different characters, styles, and moods, but each plot hinges on a blue library card and the funny tales of the life-changing effects the library card has on the four kids who discover it.
New York: Scholastic, 1998.

have learned, and even sequences of events (Rumelhart, 1980, 1984). The central function of this schema is the "interpretation of an event, object, or situation—in the process of comprehension" (Rumelhart, 1984, p. 3). Activation of the schema we hold for a given situation enables us to comprehend the situation. For example, we feel very comfortable when we check into a Holiday Inn Express during a long road trip because our schema for Holiday Inn is quite complete. We know what to expect from the desk attendant and what will be in our room. As we walk into the room we *expect* to see familiar objects—beds, a color TV, drapes on the window, and a table. We also expect to find certain things in the bathroom—clean glasses wrapped in paper or plastic, towels, soap, and perhaps even a plastic shower cap. We have learned these things about motel rooms by experiencing them firsthand, by watching television commercials, or perhaps through reading.

Schemata are constantly being updated and revised. For example, one day we went tuna fishing off the coast of Maine and, during the course of the day, drastically altered our schema for tuna. Having never seen a live tuna before, we had been influenced by the "Charlie the Tuna" ads on television. To our surprise, however, we found that fishing poles and hooks were not used to catch the tuna, but harpoons! The fish harpooned that day were the size of small cars, not the 10-inch fish that existed in our schema. The result of the fishing trip was a revised schema concerning the size of tuna. Now that you've read this story, you too may experience a change in schemata.

What is the importance of schema theory to the classroom teacher? The answer is quite emphatic: Readers comprehend text when they are able to "find a configuration of hypotheses (schema) which offer a coherent account for the various aspects of the text" (Rumelhart, 1984, p. 3) and then activate that schema. When readers fail to find such a configuration, the text appears incomprehensible. However, when those configurations are recognized, comprehension occurs as new information enters the reader's cognitive realm and interacts with an existing schema. This enables readers to form a framework of "known information" so they can hook the "new" information into it. The result is an understanding of the passage and an expansion of the existing schema.

What about you? What happens when you activate a schema? Let's try an experiment. First, read the following passage and rank your understanding of the passage from 1 to 10, with 10 signifying that you have a complete and thorough understanding of the passage and 1 designating that you don't have a clue concerning the meaning:

> The procedure is actually quite simple. First you arrange things into different groups. Of course one pile may be sufficient depending on how much there is to do. If you have to go somewhere else due to lack of facilities that is the next step, otherwise you are pretty well set. It is important not to

overdo things. That is, it is better to do too few things at once than too many. In the short run this may not seem important but complications can easily arise. A mistake can be expensive as well. At first the whole procedure will seem complicated. Soon, however, it will become just another facet of life. It is difficult to foresee any end to the necessity for this task in the immediate future, but then one never can tell.

After the procedure is completed one arranges the material into different groups again. Then they can be put into their appropriate places. Eventually they will be used once more and the whole cycle will then have to be repeated. However, that is part of life. (Bransford & McCarrell, 1974, p. 206)

Now answer these comprehension questions about this passage:

1. What are the "things" discussed that you must arrange into different groups?
2. Why must you arrange them into groups?
3. Why is it better to do too few things at once rather than too many?
4. Why would making a mistake be expensive?
5. Why is this a task that will never end?
6. Why must you rearrange the material into different groups when the procedure is finished?
7. Where is the "appropriate" place you are to put these materials when the process is complete?
8. Why must this cycle be undertaken again?
9. What type of person would not have to be concerned with these procedures?

How did you do? We find that most readers either make an A+ or an F on this test! What's the difference between these readers? It's quite simple—readers who have activated the correct schema have no problem at all comprehending this passage or answering these questions.

Still puzzled? Perhaps if we tell you that the title of the passage is "Washing Clothes" things will become crystal clear to you!

Now, reread the passage and rank your understanding by using the same numerical system you did previously. Did the number of correct items signifying your comprehension increase? What made the difference? If your score increased, it was due to the activation of your schema. Once you were given the title "Washing Clothes," you were able to construct a framework of "known" information. That in turn facilitated your ability to connect the "new" information in the paragraph to the "known" information in your schema and understand the passage. Scenes probably "played in your mind" as the text triggered experiences of personal laundry drudgeries, successes, or disaster, which increased your comprehension of the text. Your lack of understanding during the first reading was not due to lack of decoding skills, it was because you were unable to activate your schema; therefore, you were only "calling words" and optimum comprehension was circumvented.

Teachers must remember the importance of facilitating conceptual development in students and provide them with opportunities for schema activation and expansion. Above all, we must demonstrate to students that reading involves a semantic transaction with text, that a passage does not have a meaning by itself: Meaning must be created by the students through interaction with the material they read.

America's Finest
Kandice Ramos

Teacher~to~Teacher

Megan Connell teaches first grade in Grand Rapids, Michigan. She knows that good readers activate schema and make connections with the text to enhance their understanding. Therefore, she consistently models this process as she reads aloud to her students.

Megan was aware that some of the children in her class had never been to a circus. Therefore, before reading *Star of the Circus* (Sampson & Sampson, 1997), she shared the name of the book with the children and asked them what they thought it might be about. Some children responded with "the circus!" and she asked them to close their eyes and pretend they were at a circus and imagine what they would see and hear.

Her goal was twofold—to activate and to build schema—so she then asked students to "partner" with another child, talk about their "imaginings," and decide on one thing to share with the class. She told the children they would have three minutes to talk to each other and decide on one thing to share. She set a timer and the students engaged in "partnering" and "sharing."

Megan's students often engage in paired discussion and then sharing with the class. To ensure that both children in the pair will be ready to share with the class, she typically waits until the end of the "partnering" time to designate which child will report. This time, at the conclusion of the three minutes,

she stated, "Today, the partner who is wearing the most buttons will share," and gave the children one minute to decide who that would be. As she recorded the responses of each pair of students on a chart, she engaged the class in conversation to extend and support the development of schema concerning the circus.

Since *Star of the Circus* focuses on the animals in the circus, she then led the students through a rereading of their ideas on the chart with the purpose of circling any animals they mentioned. Next, she asked them if they could think of other animals they might expect to see in the circus. As the children responded, she added the names to the chart. She then showed the children the cover of the book and the children noted the animals on the cover they had listed on their chart. Megan put a star by the words "elephant" and "lion," and the children decided they wanted her to continue to "star" animals she had recorded on the chart that were characters in the book and add animals they had not "thought of." They decided that they wanted to do this after she read the book aloud because they first wanted "to find out what all of these animals were doing!" Megan began reading the book to her first-graders knowing they had "activated/ extended their schemata" concerning the circus; therefore, their comprehension should be enhanced.

Textual Factors

Teachers must be aware that other factors also affect the reading comprehension of students. Often comprehension is hampered because of poorly written text, sometimes referred to as *inconsiderate text*—passages written in ways that disrupt the natural flow of language and thought and are incompatible with the language of the reader. The preprimers of most basal series are texts with very restricted vo-

© 2001 Bill Lisenby

Computers afford special opportunities for nonprint reading.

cabulary and awkward syntax. The same is true of basal reading programs that provide "decodable" text for first-graders. Students have more difficulty comprehending such simple, dull material than they do reading and understanding more complex, but better written material (Sampson, 1982).

Writers can help readers comprehend by providing headings, overviews, subheadings, summaries, definitions, graphs, and tables. And teachers can help students by demonstrating the usefulness of such textual aids.

Contextual Setting

Reading and reading comprehension always occur in the rich context of a literacy event. Reading events are multisituational and ever changing. The same book being read by a fourth-grade student on the sofa of his or her living room will be read in a different manner when the context is changed to the student's classroom at school. The reading event is different not only because of the location change but also because of emotional or physical changes within the reader. Thus a poem read in the morning will be read differently in the afternoon. Different schemata will be engaged, and different interpretations reached. This phenomenon of the language setting and mental setting interacting to create divergent environments is well documented (Harste et al., 1982; Harste & Carey, 1979; Rosenblatt, 1978, 1983).

Author Study

2

Meet the Author

Brian Pinkney

Brian Pinkney

1. *Which book of yours has given you the greatest pleasure?*

Max Found Two Sticks, because it's really about me. I read it a lot, and each time I find out a little bit more about myself.

2. *Which book has surprised you most in terms of its public reception?*

Duke Ellington keeps coming up. People use it in a lot of ways to teach about jazz and music. Parents keep talking about it.

3. *What would you like people to remember about your work?*

The energy and rhythm that go into making a book are the same energy and rhythm I would like people to feel when they look at my artwork.

4. *What impact do you hope your work will have on children?*

I hope to encourage them to want to read and make their own art. I also hope I introduce them to different people that they might not know about.

Brian Pinkney is known for his intelligent stories and his interesting artistic style. Using a scratchboard technique, he sculpts positive images of African Americans whom young readers may not know. His works include *Duke Ellington: The Piano Prince and His Orchestra, Max Found Two Sticks, Bill Pickett: Rodeo Ridin' Cowboy, The Adventures of Sparrowboy,* and *The Faithful Friend* (a Caldecott Honor Book).

Reprinted with special permission of Brian Pinkney.

Strategies for reading also change from situation to situation and from reading to reading. Sampson and White (1983) found that children read school-type materials differently from story-type materials. Interestingly, the students used more effective strategies when reading was removed from the formal school environment. Figure 5.2, which details our total literacy view of contextual reading, gives the likely explanations for this.

The term *language setting* applies to both oral and written language and describes the many cues (linguistic, situational, cultural) that may be processed. These, in turn, modify the mental setting. The mental setting alters the schema the reader uses, which in turn determines the strategy of the reader (Harste et al., 1982).

Comprehension Modes

Related to the discussion of language setting and context is Rosenblatt's (1978, 1983, 1991) theory of *reading stance*. She states that all readers select a purpose or mental

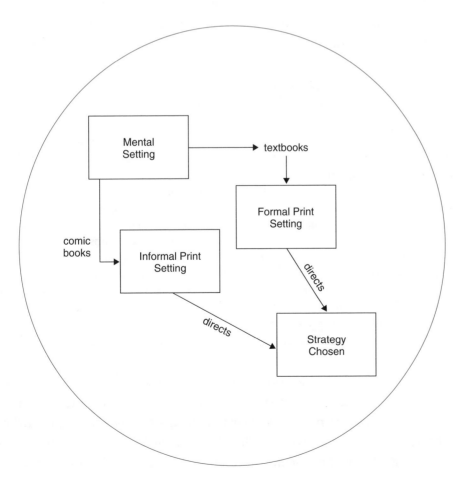

FIGURE 5.2
Situational influence on strategy selection

set for reading that determines what they seek to comprehend in the reading session. These positions vary along a continuum, ranging from an efferent to an aesthetic stance. *Efferent reading* focuses on factual meaning and includes information to be remembered, conclusions to be drawn, and propositions to be tested. Thus the reader's attention is on what is to be retained or applied after the reading.

In contrast, *aesthetic reading* focuses on what is being lived through *during* the reading. The reader's attention is expanded to include the images, feelings and associations that make the reading enjoyable, and an awareness of the sound and rhythm of the language as it resounds in the inner ear. Rosenblatt (1978, 1983) terms the comprehension that results from this type of pleasurable reading act a *poem*.

When students read, they may adopt an efferent stance, an aesthetic stance, or some position on the continuum between the two. The previous discussion of schemata detailed the importance of readers' tapping their schema during the comprehension process. Efferent reading, however, tends to place more emphasis on what is on the page and less on what is within the reader. Thus the teacher's goal is to promote the aesthetic stance by freeing students to contribute personal knowledge as they seek to comprehend. Instructional practices that encourage this reader contribution, such as Directed Reading–Thinking Activities (DR–TA), are discussed in Chapter 7.

Teacher-to-Teacher

Lisa Reeves is a fifth-grade teacher in Southern California. Her goal is to prepare her students for the many kinds of reading they will use in the "real" world. She does not concern herself with an efferent versus aesthetic debate but instead engages her students in both types of reading.

She uses cookbooks to point out to students that at times they need to take a text-centered perspective, or efferent mode, when reading. She encourages students to leave out ingredients in the fudge recipe and test the product through taste. She points out that sometimes we need to read slowly and carefully.

She contrasts efferent reading to aesthetic reading by sharing poetry. As students read Robert Louis Stevenson's "Windy Nights" (Martin & Sampson, in press), they are carried away by the images and power of the poem. The poem becomes more than the words on the page as students visualize tossing seas and galloping horses.

In summary, aesthetic reading and creating personal comprehension requires a context or reading environment that allows freedom for the reader to contribute to the text. However, many school environments stress the exact reproduction of the story as the child reads orally. This places the student in the efferent stance and discourages the aesthetic stance. Such practices focus on what students *do* comprehend instead of tapping what they *mig*ht be able to comprehend if they were given more freedom while reading (Tuinman, 1979).

Comprehension Instruction and Assessment

Comprehension has typically been taught through the presentation of various skills exercises. Such instruction does not usually take into consideration the contribution language users have to make to the process of reading comprehension. In fact, research indicates that basal readers and their subskills approach to comprehension instruction have a very serious shortcoming—they assess, rather than teach, reading comprehension (Durkin, 1978–79, 1981, 1983).

Distinctions must be made between the practice of asking students questions about what they have read (comprehension assessment) and teaching students how to comprehend (comprehension instruction). Because basal reader series and commercially prepared materials often equate the two, teachers must use alternative strategies if they are to show students that comprehension is a process in which meaning is created rather than a recall test of what students have read.

The most effective way of evaluating students' comprehension is through teacher observation, not testing. These teacher observations are less expensive than standardized tests and provide better information. Yetta Goodman (1985) has called these informal observations *kid watching*. The thrust of such observation is to answer two questions: (1) What evidence is there that comprehension is taking place? and (2) Do students' actions, such as choosing to do independent reading, indicate that they are successful in the classroom reading environment? The latter is easily answered by simple observation of student choices during free times. The first question may be answered by observing students as they encounter the comprehension activities described in Chapter 7.

FURTHER WORDS

 From InfoTrac College Edition

Let the Words Work Their Magic (excerpt from *The Art of Teaching Reading*), Lucy Calkins, *Instructor (1990)* Oct 2000 v110 i3 p25

Just a Matter of Time (giving enough time to slower students), Frank Smith, *Phi Delta Kappan* April 2001 v82 i8 p572

Parental Involvement in the Development of Children's Reading Skill: A Five-Year Longitudinal Study, Monique Sénéchal and Jo-Anne LeFevre, *Child Development* March–April 2002 v73 i2 p445(16)

Sustained Silent Reading: Try It, You'll Like It! Cynthia Anderson, *The Reading Teacher* November 2000 v54 i3 p258

Matching Texts and Readers: Leveling Early Reading Materials for Assessment and Instruction (the authors describe a book leveling system developed to support emergent literacy in one Canadian school district), Lori Jamison Rog and Wilfred Burton, *The Reading Teacher* December 2001 v55 i4 p348(9)

The Four-Square Strategy (teaching ideas), Michael Brunn, *The Reading Teacher* March 2002 v55 i6 p522(4)

Making It Sound Like Language: Developing Fluency (Center for the Improvement of Early Reading Achievement), Steven A. Stahl and Melanie R. Kuhn, *The Reading Teacher* March 2002 v55 i6 p582(3)

From Professional Journals and Publications

Goodman, K. S. (1985). Reading: A Psycholinguistic Guessing Game. In M. R. Sampson, J. H. White, K. M. Feathers, and I. L. Rorie (Eds.), *Literacy and Language Instruction* (pp. 14–22). Lexington, MA: Ginn Press.

Luke, A. (1995). When Basic Skills and Information Processing Just Aren't Enough: Rethinking Reading in New Times. *Teachers College Record, 97,* 1, 95–115.

Rosenblatt, L. M. (1983). The Reading Transaction: What For? In R. P. Parker and F. A. Davis (Eds.), *Developing Literacy. Young Children's Use of Language* (pp. 118–136). Newark, DE: International Reading Association.

Whitmore, K., and Goodman, K. (1996). Practicing What We Teach: The Principles That Guide Us. In K. Whitmore and Y. Goodman (Eds.), *Whole Language Voices in Teacher Education.* Urbana, IL: National Council Teachers of English.

Summary

We examined the reading process and found it to be an artifact of the other communicative processes. Reading and writing are based on language and are driven by the human need to communicate. Reading is a process that involves a transaction between a reader intent on establishing meaning and a text. This search for meaning will be directed by the ever-learning mind of the reader and involves a transaction between language and thought.

Teachers must aid students by helping each child conceptualize the truths about language in the comprehension processes that have been discussed in this chapter. In addition, teachers have a fundamental responsibility to establish a conceptual framework that will serve as their guide in selecting activities, experiences, materials, and evaluative procedures.

Total Literacy Anchors

- ◆ The student appropriately utilizes semantic, syntactic, and graphophonic cues.
- ◆ The student samples, predicts, confirms, and corrects while reading with meaning or "making sense" as a basis for continuing the process.
- ◆ The student is more concerned with getting meaning from the text than with decoding each word.

- The teacher views children as emerging learners.
- The teacher realizes that students learn to read and become proficient readers by having many opportunities to interact with meaningful texts.
- The teacher does not indiscriminately correct all miscues but looks on them as "windows on the reading process" and makes instructional decisions based on this information.
- The teacher provides an instructional environment that emphasizes that the foundation of reading is not just "to say the right word" but to get meaning from the print.

CHAPTER 6

Basal Readers

As You Read . . .

- What memories do you have about learning to read from a basal reading program?

- What are the major positive features of basal programs?

- What are the major limitations to basal programs?

- Why are basal programs so common in U.S. schools?

- Where do you currently see yourself as a user of basal programs and materials?

- If you do not use or do not intend to use a basal reading program, how will you answer questions from parents and school administrators about why you are not using the basal that has been provided for you by the school?

If you are new to reading education you probably have not heard the phrase "basal readers," or "basals." This unusual term is unfamiliar to those outside of elementary and middle school education. Yet for those involved in teaching children to read, basal readers is a very familiar term— one that is often greeted with either acceptance or disdain.

Basal reading programs or textbooks are comprehensive systems published by educational publishing companies for teaching reading in schools. Most commonly found in the elementary grades, basal programs are actually available in all grade levels. Most are designed for use with normally developing students; however, in recent years basal reading programs have been designed for students who experience significant difficulty in learning to read. Basal reading programs are the most commonly found platform or framework for elementary reading instruction in the United States. A majority of primary grade classrooms use basal reading programs, and most of the elementary classrooms (K–6) incorporate some aspect of basal designed instruction (Snow, Burns, & Griffin, 1998).

The term *basal* itself is not esoteric or ancient, nor is it a word obtained from some unusual teaching technique. Rather, *basal* is derived from the word *basic* and refers to the notion that, in their original forms, basal reading programs offered

Basal readers are used in virtually every elementary school in America.

teachers and schools a basic or foundational approach to reading instruction. In the days when not all teachers were fully prepared to teach reading, a basal reading program ensured that the basics of effective reading instruction, as they were known at the time, were provided to every child. This ensured an equitable, effective, and basic reading instructional program for all students.

Perhaps the most famous of all basal readers was Scott Foresman's "Dick and Jane" series. This series was developed in the 1940s and remained a mainstay in reading instruction through the 1960s. The generation of children born after World War II, the largest in U.S. history, learned to read via the now famous refrains of "See Dick. Run, Dick, run" or another basal very similar in nature to the Scott Foresman program. Perhaps you or your parents have memories of reading the basal textbook of that time.

Elements of a Basal Reading Program: Framework for Teaching Key Skills and Strategies

Basal reading programs are described by their publishers as complete systems for teaching reading within and across a number of grade levels. Published basal programs are usually geared to provide reading instruction to students in kindergarten through grade 6 or beyond. Because a basal program cuts across grade levels and does so through a series of textbooks, basal programs are also known as basal series.

At the heart of any basal program are the various component skills and strategies that are taught. The authors of the basal program assume that the instructional skills and strategies that they have identified are important for learning to read. Different basal programs have different sets of skills and strategies. In general, however, regardless of the publisher or the author, the skills and strategies incorporated in basal reflect current knowledge about teaching reading and the current policies of state governments and the federal government for teaching reading. The corpus of skills and strategies embodied in any given basal goes by the term *scope*.

Authors of basal programs not only identify the skills and strategies inherent in their program, they also identify the order (grade levels) in which those skills and strategies are introduced and reinforced. For example, phonics and decoding skills and strategies are usually emphasized before vocabulary (word meaning) skills and strategies are taught. Moreover, within phonics and decoding skills and strategies, short vowel sounds and letters that represent short vowel sounds are typically taught prior to long vowel sounds. Sounds represented by one letter are taught before sounds represented by two letters. This ordering of skills and strategies is termed *sequence*.

Basal programs usually bundle the skills and strategies into sets of related skills called *strands*. Thus, a basal reading program usually has strands that contain skills and strategies for phonemic awareness, phonics and decoding, vocabulary, comprehension, study skills, and others. To communicate the strands of skills and strategies that are part of its basal program, as well as the order in which they are taught, publishing companies provide this information in a chart or booklet called the *Scope and Sequence*. When orienting yourself to any basal program, look over the Scope and Sequence material to determine exactly what skills you will be responsible for teaching students and what materials and methods you have in your own repertoire that may be useful in teaching those skills.

Regardless of the publishing company, most basal reading programs are made up of a fairly common set of materials: textbook or anthology, big books, supplemental books, workbooks and worksheets, English language learner materials, assessment materials, parent materials, technology and multimedia materials, and a teacher's guide (Figure 6.1).

Textbook

At the heart of any basal reading program is the collection of stories, poems, and other reading passages that constitute the reading material for students. This collection is known as the basal textbook or anthology. Publishers ensure that the texts reflect the reading level of the grade for which they are intended by measuring the *readability* of each passage (see Figure 6.5 on p. 167 for more on readability). Individual passages within a grade are often grouped by theme or topic into units of study. The reading material in the textbook also reflects the various skills that are being taught at the time at which the passage is introduced. If a phonics skill or generalization is being taught, the passage will likely contain many words that reflect that skill. If sequential comprehension is under study by students, the passage will include elements that lend themselves to sequencing time events.

Big Books

Big books are enlarged texts that are used primarily at kindergarten and first grade. The books are usually displayed on an easel. Teachers use big books to guide large groups of students through an entire text using a technique called shared reading. Teachers point to the text, word by word, as they read it to the children. Later they will invite students to read the big book with them. As children come to master the story, the teacher will invite individual or small groups of children to read the big

Older Readers

***Number the Stars*, by Lois Lowry.**
The story of how a Danish girl and her family hide her best friend—a young Jewish girl—during the Nazi occupation of Denmark in 1943.
Boston: Houghton Mifflin, 1989.

***The Mysteries of Harris Burdick*, by Chris Van Allsburg.**
The book begins with a letter stating that the author does not know the origin of the photos and continues with a series of mysterious pictures each having a caption that inspires the reader to create her own story.
Boston: Houghton Mifflin, 1984.

***Toliver's Secret*, by Esther Wood-Brady.**
Ellen's grandfather is injured and she takes his place to smuggle a top-secret message to General George Washington.
New York: Crown, 1976.

***The Pushcart War*, by Jean Merrill.**
New York City's streets are in chaos—the pushcarts have declared war with the truck drivers!
New York: Peter Smith, 1987.

Regardless of the publishing company, most basal reading programs are made up of a fairly common set of materials.

Textbook or Anthology   This is the book that each student receives. It is made up of a collection of reading selections that are at the same level of difficulty (readability) and represent a variety of genres, from narrative to exposition to poetry.

Big Books   Big books are enlarged books that set on an easel. They are intended for group or shared reading by younger students, usually students in kindergarten through grade 2.

Supplemental Books   Students need something to read when they finish the passage in their textbook. Supplemental books represent further readings for students on the topics found in the textbook.

Workbooks and Worksheets   These materials provide students with opportunities to practice the various skills and strategies covered by the teacher in a lesson. They also are meant to keep students busy while the teacher works with other students.

English Language Learner Materials   These materials help students whose first language is not English make the transition from their native language to English. The materials may include storybooks, workbooks, and worksheets.

Assessment Materials   The assessment materials provide teachers with approaches for monitoring student progress in reading and mastery over various skills and strategies and units of study from the textbook.

Parent Materials   Research indicates that making connection with the home benefits students' progress in becoming fully literate. Most basal programs now provide teachers with books, materials, and ideas to share with parents and extend the learning that takes place in the school.

Technology and Multimedia Materials   No basal program would be complete without materials that require a computer or other piece of technological equipment. These may include practice programs for the computer, computer books, programs for monitoring student progress, Web connections, books on audiotape, videotapes to build background knowledge on covered topics, and so forth.

Teacher's Guide   This is the nerve center for the basal program. It provides teachers with the global and specific guide for teaching literacy. It guides teachers in the use of all the materials listed above. It indicates specific procedures for implementing comprehensive literacy lessons associated with each passage in the student textbook.

FIGURE 6.1

Basal reading program materials

book independently. Following group reading of the big book, the teacher will often ask children to identify individual words or other components of the text.

In many basal reading programs, the story portrayed in a big book is also produced in normal form and in multiple copies. Once read and mastered as a group, the smaller version of the big book provides students with the opportunity to continue reading the passage on their own in school or at home.

Supplemental Books

An increasingly popular component of basal reading programs are the supplementary books that follow up on the stories that are part of the main textbook or anthology. Supplemental books in a basal program are multiple copies of trade books that share or extend the skills and strategies, words, theme, genre, action, characters, or author with a story read in the textbook. In the initial stages of a basal program, when students are learning to decode words, the supplemental books are made up of stories that contain many of the same words that are part of the instructional lesson and the textbook story that accompanies the lesson.

When the focus is more on comprehension skills and strategies, the supplementary books deal with themes, plot structures, types of comprehension, vocabulary, and competencies covered in the instruction and textbook passage. Supplemental books allow students to read independently and reinforce previously taught skills and strategies. The textbook passage builds interest and background for the supplemental book. Because they have some degree of background through the textbook reading, students should be able to independently read, understand, and enjoy the supplementary book.

Workbooks and Worksheets

Materials used to provide practice in the various reading skills taught are found in the form of workbooks and worksheets. Workbooks are softback consumable books given to students at the beginning of the year. Worksheets are individual consumable pages (blackline masters) that supplement the workbook. The teacher duplicates the master set of worksheets at her own discretion, assigning workbook and worksheet pages that correspond to the skill or strategy under current study as well as the story that has been read. Skills and strategy strands normally developed through worksheet activities include phonics and decoding, vocabulary, comprehension, writing, and study skills.

Workbooks and worksheets also serve a management purpose for many teachers. While the teacher works with a small group of children, other students can work on assigned workbook pages and worksheets. These pages and sheets give students practice in the skills and strategies the teacher is covering; they are designed to keep students productively and independently engaged and relatively quiet while the teacher works with another group of students.

Basal programs also provide teachers with overhead transparencies for teaching skills and strategies, and some include copies of workbook or worksheet pages so that teachers can model how to complete particular assignments.

2

America's Finest

Ceretha Levingston

Choosing Diverse Children's Literature

As you plan and implement reading beyond basal reading stories for your students, it is critical that the stories, content textbooks, and trade books in your classroom provide children with a diverse view of the world. We ask you to expand your concept of multicultural literature beyond the portrayal of different cultures and peoples to include the interaction and likenesses between multiple cultures and peoples. It is important that children have exposure to the unique aspects of various peoples and cultures, but it is also critical that learners have the opportunity to explore their similarities. As we recognize and celebrate diversity, we must also ensure that children do not develop stereotypes regarding certain groups. We must ensure that the following situation does not occur in our classrooms:

> Apparently we had unwittingly told our students to emphasize differences rather than similarities between cultures; therefore, our students' first intuition in creating what we called a "multicultural classroom" resulted in a culturally assaultive classroom. (Clark, DeWolf, & Clark, 1992, p. 5)

Remember that the term *diverse groups* refers to a wide variety of classifications including, but not limited to, gender, ethnicity, race, religion, exceptionality, and culture. Therefore, as you share both textbooks and trade books with your children—

and as you build a classroom library—keep the following criteria in mind:

- Are individual members of diverse groups portrayed as unique individuals with personal thoughts, emotions, and philosophies rather than representatives of a particular group?

- Are stories available that portray characters representing diverse groups resolving problems, making decisions, and achieving success without requiring the paternalistic help of someone from a culture that is perceived as superior or more advanced?

- Are stories available that portray diverse characters in authentic and understandable settings?

- Are stories shared that portray diverse groups in different time periods and in different roles? (For instance, is literature available that portrays Native Americans in today's time period—not just as living in teepees and wearing headdresses? Are physically impaired children and adults portrayed as capable, valuable, contributing members of society?)

- Are illustrations void of stereotypically exaggerated physical and facial characteristics?

- Does the collection of books contain portrayals of characters representative of diverse groups in a wide range of settings, occupations, educational backgrounds, living conditions, socioeconomic statuses, and lifestyles?

English Language Learner Materials

Recognizing that many of the children in elementary classrooms today are not native speakers of English, most basal programs include supplementary storybooks, workbooks, and worksheets designed to help English Language

- If dialect or another language is used in the story, is it a positive portrayal? Does it support the story and the understanding of the character? Derogatory terms for groups should not be used unless they are in historical context or are essential to the conflict.

- Are stories available that portray characters from diverse groups interacting in collaborative and positive ways in realistic situations to resolve problems, make decisions, and achieve success?

- Does the portrayal of diverse groups include a variety of literature genres? For instance, folktales often portray a stereotypical view of groups based on gender and culture. It is important that children be exposed to diverse groups through all literature genres including contemporary realistic fiction, poetry, historical fiction and biography, informational stories, and fantasy stories.

In addition to these criteria, as you strive to share literature with your students that portray a range of diversity and enhance their understandings of their own experiences and the experiences of others, it is important to be aware of Rudine Sims Bishop's (1992) three classifications of literature that depict diversity:

Culturally neutral   In these texts, diversity is depicted only *incidentally*. The topics or themes are not identifiable with any particular group. For instance, diversity may be depicted in the illustrations, but the story does not require characters to be a member of a particular group.

Culturally generic   Characters from a diverse group are purposefully and primarily featured in situations that are universal—not specific to one group. For instance, *Everett Anderson's Good-bye* (Clifton, 1988) portrays a young African American boy's progression through the stages of grief as he copes with the loss of a parent—a traumatic experience for any child.

Culturally specific   The experiences of one particular group including areas such as language use, values, beliefs, attitudes, interactions, and setting are accurately portrayed. The conflict is authentic to the represented group. For example, *Be Good to Eddie Lee* (Fleming, 1993) portrays the struggles and strengths of a young boy with Down's syndrome.

Even though textbook publishers have dramatically increased the representation of diverse groups within the last thirty years, it is unlikely that one book, story, or even textbook will address all of these issues. However, your awareness of and commitment to the importance of sharing stories with your students that depict a wide range of diversity will support them as they gain appreciation for themselves and others. In addition, they will learn to celebrate both their areas of diversity and those of convergence.

Learners (ELL) transition from their native language to English. In many cases, the ELL materials include patterned storybooks in English to be read in school and the very same books in Spanish for the students to read at home with their parents.

Assessment Materials

A complete program for reading instruction needs to provide teachers with materials for assessing student learning and performance. Thus, basal programs also contain a variety of assessment materials including assessments of the student's mastery of individual passages or a collection of passages within a textbook. Also included in the assessment package are materials for placing students, measuring progress within individual skill and strategy strands (for example, phonics), and diagnostic tests for assessing areas of particular weakness or strength.

Parent Materials

With the increased recognition that home involvement is critical to student success in literacy, basal programs provide teachers with materials to extend the reading instruction experience at home. Parent materials may include newsletters that provide information on the overall program as well as various themes or units within a grade level. Duplicated worksheets that reinforce lessons in school are also a common part of the parent materials package. English and Spanish versions of these materials are often made available to teachers.

Technology and Multimedia Materials

As instructional technology evolves, basal reading program publishers ensure that the latest technological and multimedia materials and features are available for their programs. Audiocassette recordings of passages in the textbook are an excellent way for students, especially those who struggle in reading, to continue reading a text without the aid of the teacher, parent, or a classmate.

Instructional videos may also be available to explain the basal program itself or various aspects of it to teachers or parents. Videos are also used to explain and expand on readings and lessons for students. CD-ROMs and Web sites are among the newest technological features that have been added to basal programs to expand and enhance the quality of the reading education experience for students.

Teacher's Guide

Perhaps the most important part of any basal reading program is the teacher's guide (TG). This is the nerve center for the basal program, and it provides teachers with both a global and specific guide for teaching literacy. The TG connects the various and diverse elements of the program and explains to teachers how these elements come together to provide effective instruction, monitoring, and management over students' learning to read and the various skills and strategies associated with learning to read.

The TG normally comes in the form of an oversized, spiral bound book. It provides the teacher with an overview to each story and lesson, information on how to teach the story and skills and strategies within the story, correct answers for workbook and worksheet activities, and ideas for projects that extend each reading experience for students to provide additional skill and strategy practice or to allow students to respond to the reading in a creative manner. The students' textbook, workbook, and worksheet pages are also reproduced in the TG.

The TG provides information on coordinating the core program with supplemental books and multimedia features of the program. It also provides guidance to the teacher on periodically assessing student progress and diagnosing specific problems in students experiencing difficulty in learning to read. In short, the TG provides the teacher with all the information necessary for implementing the program, as intended by the authors, using all the main and ancillary materials and features, and assessing student progress within the program itself.

Teaching with a Basal

Basal reading programs are more than simply sets of materials for teaching reading. They also come with an embedded approach or generic lesson plan for teaching reading. Originally the lesson was called the *Directed Reading Activity* (Betts, 1946). Today, most professionals use the term *Guided Reading Lesson* to describe lessons that are part of basal reading programs. Regardless of the name, the lesson format is generally the same across all basal programs and is organized around prereading, guided reading, postreading response to text, skill and strategy development and practice, and extension and enrichment activities (Figure 6.2).

Prereading

In the prereading phase, the teacher introduces students to the text to be read by building background knowledge, introducing and reviewing key vocabulary words, and pointing out other key features of the passage. Often, this part of the lesson is embedded in a book walk. In a book walk, the teacher may introduce students to the title and author for the story and ask students what they may know about the topic implied in the title or what they may know about the author. The information that students share may be listed on the chalkboard or on a chart. Then the teacher may give a quick overview to the text, highlighting key events and characters and making sure students are familiar with any important or unusual words that will be encountered in the reading. Pictures and illustrations are shared,

Basal literacy programs are more than a set of materials for students and teachers. They also include specific suggestions for teaching with the materials. This is done through the Directed Reading Activity, more commonly known as "guided reading." The steps in all Directed Reading Activity lessons follow a similar a format:

Prereading   During prereading phase the teacher prepares students for the actual reading of the textbook selection. This includes building and eliciting background knowledge, introducing vocabulary, making predictions, and entertaining questions related to the passage.

Guided Reading   During the guided reading phase students actually read the passage—orally, silently, chorally in a group, or in some combination. Periodically through the reading students may stop to talk about the meaning of the selection as it develops.

Postreading Response to Text   When the actual reading is finished, the teacher invites students to consolidate their understanding of the passage by responding to the text in some way. This is often accomplished through discussion groups but may also include responding through writing, visual arts, movement, or other form of meaning representation.

Skill and Strategy Development and Practice   At this phase the teacher turns students' attention toward specific skills and strategies in reading that need to be taught. These skills and strategies may include phonics skills, study strategies, vocabulary development, or many other component skills in reading and writing. A brief lesson is usually followed with independent practice in the workbook or with a worksheet.

Extension and Enrichment   At this final, and often optional, point in the lesson, students are encouraged to expand their horizons with the passage read or with any of the skills covered. Students may write their own version of the story, develop a public debate about issues in the reading, represent meaning from the text in a novel manner, or use their creative energy in some other way to represent or extend the meaning of the passage just read.

FIGURE 6.2
Guided literacy lessons basal style

and the teacher introduces students to any figures, diagrams, charts, graphs, tables, or other features that they may need some help in interpreting.

The prereading period may also include activities designed to build students' interest in and motivation for the topic to be read. These may include role-playing activities, demonstrations, and hands-on activities to actively engage students in considering the ideas and topics to be presented in the text.

Finally, the teacher may ask students to make and share predictions about the content of the passage. Students may also be asked to come up with questions that may guide their reading of the passage. Or, in some cases, the teacher may provide a set of questions or provocative statements that will elicit interest, curiosity, and engagement in or with the text.

Guided Reading

During the reading phase of the lesson, the major task of students is to read the assigned selection. Beyond the initial stages of reading, the story is usually read silently by students and section by section. When working with beginning readers, the teacher may read the text with the children in a more guided manner. First, the teacher may read the passage to the students while the students follow along. Next, students may read the text chorally with the teacher. Finally, individual students may be asked to read the passage. Guided reading can be quite effective when the teacher creates a classroom context for focused and strategic reading (Broad, 2001).

It is normally during this reading period that teachers at all grade levels sometimes engage in round robin reading of the passage with students. Round robin reading is characterized by the teacher calling on individual students to read sections of the passage aloud while other students follow along silently. This activity ostensibly gives all students a chance to read, allows the teacher to monitor each child's reading, and provides the teacher with a method for managing student activity. We do not encourage round robin reading, however, because it is not a very authentic form of reading. Only in classrooms do we normally find this form of reading taking place.

A very important rule of thumb for oral reading is not to ask students to read something orally without giving them a chance to rehearse it silently. In round robin reading, students are normally asked to read a passage "cold," without the opportunity to preread their assigned section. Knowing this, many children who are not reading aloud find themselves looking ahead in the reading, trying to look over the portion of text they may be asked to read by the teacher. Although this is a very logical thing to do, it results in students not following along with the teacher and the reader, and it usually disrupts the meaning making that should occur during this reading period. There are many reasons and occasions for students to read orally, but round robin reading is not one of them.

At predetermined stopping points in the silent reading, students are often led in a discussion of that portion of the text by the teacher. The teacher may also ask students to identify and clarify any misconceptions that have developed and to consider the predictions they made earlier in the text and revise them or make new predictions before moving on to the next section of the passage. Although it may be wise to stop students to ensure appropriate processing and understanding of the text, too many disruptions in the reading of the entire text may disrupt readers' construction of meaning as well as their overall enjoyment of the text.

Although most of the text is read silently, there is plenty of room for variation in the reading phase. The teacher may begin by reading a brief opening portion of the passage aloud while students listen or read along silently. The teacher does this to develop a sense of fluency, meaning, and interest in the reading. Once primed by the teacher, the students are more likely to continue reading on their own. The teacher may also ask the entire group of students to begin reading the beginning of the selection in a choral manner to get everyone started on an equal footing and to develop the sense of community that should be part of the reading group. The teacher might also assign individual sections of the reading selection to individuals or pairs of students. The students then practice their assigned readings and then perform their portion for the reading group at the next class meeting.

Postreading Response to Text

Following the reading of the selection, students engage in responding to the text to consolidate and share their understandings of the passage. Traditionally, this has occurred through a brief discussion initiated and led by the teacher. In these instances, the teacher simply directed the questions that were included in the TG to specific students. Most of the questions tended to be of the literal type: Who were the main characters? What was the city in which the main character lived? The intent of these discussions is oriented more toward evaluation of student literal understandings than toward developing and nurturing those understandings.

More recently, the nature of the response to the reading has changed in basal texts. More inferential and critical level questions have been added to the mix of questions asked by the teacher: What do you think would have happened if . . . ? What did you like about this character and why? Would you have done the same thing if you were in the position of the main character?

The response activity itself has changed in many classrooms. In some classrooms, teachers ask students to write out their thoughts in response to the reading in a special journal for student response. In other classrooms, students may draw a picture and share their drawing with classmates to ignite talk about the text. Alternatively, in some classrooms students engage in discussions that are largely run by the students themselves. These have been called literature discussion groups, book clubs, or grand conversations. Although such discussions may look a bit different from classroom to classroom, the intent is to have students engage in the same type of self-sustaining, engaging, and enlightening discussions that adults participate in when they are part of a book club or a study group.

Teachers often guide younger students or students not familiar with this form of response by assigning one or more roles to students in the group. The roles can range from discussion leader to finding and defining interesting words in the passage just read. These roles give each student a very definite task in the discussion and something tangible to share with the group. As students become more comfortable with their discussion groups, the specific roles can melt away and become the responsibility of all students in the group.

Skill and Strategy Development and Practice

Next up in the Directed Reading Activity is a focus on reading skills and strategies. Remember earlier that we mentioned the scope and sequence of reading skills and strategies that are part of every basal reading program. It is in this phase of the lesson that specific skills and strategies are taught. The focus here may involve words from the reading, comprehension of the passage itself, specific skills and strategies that can be employed to negotiate the passage, and some of the literacy qualities or features found in the text. Usually a brief lesson on some skill, strategy, or other learning objective, using the passage as the context within which the skill or strategy is illustrated, is followed by the assignment of one or more pages from students' workbooks or worksheets. These pages give students practice in the skills and strategies taught and keep students busy, quiet, and, it is hoped, productively and academically engaged while the teacher works with another group of students. The assigned sheets are usually corrected at the next reading group meeting.

Extension and Enrichment

The final phase of the Directed Reading Activity provides students with the opportunity to explore topics and ideas covered in the passage and the previous part of the lesson. At this final, and often optional, point in the lesson, students are encouraged to expand their horizons with the passage read or with any of the skills covered. Students may write their own version of the story, develop a public debate about issues in the reading, represent meaning from the text in a novel manner, or

Students at work on a basal extension activity.

use their creative energy in some other way to represent or extend the meaning of the passage just read. Here are some ways students can extend their learning:

1. Write a sequel to or another version of the text.
2. Dramatize the text in some way.
3. Create an artistic representation of the text.
4. Make connections of the text to other areas of the curriculum such as writing, music, science, or social studies.
5. Read other materials or genre related to the topic or theme of the text read.
6. Study new words related to words found and studied in the passage read.

Students often find the greatest personal enjoyment and satisfaction in this portion of the lesson. Unfortunately, this portion of the lesson is identified as optional, and due to time constraints it is often skipped over by teachers who feel the need to move on to the next story and next set of reading skills and strategies to be covered.

Teacher-to-Teacher

Sally Houser has been a fifth-grade teacher for eight years. Before that she taught second grade. Her classroom is filled with trade books for student reading and centers for their independent exploration of topics of interest. In her classroom and out in the hallway, her students' work is proudly on display—written stories and essays, results of science projects and experiments, artwork, dioramas and more.

Although Sally identifies herself as a teacher who teaches reading with trade books, she readily admits that she uses material from the basal reading program provided by the school district. "Sometimes I need some materials to reinforce a particular concept that I have taught. I check in the basal guide and find that it has some workbook pages that meet my needs exactly. It would probably be better if I developed my own materials, but often I just don't have the time. The basal is a very useful resource for me."

Sally also admits that when she first began teaching and when she first moved to fifth-grade she relied more heavily on the basal. "As I have become more comfortable with the needs of children in the fifth grade and with the content I am required to cover, I have moved further away from the basal program. Personally, I like to teach my own curriculum. When I develop my own materials and assignments for students, I know what I am trying to emphasize. I don't always have that feeling with the basal materials I use."

Background to Basals

Basal reading programs were developed to reflect the best knowledge that was available in teaching reading. Basal programs of the 1940s through the 1960s incorporated what has been called the "look say" method, in which students look at a whole

Daniel Self — Name

I am eleven years old — Age

space exploration, exercize and debating. — Interests

What do you like most about school?

I like School because the way our classroom run. My teacher is a humorous guy and a good teacher.

What's your favorite subject? Why?

My favorite subject is the history simulation because it's an exciting experience whith many twists and I absolutely love it.

What's your favorite book? Why do you like it?

My absolute favorite book is Phantom Tollbooth it's a wonderfully colorful book with a wonderful ending and an endless amount of classic literature.

What advice do you have for teachers?

My advice would be to listen to the children because we have good ideals.

word and say it. The essential notions this approach was based on were sight vocabulary and analytical phonics. This approach to reading teaches children to read by learning a set of phonics generalizations and patterns, such as initial sound–letter correspondences and word families, after having learned a set of sight words that are subsequently applied to other words. This is called *analytical phonics* (Harris & Hodges, 1995). Most adults recognize the words they encounter in reading automatically, or by sight. That is, they do not have to think about, analyze, or sound out most of the words they encounter. How do adults develop their sight vocabularies? The answer is, through repeated exposures to the words they read. After many readings of a particular word, the word is stored in the reader's memory and becomes a sight word.

Basal programs of the 1940s through the 1960s attempted to capitalize on this understanding about how adults read by exposing children to a limited set of words over and over again through the books they read and through worksheets focusing on initial sounds and word families. The words were controlled for length and frequency—the highest frequency, or most common, words and words that were phonetically regular were presented first. Over time, the number and difficulty of the words introduced through these readers increased, and more and more words that did not follow the rules of phonics were presented. Figure 6.3 shows an analytical phonics lesson from a typical basal reader.

VOWEL SOUNDS—O

You know that each of the vowels stands for more than one sound.

As you say the words **not, hop,** and **dollar,** listen for the sound the letter **o** stands for. We call that sound the short **o** sound.

In which of the following words do you hear the short **o** sound?

top	know	lock	pocket
box	stop	snow	golden

As you say the words **open, both,** and **cold,** listen for the sound that the letter **o** stands for. We call that sound the long **o** sound.

In which of the following words do you hear the long **o** sound?

post	goat	over	got
bottom	snow	pop	throw

As you say these words, listen for other sounds the letter **o** stands for:

brown	come	once	trouble
do	sound	strong	scooter

In the following lines the words in very black letters may be strange to you.

1. Use the sounds the letters stand for and the sense of the other words to find out what the new words are. Put on your hat and **coat** before you go out to play.
2. The little black horse **trots** faster than any of the big horses.
3. We had a bag race and a peanut race and Jack **won** both of them.
4. Mother **bought** a big jar of lemonade at the store.
5. Look both ways before you **cross** the street.

FIGURE 6.3

Analytical phonics instruction in early basal reader programs

In the 1950s the "look–say" approach was challenged in an influential book by Rudolph Flesch entitled *Why Johnny Can't Read* (1955). Flesch argued that the "whole word" or "look–say" approach did not give all children a good start on learning to read. He argued that American children were not reading as well as children from the Soviet Union because American schools did not teach phonics. (The approach to reading that teaches children to read by focusing on letter-sounds is synthetic phonics). Flesch noted that embedded in words themselves are clues for decoding unknown words; those clues are the letters and letter combinations that represent the sounds of language. He argued that most words in English have some regular letter-sound relations embedded in them and that many words, particularly the shorter words that beginning readers encounter, can be "sounded out" almost entirely through letter–sound correspondences, or *phonics.* Flesch presented his argument in a convincing manner to politicians and parents through this mass marketed, bestselling book. Yet despite his charges, "most basal programs had always included some phonics instruction" (Graves, Juel, & Graves, 2001, p. 68).

With the civil rights movement of the 1950s and 1960s, reading scholars began to note that basal readers provided readers with a fairly stereotypical view of society. Dick and Jane were white children who lived in a fairly comfortable suburban white community in which the father worked and the mother was a housewife. That may have reflected the circumstances of some children, but it certainly did not reflect the lives of many other children. Basal reading programs were criticized for promoting and institutionalizing a view of society that was far from reality for most children.

In the face of these concerns, did basal reading programs disappear? No, they simply evolved, or shifted in their emphasis. They began to portray more children of color and other ethnic and cultural backgrounds, and they began to provide alternative views of family backgrounds, lifestyles, and careers for women and men.

Similarly, basal programs moved away somewhat from a whole word approach and toward a phonics approach. Basal readers that incorporated a stronger phonics strand—often through a phonics workbook and with stories that incorporated words that reflected the phonics teaching—began to enter the market in the 1960s and 1970s.

Linguistic basals were also developed during this time period. Linguistic basals focused children's attention on the relationship between sounds and print. However, the print unit used in linguistic approaches was usually longer, consisting of letter strings of vowels and consonants such as *-at, -an, -ip,* and so on, which we call word families, phonograms, or rimes. Instead of letter-by-letter decoding, a reader could examine a word for the longer linguistic units or chunks. Moreover, word families or phonograms were fairly consistent in the sounds they represented. When the phonogram -at appears in a one-syllable word, it always represents /at/, the sound heard in cat.

Students in basal programs incorporating a phonics or linguistic approach to early reading instruction read stories with words that reflected the phonics generalization that was being taught at the time. When short a was taught, students read stories with plenty of short a words. When the phonogram -an was the focus of instruction in a linguistic reader, students read stories about *Dan the man who ran and ran.* Clearly, stories written to provide multiple exposures to high-frequency words, practice in short a words, words that contain the consonant digraph *sh*, or repeated decodings of words that contained a particular linguistic unit such as -an are going to be limited in the quality of the story that can be presented. There are only so many ways a writer can use the word *look* or *run* in a story before the story begins to become tedious and uninteresting.

The next change in the evolution of basals occurred when critics of "whole word" and "phonics" approaches to reading instruction noted that students were being asked to read stories of questionable quality. Critics also noted that in some cases classic and very familiar stories were incorporated into basal reading programs. However, the stories were altered so that particular word features were stressed (for example, short a words) or to meet a particular readability level (see Figure 6.5 on p. 167 for more on readability). Critics of this practice noted that children were being asked to read stories that had been fundamentally altered or "engineered" so that much of the endearing qualities of the original texts were removed. Children were reading versions of *Goldilocks and the Three Bears* that were unlike the versions that had been read to them at home.

Psycholinguistics is the science of how the mind processes language. This school of thought has had a profound effect on reading education by broadening reading instruction to include strategies beyond memorizing words and using sound-symbol relationships. The psycholinguists noted that information to assist in decoding words can be found in the syntactic (grammatical arrangement) and semantic (the meaning being communicated) systems that are part of language. For example, when a reader encounters the word *the,* the reader knows that the next word will likely be either a noun or a word that modifies a noun (the man or the big red truck). This knowledge of syntax reduces the possibility of other words that could follow *the.* Similarly, when reading about eating a meal at a fast food restaurant, a knowledge of semantics tells the reader that the text will likely not have words such as *waiter, entrée, wine,* or *tip* included in it. It is more likely that the words *hamburger, shake, French fries,* and *drive thru* will appear in the text. Syntactic and semantic knowledge doesn't always provide the reader with the precise word that is to be read. It does, however, help the reader to make good predictions about the words to be read—words that will most likely fit the overall meaning of the passage.

Key, then, to the psycholinguistic approach to reading is the notion of prediction. Readers often predict words using the semantic and syntactic information embedded in an authentic (not altered or "engineered") and well-developed story. Thus, advocates of a psycholinguistic approach to reading, which has come to be called "whole language," note that readers need to read authentic texts—the very kinds of stories that have been to read to them at home since they were born.

In the face of these concerns, did basal reading programs disappear? No, they simply evolved, or shifted their emphasis, once again. In the 1980s and through the early 1990s, basal readers shifted dramatically away from "engineered" stories, stories developed for the sole purpose of teaching "whole word" or phonics-oriented decoding. Basal reading textbooks came to be called *anthologies,* collections of authentic and previously published stories by children's authors.

Although the quality of the stories children encountered in their reading books increased dramatically, many teachers around the country began to note that the stories also were more difficult for many children. By not controlling text difficulty through word repetition or focusing on phonic elements, some stories became more challenging. Stories could be made easier to read by adding an element of predictability. Predictability comes from the inclusion of rhyme, rhythm, and repetition of phrases or sentences in a text. Perhaps the classic predictable text is Bill Martin Jr's *Brown Bear, Brown Bear, What Do You See?* (1967):

Brown Bear, Brown Bear, what do you see?
I see a red bird looking at me.
Red bird, red bird, what do you see?
I see a yellow duck looking at me.

The text continues through a variety of animals of various colors, following the familiar pattern throughout.

Children can learn to read, and certainly enjoy, predictable or patterned texts after just a few repetitions, but some critics (Osborne, 1997) argue that students who can read the words in the context of the predictable text would have difficulty recognizing the same words in less predictable passages or in isolation. Furthermore, Osborne claims that when students read predictable text they do not develop true decoding skills. However, research in first-grade classrooms suggests that when students learn to read using predictable texts they rapidly develop and internalize phonic skills (Sampson, 1997).

Critics of the whole language approach, while applauding the significantly improved literary quality of texts children were asked to read, raised concerns about children making adequate progress in early reading achievement, especially those children who did not have the rich literacy background that exposed them to good literature for children in their preschool days. At the same time, educational leaders and policy makers noted that, among some measures of reading progress, students in the United States had remained fairly static in their levels of reading achievement over the past two decades. Another change in reading education was called for.

And so, in the face of these concerns, did basal reading programs disappear? No, they simply evolved, shifting in their emphasis to reflect the current understandings of how children learn to read and what policy makers feel is most important to emphasize in literacy education.

Some critics of whole language define whole language as immersing children in a rich environment of language and literature. They ridicule the notion that learning written language is like learning oral language—that when immersed in a sea of print children will learn to read and write just as easily as they learn to speak and listen. These critics claim that whole language teachers never directly teach skills.

Not all whole language advocates would agree with this characterization. They point out that the word *whole* in whole language means that all three cueing systems are taught in whole language classrooms. We certainly believe that whole language, when done by the best teachers, incorporates a lot of direct instruction. Nevertheless, the perception of whole language not advocating direct instruction of students has resulted in the current basal reader approach embedding a very definite direct and systematic approach.

The newest generation of basal programs has seen a return to stories specifically written to feature a strong phonics emphasis. In the primary grades, stories are made up of what has been called "decodable texts." Decodable texts are texts that contain words that reflect what has been taught in decoding in phonics. At the same time, publishers of basal programs have attempted to maintain the diverse view of society that has evolved through previous generations of basals, and they have attempted to keep the high-quality literature, especially beyond the initial stages of reading, that was a main feature of basals that reflected a more whole language approach. However, it should be clear that highly decodable texts and high-quality authentic literature may be goals that are at odds with one another and that they may be very difficult to obtain.

No doubt basal reading programs are here to stay. They have existed through a variety of revisions of thought about the way effective early reading instruction should be delivered, and they have adapted to those changes in philosophy and emphasis. As you begin your career in teaching reading, it is safe to say that published basal reading programs will likely be around throughout your career. However, what they look like in twenty years may be quite different from the way they look

Excerpts from stories in basals can lead students to read the entire book.

and approach reading today. How do you think the next generation of basal readers will look? What changes in society, technology, and teaching will inspire changes in teaching literacy and in basal reading programs?

Using Basal Programs

As you can see from our brief presentation on basal reading programs, they can be quite complex and involved. But the purpose of basal programs is to make the teaching of reading easier and more consistent within and across grade levels and schools. Rather than having to determine what skills and strategies need to be covered within a particular grade level, finding reading materials for students to read at the appropriate level of difficulty, developing specific lessons that cover all the requisite skills and strategies, and developing assessment materials to determine students' mastery of the content, basal reading programs provide teachers with a ready-made set of competencies to be mastered, a source of texts, instructional materials, and lessons for teaching the texts and competencies. Wiggins (1994) notes that teachers are comfortable with basals because they provide specific activities for teaching, reteaching, and reinforcing requisite skills and strategies and because they provide a concrete means for monitoring student progress. See Figure 6.4 for more on how to structure discussion groups and Figure 6.5 for determining readability of materials you are using.

A hallmark of basal reading programs is the discussion that follows the reading of a text selection. The traditional approach to basal discussion groups places the teacher as the leader of the discussion (the teacher asks students questions from the teacher's guide and evaluates students' responses), but newer, more student-centered approaches have emerged. One of the more popular approaches is Literature Circles (Daniels, 1994).

In the Literature Circles approach, specific roles are assigned to students in the reading group. Students then use these roles as a vehicle for participating in the discussion of the text. Some of the more popular roles are these:

Discussion Director   This student leads the discussion. She calls the group to order, keeps the group's discussion focused, calls on students to participate, and ensures that all students participate.

Connector   This student makes connections between events or characters in the text read and other stories or events in his own life.

Word Wizard   The word wizard searches the passage for interesting words and shares them along with a brief definition and other relevant information with the rest of the group.

Illustrator   The illustrator creates an illustration that reflects a significant event in the text. The illustrator shares the illustration with the group as well as a presentation of the significance of the information portrayed in it.

Passage Picker   The passage picker searches the passage for a segment of the selection to read aloud. The passage picker shares her reason for her selection, for example, a critical event, literacy style, or imagery conveyed.

Summarizer   The role of the summarizer is to summarize the information in the text and to summarize the discussion that takes place during a circle meeting.

The roles in the Literature Circle format were intended to help students learn to participate in discussions about trade books, but the format works equally well with selections from basal reading programs. Discussions of this sort allow students to take more of the responsibility for engaging, in-depth discussions that lead to greater understandings and insights for the participants. Literature Circles are discussed in greater detail in Chapter 13.

FIGURE 6.4
Text discussion groups

Basal Programs as a Foundation for Instruction

Imagine yourself as a brand new teacher. You are probably a bit unsure of yourself. You may really know that you enjoy working with children and find that you can be successful in helping children learn. But with only a few months in a classroom as a student teacher and only a few classes on effective instructional approaches, you probably (and rightly so) do not feel that you are as good a teacher as you would like to be. Moreover, once you are assigned a classroom, you could feel over-

A key feature of basal programs is matching students in assigned grade levels with texts that are written at a level of difficulty that matches their grade placement. Determining the difficulty of texts is called determining *readability,* but more recently teachers and publishers have been using the term *leveling* to indicate the appropriate level of reading difficulty for a particular text.

First off, let's realize that determining text difficulty or readability is an inexact science. Traditionally, developers of readability measures have focused on two aspects of text difficulty: word difficulty and sentence difficulty. *Word difficulty* is usually measured by length of words or the relative rarity of words in passages. *Sentence difficulty* is a function of sentence length, with longer sentences assumed to be more difficult to read and understand than shorter sentences. These two features have found their way into most measures of readability.

Leveling books for determining text difficulty often examines other elements that may make a text difficult. Elements such as supporting graphics and illustrations, font and font size, spacing, predictability of words within sentences, and so forth are added to the determination of text difficulty.

Both of these approaches work to some extent. However, both omit the most important factor in determining text difficulty—the reader. A reader brings various dispositions, skills, interests, and attitudes to the reading that will make a given text more or less difficult to read. Two readers who read at exactly the same level as determined by testing may find the same text quite different in difficulty. If one reader is interested in the topic, familiar with the words, and has good background knowledge for the text, she is likely to find it easy. The other reader, at the same reading level, finds that he is not interested in the topic, is not familiar with the words, and has little background for the text. This reader is likely to find the same text relatively difficult. Although readability determination and leveling provide us with a ballpark estimate of a text's difficulty, we will never know for sure how difficult it may be for a particular reader without knowing the reader. In judging difficulty of texts, teachers need to be very aware of their students and their interests and backgrounds.

It is a good idea to have a sense for the difficulty level of texts students may be asked to read, and in basal reading programs the readability has already been established. But what do you do when you have reading materials that are not part of a basal program? The answer is to determine readability level on your own.

A number of formulas, readability graphs, and protocols can be used to determine readability. However, we find that the easiest way to determine readability is right at your fingertips. Most word processing programs have built into them a program for determining readability (it is usually found within the *tools* menu). Here is how it works. Simply type in the text for which you wish to determine readability level. If the text is lengthy, type in a section of the text. You may wish to enter several selections of approximately 100 words or so. Once you have entered the words, click on the readability item in the tools menu of the word processing program. Instantaneously, the program will give you a traditional measure of readability (in grade level increments) that is based on word difficulty and sentence difficulty.

Remember, as you determine readability in this manner, it is only an estimate. The ultimate determination of readability comes when individual readers are asked to read selected texts. Nevertheless, traditional measures of readability can assist you in leveling the books and other reading materials in your classroom or in finding books that you feel may be instructionally appropriate for your students.

FIGURE 6.5

Readability: Determining the difficulty of texts

Steven Kellogg

Meet the Author

Steven Kellogg

1. *Which book of yours has given you the greatest pleasure?*

Making a book is like making a friend. Each one is different, each one is special, and it is very difficult to choose a favorite. I have received enormous pleasure from all the books I've worked on, but two that I could mention are Margaret Mahy's *The Boy Who Was Followed Home*, which was a particularly magical story to illustrate, and *A Beasty Story*, which gave me the chance to work with my dear friend Bill Martin Jr.

2. *Are you sometimes surprised by the way your work on a book evolves?*

The element of surprise is an important ingredient in a book. Literature, like life, is most compelling when it confronts us with the unexpected and demands a spontaneous reaction. These experiences challenge us to grow and to expand our personal horizons. In writing and illustrating a book, I am never sure exactly where the characters or their story are going. There is a constant series of surprises for me as the words and pictures go together, and that is an important part of the fun.

3. *What would you like people to remember about your work?*

I would like people to think of my books as a feast for the eye and a feast for the ear, and I hope that they will be happy that my stories and pictures have been, for a brief period, a part of their lives.

4. *What impact do you hope your work will have on children?*

I want the time that the young reader shares with me and my work to be an enjoyable experience—one that will encourage a lifetime association with pictures, words, and books.

Steven Kellogg's almost hyperkinetic illustrations threaten to jump off the page and run amok. Certainly his characters do run wild in the imaginations of millions of children because of books such as *Best Friends, Island of the Skog, Christmas Witch, A Rose for Pinkerton, Behave!,* and tall tales featuring American legends Mike Fink, Johnny Appleseed, Pecos Bill, and Paul Bunyan.

Reprinted with special permission of Steven Kellogg.

whelmed if you have to determine the various skills, strategies, and other competencies that must be taught in your grade level, find materials to accompany those competencies, and then develop creative lessons and instructional routines to teach students every day.

In all likelihood you would find a basal reading program very comforting. This one program identifies what you need to teach and provides the materials you need to do the teaching and assessing and the lesson formats for doing the teaching. Many new teachers have survived their first year or two of teaching by sticking close to the basal reading program.

From a parent's or a school administrator's point of view, use of the basal program provides some assurance that requisite skills are being covered in a way endorsed and validated by at least some literacy experts. Some degree of quality in teaching and learning is assured through the use of the basal reading program.

Belinda Zimmerman has taught first through third grades. She says that when she left her undergraduate teaching program she felt very confident in her ability to teach reading her own way. "Even as a new teacher I knew how to teach reading. Even so, the school required that I use the basal program. I was so disappointed. After the first year, I developed a detailed plan for teaching reading without the basal and submitted it to the district. They approved the plan, and in my second year of teaching I was able to teach reading the way I wanted to." Belinda has never looked back. She has been trained as a Reading Recovery teacher, has earned her master's in reading, and is currently working on her doctorate. She also teaches other teachers in undergraduate courses, reading clinics, and professional development courses. She is a master teacher.

Belinda does admit, however, that she has occasionally used some of the stories from her school's basal anthology with her students. "The basals had the original stories that I wanted to use with my first-graders. And so I used them." Belinda adds that "the current basal programs are not bad. They provide good ideas for teaching reading in an effective manner. The only thing is, the basal may be a good program, but it's not *my* program. When I teach using my own methods and ideas, I make sure that my students learn."

Now, put yourself in the role of a more veteran teacher, say, someone who has been teaching for five years. You have used the basal program, and you know it well. You have also been taking graduate courses in teaching reading, learning from your colleagues in your building and school district, and reading professionally. You feel that you have more to offer your students than what is contained in the basal program. Perhaps you feel that some of the approaches in the basal reading program don't really match up well with your own style of teaching. You feel you can cover the same content and competencies using other reading materials or other methods of instruction. Should you be allowed to do so? We think so.

We feel strongly that teachers should be allowed to make choices about how they teach literacy. A basal reading program can be an effective approach to teaching reading if it engages students with stories and strategies for comprehending. If it is effective, it is most probably because of the teacher, not the materials or the methods. It is the teacher that makes the difference. So, if a teacher feels that she can best teach reading using a basal program as a foundation for instruction and supplementing it with other materials and methods she has found from her past five years in the field, we would agree.

If, on the other hand, a fifth-year teacher has decided that she wants to make a change in the way she approaches reading—moving from stories in the basal program to a more trade book orientation; moving from the Directed Reading Activity to other lessons that best fit her style of instruction, again we would agree.

Basal reading programs offer teachers and schools one approach to teaching reading. However, to dictate that one approach for all schools or teachers or students is to deny the fact that we all have individual differences in the way we teach and learn. In reviewing research on effective instruction in reading, the National Reading Panel (2000) has noted that some programs work well for some students and other programs work best for other students. "One size fits all students" simply does not work when in comes to teaching literacy.

Inherent in basal programs is the notion that one basic approach, one series of passages, one level of difficulty, is best for all students regardless of their interests, background, and level of development. Teachers must be given considerable freedom in creating the kind of curriculum that works best for them and their students. In some cases, it will be the basal reading program. In other cases, it may a different approach.

While stating the need for great choice, we also recognize the need for some degree of consistency in the curriculum within and between grade levels and also the need for accountability for student learning. Curriculum consistency—knowing what we are going to teach and when it will be covered—can be developed through ongoing dialogue and negotiation between teachers, parents, and school administrators. Accountability ensures that students learn what they are supposed to learn. Ways to determine accountability can also be determined and developed through the same interactive process that leads to curriculum consistency.

Curriculum and accountability must cut through and across all grade levels. How teachers tackle the curriculum and how they achieve accountability needs to be a decision that is arrived at largely by professional teachers themselves who have the support and encouragement of their administrators, colleagues, and other professionals in the field.

Resource, Guide, or Prescription?

The ways basals are ultimately used depends on the way they are viewed by teachers and schools. At one end of the spectrum is the notion that basal reading programs are self-contained approaches to teaching reading designed by experts and should be followed by teachers in the manner prescribed by the Teacher's Guide using the materials accompanying the program.

Advocates of such an approach argue that if all teachers used the program as outlined in the TG, a sound and consistent program of literacy education would be provided by all teachers. It would also remove the teacher variable from the educational equation. All teaching, regardless of the teacher, would be reduced to a common denominator. Less able and less prepared teachers could provide the same level instruction as the best teachers . . . or so the thinking goes.

We recognize that basal reading programs are a fact of life in American schools. There is little likelihood that they will be replaced by a radically different approach. With this in mind, teachers and schools need to determine how best to use basal programs to provide the best instruction possible to students. If basals are to be used, we feel that they are best used as a guide or resource for informed teaching (Durkin, 1993; Spiegel, 1992). Decisions on how to teach reading should be made by the teacher, not by an instructional program.

If schools subscribed to the notion that basal reading programs should be followed in a prescriptive manner, then you might find yourself learning about basal reading programs in a technical college, not a college or university that invests itself in teaching students to be informed thinkers and decision makers. If all that is needed to be an effective teacher of reading is to follow the script offered by a basal program, then the most appropriate place to teach reading would be in a technical college where the focus is on gaining skill and expertise in implementing and operating technical programs and equipment.

The fact that you find yourself reading this book and learning about basal programs in a college that is part of the liberal education tradition suggests to us that the American system of schooling believes instruction is most effective when it is delivered by teachers who are knowledgeable about children, literacy, and instruction and are able to make informed decisions on how to provide instruction in literacy to the children with whom they work.

So how should you use the basal reading program in your classroom? That decision depends on you. How comfortable do you feel in developing your own program in teaching? Do you feel more comfortable relying on an already established program? If your answer to the last question is "yes," then you should feel comfortable using the basal program as your main guide in teaching reading. However, remember always that you are the teacher, and you are ultimately responsible for what happens in your classroom. If you decide to rely on the basal, feel free to deviate from its recommendations whenever you feel that such changes would increase your students' literacy learning.

If you are a teacher with a bit of experience, or even a new teacher who is confident of your knowledge of literacy learning, we recommend that you use the basal reading program as a resource for your literacy curriculum and instruction. You may choose to use selected texts, selected lessons, selected worksheets or workbook pages, or make use of other items that are part of the basal program. You determine the literacy program, and you determine what best meets the needs of your students within the program that you have developed. The basal program, then, becomes one more resource at your disposal for providing the very best instruction in literacy possible.

We hope all teachers find themselves moving toward independence from the basal reading program, but these programs do have an important place in contemporary American reading instruction. Just as teachers talk about providing scaffolding for student learning, basal reading programs provide teachers with a personal scaffold in their development as effective and independent teachers of literacy to all students.

FURTHER WORDS

 From InfoTrac College Edition

An Analysis of Changes in a Selected Basal Reading Series, Bennie G. Barron, Martha Henderson, and Linda Edwards, *Education* Summer 1992 v112 n4

Ruffles and Flourishes (how publishers of basal reading texts eliminate the spice in stories by using simple vocabulary) (column), Susan Ohanian, *The Atlantic* September 1987 v260 p20(2)

What Makes Intermediate-Grade Students Want to Read? (the intermediate grades), Jo Worthy, *The Reading Teacher* March 2002 v55 i6 p568(2)

Retooling the Reading Lesson: Matching the Right Tools to the Job, Ruth A. Short, Mary Kane, and Tammy Peeling, *The Reading Teacher* November 2000 v54 i3 p284

Should We Replace Basal Readers with "Real Books"? (debate), Fredrick R. Burton and Frances Sumake, *NEA Today* November 1984 v3 p23(1)

Leveled Text: The Good News and the Bad News. (Questions and Answers), Edna Greene Brabham and Susan Kidd Villaume, *The Reading Teacher* February 2002 v55 i5 p438(4)

Questioning the Text (nice comprehension strategies with classroom pictures), Stephanie Harvey, *Instructor (1990)* May 2001 v110 i8 p16

Tackling TOUGH Words (includes strategies), Laura Robb, *Instructor (1990)* October 2000 v110 i3 p35

Multiple Readings of a Picture Book, Greer Johnson, *Australian Journal of Language and Literacy* October 1999 v22

From Professional Journals and Publications

Blachowicz, C. L., & Fisher, P. (2000). Vocabulary Instruction. In M. Kamil, P. Mosenthal, P. D. Pearson, & R. Barr (Eds.), *Handbook of Reading Research* (vol. 3, pp. 503–523). New York, NY: Longman.

McKenna, M. C., Stratton, B. D., Grindler, M. C., & Jenkins, S. J. (1995). Differential Effects of Whole Language and Traditional Instruction on Reading Attitudes. *Journal of Reading Behavior, 27*(1), 19–44.

Raphael, T. (1992). Question-Answering Strategies for Children. *The Reading Teacher, 36,* 186–190.

Summary

Basal reading programs are commercially developed, complete programs for teaching literacy to students primarily in the elementary grades. Basal programs consist of an extensive set of reading passages, practice sheets, assessments, and other materials at a level of difficulty appropriate for the grade level for which it is intended. Basal programs also have embedded within them a lesson format that provides students and teachers with support and instruction before, during, and after the reading of each passage selection. Individual skills and strategies related to becoming a proficient reader and the order in which they are taught within a basal program are identified through the scope and sequence chart.

The basal approach to teaching literacy dominates literacy instruction in the United States. Although it has evolved over time in tune with current thinking about effective instruction in reading, basal readers are likely to a part of the American educational system for years to come. Rather than accept or reject the notion of basals, we recommend that teachers view basal literacy programs in light of their own needs in teaching reading. Newer and less confident teachers should view basals as a guide to their literacy curriculum and instruction. More seasoned teachers should view the basal program as one of many possible resources for developing their own curriculum and instruction for students. In this latter case, the basal is a resource in which certain and selected elements may be used whenever the teacher feels it necessary. In no case, however, do we feel that a basal should be viewed as prescription for literacy instruction. Effective teaching comes from a thorough knowledge of learners, literacy, and instruction. Basal programs cannot offer knowledge of learners and the instructional needs of learners. Only teachers have that knowledge, and only teachers should be trusted with making the ultimate decisions for how teaching occurs in classrooms.

Total Literacy Anchors

- The teacher uses workbooks and worksheets and assessment materials to evaluate student learning.
- The teacher encourages parents to become involved in the parent materials sent home.
- The teacher incorporates technology and multimedia materials and employs suggestions from the teacher's guide that will help students learn.
- The teacher involves students in prereading, guided reading, and postreading activities.
- The teacher encourages student skill development and strategy development through story extensions and story enrichment activities.

CHAPTER 7

Reading Comprehension Strategies

As You Read . . .

- Why is it important to involve students in the process of thinking and predicting during reading?

- How can a total literacy curriculum capitalize on the diverse schemata students bring to the classroom?

- How can teachers shift their students' comprehension stance from efferent to aesthetic modes?

- What are the advantages of students' mastering reader-based strategies?

- What is the value of students' creating conceptual maps?

Author Words

Mary Beth Sampson

In Chapters 5 and 6 we explored the reading process and students' interactions with text. This chapter focuses on strategies that help children comprehend text. Some of the strategies are teacher initiated; others are student initiated. Above all, we must remember that the value of a strategy should be evident to the students. Reading should never be a chore; instead, we should strive to make reading a delight. Thus reading strategies should be a resource children can call on when they need help in understanding text. They should be a means to the end of better comprehension; they must never become an end in themselves.

As you examine strategies, it is important to focus on the process rather than the individual steps of the strategy. Ask yourself, "Does this strategy allow my students to 'act like real readers'?" Think about the processes that "real" readers are involved in, and determine if the strategy provides opportunities for your students to engage in those processes. Does the strategy engage students in active interaction with the text? Do students have opportunities to predict and revise, confirm, or reject their predictions? Does the strategy enable students to determine purposes for reading and then read to fulfill those purposes? Are students involved in forming questions about the text and searching for answers to those questions? Do students have the opportunity to share and discuss their views? These and other questions must be asked as you determine if a strategy will be worthwhile for your students.

Your examination and decision-making process is rather like the old story about a sculptor and an elephant. When asked how he was able to sculpt such a realistic elephant out of granite, the sculptor replied, "Well, I just decide what an elephant looks like, look at the block of granite, and chip away everything that doesn't look like an elephant." As a teacher, your challenge is to decide what real readers look like and chip away everything from your reading program that does not help your students to "look like" or "act like" real readers.

Teacher-Directed Strategies

PRAISE

For decades educators have pointed to the value of positive reinforcement on student well-being and academic achievement. Consequently, if all this strategy entailed was praising students—as the acronym "PRAISE" suggests—it would still be a good strategy to use with children. As humans, we strive for recognition and acceptance. As learners, we rejoice when we receive a "pat on the back" and hear the words "well done!"

Ceretha Levingston uses the PRAISE strategy with her second-graders.

Sampson and Sampson (2002) developed the PRAISE procedure to provide positive feedback to students and to strengthen their vocabularies and writing skills. The letters in PRAISE represent the steps in this strategy:

Predict the words you would expect to find in a book about _____.

Read the story to the students.

Analyze the predictions with the words actually found in the story.

Involve the students in an innovation to the story.

Share your innovation, or writing, with the class.

Explain what the story means to you.

The Teacher-to-Teacher feature describes how the PRAISE technique works. You'll note that the technique moves students through all the steps of the reading process (prereading, reading, postreading) as children move from schema activation to listening to writing to sharing.

Pam Cheatham teaches first grade in Commerce, a small college town about sixty miles east of Dallas, Texas. Realizing that many of her nonreaders are avid football fans, she uses PRAISE to share a story about a future Super Bowl game between the Dallas Cowboys and the Kansas City Chiefs. Here are the steps she follows.

Predict

She begins by asking her class this question: "What words do you think the author will use in a book about football?" As the excited students share, Pam takes dictation—calling out the name of each letter as she writes the words on the board. Pam is excited that several of her lowest achieving students—who suffer from low self-confidence—shine as experts as they know more football vocabulary than anyone else in the class. Pam also notices that Si Won, who just moved to Commerce from Korea, is very interested in these new football words. After five minutes, the board is filled with football jargon. The children came up with these words:

football	coach	Super Bowl
cheerleaders	linebacker	penalty
huddle	tackle	pass
quarterback	referee	fumble
whistle	cheer	interception
dance	TV	touchdown
flag	tight end	blimp

"Great, boys and girls," Pam says. "Now listen as I read you *The Football That Won* by Michael Sampson (1999). Listen to see if the author used any of your words in his story."

Read

Pam then reads the story, which is a cumulative pattern based on the story model used in *This Is the House That Jack Built*. The children listen with rapt attention and increasing excitement until Pam reads the final page—which includes the accumulation of all the prior pages.

Analyze

Then the young arms explode as they shoot to the sky—eager to tell Pam what they think of the story and their matching words. One by one, children come to the board and point to words they had predicted might be in the story—and that actually were. Pam is pleased that the children are matching words they know orally with the way the words appear in print.

Innovate/Involve

Pam then asks, "What words did the author leave out that you thought he might have used in the story?" After the students point out words like flag, dance, and referee, which were not found in the story, Pam shares "notice that the author used the THIS/THAT pattern to write this book—**THIS** is the quarterback **THAT** fumbled the football; **THIS** is the blimp **THAT** floated and flew; **THIS** is the safety **THAT** crunched the quarterback." She then breaks the class into small work groups and asks them to write new pages for the book, using words the author did not use. She points out their dictated list of football words on the board, and tells them they can add new words to that list if they wish.

Share

Pam circulates as the children write their innovations to the text. She notes that some groups create three or four new pages, and some groups only one. Next, she asks each group to *share* their innovation with the class. She is pleased to notice that several nonreaders proudly stand and read the page their group has crafted.

➤ ➤ ➤

Explain

To close the PRAISE activity, Pam asks the students to evaluate the book by "explaining" their rating of the book to other students. Some students rate the book on a scale of 1 to 10; others give the book a thumbs up or thumbs down. Pam points out to the class that some students liked the book more than others did, and that is true of all books—individuals are drawn to different subjects and stories.

Pam recognizes the importance of vocabulary to reading comprehension. When children brainstorm as a class, they are in effect sharing their vocabularies with one another. She realizes that as she takes dictation she is modeling how the sounds of the words track to print, and the correct spellings of words. She loves the innovation phase of PRAISE because it allows her students to naturally flow into the writing process in a fail-safe mode. She is pleased that even nonreaders can participate successfully and come to understand that reading is "talk written down" as they write and share what has been written. She likes the "evaluation" in PRAISE because she wants her students to get in the habit of being "book critics" so they can do a better job of self-selection of the books they will read independently. But most of all, Pam enjoys the many opportunities the procedure affords her to PRAISE her students.

RISE

Teaching Strategies
RISE

Gardner (1991a, 1993, 1999) has identified eight intelligences, or ways of being smart. Educators today are recognizing that to think of intelligence simply in terms of linguistic skill is misleading. In a total literacy classroom, teachers include all of Gardner's intelligence areas as they strive to reach all learners. These multiple intelligences include linguistic intelligence, logical-mathematical intelligence, spatial intelligence, bodily-kinesthetic intelligence, musical intelligence, interpersonal intelligence, intrapersonal intelligence, and natural intelligence.

In the PRAISE strategy, the instructional and multiple intelligence focus is on linguistic intelligence. Now we shift to a strategy that involves spatial and bodily-kinesthetic intelligence as we discuss the RISE procedure (Sampson & Sampson, 2002).

It has been said that comprehension is "making pictures" in your head. Advocates of multiple intelligences would agree and point to spatial intelligence as one of the key correlates of comprehension.

When children begin the school program, they love to draw. But by the end of third grade, drawing is a forgotten art. RISE encourages children to think visually and to demonstrate their personal comprehension of story through their drawings. Here are the steps for using the RISE strategy:

Read the story. In the primary grades, teachers may choose to read aloud stories that are too complex for children to read independently.

At the intermediate and middle school levels, students may read independently or listen as the reader reads.

Illustrate the story. Have students illustrate a "strong" image they have from the story. Don't worry about expertise as an artist; stick figures can represent images adequately.

Sequence the sketches. After the students share their sketches with the class, break the class into groups of six. Ask each group to examine their six sketches and place them in order according to the sequence of the story. Then have each group come to the front of the room—standing and displaying their pictures in sequential order.

Enact the story. Ask each group to select one sketch and work up a way of sharing that scene through a skit or play. As the children act the scene out, the rest of the class can predict which scene it is.

RISE involves students in important literacy skills, such as sequencing events, and takes advantage of several multiple intelligences students possess. Poor readers are often great at drawing, and this affords them an opportunity to encounter success in the classroom. Nonreaders are often nonverbal but excel at kinesthetic activities such as drama. But best of all, RISE demonstrates that students' comprehension varies and that the same story will mean different things to different students. By sharing through art and drama, all students will benefit by an enriched, more-encompassing comprehension of the story. The whole class comprehension is greater than the individual parts.

Think-Alouds

In think-alouds, teachers reveal the mental processes they are engaging in while reading by sharing their thoughts about the text and their comprehension while reading orally to their students. This strategy was devised by Beth Davey (1983) and involves teachers modeling a process they hope their students will internalize. The strategy consists of the following steps:

STEP 1   Select a text to read aloud to your class. Decide which places in the text you consider important, and then pause at those places.

STEP 2   When you pause, predict what you think will happen next. Verbalize the process you went though to make those predictions. What in the text triggered your response?

STEP 3   Describe the "picture" the text has painted in your mind. Tell children how that picture changes as you receive more information from the text. Talk about how the mental picture stays in your mind throughout the story.

STEP 4   As you continue to read, talk about the schemata the text has triggered. If the story reminds you of particular people, events, scenes, or other stories,

Ted Rand

1. *Which book of yours has given you the greatest pleasure?*

Cabin Key, which began as a conversation with an editor. My wife, Gloria, and I were telling her about a mountain cabin that has been in our family for four generations, and the editor suggested that there was a book there. Writing and illustrating the book turned out to be a labor of love. We first took our children to the cabin when they were in diapers, and now they are taking their children there.

2. *Which book has surprised you most in terms of its public reception?*

Knots on a Counting Rope. We were apprehensive at first because the Native American boy in the story is blind, and we wanted to handle that with sensitivity. That book has been so well received and is used by many teachers in talking about attitudes toward people with handicaps.

3. *What would you like people to remember about your work?*

I want people to remember the authenticity. We do a lot of research so our artwork accurately represents the images in the text. Our goal is to thoroughly connect words with pictures, to so interlock text and illustration that they cannot be separated.

4. *What impact do you hope your work will have on children?*

More than anything, we want to produce books that children will love in the hope that they will come to love reading itself.

Ted Rand excels in portraying the emotions of the characters in his books. His paintings are painstakingly researched and accurately rendered, and his masterful use of light and darkness brings a magical quality to his work. His books include *The Night Tree; The Football That Won . . . ; Once Upon a Farm; Knots on a Counting Rope; Barn Dance; Ghost-Eye Tree; Homespun Sarah; Country Kid, City Kid;* and *All Kinds of Kids.*

Reprinted with special permission of Ted Rand.

tell the students what you are thinking about and why. You may want to use analogies to explain your comprehension by stating, "Oh, I understand, this is like (*give an example or illustration*)."

STEP 5   Stop occasionally and share a comprehension problem with the class such as something that has puzzled you or that you don't understand. Elicit students' help in formulating a plan of action that will aid in clarifying your confusion or "fixing" the problem. Talking about comprehension problems is a very important part of a think-aloud. The teacher and students have the opportunity to explore varied ways to aid in the comprehension of a text, and then to discuss what was effective and what wasn't. Students will also learn that sometimes it is effective to just keep on reading. The point of confusion will often become clearer as the reader moves on in the text.

Modeling the strategy is important, but students need the opportunity to practice verbalizing their interaction with the text. Students may work in pairs and "talk through" text as they monitor their understanding.

Shared Book Experience

Shared book experience originated in New Zealand in the late 1960s to provide emerging readers with the opportunity to have successful, meaningful interactions with text (Holdaway, 1979). Big books containing enlarged pictures and text are used so children can visually and auditorially experience the book as the teacher shares it. Patterned or predictable stories are often used so children may participate in the sharing experience by repeating patterned lines and predicting story development. These are the stages in using a text for shared book experience (Ward, 2001b):

Discovery   This is the introduction of the text to the students. This presentation includes sharing the title and author, previewing and discussing the book, and providing opportunities for students to use their prediction skills. This phase includes an enthusiastic reading of the text during which the teacher points to the words; the children have an opportunity to see the words as they are being read. In addition, this is an opportunity for the teacher to verbalize predictive aspects of the story with phrases such as, "Do you think his parachute will open?" or "What makes you think that?" or "What do you think will happen next?" or "What in the story makes you think that?"

Exploration   This stage may involve many visits to the text for varied purposes. From the literacy transaction model, you might incorporate Strand 1 (self-expression) activities such as unison reading, role playing, or dramatization during this phase. Strand 3 (conventions) activities such as examining textual features or print details or identifying and categorizing letter–sound relationships are also possibilities. Favorite words and phrases could be identified and added to the Word Wall. It is important to remember that all of these activities use the text, not worksheets.

Independence and Expression   This phase intertwines with the second. Many Strand 1 activities fall in this category as children bring their own understanding to the text. Activities such as dramatization, independent writing, art and music activities, contrast and comparison with other texts, and innovations on the text provide opportunities for children to demonstrate and anchor their knowledge of the text.

These phases represent how one book might be shared with a class; when you use shared book experience in your classroom, the phases may overlap as you continually expose your children to new books. The classroom Teacher-to-Teacher feature shows how one teacher used the suggestions by Geoff Ward (2001b) for a shared book experience in her classroom.

Sue Smith wishes that all of her 5- and 6-year-old students had the opportunity to sit in the lap of a loving caregiver and interact with a book as it is read aloud. Sue believes the opportunity to see and hear the text simultaneously and make comments, ask questions and receive answers, repeat favorite lines as they are underlined with the finger of the reader or listener, and have a joyful, meaningful interaction with a book are critical components of the literacy development of her students. Because not all of her children have this opportunity in their homes and Sue cannot pull each child onto her lap and share a book with that child, Sue has done the next best thing.

She has made it a priority to acquire numerous big books with enlarged text and pictures. In addition, she has collected favorite songs, poems, finger games, and chants, and she has written the text of these favorites in enlarged print on charts. Many of these charts have appropriate illustrations cut from magazines, and some have pictures drawn by her students attached to them. Sue continually adds to her collection of enlarged texts that she can share with her children.

Sue values time for her class to "tune-in" to language. She uses the charts with favorite poems, songs, chants, and finger games that the children have been exposed to throughout the year as a joyful warm-up time of unison chanting and reading.

After the warm-up, Sue usually rereads a favorite story from a big book or chart that has been introduced in previous sessions. During this time, the children have the opportunity to explore meanings, textual features or print details, language patterns, or any feature of the text that intrigues them. Children may explore particular letter–sound relationships in the familiar text, and Sue may facilitate this discussion by using flaps of paper to cover up parts of words to observe patterns. She often invites her students to discuss possible innovations on the familiar text. Verbalizing these innovations often leads to individual or collaborative writing projects.

She then introduces a new big book or chart, and children have an opportunity to

Directed Reading–Thinking Activity (DR–TA)

DR–TA was developed by Russell Stauffer (1976) to involve students more actively with the material they read. The procedure involves the students in divergent thinking by asking them to read, make predictions, and think about what they are reading. DR–TA motivates students because it arouses their curiosity and lets them become involved in stimulating explorations of plot developments.

The teacher can adapt DR–TA for most types of reading material and for just about any grade level. While the procedure may also be used with individual students, Stauffer (1980) suggests the procedure is most effective when used with a group. DR–TA attempts to develop several abilities:

- ◆ Determine purposes for reading.
- ◆ Extract, comprehend, and assimilate information.

engage in the discovery phase of the book by using their predictive skills. During the initial reading, the children begin to chime in and say predictable phrases with her. She sometimes uses small pieces of paper to cover up words or parts of words and encourages children to discuss how they can determine which word is covered. Children use the semantic, syntactic, and graphophonic cueing systems in unison during this contextualized activity. If the children are enthusiastic about the book, Sue reads it with the class again, and children volunteer to dramatize portions of the book during reading. This often leads to expressive activities centered around the book: innovations on the text, art activities, thematic studies, musical adoptions of the text, Reader's Theater presentations, contrast and comparison with other texts, or other activities determined by collaboration between the teacher and students. Not every text becomes an extended study for every student. The students continually have voice and choice in determining texts that spark their interest.

Sue weaves a time for independent reading into every day. Some children may revisit books or charts that have been shared in big book format and have become old favorites. Other children may work in self-chosen small groups. During this time, Sue has the opportunity to observe the children's reading and record her observations. She occasionally joins in or provides assistance, but she is careful not to destroy the self-monitoring reading behavior that the children are developing during this time.

Sue may vary the order and grouping of the instructional activities. For instance, the independent reading time may occur earlier in her schedule so she will have an opportunity to work with small groups who have shown a need for minilessons in specific areas. At times, some children might be working on expressive activities inspired by a specific text while others are engaged in independent reading of favorite texts. Some text receives such an enthusiastic response that the entire class collaborates to write an innovation. Sue strives daily to provide her emerging readers with depth and breadth of exposure to a variety of texts through the flexibility of the shared book experience.

- ◆ Examine reading material based on purposes for reading.
- ◆ Suspend judgments.
- ◆ Make decisions based on information gleaned from reading (Tierney & Readence, 2000).

A group DR–TA is conducted in the following manner:

STEP 1　The teacher begins the lesson by sharing the title of the selection to be read, asking, "What do you think a story with this title might be about?" The teacher then accepts the answers of four or five students before proceeding. The teacher may want to write these predictions on a chart or overhead transparency or may choose to share them at the oral level.

STEP 2　The teacher invites the students to read the first paragraph or to the point that the predictions will be confirmed, rejected, or modified. Asking students if they still think the same as they did earlier, the teacher may focus on specific responses. "Do you still think the story is about a bank robber?" After students have responded, new predictions are elicited.

STEP 3   Students continue through the text—predicting, reading, and reacting to their predictions. The teacher continues to ask questions such as "Were you correct?" or "What do you think now?" or "What do you think will happen?"

At this point the teacher has completed the first phase of the DR–TA, stimulating the reading/thinking of the students during the story. Now the emphasis changes to specific skill development and a reexamination of the story. Stauffer (1969) refers to this stage as "skill training of a different kind" (p. 64). The format of this stage may vary, but components usually include concept clarification, personal reflection, and semantic analysis (Tierney & Readence, 2000).

Vocabulary extension comes during this final stage rather than before the reading of the story. The teacher asks questions like "Was there something you didn't understand in the story?" Some students will bring up concept level questions, and others will ask about specific vocabulary words encountered in the story. This method of vocabulary study makes more sense than the preselected method used in the directed reading activity because it allows for self-selection by the student and vocabulary discussion in context. Furthermore, this discovery technique of vocabulary development is more effective because the words are encountered in the context of the story rather than in isolation (Cunningham, Moore, Cunningham, & Moore, 1983).

The teacher's role is quite different in a DR–TA than when presenting a directed reading activity. In a directed reading activity, the teacher operates from a script provided by a basal reader and serves as questioner and judge of the students' answers. In contrast, the role of the teacher during a DR–TA is as moderator and "intellectual agitator" (Petre, 1969).

Directed Listening–Thinking Activity (DL–TA)

The Directed Listening–Thinking Activity follows basically the same process as the Directed Reading–Thinking Activity except that instead of the students reading the text, the teacher reads the text aloud to the students. Step 1 of the process is the same as that described for DR–TA. Steps 2 and 3 copy Steps 2 and 3 of DR–TA except the teacher is reading the text aloud instead of the students silently reading the text. The discussion and the opportunity to confirm, reject, extend, or offer a prediction engage children in the interactive process with text offered by the DR–TA. Vocabulary extension is addressed in the same way for a DL–TA as for a DR–TA.

Eli W. Rabb — Name

I am 10 years old. — Age

My interests are Soccer, — Interests
basketball, and animals.

What do you like most about school?

What I like most about school is that I can debate over the revolution... it feels as if I'm really back then.

What's your favorite subject? Why?

My favorite subject is Writing because my teacher lets us write about fiction and about facts on different topics... I mean we have so many things to choose from.

What's your favorite book? Why do you like it?

My favorite book is "Hatchet" because it describes a boys emotions and thoughts well while he is fighting for his life in the wilderness.

What advice do you have for teachers?

My advice for teachers is if you are doing a subject make it fun, you also need to always put humor into things... never stop a student from reading with the exeption of supposed to be doing something. else

Students have the opportunity to identify words and phrases that captured their attention by puzzling them or saying things in a new way.

DR–TA and DL–TA place a major emphasis on the relations among reading, thinking, and predicting. Because they encourage students to initiate their own reading goals, reading becomes more meaningful and comprehension is facilitated. DR–TAs are a useful alternative to directed reading activities and are claiming larger shares of instructional time in elementary classrooms. DL–TAs help teachers engage their students in the processes of predicting and then confirming, rejecting, extending, or revising those predictions based on information revealed in the text when the teacher is reading aloud.

Prevoke

One of the key ingredients in DR–TA is prediction—having students use their background knowledge to infer predictions about upcoming portions of the text they will be reading. By making personal predictions, readers are more likely to stay actively engaged in trying to make sense of the passage they are reading.

The prevoke or predictogram strategy is a vocabulary activity that also requires students to make predictions about the text (Blachowicz & Fisher, 2000). We prefer the term "prevoke," because it helps us to remember that prediction (pre) based on vocabulary (voke) is at the heart of this comprehension activity.

The first step in the prevoke strategy is to identify and select a set of key words from a passage to be read by students. Once the words are selected, the teacher displays them for students and provides a quick overview to the words and their meaning. Then she puts the students to work. Students are asked to sort the words into categories. They can be meaningful categories supplied by the teacher (for example, words that describe characters, words that describe the setting, words that suggest the plot) or categories determined by the students. The sorting activity helps students think about the meaning of the words and how they may fit into the upcoming story.

Once the words are sorted and the sorts discussed, the teacher asks students to work in groups of three or four to predict the nature and events of the story they will soon be reading. Creating the prediction becomes a bit of a mystery as students use the limited clues provided by the teacher to come up with a plausible series of events that tell the story. The predictions are shared and recorded and are used as the basis for discussing the story once it has been read.

We have found that students thoroughly enjoy this activity. It puts them in control of reading and puts them in a position of creating meaning, which is what comprehension is all about. Many times, the predictions made by students are more interesting than the stories themselves. In those cases, students can be asked to elaborate on their predictions by writing a new story based on the words that were given.

Brainstorming

The importance of a reader activating his or her schema or background knowledge before reading in order to maximize comprehension has been discussed previously. Brainstorming is one of the simplest ways to aid children in activating their schemata or prior knowledge before reading. This "what-do-you-think-of-when-I-say _____" activity is the cornerstone for many of the more sophisticated prereading activities, such as conceptual mapping or K-W-L (described later in this chapter). As the teacher records students' responses, assessment of the knowledge base of the students is possible. As students brainstorm items, the teacher may extend concepts or define terms the students will encounter when reading the text. Because brainstorming is a flexible strategy that requires marginal manipulation of information, it is useful when students have little prior knowledge of a subject. The Teacher-to-Teacher feature about Laurie Mattox's class illustrates this point.

Teacher-to-Teacher

Laurie Mattox frequently uses brainstorming with her sixth-graders before they read science texts. One lesson dealt with the physical characteristics of eagles, their habitat, and the problem of eagles becoming an endangered species because the chemical thallium sulfate weakens the shells before the eaglets can hatch. She was concerned that students would not be familiar with some of the terminology used in the text although they might have heard the concepts referred to in different terms. Therefore, she asked students to close their eyes and think about "eagles"—any places they had ever seen eagles, how they would describe an eagle to someone who had never seen one, and any information they had read or heard about eagles. After two minutes of thought time, she asked students for their ideas. She recorded the in-

formation on an overhead as students shared (Figure 7.1).

When all of the responses were recorded, she asked students if any of the terms seem to refer to the same thing or category of things. Students identified words and phrases that seemed to address the same topic and assigned the following categories: feeding habits of eagles (carnivorous, eat rodents, hunters); descriptions of eagles (claws, beak, long wings, strong, powerful, not really bald but white feathers, feathers, large wingspan, majestic, soar, fly high); different types of eagles (bald, golden); where eagles lived (mountains, big nests); ways eagles are used as symbols (symbol of freedom, symbol of USA, national bird, on Mexico's flag, on

➤ ➤ ➤

USA money); threats to the eagles (endangered, pollution harmful to them, being poisoned by chemicals); and other information. As the students categorized the information, Laurie wrote it on another overhead (Figure 7.2).

When the students had finished their categorizations, she said, "I am impressed. It is obvious you already have a lot of knowledge about eagles. The pages you are going to read tell about three things you have generated information about: what the eagles look

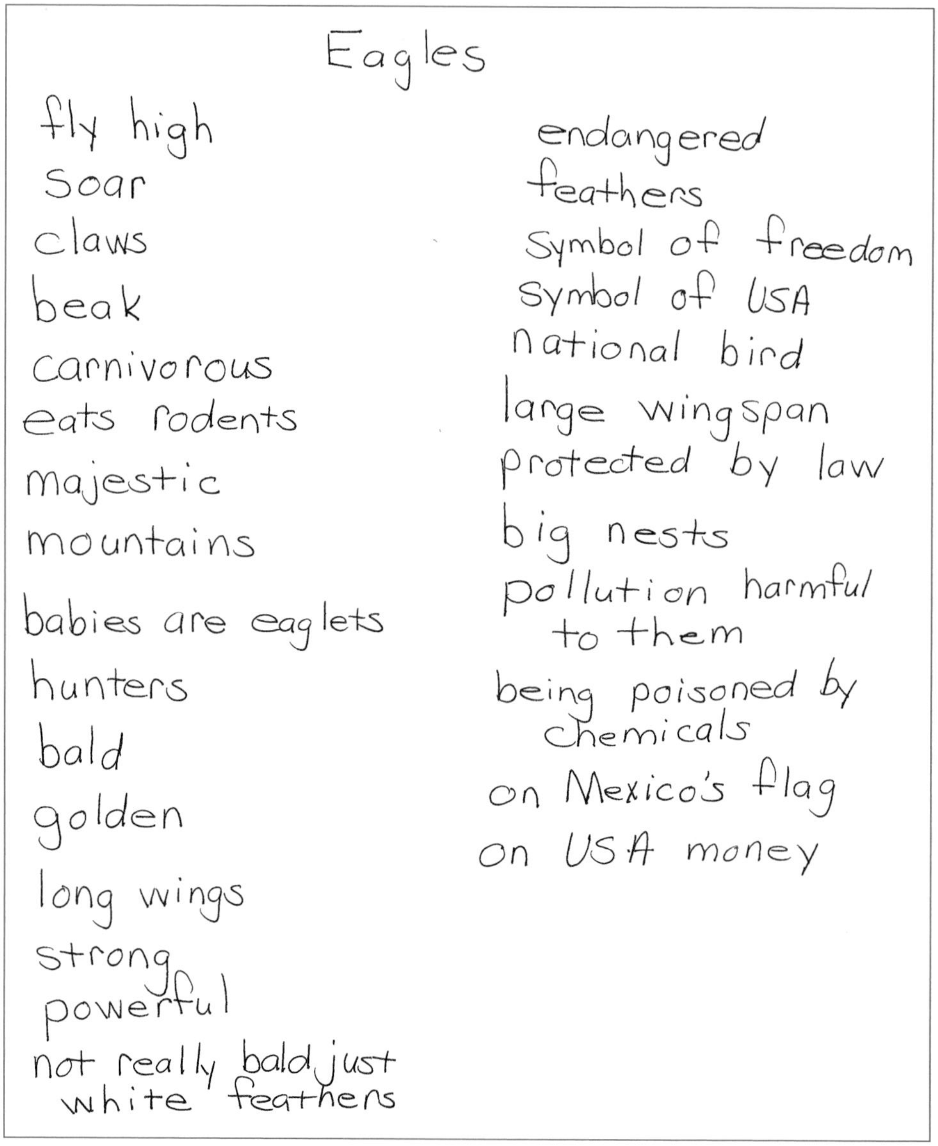

Eagles

fly high
soar
claws
beak
carnivorous
eats rodents
majestic
mountains

babies are eaglets
hunters
bald
golden
long wings
strong
powerful
not really bald just
white feathers

endangered
feathers
symbol of freedom
symbol of USA
national bird
large wingspan
protected by law
big nests
pollution harmful
to them
being poisoned by
chemicals
on Mexico's flag
on USA money

FIGURE 7.1
Students' initial ideas about "Eagles"

like, where they live, and what is causing them to become endangered. Let's look at what you said."

Laurie then used the students' knowledge as a basis for extension. "You talked about 'where the eagles live.' When you read your text, the authors are going to use a word that means the same thing. Does anyone have an idea about what that term might be?" When a student volunteered "habitat," Laurie wrote it by the appropriate phrase. She then commented, "The book is also going to describe the eagle's claws, but we will use another word that means the same thing as claws. Remember that word and we will talk about it later," and she drew a line by "claws" to provide a reminder to write the new term on the overhead. She mentioned that the text would give many details con-

cerning the way eagles look, but it would be referred to as "physical characteristics" in the text, and then she wrote that label on the overhead. She continued, "You will also find out more information about why some eagles are endangered species. One chemical that will be talked about is thallium sulfate. Be sure to note why this chemical is dangerous to eagles, and she wrote the term by the comment "being poisoned by chemicals."

Laurie concluded by stating, "I will leave this overhead up during your reading so you can jot down anything you want to add to the information we have. If you read something that confirms information we have listed, be sure to note the page number so we will have it for a reference. We'll have a chance to see if our information is the same as the book's."

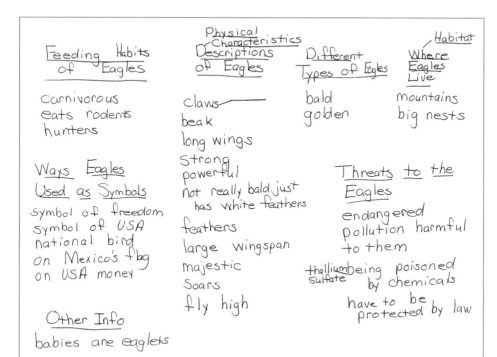

FIGURE 7.2
Categorizing ideas about "Eagles"

By using brainstorming as a prereading strategy, Laurie involved her students in activating their schemata concerning eagles. Because she used the children's information as part of her instruction, the students realized that their input was valued. By using the words the children had originally brainstormed as a basis for the introduction of new terms and concepts, a framework of "known" information was formed to "hook" the "new" information onto so it would be easier to understand and remember. Because the brainstorming was recorded on overhead transparencies, the information was available throughout the study for refinement and extension.

Laurie's framework for brainstorming is that thinking and creativity are the keys. Therefore, all brainstormed information will be recorded and will never be challenged or ridiculed. However, the class is not allowed to accept *any* information as fact until it can be documented. Therefore, as students find information that proves brainstormed information, they jot down the source and page number and that data is added to the overhead. Then—and only then—will that information be stated as factual. Laurie has found that this has motivated her students to continue their exploration of a topic beyond the time spent in class and outside of the school environment. Students often bring in magazines, books, or newspaper articles that "document" a brainstormed item as factual. By extending and refining brainstormed information, students become aware that learning is not confined to the classroom but is a lifelong journey!

Link

Link is a variation of brainstorming. The strategy was developed by Joseph Vaughan and Thomas Estes (1986) and is ideal when you suspect that only some of your students have background knowledge on the topic. Here are the steps:

STEP 1　Write the topic or key term on the board or overhead transparency. Then give students three minutes to *list* what they know about it in brainstorm fashion on their own paper.

STEP 2　Go around the room, and let students share their responses. Write these responses on the board or overhead transparency. After all responses are given, invite the students to interact with students who provided items to *inquire* and ask for clarification about the items.

STEP 3　Repeat the first step, but limit the time to one minute (students usually write more). Have them note all they now *know* about the word based on the previous discussion.

This format incorporates writing before students share and encourages students to explore the reasons behind certain contributions. The opportunity for discussion, reflection, and clarification enhances students' understandings of the topic and usually enables them to think of more information when they move to Step 3.

Courtesy of Michael Sampson

Kim Henderson introduces the "circle of questions" procedure to third-graders.

Circle of Questions

Circle of questions is a strategy that was developed to engage students in brainstorming, predicting, generating questions about text, categorizing, and interacting with text to answer those questions (Sampson, Sampson, & Linek, 1994). When used with content material, the steps are as follows:

STEP 1 Divide students into groups of four. Groups should have a Timekeeper, a Recorder, a Reporter, and a Leader. Introduce the topic, and give students three to five minutes to brainstorm questions they have about the topic.

STEP 2 Draw a circle on a chart, an overhead, or the board. Give students two minutes to rank-order their questions from most important to least important.

STEP 3 Each group then shares their most important question, and the teacher draws a line from the circle and writes the question. If a group's number one question has been shared, the group shares their number two question. The sharing and recording of questions continues until all of a group's questions have been shared by that group or another one. The group may then "pass." Recording of questions continues until all groups have "passed."

STEP 4 The questions are reviewed and examined to determine categories. The teacher may use colored markers or chalk to designate items that belong in specific categories.

STEP 5 Each group then chooses a category to become an "expert" in. As they read, they search for answers to the questions in that particular category. The Recorder writes their answers and where they were found in the text and shares the information with the class. The teacher then writes the answers and where they were found by the appropriate question. Discussion concerning the answer and whether the text adequately addresses the concern ensues. Sometimes students may decide that additional research is needed.

Try this strategy *after* students have read a challenging or controversial text. Students can divide into groups and generate questions they have about the text after reading it. The procedure can then continue with Step 2.

As students engage in this strategy, they begin to realize that not all questions are answered by a particular text, and sometimes more questions are raised. Even more important, they are actively constructing their own questions about a topic and exploring the text to find answers, just as "real readers" do.

Conceptual Mapping

Because reading is a transaction between a reader and a text, comprehension may be facilitated when students think about what they are about to read. *Semantic* or *conceptual mapping* is a strategy that enables students to associate what they know with what they read, thus bringing stories to life (Heimlich & Pittelman, 1986; Hittleman, 1988; Pittelman, Heimlich, Berglund, & French, 1991).

Conceptual maps may involve groups or individual students; the procedure is appropriate for use with ages ranging from preschool to high school. Matthew, a 5-year-old with an interest in dinosaurs, received a copy of *Dinosaurs and Other Prehistoric Animals,* by Darlene Geis (1982), for his birthday. His mother Pat had just studied conceptual mapping in an education class and tried out the procedure with him. She started by writing "DINOSAURS" on a large sheet of paper, and then asked Matthew to think about dinosaurs and how they lived. Matthew quickly took charge of the "lesson" by stating, "They had a lot of different names." After Pat wrote the word "NAMES," Matthew asked how to spell Hesperornis and insisted on writing down the letters himself, one by one. He then allowed his mother to print Coelophysis, Plateosaurus, and Teratosaurus. He then brainstormed about where the dinosaurs traveled, how they died, where their bones and fossils are found today, and much more. From time to time, Matthew insisted on printing letters and adding pictures to the conceptual map. Figure 7.3 shows the completed map.

Matthew was now prepared to read his new book, with all of his stored knowledge about dinosaurs at hand to assist him when the book presented new information about dinosaurs and their lives. When the story was over, Matthew wanted to add new categories and information to his dinosaur "map."

When conceptual maps are created in group situations, students can assist in organizing their knowledge about the subject. The creation of the map brings out the key vocabulary words and concepts, enabling many students to learn about the subject even before they read.

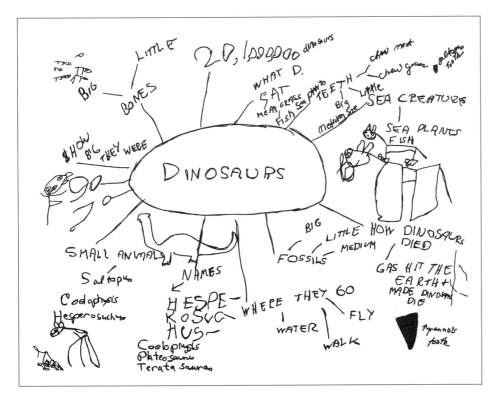

Conceptual maps are also excellent postreading activities. After reading, constructing conceptual maps helps students remember and represent graphically the information read, and it involves the movement from linguistic to spatial intelligence. In addition, if students have constructed conceptual maps before reading, they have the opportunity to extend and refine those maps with information they gleaned from the text. Such mapping gives the class a tool for "combining individual efforts" (Calfee & Patrick, 1995, p. 79). If desired, information that has been confirmed by the text can be highlighted and page numbers can be noted. These maps reveal significant information concerning students' comprehension and their conceptual organization of the text and often encourage children to engage in further study concerning a particular topic or character.

Story Maps

Story maps involve students in constructing "a basic framework for organizing and storing information" (Idol-Maestas & Croll, 1985, p. 4), which in turn anchors and extends their comprehension (Gordon & Pearson, 1983; Short & Ryan, 1984; Singer & Donlan, 1983). Story maps can consist of a very basic format in which students draw, write, or do a combination of both to represent their understanding of the beginning, middle, and end of a story. They may be developed to portray the different elements of story grammar that refer to the components of a story: characters, setting, problem, series of problem-solving events, and resolution. Or, as demonstrated in the Teacher-to-Teacher feature, a story map may portray a child's conceptualization of a story and character relationships.

Teacher-to-Teacher

Dee Finley, a third-grade teacher, became interested in story maps as a "window" through which she could view her students' comprehension. Before reading a version of "The Three Little Pigs" in the basal reader, she asked her students to share what they remembered about the classic story. This information was organized into a conceptual map as the students shared. Next, Dee provided the students with time for silent independent reading of the story. Finally, students created their own story maps. Figure 7.4 shows Shannon's conceptualization of the story.

Interestingly, the map clearly shows the major characters in the story and their rela-

tionships with one another. The map demonstrates to Dee that Shannon has comprehended the story. In addition, the creation of the map probably deepened Shannon's knowledge of story structure and should help him the next time he creates a story of his own.

Dee often uses mapping as a prewriting activity with her third-graders. In response to her assignment to create a "Just Thinking About You" card to a loved one, Jonathan created a birthday card for his father (Figure 7.5). Note his brainstorming list of adjectives (right side of card), which assisted him in the actual writing of the card.

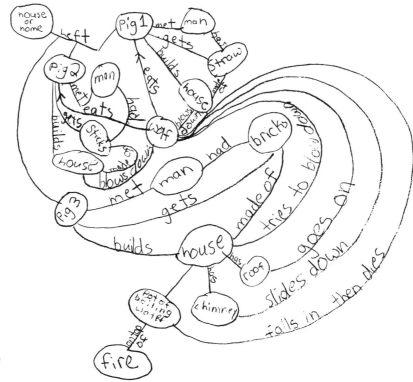

FIGURE 7.4

A story map of "The Three Little Pigs"

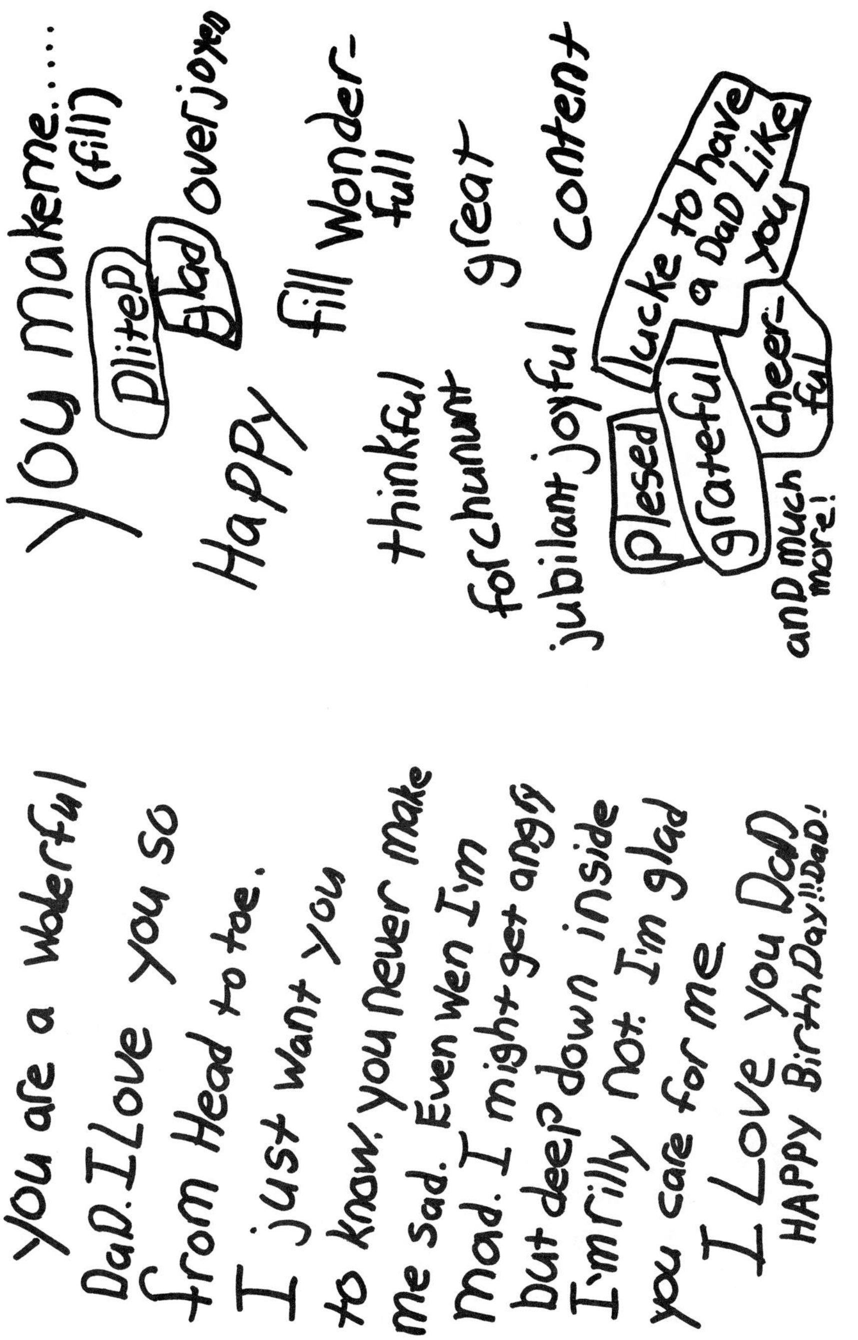

You makeme.... (fill)

Dlited

Glad overjoyed

Happy fill Wonder-
full

thinkful

forchunint great

jubilant joyful content

lucke to have
a Dad Like you

Plesed

grateful

Cheer-
ful

anD much
more!

You are a woderful
DaD. I Love you so
from Head to toe.
I just want you
to know, you never make
me sad. Even wen I'm
Mad. I might get angy
but deep down inside
I'mrilly Not. I'm glad
you care for me
I Love you Dad!
HAPPY BirthDay!!DaD!

FIGURE 7.5
Jonathan's
birthday card

K-W-L

K-W-L is a strategy that involves students in activating their mental schema concerning a topic, developing questions about and a purpose for exploring information concerning the area, and recording information they gleaned from the exploration that answers their questions and concerns. Developed by Donna Ogle (1989), this strategy models processes that proficient readers use when attempting to learn from text. Here is a list of the steps for implementing K-W-L with a class:

STEP 1 Introduce the new topic and solicit what students *know* about the subject through brainstorming. The teacher divides a chart or overhead into three categories:

K—*What We Know*
W—*What We Want to Know*
L—*What We Learned*

The teacher then writes the brainstormed information in the column labeled **K**–*What We Know* on the chart or overhead so it can be used throughout the study. It is important that *all* brainstormed information be recorded on the overhead or chart—this is not the time to correct misconceptions but for students to activate their background knowledge base concerning the topic. Students may be given a sheet with the K-W-L categories so they can record their personal brainstorming.

STEP 2 Pose the questions "What do you have questions about?" "What do you want to learn more about?" and "What do we need to find out about this topic?" As students begin to generate questions, the teacher records these on the chart or overhead in the column labeled **W**–*What We Want to Know*. This questioning process models what lifelong learners are consistently doing—developing questions and purposes for reading. If students have been given a personal K-W-L sheet, they should be encouraged to write questions they have about the topic.

STEP 3 To extend students' readiness to read the text or explore a topic, it is valuable for the teacher to ask students to look at the information they have brainstormed and think of ways to form categories. For instance, if the topic is spiders, younger students might sort their brainstorming into categories such as different types of spiders, what they look like, what they eat/how they get their food, and how they protect themselves. Older students may use more sophisticated categories such as physical appearance, habitat, diet, poisonous/

toxicity, nonpoisonous, and types of webs. The teacher should organize the categories on a chart to aid students in organizing information as they explore the topic.

STEP 4   The students then explore the topic. The K-W-L chart provides a purpose for the explorations, but the exploration may proceed in a variety of ways. It may be implemented with a whole class, or a small group. Children may examine a variety of materials, or the same text. Students might look for information that answers all of the questions, make notes, or add to individual K-W-L charts, and then share the information during whole class discussion to extend the class chart. Individuals, pairs, or small groups may choose to focus on one particular category, explore the topic, and write information on individual or group K-W-L charts to share with the larger group. The strategy may be implemented by the teacher taking dictation on a class chart during the **K**–*What We Know* and **W**–*What We Want to Know* segments, reading text to children, and taking dictation during the discussion phase of **L**–*What We Learned.*

As with all strategies, it is important to focus on your students and adapt the strategy to meet the age and instructional needs of the learners. One adaptation evolved from concern when students initially brainstormed information that was incorrect and we wrote it under the **K**–*What We Know* column. As teachers, we did not want to correct the incorrect information because we knew it would stop the brainstorming. However, that meant the incorrect information remained on the class chart throughout the topic exploration. This dilemma resulted in a K-W-L adaptation that is called "Confirming a K-W-L" (M. B. Sampson, 2002). The K column shifts from *What We Know* to *What We Think We Know.* During the brainstorming process, it is important to discuss the concept that we cannot accept anything as a "fact" or place it in the **L**–*What We Learned* column until we can "confirm" it with reliable/valid sources. Since the number of sources and what is considered reliable/valid are dependent on the age of the students and the availability of resources, it is important to reach consensus concerning those areas during class discussion.

Although the process of topic exploration may proceed in a variety of ways, as in the original K-W-L, there are differences in the students' purposes. In addition to searching for information that answers their questions or that they consider important/interesting, students are also looking for sources that "confirm" items that were brainstormed in the **K**–*What We Think We Know* column. Students must note the source of the information. We have found it useful to give students small sticky notes during their exploration of text to "mark" items that confirmed statements of knowledge, answered questions, or provided important information. An item cannot receive a "check" in the Confirmed column until the previously agreed upon number of sources have been found.

After the students have explored the topic, debrief with the class. Ask them to share the answers they found to questions in the **W**–*What We Want to Know* column, and the information they were able to confirm in the **K**–*What We Think We Know* column. Record the information and the sources on the class K-W-L chart. Continue the process by asking students to share any new ideas and information they found in the text that was unexpected. Record the information and sources on the class K-W-L chart under the **L**–*What We Learned* and Source column. This process of confirming, rejecting, and /or extending information brainstormed in the K column demonstrates to students that revision and extension of knowledge is part of the learning process. In addition, it highlights the importance of critically evaluating information before accepting it as factual. Figure 7.6 shows both the original K-W-L chart and the "Confirming a K-W-L" format.

K *What We Know*	W *What We Want to Know*	L *What We Learned*

Chart Format for "Confirming" a K-W-L

What We Think We Know	Confirmed	Source	What We Want to Know	What We Learned	Source

FIGURE 7.6
Chart format for
K-W-L strategy

Anticipation-Reaction Guide

Anticipation-reaction guides are designed for prereading anticipation and postreading contemplation (Head & Readence, 1986). They consist of a series of teacher-prepared statements related to the topics of a book or chapter. Students agree or disagree with the statements *before* reading, and discuss the reasons for their answers. (Students might write down their reasons, in pairs, before discussing them as a group.) After reading, students decide what they think are the author's feelings or thoughts about the statement, and what in the text makes them attribute this viewpoint to the author. During class discussion, they compare their responses with their classmates and have the opportunity to reread and cite evidence that supports their responses. Figure 7.7 is an example of an anticipation-reaction guide based on Who *Put That Hair in My Toothbrush?* (Spinelli, 2000).

Using this technique, students draw on their background experiences and knowledge in responding. Prereading discussions are facilitated because there are no right or wrong answers. A framework is formed by the activation of students' schemata for new information to "hook" onto. As students compare and contrast their views with the views they perceive to be those of the author, they have the opportunity to discuss what passages in the text support their beliefs. Because there are no "right" or "wrong" answers, students have the opportunity to discuss text and defend divergent viewpoints.

Anticipation-Reaction Guide
Who Put That Hair in My Toothbrush?

Read the statements. Write *yes* if you agree. Write *no* if you disagree.

What I think		What the author thinks
_____	It is difficult to be a middle child.	_____
_____	Parents treat all their children fairly.	_____
_____	Sometimes getting what you wished can be painful.	_____
_____	Sibling rivalry is natural.	_____
_____	Treating others like you want to be treated is very important.	_____
_____	Sometimes it is difficult to be a parent.	_____

FIGURE 7.7
Anticipation-Reaction Guide for *Who Put That Hair in My Toothbrush?*

Young Readers

It's Simple, Said Simon, **by
Mary Ann Hoberman.**
A young boy takes a walk,
meets numerous animals, and
finds it "simple" to meet their
requests—until he meets a
cunning tiger and finds it necessary to use his wits.
New York: Knopf, 2001.

I Remember Papa, **by
Helen Ketteman.**
A grown man tells the heart-
warming story of when he
learned that the actions of
love speak louder than words
when his father took him on a
trip to see the Cincinnati Reds
play baseball.
New York: Dial, 1998.

Swish! **by Bill Martin Jr.
and Michael Sampson.**
The energetic text features
two multiracial teams of girls
racing up and down the basketball court. Children will
enjoy chiming in with the author's repetition of "dribble,
dribble, dribble" and "Swish!"
New York: Henry Holt, 1997.

Cows Can't Fly, **by
David Milgrim.**
A young boy draws flying
cows—and a herd of cows
takes flight. He is enthralled
but is the only one to see
them since everyone else is so
busy looking down.
New York: Viking, 1998.

Conferencing about Text

As we have discussed earlier, it is important for students to have the opportunity to talk about the text they are reading. This is a literacy activity that people who love to read naturally engage in. They are always telling you about the book they are reading, the new author they have discovered, the interesting article they just read—and the list goes on. When reading is an interesting and integral part of our lives, we want to share our excursions into text with others. Conferencing enables students to engage in this behavior in the classroom.

Students may conference with a peer or with the teacher. If a child is confer-
encing with a peer, the conference may be recorded so the teacher can sample bits of the conference to determine what interactions with the text were being dis-
cussed. Older children can use Carolyn Burke's strategy of written conversation to conference and write their conversation rather than discussing orally (Harste, Short, & Burke, 1988). To accomplish this, a student would write a comment or question about the text on a piece of paper and hand it to a partner. The partner reads the question or comment, responds in writing, asks a new question, and returns the paper to the first student. The process continues in this manner with students alternating roles of questioner and responder. Here are some sample questions that aid in oral or written conferencing about stories:

1. Who are the most important characters? Why do you think so?
2. Describe the kind of place where the story happened.
3. What is the main problem or conflict in this story? How was it solved? Can you think of another way it could have been solved?
4. Who do you think is the main person in the story? Why?
5. How does the main character change, or how is the character different at the end of the story? What do you think caused this change?
6. What do you think is the most important event in the story? Why?
7. Would you recommend this book to other readers? Why or why not?
8. If you were the author of the story, would you rewrite any parts? Why?
9. Does this story remind you of any other stories you have read? Why? What parts?
10. What is your favorite page? Why?

   Sample questions for use with content text include these:

1. What was the most important thing you learned from this text? Why do you think it is the most important?
2. What was the most confusing part of the text? What seemed to cause it to be confusing?

3. What new terms did you find in the text? Were you able to figure out what they meant? How did you do this?

4. Was there information you already knew? What was it?

5. Was there anything you thought you knew, but the text had different information? What was it? Do you believe the text is right? Why or why not?

6. What would be a good question about this text? What is the answer?

7. What in the text would you like to know more about? Where do you think you might find the information?

As children engage in oral or written conferencing, they have the opportunity to explore their perceptions of the text and gain exposure to the perceptions of others.

Reciprocal Questioning Technique

Are you interested in ways to involve your students in the reading process—to help them interact mentally with the printed page in such a way that the text becomes more than mere words on paper? One strategy proven effective in facilitating this interaction is the **R**eciprocal **Quest**ioning **T**echnique (ReQuesT), which enables students to approach reading with an inquiring attitude (Manzo, 1969). This strategy is particularly effective for students with poor comprehension skills. ReQuesT can be used at any level, from first grade through university classrooms (Tierney & Readence, 2000). The basic steps of the procedure remain the same, regardless of the class grade level. The teacher simply adjusts the difficulty of the material and length of the text according to the abilities of the students. Originally, ReQuesT was designed to be used on a one-to-one basis, but the procedure has proven to be equally effective with groups ranging from two to eight students. However, participants in the group must have approximately the same reading level because they will all be reading the identical passage.

The first responsibility of the teacher when using ReQuesT is to select well-written and level-appropriate reading material. Contrived basal stories that contain no real plot are ineffective. However, some basal stories are perfect candidates for ReQuesT. Other material sources include content-area textbooks, newspaper articles, and magazine pieces. After selecting the material, the next step is to identify good break points within the story where the group will pause from their reading and ask questions. When using ReQuesT for the first time, it is very important to explain to students what is expected of them. Most students have had very little instructional variation from the traditional directed reading activities that accompany basal readers. Therefore, students should be told they will be reading the story in a different way and that the purpose of the lesson will be to improve their understanding of what they read. In addition, students will be told that they will be required to ask both the teacher and the other students questions about the passage. Further, these should be the thought-provoking kinds of questions that teachers ask. At this point the teacher is ready to begin and should adhere to the following basic steps:

STEP 1   Teacher and students silently read the first section of the material. This section might be as short as a few sentences for second-graders, or as long as several pages for high school students.

STEP 2   When all have completed the section, books are turned face down and the questions begin. As originally designed by Manzo (1969), one student asks the teacher as many questions as desired. Then the teacher asks that same student questions. However, Tierney and Readence (2000) recommend that a good alternative to this procedure is to have the roles of questioner and respondent either alternate around a circle or proceed at random within the circle. This works quite well, resulting in intragroup discussions about the quality and appropriateness of certain questions and responses. The teacher's role during this question-and-answer time is to model more provocative questions and to provide positive feedback to students by commenting on their questions. Such comments might include "Good question" and "That's a good way of thinking about that." If a question is not clear during the question–answer procedure, the student can ask for clarification. An answer of "I don't know" is unacceptable. The student (or teacher) must at least try to explain why he or she doesn't know the answer. If necessary, the question can be rephrased and reference to the text can be used to justify an uncertain response. Should the question a student intended to ask be posed first by someone else, that student is allowed to refer back to the material and select another question. Teachers must, of course, be sure to have the students read the next section of the story when it appears the material has been "milked" of all useful information.

STEP 3   The students and teacher proceed from section to section, following the same procedure. This continues until the teacher observes that questions are being asked that show the students are in command of their comprehension of the story. At this point, the teacher moves the group from the development of questioning behaviors to the development of student predictive behaviors. The teacher can make inquiries such as "What do you think will happen next?" and "Why do you think so?" Such questions guide the silent reading of the students as they read the next section of the story. After reading the section, the teacher discusses individual predictions of the students. Questions like "Did your prediction occur?" and "Do you still think . . . ?" help stimulate further consideration of the text. This process is modeled through several sections of the book, or until the teacher feels the students are making sensible predictions and comprehending the text. From this point, the remainder of the selection is read silently, with the teacher offering assistance to students when necessary without interfering with their reading.

STEP 4   Once the selection has been completed, the students and the teacher may discuss specific predictions that were made by members of the group. Information or concepts not understood in the story may then be clarified. Through this interaction, students often gain a clearer understanding of the selection.

Students who participate in ReQuesT will quickly assume more responsibility in asking questions. Searfoss and Readence (1985) state that the ReQuesT procedure "provides a format to fill the gaps between instructional lessons in which teachers direct children's comprehension processes by questioning, and lessons that allow for children to direct their own learning through active comprehension" (p. 246).

When using ReQuesT for the first time, some teachers make the common error of dominating the discussion. The teacher should be patient with the students and allow them to create and answer the questions at their own pace. Group interaction is essential. The silence that may occur during this procedure could be an indication that the students are thinking, and that's what they must do to comprehend. Jenkins's (2001) research indicates that our schools are in critical need of instructional practices that provoke students to think. The ReQuesT procedure offers an important step toward that goal.

Cloze Procedure

The cloze procedure requires readers to respond to a reading passage by supplying words that have been deleted from the text. It demands that the reader search for information clues to predict what word or type of word would be syntactically and semantically appropriate for the deletion. Thus students are required "to complete a familiar—but not quite finished pattern—to 'see' a broken circle as a whole one . . . by mentally closing the gaps" (Taylor, 1953, p. 415). As a teaching technique, cloze may be used to encourage the use of contextual clues, strengthen vocabulary, encourage divergent production, and improve reading comprehension (Bortnick & Lopardo, 1976; Rankin, 1977; Sampson, Valmont, & Allen, 1982; Ward 2001a).

The cloze procedure is appropriate for use with students of all ages. The materials selected should be relatively easy reading for the students. Selections may be taken from poems, stories, subject matter texts, or even from language experience stories (Tierney & Readence, 2000).

After selecting the passage the teacher wants to develop into a cloze exercise, he or she will need to determine instructional objectives before making the cloze deletions. Adjectives or some other part of speech may be deleted, but whatever is decided, the difficulty of the passage will be affected. (An example of a cloze activity is shown in Chapter 11.)

The passage may be read and completed individually by the students. However, it is important that the students come together in small groups to discuss the various words selected to complete the cloze blanks. Such discussions should focus on the variety of answers that could be used in most cloze blanks and on the reasons for a particular response within the context surrounding the deletion (Sampson et al., 1982). Semantic consistency should be the determining factor concerning the appropriateness of the responses (Sampson & Briggs, 1983).

Cloze is a worthwhile instructional activity when used appropriately. However, cloze lessons must include more than just the completion of cloze deletions. Group discussions are imperative. Comprehension and vocabulary improvements will result only when student involvement and teacher follow-up are included.

Reader-Directed Strategies

Students who excel in school usually share a common characteristic—they are good readers. What is a good reader? Examining characteristics of successful readers reveals the answer to this question. Good readers know how to extract information from their textbooks, to evaluate its importance, and to link new information with old. In addition, they monitor their understanding and retention and evaluate their progress in terms of their purpose for reading.

Unfortunately, content-area materials may be quite difficult for some students to comprehend. Consequently, students may experience continual frustration from their inability to understand their text. Their study time often involves nothing more than passive—sometimes desperate—rereading.

What can a teacher do to help students learn from reading? One answer is to provide them with workable strategies to guide their reading. This section of the chapter details several techniques that have been proven successful in improving the comprehension of individual readers.

SMART

Study strategies for content reading have been available for years. However, most of these strategies share a common fault: They stress remembering and place little emphasis on understanding. The self-monitoring approach to reading and thinking (SMART) was developed to emphasize understanding and, as a by-product, remembering (Vaughan & Estes, 1986). The strategy is effective because remembering naturally follows understanding, and understanding often eliminates the need to memorize.

The steps involved in SMART are discussed next. We recommend you try out this procedure with your next reading assignment. These instructions are addressed to the students:

STEP 1 Survey the material to get a general idea of what the passage is about. When surveying, look at the title, subheadings, pictures, graphs, and summary of the section. Identify and note logical breaking points; you will be stopping at these points to check your understanding. These breaking points often are between subheadings in the textbook.

STEP 2 Read each segment of the text, placing a plus (+) by material you understand (place this "+" in the margin in pencil, using a separate sheet of paper if marking in the book is not permissible or use small sticky notes). Place a question mark (?) in the margin beside material you do not understand.

STEP 3 As you read each section, pause to clarify your understanding. Do so by completing the following steps:

◆ Explain to yourself in your own words what you understand. Looking back at the material as you do so is allowed.

◆ Examine what you do not understand using these steps:

   a. Reread the portions you do not understand.
   b. Identify what might be causing the problem. It might be a word, a phrase, or a relationship.
   c. Think of something that might help you to understand, such as reviewing similar information in another portion of the text, using the glossary, or perhaps examining graphic aids and illustrations.
   d. Try your idea out. If it works and you now understand, change the question mark (?) in the margin to a plus (+).
   e. Explain to yourself what you do not understand (for example, "I still don't understand how investment casting of metal is done.").
   f. If a formula is creating the problem, reread the explanation of the formula. Next, reread the example that illustrates the formula; this will often clarify hazy notions you might have. Your goal should be to comprehend the formula, the example of the formula and its answer, and, most important, the generalization or conclusion at the end of the section.

STEP 4 Go on to the next segment of the text. Repeat Steps 2 and 3.

STEP 5 As you proceed through each section of the reading assignment, turn back and reexamine concepts you did not understand earlier. Ask yourself, "Does it make sense now?" If it does, it is probably because you learned something new as you read the latest section or were able to relate the new information to information you already knew. If the content still does not make sense to you, don't be concerned. Just keep reading.

STEP 6   After reading the entire assignment, do the following:

◆ With your book closed, explain to yourself what you understand about what you read.

◆ Open your text and look back over the material to refresh your memory. Do not be concerned about things you don't understand. You can ask a classmate or your teacher about them later.

◆ Rethink what you do not understand. What could they mean? Are they related to other things that you do understand?

STEP 7   With the book closed, explain to yourself one final time what you do understand.

Patty Engle listens as a fourth-grader shares a REAP annotation.

Courtesy of Michael Sampson

Content-area materials are often difficult for students to read. Their difficult readability levels and complex explanations of concepts, formulas, and procedures frustrate many students. Consequently, many students decide that taking notes and observing the teacher are the best ways to obtain information about content. The solution to the problem is for you to help students overcome their fears of their texts. SMART is an excellent first step toward that end. As students learn to monitor their own comprehension and learn *what* to do when they don't understand, they will develop a new respect for their text and their ability to manipulate it. The result will be successful students who learn from reading.

REAP

The read, encode, annotate, ponder (REAP) technique is based on the premise that comprehension is facilitated when students have to communicate their understanding of text to others. Specifically, the procedure is designed to improve the comprehension skills of students by having them synthesize an author's message in the form of annotations (Eanet & Manzo, 1976). Research indicates that comprehension is significantly improved by this postreading activity (Eanet, 1978). However, Vaughan (1982) cautions that the technique requires students to become "adept at constructing" the various types of annotations if the activity is to be of value.

REAP is appropriate for use with intermediate-grade students and higher and is most effective when used with text that stimulates diverse opinion. The activity consists of the following four stages:

Read to uncover the ideas of the author

Encode the ideas of the author into the student's own language

Annotate those ideas into written form

Ponder the significance of the annotation

When your students write annotations, they will be interacting with the ideas of the author, synthesizing those ideas into their own language, and putting that synthesis into writing. This demands interaction with the text, which results in comprehension.

Students may use several different forms of annotations, including heuristic, summary, thesis, question, intention, motivation, and critical annotations (Eanet & Manzo, 1976).

To provide examples of the various annotation styles, we'll share the following editorial piece, which was published in the *Dallas Morning News* in 2001, and then construct appropriate annotations for it:

What's Wrong with *Charlotte's Web?*
Michael Sampson, Ph.D.

The children of Texas were dealt a terrible blow last week. That blow came from a well intentioned but sadly misinformed Texas State Board of Education, who in the interest of promoting phonics instruction, mandated reading textbooks that restrict children's access to interesting and challenging language.

The board called for stories in beginning reading textbooks to be restricted to simplistic, phonetically regular words and passages. With a wave of the board's magic wand, children's stories in textbooks are being transformed—from real stories to phonics-based stories. In fact, the state board set the magic number of phonemically regular words that must be used at 80 percent.

As a writer of books for young children, I'm appalled at the thought of being asked to restrict my language, and the language children are allowed to read, to mostly phonemically regular words. Since our English language is only 65 percent phonemically regular, that means that I would have to drop about 4 of every 10 words from the vocabulary I share with children. And vocabulary is the building block of a story—interesting language begets interesting stories.

Real stories by real authors will not meet this new criterion. Censored would be the classic stories from my generation—the Hardy Boys, Nancy Drew, *Lad a Dog.* Wilbur of *Charlotte's Web* fame would be excluded, as well as today's Harry Potter books that children everywhere want to read. But the real question is about phonics. But how does a child learn phonics? Although isolated drill and worksheets may be useful, children truly learn phonics by reading. And children want to read interesting, engaging stories—not simplistic, uninteresting ones.

Ironically, learning to read is joyously simple when children read stories they are interested in. Conversely, research studies indicate that simple, uninteresting stories are harder for children to read than more complex, engaging ones.

By using the whole brain and what they know about the topic being read, children can read material that is more complex than they might be able to read by simply "sounding out" words. As children read "real books," they internalize the sounds of language by hearing the words in their mind's ear as they read. This internalization allows children to apply these phonetic principles to new words they will encounter in subsequent reading material.

When adults read, they simply toss aside books or newspaper articles they are not interested in. Unfortunately, a first grade child in a classroom does not have that option when it comes to reading the state-purchased textbook.

The state board wants to be sure that children are taught phonics in a systematic manner. And they want to make sure that the textbooks children read will not "confuse" the students with words that do not agree with the rules they are being taught.

But how do we "protect" these young readers from words that dispute their phonetic rules outside of class? Do we screen all their reading material?

Do we cover their eyes with a blindfold lest they read the word colonel on a chicken billboard?

The answer, of course—is that we should not.

But the state board's action, unless overturned, has many downsides and raises several questions.

Why should we subject children who are good readers to bad stories they don't want to read? Why should we force children to read stories that will not help them grow stronger vocabularies? And why should we subject at risk students to bad stories—stories that are hard to read and that do not grow their language?

I have a 15 year old who is learning to drive. While he did spend some time studying about driving, he is really becoming a driver by driving. Drivers drive on real roads in real cars—roads that have bumps and traffic. Children must have the same opportunities and trials while learning to read. Real stories contain words that reflect our language—a language that is not bound to the rules of phonics. We must not deny our children the joys and challenges of good stories that paint pictures in their minds, make them laugh, and make them want to read more.

Like my son the driver, readers must have the opportunity to experience reading on the highways of reading—not the go cart course of phonics-based stories and psuedo reading.

Now let's examine the content of this story using a variety of annotation styles:

Heuristic annotation   The heuristic annotation depicts the essence of the author's message through a selection of the author's own words:

> That blow came from a well intentioned but sadly misinformed Texas State Board of Education, who in the interest of promoting phonics instruction, mandated reading textbooks that restrict children's access to interesting and challenging language.

Summary annotation   A summary annotation condenses the author's message as it presents a simple synopsis of his or her ideas:

> Readers of school materials should have access to stories that contain rich, vibrant, relevant language like they'll encounter in the real world.

Thesis annotation   A thesis is a precise statement of the author's point of view:

> The Texas State Board of Eduation should not restrict beginning school books to phonetically regular words—to do so would deprive children of the richness of language that exists in real books.

Question annotation   A question annotation approaches the central content of a selection in question form. Students need not provide answers to the questions they write—the answers are subject to debate:

Why did the state board make this ruling? Why should students who are good readers be made to read stories that are too simplistic for them? Why should we force children to read stories that will not help them grow stronger vocabularies?

Intention annotation   An intention annotation considers author motive—why did they write the piece and what do they believe?

The author does not believe phonics should be taught at the expense of rich reading experiences for children. He believes students will learn

Diverse Learners

Meeting the Needs of Children with Health Impairments

Ms. Jones was concerned about William, one of her first-graders. He was losing weight and going to the bathroom frequently. In addition, he often complained about being thirsty and "too tired" to participate in an activity. However, Ms. Jones was still shocked when she heard that he collapsed at home and was rushed to the hospital. His blood sugar level was 387, and further testing confirmed a diagnosis of juvenile diabetes (Type I).

After a week-long stay in the hospital to stabilize his blood sugar and for him and his family to receive training in monitoring his blood sugar and administering insulin injections, he returned to school with several items that were critical to his health. These included a glucometer (test strips and lancelet that enabled him to prick his finger, obtain a blood sample, and determine his blood sugar level), insulin and syringes, and snacks. It was necessary for him to frequently monitor the level of his blood sugar by pricking his finger to obtain a blood sample for the glucometer, take insulin injections prior to eating based on his blood sugar level, and eat snacks at certain times. In addition, his diet limited sweets and carbohydrates.

She was in the situation that many teachers find themselves in when working with students who have health impairments.

The Individuals with Disabilities Act defines *health impairment* this way:

> Having limited strength, vitality, or alertness, due to chronic or acute health problems such as heart condition, tuberculosis, rheumatic fever, nephritis, asthma, sickle cell anemia, hemophilia, epilepsy, lead poisoning, leukemia, or diabetes, that adversely affects a child's educational performance. (IDEA, Section 300, 7 [8])

Some students with health impairments are eligible for special services if the health problem substantially limits participation in one or more life activities (Brimer, 1990); however, all students with chronic and/or life-threatening impairments or illnesses need a supportive instructional environment in order to thrive. Fortunately, Ms. Jones had taken action to ensure that William felt comfortable continuing the routine that was critical to maintaining his health once he returned to school. Although William had juvenile diabetes, many of the following actions can provide needed support to children with other chronic and/or life-threatening health situations as well:

Utilize others as resources.   Collaborate with others to glean information from their expertise. School personnel, the stu-

phonics through reading as they internalize the sounds of language through reading.

Motivation annotation   A motivation annotation addresses the author's motives, biases, and preceptions:

The author writes children's books and does not want his choice of words limited by the Texas State Board. He argues that when language is restricted children's learning of language will be hampered.

---

dent, parents, and the student's classmates are available for support. Ms. Jones and the school nurse visited William at home before he returned to school. With William and his parents, they collaboratively designed a plan that would provide opportunities for William to monitor his blood sugar, take insulin injections, and eat snacks at the designated times—in addition to any time he felt weak or dizzy.

Learn about the health impairment, treatment, and the possible impact on school performance.   Ms. Jones asked for information from the school nurse, William, and his parents. She received information about items such as how to recognize an insulin reaction, the impact of exercise on blood sugar levels, and the impact of blood sugar levels on moodiness and fatigue. In addition, she went online to www.diabetes.org/ to learn more about diabetes.

Plan ahead so that the student will be included in as many class experiences/ activities as possible—and treated as normally as possible.   Ms. Jones made sure that when treats were served in class, or when she implemented an activity that incorporated food, that she either provided something William could eat—or provided choices so that he was not the only child eating a particular food.

Share nonconfidential and appropriate information about the student with classmates before the student returns to school.   Encourage classmates to be supportive and to communicate by calling, writing, or emailing when a student has an extended absence. Ms. Jones knew the students would have questions about William's extra snacks and medical supplies. Plus, they had been worried about him during his absence. During the home visit, she discussed William's classmates' concerns with William's parents. She asked his parents to list what they believed would be appropriate to share with his classmates in order to ease his return to school.

As a result of Ms. Jones' proactive and student-centered actions, William's return to school was smooth. He was not isolated or made to feel different, and he continued to be accepted as an integral part of the classroom community. Therefore, he continued to progress—physically, emotionally, and academically.

Critical annotation   A critical annotation allows the reader, or annotator, to respond to the writer:

> The author is wrong. Children must be taught phonics properly if they are ever to become good readers. No child must be left behind.

The selection being read may limit the types of annotations that are suitable. Tierney, Readence, and Dishner (1995) recommend that the teacher preview the material to decide which types of annotations will work best.

The Ponder stage of REAP involves the use of annotations for classroom activities or personal study. Eanet and Manzo (1976) suggest several possible uses of annotations. Students might write annotations of library books they have read. These annotations can be filed in the library as a source of review for prospective readers of the book. Another possibility is for students to review past reading assignments by consulting their annotations and the annotations of others.

REAP does a good job of interrelating reading, writing, and thinking. When used selectively, it can facilitate reading comprehension and improve study skills.

Sketch to Stretch

The sketch to stretch strategy was devised by Jerry Harste and his colleagues at Indiana University and provides students with an opportunity to represent the most important "picture" that played in their mind when they read a selection (Tierney & Readence, 2000). It also gives students the chance to view the varied meanings constructed by different class members as they share and discuss their drawings. The strategy is useful for both content and narrative texts and consists of the following steps:

STEP 1   Students read text. (If desired, students may divide into groups of four to five and read the same selection. This strategy may also be implemented with a story the teacher reads aloud to the class or to a small group of children.)

STEP 2   Draw a sketch of "the picture you see in your mind when you think of the story." Remind students there is not a "right" or "wrong" picture. There are many ways of depicting the meaning of an experience.

STEP 3   If all students have been reading the same text, they should divide into groups of four or five after completing their sketches. Each person shows his or her sketch to the others in the group. Group members have a chance to express what they think the artist/student is trying to say.

STEP 4   After all group members have had the opportunity to indicate what they think the drawing represents, the artist/student gets the last word.

STEP 5   All of the groups share. Groups may collaborate and construct a group sketch after sharing, choose one from the group to share, or share all of the sketches. Sketches may be put on the overhead projector or displayed on poster board.

This strategy provides students with an opportunity to discuss the impact the text had on them by deciding on and then sharing the most important mental image that was formed as they interacted with the text. During this sharing, the concept is reinforced that reading text is much more than just "saying the words." Mental images must be formed.

Save the Last Word for Me

Save the last word for me is a strategy that was developed to involve students in making decisions about text and sharing the basis for those decisions (Harste, Short, & Burke, 1988). As students discuss their views, they are exposed to the concept that there is not one "right way" to comprehend. Save the last word for me consists of the following steps:

STEP 1   Students are given 3-x-5-inch cards and instructed to read the text.

STEP 2   As they read, they are encouraged to write any words, phrases, or segments from the text that they feel are particularly important, interesting, surprising, or warrant further discussion. We have found it useful to limit the number of cards so children are involved in making decisions about text. Otherwise, children begin writing everything down and do not have time to complete the reading. The number of cards you give will depend on the grade level of the students, but we usually limit it to five. We also ask children to write the page number where the segment of text was found so it will be easy to find the portion for future reference.

STEP 3   On the back of the cards, the children compose what they want to say about the segment of text they selected. Figure 7.8 shows some student reactions to the Newbery Honor Book *Hatchet* (Paulsen, 1996).

STEP 4   Students rank-order their cards from most important to least important.

STEP 5   Students divide into small groups and share their number one quote. During this time of sharing and discussion, if another student has shared a student's number one quote, he or she shares the second ranked quote. As each student shares, the other students in the group react to the segment of text. After students have responded, the sharer of the quote has the "last word" and reads from the back of the card what he or she wrote as the reason for choosing that particular segment of text. The process continues until all quotes are shared or time runs out.

STEP 6   Students in the group may collaborate and rank-order several quotes they would like to share with the entire class and develop reasons for their choices. The same procedure for group sharing as for individual sharing

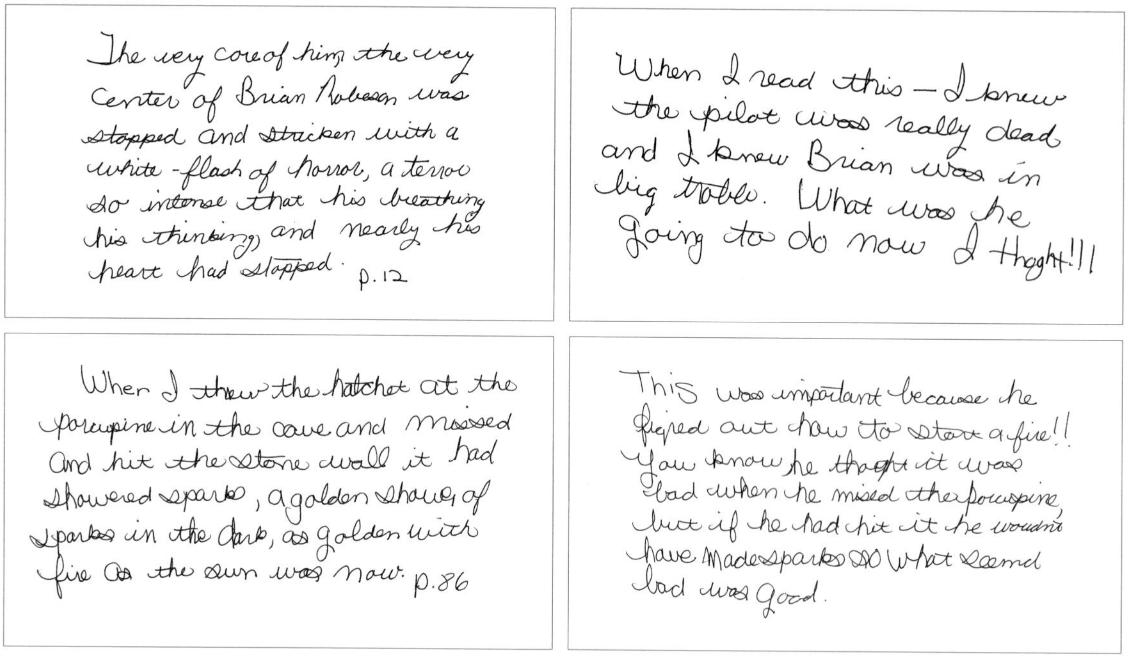

> The very core of him, the very center of Brian Robeson was stopped and stricken with a white-flash of horror, a terror so intense that his breathing, his thinking, and nearly his heart had stopped. p.12

> When I read this — I knew the pilot was really dead and I knew Brian was in big trouble. What was he going to do now I thought!!!

> When I threw the hatchet at the porcupine in the cave and missed and hit the stone wall it had showered sparks, a golden shower of sparks in the dark, as golden with fire as the sun was now. p.86

> This was important because he figured out how to start a fire!! You know he thought it was bad when he missed the porcupine, but if he had hit it he wouldn't have made sparks so what seemed bad was good.

FIGURE 7.8

Reactions to *Hatchet* by Gary Paulsen using the "Save the Last Word for Me" strategy

would be followed. After the other groups have given a group response to the shared quote, the sharing group would have the "last word."

As students engage in this process, they have the opportunity to make decisions about text, justify those decisions, and then discuss them. When this process occurs, students are actively involved in bringing personal meaning to text, as evidenced by the student comments in Figure 7.8.

Making Strategies Work for You

We hope you are thinking of ways you could adapt or modify some of these learning strategies in your classroom. Once again, the emphasis must be on involving your students in the *process* of "acting like real readers." Activities must place students in the position of actively interacting with the text, synthesizing the material, and producing something that demonstrates *their* understanding rather than being in the position of answering questions they never asked. Here are some activities students might do that would provide avenues for reflection, sharing, and discussion:

1. Make a newspaper out of the important events of a story or a selected part of the newspaper such as a comic strip, editorial cartoon, want ad, lead story, editorial, help wanted ad, classified ad, or letter to the editor—the list goes on and on.

2. Write to the author about his or her story, write to a character in the story, assume the role of a character in the story and write to a classmate, assume the role of one character and write a letter to another character in the story, assume the role of a character in one story and write to a character in another story, assume the role of a character in the story and write a letter to the editor of a newspaper—once again you are limited only by your imagination.

3. Make a wall story out of the story. Select the important events that tell the story and illustrate and write a short description and attach these segments to the wall or bulletin board in sequential order. This project could be done in groups.

4. Create time lines from a story, or chart the sequence of important story events.

5. Illustrate favorite scenes and characters from the story, and write or tell why they were chosen.

6. Rewrite a story into a play or Reader's Theater script.

7. List alternative solutions for a problem in a story.

8. Create puppets for a dramatization. Dramatization may be impromptu, or students may write a script.

9. Do writing activities on the story, for example, journal responses, letters, poems, patterned books, or critiques.

10. Write a "concise summary" of the story. Teacher and students should collaborate to determine the maximum number of words that may be used. This limitation causes students to write precisely with words of high imagery. Students may edit their summaries, illustrate them, and make a class book.

11. Have a panel discussion. Some likely topics are the actions of a character, alternative endings of the story, believability of the story, contrast and comparison with other stories, or writing style. Topics would depend on story and age of students.

12. Prepare a book jacket that would represent the story.

13. Decide on three new titles for the story. Give a rationale for your decision.

14. Write a publisher's blurb or advertisement for the story.

15. Create a poster advertising the story.

16. Write a review of the story. Bring in book reviews from magazines and newspapers so students can become acquainted with the critical style of writing. Students may also follow a pattern such as (a) title; (b) author; (c) where and when the story takes place; (d) main characters; (e) the most interesting thing that happened; (f) if you did or did not enjoy the story—why or why not; (g) would you recommend this story to someone else—why or why not?

17. Write a letter recommending the story to a friend.

18. Assume the role of a character in the story and write a letter to a friend or family member describing your situation/problem.

19. Create a personality sketch of one of the story characters.

20. Compose a "rap" about a story character.

21. Construct a mobile of the story characters. On the back of each character, write five adjectives that describe the character.

22. Construct a flip chart depicting the important scenes in a story. Students may also write a one- or two-sentence description on each page.

23. Think of a new character that could be added to the story and assume the role of that character. Then write to or discuss these issues: What would the character do? How would the character fit into the story? What would the character contribute?

24. Write a sequel or prequel to the story. What happens to the characters?

25. Identify the turning point in the story and rewrite it. Then finish the story with the new ending.

26. Write an interview between a character in the story and the author, between a student and a character in the story, between a student and the author, between two characters in the story—once again the list goes on and on.

27. Play story charades. Put the names of the various stories already read and their characters into a box. Draw the titles of the stories or names of characters out of the box and pantomime actions to convey the answer.

28. Try the "never-ending story review." Start a sheet of paper around the room and ask each student to add a one-sentence response to the story. Sentences cannot be duplicated.

From InfoTrac College Edition

Comprehension Instruction: Beyond Strategies (questions and answers), Susan Kidd Villaume and Edna Greene Brabham, *The Reading Teacher* April 2002 v55 i7 p672(4)

Get Real about Reading, Lucy McCormick Calkins, *Instructor (1990)* May–June 1997 v107 n8 p37(5)

Confirming a K-W-L: Considering the Source (teaching ideas), Mary Beth Sampson, *The Reading Teacher* March 2002 v55 i6 p528(5)

Comprehension through Characterization: Enabling Readers to Make Personal Connections with Literature (teaching ideas), N. Alexandra Bluestein, *The Reading Teacher* Feb 2002 v55 i5 p431(4)

From Professional Journals and Publications

Blachowicz, C. L. & Fisher, P. (2000). Vocabulary Instruction. In M. Kamil, P. Mosenthal, P. D. Pearson, and R. Barr (Eds.), *Handbook of Reading Research,* vol. 3, pp. 503–523. New York, NY: Longman.

Harvey, S. (2001). Questioning the Text. *Instructor, 110*(8), 16.

Johnson, G. (1999). Multiple Readings of a Picture Book. *Australian Journal of Language and Literacy, 22.*

Raphael, T. (1992). Question-Answering Strategies for Children. *The Reading Teacher, 36,* 186–190.

Robb, L. (2000). Tackling TOUGH Words. *Instructor, 110*(3), 5.

Sampson, M. B. (2002). Confirming a K-W-L: Considering the Source. *The Reading Teacher, 55,* 528–532.

Summary

Comprehension should be the major focus in all language activities. Because it involves a transaction between language and thought, instructional activities must be meaningful and representative of the kinds and types of language experiences students encounter in life. Contrived language and instructional practices are confusing and counterproductive for students.

We must shift instructional priorities from regurgitation of information to demonstration that what is important in reading is the personal meaning created when a reader and a text interact. The comprehension strategies presented in this chapter were developed toward that end. They will serve as a valuable resource as you seek to build and enhance the reading comprehension skills of your students.

Total Literacy Anchors

◆ The student applies personal experiences and background knowledge to text to facilitate comprehension.

◆ The student adjusts comprehension mode and uses various strategies based on the purpose for reading and the difficulty of the text.

◆ The student monitors his or her own understanding of the text and takes appropriate measures when comprehension breaks down.

◆ The teacher has a repertoire of teacher-directed and reader-directed strategies that may be modeled to assist students in comprehending text.

◆ The teacher realizes that students have individual schemata or background experience, which affects their comprehension of a text.

CHAPTER 8.

The Writing Process

As You Read . . .

◆ How does a teacher's definition of writing affect the way she or he teaches writing?

◆ What happens to students' self-concept when they view themselves as authors?

◆ How does research suggest writing should be taught?

◆ How does literature influence personal prose writing?

◆ What is the value of journals in developing personal writing styles?

◆ How can technology aid writing?

Author Words
Michael Sampson

Allchildren are writers. In this chapter we share numerous examples of the stories and poems children have written. In Chapter 9 we look at literacy structures that provide formats for children's stories. We close our writing section with Chapter 10, which examines different ways to manage the writing classroom.

More than anything else, this chapter is about freedom—freedom to write without fear or embarrassment; freedom to take risks; freedom to experience growth in literacy. We share stories that illustrate the literacy growth of students as they write to convey information, as they share personal observations, as they use their imaginations, as they share feelings about themselves and life, and as they reflect the influence of literature on personal language and writing.

The scribbles of preschool children represent the first stage of writing. They convey meaning through these markings, and children can usually explain just what their writing "says." These messages may be refined into alphabetic writing as children move into meaning-centered classrooms that value self-expression through writing.

Young children must not feel they have to write correctly in order to begin. Eventually, however, children realize that writing involves requirements not encountered in oral expression—handwriting, spelling, punctuation, and other elements of composition—and they must master these skills if they want others to easily read and understand their ideas. If we begin too early to stress the mechanical and formal elements of writing or if we stress them at the expense of the quality of creative thought, we may create a distaste for writing. Our aim should be to develop genuine interest in writing and to promote as much writing as we can. Correct form must serve—never rule—writing.

By reading the writing of others in which standard forms of expression are encountered, children come to incorporate these forms into their own patterns of writing (Chatton & Collins, 1999; Graves, 1981, 1994; Martin & Sampson, 1994). As teachers, we must emphasize both writing and reading. They reinforce each other.

Understanding Writing

Our understanding of the writing process has been significantly influenced by the theories of Lev Vygotsky. Vygotsky believed speaking and writing are linked; in fact, that oral language is the springboard for writing. He observed that children's development of communication skills, including writing, evolved and matured from social speech (Vygotsky, 1962). This social speech includes what Vygotsky termed *communicative speech* and *egocentric speech.* Children use communicative speech for telling their mother they are hungry, writing a letter, or asking what time it might be. Egocentric speech is used as children plan and carry out activities. Egocentric speech helps students express, and sometimes overcome, difficulties: Two-year-old Bradley was overheard saying, as he was slipping off a tree limb, "This boy's gonna fall, this boy's gonna fall!" He wasn't calling for help; he was merely vocalizing his thoughts.

Vygotsky (1962) viewed egocentric speech as a transition from vocal to inner speech. Inner speech is shortened and transformed speech—bursts of thoughts and insights that equate to pure meanings. These meanings or thoughts are a prerequisite to written communication. Writing takes place through the translation of inner speech into scribbles, drawings, words, or phrases. Figure 8.1 diagrams the relationships between inner speech and its forms of expression—oral and written communication.

Inner speech may be used for many types of expression or communication. The expression may be in the mode of oral speech, thinking, or writing. Writers often use inner speech to "think out loud" or to "talk through" what they want to express in written communication. Ideas may begin with images, but images soon are represented in inner speech with voice. Moffett (1981) asserts that writers must discover their "stream of consciousness," which is, in essence, their inner voice. Donald Murray (1989), an accomplished writer, says, "I will not start writing until I hear or sense the voice of the text" (p. 85).

We often interfere with the natural cycle of self-expression by asking children to write about something they don't want to write about, or demanding that they write before they are ready to write. Vygotsky's theories have something to say to us here too. In *Whose Language? What Power?* Frank Smith (1993) summarizes

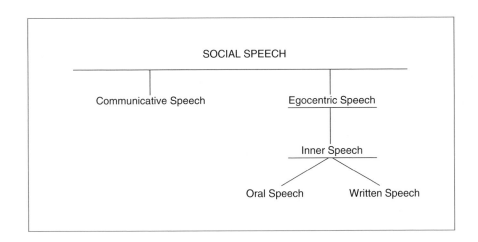

FIGURE 8.1
From thought to communication

Poetry books to share with students to celebrate the rhyme and rhythm of language.

Young Readers

Timothy Tunny Swallowed a Bunny, **by Bill Grossman.**
Hilarious poems describing people in ridiculous situations.
New York: HarperCollins, 2001.

Honey, I Love (Let's Read Aloud), **by Eloise Greenfield.**
Originally published as part of a collection in 1978, this full-color rendition of the classic *Honey, I Love* poem explores the love, laughter, and joy of a young girl's everyday life.
New York: Harperfestival, 1995.

Barking Spiders and Other Such Stuff: Poetry for Children, **by C. J. Heck.**
A collection of poetry for all ages written from a child's point of view concerning the joys and traumas of growing up.
Pittsburgh, PA: Sterling House, 2000.

Here Comes Mother Goose, **edited by Iona Archibald Opie.**
Rosemary Wells's beautiful watercolor illustrations bring this collection of favorite nursery rhymes to life with whimsical animals.
New York: Candlewick, 1999.

Vygotsky's position clearly: "Anything the child can do with help today, the child will be able to do alone tomorrow. There is, therefore, no point in teaching anything a child does not immediately understand or find relevant" (p. 66).

Children as Authors

When children view themselves as authors, they begin to value their literacy talents and become critical readers and writers. In one important study, Graves and Hansen (1983) examined first-graders' concepts of authorship and of the relation between reading and writing. They did so through the use of the Author's Chair, a place where the children shared their "published work" or the work of a professional writer. After reading a self-authored book, the student author receives acceptance from the listeners: "I liked the part where you found the gold." "I liked the way the story ended!" Then the questions begin: "Why did you choose this topic?" "Why did the spaceship blow up?" When a trade book is read and the author is not present, the questions are still asked as the teacher and children speculate on the answers the author might have provided. Through the use of the Author's Chair, Graves and Hansen (1983) observed that children grew into an understanding of the author concept.

A student author shares his work in the Author's Chair.

Courtesy of Michael Sampson

Graves and Hansen broke the process of assimilating the author concept into three phases. The first phase, *replication*, involved understanding that authors write books. In this phase this vague understanding is refined as students do what authors do—write books. As the children struggle to put their thoughts on paper, they experience what authors experience. As they read and listen to stories being read from the Author's Chair, they question the formation and meaning of stories and learn better how to communicate as authors.

The second phase, *transition*, is marked by the child's developing concept of "I am an author." The children's books are displayed alongside those of professional authors. The children become more aware of the options they have as writers because of the questions they are asked as they sit in the Author's Chair.

The third phase, *option-awareness*, grows out of these questions. Students are aware of the content they want to include and the organization that will be needed to express their message. In addition, they become better readers because they become more assertive in dealing with other authors. Graves and Hansen clearly describe this process: "At first an author is distant, then an author is self, finally the self-author questions all authors and assertive readers emerge" (p. 181).

The results of a two-year study at Mast Way School in New Hampshire led Graves (1986) to focus on two capstones of highly successful classrooms: the role of the teacher as a literate leader or mentor in literacy, and the conditions for literate occasions that teachers set up in their classrooms.

In discussing the first capstone, Graves states, "It is the literate lives we lead, far more than methodology, that we bring to children." Teachers, then, must value literacy as a way of life, remaining active as readers and writers themselves.

In considering the second capstone, Graves calls on teachers to take an "inside-out" look at their classroom environment. This process involves a careful examination of teaching methods, student interactions, and literacy materials. Examination should lead teachers to a knowledge of what they need to do to "nurture, sustain and extend the literacy environment" in their classroom. Graves emphasizes that, just as certain plants grow better in certain climates, different students and teachers learn together in different ways.

Consequently, all teachers must create their own classroom environment, adapting what they have learned from others to capitalize on their own teaching strengths. From the first year in school until the last, every student needs to feel the thrill of authorship. Individual contributions to writing should be treated with appropriate mountings and bindings and displayed to foster a feeling of authorship. Students who experience authorship many times are likely to be those most interested in other authors. They appreciate vivid descriptive passages, the beautiful language of good poetry, and characters who seem to live. They can muse with an

Life Doesn't Frighten Me, by Maya Angelou.
The message and language used as the poet confronts real and imaginary fears speaks to all ages.
New York: Stewart Tabori & Chang, 1998.

The Bookworm's Feast: A Potluck of Poems, edited by J. Patrick Lewis.
Alliterations, puns, word plays, and tongue-twisters organized by categories such as "Sumptuous Side Dishes" and "Delectable Desserts."
New York: Dial, 1999.

Older Readers

It's Raining Pigs & Noodles, by Jack Prelutsky.
Younger children will also enjoy the silliness, mazes, and shapes, but it is older readers who will truly appreciate and understand the wit, word play, and puns.
New York: Greenwillow, 2000.

Polkabats and Octopus Slacks: 14 Stories, by Calef Brown.
Even though the title may contain the word "stories," the book is a collection of fourteen rollicking and zany rhymes that will cause children to associate the term "poetry" with "laughter."
New York: Houghton Mifflin, 1999.

The Pig in the Spigot: Poems, by Richard Wilbur.
Fun with poetry—and words— as small words are found in larger ones.
New York: Harcourt Brace, 2000.

CLASSROOM
LITERATURE
CONNECTIONS
CONTINUED

The Great Frog Race and Other Poems, by Kristin O'Connell George.
Beautiful language brings the reader into the world of a young girl who lives in a picturesque rural area, yet deals with many of the struggles and emotions that most children face.

New York: Clarion, 1997.

Insectlopedia: Poems and Paintings, by Douglas Florian.
A clever collection of poems about spiders and insects.

New York: Harcourt Brace, 1998.

author rather than always seek to be amused. They know that good writing is not easy. The satisfaction of having personal ideas accepted, enjoyed, and appreciated builds a strong desire for contact with other authors. The discussions and Teacher-to-Teacher features in this chapter will give you ideas for engaging your students in learning to write—by writing. The reading/writing connection supports children's overall literacy growth (Hansen, 2001), so be sure to note how many "reading skills" children are learning as they write.

The Writing Process

Graves's ethnographic studies of young writers (1975, 1983, 1986, 1994, 1999) in classrooms confirmed that students are creative artists who have both the ideas and the language necessary to communicate through writing. Students need an oppor-

A first grader proudly displays his published book.

tunity to work independently as they conceive and plan their manuscripts, write drafts, revise, and refine to the point that the material is ready for classroom publication. Throughout the process, students may call on peers for advice and help. The teacher functions as an additional resource in encouraging the students to refine and elaborate their manuscripts.

Regardless of the terminology, it is crucial to realize that the writing process is rarely a linear progression through a series of "steps." Writing is recursive in nature, and writers often "revisit" their writing: understandings and ideas evolve as writers read and reread their writing (Atwell, 1998; Graves, 1994; Perl, 1994). An author may write an ending to a manuscript before the beginning is completed. The main

Diverse Learners

Ralph Sanders, principal of an Intermediate School in Greenville, Texas, seeks to promote an environment in his school that celebrates the diversity of the people of the United States. Teachers have formed a multicultural awareness committee that is proactive in promoting knowledge about cultures. The committee meets every two weeks to talk about school events and issues and to mentor new teachers into the culture of their school and its learners.

The committee offers new teachers to the building these tips about cultural understandings:

♦ Be aware of different cultures and be sensitive to their beliefs.

♦ Remember that all students, regardless of color, have the same needs—to be loved, to be valued, and to be respected.

♦ Children from different cultures may react differently to discipline. For example, Anglo children may look the teacher in the eye as a sign of respect; African American children may avoid eye contact as a sign of respect.

The Multicultural School

♦ Don't emphasize color. Don't identify a child by color by saying things like "that black child" or "that Chinese girl."

♦ Respect children's names. Learn to pronounce them; don't shorten or "Americanize" children's names.

♦ Be accepting of children's dialects.

♦ Celebrate the holidays of the cultural groups in your room.

♦ Assign new children a "buddy." An English-speaking buddy can help orient new LEP students in school situations (such as the lunchroom, playground, music, or recess activities).

Children who speak little or no English, perhaps more than any others in school, are at the mercy of their teachers and classmates. The teacher's sensitivity, respect, attitude, and common sense can make the difference between a classroom climate permitting students to thrive and develop or one in which students languish and retreat into their own private shells. For students to acquire English and a comfort zone in a new culture, the affective domain must be addressed as vigorously as the cognitive domain.

idea of the piece may evolve as the author writes. The author may put the writing aside for a time and begin work on a new manuscript. You will find a detailed description of the implementation of the writing process in Chapter 10.

The writing process generally includes *prewriting, drafting, revising, editing,* and *celebration/sharing/publishing.* Let's examine each of these phases, but keep in mind that writing is not a linear process. Your students may skip some phases, get stuck in others, and at times put the whole project aside.

Prewriting

Prewriting provides an opportunity for writers to think about the reason or purpose for writing and who their audience will be. This leads to decisions concerning the form of the writing such as a letter, poem, story, or set of instructions. Teachers often provide support for writers during this time by group discussion and brainstorming. In addition, minilessons exploring various aspects of writing: different genres of writing, leads for various genres, different ways authors portray setting, and high imagery words all provide resources for writers. The latter part of this chapter includes topics and types of writing that would be valuable for minilessons.

Children are encouraged to keep a writer's notebook where they collect writing "resources" from brainstorming or minilessons such as ideas for manuscripts, various formats for writing, interesting or intriguing words and phrases, attention-grabbing leads, unique settings, experiences, discoveries, emotions—the possibilities are limitless (Fletcher, 1992, 1996). Calkins's (1991, 1994) work highlights the significance of students' personal notebooks as a think-tank for manuscript development. Ralph Fletcher (1996) stressed the importance of a writer's notebook as a "place to live like a writer" by keeping a written record of the things that trigger strong emotions such as happiness, sadness, anger, or amazement: the things you have noticed and want to remember . . . or perhaps would prefer to forget. He notes that this recording of experiences, emotions, and observances should occur not only in school but any time of the day and in any place you find yourself.

Prewriting models the collection and extension of ideas that writers continually engage in. As teachers model this process, children begin to internalize this practice as they begin to "think like writers."

Drafting

Once writers have developed some ideas concerning purpose, form, and audience, they need to spend time getting these thoughts on paper. It is important that students realize that writers "revisit" and refine their writing. Therefore, they should spend time at the beginning of the process just letting the ideas

Meet the Author
Ralph Fletcher

flow. Naturally, writers will want to spend enough attention on the draft so they can read their own work in the revision stage (Ward, 2001), but the focus of this first draft is not on the mechanics such as spelling or punctuation—or neatness—but on getting their "thinking on paper." William Faulkner's advice to writers was specific about initial efforts, "Get it down. Take chances. It may be bad, but it is the only way you can do anything really good." As writers begin to read and reread their writing, they will refine and extend their ideas. It is helpful to label these initial drafts with a term such as "First Draft" or "Work in Progress" and the date.

Revision

Revision focuses on clarifying the meaning of the writing. As writers read and reread their own writing, they sometimes discover they need to adjust earlier decisions concerning the purpose, form, or even the audience of their piece. This will result in revisions to their initial drafts. After writers have read and reread their pieces to determine if it "makes sense to them" or "paints a picture in their minds," it is helpful to determine if the text paints the same picture in the mind of someone else. Revision is not a solitary process. The reactions and comments of other writers support the revision process by providing feedback concerning whether or not the writing is clear, engaging, and understandable (Sommers, 1994).

Conferencing with writers aids in the revision process. Lucy Calkins (1986) documented the importance of conferencing with writers as they write in the Manhattan Writing Project. One way to implement peer conferencing for revision is for the writer to find a partner and read the manuscript to that person. When the writer reads to the partner, the partner focuses on the meaning—not the mechanics.

Editing

Editing provides an opportunity to address the mechanics of the piece—the "correctness" of the grammar, punctuation, and spelling. By this time the piece should have undergone revision for meaning; the author now feels the piece conveys a message that others would want to read. Writers understand that another reader may not have access to the author to clarify anything the reader does not understand about the text; therefore, neatness and correct punctuation, spelling, and grammar are a necessary courtesy to the reader.

During the process of revision and editing, writers should not be required to copy and recopy drafts. When given materials such as fine-tipped markers of different colors (to mark over text), masking tape (to "cover" text they want to change and write over it), and scissors and tape (to rearrange and add text), the revision of drafts becomes a time-efficient, manageable—and even enjoyable—process. If students have access to a computer with a word processing program, this facilitates the revision and editing of drafts.

Publication/Celebration/Sharing

The most important finding of process writing research is that writers need an audience (Atwell, 1987, 1998; Calkins, 1994; Thomason, 1993). Nancy Atwell (1987) expresses it clearly: "A sense of audience—the knowledge that someone will read what they have written—is crucial to young writers" (p. 265). Children readily assume the role of authors when their writing is shared, read by others, displayed, and valued. When their efforts are treasured in this manner, children produce more writing and develop pride and confidence in their ability. We share ways in which you can honor your young writers in Chapter 10.

Think of your writing program as an exquisite tapestry. The most beautiful—and valuable—tapestries have a myriad of colors, textures, and designs interwoven throughout. Thus you must have a variety of writing experiences for your students. Your students may carry some pieces through the entire process to publication/celebration, while other writing may not progress beyond the draft form. Some writing may be collaborative with you serving as a scribe for your students' language, other pieces may involve you and students "sharing the pen." The purpose of some writing may be "writing for thinking" in journals and remain unedited. In the following sections, we share ways for you to "weave a tapestry" of writing experiences for your students.

Collaborative Writing

Dictation and the Language Experience Approach

As children experience writing as a form of self-expression and are freed from the requirement of producing error-free work, they can and do write effectively. This writing is produced by preschoolers as well as elementary school students. This fact raises an important question: Is there a need for dictation (teachers operating as scribes for children), since students can write their own stories independently? The answer is "yes." Dictation, as defined by the language experience approach (Allen, 1999), involves different processes and has goals different from those of independent writing. Teachers don't take dictation "because children cannot write; they are using dictation as another form of writing" (Sulzby, Teale, & Kamberelis, 1989,

p. 75). Dictation provides and demonstrates an important link among thought, language, writing, and reading for many children (Cramer, 2001; M. R. Sampson & Sampson, 2001). In addition, dictation provides opportunities for teachers to reinforce the meaning and importance of writing skills, to offer alternatives to grammar, to demonstrate standard spelling, and to encourage elaboration that leads to clarity and interest.

We model reading by reading to children because we want them to read. In the same manner we model writing by writing down what children have to say because we want them to write. We validate the child when we take dictation; we enhance self-esteem as we accept the child's language and contributions to individual or group efforts. Furthermore, some children have not had many opportunities to write or scribble at home and really do not understand or value writing. Jacque Wuertenberg (1990) expresses the importance of dictation in school programs best: "Until you see your language valued through dictation you may not have the courage to write something down. Once you see your language written down you can't help but to want to write for yourself."

Independent writing can be slow because of the time it takes students to form letters and explore spelling. Dictation provides a technique that enables a writer to have his or her thoughts quickly turned into print, thus enabling the author to focus on a stream of thoughts instead of the surface features of print. Murray (1989), in discussing his own writing, takes note of the occasional need of authors to quickly capture their thoughts. Murray sometimes tapes his first draft to avoid the delays that letter formation entails. "Dictating is marvelously helpful, because it allows me to write at greater speed, and fast writing is extremely important for me" (p. 86).

Dictation is an efficient technique teachers can use to help students "discover" certain truths about language, writing, and reading. When children write independently, they represent their thoughts with spellings that may be unconventional or "invented." Over time, spellings become standard as children have repeated experiences with reading and writing. Dictation is one experience that aids in the acquisition of standard spelling.

Teachers should be careful to balance dictation opportunities with opportunities for children to write independently. In independent writing, children should be encouraged to write without worrying about standard spellings. Yes, teachers should avoid "telling" children standard spellings when students are involved in independent first-draft writing. To do so only makes children dependent on the teacher, or in the words of Donald Graves (1994): "If children had to wait for full spellings from the teacher, the teacher would have to don track shoes and sprint around the room accommodating every child" (p. 257). Plus, when the teacher simply tells children standard spellings, they have little incentive to try on their own and to discover how sounds track to letters and letter patterns. Children will have many opportunities to "see" words spelled in "book" language—from word walls, environmental print, and dictation.

Thus a combination of independent writing and writing through dictation is recommended. Both are effective avenues to self-expression.

The Dictation Process

Procedures vary in instructional programs that help students progress from talk to writing, but a few basic steps are recommended. The process is described in detail in the Teacher-to-Teacher feature.

Teacher~to~Teacher

Jane Good describes a dictation procedure that works for most students. She follows seven steps.

STEP 1 Students talk about paintings they have made or experiences they have had. After the talk, Jane writes one or two things the student chooses for recording. As she writes, she talks to herself, not teaching directly but reminding herself in audible sound about important aspects of writing:

She is using alphabet symbols that have names.

Some of the words use capitals for the first letter.

The same letters are used over and over as first letters in words.

Some words appear again and again.

Some ending sounds tell how many and when.

This talk is about the symbol system and how it works in writing.

STEP 2 Jane reads what has been written and checks it with the student who said it. If it is appropriate, she asks the student to read it with her.

STEP 3 Paintings with dictation are displayed around the classroom at levels that students can reach. With felt-tipped pens, students identify language characteristics such as these that are essential to understand for independent writing:

Words that are alike (usually words of highest frequency)

Words that begin alike

Words with capital letters

Punctuation that is the same

Rhyming words

Other topics appropriate to what is displayed

Students mark each category with colored pens. Usually two, and not more than three, categories are used at any one time.

STEP 4 Words that appear five or more times are collected for a chart, "Words We All Use." This chart becomes a major resource for spelling in the Writing Center.

STEP 5 When a student indicates an interest in writing, the dictation is recorded very lightly, and the student traces over the letters. A model alphabet with arrows to show

Interactive Writing

Interactive writing is a process "in which a teacher shares a pen—literally and figuratively—with a group of children as they collaboratively compose and construct a written message" (McCarrier, Pinnell, & Fountas, 2000, p. 4). The process is similar to that of dictation. The teacher engages in dialogue with the children to collaboratively construct a common text. In this process, the teacher and students talk about writing the text. The teacher usually begins the instruction by acting as scribe. However, as the writing progresses, the teacher issues invitations to "share the pen." These invitations are based on the instructional needs of the students and the "teaching points" the teacher wants to emphasize. This is not intended to be a laborious process. Based on their writing level, chil-

directions for strokes in writing is available in the Writing/Publishing Center.

STEP 6 Dictation is recorded with space beneath each line for copying. The writing is large enough so students have no difficulty copying beneath what the teacher has written.

STEP 7 Students write on their own, using resources from the Writing/Publishing Center such as spelling lists of words of highest frequency and special lists of words for color, size, shape, smell, sound, texture, and motion.

Jane finds that with these procedures most of the students in her class improve as independent writers. In addition, when talking about writing, they can use names of the letters of the alphabet, can spell words and understand when someone else spells, and can talk about capitalization, punctuation, and other fine points involved in the writing process.

Charlene Chambers, a first-grade teacher, takes dictation from her students on a chart tablet that hangs on an easel.

Sometimes, a student is chosen ahead of time and comes prepared to tell about a real experience or to tell an imaginary story. The whole story is told orally, and then Charlene asks the author to select one or two things from the story for her to write. She wants young students to realize that what is written in most books for them to read is not all the author had to say. It is only a part of the whole story. In this way she helps them across the most difficult time in reading instruction when stories are short and incomplete and meanings are scarce.

As she writes, she chats about those characteristics of written language that everyone must know in order to be literate. This indirect teaching has an influence on students who would be reluctant to try to understand if they were confronted with the same information on a worksheet. She does this effective teaching of writing skills with materials that are understood by the learners. Comprehension is assured because the story comes from the students, not from an author who is not present.

dren may insert a letter, a word, or perhaps a phrase in the collaborative text. Emergent writers may illustrate spacing between words.

It is necessary for the teacher to make strategically planned "invitations" and point out key points that will "scaffold" children's literacy development—in both reading and writing (Button, Johnson, & Furgerson, 1996). This is an "apprenticeship" process for the children (McCarrier et al., 2000) and, as with dictation, is not limited to stories. Interactive writing may be used with text such as lists, questions, labels, letters, recording of information, names—all are opportunities for the teacher to share both the function and form of writing with students. The collaborative text is also an excellent source of reading material.

Understanding Conventions through Collaborative Writing

Children, like adults, like to talk. The discussions children have represent excellent beginnings for collaborative writing with the teacher. Writing a collaborative composition via dictation or interactive writing is an excellent opportunity to learn many conventions that carry over to the independent writing of students. Because the text is one that children will read and reread, it is important that it is edited for mechanics such as spelling and punctuation. As teachers or students point out that it is important to capitalize a title or the beginning of a sentence, leave a margin, and supply quotation marks, they call attention to these literacy conventions. Thus conventions are learned as a natural part of writing, along with content and organization. These are valuable instructional opportunities addressing conventions that are interwoven into meaningful literacy experiences involving expression and impression. In a meaning-centered classroom, the effective teacher does not question whether or not to teach the conventions of language but how and when to teach them (Dahl et al., 2001; Dudley-Marling & Dippo, 1991; McIntyre & Pressely, 1996).

As teachers and students engage in talk about writing from group dictation or interactive writing, many opportunites for addressing writing and reading skills emerge. Here are five important characteristics of writing you can address:

1. *Some words are used over and over, and others are not used very often.* Words that occur most frequently in group and individual compositions at any level in school are the same words that occur frequently in most writing. These are usually determiners (words such as "the," "this," "that," "those"), prepositions (words such as "to," "from"), pronouns (words such as "I," "you," "he," "she"), conjunctions (words such as "and," "but"), question words (words such as "who," "what," "where," "when," "why"), auxiliaries (words such as "be," "have"), and an assortment of other words such as negatives and words of courtesy. These high-frequency words often are not phonetically regular. Stu-

Ian Morehouse — Name

11 years — Age

Math, reading, watching T.V., computer games, football, playing with my friends — Interests

What do you like most about school? What I like about school is having games for our study. I also like it when we do reading for an hour. School is also fun when you get to have a structured activities to start the day off.

What's your favorite subject? Why? My favorite subject is Math because we get to play games and it is fun. Math is also tied with Reading to. I like Reading because you can learn so much from the books that you read.

What's your favorite book? Why do you like it? My favorite book is The Treasury of Roald Dahl. I like it because it told me about life and what will happen to us.

What advice do you have for teachers? The adice I have for Teachers is you need to be felxible with the kids. You also need to have activities for almost all of your subjects so the kids can learn better.

dents should be made aware of the need to learn standard spelling for these words and to learn to use the spelling aids provided in the classroom.

Other words that occur frequently in some compositions but not in all compositions may be nouns and verbs. Sometimes they are adjectives and adverbs. When students are writing compositions with the frequent use of the same word or words, the spelling should be furnished in a place that is easy to see, such as on a Word Wall.

America's Finest
Leigh Walker

2. *Some words begin alike.* The letters of the alphabet are used over and over in the initial position of words. If the first sound of a word is written with a single consonant, it is likely to be the same sound–symbol relation for most words beginning with that letter (except for *c* and *g*). This is dependable information for writing—and reading.

3. *Some words end alike.* The endings that occur most frequently (*-s, -es, -ed, -ing, -er, -est, -ful,* and *-ly*) change the meaning of root words and may shift their positions in sentences. Recognizing them and understanding their significance are essential to the finer points of meaning. It is through writing, much more than through reading, that students come to grips with this aspect of language structure.

4. *Only twenty-six letters are used to write all the words we use.* Each of the letters has a name that is useful in talking about spelling and in doing reference research. Each letter can be written with numerous configurations and must be recognized in its many forms. Each letter represents one or more sounds when used in writing. Consonants represent fewer sounds than vowels. Knowing the alphabet and being able to talk about the names of all the letters are useful in writing.

5. *Some syllable types occur over and over in the language.* These syllables are known as phonograms or "rimes." When different consonants or onsets (consonants that precede the vowel in a syllable) are placed at the beginning of these syllables, new words are formed. The following thirty-seven rimes are part of approximately 500 words typically found in primary grade reading materials (Adams, 1990, p. 85).

THIRTY-SEVEN RIMES THAT MAKE UP APPROXIMATELY
500 PRIMARY GRADE WORDS

-ack	-all	-ain	-ake	-ale	-ame	-an
-ank	-ap	-ash	-at	-ate	-aw	-ay
-eat	-ell	-est	-ice	-ick	-ide	-ight
-ill	-in	-ine	-ing	-ink	-ip	-ir
-ock	-oke	-op	-ore	-or	-uck	-ug
-ump	-unk					

These rimes are useful in the analysis of unfamiliar words for reading, writing, and spelling. Students enjoy games that contrast beginning sounds with these high-frequency syllables. After finding as many words as possible by changing beginning consonants and consonant clusters, students can add endings. For more mature students an added challenge might be to make columns and list words that become nouns, verbs, adjectives, and adverbs by changing the endings.

It is impossible to implement dictation or interactive writing in your classroom without illustrating the five characteristics of writing and spelling just described. The concepts related to these five must be understood and developed to support independent writing. However, too much emphasis on conventions without allowing for the personal, dynamic ideas of students may result in writing becoming a chore, not a joy.

In addition, dictation and interactive writing provide students with an opportunity to explore the strong relationship that exists between speech and writing. However, they also learn that writing, until it is refined through revision and editing, is an imperfect representation of speech. It frequently lacks pitch, tone, emphasis, pause, and juncture. Whereas speech is highly perishable, written records have a degree of permanence. Refined writing represents the communication of thoughts with word order and patterns that are not characteristic of spontaneous expression; it raises language to a literary level.

Freeing Students to Write

One of the most exciting aspects of teaching is the delight you feel when you read the stories your children write. Teachers are like sculptors—they have an opportunity to create beautiful treasures of art. Our creations are the manuscripts the children produce, expressed through the genres of books, research reports, personal observations, aspirations, imagination, and self-concept pieces. You, too, can free students to write in personal ways that reflect their interests and concerns.

Journals

As with most literacy skills, writing is best learned by writing, not by studying about how to write. One of the best ways of getting students involved extensively in writing is through journals. A journal is simply a notebook or tablet in which students express themselves by writing about their thoughts, their ideas, their feelings. Journals let writers explore the writing process. Because journals are never corrected or edited, they represent the "least threatening of all writing activities" (Unia, 1985, p. 72).

As students write about what is happening in their lives outside the classroom, teachers can monitor children's experiences and discover how they are growing as individuals.

Becky Chavarría-Cháirez

1. *Which book of yours has given you the greatest pleasure?*

Each is special like each and every child, I suppose. But, if I had to choose I'd have to say it is *Magda's Tortillas ~ Las tortillas de Magda*. I had many dreams and wishes for my first book in this series of fully bilingual children's picture books. I wanted this fictional character to be as believably alive and curious as the 7-year-old that she is and one who is also living, growing, and emulating a bicultural Hispanic experience—reflecting the lives of millions of U.S. Hispanic children. And *Magda's Tortillas* has accomplished that and more. The book has received critical acclaim, award nominations, and been a finalist for a national children's book award. But I derive immense pleasure from hearing parents and teachers share how this 32-page book has inspired their *niños*—boys as well as girls—to seek their own, one-on-one tortilla-making lesson. By design, I did not include a tortilla recipe, so that readers young and old would need to seek a recipe, the secret to making tortillas, from someone they know. Now that I think of it, *Magda's Tortillas*, my first book, is about as infinitely special as a first child.

2. *Which book has surprised you most in terms of its public reception?*

I am so appreciative to how people of all ages have responded to my first book, *Magda's Tortillas ~ Las tortillas de Magda*. I wrote the story for my older daughter, Carina—who would never know my grandmothers. Children love the story but *las abuelas* and grandmas are among the biggest fans. The appreciation and recognition of the story comes from grown women who outnumber the children who line up to buy the book. The book allows them to remember their first tortilla-making times and helps pique their interest in tortilla making so that they will seek and carry on the tradition of hand- and home-made tortilla making. And, many of these grandmothers are not Hispanic. They are often on a personal bicultural family mission, wanting to demonstrate to their Hispanic/Anglo grandkids that their Latino roots are precious. They use the book to keep their cultures side by side—blended and equally shared and honored.

3. *What would you like people to remember about your work?*

I hope people will recognize the unique position that Hispanic children in the Americas

---

Many teachers use journals as a means of responding to literature. Fuhler (1994) cites journals as an opportunity for students to mesh in a "thoughtful, personal engagement with trade books" (p. 400).

Although we generally think of journals as simplistic notebooks in which students jot their thoughts, teachers can use journals in a number of targeted ways in a total literacy curriculum. Here are a few examples:

Dialogue   The teacher and the student, or a student and a student, maintain a written conversation over time. The style is informal and friendly and results in students tapping another source of information—the teacher or fellow students.

Learning Logs   A written record of observations about content learning or musings about readings, Learning Logs enable students to make connections and organize their knowledge.

are in—they are extremely rich—they always have been. And now children's books like Magda's adventures are telling their stories—although fiction, they are so true.

4. *What impact do you hope your work will have on children?*

First, I want these stories that are steeped with my Mexican American experiences to seep into the mainstream U.S. culture. My bilingual books are designed for ALL children, not just Mexican American or Hispanic kids. The Magda books are created with much love and designed to entertain and enlighten children—Hispanic, non-Hispanic, English- and/or Spanish-dominant readers and those who are living, playing, and learning in fully bilingual environments—the way I was raised.

Second, for Hispanic youngsters, I want them to derive a sense of belonging and an affirming boost to their self-esteem. When I meet students and read to them, I marvel at the immediate impact, the physical reactions I see in them. Their body language reveals that they are entranced by Magda making tortillas or creating piñata magic for her little brother and hearing the blending of English and Spanish. The body language is strong:

Kids' pupils dilate and they hang on to every word. For Hispanic children, these stories validate them and will build their cultural self-awareness and personal self-esteem. Who knows, this new genre in children's books could very well be the supplemental link that communities have been seeking to help Hispanic students stay in school and celebrate who they are. *Vamos a ver.* We shall see.

And last, for non-Hispanic children, I want them to discover the universal themes and emotions in each story. Magda Madrigal is like millions of Latino children in the United States and accurately captures a glimpse into their lives including Spanish language, family traditions, food customs—the universal elements of culture. This story underscores the universal connections we can all share.

Becky Chavarría-Cháirez is an award-winning broadcast journalist, freelance writer, speaker, and multiculturalist. Her children's books include *Magda's Tortillas ~ Las tortillas de Magda* and *Piñata Magic ~ Magda y la piñata mágica.*

Reprinted with special permission of Becky Chavarría-Cháirez.

Double Entry   The first column might contain details about events that are occurring in the students' life, and the second column might contain the students' reactions to them. Or the first column might contain facts about a book being read, and the second column might contain personal commentary.

Response   Sometimes called Reading Logs, response journals afford students the opportunity to respond to literature with personal comments and feelings. For example, second-graders listening to their teacher read *Joey Pigza Loses Control* (Gantos, 2000) have the opportunity at the end of the read-aloud period to respond to the story. Sometimes that response is an implicit reaction to the text; at other times it might be a specific response to a teacher question such as "How do you think Joey felt when his father threw his medicine away?"

Regie Routman (1991) shares that journals are a "non-threating place to explore learnings, feelings, happenings, and language through writing" (p. 197). Routman (1995) sees the following benefits when teachers engage students in journal writing:

◆ Promotes fluency in writing

◆ Promotes fluency in reading

◆ Encourages risk taking

◆ Provides opportunity for reflection

◆ Validates personal experiences and feelings

◆ Provides a safe, private place to write

◆ Promotes thinking and makes it visible

◆ Promotes development of written language conventions

◆ Provides a vehicle for evaluation

◆ Provides a personal record for students

In summary, journal writing is an important tool in the total literacy classroom. It provides an excellent opportunity for writing to be demonstrated as a meaning-centered process. In addition, journal writing helps teachers understand their children in personal as well as academic terms. (See Teacher-to-Teacher box on pp. 239–240.)

Individual Stories

It is essential that children be given the opportunity for self-expression through writing every day. When children are encouraged to write, you'll see their vocabularies spring to life. Consider Kelly, a bright first-grade student who wrote this:

See the lightning!
Seagulls were twirling like kites.

At work on a story.

Courtesy of Michael Sampson

Linda Lewis-White teaches third grade. Her students are in a bilingual program that recognizes that literacy develops as students have opportunities to communicate in both their native language and English. She uses journal writing as the cornerstone of her writing program. On the first day of school, Linda shares with her students that the purpose of keeping journals is to record their ideas, experiences, and feelings. She tells students that spellings do not need to be correct—they can invent spellings for words they don't know how to spell. In addition, she promises not to mark or correct their journals. Instead, she explains that she will read what they have written and write a response to their message.

As the year progresses, Linda fosters dialogue with her students through their journals. She uses the opportunity to demonstrate through her responses how written language conveys meaning. She may demonstrate standard spellings of the words a child might have spelled functionally by using the word or words in her response to the child. Sometimes the student notices her standard spelling and may say, "So that's how you spell that word!" Usually, however, the entries are received without comment.

Students generally start their journals in their native language but move to English by November. Linda usually responds to the students in English, demonstrating English syntax and construction. The journal entries start out very brief, but increase in length as the year progresses and the students gain confidence in their abilities to communicate their ideas through writing. The sample journal entries shown in Figure 8.2 demonstrate the interaction between Linda and Jerry.

Journals provide a valuable opportunity for students and teachers to learn more about each other and the writing process. Students have an opportunity to write on a near daily basis and to receive quick feedback centered on the meaning of what they have written. Individual teachers adapt journals to the context of their classrooms and use them in many ways. Some teachers leave them as private writing, never responding to or reading them. Other teachers respond only when the student requests a response (Newman, 1984). Responding to journals is time consuming, but it is a good investment of time. Linda altered her journal schedule so the students wrote every Monday, Wednesday, and Friday. This enabled her to give back the journals Tuesday, Thursday, and Monday mornings.

9-2 Today was the frst day of skul, I was Japy dat I was in 3 grad.

I am very happy that I am teaching third grade – and that you are in my class!! Welcome!! Welcome!!!

FIGURE 8.2
Sample journal interaction

➤ ➤ ➤

9-3 I always lak to wach tom and Jenny rhe in the monnin. It always maks me laf.

You'll never guess what my favorite show is! It is Good Morning, America! Of course, sometimes they make me laugh.

9-4 I alwas lak to rede Buks we I am in the libere at skul.

I am always reading and looking for new books to read. I just finished The River by Gary Paulsen. What are you reading? Any suggestions for a new book for me?

12-1 In cristmas I am going to have Legu toy, I want it becas it cud bild a lots of things.

Christmas is wonderful! There is always so much excitement and suspense.

It sounds as if you know what you want. There are so many different Lego sets; which one do you want? What are you planning to build?

1-18 Today at shcool at 8:30 we went ro the libere we met a nan hou wenrks in a libere. And he told us hao to get a libere card. And he had a dog and ha told us about his fiusher.

Sounds as if you had a wonderful time! The library is one of my favorite places, and it seems as if it is one of your favorite places also. We have a lot in common.

Are you planning to get a library card? My library card is like my "ticket" to many new people and places!

The power of imagination is revealed in the pieces children write. Consider Carolyn's story:

THE ELEPHANT HAD A TOO-LONG TRUNK!!
Once there was an elephant with a very long trunk. In fact, it was too long.
One day he heard about a contest.
The next day he saw a sign about it.
CONTEST!
The elephant that can eat the
most peanuts will win a trip
to Africa. For more information
call 886-8844.
He thought, oh I must enter that contest, so he called 886-8844.
The man who answered the phone was friendly. The man told the rules and that the contest was the next day.
The next morning the elephant with the too long trunk got up early and went to the contest spot. And to his surprise he won.
The next day he went to Africa. He had lots of fun playing tag with the snakes. He also had fun swinging from tree to tree with the monkeys. He stayed for a month and then he had to go home. He was very sad but he knew he would be back again.
The End
CAROLYN, AGE 9

Teacher~to~Teacher

Katie Hart read a Bill Martin Jr. book to her class. Students liked it so much that she suggested they write one of their own using the same language pattern that was used in *My Days Are Made of Butterflies* (Martin, 1989). They decided on a title, *Spring Days Are Made of Blooming Flowers,* and composed the first page of the book. On days that followed, students contributed to the book. It was edited, illustrated, and bound. Katie duplicated copies for every student. She left the space for illustrations blank for each student to fill in.

Spring Days Are Made of Blooming Flowers
(Adapted from My Days Are Made of Butterflies, *by Bill Martin Jr.)*

   Spring days are made of blooming flowers in my garden. Joel
   Spring days are made of baby birds chirping in the trees. Marcia
   Spring days are made of working bees collecting nectar in the desert. Thomas
   Spring days are made of whispering breezes and waving leaves. Maria

➤ ➤ ➤

Katie believes she should permeate the learning environment with lists of words that help students say and write their observations and feelings in poetic language. Here are some categories she finds useful:

Color Words	Taste Words
Size Words	Smell Words
Shape Words	Rhyming Words
Texture Words	Similes
Sound Words	Metaphors

Katie knows that the lists must be kept open so additions can be made. She pauses when reading to students to savor a beautiful way of saying something. She keeps a Poet's Corner available on a bulletin board so students can pin contributions on it. A branch from a tree is "planted" in a clay pot and labeled the "Poet's Tree." It is available for students to hang poetic expressions on for others to read.

Most students have tremendous language power that is never tapped for written self-expression. "Correctness" as the initial goal forces students to rely on available materials and safe ideas. Teachers must create opportunities for students to express themselves through many genres and purposes (Evans, 2001).

Teacher-to-Teacher

Julia Gore was aware of some students' interest in football just before a Super Bowl game. She used this interest to invite groups of students to dictate to her their perceptions of "How to Play Football." The collaborative compositions were good enough that she duplicated them for students to take home. The parents of the kindergarten children encouraged her to submit the work of the students to the local newspaper for a Sunday edition special page. All of the compositions were published. Two are reproduced here.

How to Play Football

by Brian, Meredith, Gunnar, Eddie, Sharon, Heather, and Larry

First you get 6 or 7 or 20 or 38 people on your team.

You wear helmets and sport shirts and knee pads and arm pads.

You need poles so you can make a goal.

You hold the football and you run and kick and you throw the ball to one of your friends if someone gets too close.

You throw the ball to the other team to score points.

There is a defense, outfielders, front runners, offense, infielders, tackles and a scorpion.

You try to throw the football over the poles to make a goal.

Whoever gets the most points, wins and gets a cup and a treat and a free lunch.

How to Play Football

by Julie, Scott, Todd, Jenny, Monty, and Chase

They put on helmets, shoulder pads, knee pads and shoes with bumps.

All the heads go the same way and they hike the ball. They run and try to catch the ball. Then they jump all over each other.

They go back and do it all over again and try to make a touchdown.

Chapter Books

Students who begin to read whole books are aware that they are printed on numbered pages. When they begin to write longer stories, they enjoy paging their manuscripts. Eight-year-old Jonathan discovered another division of stories—episodes. Figure 8.3 contains two episodes from his story "The Silly Little Fish."

Arrangement into chapters is another development in prose writing. Long compositions should have some breaking points to keep a plot sequenced and to take care of increasing complexity, which develops as stories lengthen and deal with many characters.

Research Reports

As students travel the road to total literacy, they are on a never-ending journey. They will always be writers, and they will always be doing research to support what they write. Or, as Lucy Calkins (1986) explains, "The writers begin with what they know, they learn more about the topic, and they teach their content to readers" (p. 274). It is important for elementary students to have the oppor-

Courtesy of Mary Beth Sampson

A study group goes online to research a topic.

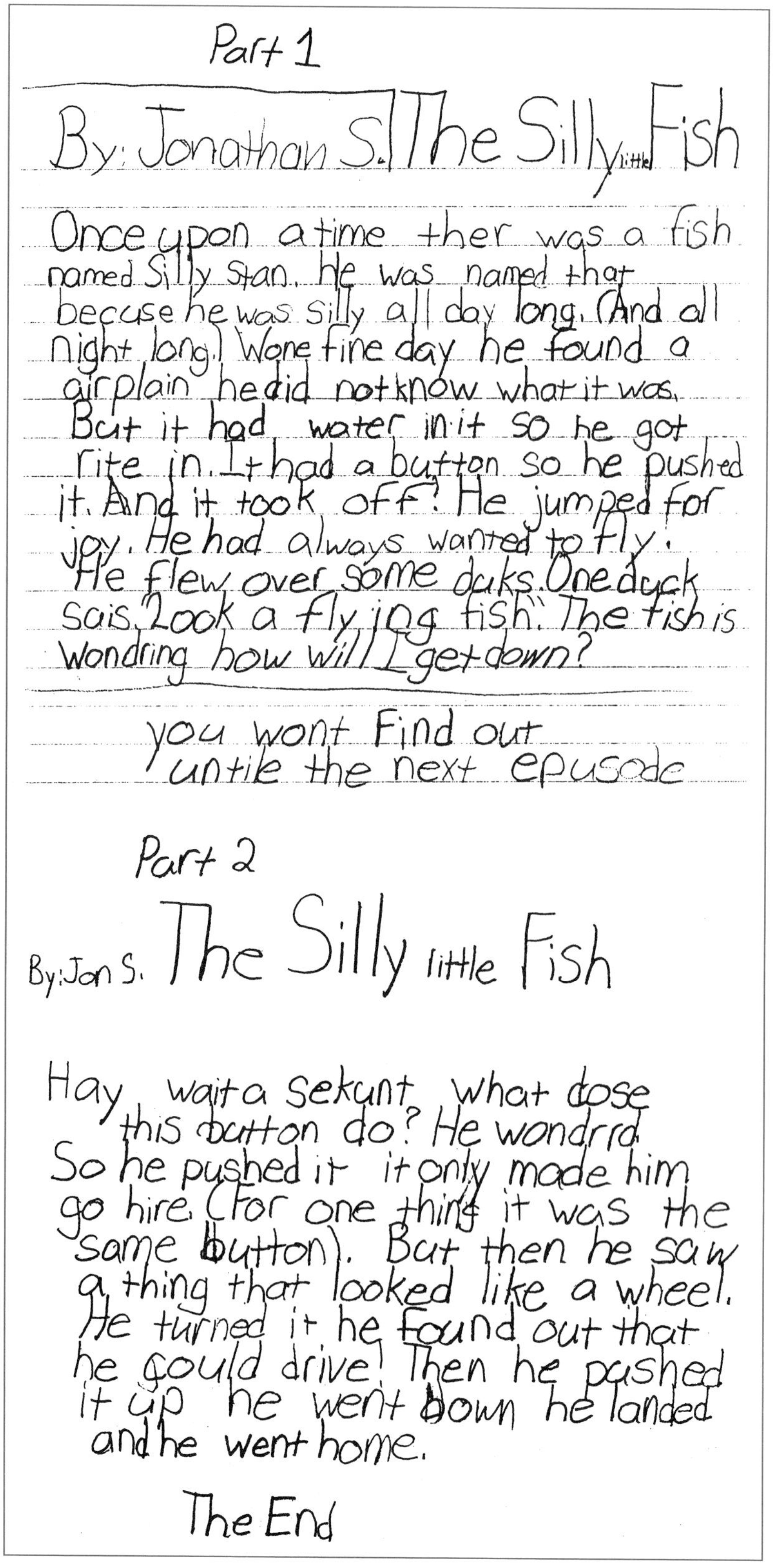

Part 1

By: Jonathan S. The Silly little Fish

Once upon a time ther was a fish named Silly Stan. He was named that becuse he was silly all day long. (And all night long.) Wone fine day he found a airplain he did not know what it was. But it had water in it so he got rite in. It had a button so he pushed it. And it took off! He jumped for joy. He had always wanted to fly. He flew over some daks. One duck sais "look a fly ing fish". The fish is wondring how will I get down?

you wont Find out until the next epusode

Part 2

By: Jon S. The Silly little Fish

Hay, wait a sekunt, what dose this button do? He wondrrd So he pushed it it only made him go hire. (for one thing it was the same button). But then he saw a thing that looked like a wheel. He turned it he found out that he could drive! Then he pushed it up he went down he landed and he went home.

The End

FIGURE 8.3
An 8-year-old's story

tunity to explore factual information and then use their new knowledge as a basis for writing. This learning sequence, from research to writing, can begin in the elementary school (Duthie, 1994; Graves, 1989b). The Teacher-to-Teacher feature shows how this happened for one student as he researched and wrote about Davy Crockett.

Teacher-to-Teacher

Jonathan Schmidt, a student in Linda Allen's fifth-grade class, became interested in Davy Crockett. In preparing a report to the class on Crockett, Jonathan demonstrated what he had learned about researching the writing process. During a minilesson focusing on the information needed in a report about a "real person from the past," the class decided that at least four main ideas should be included in a report: (1) when and where the person was born and something about his family; (2) at least three interesting things about the person when growing up; (3) at least three reasons the person was famous/important; and (4) what happened to the person. These four areas provided a focus for gathering information.

Jonathan checked out books from the library on Davy Crockett. He read reports from an encyclopedia. He used the classroom CD-ROM multimedia encyclopedia and conducted an Internet search. Jonathan kept notes of what he was discovering about Crockett and used these notes to create a semantic web (see Chapter 7) addressing the four areas that the class had decided were important. Finally, he wrote the following report.

DAVY CROCKETT

On August 17, 1786, Davy Crockett was born in the wild disputed frontier territory of Tennessee. Davy's mother and father, from the outside, looked pretty ordinary. They had a normal log cabin like anyone else. They ate normal food like anyone else. They even had a normal plot of land like anyone

else. Yet, the Crocketts were far from ordinary. They had great talents and lived in a great place.

Davy learned how to do many things such as tell the weather for tomorrow by the signs of today, and to make animal like noises of almost any animal you can name. Davy also learned how to flip a tomahawk anywhere, and it would land any way he wanted it to.

To finish training Davy, the Crocketts had the best marksmen in the valley teach him all they knew about hunting. Along with the lessons, Davy figured out some ideas of his own. Then he finally made up a rule for the best way to shoot. The rule was: Be sure you're right, then go ahead and pull the trigger.

When Davy grew up, he finally got his first true love. You can take your choice of two stories about Davy's first sweetheart. His neighbors say that his first true love was the "pride of Old Kentucky." She lived up in Gum Hallow on Goose Creek. Every winter she got so plump on bear's meat that by the spring she was bigger around than a barrel. Some say that when she sneezed it took the hens right off of their eggs. There was never a girl who liked anyone the way that she did Davy.

Of course, Davy's story of his first sweetheart was very different. He said that he didn't like girls very much until he was about eighteen. This may have been because he had three sisters of his own. But after a time, he fell in love. He had been working for a trustworthy old Quaker, John Kennedy, who lived about fifteen miles from the Crockett cabin. When the Quaker's niece came back from North Carolina to pay the Kennedys a visit, Davy soon found himself head over heels in love. "I've

➤ ➤ ➤

heard people talk about hard loving," said Davy, "but I reckon no poor devil in all the world was ever cursed with such hard love as mine. I thought if all the hills about there were pure gold and they all belonged to me, I'd trade them if I could only talk to her the way I wanted to." But Davy was too afraid to say anything to her because he was afraid he might say it wrong. Yet, Davy knew he had to talk to her. So he went and told her how much he loved her and how beautiful she was, but she was honest and said she was engaged to her cousin, the son of the old Quaker. This was even worse news for Davy than anything she could have told him. Fortunately, he finally got over her, and since he had heard that women liked men with an education, he went to school to get educated.

Then his life got onto a famous track. First, he fought in a few wars. Then when he returned, he decided to do something for the law. At first, he just wrote warrants and other documents as a scribe. But through the years he progressed until he became the colonel of the militia. Then Davy got elected to the legislature. He learned a good deal about the government and served his district well. We know he did well because when he moved to a new place where he thought his neighbors didn't even know him, they elected him to the legislature just as soon as an election came around.

When Davy went to Washington he had many interesting times there, but that is not the reason he is famous. During reelection he reportedly told voters in his district, "Elect me or not, if you don't, you can go to h---, and I'll go to Texas." I don't know if this is true or not, but it is a fact that before long, ex-congressman Crockett was going to Texas and the Alamo.

Texans by then were yearning for their independence. Davy did not go to Texas to get in a war, but to "look things over." When Davy got to Nacogdoches, he heard that the Texans had their revolution rolling and that they were asking Americans to come help. Davy decided to join the Texans and headed for the Alamo.

When Davy entered the gates of the Alamo, a young man came up to shake Crockett's hand. Crockett introduced himself, but the man explained that he needed no introduction. This man had a soft southern accent, and now Crockett knew why the newspapers called him "the gallant Travis." Just a little talk proved that the Texans were in a fix, but all of the Texans stayed to defend their country.

The battle of the Alamo continued until March 5, and then the soldiers of General Santa Anna caught the Texans off guard as they mounted a full attack. Every man tried to get to his post, but it was hopeless against the swarm of soldiers. Davy and his men held up their posts as long as they could.

They were the last to be penetrated. As we know, the people of the Alamo died that day, but they still live on in our minds.

Personal Observations

Some students fail to respond to instruction in how to read and write and are classified as nonreaders/nonwriters, "at risk" or "below grade level." This happened to Danny in school. His teacher tried to relieve him of the feeling that he couldn't read and write. She showed Danny that he could "read" from his personal observations. He grew to the point that he could tell and dictate stories from real life and from imagination. The first story that he wrote independently and made into a book reveals he had been reading much nonprint during the time he was failing to read printed material in school. It had never occurred to him that he could write about what he observed and talked about. One of his stories in his language follows.

MY VERY OWN DOG

BY DANNY

One day my dog he got sick.
He sneezed a lot.
We gave him a lot of milk and he got well.
He played with us.
Then every day he went out looking for a girl friend because he wanted to see some baby dogs,
Then he found one.
Then he was the father of the dogs.
I don't know how many puppies.
Then one day this truck came by and ranned over him.
Then he had a broken leg.
We took him in the house and my father got a ruler and
broke it and put it on his leg.
My dog is still alive—but he's tired of looking for girl friends.

Where did a "nonreader" and "nonwriter" like Danny get the information for his story? How is it that he could read this story but could not read a preprimer in a reading series?

The answers lie in the ability of one special teacher to release Danny to say what he had to say in his own language patterns and with his own vocabulary. The writing process, though laborious to Danny, helped him internalize the vocabulary he used in talking so the printed forms were meaningful. Together, he and the teacher edited the story, paged it, illustrated it, copied it, and then bound it into the first whole book Danny ever read although he had been in school for four years.

Aspirations

Inside many young students is the desire to be something—to be a contributor rather than always a consumer. Teachers need to know the aspirations of students, but they never have access to that information when the daily routine consists of the exact replication of printed material followed by simple comprehension questions.

One way to assure some understanding of aspirations is to encourage self-expression through writing. Frequently this writing will reveal inner feelings and high aspirations. With this informal contact, teachers can respond, support, and encourage growth. First, let's consider the aspiration of Julie, a 7-year-old. She writes, *"I want to be a teacher. And why I want to be a teacher is to make your desire come true."* Figure 8.4 is a copy of the piece; note her invented or developmental spellings.

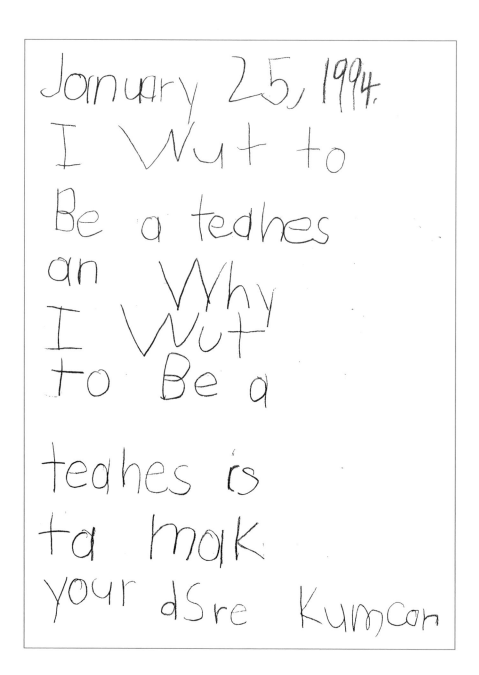

FIGURE 8.4
Julie's aspiration

Now let's look at the work of a third grader, Lisa. She attended a school where she had many opportunities to experience authorship. Her teacher organized the learning environment to promote self-expression through art, drama, and writing. This teacher felt she had to have more information than that provided by test scores to do an intelligent job of grouping students for instruction in reading. Lisa wrote her book *When I Won $100,000,000.00* during the second week of third grade. Her book told the teacher much about Lisa. She was observant; she was interested in ecology, health, and peace; she gathered information from sources outside of school; she had some contact with classical literature. But most of all, Lisa was a child with high aspirations that would be useful in her school program. Here is the text of Lisa's book without her illustrations and attractive binding.

WHEN I WON $100,000,000.00

BY LISA

When I won $100,000,000.00 I thought I was the president of the United States. Imagine me winning $100,000,000.00.

I bought two of the most expensive cars, ten large color television sets, five of the largest mansions, the Grand Canyon, ten bicycles, found a cure for muscular dystrophy, and gave our land freedom.

I stopped pollution and forest fares. I have a chauffeur-driven car.

Wow! It's a great feeling to win $100,000,000.00. I wish I could do more to help my country do the things it needs to do, but I ran out of money.

The greatest thing I won since the $100,000,000.00 was winning a teacher named Mrs. Allen. I think she's great! (And just like Shakespeare said, "Money doesn't grow on trees.")

Lisa could never have revealed her high aspirations through diagnostic testing or by giving correct answers to an endless number of questions that she did not ask.

Imagination

Perhaps the richest source for writing is the unlimited imaginations of children. The bulk of writing that children do is from this genre. Why is this so? Our theory is that this genre frees children from the requirement of being correct. After all, it's their imagination, and who can say something could or could not occur? Consider the story "The Time Machine" by 10-year-old Josh Santana (Figure 8.5).

Students who are reluctant to engage in writing from imagination can be teamed with other students for co-authored selections. Others can become illustrators for books produced by their classmates. This process is explored in Chapter 10.

Self-Concept

Students reveal much of themselves as they write. The information, though subtle, helps teachers develop expectations for individuals. Johnny Gonzales revealed much about his basic character when he wrote "Why I Like Me." His teacher modified her feelings about Johnny after she read it. English was

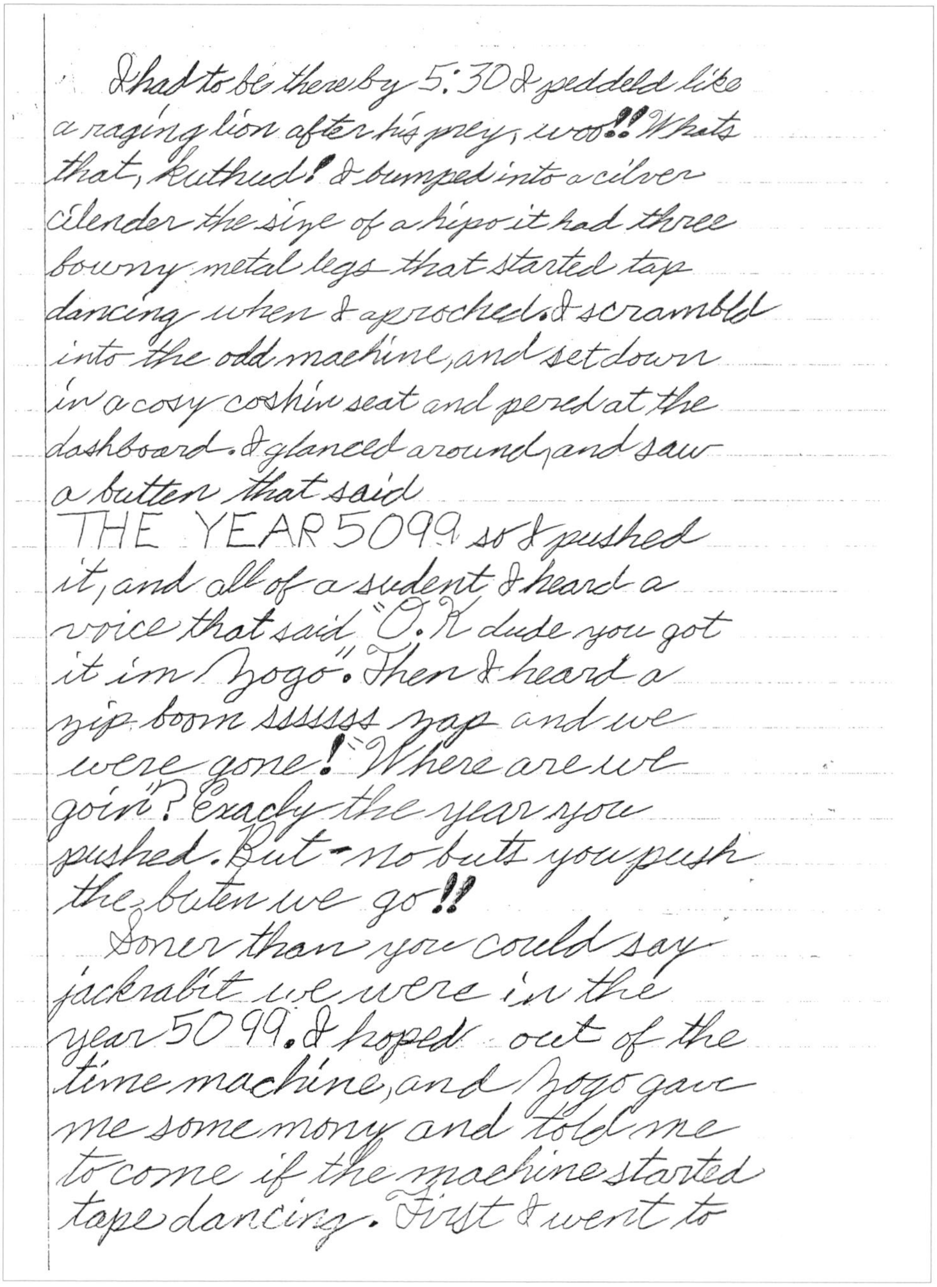

FIGURE 8.5
"The Time
Machine"
by Josh Santana

> I had to be there by 5:30 & peddeld like a raging lion after his prey, wooo!! Whats that, kuthud! I bumped into a cilver cilender the size of a hipo it had three bowny metal legs that started tap dancing when I aprocked. I scrambld into the odd machine, and set down in a cosy coshin seat and pered at the dashboard. I glanced around, and saw a butten that said THE YEAR 5099 so I pushed it, and all of a sudent I heard a voice that said "O.K dude you got it im Yogo". Then I heard a zip boom ssssss yap and we were gone! Where are we goin? Exacly the year you pushed. But — no buts you push the buten we go!!
>
> Soner than you could say jackrabit we were in the year 5099. I hoped out of the time machine, and Yogo gave me some mony and told me to come if the machine started tape dancing. First I went to

Johnny's second language, and he had some difficulty with exact replication of the language in the reading curriculum. After knowing about Johnny's strong self-concept, she was able to help him without being concerned about fleeting errors in word recognition and in spelling. She trusted Johnny and his natural ability as a learner.

C. D Shak, and bought two hover boards. Then I started looking around out of the store & got a pump up cape, and a pair of rocket shoes. Then I saw a neat clock that sounded like it was tape dancing then I realised that it was my time machine. I bosted of and landed in the machine hoyo took me to my freands party only I forgot a present but then I rememberd I bought two hover boards so I gave him one. Every body wanted to try it. Finaly I went home. I brushed my teeth, and washed my and went to bed.

When I woke up I thought the bazare thing was all a crazy dream then, I sliped my hand into my pocket and jerked out a penny that said the year 5099.

WHY I LIKE ME

BY JOHNNY GONZALES, AGE 7

Page 1: *I like me because I clean the table and it makes me feel happy.*

Page 2: *Also I like me because I help my mom with the baby at night when she is tired.*

Page 3: *I like me when I understand my mom and dad speak Spanish, and I'm proud I speak English, too.*

Page 4: *I can make bookshelves all by myself, and my mom uses them, and when I'm finished my mom hugs me, and says, 'That's great!'*

Page 5: *I like me because I finish my homework when my teacher tells me.*

Page 6: *I like me because I know how to drive a car. I learned from watching my dad drive.*

Page 7: *I like me because I am big and I could do almost anything my dad could do.*

Page 8: *Also, I like me because I do anything my mother says, and that makes me feel good.*

Page 9: *I like me because I like dogs and cats. I'm kind to them.*

Page 10: *And most of all I like me because I'm me.*

Page 11: *THE END*

Response to Experiences

Becky Davis took her first-grade class to the Shamrock Dairy. Something very interesting occurred while the class was there. See Figure 8.6 for Carson's written response to the experience.

Here's how Carson read his story to the class during Author's Chair:

We went to the dairy and I saw a baby cow be born. The mother cow just stood in her stall and mooed, and was she surprised when she turned around and saw her baby.

There was the baby, all wrapped up in a plastic sack, and the mother started to lick it off. I didn't know that baby cows came in plastic sacks! It was so cute!

The lady at the dairy didn't know that the cow was going to have her baby while we were there.

Boy, were we glad she did!

Three wonderful things had occurred. First, the children experienced a delightful trip to the Shamrock Dairy. Second, Carson had an opportunity to write his story using his language expressed with his own invented or developmental spellings. And third, Carson's story was honored as he shared it in the Author's Chair.

Descriptive

One of the signposts we observe in developing writers is an attention to detail. Kyle Smith received a pet lizard for his eighth birthday. The next day, during Writer's Workshop, he described the lizard in great detail (Figure 8.7).

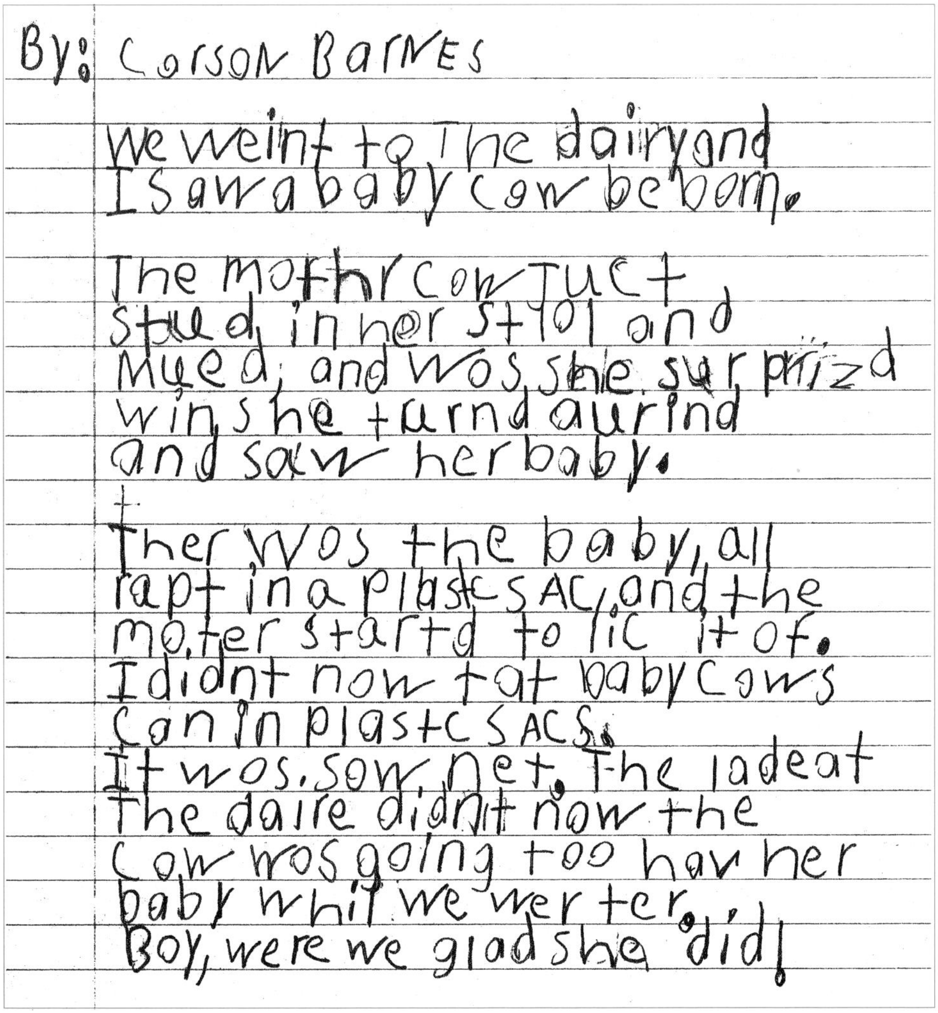

By: Corson Barnes

We weint to The dairy and
I saw a baby cow be born.

The mothr cow Tuct
stud in her sttol and
Mued, and wos she surpriizd
win she turnd aurind
and saw her baby.

Ther wos the baby, all
rapt in a plasts sac, and the
moter startd to lic it of.
I didnt now tat baby cows
can in plastc sacs.
It wos sow net. The lade at
The daire didnt now the
cow wos going too hav her
baby whil we wer ter, did
Boy, were we glad she did!

FIGURE 8.6
Carson's experience
at Shamrock Dairy

Current Interest

Students like to write about what is on their minds. While 8-year-old Kyle is excited about his new pet lizard, 13-year-old girls are daydreaming about other things (Figure 8.8).

Students should be given the freedom to write about what they want to write about. Research has shown us that the more children write, the better they become at writing. Thus current interests are a rich area for manuscript production.

Personal Poetry

Because of its color, rhythm, and fresh approach to reality and fantasy, poetry has a natural appeal. Poetry encourages children to try out language characteristics used by many authors. These writing experiences move them closer

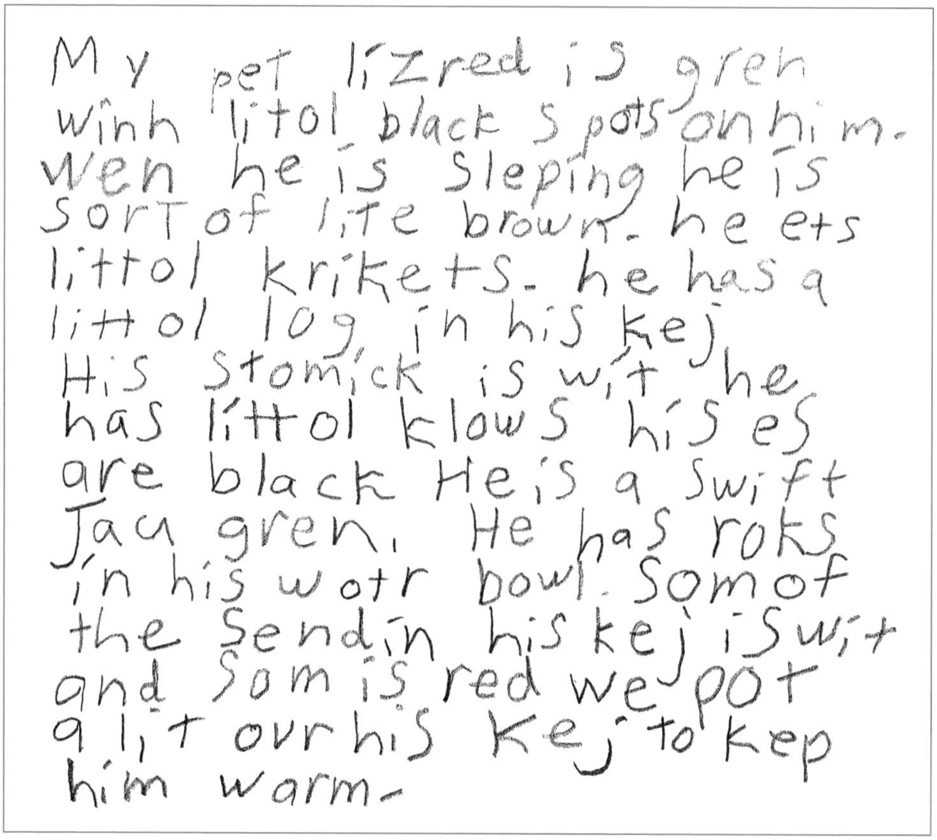

My pet lizard is green with little black spots on him. When he is sleeping he is sort of light brown. He eats little crickets. He has a little log in his cage. His stomach is white. He has little claws. His eyes are black. He is a Swift Jade Green. He has rocks in his water bowl. Some of the sand in his cage is white and some is red. We put a light over his cage to keep him warm.

FIGURE 8.7
Kyle's birthday present

and closer to the realization that much, if not most, of their writing is an extension of their own personal language.

As noted by Irene Fountas and Gay Su Pinnell (2001), "Poetic writing involves using written language as art. The writer may express feeling (as in expressive writing), but the feelings are arranged and ordered into a pattern that is pleasing in itself. . . . The poetic writing pleases and satisfies the writer, and, as a result, the reader. It stands alone and does not become dated information" (p. 5).

How do we develop poets in our writing program? We believe two major emphases are key:

◆ *Read poetry daily in your classroom.* Children internalize the structure and flow of poetry by hearing it through their ears. Be sure to read a variety of styles—from fun to serious—and a variety of authors as well.

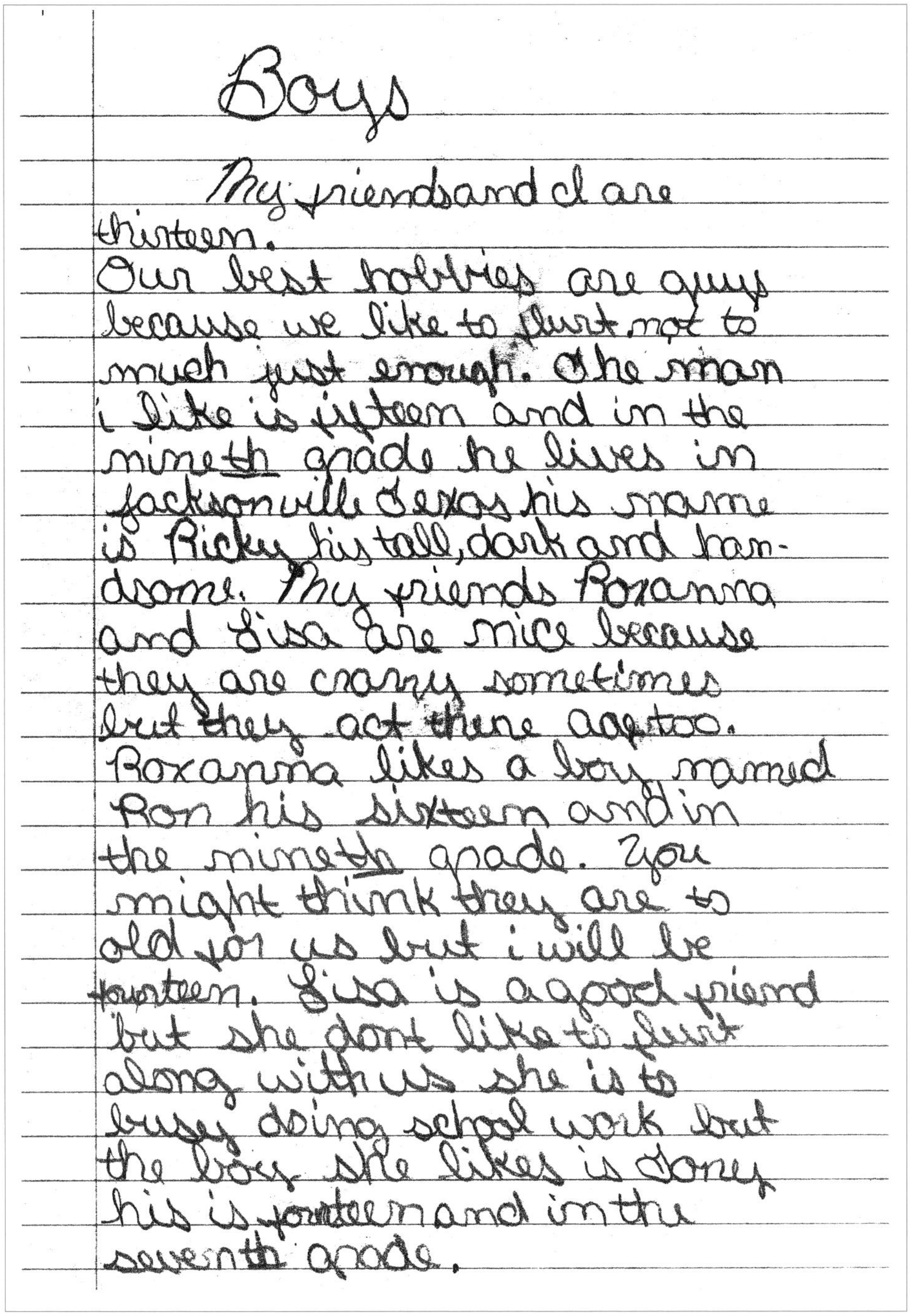

Boys

My friends and I are thirteen. Our best hobbies are guys because we like to flirt not to much just enough. The man i like is ifteen and in the nineth grade he lives in Jacksonville texas his name is Ricky his tall, dark and handsome. My friends Roxanna and Lisa are nice because they are crazy sometimes but they act there aqe too. Roxanna likes a boy named Ron his sixteen and in the nineth grade. You might think they are to old for us but i will be fourteen. Lisa is a good friend but she dont like to flirt along with us she is to busy doing school work but the boy she likes is Tony his is fourteen and in the seventh grade.

FIGURE 8.8

Boys on the brain

◆ *Bring poetry to life by acting it out.* Chapter 3 contains suggestions for encouraging children to perform poetry.

Nancy Larrick (1991) believes children come to poetry when teachers bring poetry to children. In *Let's Do a Poem: Introducing Children to Poetry*, Larrick examines (1) the music of poetry, (2) the language of poetry, (3) the movement and dance of poetry, and (4) the drama of poetry. Larrick believes oral performance is the key: "Like a song, a poem is meant to be heard. Often the appeal of the song depends on the singer. We are captivated when the song flows melodiously, when the words are enunciated clearly, when the timing and tone seem to fit the mood. Once we hear the song from an appealing voice, we want to hear it again, even to try ourselves" (p. 2).

Poetry has a rich oral history (Cramer, 2001). When students can enjoy hearing poetry and discussing what it means to them, they are interested in writing creative verses on their own (Graves, 1989). Class groups compose poems to describe or summarize a common group experience, but the heart and soul of poetry writing is in individual production. Individual compositions may first occur accidentally when young children are dictating their thoughts to the teacher. Simple poems of two lines occur in young children's compositions when their full free language is used in self-expression. As they work in a nonthreatening language environment, they use language that is seldom used except in writing poetry.

Most students begin to write their thoughts in poetic forms when they live in a rich environment of poetry. From simple beginnings they want to express more and more of their thoughts and feelings in the poetic language they have been hearing and reading.

Teachers should bring poetry of many types into the classroom. Student interest in poetry is broadened by exposure to varied selections. Children move naturally from hearing poetry to writing poetry. Students often reduce complexity to simplicity, as Susan does here:

The Old House
The house is old and dark
the trees are like a park.
It is damaged with no care.
Stillness is in the air.
The porch roof sags
And the window shades are just torn rags.
But the house has had its day!
Most things happen that way.

You'll also receive some poems that will surprise and maybe even shock you. Consider this collaboration by seventh graders Susie and Kendra:

The Kiss
A peach is a peach,
A plum is a plum,
but a kiss ain't a kiss
unless there's a tongue!

Poetry writing brings together elements of style and form that lift ideas above communication of the common reporting type. It frees students to explore and experiment with language. Fears of being wrong are minimized. The language of poets is valued along with their ideas.

Teachers as Writers

The greatest leaders lead by example. It's one thing to tell children that writing is important and fun; it's even better to demonstrate that writing is important and fun by writing yourself. Writing will be valued where writing is honored. And we value writing when both students and teachers write together.

Teachers must be writers because only writers understand what writing is like (Barbieri & Reif, 1994; Wickwire, 1990). We must keep in touch with the writing process through writing, for when we cease to write, we cease to understand the toils, frustrations, and joys that writing entails. Or, as Newman (1990) has said, we need to understand writing from inside the process.

How do we start writing again? Murray (1989) says it is simple: "Writing begins when teachers give their students silence and paper—then sit down to write themselves" (p. 19). So remember to experience and discover with your students the joys of writing. Donald Graves (1994) echoes the importance of the teacher as writer when he states, "Writing is a studio subject, I invite children to do something I am already doing" (p. 47).

For a jump-start, we recommend an excellent book by Tommy Thomason (1993), *More Than a Writing Teacher.* The book is designed as a writer's workshop for teachers and includes sections ranging from "The best excuse" to "Time to write." Thousands of teachers credit Thomason's book with moving them from talking about the need to write to actually writing. In addition, Figure 8.9 lists our favorite writing books; read them. Implement their advice in your classroom, and you will also become a better writer by putting into practice the very things you tell your students to do. The writing process is the writing process—whether you are 11 years old or 20 or 50. So—write, write, write!

Our Favorite Books about Writing

The Must-Reads

Atwell, Nancie. *In the Middle: Writing, Reading, and Learning with Adolescents,* 2nd ed. Portsmouth, NH: Heinemann-Boynton/Cook, 1998.

Calkins, Lucy. *The Art of Teaching Writing*. Portsmouth, NH: Heinemann, 1994.

Graves, Donald. *Writing: Teachers and Children at Work*. Portsmouth, NH: Heinemann Educational Books, 1983. After that book, try another Graves, *A Fresh Look at Writing*. Portsmouth, NH: Heinemann, 1994.

Lane, Barry. *After the End: Teaching and Learning Creative Revision*. Portsmouth, NH: Heinemann, 1993.

Books about Writing

Amberg, Jay & Larson, Mark. *The Creative Writing Handbook*. Glenview, IL: Good Year Books, 1992.

Ballenger, Bruce, & Lane, Barry. *Discovering the Writer Within: 40 Days to More Imaginative Writing*. Cincinnati, OH: Writer's Digest Books, 1989.

Brande, Dorothea. *Becoming a Writer*. Los Angeles: J. P. Tarcher, 1934.

Bryant, Jean. *Anybody Can Write: A Playful Approach*. San Rafael, CA: New World Library, 1984.

Elbow, Peter. *Writing with Power: Techniques for Mastering the Writing Process*. New York: Oxford University Press, 1981.

Fletcher, Ralph. *What a Writer Needs*. Portsmouth, NH: Heinemann, 1993; *Keeping a Writer's Notebook,* Portsmouth, NH: Heinemann, 1996.

Goldberg, Natalie. *Wild Mind: Living the Writer's Life*. New York: Bantam, 1990; *Writing Down the Bones: Freeing the Writer Within*. Boston: Shambhala, 1986.

Gould, June. *The Writer in All of Us: Improving Your Writing Through Childhood Memories*. New York: E. P. Dutton, 1989.

Graves, Donald. *A Researcher Learns to Write*. Portsmouth, NH: Heinemann, 1984.

Klauser, Henriette. *Writing on Both Sides of the Brain*. San Francisco: Harper & Row, 1986.

Mack, Karin, & Skjei, Eric. *Overcoming Writing Blocks*. Los Angeles: J. P. Tarcher, 1979.

Stein, Sol. *Stein on Writing*. New York: St. Martin's, 1995.

Thomason, Tommy. *More Than a Writing Teacher: How to Become a Teacher Who Writes*. Commerce, TX: Bridge, 1993.

Ueland, Brenda. *If You Want to Write*. St. Paul, MN: Graywolf Press, 1987.

Zinsser, William. *On Writing Well*. New York: Harper & Row, 1985.

Books about Writing in the Classroom

Avery, Carol. *. . . And With a Light Touch*. Portsmouth, NH: Heinemann, 1993.

Calkins, Lucy. *Lessons from a Child: On the Teaching and Learning of Writing*. Portsmouth, NH: Heinemann, 1983.

Carrol, Joyce Armstrong & Wilson, Edward E. *How to Teach Writing*. Englewood, CO: Teacher Ideas Press, 1993.

Collerson, John, ed. *Writing for Life*. Rozelle, NSW, Australia: PETA, 1988.

FIGURE 8.9

Cullinan, Bernice E., ed. *Pen in Hand: Children Become Writers*. Newark, DE: IRA, 1993.

Elbow, Peter, *Writing Without Teachers*. New York: Oxford University Press, 1973.

Frank, Marjorie. *If You're Trying to Teach Kids How to Write, You've Gotta Have This Book!* Nashville, TN: Incentive Publications, 1979.

Gordon, Naomi, ed. *Classroom Experiences: The Writing Process in Action*. Portsmouth, NH: Heinemann, 1984.

Harste, Jerome C. et al., eds. *Creating Classrooms for Authors: The Reading-Writing Connection*. Portsmouth, NH: Heinemann, 1988.

Nathan, Ruth, et al. *Classroom Strategies That Work: An Elementary Teacher's Guide to Process Writing*. Portsmouth, NH: Heinemann, 1989.

Newkirk, Thomas, & Atwell, Nancie, eds. *Understanding Writing: Ways of Observing, Learning, and Teaching*. Portsmouth, NH: Heinemann, 1988.

Noguchi, Rei R. *Grammar and the Teaching of Writing: Limits and Possibilities*. Urbana, Ill: National Council of Teachers of English, 1991.

Parry, Jo-Ann, & Hornsby, David. *Write On: A Conference Approach to Writing*. Portsmouth, NH: Heinemann, 1985.

Parsons, Les. *Writing in the Real Classroom*. Portsmouth, NH: Heinemann, 1991.

Romano, Tom. *Clearing the Way: Working with Teenage Writers*. Portsmouth, NH: Heinemann, 1987.

Thomason, Tommy. *Writer to Writer: How to Conference Young Authors*. Norwood, MA: Christopher-Gordon, 1997.

Thomason, Tommy, & York, Carol. *Write on Target: How to Prepare Young Writers for Success on State Writing Achievement Tests*. Norwood, MA: Christopher-Gordon, 2000; *Absolutely Write!* Norwood, MA: Christopher-Gordon, 2002.

Note: Our appreciation goes to Tommy Thomason for his advice and input on this list.

FURTHER WORDS

 From InfoTrac College Edition

All "Journaled Out?" Try These Strategies (student writing activities), Brenda Power, *Instructor (1990)*, March 1997 v106 n6 p48(2)

Process Writing in the Classrooms of Eleven Fifth-Grade Teachers with Different Orientations to Teaching and Learning (statistical data included), Marjorie Y. Lipson, James Mosenthal, Patricia Daniels, and Haley Woodside-Jiron. *The Elementary School Journal*, November 2000 v101 i2 p209

Interactive Writing with Young Children, Nigel Hall, *Childhood Education*, September 15, 2000 v76 i6 p358

The Craft of Telling (Off the Cuff column), Donald M. Murray, *The Writer*, June 1994 v107 n6 p7(2)

From Professional Journals and Publications

Barlow, B. (2001). Boost Writing Skills with Everyday JOURNALING. *Instructor, 111*, (1) 44.

Bugeja, M. (2001). Clean Up Your Copy. *The Quill, 89*, (1), 56.

Dahl, K. L., & Freppon, P. A. (1995). A Comparison of Innercity Children's Interpretations of Reading and Writing Instruction in the Early Grades in Skills-Based and Whole Language Classrooms. *Reading Research Quarterly, 30*, 50–74.

Dyson, A. H. (1995). The Courage to Write: Child Meaning Making in a Contested World. *Language Arts, 72,* 324–333.

Graves, D. H., & Hansen, J. (1983). The Author's Chair. *Language Arts, 60,* 176–183.

Lipson, M. J., Mosenthal, J., Daniels, P., & Woodside-Jiron, H. (2000). Process Writing in the Classrooms of Eleven Fifth-Grade Teachers with Different Orientations to Teaching and Learning. *The Elementary School Journal, 101* (2), 209.

Martello, J. (2001). Talk about Writing—Metalinguistic Awareness in Beginning Writers. *Australian Journal of Language and Literacy, 24,* (2), 101.

Summary

Teachers in a total literacy environment use various methods and materials to stimulate students to develop as writers. They never set out to teach how to write by a prescribed system. They think of students as having the basic ingredients of writing and reading inside. They interact with students to help each one discover nonprint and printed forms of communication. When the ability to write independently is achieved, teachers do not say that they have taught the student how to write. They know what they did was to release something in the student that had always been there.

Total Literacy Anchors

- Students use personal observations as a source for writing poetry and prose.
- Students draw on imagination as a source of topics for writing.
- Students share aspirations through interesting topics and artful ways of writing.
- Students reflect the influence of good literature when writing.
- Students write on a variety of subjects in interesting and creative forms.
- Students see possibilities for artful writing in ordinary experiences.
- Students experiment with style and form in poetry writing.
- Students contribute copies of books to school and public libraries.
- Students write, write, write!

CHAPTER 9

Writing Patterned Stories AND Poetry

As You Read . . .

◆ What are literary genres?

◆ How do genre models make writing easier for students?

◆ What is the value of genre poetry writing in a total literacy program?

Author Words

Mary Beth Sampson

What's the difference between the lyrical refrain of *Brown Bear, Brown Bear, What Do You See?* and the spellbinding tale *Where the Wild Things Are?* The answer lies in the linguistic structures, or genres, Bill Martin Jr. (1967) and Maurice Sendak (1963) used to weave these two classic children's stories. Some examples of genre are fiction, historical fiction, nonfiction, folktales, fantasy, poetry, and predictable stories. Within genres are subgenres. In this chapter, we explore the subgenres of predictable stories and patterned poetry. We start with the story patterns of the repetitive language subgenre, the rhyming language subgenre, the interlocking subgenre, the color subgenre, the cumulative subgenre, the culturally familiar subgenre, and the circle subgenre. Then we move to the poetry subgenres of haiku, senryu, snapshot, tanka, sijo, couplet, cinquain, terquain, diamante, renga, limerick, and shape patterns.

These subgenres are important because they provide an excellent outlet for children's self-expression. In Chapter 8, student stories illustrated what young authors can create when given an opportunity to develop their thoughts through stories and poems. In this chapter, through genre study and analysis, we see how students can go beyond their own personal writing styles.

As students read well-written materials that reflect the ways authors express themselves in beautiful language, they will see how others write. Students can then use these patterns when expressing their own thoughts and feelings. They'll notice that professional writers often use these patterns or genres in their writing. For example, 9-year-old Melissa was excited to discover she had something in common with the writer/illustrator team of Bill Martin Jr and Steven Kellogg—both had used a combination of color and rhyming subgenres in their latest books. Melissa had put the two subgenres to work in her book *Lost in the Woods;* Martin and Kellogg (1999) had used the genres in their bestseller *A Beasty Story.*

What is the value of genre patterns? Students are constantly learning, and the materials they read "demonstrate" to them what writing can be like (Smith, 1985). Consequently, students benefit when they come under the influence of a variety of writing styles and forms, including artful forms of expression such as predictable genre stories and genre poetry.

When students write using the forms and linguistic patterns of others, they develop new means of self-expression—saying things differently than they normally do. And even though the patterns can be restrictive, the writer does have choices and options of words and ways of combining words to express ideas.

Although the focus of this chapter is on self-expression and the influence of other language styles on personal language, embedded within the process are elements of form such as spelling, punctuation, capitalization, grammar, handwriting, and sentence sense. These elements of form apply to the productive writing of students and are supports for clear and effective communication—not instructional lessons in themselves.

The teacher plays a crucial role in all aspects of the writing program. In a total literacy classroom, the teacher does not dictate standards and pass judgment on students' creative productions but suggests and illustrates alternatives so students increase their awareness of variety in style and correctness in form. The teacher provides many models that give a measure of security to students who are exploring their communicative powers. This chapter describes some models teachers may use to stimulate writing and literacy growth.

Predictable Subgenre Stories

Research has shown that stories featuring patterned literary structures are easy for students to read (Bridge, 1979, 1986; Rhodes, 1981; Yellin & Blake, 1994). Such structures are sometimes called predictable books or structured language books. We use the term *predictable books* to highlight the patterns or genres contained in these books. When a story has an understandable structure, students are free to use

America's Finest
Frankie Jarrell

Courtesy of Michael Sampson

Students collaborate on a story.

their knowledge about language to predict many of the events in the story. Such stories furnish an excellent pattern for young authors to emulate as they write stories for themselves and classmates. Many children will take the first step toward divergence in their writing as the pattern encourages them to go beyond their own writing style and adopt the style of the pattern.

The following genres can be used to stimulate writing selections that have predictive characteristics. Such patterns extend students' writing beyond the personal styles discussed in Chapter 8.

The Repetitive Language Pattern

Many stories for young readers feature a literary device called repetitive structure. Such stories present a pattern and repeat it, time after time, with only slight variations throughout the book. Bill Martin Jr. and Michael Sampson (in press) provide such a structure in their *All Kinds of Kids:*

2–3) Some kids are boys.

Some are not.

4–5) Some kids are little.

Some are not.

6–7) Some kids are friendly.

Some are not.

8–9) Some kids live near you.

Some do not.

32) WHAT KIND OF KID ARE YOU?

After reading and enjoying *All Kinds of Kids,* 7-year-old Angie used the pattern to write about her first love—horses.

Some horses neigh.	Some horses run.
Some do not.	Some do not.
Some horses eat flowers.	Some horses roll in dirt.
Some do not.	Some do not.
Some horses are spotted.	Some horses buck.
Some are not.	Some do not.
What kind of horse would you like?	

Angie's story is one that even students who are considered nonreaders can read and is one of the most popular books in the classroom library. Note that

Angie changed the pattern to "Some are not—to match the linking verb in the previous line. Her metalinguistic knowledge of language and her intuition told her to do so. Even nonreaders alter the pattern to make the language correct when they come to this section of the story. Repetitive structures like this one provide an excellent model for readers and writers.

The Rhyming Language Pattern

Both the sound and syllabication of words are communicated to children when they encounter a story that uses a rhyme scheme. A story that has such rhyme and rhythm is the traditional *Whistle, Mary, Whistle*. It begins:

> Whistle, Mary, whistle.
> And you can catch a cow.
> I can't whistle, Mother.
> I just don't know how.

A fifth-grader's innovation about this story concerns reading.

> Read, Meredith, read.
> And you will have some fun.
> I can't read, Teacher.
> I'd rather skip and run.
> Read, Jonathan, read.
> Of kings and queens and joy.
> I can't read, Teacher.
> I'm just a little boy.
> Read, Darcy, read.
> The frog just caught a rat.
> I can't read, Teacher.
> This book is just too fat.

> Read, Stephanie, read.
> Of travels to the zoo.
> I can't read, Teacher.
> I chose this book for you.
> Read, Joshua, read.
> Of trips to outer space.
> I can't read, Teacher.
> Its just too fast a pace.
> Read, Johnny, read.
> I've found a book for you.
> Oh, boy! Monsters!
> I want to read now, too.

Predictable patterns that have a rhyme scheme are essential for the development of sensitivity to ending sounds that are alike. Most students can respond to rhyming whether they are good readers or not. They enjoy and benefit from selections that include rhyming.

Rhyme adds a poetic quality to text. However, rhyming schemes, regardless of position within the story, should not detract from the beauty or flow of the story being told. Art can also support the rhyme as demonstrated by Newbery award-winning illustrator Richard Egielski in Bill Martin Jr's *"Fire! Fire!" Said Mrs. McGuire* (1996).

The Frog Principal, by **Stephanie Calmenson.** The adventure begins when a bumbling visiting magician accidentally turns the school principal into a frog. *New York: Scholastic, 2001.*

Wait! No Paint! by **Bruce Whatley.** This whimsical rendition of *The Three Little Pigs* includes a careless illustrator who spills his orange juice and runs out of red paint. *New York: HarperCollins, 2001.*

Older Readers

The Girl Who Spun Gold, by **Virginia Hamilton.** This West Indian version of the little-man (Rumpelstiltskin) traditional folktale includes a spirited heroine. *New York: Blue Sky, 2000.*

Sleeping Ugly, by **Jane Yolen.** First published in 1981, with a reprint in 1997 and a library edition in 1999, this tale of Plain Jane, Princess Miserella, and a fairy falling into a deep sleep and a prince deciding who to awaken with a kiss causes one to rethink the traditional definition of beauty. *New York: Coward, 1981.*

Just Ella, by **Margaret Peterson Haddix.** A continuation of the Cinderella story, but with a "twist" regarding what "happily ever after" really is. *New York: Simon & Schuster, 1999.*

Meet the Author
Richard Egielski

The Interlocking Pattern

An intriguing variation of repetitive form is the interlocking pattern. Interlocking structures connect segments of the text and enable children to read each succeeding episode with confidence. One of the best known examples of interlocking structure was developed by Bill Martin Jr and is featured in his interlocking texts *Brown Bear, Brown Bear, What Do You See?* (1967) and *Polar Bear, Polar Bear, What Do You Hear?* (1991) Notice how Martin (2003) uses the interlocking pattern in his third bear book, *Panda Bear, Panda Bear, What Do You See?* (2003) which features the movements of endangered creatures.

> Panda Bear, Panda Bear, what do you see?
> I see a Bald Eagle soaring by me.
> Bald Eagle, Bald Eagle, what do you see?
> I see a Water Buffalo charging by me.

Teacher-to-Teacher

Joy, a second-grade student, used the *Polar Bear, Polar Bear, What Do You Hear?* interlocking pattern to create her own story, which she named *Woolly Lamb, Woolly Lamb*.

Woolly Lamb, Woolly Lamb, what do you hear?
I hear a green frog croaking so near.
Green Frog, Green Frog, what do you hear?
I hear a shaggy wolf howling so near.
Shaggy Wolf, Shaggy Wolf, what do you hear?
I hear a wild goose honking so near.
Wild Goose, Wild Goose, what do you hear?
I hear a sneaky snake hissing so near.
Sneaky Snake, Sneaky Snake, what do you hear?
I hear a little mouse squeaking so near.
Little Mouse, Little Mouse, what do you hear?
I hear a barn owl hooting so near.
Barn Owl, Barn Owl, what do you hear?
I hear a red rooster crowing so near.

Red Rooster, Red Rooster, what do you hear?
I hear a gentle donkey braying so near.
Gentle Donkey, Gentle Donkey, what do you hear?
I hear a woolly lamb bleating so near.
Woolly Lamb, Woolly Lamb!

Joy could write *Woolly Lamb, Woolly Lamb, What Do You Hear?* because she knew so well the pattern of *Polar Bear, Polar Bear, What Do You Hear?* She knew the rhythm and the language well enough to make it her own. It is easy to see that she could add many more stanzas, or she could change the focus to "What do you feel?" or "What do you smell?" or to other topics such as vehicles, insects, or bodies in space. This pattern is very useful in helping students extend from their home-rooted language to literary language.

Students organize a predictable book manuscript for presentation to the class.

The Cumulative Pattern

Cumulative story sequences enable students to hold lengthy phrases in short-term memory while concentrating on one new episode on each succeeding page. The Mother Goose tale "The House That Jack Built" is a well-known example of a cumulative structure.

PAGE 1   This is the House that Jack built

PAGE 2   This is the Malt,
              that lay in the house
              that Jack built.

PAGE 3   This is the Rat,
              that ate the malt,
              that lay in the house
              that Jack built.

The pattern continues with an additional episode each page for an additional eight pages.

Crescent Dragonwagon uses the "Jack" pattern in *This Is the Bread I Baked for Ned* (1999): "This is the Bread I baked for Ned, baked for Ned in the morning." Likewise, Michael Sampson (1999) uses the same pattern in *The Football That Won . . .*: "This is the linebacker that sacked the quarterback that fumbled the football that won the Super Bowl."

Donald Crews

1. *Which book of yours has given you the greatest pleasure?*

Bigmama's. This book meant a great deal to me personally and to my family. It was especially gratifying to me to see how excited my mother became over the book. A video was done on the book, and Mom and I got to travel back to where she grew up. It was fulfilling for me to share her feelings and her pride.

2. *Which book has surprised you most in terms of its public reception?*

Freight Train. I had done several books before, but this book was special from the beginning. Now there is a whole new crop of kids who have discovered the book. It was published in 1979, but for them the book was just done yesterday.

3. *What would you like people to remember about your work?*

I want people to look at individual books and see that I have found ways to make the material exciting—and that it's not the same way all the time.

4. *What impact do you hope your work will have on children?*

Especially for black children, I want them to see that they can achieve a level of success by hard work and dedication. They have role models in sports, but I want to present another option for their talents so they can find another way to achieve.

Donald Crews won the Caldecott Medal with *Freight Train* and has produced many stunning early childhood picture books. With *Bigmama's* and *Shortcut,* he has become a storyteller as well as an accomplished graphic artist. His books include *Ten Black Dots, We Read A to Z, Parade, Bicycle, Truck, School Bus, Each Orange Had 8 Slices: A Counting Book,* and *Inside Freight Train.*

Reprinted with special permission of Donald Crews.

Another example of the cumulative pattern can be seen in Bill Martin Jr's *Old Devil Wind* (1993); still another is evidenced in Audrey Wood's (1984) *The Napping House.*

The Chronological Pattern

This pattern uses enumeration to foster predictability and may use alliteration to support predictability. Eric Carle's (1987) *The Very Hungry Caterpillar* is perhaps the most famous example of this genre:

> In the light of the moon a little egg lay on a leaf.
> One Sunday morning the warm sun came up, and . . . pop!
> Out of the egg came a tiny and very hungry caterpillar.
> He started to look for food.
> On Monday he ate through one apple. But he was still hungry.

It can be extended with other stanzas, made into books, and read by students in their own classes and in other classes. Older students enjoy writing with this pattern to create books for kindergarten classes.

Rosalinda Flores, a fifth-grade teacher in Dallas, Texas, uses patterned books as a mainstay of her writing program. She has developed a technique for using patterned language selections for literacy development that has become a model for other teachers in her school. She follows six basic steps (see Figure 9.1) that enable her students to produce beautiful adaptations of well-written books. Rosalinda believes quality is more important than quantity; consequently, she carefully orchestrates the movement of a patterned book from its introduction to its output as a new book.

When a new patterned book is introduced to the classroom environment, by students or by Rosalinda, she takes time to ensure that the children have internalized the pattern before they attempt to adapt it. She shares the book with the students through choral reading and unison reading. The students do Reader's Theater presentations of the story. At some point, it becomes evident that the children have claimed the pattern as their own.

Then the fun continues. Rosalinda invites the class to modify the pattern and create new books. Often one book is written from the pattern as a whole class activity. After

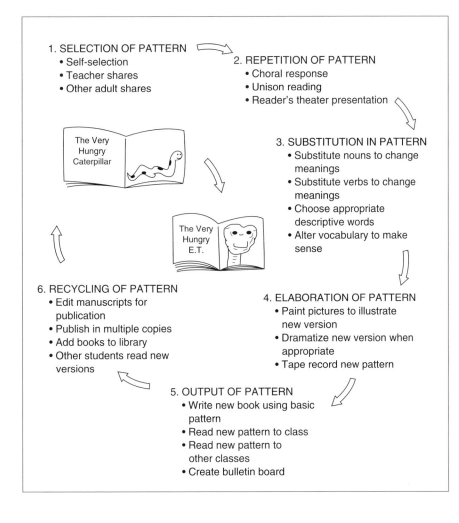

1. SELECTION OF PATTERN
   • Self-selection
   • Teacher shares
   • Other adult shares

2. REPETITION OF PATTERN
   • Choral response
   • Unison reading
   • Reader's theater presentation

3. SUBSTITUTION IN PATTERN
   • Substitute nouns to change meanings
   • Substitute verbs to change meanings
   • Choose appropriate descriptive words
   • Alter vocabulary to make sense

4. ELABORATION OF PATTERN
   • Paint pictures to illustrate new version
   • Dramatize new version when appropriate
   • Tape record new pattern

5. OUTPUT OF PATTERN
   • Write new book using basic pattern
   • Read new pattern to class
   • Read new pattern to other classes
   • Create bulletin board

6. RECYCLING OF PATTERN
   • Edit manuscripts for publication
   • Publish in multiple copies
   • Add books to library
   • Other students read new versions

The Very Hungry Caterpillar

The Very Hungry E.T.

FIGURE 9.1
Using patterned language selections for literacy development

sharing Eric Carle's (1987) *The Very Hungry Caterpillar,* the class decided to write a book called *The Very Hungry E.T.* Verbs in the pattern were substituted to change the meaning in alignment with the new focus. Appropriate descriptive words were added and the vocabulary altered to make sense. After two drafts, the book was complete. Pictures were painted to illustrate the new version, and a Reader's Theater performance held. That was just the beginning. A host of authors started independent productions of new versions of the pattern. Within a week, Scotty, Yolanda, Stacey, and Mark had written and illustrated *The Very Hungry E.T.* Scotty had watched the movie *E.T.* ten times and was the content expert of the group. Yolanda did most of the editing of the version, and Mark illustrated the book. It became the talk of the school and was featured on the community's cable television channel.

The Very Hungry E.T.

In the light of the moon, a little man stood in a field.
One Sunday morning the warm sun came up and—
POP—out of a storeroom came a very hungry E.T.!

He started to look for food.
On Monday he ate one Reese's pieces . . .
BUT HE WAS STILL HUNGRY!
On Tuesday he ate two bowls of cottage cheese . . .
BUT HE WAS STILL HUNGRY!
On Wednesday he ate three pizzas . . .
BUT HE WAS STILL HUNGRY!
On Thursday he ate four slices of bread . . .
BUT HE WAS STILL HUNGRY!
On Friday he ate five bananas . . .
BUT HE WAS STILL HUNGRY!
On Saturday he ate a piece of lemon pie, a candy bar, one apple, a slice of meat . . . and a piece of strawberry shortcake!
That night he had a stomachache.
The next day was Sunday again and he drank a Coke and felt much better.
Now he wasn't hungry anymore—he was a BIG, FAT, E.T.!
E.T. went to Elliot's house and stayed for a month and then he went . . . H O M E !!!

Rosalinda varies the procedure from time to time and always allows students freedom to choose what writing projects they wish to become involved in.

The Culturally Familiar Pattern

This pattern involves using stories children will already be familiar with because they are a part of their lives and culture. We can't provide a list of such books because what's familiar to one culture may not be familiar to another. However, to many children in the United States, *Little Red Riding Hood, The Three Little Pigs, Jack and the Beanstalk,* and *The Night Before Christmas* will be culturally familiar stories. Steven Kellogg has illustrated a number of these books for today's readers.

The Circle Pattern

Another noteworthy pattern for writers to emulate is the circle pattern. This pattern ends with a return to the first event of the book, hence the name circle pattern. Laura Numeroff's (1985) *If You Give a Mouse a Cookie* is the classic example of this pattern. The story begins with a little boy who encounters a hungry little mouse.

Students study the patterned used by author Robert Kraus (1989) in *Where Are You Going Little Mouse?*

He gives the mouse a cookie, then he has to give him milk to go with the cookie. The mouse and boy proceed through a series of cause/effect events that culminate with the mouse wanting milk. The last line reads "and chances are if he asks for a glass of milk, he's going to want a cookie to go with it." Children enjoy composing books that feature this pattern, as illustrated in the teacher-to-teacher feature.

Teacher-to-Teacher

Deeanne Barker's second-grade class enjoyed reading *Star of the Circus* by Michael and Mary Beth Sampson (1997). Their circle pattern features a mouse who stands in the center ring singing, "I'm the star of the circus, I'm the star of the circus," only to be replaced in the center ring by larger and larger circus animals who sing the same song.

Deeanne's class incorporated this pattern into a book they wrote during their study of a thematic unit on pets. As children brainstormed different breeds of dogs, Deeanne recorded their dictations in the form of a conceptual map (conceptual maps are described in Chapter 7). The children then ranked the breeds according to size and incorporated them into the circle pattern of the book they called *Dogsong*.

➤ ➤ ➤

Poodle stands on top of the doghouse and sings,
  "I'm the king of the backyard,
  I'm the king of the backyard!"
Dachshund pushes Poodle off the doghouse and says,
  "Now who is the king of the backyard?"
  "You are, big Dachshund," says Poodle.
Dachshund stands on top of the doghouse and sings,
  "I'm the king of the backyard,
  I'm the king of the backyard!"

The book continues as it features a chow, a cocker spaniel, a german shepherd, a rot-tweiler, and a doberman. This is how the children closed the pattern:

  Poodle was watching from behind a tree.
  He sneaks up behind the doghouse and barks
"Bow Wow Wow,"
  and scares the Doberman away.
  Poodle stands on top of the doghouse and sings,
  "I'm the king of the backyard,
  I'm the king of the backyard!"

The children edited, illustrated, and published the book. *Dogsong* is one of the most popular books in the library, and one that can be read by all of the students.

The Value of Genre Writing

The use of highly predictive selections is a sure way to develop oral language abilities that are not natural in home-rooted language. These literary-level language abilities gained from reading predictable materials permit students to move into the reading and writing of sophisticated literature at a much faster rate. When stories with predictable language patterns are read with students, the patterns become a part of the students' language repertoire. What students hear and say can be used as a basis for writing, and patterns provide a framework for putting ideas into print.

Children who move toward self-selection of reading must have some prior experience in dealing with language that has characteristics of a predictive sequence. They must recognize the value and artistry of writing in comparing and contrasting patterns. They must know that many authors take a simple idea and elaborate to extend meaning. They must appreciate and enjoy the rhythm of language rather than be concerned at all times about recognition and comprehension abilities. Stories that are crafted with such patterns demonstrate to children what good writing is like and serve as an invitation to the student to emulate such a style.

Patterned Poetry

America's Finest
Reggie Dixon

In Chapter 3 and throughout this book we have shared our love of poetry and the way poetry makes language alive and beautiful. We have shared our favorite poets with you—Shel Silverstein, Jack Prelutsky, and, of course, Robert Frost. But now we move to a different type and style of poetry, patterned poetry. You will find these patterns to be powerful tools for use in your writing classroom. They afford young authors an easy and successful entry into the world of poetry. They'll be amazed at the beauty of their langauge—and so will you.

These poetry patterns provide form while offering openness to students' creativity. They are useful in launching children into new styles of talking and writing; here are some useful poetic patterns for children to use in the elementary and middle grades:

Haiku

Senryu

Snapshot

Tanka

Sijo

Couplet

Cinquain

Terquain

Diamante

Renga

Limerick

Shape patterns

These patterns require children to identify syllables in words, to rhyme, and to select predetermined forms of words such as nouns, verbs, and descriptors. In these forms the syllable is highlighted more than in some others. Its significance in studying language is summed up by Durkin (1983) when she states, "It is the syllable to which all [word study] generalizations refer" (p. 164). The patterns of writing illustrated in this discussion suggest ways in which children can express their own observations, feelings, and imaginations with styles and forms they have not previously used at home or at school. These patterns offer enough literary quality to help children appreciate the work of artist-authors who write in disciplined forms.

Haiku

The pattern of haiku is three lines, seventeen syllables, nonrhyming:

Line 1:   five syllables

Line 2:   seven syllables

Line 3:   five syllables

Haiku is an Oriental verse form of ancient origin. Its simplicity encourages children to say beautiful things in a new way. It is used to express observations and feelings about nature and the seasons. This form highlights the use of words of the form classes nouns, verbs, adjectives, and adverbs. It is worth noting that Japanese syllables are different from English forms in that they are all short. It is acceptable to write Haiku in three short lines with the second slightly longer than the first and third. However, fitting thoughts into a structure of 5–7–5 syllables often gives children a secure place to start writing. Here are two examples of haiku:

Winter's icy breath
Blows against the windowpane
Seeking warmth inside.
JOSE

Beautiful mountains
Shimmering in the sunset
Day is leaving Earth.
MIKE

Teacher-to-Teacher

Once Deeanne Barker is sure most of her 8- and 9-year-olds can write their own ideas in language that is close to their talk, she combines brainstorming and dictation to illustrate other ways of saying things. She suggests rhyming words and records some the children know. She then introduces rhyming couplets, triplets, and quatrains. Rather than assign children to write in these patterns, she provides a common experience such as a picture or a film without words and then takes dictation from the group to illustrate the features of the patterns. Revisions are easy to make on the chalkboard, and the children suggest changes from original presentations until a satisfying pattern is illustrated. Nonrhyming patterns such as those of haiku and some cinquains are shown. Deeanne hopes that from the experience the children will gain confidence to use new writing patterns on their own—and they do. They experience oral composition first and then move to writing.

She brought to the class a picture of a high mountain waterfall. It was a beautiful sight that inspired students to say things that were extraordinary. After talking for a while, she recorded on the chalkboard some of the things individuals dictated. After she had seven or eight statements, she directed the attention of the class to the composition of a haiku to attach to the picture when it was put on the bulletin board. They had written haiku before and knew the basic structure. Deeanne knew a lot about the artistry of haiku, but she did not try to teach that at the time of composition. From all their dictated statements, these were chosen to represent the picture of the waterfall:

Slender waterfalls
From vast snow fields trickle down
Like long silver threads.

This composition was satisfying and treasured by members of the class. They read it to each other and to visitors. Some students copied it in books of poetry that contained other poems they were collecting.

Senryu

The pattern of senryu (sin ah rue) is the same as haiku—three lines, seventeen syllables, nonrhyming. However, senryu is used to communicate topics that are not about nature and the seasons. Here are two examples of senryu:

The ferris wheel turns　　*Old Fisherman sits*
Taking me into the sky.　　*On the pier early in day*
I can see the World!　　*Catching his dinner.*
BLAKE　　**MEREDITH**

Snapshot

The snapshot is a verse form developed by Claryce Allen to "freeze" a moment in time. It gives writers more freedom than the haiku or senryu. Snapshots can be on any topic and "flow" more smoothly than haiku or senryu.

The pattern of a snapshot is three lines, nineteen syllables, nonrhyming:

Line 1: seven syllables　　*The ocean waves lapping at*

Line 2: five syllables　　*My feet come and go,*

Line 3: seven syllables　　*Taking sand from between my toes.*

　　　　　　　　　YVONNE

Now here is a double-take example:

Late summer: six pelicans
Led by two small birds
Skimming over morning waves,
Flying so low that each move
Of birds is mirrored
On the rippling gray-blue waves.
BRYANT AND JOSHUA

　　　Haiku, senryu, and snapshots use only a few syllables to express a thought that could become the main idea for an essay, a story, or a lyric. Children who have never expressed their thinking in those three complex forms profit from the experience of writing in the understandable, simple forms of a known pattern.

　　　These forms, as well as other syllabic patterned poetry, require a functional understanding of structural analysis—syllabication, prefixes, suffixes, synonyms, and contractions. The students must learn to eliminate many words of structure and depend on the reader to fill in the omitted words when they are useful for the flow of ideas. They focus on the words that carry the heavy load of meaning in communication and thus build skills necessary for silent reading at a rate faster than speech.

Snapshots are written every day by the first-grade students in Lila Bruton's language arts class. Lila has found several procedures that help her young authors write snapshots. The children construct viewfinders by punching a pinhole in a piece of writing paper. They look through the hole and find something of interest. After writing down three things about what they have in focus, they edit those thoughts and create a snapshot. Another effective technique is Lila's Snapshot Box. It contains good photographs that focus on one interesting thing or idea. Students constantly bring in photographs that are added to the collection, and the snapshots that result are outstanding.

Tanka

The pattern of tanka is five lines, thirty-one syllables, nonrhyming:

Line 1:   five syllables

Line 2:   seven syllables

Line 3:   five syllables

Line 4:   seven syllables

Line 5:   seven syllables

Tanka is another ancient Oriental poetry form. It is a haiku plus two lines of seven syllables each. Actually, the tanka is older than the haiku, and it is believed the more popular haiku is just a shortened form of tanka. The author of a tanka usually, but not always, expresses five thoughts on a topic. They may include the following:

The name of something

Its actions

Its location

Its usefulness

Its beauty

Something distinctive or unusual about the subject

A comparison

The color, size, shape, sound, and other features

Here are some examples of the tanka:

At morning sunrise
The ranch hands discuss the day.
Their work never ends:
Riding the rugged hillsides
Weathered crackling skin.

CAMI

Gentle flelds embrace
Chromatic-winged butterflies
On soft springtime days.
Their fluttering extension
Brings harmony to mankind.

MARCIA

Kim Pearce uses tanka as group projects with her third-graders. She encourages students to proceed in this way:

- Think about the topic.
- Write what they think about the topic.
- Edit, deleting words not required for meaning.
- Add descriptive nouns.

- Count syllables and change words to get more or fewer syllables.
- Consult a thesaurus when new words with the same meaning are needed.

 Kim collects tanka from several authors. The students illustrate them, bind them into a book, and place the book in the classroom library.

In guiding authors to try the tanka, haiku, and senryu, teachers can encourage children to record their observations in natural ways. Then they count syllables. They will be surprised at how many natural utterances occur in phrases and sentences of five and seven syllables. Most of what is said can be recorded in measures of five or seven syllables, with a few adjustments. It is as natural for kindergarten children to dictate in these patterns as it is for older children to write in them.

Sijo

The sijo pattern consists of six lines, six to eight syllables per line, forty-two to forty-eight syllables total, nonrhyming, no limitation on topics.

Sijo (pronounced "she-djo") is a beautiful poetry form that was developed during the Yi Dynasty in Korea during the fourteenth century. In the simplified form popularized for school use by Lee Bennett Hopkins, it is much like the haiku and tanka but is not as restrictive (Allen, 1976). Although it is nonrhyming, sijo includes internal rhymes that occur frequently in Korean verse. Alliteration is used to produce a poetic quality. Observations can be recorded on almost any topic and then edited for the six lines of six to eight syllables each. Here are examples of the sijo:

A wonderful time of year	*Intelligent, loving eyes,*
Families coming together	*Eyebrows expressing thoughts,*
Exchanging their gifts of love,	*Tails wagging and thumping,*
Enjoying the sights and sounds	*Bodies wiggling and hopping,*
Of a special celebration.	*Barking, whining, sighing,*
Christmas time is wonderful for all.	*My labradors speak to me.*
FRED	**CHRISTINA**

Cultural Festival

Our American cities have become havens for the peoples of the world. Hundreds of thousands of refugees have immigrated to the United States from Southeast Asia and are proud of their new homes.

But American schools, and our culture, often misunderstand the diversity of these Vietnamese, Cambodian, Laotian, Hmong, and other Southeast Asian immigrants. "We have different backgrounds, cultures, and politics back home, but here people tend to lump us together as Southeast Asians," said Van Lam. "We don't speak the same languages and our beliefs are very different" (as cited in Hendricks, 2002, B1).

Indeed, Americans don't realize the friction that exists within these very different cultures. For example, the Vietnamese and Cambodians have historically been enemies and continue to feel reservations about being grouped together—even in the United States.

The same problems hold true for immigrants from Latin America—including Salvadorans and Mexicans. "Some Mexicans just see us as 'Oaxaquitas'; there's a kind of discrimination against us as an indigenous people," said Concepción Pacheco, an immigrant from Oaxaca (Hendricks, 2002, B2).

So what can the school, the community—and the classroom teacher—do about these problems? We must find opportunities for students—and parents—to find out that they are more alike than different. In Fresno, California, an annual festival is held to celebrate the diverse cultures of California's Central Valley. The festival was organized by community leaders and schools who were troubled because their immigrant communities lived in isolation from each other and were often misunderstood by the larger community. The festival features food, handicrafts, and dance from the many cultures of the valley.

After attending the festival, Pacheco said, "I used to think of blacks as people who didn't work and got into trouble, but here I can see their music and their culture. Our cultures cross the street a lot, but here we learn more about each other" (Hendricks, 2002, B2).

Children come to school with many of the prejudices held by their parents toward other cultural groups. Interaction, and working together on common projects, is the key to understanding people who appear to be different than they are. To this end, the classroom teacher has a marvelous opportunity to bring cultures together through the havens of love and acceptance created by the total literacy classroom.

Writing the sijo gives children practice in elaborating, sequencing, and comparing. All of these abilities are prerequisite to comprehending when reading what others have written. Besides that, the sijo is a literary form that is easy and pleasurable.

Poetry Patterns That Feature Form Class Words

Writing activities that require children to know classes of words to fit into a predetermined pattern are useful in vocabulary expansion. Children have the security of the pattern as a guide, but they are free to use any words they know to fill in the pattern. The couplet, cinquain, terquain, and diamante are examples.

Couplet

The noun-verb patterns in sentences can be demonstrated with couplets. If students do not know what couplets are, assure them the meaning is about the same as "couple." Most of them will know the meaning of the word and predict that "couplet" means "two." A couplet is a short poem or part of a poem that has two lines that rhyme. A "quick couplet" is an easy way to introduce this rhyming verse form. Here are two examples of couplets:

Joshua cries   *Bears growl*
With his eyes.   *On the prowl.*
MARSHA   TERRI

After children read, write, and enjoy couplets, the transition can be made to reading sentences with an effort to see the noun-verb pattern without looking at the other words. This is an introduction to skimming, but it also forms a basis for evaluating effective, clear writing.

Teacher-to-Teacher

Linda Crane uses couplets with her kindergarten students starting from the first day of class. She uses the words the children generate from writing couplets in various ways, including these:

♦ She lists many of the words that are used as names in couplets on a chart called Nouns We Have Used.

♦ She lists many of the words in the first lines that are words of action on a chart called Action Words. Students add rhyming words to these to generate new couplets.

♦ She values couplets by collecting and binding them into books of couplets.

Cinquain

The pattern of the cinquain (sin cane) is five lines, nonrhyming.

Line 1:   one word, the name of something
           two syllables

Line 2:   two words that describe line 1
           four syllables

Line 3:   three words, an action for line 1
           six syllables

Myra Crump conferences with a young poetry writer.

Courtesy of Michael Sampson

Line 4: four words, a feeling about line 1
eight syllables

Line 5: a synonym or a word referring back to line 1
two syllables

The first cinquains were written by Adelaide Crapsey (1914). This American form has been widely used in schools because of its simplicity. The original form had syllabic control and no requirement for particular parts of speech. However, the following structured form is usually used with younger authors:

Line 1: one word, a title

Line 2: two words, description of the title

Line 3: three words, an action

Line 4: four words, a feeling

Line 5: one word, reference to line 1

Only eleven words are required to express the thought with a cinquain. Children who use it know when they have achieved their goal. Kindergarten children can dictate cinquains as group compositions, or individuals can dictate their own. Sixth-grade students enjoy writing them in the modified form as well as with the syllabic requirement.

Cinquain enables students to create beautiful and poetic language. Here are two examples of cinquains:

Rabbit
Furry, quiet
Wiggling, listening, hopping
Cute and cuddly friend
Pet
LISA

Football
Rough, rugged
Catching, crunching, collapsing
Fans are joyfully shouting
Fall
CINDI

Cinquain writing maximizes the use of nouns, verbs, and adjectives. It minimizes the use of words of structure. Children can compose them in group situations or on an individual basis before they have mastered English syntax. They are especially useful for children learning English as a second language because they can be used early and can be beautiful expressions of self.

Terquain

The terquain is a simplified form of cinquain that was developed for recording artful language of young children who possess very little English. However, the form is excellent for all types of students. The pattern consists of three lines, four or five words, nonrhyming:

Line 1: one word, the subject

Line 2: two or three words, description of the subject

Line 3: one word, a feeling about or a synonym for the subject

Here are two examples of terquain:

Children
Running, jumping
Playmates
JENNY

Snow
Falling and drifting
Winter
PAUL

Diamante (Diamond Poetry)

The pattern for a diamante is seven lines, nonrhyming:

Line 1: one word, a noun

Line 2: two words, adjectives

Line 3: three words, participles

Line 4: four words, nouns

Line 5: three words, participles

Line 6: two words, adjectives

Line 7: one word, a noun

Lines 1 and 7 are opposites or contrasts. Lines 2 and 3 and half of line 4 describe the noun of line 1. Lines 5 and 6 and the other half of line 4 describe line 7. A diamante challenges the writer to shift the description of one thing to its opposite within a pattern. It brings into play synonyms and antonyms and extends them with descriptive words. Line 4 is a transition line, and frequently the two middle nouns refer to both lines 1 and 7. Some examples of diamantes follow. Note that the line lengths convert the shape of the poem into a diamond.

Elephant

huge, gray

trumpeting, stomping, rearing

giant performer / midget rodent

scurrying, scampering, squeaking

small, furry

Mouse

BRYANT

Day

Bright, warm

Playing, working, swimming

Sun, clouds, stars, clear

Resting, sleeping, snoring

Dark, cool

Night

SHEILA

Teacher-to-Teacher

Shan Palmer, a resource teacher in Green Valley, Arizona, frequently uses terquains to record the language of her students. Shan introduces the form by composing terquains with the children as they make suggestions. They notice that everything around them has a name and can be described with language. They quickly move to composing their own terquains independently. Shan collects the poetry and uses it for bulletin board displays and classroom reading material. Because the focus of terquain writing is on nouns and descriptive language, Shan notices the language level of her students increases rapidly.

George Gallegos frequently uses diamantes with his fifth-grade students. He leads them to talk about antonyms and how they form the key meaning of a diamante. He lists words of opposite meaning that students can use when they write diamantes.

The students learn that participles describe nouns and function as adjectives. They discover that the root words of participles are usually found in verb slots in sentences and that participles have *-ing* endings.

George guides his students as they edit diamantes, using alliteration in some of the lines and progressing from fewer syllables to more syllables in lines 2, 3, 5, and 6. The class uses diamantes for choral reading. They enjoy reading half of the diamante in happy voices and the other half in sad voices when the subject is work/play or summer/winter.

George recognizes that diamantes are excellent as the basis for expansion to paragraphs. The students often expand diamantes in this manner and remark that the key difference between a diamante and a good paragraph is that words of "empty" meaning or structure are needed in sentences, but not in diamantes.

Renga

Renga is a chain of poems written by multiple authors. The first author writes with a pattern that the other authors are to follow. The first poem provides the topic. Some possibilities follow:

- Haiku linked to haiku extended to tanka (tanka for two)
- Tanka linked to sijo
- Couplets linked to couplets

Here are some examples of haiku linked to haiku:

Bare branches outline	*Snow begins to fall*	*Blankets of snow melt*
Against a flaming sunset	*Like a blanket of winter*	*As winter turns to springtime*
Winter's calm goodnight.	*Lasting until spring.*	*Year after year after year.*
CHRISTI	**ELLIE**	**ELLIOT**

Here are two examples of couplet linked to couplet:

Owls who,	*Rabbits run,*
In the zoo.	*In the sun.*
SHANE	**AMBER**

Limerick

The limerick pattern is five lines, thirty-four to thirty-nine syllables, rhyming:

Line 1: eight or nine syllables, Rhyme A

Line 2: eight or nine syllables, Rhyme A

Line 3: five or six syllables, Rhyme B

Line 4: five or six syllables, Rhyme B

Line 5: eight or nine syllables, Rhyme A

Usually a limerick follows the syllable pattern of 8-8-5-5-8 or 9-9-6-6-9, but other combinations can be used. These fit a pattern of three-beat and two-beat lines. The rhyming scheme requires three words that rhyme and two words that rhyme. It is a triplet split by a couplet. Because limericks are written for fun and nonsense, rhyming words can be created. Some limericks follow.

There once was a farmer from Maine	*There once was a puppy named Prince,*
Whose cow was in terrible pain.	*Who guarded his owner's back fence.*
He went to the vet	*He barked at the man*
To care for his pet.	*Who picked up the can*
But then he got caught in the rain.	*Stealing garbage just didn't make sense!*
CAROL	**MIKE**

Writing limericks can create an interest in reading nonsense verse like that written by Edward Lear and Dr. Seuss. Students who write limericks will benefit from lists of rhyming words, which may be kept in the Writing/Publishing Center.

Shape Patterns

Writing patterns designed around shapes have been developed by Iris M. Tiedt (1983). Among those that bring new style and a dependable form to children's writing are the triangle triplet and the quadrangle.

Triangle Triplet

The triangle triplet pattern is three lines, rhyming. The three lines can be read by beginning at any point of the triangle. The challenge is to say three things on one topic that can be read in any order with essentially the same meaning.

Quadrangle

The pattern of a quadrangle is four lines, a quatrain. Rhyming schemes can have any of the following forms:

AAAA

ABAB

ABBA

ABAC

AABB

ABCA

The lines are arranged around a quadrangle. They can be read beginning at any corner. The meaning remains essentially the same regardless of where the

Michael Naizer — Name

9 years old — Age

Playing computer games, Watching TV, and Drawing — Interests

What do you like most about school?

What I like most about school is being able to read a lot and talking to my friends.

What's your favorite subject? Why?

My favorite subject is Science, because there are many different kinds of science and I like reading because it's like watching an invisable movie.

What's your favorite book? Why do you like it?

My favorite book is Mrs. Frisby and the Rats of NIMH because it was exciting and it had parts were everything sounded bad but it was good at the end.

What advice do you have for teachers?

Make up fun sayings about how to do something and tell them to your kids to help them remember things.

reading begins. The form requires a great deal of editing unless the author is lucky. This is a useful form for group writing as well as for individual authorship. An example follows:

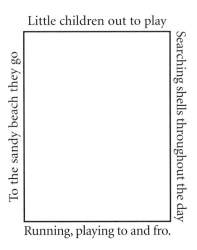

Little children out to play

To the sandy beach they go

Searching shells throughout the day

Running, playing to and fro.

FURTHER WORDS

 From InfoTrac College Edition

Children's Books as Models to Teach Writing Skills, Susan Anderson McElveen and Connie Campbell Dierking, *The Reading Teacher* December 2000 v54 i4 p362

Poetry, Diane Miness, *The Reading Teacher* April 2001 v54 i7 p718

Be a Better Writing Teacher (cover story), Donald H. Graves, *Instructor (1990)* November–December 1994 v104 n4 p43(3)

The Power of Dialogue, Sol Stein, *The Writer* February 2000 v113 i2 p16

From Professional Journals and Publications

Durham, J. (1997). On Time and Poetry. *The Reading Teacher, 51*, 76–79.

Larocque, P. (2001). Show, Don't Tell. *The Quill, 89*(3), 50.

Perfect, K. A. (1999). Rhyme and Reason: Poetry for the Heart and Head. *The Reading Teacher, 52*, 728–737.

Routman, R. (2001). Everyone Succeeds with Poetry Writing. *Instructor, 111*(1), 26.

Strickland, D., Bodino, A., Buchan, K., Jones, K. M., Nelson, A., and Rosen, M. (2001). Teaching Writing in a Time of Reform. *The Elementary School Journal, 101*(4), 385.

Vacca, R., and Linek, W. M. (1992). Writing to Learn. In J. W. Irwin and M. A. Doyle (Eds.), *Reading/Writing Connections: Learning from Research* (pp. 145–159). Newark, DE: International Reading Association.

Summary

Students' writing abilities are extended when they have opportunities to express themselves in one of the genres discussed in this chapter. Students and teachers alike will be amazed at the beauty of the expression that comes forth when one writes in patterned format and verse.

Total Literacy Anchors

- ◆ The student elaborates basic sentences with descriptive words and phrases to denote:

Color	Sound
Size	Smell
Shape	Taste
Texture	Touch

- ◆ The student collects words and phrases from authors that may become a part of personal speech and writing.

- ◆ The student expresses his or her own thinking in predictable story and poetry genres.

- ◆ The student is influenced by predictable language stories and becomes more self-expressive as an author.

- ◆ The student is the author of books that are shared with a wide range of readers.

CHAPTER 10

Organizing AND Managing THE Writing Classroom

As You Read . . .

- What is involved in orchestrating a writing program?

- How can teachers build a psychological environment for young student authors that encourages children to be risk takers?

- What is the value of conferencing with young authors?

- How does the physical environment affect students' writing?

Whhen an orchestra plays together, the music it creates collectively is much more beautiful than what any single musician makes. But there is one person who doesn't play at all. That person is the conductor. However, the conductor performs a very important role: She or he inspires the musicians to their ultimate level of performance.

And so it is with the writing classroom. The teacher serves as the conductor, inspiring children to new heights in writing. But unlike the orchestra conductor, the teacher-conductor gets to participate. Writing classrooms feature children and teachers writing together. In this chapter, we examine the roles of children and teachers in the orchestra of the writing classroom. We'll see classrooms where writers write and teachers and students learn together.

The last two chapters were about the writing process. Chapter 8 examined the theoretical base, provided a brief description of the writing process (prewriting, drafting, revising, editing, publishing/celebration), and described the essays, stories, journals, books, and poems that can be produced when students are given the freedom to write creatively. Chapter 9 revealed the influence of genres or patterns on students' literacy development. In this chapter, we describe how teachers can build environments where such writing can take place. We discuss multiple ways to implement the stages of the writing process through practices such as brainstorming, teacher conferencing, collaborative student committees, and the orchestration that takes place between students and teachers in language-based writing classrooms.

The Writing Classroom

In the total literacy classroom, students have freedom to experiment with language. In fact, experimentation is essential if students are to reach their potential as language users and authors. Every oral exchange, every writing effort is an experiment in which students learn something about the effectiveness of that particular communication. In many classrooms, learning to be a successful language user is a trying situation and is very risky to students' self-esteem. Moreover, when the cost of making mistakes becomes too great, students stop taking risks and lose opportunities for growth. The opposite is true in total literacy classrooms: Experimentation is the vehicle that carries students toward literacy. Students must feel free to try; otherwise, there is nothing to refine, guide, or develop. Budding authors need teachers who are open to children's efforts, accepting invented or exploratory spelling and early attempts at punctuation and sentence structure. Students must be able to experiment with what they want to say and how they want to say it. Creative efforts like the one shown in Figure 10.1 may enter the classroom on scraps of paper, sometimes with supporting illustrations.

Students sometimes develop generalizations about sound–symbol relations that, when applied, result in misspellings. Bobby furnishes an example in Figure 10.2. To tell Bobby, age 7, that he misspelled the words *no* (know), *iny* (any), *thay* (they), *led's* (lettuce), *carits* (carrots), and *hi* (high) is in effect telling him that correct spelling is more important than content. At this stage, acceptance and encouragement are high priorities. Writers must produce manuscripts before they can refine them.

Some writing is difficult to interpret. Spelling often gives minimum clues, but with the author present to do the reading, comprehension is possible. Salvador gave a good example when he wrote, “dess June he is sic picos du munsr mk hm

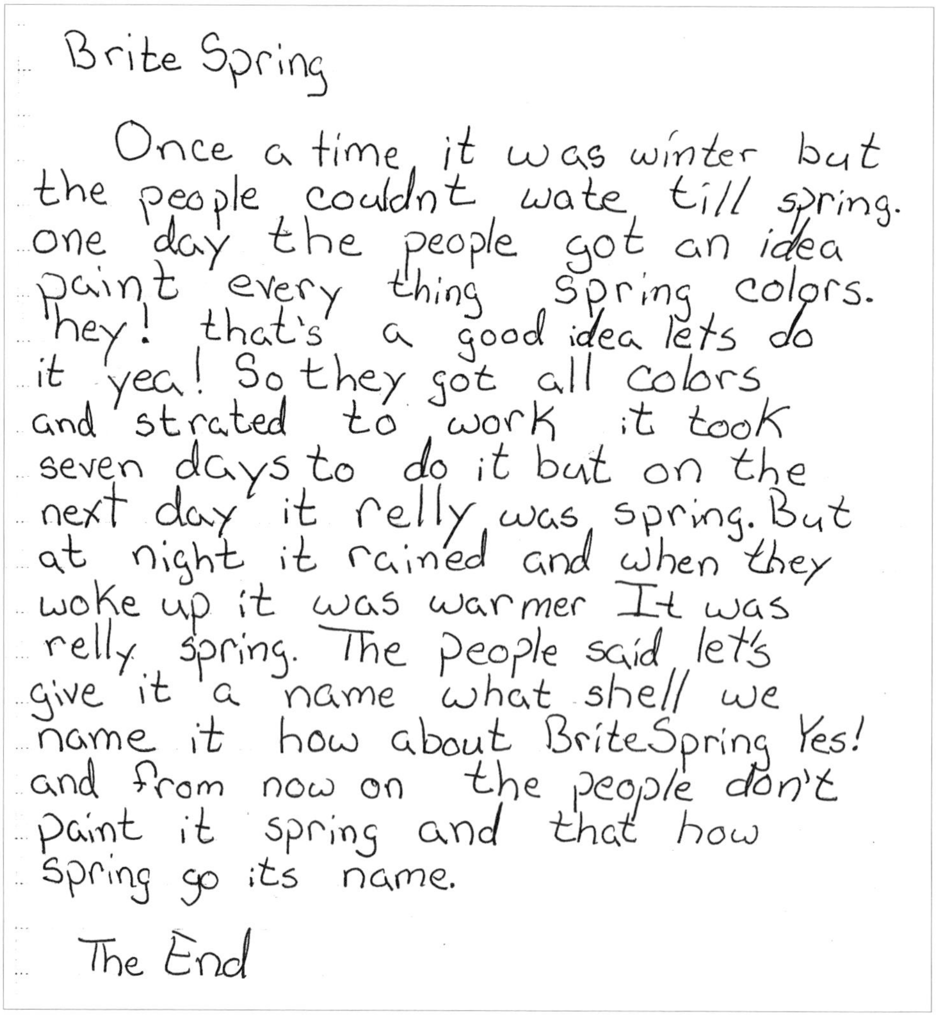

Brite Spring

Once a time, it was winter but the people couldnt wate till spring. one day the people got an idea paint every thing spring colors. hey! that's a good idea lets do it yea! So they got all colors and strated to work it took seven days to do it but on the next day it relly was spring. But at night it rained and when they woke up it was warmer It was relly spring. The people said let's give it a name what shell we name it how about BriteSpring Yes! and from now on the people don't paint it spring and that how Spring go its name.

The End

FIGURE 10.1
Painting spring

sic." When he read the story, the sound–symbol relation became clear. He read, *"This is Johnny. He is sick because the monster makes him sick."*

A group of children wrote and illustrated stories following a seal show. During prewriting, they created the word cluster shown in Figure 10.3.

In addition to the 14 words the children suggested following the show, a list of about 100 words of highest frequency was visible from any place in the classroom. Abel wrote, "I sw a seal played wriz a ball and he make tricks." He read, *"I saw a seal play with a ball and he makes tricks."*

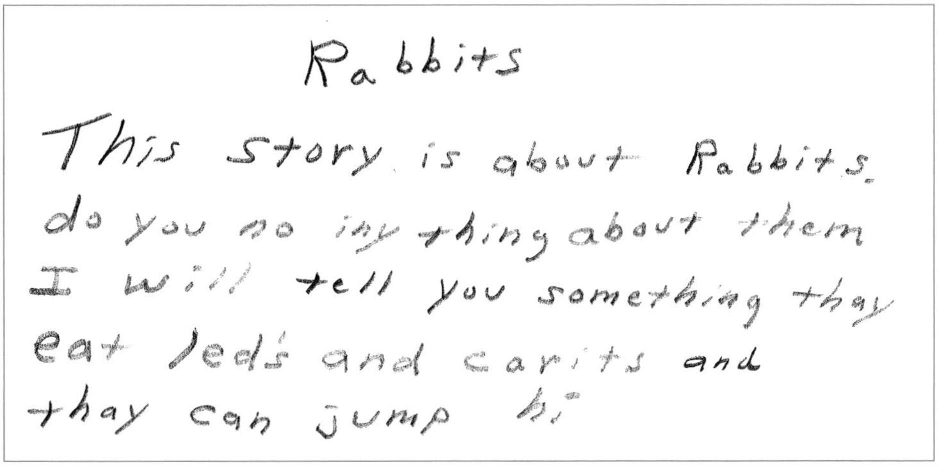

Rabbits

This story is about Rabbits.
do you no iny thing about them
I will tell you something thay
eat leds and carits and
thay can jump hi

FIGURE 10.2
Bobby's story about rabbits

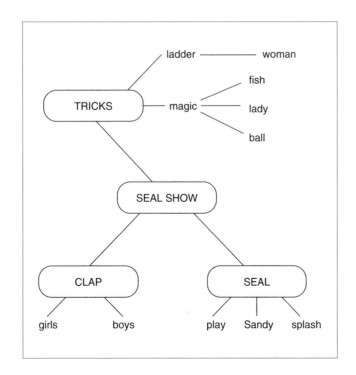

FIGURE 10.3
The seal show story word cluster

Harold wrote, "The seal was duen some trics. And the lade sent ot got a nedr seal. And the seal did not no trecs. And the lade hed some segy from the seal. Adn the seal clap hes hons. the seal got up on hes set the seal et fsh. the fehes wer ded."

Harold's story is easy to read with his invented spelling. The only word that might give an adult reader trouble is *segy* (sausage). He made minimum use of the resources provided for spelling. At this point, he was personally involved to the extent that his own resources seemed adequate—and they were.

Isabel wrote, "The seal had a ball on his nos. They he went up the ladder and down the ladder. The seal aet fish and all the doys and girls wour claping." Isabel used the resources but still had a problem copying from one place to another.

From this writing lesson in a class of bilingual children, the teacher has achieved a great deal. Consider these accomplishments:

- Most students felt comfortable writing independently.
- A common experience, the seal show, provided a base for building a speaking, writing, and reading vocabulary.
- Every child could read his or her own writing.
- Children who volunteered their stories had them edited and published in a booklet with their own illustrations.
- Children used writing resources that were developed in the classroom to free themselves for independent writing.

Interaction in the Writer's Workshop

Stephanie Noland tells of the time Bill Martin Jr visited her multiage classroom. After spending the day watching her and her students interact, he said, "Do you

First-graders collaborate at the Writing Center

Courtesy of Lisa Bartlett

Jarred Turner — Name

11 years — Age

playing very physical sports, and reading — Interests

What do you like most about school?

The thing I like most about school is the way we do things. We dont use text books so there is usually never a dull moment and we're always having fun.

What's your favorite subject? Why?

My favorite subject would have to be Math. I dont know why its my favorite I've just always liked it and I'm always happy when we have to do it. I'm also always willing to learn anything I can, anytime.

What's your favorite book? Why do you like it?

My favorite book would have to be Harry Potter and the Goblet of Fire. I like it because there are no boundries and it gets me thinking what if something like that could really happen.

What advice do you have for teachers?

My advice for teachers would have to be that when your teaching dont just give them some pages to do in class and if they dont finish to do it for home work. Make it fun, do them a favor by adding a little imagination.

know what makes you such a great writing teacher?" Stephanie waited for Bill to continue, anticipating he would mention her knowledge base, her commitment, or perhaps her sensitivity to children. Instead, he said, "Because you're so extraordinarily organized!"

Bill was right—Stephanie's classroom writing procedures are organized. Every child is familiar with the system the class uses, and every child is independent of her. They simply "get to work" on writing when they arrive in the morning, picking up where they left off the day before. They can do so because of the predictable nature of her Writer's Workshop procedures. In discussing their work with children in New York City, Lucy Calkins and Shelley Harwayne (1987) express the same concept. "In the writing workshop, both the schedule and the expectations are simple and predictable. Students can become strategic learners because they know when they will be writing, which supplies will be available, and what their writing time will be like" (p. 33).

What is Writer's Workshop? It means different things to different people, but in general, it's simply a time when writers work. Their work may include journal writing, brainstorming ideas during prewriting, writing initial drafts, collaborating with other authors, conferencing with student committees or the teacher, illustrating manuscripts, and celebrating authorship. There are many ways to organize Writer's Workshop; the Teacher-to-Teacher feature shows how one teacher does it.

Teacher-to-Teacher

Bob Nottingham believes writers write best when they have time—time to work, time to share, time to dream, and time to turn their dreams into manuscripts. Here's his Writer's Workshop schedule:

Time	Activity
10 minutes	Journals
20 minutes	Uninterrupted writing
20 minutes	Committees meet
	Conferencing
	Writing seminars or minilessons

10 minutes	Celebration of writing
	Author's Chair
	Whole group share

Bob believes two factors are of great importance in the writing classroom: Children must have time to write every day, and the writing his children do must be recognized. To that end, the classroom runs an "in-house" Publishing Center. His children work together in collaborative committees to receive, edit, and publish the writings of the children. You will read more about these collaborative committees later in the chapter.

Minilessons in the Writer's Workshop

Minilessons are short presentations on skills, strategies, and processes writers need and will use during their writing. They are generally presented just before the writing phase of Writer's Workshops. Most teachers who use minilessons effectively make them short, focus them on one topic at a time, present them as options skilled writers frequently use (not mandates from headquarters), and tailor them to specific needs of the writers in the class at that time.

Mary Ellen Giacobbe (1991) identifies four categories of minilessons:

1. *Procedures.* The operations and management of the writing process, such as a minilesson on how to select a story for publication and the steps you must take to prepare a piece to "go to press."

2. *Strategies.* These include techniques real writers use, such as how to gather and organize thoughts and ideas for writing in a writer's notebook, how to select a topic, or what to do when you have writer's block.

3. *Qualities of good writing.* These include practical topics, such as writing strong leads, eliminating clutter, focusing the piece, and so on.

4. *Skills.* These include English conventions such as capitalization and punctuation.

The Teacher-to-Teacher feature provides an example of one type of minilesson, writing strong leads.

Teacher-to-Teacher

Debby Johnson read *Absolutely Write!* (Thomason & York, 2002) while on a beach in Mexico during her spring break, and Chapter 6, "Crafting Engaging Leads," ruined her vacation! An idea for a minilesson on story leads for her fourth-graders came to her, and she could think of nothing else for the next two days. She racked her brain, trying to remember how her two favorite chapter books—*A Year Down Yonder* (Peck, 2001) and *Gathering Blue* (Lowry, 2000)—began. She went to every bookstore in Cancun, but alas, no English-language adolescent books were on the shelves. So she did what she had to do—she rebooked her flight and returned home early. And on Monday morning of the following week, she began the first of five minilessons on writing engaging leads.

She showed her students leads from their favorite chapter books, and the students discovered that there is no one right way to do a lead. But the students noticed that writers sometimes begin a piece in one of these three ways:

◆ **A problem** "One day grandfather wouldn't get out of bed. He just lay there and stared at the ceiling and looked sad" (John Reynolds Gardiner, *Stone Fox,* 1980, p.3).

➤ ➤ ➤

- **A description** "One dark and windy autumn night when the sun had long gone down" (Bill Martin Jr & John Archaumbault, *The Ghost-Eye Tree*, 1985, p. 3).

- **Dialogue** "Tom?" No answer. "Tom!" No answer. "What's gone with that boy, I wonder? You, Tom!" (Mark Twain, *The Adventures of Tom Sawyer*, 1987, p. 1).

Two months later, Debby Johnson's students had evolved as writers to the point that their leads usually grabbed the reader's attention. Ms. Johnson knew her work had paid off when she read the first few sentences of *Teacher Beware!* by Sarah, Nicole, and Lisa.

"She was a good teacher—too good, perhaps. She should never have gone down to the sandy, sun-splotched, Mexican beach that day. Or at least she should have left the book behind. The awful book that was to bring her torment and ruin her vacation . . ."

Tommy Thomason (2001) recommends that minilessons fit the writing needs of the students. Here are some of his ideas for possible minilessons:

- Establishing procedures for the Writer's Workshop
- Managing your time in Writer's Workshop
- Editing your work
- Establishing procedures for illustrating a book
- Working in peer editing groups
- Choosing a topic
- Using books as inspiration for topic choice
- Rereading for clarity and completeness
- Determining the focus of the writing
- Avoiding plagiarism
- Writing from another point of view
- Sequencing information by cutting and pasting
- Writing descriptions
- Writing conversation
- Adding information for clarity
- Eliminating excessive adjectives
- Writing effective titles
- Writing good leads
- Learning how to show, not tell
- Using capital letters

- Using a dictionary
- Using exclamation marks
- Using question marks
- Using possessives
- Choosing plurals versus possessives
- Using contractions
- Using nouns as antecedents for pronouns
- Writing a letter with proper form
- Using synonyms

Minilessons may be whole class or small group. Students who lack confidence in making decisions about their own writing and that of others have opportunities to listen and participate without being graded. Minilessons result in improved writing by the students and an increased ability to appreciate effective writing by other authors.

Conferencing

Young authors learn more about writing through the actual process of writing and collaborating with other authors than by any other method. However, conferencing remains a very efficient method of guiding authors and their writing. Conferences have been misused in the past because they were inflexible and teacher-centered with set schedules. Avoid using a plan such as this:

Teaching Strategies

Writing Conferences

> Choose topics and write first draft on Monday; Tuesday revise; Wednesday conference with teacher; final draft due on Thursday.

This does more to damage fluency than to build writing strengths. Some papers do not need revisions; other papers need multiple revisions. Or, as Donald Graves and Virginia Stuart (1985) say, "It is just as hard to apply one timetable to twenty-five papers as it is to fit one assignment to twenty-five hearts and minds" (p. 22). Thus conferences must be individual matters and should be handled differently according to the context of the situation.

Powerful demonstrations stem from conferences. What the teacher emphasizes during the conference will affect how students approach the writing act. In addition, teachers must be careful not to try to accomplish everything in one conference. Children will be overwhelmed if the teacher tries to address all the issues from punctuation to content in one setting. In some classrooms, teachers have overcome this problem by having different types of conferences, ranging from content conferences to editing conferences. Research has indicated that children learn best in classrooms where they have opportunities to talk with each other—not just to the

Teaching Poor, Culturally Diverse Urban Children

Sadly, a culture of poverty exists in America today. Teachers in inner cities often work with children who live in shelters or other poor living conditions. Many of these students do not speak English, or speak English as their second language. Lisa Delpit (1995) has developed the following principles for working with such poor, urban children.

♦ **Teach more—not less.** We often underestimate our students because a child is poor and experiencing the shock of poverty, or because a child does not speak English well. We react by simplifying our curriculum. Instead, we need to teach such children even more—using the total literacy techniques found throughout this book to deliver meaningful content in meaningful ways.

♦ **Focus on critical thinking.** We often react to children who are oppressed by poverty by viewing them as being less intelligent than other students and react by teaching less content and less complex ideas. But children of poverty are even more in need of critical thinking skills than are other students. Include opportunities for critical reasoning through the stories that children read and in their reactions to stories.

♦ **Develop basic skills and conventions.** It's true that children of poverty need more than basic skills, but they do need to master basic skills that are essential to success in American education. In a total literacy program, these conventions of language are mastered from whole to part as children move from expressing their ideas to communicating these ideas to others using standard spellings and grammar.

♦ **Overcome racism and class discrimination.** An unfortunate result of racism is that children come to believe they are less intelligent than other students and that they will never be able to reach their dreams. Such low expectations—from both student and teacher—become a self-fulfilling prophecy. What can the teacher do? Show children how smart they are by helping them succeed in literacy tasks. From that success, the teacher can praise the learner and focus attention on his or her accomplishments.

♦ **Build on strengths.** It's important for all children to experience success—but children of poverty need success even more than other students because they are often treated as if they are failures. Thus it is important that such children have an opportunity for success in school. Explore what each child is "good" at and allow him or her to experience success through that activity. As their self-esteem grows, children can move from one success to

teacher (Atwell, 1987, 1990, 1998; Calkins, 1994; Dyson, 1987). Such collaborative talk and learning take place in peer writing conferences. Bissex (1985) suggests that teachers model conferences by leading them to demonstrate the conference process. Once children have internalized the process, they can conduct their own conferences, freeing the teacher to circulate and listen and serve as a resource if needed.

We find it best to do conferencing on an informal basis, giving feedback to students as we move through the room and as their questions arise. The

another as teachers lead them from things they can already do to things they are learning to do.

♦ **Teach through examples and experiences from the child's world.** Total literacy teachers realize that children come to the classroom with diverse experiences. They study the cultures of their classroom and teach from their understanding of how children from various backgrounds view the world. They use that knowledge to integrate the background knowledge the students possess into the teaching/ learning process.

♦ **Make your classroom into a caring, "family" unit.** Make all the students feel special—make them feel valued by the teacher and by classmates. Publish a class newsletter that highlights the individuals in the class; celebrate children's birthdays, take dictation from the children that features good things about one another; give your class a nickname, such as Ms. Martin's Marvels (Delpit, 1995) to show the children that someone really cares for them.

♦ **Monitor your students to discover which instructional strategies will work best with them.** The teacher should be a "kid watcher." Don't make the mistake of labeling children of poverty as all being alike—they are not. Although they do have some common needs, their learning styles vary tremendously. Discontinue inappropriate instruction and deliver individual instruction that meets the specific needs of the individual learner.

♦ **Value and honor the child's culture.** Support the child's home culture and values of the children you teach, and help them to maintain their cultural identities. Search for children's literature that represents every cultural group in your classroom, and place these books in your classroom library. Celebrate the holidays from the various cultures in your classroom. Respect the home-rooted language and dialects of your students.

♦ **Focus on service to others.** Delpit encourages classroom teachers to convey to students that they owe a debt to their communities. Invite guests who have gone on to be productive community leaders to share with your students. From professional athletes to elected officials to volunteers, these leaders share through example that going to school and succeeding in school is one step toward having an impact in our communities and making the quality of life better for everyone.

important thing is that the first focus must be on content, with organization and conventions coming at a later time.

What Do I Ask during Writing Conferences?

Thomason (1997) cautions that "every conference is different," and the types of questions writing coaches might ask during conferences depend on the stage of the process the student is currently working through. To get a feel for the types of questions you might want to ask, let's look at Thomason's suggestions for questions you might ask at two different stages of the writing process:

AT THE PREWRITING STAGE

1. What do you think you'll write about?
2. Why did you choose that?
3. Where will you start? What will your lead be about?

AT THE FIRST DRAFT STAGE

1. Do you have more than one story here?
2. Underline the part that tells what this draft is about.
3. What is the most important thing you're trying to say here?
4. Explain how your title fits your draft.
5. Can you tell me more about this?
6. This part isn't clear to me. Can you tell me what you mean?
7. Can you describe this for me?
8. What's next?
9. Are you happy with your lead/ending?
10. How does your lead grab your reader's attention?
11. Can you be more specific here?
12. Is this the best word here?
13. Can you think of a different way to say this?
14. What do you think you can do to make this draft better?
15. What works so well you'd like to try to develop it further?
16. What did you learn from this piece of writing?
17. Can you think of something you tried in this draft that you've never tried before?
18. How can I help you with this piece?

Notice that the questions guide the writer to reflect on the writing and take ownership in making decisions concerning the manuscript. That is crucial to successful teacher/writer conferences and probably one of the most difficult aspects. As teachers, we are often tempted to specifically state what we think should be done to the piece. This shifts the focus to the improvement of a particular piece of writing rather than the writer learning to make decisions about revision that will contribute to the individual's growth as a writer. Lucy Calkins (1994) addressed this dilemma by noting, "If we can keep only one thing in mind—and I fail at this half the time—it is that we are teaching the writer and not the writing. Our decision must be guided by 'what might help this *writer*' rather than 'what might help this *writing*.' If the piece of writing gets better but the writer has learned nothing that will help him or her another day on another piece, then the conference was a waste of everyone's time. It may even have done more harm than good, for such conferences teach students not to trust their own reactions" (p. 228).

What Do I Ask during Preparation for Publication?

At this point, writer's conferences usually deal largely with form and mechanics. Ask what things need to be checked to get a piece ready for publication. You might ask the child to go back through the piece and circle all the words he or she thinks might be spelled incorrectly, box areas with punctuation and capitalization problems, and so on. You can use publication conferences to show the child progress made in spelling or show various rules the writer needs to know. After the writer has edited, you might have the piece passed on to an editing committee or to other writers who might specialize in spelling or capitalization, for example.

Teacher-to-Teacher

Authors at Ben Franklin Elementary School who want to be published move through a four-part process:(1) romancing the idea, (2) initial draft, (3) revision, and (4) editing. *Romancing the Idea* involves brainstorming and playing with the language that might be a part of the story. In the *Initial Draft*, students record the images and ideas that flow from their imaginations without concern for proper mechanics and spelling. Conferencing comes in the third step, *Revision*. The writer shares the story with the teacher or others in the class. The primary purpose of this sharing is to determine if the audience understands the story and its message. In the last phase, *Editing*, the classroom teacher assumes the role of editor-in-chief and conferences with the author, checking for both content and convention. Collaborative decision making takes place between author and teacher. After its completion, the work may be considered for publication by Beat Street Station, the school's parent-run publishing house.

It is crucial that children have avenues available to publish their art and writing in ways that value and honor their work. When you have children who are ready to engage in revision of their manuscripts, it is important to remember that there are many ways to implement the process (Chihak, 1999). It may be effective for children to collaborate with revision/editing partners. The Teacher-to-Teacher feature demonstrates how one teacher implemented peer revision/editing in her classroom. This process—or an adaptation of it—may be useful in your classroom.

Caroline Ashley believes peer editing is an integral component of the writing process. She conducts a minilesson, asking students to brainstorm what helps us read and understand the writing of other authors. She takes dictation on a large chart as her students contribute their ideas. When they have finished responding, she gives them a piece of paper and asks them to vote for the item they considered most important in helping read the work of other authors. After the votes were tabulated, the "top four" were "It makes sense/It causes a picture to play in our mind" "We know where the sentences start" "We can tell where sentences end" and "The words are spelled right." She explained that all of the brainstormed items were important, but they were going to focus on the top four today and revise their sentences into a checklist that they could use for revision and editing. During class discussion, the following revision/editing checklist was collaboratively designed. She then made copies for the students.

Name _____

Revision/Editing Partner _____

Manuscript Title _____

Date _____

1. _____ Does this make sense
   (my initials) to me? (if yes, initial)

2. _____ _____ Does this make sense
   (my initials) (partner's initials) to my revision/editing
   partner? (if yes, initial)

3. _____ _____ Do all sentences begin
   (my initials) (partner's initials) with a capital letter?
   (if yes, initial)

4. _____ _____ Do all sentences end
   (my initials) (partner's initials) with something (. or ?
   or !)? (if yes, initial)

5. _____ _____ Have I circled all the
   (my initials) (partner's initials) words I need help
   spelling or I am not sure
   about? (if yes, initial)

The class agreed on the following process when someone was ready to revise a manuscript.

First, the author must read the manuscript and determine if it "makes sense." If so, the author should put initials on the line by number 1.

Second, the author collaborates with a revision/editing partner by reading it to the partner. (It is the teacher's decision whether editing/revision partners are self-selected or teacher-selected. This may shift as determined by the needs and developmental level of the students. In addition, it is important that the author read the manuscript to the revision/editing partner. This keeps the focus at this point on the meaning of the manuscript rather than the mechanics.) When the revision/editing partner agrees that the manuscript "makes sense," the author and revision/editing partner both initial on the appropriate lines by number 2.

When the author and revision/editing partner have both agreed that the manuscript "makes sense," they move to numbers 3, 4, and 5. During this time, they should use resources in the classroom to aid with mechanics. One of the resources they have

Collaborative Committees

Students learn best when they are involved as editors and participants in the classroom publishing process. Collaborative committees are one avenue to this involvement. As students serve on committees, they internalize the fine points

is an "editing notebook." Each page contains one letter, a list of high-frequency words beginning with that letter, and lines to add words they "need help" spelling. Here are examples of the pages for "Aa" and "Bb."

A a	B b
a	baby
about	back
after	ball
again	be
all	beautiful
along	because
also	been
always	before
am	big
an	black
animal	book
are	both
another	box
around	bring
as	brown
ask	but
asked	by
at	————
ate	————
August	————
away	————
————	
————	
————	

Caroline asked the students to alert her by a prearranged signal if the author and revision/editing partner had circled a word and could not find it in the classroom resources. As she moved around the room, she would stop briefly by the pair, they would show her the word, she then wrote the correct spelling of the word on a sticky note, gave it to them, and moved on. The team was then responsible for editing the manuscript—and adding the word to their editing notebooks on the appropriate page. Caroline found this to be an efficient way of rapidly meeting the needs of many students while engaging them in the responsibility for revision and editing.

As the students became proficient in revision/editing using the checklist they had devised, they periodically revisited it during minilessons and added additional components. Caroline then made copies of the revised form, and students used it during the revision/editing process.

During this process, Caroline found that her students explored many different components of effective writing. The use of adjectives, interesting ways to begin stories, making sure the title "fits" with the story, and using different words (synonyms) throughout the piece so it "doesn't get boring" were just a few of the items discussed during minilessons. Each time she asked the class to "vote" on what they considered most important, and they added one thing to the list. She found that the process of developing the checklist was a valuable learning experience. In addition, because the students had invested time and thought in the checklist, it was a valuable support for peer editing/revision.

of writing and develop an appreciation for the way other authors express themselves in beautiful language. Some committees on which students can serve include editorial, illustrating, and binding.

The Editorial Committee

One way for a student to experience the learning involved with revision of text is to be part of an editorial committee. The editorial committee accepts original manuscripts and reads them to identify mechanical and technical errors and to make suggestions for improving style and form. Some committees divide responsibility by assigning each member a specialty such as story sense, spelling, capitalization, punctuation, sentence sense, or paragraphing. Each specialist reads the manuscript and notes suggestions. Then the committee calls a conference with the author to review the suggestions. The author accepts or rejects the suggestions in terms of the purpose of the manuscript. In some cases the author then takes the manuscript to the editor–in-chief, who is usually the teacher. After review by the editor-in-chief, necessary revisions are made. Rewriting is often desirable before preparing a manuscript for duplication.

Editing newspapers and magazines may involve other procedures. Contributors may place their rough drafts in designated places for editors to review. There may be editors for stories, reports, comics, sports, fashions, entertainment, editorials, interviews, puzzles, and any other sections included in the publication. In addition to attending to technical errors, editors have to plan the use of assigned space and recommend alterations to fit the spaces.

Reading rough drafts may be used as an editing technique for contributions to a class book. Groups of five or six can read each other's manuscripts, marking anything that needs to be changed. When a manuscript is returned to the author, it will have been reviewed by every editor and will be ready to be rewritten in a refined version.

The teacher should not serve as the *grader* of papers, mandating suggestions for corrections to be made when a manuscript is copied. Rather, the teacher serves as an editor working *with the author;* the author then makes the final decision or choice concerning revisions. Choices of topic, revisions, and illustrations lead to a sense of student accomplishment and pride (Hubbard, 1985).

The Illustrating Committee

Authors may do their own illustrations, or they may seek help from members of the illustrating committee in the Publishing Center. Children on the committee can offer suggestions for illustrations and read paged manuscripts to make certain the text suggests an illustration at the point that space is provided for it.

Some members of each illustrating committee should understand the following points:

1. Nouns can be illustrated more easily than any other class of words. Because nouns carry the heaviest load of meaning in passages, good illustrations aid in

Courtesy of Lisa Bartlett

A committee at work.

word recognition and prediction of words and phrases. For easy reading materials, all nouns not on lists of words of highest frequency should be illustrated.

2. Color, size, and shape words can be illustrated. Illustrations can reduce the difficulty of the story and can add to an author's meaning.

3. Texture words can be illustrated with collage materials and with brush strokes. The tactile experience available from collage illustrations extends vocabularies whether the words are printed or not.

4. Taste and smell words can only be implied in most illustrations. (Some "scratch and smell" books are available commercially.)

5. Leaves, dried flowers, feathers, and other thin materials pressed between waxed paper with a warm iron make attractive illustrations.

6. Abstract designs such as string paintings, sponge prints, and thumbprints are sometimes as effective as realistic representations.

7. Crayon rubbings on topics of interest such as Christmas can make "instant illustrations."

8. Computer art is an option for authors who wish to "do" their art via computer applications. Programs such as Kid Pix or Illustrator may also be used. Likewise, photos made with a digital camera are easily incorporated into the manuscript.

Some children like to take their manuscripts home for others to illustrate. The family team is a good unit for working on a publication.

In many classrooms, book-length publications are produced for every member. Spaces for illustrations are left blank during duplicating and binding. Each student does his or her own illustrations after receiving the book. Copies for the library are prepared by the illustrating committee.

The Bindery Committee

Many students volunteer for the bindery committee. They enjoy the process of assembling, sewing, stapling, cutting cardboard and cloth to size, gluing, and pressing. Most publishing areas have models of different bindings with step-by-step procedures to accompany them. An example of how to produce a bound book is detailed in Figure 10.4.

Explanations of several types of bindings should be available. Simple flexible bindings are useful, but they do not last long in libraries. Volunteer parents are very useful in the bindery. They can furnish materials and assist in making covers. A supply of covers for standard-sized paper can be made in advance, and the author can choose the binding and attach the book.

A publication program does not need to wait until a Writing/Publishing Center has been established. Stapling a simple text to a painting for display on the chart rack or on a bulletin board is a simple way of recognizing student language productivity. Attractive bindings can be made of construction paper. Stories written on the chalkboard can be copied and placed in a folder and left unbound. Authors can read unbound and unedited stories to the class.

A Physical Environment for Authors

Some physical characteristics are helpful if productive efforts are to be attained with minimum help from a teacher or other adults. A well-supplied Writing/ Publishing Center enhances the efforts of young writers.

The Writing Center

The Writing Center is a part of the Writing/Publishing Center where students go to write. It can also be a place where materials are stored for students to check out and use in a variety of locations. The ideal Writing Center is developed cooperatively by students and teachers as they work together as authors. Some supplies and components can be planned and provided for before a class group is formed.

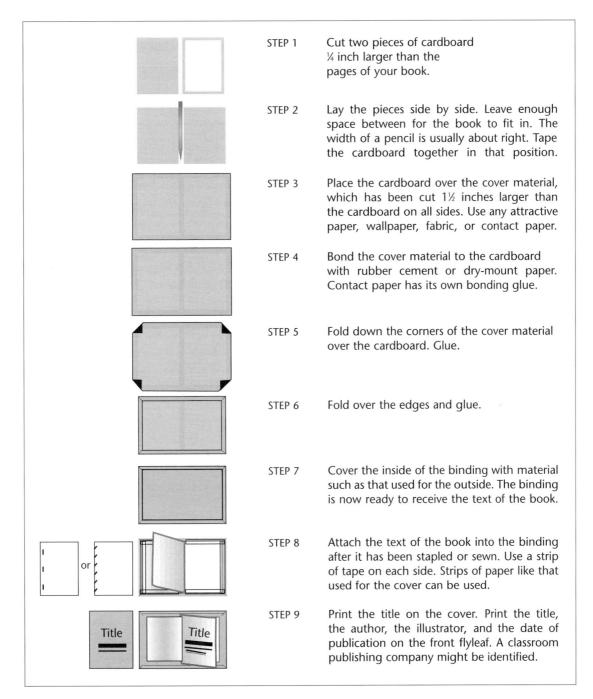

STEP 1 Cut two pieces of cardboard ¼ inch larger than the pages of your book.

STEP 2 Lay the pieces side by side. Leave enough space between for the book to fit in. The width of a pencil is usually about right. Tape the cardboard together in that position.

STEP 3 Place the cardboard over the cover material, which has been cut 1½ inches larger than the cardboard on all sides. Use any attractive paper, wallpaper, fabric, or contact paper.

STEP 4 Bond the cover material to the cardboard with rubber cement or dry-mount paper. Contact paper has its own bonding glue.

STEP 5 Fold down the corners of the cover material over the cardboard. Glue.

STEP 6 Fold over the edges and glue.

STEP 7 Cover the inside of the binding with material such as that used for the outside. The binding is now ready to receive the text of the book.

STEP 8 Attach the text of the book into the binding after it has been stapled or sewn. Use a strip of tape on each side. Strips of paper like that used for the cover can be used.

STEP 9 Print the title on the cover. Print the title, the author, the illustrator, and the date of publication on the front flyleaf. A classroom publishing company might be identified.

FIGURE 10.4
Step-by-step book binding

Paper should be available in a variety of qualities, sizes, and colors. Handwriting paper can be in supply for practice in handwriting skills, but it must not be a paper prescribed for authors to use. At all levels authors need a choice of paper suitable to what is being written. Large quantities of newsprint are handy for first drafts. The blank sides of printed sheets can be used for original manuscripts. Others supplement the school supply with end-of-roll newsprint from newspaper publishers and with printer's scrap from a print shop. Oversized paper for big books is a definite bonus.

Markers of many sizes and colors should be available. Different kinds and colors of pencils, felt-tipped pens in a variety of colors, and crayons of all sizes and colors are needed so authors can get the desired effect for their manuscripts.

Writing models that show several configurations of capital and lowercase letters can be useful when authors are ready to refine and edit manuscripts.

Spelling aids should be available in a variety of forms and in several places. Word lists such as these are useful resources for student writers:

- High-frequency and frequently misspelled words that develop as children analyze their own dictation and writing to discover the words all authors use (see Figure 10.5)
- Name words that accumulate for specific topics or that are used frequently by many students
- Descriptive words such as color, size, shape, texture, smell, taste, and touch
- Words of movement that are used as verbs in sentences
- Proper names useful for special seasons and projects

In addition to these lists, resources such as these are also needed by student authors:

- Picture dictionaries that might grow from children's own language
- School dictionaries that offer a major resource for more mature authors
- Computer spell check programs

Idea starters—a sentence or story line or idea—tend to stifle children's creativity and freedom of choice as writers and have been misused by some teachers (Calkins, 1983). However, a new form of literacy is emerging as high-stakes testing has become a reality over the past few years. Even in writing, tests are used to judge how good children are as writers and how effective writing programs are (Thomason & York, 2000). Unfortunately, these tests are usually essays that children write cued by idea starters.

In such tests, children are given no choice; they must write an essay based on a picture or sentence stimulus. Good writers can fail such a task if they are not familiar with the form of such tests. Therefore, school writing programs must

a	between	daddy	fellow	guess	is
about	big	dark	few		it
after	black	day	fifth	had	its
again	blue	dear	finally	hair	it's
all	body	did	find	half	
almost	book	didn't	fine	hand	jet
along	both	died	finished	happened	jump
alphabet	box	different	fire	happy	just
also	boy	do	first	hard	
always	bring	does	fish	has	keep
am	brother	dog	five	hat	kept
an	brown	done	fly	have	killed
and	but	don't	foot	having	kind
animal	buy	door	for	he	knew
another	by	down	found	head	know
any		drama	four	heard	
are		draw	fourth	help	language
around	cafeteria	dress	friend	her	large
art	call	drink	from	here	last
as	came		front	high	late
ask	can	each	full	him	laugh
asked	can't	early	fun	his	learned
at	car	ears	funny	hit	leave
ate	cat	eat		hold	left
aunt	chair	egg	game	home	legs
away	children	eight	gave	hope	let
	Christmas	end	get	hot	letter
baby	city	enough	getting	house	light
back	class	even	girl	how	like
bad	clean	ever	give	hundred	lips
ball	close	every	giving	hurt	little
be	coat	everyone	glad		live
beautiful	cold	everything	go	I	living
became	come	eye	goes	ice	long
because	coming		good	if	look
bed	cook	fall	got	I'll	lots
been	could	far	grade	I'm	love
before	couldn't	farm	gravel	important	
began	country	fast	great	in	made
best	cow	father	green	interesting	make
better	cut	feet	grow	into	man

many	oh	rain	sometimes	time	went
may	old	ran	soon	to	were
me	on	read	spring	today	what
meet	once	reading	start	together	when
men	one	ready	stay	told	where
might	only	real	stop	tongue	which
milk	open	red	story	too	while
mine	or	rest	street	took	white
minutes	orange	ride	study	top	who
Miss	other	right	such	town	why
money	our	room	summer	tried	will
more	out	round	sun	trip	window
morning	outside	run	supper	try	winter
most	over		sure	turn	wish
mother	own	said	swim	two	with
mouth		same			without
Mr.	paint	saw	table	under	woman
Mrs.	painting	say	take	until	women
Ms.	paper	school	talk	up	won't
much	part	second	teacher	upon	wood
music	party	see	teeth	us	world
must	pass	seen	tell	use	would
my	past	send	ten	used	wouldn't
myself	pay	sent	than		write
	people	seven	thank	vacation	writing
name	person	shall	that	very	wrong
near	pet	she	the	visit	wrote
never	pick	should	their	vocabulary	
new	pig	show	them		yard
next	pink	sick	then	walk	year
nice	place	side	there	want	yellow
night	play	since	these	war	yes
no	please	sing	they	warm	yet
nobody	pretty	sister	thing	was	you
none	principal	sit	think	wash	young
north	pull	six	third	wasn't	your
not	purple	sixth	this	water	yours
now	put	sleep	those	way	
		small	thought	we	zipper
of	quick	so	three	weather	zoo
off	quiet	some	through	week	
often	quite	something	till	well	

FIGURE 10.5

Allen list of words for spelling and editing

CLASSROOM
LITERATURE
CONNECTIONS

Books that encourage writing.

Young Readers

Aunt Isabel Tells a Good One,
by Kate Duke.
Penelope's Aunt Isabel constructs a delightful story that
includes a discussion of story
structure.
New York: E. P. Dutton, 1992.

Aunt Isabel Makes Trouble,
by Kate Duke.
Aunt Isabel mouse continues
her story-within-a-story tradition by spinning a fanciful
naptime story while discussing
story elements.
New York: E. P. Dutton, 1996.

*Nothing Ever Happens on
90th Street,* **by Roni Schotter
and Krysten Brooker.**
Eva's homework assignment is
to write about what is around
her, and she is convinced that
nothing is happening until she
receives writing advice from
neighbors and begins to really
observe.
New York: Scholastic, 1999.

Older Readers

*Abraham Lincoln the Writer:
A Treasury of His Greatest
Speeches and Letters,*
by Harold Holzer.
A compilation of Lincoln's
writings from age 16 to a
speech he wrote a month before his death.
Honesdale, PA: Boyds Mills, 2000.

include activities that will enable students to succeed with this genre. Story starters may occasionally be used and serve as one aspect of the writing program. Here are some ways you might include them in your classroom:

- Children may "jot" down ideas for stories in their writer's notebook, saving them for future writing workshop sessions.
- Story beginnings can be copied on cards with just enough story to suggest characters, setting, and a hint of plot.
- Story middles, copied on cards, can be developed in both directions to tell stories.
- Story endings, copied on cards, can give a hint of what might have happened in entire stories.
- Story pictures can be filed for personal interpretation by authors.
- Examples and explanations for riddles and jokes can be used as models.
- Headlines from newspapers, mounted on cards, can be used as ideas for stories and poems.

In his excellent book *A Fresh Look at Writing,* Donald Graves (1994) discusses the issue of providing topics for writers. While still advocating that children need to have multiple opportunities to select their own topics in order to have "ownership" of their writing, he states, "Sometimes topic assignments are helpful and even necessary. Students do make bad choices and experience writer's block, or they need to shift to new topics after exhausting their usual few" (p. 108). He provides another keen insight for teachers by stating, "You may even find it useful to ask students to assign you a topic in order to show them how you work on assignments" (p. 108).

Vocabulary enrichment resources must grow as the Writing Center is used or there will be little improvement in the quality of writing. Lists, files, and posters can be started for enrichment resources. Here are some possibilities:

- Figurative language files with examples of similes, metaphors, and personification as used by other authors
- Lists of synonyms and antonyms, especially examples of words of two, three, and four syllables that are useful in writing poetry with controlled syllabic patterns
- Alliteration aids such as a list of words beginning with the same sound
- Rhyming aids that include lists of two, three, and four words that rhyme
- How to say "said" in many ways as an aid to writing conversation that emphasizes characterization
- Nonsense words that can be used or can serve as examples for making up new words for nonsense writing

Students should be encouraged to contribute to the resources in the Writing Center. It is their source of help and inspiration, and they must understand what is there and how to use these resources.

As students mature as authors, each one should develop a personal writing handbook that contains many of the helps just listed for the Writing Center but features aids each author uses frequently. The main value of the writing handbook is that it serves as a place where students can jot down ideas for stories, leads for stories, or other ideas.

The Publishing Center

The Publishing Center, a part of the Writing/Publishing Center, is a place in a classroom or school where students process their original manuscripts through editing, illustrating, paging, copying, and binding into forms for others to use. It may be an integral part of the Writing Center, or it may be at a separate location. Some schools with many authors maintain a Publishing Center for the whole school and invite parents to assist in the operation by supplying materials, typing, and helping with the binding process. In these schools, simple binding is done in the classrooms, and only manuscripts that are selected for production in multiple copies go to the school Publishing Center.

At Ben Franklin Elementary School, the students have established Beat Street Station, an area in the school's foyer that features the very finest of "Be Authors Today," their school's publishing house. This is a place for browsing, reading, and sharing. The process of selecting manuscripts to be published in multiple copies should be well understood by students. A committee might develop criteria and publish them. It should emphasize that everything that is written does not need to be published in multiple copies. Single original copies are enough for most of what is written.

Publishing is the peak experience in a total literacy classroom. It truly integrates writing, reading, speaking, and listening. It brings into focus the mechanics of language. It draws on influences from many authors and publishers. It uses graphics as an essential ingredient in the language arts. It can be extended and interpreted through dramatization and choral reading. A total literacy classroom is impossible to maintain without publishing individual books, class books, individual story charts, newspapers, magazines, catalogs, and recipes. For these publications, these supplies and aids, which may not be typical of other communication and writing programs, are required:

- Scraps of cloth, cardboard, wallpaper, braid, yarn, and leather for covers and illustrations
- Contact paper to use in bindings of hard-cover books

The Great Green Notebook of Katie Roberts—Who Just Turned 12 on Monday, **by Amy Hest.**
Readers learn about Katie through her notebook, sketches, and letters.
Boston: Candlewick, 1998.

All Ages

From Pictures to Words: A Book about Making a Book, **by Janet Stevens.**
Janet Stevens discusses the creative and practical processes of writing/making a book.
New York: Holiday House, 1995.

Author: A True Story, **by Helen Lester.**
Helen Lester shares the joys and struggles of her journey as an author from age 3 until the present in a lighthearted yet reassuring way.
New York: Houghton Mifflin, 1997.

If You Were a Writer, **by Joan Lowery Nixon.**
Melia's mother is a writer—so Melia wants to write. Her mother shares information and soon Melia finds she is writing!
New York: Simon & Schuster, 1995.

What Do Authors Do? **by Eileen Christelow.**
Cartoon panels share the creative process of two writers who have viewed the same event but one is writing a picture book and the other a chapter book.
New York: Clarion, 1995.

What Do Illustrators Do? **by Eileen Christelow.**
Two illustrators are portrayed in cartoon panels as each illustrates *Jack and the Beanstalk* from their individual perspective.
New York: Houghton Mifflin, 1999.

*The Young Journalist's Book:
How to Write and Produce
Your Own Newspaper,*
by Nancy Bentley and
Donna Guthrie.
Step-by-step information con-
cerning what a journalist does
and how to publish your own
newspaper.
Brookfield, CT: Millbrook, 2000.

How a Book Is Made, by Aliki.
Aliki, the author and illustrator of more than fifty books,
shares a clear description of
the authorship process from
the genesis of an idea to the
finished book.
New York: HarperCollins, 1991.

- Sewing equipment that includes a sewing machine, hand-sewing needles, an awl, and thread
- A laminating machine or iron to use with laminating paper
- Computers and printers, especially when making multiple copies

Computers and Writing and Publishing

The Internet and other computer applications are changing the world (Karchmer, 2001). More than twenty years ago, at the advent of the computer age, Toffler (1980) warned that "an information bomb is exploding in our midst, showering us with a shrapnel of images and drastically changing the way each of us perceives and acts upon our private world" (p. 156).

But even Toffler would be shocked at how far-reaching the changes have been. Research has been greatly simplified as children move to search engines and type in key words and are immediately rewarded with multiple Web pages or links to the topic (Karchmer, 2001). This "explosion" is also clearly visible in writing classrooms across the country today as children receive ongoing feedback on spelling and grammar as they compose. Virtually every school district has invested in computers to keep pace with the changing world of technology. Literacy is being redefined as new technologies impact not only learners but teachers as well (Leu, 2000).

Teachers must make wise use of the computer, being careful it does not replace creative teaching and child-to-child interactions. Computers support children's growth as readers and writers, but they cannot teach language or reading. Children learn language and literacy in the process of meaningful communications with the world around them. The computer is but one tool that may be used to provide these literacy interactions.

Word Processing and the Writing Process

One of the key advantages presented by computers is word processing. Many students are reluctant to write because of both their poor handwriting and the tediousness of recopying their stories and papers to make them neat. In addition, good writing requires editing and rewriting, which results in even more recopying. When asked why his stories were so short, one third-grader replied, "I don't wanna write too much 'cause it takes too long to recopy." But writing is becoming less difficult because word processing enables text to be easily manipulated. It may be adapted, deleted, inserted, or moved about with ease (Broad, 1999; Downes & Fatouros, 1995; Dudley-Marling, 1985). Inexpensive printers provide students with nicely typed copies of their work. Zaharias (1983) reported that children are more willing to take risks as writers and to make more revisions when writing with a word processor. Perhaps the greatest contribution computers are making is the freedom they provide young writers through word processing.

Web Books

The power of the Internet can be captured in writing programs as children write and publish digital books, called *webbes* (**Web** Books for Everyone). Developed by Condon and McGuffee (2001), webbes are simple nonfiction picture books. Classrooms that have access to a computer, word processor, digital camera, and the Internet can quickly be transformed into "publishers." Even better, their publications can be shared with other students and classes worldwide.

Step-by-step procedures for creating webbes have been created by Michael McGuffee (2001). These specific instructions and periodic updates can be found at www.realebooks.com.

America's Finest
Michael McGuffee

Teacher-to-Teacher

Margaret Blankenship's third-grade classroom is filled with children who love computers and computer software. In contrast to many classrooms, the computer is integrated into the content areas of science, math, social studies, and language arts. Software is used constantly throughout the day by her students as they learn, with the assistance of the computer, about topics related to their content studies. Margaret's students delight in encountering historical figures such as Paul Revere and Joan of Arc as they solve mysteries while playing *Where in Time Is Carmen Sandiego?* Collaborative learning is evidenced as children work together in language arts and science adventures such as Sierra's *Space Quest* series.

Jason and Blake didn't want to go home one day until they had finished an exciting encounter in *Space Quest*. They finally decoded an alien space message that led to the solution of the game. Their decoded message is pictured in Figure 10.6; Jason's writing is at the top of the page and Blake's at the bottom. Notice the vocabulary generated by the

boys: *inpenetrable, deactivated, Jellow pistols.* Such interactions and collaborations are the essence of meaning-centered learning.

Josh Sonata, a third-grader, had never used a computer before his teacher asked him to write using a word processing program. Within twenty minutes he had completed the first draft of "The Adventures of Mike," which is reproduced below just as he wrote it. The computer freed Josh from concerns about his poor printing and allowed him to focus on story development. Josh corrected spelling and spacing problems in a later draft of the story. He soon became the third grade's most prolific writer.

The Adventures Of Mike
story and pictures by Josh Sonata

Once upon a time there was a sincetast his name was Mike. He had a cat named Sourpoos. He also had a dog named Wilber. As you know haveing a

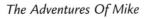

cat and a dog leads up to problems so the sincetast was not a happy one. But he was the worlds most best. He wanted to get away from the world and all the emotion. So he invented a srinking machine without knowing it. One day a day when he was esecialy curious he stepped in the srinking machine shut the door and pushed the red button and CLISH CLASH BING BANG ZINK ZANK and then he was small. Then his dog said 'What happend to the professor?'

"I do not know" said the cat.

Well now we come back to are dear old professor. HELP he cried in his strongest-weakest voice I say that becose it was weak compared to his regular voice. But no one heard him. Luckly the door was light and not locked. So out he went into the real world. He was so small that his cat didn't even see him. But his dog did. ' Hey' cried the dog look cat a rat. The professor started to say that he was the professor but he was afrad the dog might lick him. The professor happend to glance up at the clock and said 'Oh my gosh! I can not bleve the time I have class in 12 minits.' Now rember the cat he finaly found what the dog was talking about and when the professor looked up he found to his supprise he was being chsed by a cat...........TO BE CONTUED

Scott Beesley is a fifth-grade teacher in Nevada. Recognizing the potential of the computer to motivate students in writing, Scott developed, with the aid of his students, an email and instant messenger system for his school. Students wrote more than 1,000 messages to one another during the school year and had non-oral, written "chats" on a daily basis. Scott found that the children's writing fluency improved by

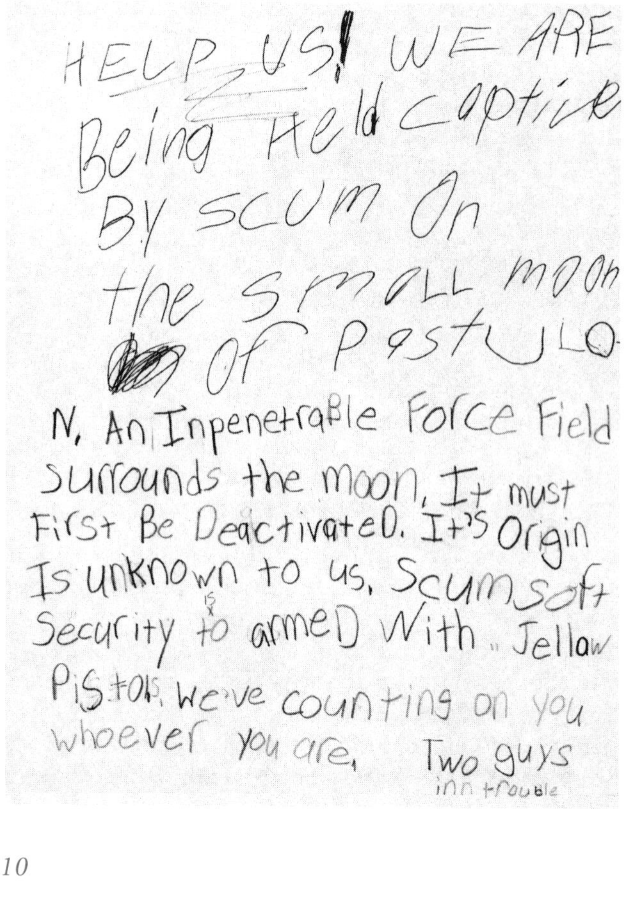

FIGURE 10.6
Story generated through student involvement in computer program

HELP US! WE ARE
Being Held coptive
BY SCUM On
the small moon
of PostuLo-
N, An Inpenetrable Force Field
surrounds the moon, It must
First Be Deactivated. It's Origin
Is unknown to us, Scumsoft
Security is to armeD with Jellow
Pistols. We've counting on you
whoever you are,   Two guys
                    inn trouble

year's end and that students made tremendous gains in spelling despite the claims of some that email and chatting deemphasizes spelling.

Gail Heather, a first-grade teacher who frequently took dictation from her children, decided to take dictation on a computer and project the image. The children were excited to see their spoken language appear on the screen, even more so than on chart paper. Students were eager to contribute their ideas to the collaborative story and to read the story when it was completed. The session was so successful that the dictation sessions using the word processor became a regular part of class activities. At the end of the year, Gail reported the following:

◆ She was able to take dictation much faster with the word processor than by hand.

◆ Stories dictated into the word processor were significantly longer than stories recorded on chart paper.

◆ Realizing how easily changes could be made, children asked for more revisions than normal.

◆ Dictated stories could easily be turned into typed class books by having the stories printed on the classroom printer and then bound.

◆ Gail no longer worried about her spelling—the spell check feature corrected her spelling as she took dictation.

Although Gail still takes group and individual dictation from children, she now has a valuable alternative for taking dictation. She reports that publishing has increased dramatically in her classroom and that the day she incorporated technology as part of the writing process was the dawn of a new era for her as a teacher.

Young Authors' Conference

Young Authors' Conferences are sponsored by many schools. They are a "grand culmination" of an author study: "For readers to meet the person who has moved them in some way through his or her literature heightens the literary experience tenfold" (Jenkins, 1999, p. 127). Young Authors' Conferences help students learn to select story lines representative of their goals for personal writing. They also help children gain the accompanying skills required for publishing. Students who are selected to represent their classrooms or school groups at areawide book fairs usually have opportunities to participate in writing seminars conducted by well-known authors and by college teachers of writing and children's literature. This experience is highly motivating and helps young writers set goals for future productions (Buzzeo, 1998).

Getting ready for a Young Authors' Conference involves much more than writing books. Parents, school administrators, and school board members are involved in planning and decision making. In the process, they come to appreciate the work of teachers and students who are involved. They discover that students have re-

Author Visit

Students listen as an author shares his book.

Courtesy of Irma Fridge

sponsibilities that are very demanding. They learn that selections are made on the basis of criteria students consider important. In applying the criteria, the young authors find out much about the mechanics of writing and publishing. A group getting ready for a Young Authors' Conference needs students with a variety of skills:

◆ Students with the attitude of scientists to check the validity of facts

◆ Students interested in the mechanics of editing

Author Study

Floyd Cooper

1. *Which book of yours has given you the greatest pleasure?*
I'll have to select two—*Grandpa's Face* and *Be Good to Eddie Lee* because of the humanity set forth so wonderfully by the authors.

2. *Which book has surprised you most in terms of its public reception?*
Satchmo's Blues was a big hit. Also *Coming Home,* my first authored title.

3. *What would you like people to remember about your work?*
I want people to know about how my art is achieved. How I use the eraser to make my paintings. I feel there may be more artists out there than we know, people who may not realize they can make art this way!

4. *What impact do you hope your work will have on children?*
I want them to realize the incredible odds I overcame to just be here. Particularly for children to know that they must persist and hold fast to their dreams.

Floyd Cooper's unique technique of using an eraser to draw his pictures yields warmly textured pictures that beautifully complement the text. Two of his books, *Meet Danitra Brown* by Nikki Grimes and *Brown Honey in Broomwheat Tea* by Joyce C. Thomas, won Coretta Scott King Honor Books for illustration. Other books by Floyd Cooper include *Miz Berlin Walks, Cumbayah, Coming Home, One April Morning, Satchmo's Blues, Shake Rag, Be Good to Eddie Lee,* and *Caddie the Golf Dog.*

Reprinted with special permission of Floyd Cooper.

- Students sensitive to language who can consult with authors about style and form
- Students who are talented as artists who can illustrate books when an author does not choose to do so
- Students who can type manuscripts
- Students who can bind books with sturdy and attractive bindings that will withstand much handling
- Students who can organize parents into working groups to support the publishing enterprise with scrap materials and needed equipment, such as sewing machines and computers
- Students who can represent the class project to the school principal and the local school board
- Students who can share their books with audiences by skillful oral reading
- Students who can contribute to writing seminars that will be helpful in setting new goals and raising aspirations for improved publications

Because a book will be shared in a Young Authors' Conference, students produce stories that represent their finest writing. This writing reflects the research and editing efforts of the students and demonstrates what happens when children extend their imaginations in new and creative ways.

Young Authors' Conferences require much work (Buzzeo, 1998), but the rewards far outweigh the costs. When children's books are honored, children are honored, and when children are honored, they will be motivated to write time and time again.

Teacher-to-Teacher

Angel Perez, a bilingual fifth-grade teacher from New Mexico, has been involved in honoring the writings of his school's young authors for many years. Consequently, Grand Vista's Young Authors' Conference is a high point of the school year.

Angel has discovered that a literacy-rich environment results when children's books are integrated throughout the school day. When students read books such as Richard Peck's (2001) Newbery Award–winning *A Year Down Yonder*, they want to write their own. An additional motivation for writing is the opportunity to have the book admired by others at the Young Authors' Conference.

One secret to a successful conference is parent involvement and support. Angel writes each parent, explaining what a young authors' conference is like and asking for their participation. A sample letter follows:

Dear Parent,
You are invited to participate in the celebration of the Longfellow Elementary Young Authors' Conference on Friday, April 28, from 8 to 11:40 a.m. It's an exciting day for students, teachers, and parents as our young writers share their books and meet Bill Martin Jr, a noted author.

➤ ➤ ➤

First, the children are placed in small sharing groups where they share the books they have written with nine other children and an adult leader for about 30 minutes.

After the sharing groups, one-third of the students will go to an assembly to meet a famous author, one-third will go to activity groups, and one-third will make new books. Each group will rotate through all three sessions. Each session will last about 45 minutes. A leader will stay with the same group all morning.

We would like to invite you to participate in the conference as a sharing-group leader and/or an activity-group leader. Sharing-group leaders will guide small groups in which students read their own books. Activity-group leaders will plan and conduct activities designed to encourage student creativity. These may include games, arts and crafts, music, drama, cooking and more. This year we want one adult for every ten students. Some of the adults may assist in an activity directed by someone else.

If you can participate, please respond below and return by Friday, April 7. We know you will be glad you did!

(Please check one or more.)

_____ I will conduct a sharing group only.

_____ I will conduct a sharing group and will stay with a group of ten students throughout the three morning sessions.

_____ I will conduct an activity group.

Activity planned _____

Number of students (circle) 10 20 30

Grade level preferred _____

Language of students preferred _____

_____
Signature   Student's Name   Teacher

FURTHER WORDS

From InfoTrac College Edition

Internet Workshop: Making Time for Literacy (exploring literacy on the Internet), Donald J. Leu Jr., *The Reading Teacher* February 2002 v55 i5 p466

From Conditions of Learning to Conditions of Teaching (conditions for literacy learning), Brian Cambourne, *The Reading Teacher* December 2001 v55 i4 p358(3)

The Nuts and Bolts of Teaching First-Grade Writing Through a Journal Workshop (teaching ideas), Lyn Wagner, Jennifer Grogan Nott, and Ann T. Agnew, *The Reading Teacher* October 2001 v55 i2 p120(6)

Suspense: Keeping Your Reader Reading (how to write suspensefully), Sol Stein, *The Writer* November 1996 v109 n11 p14(5)

From Professional Journals and Publications

Au, K. H., and Carroll, J. H. (1997). Improving Literacy Achievement through a Constructivist Approach: The KEEP Demonstration Classroom Project. (Kamehameha Elementary Education Program). *The Elementary School Journal, 97*(3), 203.

Chihak, J. (1999). Success Is in the Details: Publishing to Validate Elementary School Authors. *Language Arts, 96*, 491–498.

Isaacson, S. L. (1994). Integrating Process, Product, and Purpose: The Role of Instruction. *Reading and Writing Quarterly, 10*, 39–62.

Larocque, P. (2001). Crawl Before Running. *The Quill, 89*(1), 54.

Novelli, J. (2000). Attention-Getting Beginnings. *Instructor, 110*(3), 47.

Poindexter, C., and Oliver, I. (1999). Navigating the Writing Process: Strategies for Young Children. *The Reading Teacher, 52*, 420–423.

Summary

This chapter provided the how-to aspect of orchestrating the classroom writing program. However, the key to excellence in guiding a literacy program is not in procedures but in attitude. An attitude that values student self-expression releases authors to write in creative and beautiful ways. This freedom of expression is the ultimate goal of the total literacy classroom.

Total Literacy Anchors

SELECTING IDEAS AND PATTERNS

- Students find topics for writing in the immediate environment.
- Students find topics for writing from imagination.
- Students use classic stories as models for writing.
- Students extend the concept of the alphabet into book-length production.
- Students select a variety of literary forms to express personal ideas.
- Students choose imaginary and nonsense topics as well as real-life topics.
- Students adapt predictive language patterns to their own topics and interests.

EDITING MANUSCRIPTS

- Students assume responsibility for self-editing.
- Students participate on editorial committees in the editing of group projects.
- Students use spelling resources available in the Writing/Publishing Center.
- Students use descriptive vocabulary to elaborate simple language.
- Students page manuscripts for illustrating and printing so each page has at least one contributing idea.
- Students edit poetry for spacing and selection of print as well as for spelling, capitalization, and punctuation.

PUBLISHING MANUSCRIPTS

- Students make a variety of bindings for books.
- Students participate in the production of class publications such as newspapers and magazines.
- Students serve on committees responsible for producing finished books.

CHAPTER 11

Literacy Conventions: Words, Spelling, Grammar, AND Handwriting

As You Read . . .

- What role does writing play in spelling acquisition?

- What role does reading play in spelling acquisition?

- Why is the freedom to experiment—to use invented spellings—important in total literacy classrooms?

- What role does dictation play in the process of spelling maturation?

- Why is it important for spelling programs to afford many opportunities for writing?

- What insights into spelling do children gain through reading and writing activities in total literacy classrooms?

- What role does word study (beyond spelling) play in effective reading, writing, and language arts programs?

- Why is it important to demonstrate respect and acceptance of the home-rooted language that children bring to the classroom?

- Can grammar be taught in an informal, meaning-centered way? Or, must it, by necessity, be presented in a highly structured, specific, and predetermined sequence?

- Is handwriting instruction in the elementary grades valuable?

- How should handwriting be taught in total literacy classrooms?

- Beyond "correct" or conventional use of language in writing, what are the appropriate goals for language/literacy instruction?

Author Words
Timothy Rasinski

Spelling and the study of words is one of the most researched, most discussed language arts. Unfortunately, misconceptions abound on the topic of spelling. We take an in-depth look at spelling and word study in this chapter and leave you with suggestions that will help you free students from the fears of spelling and help them become excellent editors of their own work.

Spelling and Word Study

How do children become good spellers?—through the processes of writing and editing. Children who feel an urge to communicate, who experience the thrill of authorship, and who know the satisfaction of writing something that is important to other people are the ones most likely to develop skill as spellers. And as students become more interested in writing, they become more interested in language and want to acquire new words.

Spelling is an inseparable part of total literacy programs that keep speech, writing, and reading related in instruction. Children must learn common spellings of words they write because other students—not just the teacher—read much of what they write. Children must learn to edit their writing for correct spelling because many stories or poems are published and become a part of the instructional materials. However, as teachers, we must be sure concern for spelling does not hamper the creative composing process of the writers in our classrooms.

Thus, as children write, they should be encouraged to use whatever words are most appropriate to express the feelings or moods they wish to create, regardless of how they might spell these words. Natural or "invented" spellings are developmental in nature and are an indication that children feel, as Clark (1989) says, "free to write." Simply expressed, communication is the primary objective of writing. Correct spelling is a secondary objective, a supporting one. Children must feel secure in exploring the spelling of new and unusual words. We recommend the following ten principles for teachers concerning spelling:

1. Children learn to spell words they find personally interesting and use in their everyday writing.
2. Spelling is a developmental process. It develops along fairly consistent lines that mirror their reading development.
3. Having children work out their own invented spellings of high-frequency words reinforces their knowledge of phonics and the English spelling system and enables them to test hypotheses about how language works.

Courtesy of Michael Sampson

Standard spellings make the message easier for others to read.

4. Proficiency in spelling will develop through consistent opportunities to write for real purposes.

5. Spelling is a subset of writing. It should never become more important than writing or be taught in place of writing.

6. There is a place for direct instruction in word spelling in the language arts curriculum. There are many ways to learn to spell words (for example, memory, pneumonic devices, or patterns). Spelling instruction should help students use as many strategies as possible to learn to spell.

7. High-frequency words are good candidates for spelling instruction.

8. High-frequency spelling patterns (onset, rimes, derivations) are good candidates for spelling instruction.

9. High-frequency and high-utility semantic patterns (for example, Latin and Greek derivations) may be good candidates for spelling instruction.

10. Spelling and word study should be aimed at nurturing a love and fascination for words in students, from their history, to their meaning, to their connections to other words and concepts.

We will begin our exploration of spelling by looking at young spellers and the stages they move through on their journey to becoming conventional spellers. Then we will examine two major views of how spelling should be taught—through the processes of writing, reading, and editing or through direct instruction of specific words.

The Beginnings

America's Finest

David Brown

Young children's scribbles are a form of self-expression. This early writing is a process that will evolve as the child matures; therefore, adults should be patient with these letterlike forms that look only slightly like writing. In effect, children can write before they can read if given the opportunity. These young children use "invented spellings" (Bissex, 1980; Cambourne & Turbill, 1988) and learn to write in the same manner and for the same reasons they learned to talk.

After hearing his mother share *Read About Spiders,* 5-year-old Joshua wrote, "I LIC SPIDRS CS' SPIDRCR GUD" [I like spiders because spiders are good] (Clem & Feathers, 1986). His message reveals his understanding that writing may be used to express feelings and to record thoughts and opinions (see Figure 11.1). His story confirms what Bissex (1985) has noted: Children invent their own systematic spellings in their "active search" for the rules that govern our writing system. Joshua's experimentation demonstrates he has comprehended that letters represent speech sounds, and he is well on his way to becoming a proficient speller. The first step in spelling is to recognize its role in communication.

The importance of invented spellings and the role they play in children's pursuit of literacy has received widespread attention in recent years (Bissex, 1980; Chomsky, 1971; Farris, 1993; Henderson, 1986; Henderson & Beers, 1980; Kamil & Randazzo, 1985; Read, 1980; Yellin & Blake, 1994). This recognition is leading

FIGURE 11.1
A 5-year-old writes about spiders

teachers to the understanding of the importance of allowing young children to represent their thoughts on paper and of not correcting invented spellings because "corrections stifle children's confidence and desire to write" (Kamil & Randazzo, 1985, p. 124).

These "errors" are, in fact, a step toward the child's construction of a coherent system of spelling and writing. These representations of meaning constantly evolve toward standard forms (Bissex, 1980). In addition, it must be remembered that most writers, including adults, encode meaning on the first draft of a message without allowing spelling or grammar to interrupt the process (Harste, Burke, & Woodward, 1983).

Stages of Spelling Development

Over the past several years, we have had an extraordinary opportunity to follow a class of twenty-four children from kindergarten through fifth grade. During that time, we saw the children blossom into readers and writers. Along the way, we also observed their development and transition as spellers. We share what we learned, because teachers often only see the grade level they work with and do not have the opportunity to view children along the developmental pathways we observed.

The developmental stages we observed were (1) scribble-pictorial, (2) letter, (3) phonetic, (4) approximal, and (5) standard. Although most children follow this pattern, not all will. Figure 11.2 provides examples of these developmental stages.

The Scribble-Pictorial Stage Many children, upon arriving at kindergarten, simply scribble or draw pictures when asked to "write a story."

Stage	Characteristics	Examples
Pictoral-Scribble	Draws pictures; scribbles	Pictures children draw
Letter	Recognizes that words are made up of letters	RD for Read
Phonetic	Spells words the way they sound Uses some vowels	"sekunt" for "second"
Approximal	Many words correct Some words spelled phonetically	"wondring" for "wondering"
Standard	Spelling is usually accurate Some spelling errors made	

FIGURE 11.2
Stages of spelling development

Typically, children ages 3 to 5 tend to be in this stage. During this stage, children are becoming aware that speech can be recorded with graphic symbols, but they do not yet have a clear understanding of the relationship between sounds and letters.

The Letter Stage   Many children arrive at kindergarten in this stage. They tend to "write" using one to three consonant letters to represent each word. Often children will spell with two letters—one letter to begin the word and one letter to end it. Children in this stage have made a major leap toward literacy. They have formulated the concept of words and are attempting to represent words with letters (Raine, 1994). With some effort, you can read what these children have written.

The Phonetic Stage   You can easily read what children write in this stage. The letters in words closely resemble the way the words "sound"; "for" might be spelled *fro* and "with" may be spelled *whit*. At this stage children have started adding vowel sounds as they attempt to represent words.

The Approximal Stage   Many high-frequency words are spelled correctly; many others are almost correct. Spellings still tend to be phonetic, but editing processes have "kicked in" and almost weekly growth toward standard spellings is observed.

Standard Spelling   This level is achieved by most children no sooner than fifth grade. For some children, spelling is natural at this point, and they spell most words correctly. For many children, as with adults, standard spelling will occur through editing, not first draft attempts.

We noticed that some of our brightest students were poor spellers and that some of our weaker students were good spellers. We conclude that spelling is a tal-

_____Laheya Crosby_____ Name
_____10 years old_____ Age

_____Computers, BasketBall_____ Interests
_____roller blading_____

What do you like most about school?

What I like most about school is that we learn about things that we didn't know and we do so good at them.

What's your favorite subject? Why?

My favorite subject is Math because they are so easy especially the addition and multiplication facts. I like addition and multiplication facts because they help you learn how to add and multiply if you have a math test to take.

What's your favorite book? Why do you like it?

My favorite book is the Baby-sitter's Club books because they talk about baby-sitting. I love baby sitting because I baby sit my little cousins.

What advice do you have for teachers?

My advice for teachers is have a great time teaching children and love your job to help us get better at things we think we can't do.

ent, just as music and art are talents. However, all children can become better spellers through writing, reading, and editing. Now let's consider what happens if this philosophy is continued in later grades.

The Process-Centered View of Spelling Instruction

At the heart of any literacy program are opportunities for students to read and write for real purposes. Through their reading, students come across interesting and varied words. As they write, they use words they do not know how to spell. When attention is drawn to the spelling of those words through editing, students begin to develop competence as spellers.

Although spelling is typically taught as a subject in school, most spelling is learned outside of spelling class. Consider, for example, that the average educated adult has a vocabulary of more than 100,000 words. Spelling curricula provide thirty-six weeks of spelling lists that contain approximately twenty words each. Over eight years of instruction, students are asked to learn only 5,760 words—far short of the 100,000 they need. So how do they learn these words? As children read and write, many words and patterns are learned largely at the subconscious level, and through editing their own writing. Thus, spelling is learned through the processes of using language in reading and writing.

Teacher-to-Teacher

After five years of teaching third grade, Susan Tollison had developed a love for the language arts. She enjoyed children's literature and loved sharing her favorite books with her children. She loved music and enjoyed the daily sing-along sessions in her classroom. But there was one thing she didn't enjoy—the school's spelling program.

The very traditional program required that children be given twenty words to learn each week and that a test be given every Friday. Many of her children struggled with the test and failed the Friday quiz week after week. Other students quite easily memorized the words, scored an "A" on the test on Friday, then forgot the words. Parents complained to Susan that they would spend hours each week working with their children on the spelling list at home. Finally, after five years of having the spelling curriculum rule Susan and her students, things changed.

Susan attended a Pathways to Literacy workshop led by Bill Martin Jr. In the session, she became intrigued with process writing and vowed to change her language arts block when she returned to school in the fall. And change she did.

Spelling ceased to become a subject in school and became a part of her writing program. After one year of children writing and editing every day, Susan discovered she had a classroom filled with good spellers. But more important, she had a classroom of children who were not afraid to write. They used much more advanced vocabulary in their compositions, and the final drafts of their manuscripts contained very few spelling errors. By trusting in the children and the process, Susan transformed her classroom and triumphed over the one aspect of school she disliked the most.

Through many varied writing and publishing opportunities, students develop an internal motivation to spell in conventional ways to facilitate their audience's understanding of their message. In addition, through authentic writing experiences, students put into practice the various strategies they have at their disposal for spelling words. As a result, those strategies become internalized, and students spelling *and* decoding knowledge for the words they write is further solidified.

A spelling program that does not use real reading and real writing is not, in our opinion, effective. Learning to spell correctly without any connection to the purpose for spelling is an empty activity.

Language Experience and Spelling

In our work with young children, we have noticed one key strategy that enhances children's move toward standard spellings. We're talking about dictation—the language experience approach strategy of writing down what children say to create texts they can read. Through dictation, children can see the relationships that exist among thoughts, language, reading, and writing (Sampson, Sampson, & Allen, 1995). Dictation also demonstrates to young children the accurate spelling of words. Smith (1985) states that the first key component in learning is observation. He calls these observations "demonstrations" and says they tell the learner "this is how something is done" (p. 108). As teachers take dictation from children and write their language on the board or on the children's individual pictures, they are "demonstrating" to the children that "this is how this word is spelled." Children will receive additional demonstrations concerning spelling as they become proficient readers and see the words playing in the movie of their minds time after time. The schemata that are constructed through these demonstrations enable us to "look" at a word and, using the visual feedback, know if it is spelled correctly or incorrectly.

Some have argued that the practice of taking dictation should be replaced with the opportunity for children to do independent writing using invented spellings (Kamil & Randazzo, 1985). As discussed in Chapter 10, both practices are valuable classroom tools for the development of literacy skills—both give children an opportunity to supply the language and the words that are a part of that language. Invented spellings enable children to write independently. Dictation, however, is very efficient because it points children toward the use of standard spellings and is, therefore, a valuable part of process classrooms in the primary grades.

Spelling Resources for the Process Classroom

Children who can read words on lists are able to improve their spelling by the use of the word lists during writing and editing. Here are three lists that can be supplied on an individual basis or on charts in a total literacy classroom:

- ◆ Words for spelling and editing
- ◆ Words often spelled and pronounced incorrectly
- ◆ Roy Peter Clark's "yucky" list

The list of words for spelling and editing may be created using the Allen list of 100 high-frequency words (see Figure 10.5 on page 309). Arrange these words alphabetically so students can locate words quickly.

Words often spelled and pronounced incorrectly (Figure 11.3) is a useful editing resource because it shows children words they may think they spell correctly but don't. The "yucky" list (Clark, 1989) is a list the classroom teacher creates for each class; the list is comprised of words the teacher notices children constantly misspell. Thus, this list will be different for each grade and will change during the school year as children progress as spellers.

The Direct Instruction View of Spelling

The best classroom-based spelling programs challenge students to thoughtfully consider words through their reading and their writing. However, in reality, most schools use spelling lists and programs to teach spelling. Thus, we'll now share what we believe are the best procedures for direct instruction of spelling.

Selecting Spelling Words

Direct instruction in spelling assumes that there are words and word elements worth teaching. Although we don't subscribe to a prescribed list of words for any particular age or grade level, when direct instruction of spelling is mandated, teachers should take advantage of these key principles when selecting words:

1. Words chosen by the student or students for personal reasons. Studies of vocabulary learning have found that when students identify and choose their own words to learn, powerful vocabulary learning results. Blachowicz and Fisher (2000) describe a study of high-level vocabulary learning in which the teacher empowered her students to find interesting words in their reading, put the words on display in the classroom, and tell the rest of the class about the words they had chosen.

above	couple	give	machine	ranger	tongue
across	cousin	gives	many	ready	too
again	cruel	gloves	measure	really	touch
against	curve	gone	might	right	two
aisle		great	mild	rough	
already	dead	guard	million		use
another	deaf	guess	mind	said	usual
answer	debt	guest	minute	says	
anxious	desire	guide	mischief	school	vein
any	do		mother	science	very
	does	have	move	scissors	view
bear	done	head	Mr.	sew	
beautiful	don't	heart	Mrs.	shoe	was
beauty	double	heaven		should	wash
because	doubt	heavy	neighbor	sign	weather
been	dove	here	neither	snow	weight
behind	dozen	high	night	soften	were
believe			none	soldier	what
bind	early	idea		some	where
both	earn	Indian	ocean	someone	who
bough	eight	instead	of	something	whom
bread	enough	isle	office	sometime	whose
bright	eye		often	son	wild
brought	eyes	key	oh	soul	wind
build		kind	once	special	wolf
built	father	knee	one	spread	woman
bury	fence	knew	onion	square	women
busy	field	knife	only	steak	won
buy	fight	know	other	straight	would
	find		ought	sure	wrong
calf	folks	language		sword	
captain	four	laugh	patient		you
caught	freight	laughed	piece	their	young
chief	friend	leather	pretty	there	your
child	front	library	pull	they	
clothes		light	purpose	though	
colt	garage	lion	push	thought	
coming	get	live	put	to	
cough	getting	lived		together	
could	ghost	love	quiet	ton	

FIGURE 11.3
Words often spelled and pronounced incorrectly

2. High-frequency words that students will read and write often in their literacy interactions. A list of 600 high-frequency words is provided in Figure 11.4. According to Edward Fry, the originator of this word list, the first 300 words (along with various suffixes and inflected endings) represent approximately 67 percent of all the words students will encounter in their reading. If about 100 words per year from the list of high-frequency words are selected for instruction, all 600 words could be covered in the first six grades of school. And, at a rate of 4 words per week, all 100 words could be covered in twenty-five school weeks.

First 100 Instant Words

the	his	when	many	write	long
of	they	your	then	number	down
and	I	can	them	no	day
a	at	said	these	way	did
to	be	there	so	could	get
in	this	use	some	people	come
is	or	an	her	my	made
you	one	each	would	than	have
that	had	which	make	first	from
it	by	she	like	water	their
he	words	do	him	been	if
was	but	how	into	called	go
for	not	will	time	who	see
on	what	up	has	oil	may
are	all	other	look	sit	part
as	were	about	two	now	
with	we	out	more	find	

Second 100 Instant Words

over	things	too	put	read	away
new	our	means	end	need	animals
sound	just	old	does	land	house
take	name	any	another	different	point
only	good	same	well	home	page
little	sentence	tell	large	us	letters
work	man	boy	must	move	mother
know	think	following	big	try	answer
place	say	came	even	kind	found
years	great	want	such	hand	study
live	where	show	because	picture	still
me	help	also	turned	again	learn
back	through	around	here	change	should
give	much	form	why	off	American
most	before	three	asked	play	world
very	line	small	went	spell	
after	right	set	men	air	

FIGURE 11.4

Fry's instant word list of 600 high-frequency words

Source: Fry, E., Kress, J., and Fountoukidis, D. L. (2000), *The Reading Teacher's Book of Lists,* 4th ed. Englewood Cliffs, NJ: Prentice-Hall. Reprinted with permission of Edward Fry, copyright holder.

Third 100 Instant Words

high	city	seemed	until	once	let
every	earth	next	children	book	above
near	eyes	hard	side	hear	girl
add	light	open	feet	stop	sometimes
food	thought	example	car	without	mountains
between	head	beginning	miles	second	cut
own	under	life	night	later	young
below	story	always	walked	miss	talk
country	saw	those	white	idea	soon
plants	left	both	sea	enough	list
last	don't	paper	began	eat	song
school	few	together	grow	face	being
father	while	got	took	watch	leave
keep	along	group	river	far	family
trees	might	often	four	Indians	it's
never	close	run	carry	really	
started	something	important	state	almost	

Fourth 100 Instant Words

body	ever	during	wind	pattern	sing
music	piece	short	rock	numeral	war
color	told	better	space	table	ground
stand	usually	best	covered	north	king
sun	didn't	however	fast	slowly	fall
questions	friends	low	several	money	town
fish	easy	hours	hold	map	I'll
area	heard	black	himself	farm	unit
mark	order	products	toward	pulled	figure
dog	red	happened	five	draw	certain
horse	door	whole	step	voice	field
birds	sure	measure	morning	seen	travel
problem	become	remember	passed	cold	wood
compete	top	early	vowel	cried	fire
room	ship	waves	true	plan	upon
knew	across	reached	hundred	notice	
since	today	listen	against	south	

Fifth 100 Instant Words

done	strong	nothing	system	deep	power
English	verb	rest	behind	thousands	cannot
road	stars	carefully	ran	yes	able
half	front	scientists	round	clear	six
ten	feel	inside	boat	equation	size
fly	fact	wheels	game	yet	dark
gave	inches	stay	force	government	ball
box	street	green	brought	filled	material
finally	decided	known	understand	heat	special
wait	contain	island	warm	full	heavy
correct	course	week	common	hot	fine
oh	surface	less	bring	check	pair
quickly	produce	machine	explain	object	circle
person	building	base	dry	am	include
became	ocean	ago	though	rule	built
shown	class	stood	language	among	
minutes	note	plane	shape	noun	

Sixth 100 Instant Words

can't	subject	eggs	sat	pat	meet
matter	Europe	train	main	sign	third
square	moon	blue	winter	record	months
syllables	region	wish	side	finished	paragraph
perhaps	return	drop	written	discovered	raised
bill	believe	developed	length	wild	represent
felt	dance	window	reason	happy	soft
suddenly	members	difference	kept	beside	whether
test	picked	distance	interest	gone	clothes
direction	simple	heart	arms	sky	flowers
center	cells	sit	brother	glass	shall
farmers	paint	sum	race	million	teacher
ready	mind	summer	present	west	held
anything	love	wall	beautiful	lay	describe
divided	cause	forest	store	weather	drive
general	rain	probably	job	root	
energy	exercise	legs	edge	instruments	

FIGURE 11.4

continued

Learning about words

3. High-frequency structural word patterns. Words that have embedded in them key patterns (onsets and rimes) that will aid the student in spelling and decoding the words. Figure 11.5 lists thirty-seven high-frequency letter patterns. According to Edward Fry, this list of rimes (also known to teachers as phonograms or word families) can be used to spell and decode 654 one-syllable words.

These certainly would be good candidates for instruction. However, well over 100 rimes are useful for spelling and decoding. A basic list of common rimes is provided in Figure 11.6. Francine Johnston (2001) recommends that short vowel (consonant, vowel, consonant) patterns be taught first, followed by the long vowel patterns (consonant, vowel, vowel, consonant; consonant, vowel consonant, silent *e,* and so forth).

4. High-frequency and utility in semantic patterns. These words have embedded in them key semantic patterns (meaning-based patterns often derived from Latin and Greek roots for English words) that will aid the student in spelling, decoding, and deriving meaning from the words. A basic list of some common and useful semantic patterns is provided in Figure 11.7. The study of semantic patterns should not fully begin until students have some mastery of the basic structural patterns.

5. The study of one-syllable words should precede the study of multisyllabic words, although this may occur simultaneously as students study words of various length based on a targeted patterns.

ay	say, day	ing	sing, ring	est	best, rest
ill	hill, fill	ap	rap, cap	ink	rink, sink
ip	ship, dip	unk	hunt, bunk	ow	low, slow
at	hat, cat	ail	pail, sail	ew	few, dew
am	ham, jam	ain	pain, rain	ore	sore, more
ag	rag, sag	im	him, rim	ed	sled, Ted
ack	rack, sack	uck	truck, luck	ab	crab, lab
ank	bank, Hank	um	hum, drum	ob	rob, lob
ake	rake, make	eed	deed, reed	ock	clock, rock
ine	spine, mine	y	try, my	op	hop, stop
ight	sight, might	out	shout, pout	in	pin, win
ick	sick, lick	ug	hug, slug	an	man, can
ell	bell, tell				
ot	hot, spot				

FIGURE 11.5

High-frequency letter patterns

Teacher-to-Teacher

Jennifer Read is a second grade teacher who has developed an interesting manner for selecting words for weekly spelling study. She begins by choosing a letter pattern that needs to be covered. At the beginning of the school year, the primary grade teachers get together and chose word family patterns that should be presented and taught at each grade level. She usually chooses two. From each pattern she selects five words, two one-syllable words and three two- and three-syllable words. She wants students to be able to use their knowledge of letter patterns to spell and decode the more challenging multisyllabic words as well as the easier one-syllable words. She also chooses a couple of words that she notices students are having difficulty with in their own writing. Sometimes she chooses a couple of "hard to spell" words from a list she keeps in her spelling folder. She also adds about five words from the high-frequency word list that students are supposed to master by the end of second grade. This makes a total of about twenty words.

Finally, the students add five to ten words to the spelling list. The students choose words they like and words they want to learn.

Sometimes Jennifer reads a book or a chapter of a book and asks students to pay attention to any interesting words they hear and would like to learn. Thus, this last portion of the word list often comes from a real story the students have recently heard. This helps them to develop appreciation for the author's use of words in creating a story that students like to read or hear. Interestingly, oftentimes the words the students choose contain elements or patterns that are part of the week's study. It gives them good practice in using their knowledge about word patterns to figure out interesting and more challenging words.

From this list of thirty or so words, students choose anywhere from fifteen to twenty words they would like to study and learn throughout the week. Of course, Jennifer provides some guidance into the words the students have chosen. But the students are remarkably responsible for their own learning, and they have a good sense of how much they can handle to be successful. Jennifer feels that this approach creates a nice balance between what she determines needs to be covered and what students want to cover in their spelling.

ab: tab, drab
ace: race, place
ack: lack, track
act: fact, pact
ad: bad, glad
ade: made, shade
aft: raft, craft
ag: bag, shag
age: page, stage
aid: maid, braid
ail: mail, snail
ain: rain, train
air: hair, stair
ait: bait, trait
ake: take, brake
alk: talk, chalk
all: ball, squall
am: ham, swam
ame: name, blame
amp: camp, clamp
an: man, span
ance: dance, glance
and: land, gland
ane: plane, cane
ang: bang, sprang
ank: bank, plank
ant: pant, chant
ap: nap, snap
ape: tape, drape
ar: car, star
ard: hard, card
are: care, glare
ark: dark, spark
arm: harm, charm
arn: barn, yarn
arp: carp, harp
art: part, start
ase: base, case
ash: cash, flash
ask: mask, task

ass: lass, mass
at: fat, scat
atch: hatch, catch
ate: gate, plate
aught: caught, taught
ave: gave, shave
aw: saw, draw
awn: lawn, fawn
ax: wax, sax
ay: hay, clay
aze: haze, maze
ead: head, bread
eak: leak, sneak
eal: real, squeal
eam: team, stream
ean: mean, lean
eap: heap, leap
ear: year, spear
eat: beat, cheat
eck: peck, check
ed: bed, shed
ee: tee, tee
eed: need, speed
eek: leek, seek
eel: feel, kneel
eem: deem, seem
een: seen, screen
eep: keep, sheep
eer: beer, peer
eet: feet, sleet
eg: leg, beg
eigh: weigh, sleigh
eight: weight, freight
ell: fell, swell
elt: felt, belt
en: Ben, when
end: tend, send
ent: sent, spent
ess: less, bless
est: rest, chest

et: get, jet
ew: flew, chew
ib: bib, crib
ibe: bribe, tribe
ice: rice, splice
ick: kick, stick
id: hid, slid
ide: wide, pride
ie: die, pie
ief: thief, chief
ife: wife, knife
iff: cliff, whiff
ift: gift, sift
ig: pig, twig
ight: tight, bright
ike: Mike, spike
ile: mile, tile
ill: fill, chill
ilt: kilt, quilt
im: him, trim
in: tin, spin
ince: since, prince
ind: kind, blind
ine: mine, spine
ing: sing, string
ink: sink, shrink
ip: hip, flip
ipe: ripe, swipe
ire: tire, sire
irt: dirt, shirt
ise: rise, wise
ish: dish, swish
isk: disk, risk
iss: kiss, Swiss
ist: mist, wrist
it: hit, quit
itch: ditch, witch
ite: bite, write
ive: five, hive
ix: fix, six

Teaching Strategies
Onsets & Rimes

FIGURE 11.6
Common rimes

o: do, to, who   oon: moon, spoon   ox: fox, pox

o: go, no, so   oop: hoop, snoop   oy: boy, ploy

oach: coach, poach   oot: boot, shoot   ub: cub, shrub

oad: road, toad   op: top, chop   uck: duck, stuck

oak: soak, cloak   ope: hope, slope   ud: mud, thud

oal: coal, goal   orch: porch, torch   ude: dude, rude

oam: foam, roam   ore: bore, snore   udge: fudge, judge

oan: Joan, loan   ork: cork, fork   ue: sue, blue

oar: boar, roar   orn: horn, thorn   uff: puff, stuff

oast: boast, coast   ort: fort, short   ug: dug, plug

oat: boat, float   ose: rose, close   ule: rule, mule

ob: job, throb   oss: boss, gloss   ull: dull, gull

obe: robe, globe   ost: cost, lost   um: sum, chum

ock: lock, stock   ost: host, most   umb: numb, thumb

od: rod, sod   ot: got, trot   ump: bump, plump

ode: code, rode   otch: notch, blotch   un: run, spun

og: fog, clog   ote: note, quote   unch: bunch, hunch

oil: boil, broil   ough: rough, tough   une: June, tune

oin: coin, join   ought: bought, brought   ung: hung, flung

oke: woke, spoke   ould: could, would   unk: sunk, chunk

old: gold, scold   ounce: bounce, pounce   unt: bunt, hunt

ole: hole, stole   ound: bound, found   ur: fur, blur

oll: droll, roll   ouse: house, mouse   urn: burn, churn

ome: dome, home   out: pout, about   urse: curse, nurse

one: cone, phone   outh: mouth, south   us: bus, plus

ong: long, wrong   ove: cove, grove   ush: mush, crush

oo: too, zoo   ove: dove, love   ust: dust, trust

ood: food, mood   ow: how, chow   ut: but, shut

ood: good, hood   ow: slow, throw   ute: lute, flute

ook: cook, took   owl: howl, growl   y: my, dry

ool: cool, fool   own: down, town

oom: room, bloom   own: known, grown

FIGURE 11.6
continued

Instructional Strategies

In the past, direct instruction in spelling relied heavily on developing students' memory for words. The skill drills and worksheets were aimed at giving students practice in word spellings so that the spellings would become embedded in students' memories. While memory and practice are certainly and undeniably key elements in learning to spell, they are not the only internal mechanisms students use to enable their spelling. Pneumonics, phonics, meaning, word histories, and

Root	Meaning	Example
act	do	react
aero	air	aerate
agri	field	agriculture
alt	high	altitude
alter	other	alternate
amo, ami	love	amiable
ang	bend	angle
anim	life, spirit	animal
ann, enn	year	annual
anthr, anthro	man (people)	anthropology
aqua	water	aquarium
arch	chief	archbishop
art	skill	artist
ast	star	astronaut
aud	hear	auditorium
belli	war	belligerent
biblio	book	bibliography
bio	life	biology
brev	short	brevity
cam, camp	field	campus
cap	head	captain
cardi	heart	cardiac
center, centr	center	egocentric
cert	sure	certain
chron	time	chronological
cide	cut, kill	suicide
cogn	know	recognize
corp	body	corporation
cosm	universe	cosmonaut
crat	rule	democrat
credit	believe	incredible
cycl	circle, ring	bicycle
dem	people	democracy
dict	speak	contradict
div	divide	divorce
don, donat	give	pardon
dont, dent	tooth	orthodontist
dox	belief	orthodox
esth	feeling	anesthetic

FIGURE 11.7
Semantic patterns

Root	Meaning	Example
fac	make, do	factory
flex, flect	bend	reflex
form	shape	uniform
fract, frag	break	fracture
frater	brother	fraternity
fric	rub	friction
gen	birth, race	generation
geo	earth	geology
gon	angle	pentagon
grad	step	gradual
gram	letter, written	telegram
graph	write	telegraph
grat	pleasing	gratitude
homo, hom	man	homicide
hydr	water	hydrant
ject	throw	reject
junct	join	juncture
jud	law	judge
jur	law, swear	perjury
jus	law	justice
lab	work	labor
lat	side	collateral
liber	free	liberty
loc	place	location
luc	light	elucidate
lum	light	illuminate
luna	moon	lunar
lust	shine	luster
man	hand	manual
mand	to order	command
mania	madness	maniac
mar	sea	marine
mater, matri	mother	maternity
max	greatest	maximum
mech	machine	mechanic
ment	mind	mental
meter	measure	thermometer
migr	move	migrate
min	small, lesser	minimize
mob	move	automobile
morph	shape	polymorphous

FIGURE 11.7

continued

Root	Meaning	Example
mort	dealth	mortal
mot	move	motor
mut	change	commute
narr	tell	narrate
nat	born	innate
nav	ship	naval
neg	no	negative
neo	new	neoclassic
nov	new	novel
ocu	eye	binocular
opt	eye	optometrist
opt	best	optimal
onym, nym	name	pseudonym
orig	beginning	origin
ortho	straight, right	orthodontist
pater	father	paternal
path	feeling, suffer	sympathy
ped	foot	pedal
phil	love	philosophy
phob	fear	claustrophobia
phon	sound	phonograph
photo	light	photograph
phys	nature	physical
plur	more	plural
pod	foot	tripod
poli, polis	city	metropolis
pop	people	popular
port	carry	transport
pos	place	position
psych	mind, soul	psychology
pug	fight	repugnant
quer, ques	ask, seek	inquiry
scend	climb	ascend
sci	know	conscience
scop	see	microscope
scribe, script	write	inscribe
sect	cut	dissect
serv	save, keep	reservoir
sign	mark	insignia
son	sound	unison
soph	wise	philosopher

Root	Meaning	Example
spec	see	inspect
spir	breathe	spirit
stell	star	constellation
struct	build	structure
sum	highest	summit
tact	touch	contact
temp	time	temporary
terr	land	terrain
tex	weave	texture
the, theo	god	theology
therm	heat	thermos
tract	pull, drag	tractor
urb	city	suburb
vac	empty	vacant
vag	wander	vagrant
var	different	variety
ver	turn	convert
ver	truth	verify
vict, vine	conquer	victory
vid	see	video
viv, vit	live	survive
voc, vok	voice	vocal
void	empty	voided
volv	roll	revolver

FIGURE 11.7
continued

interest play important roles and should be part of any effective instructional routine in spelling. In the following sections we describe several key instructional elements teachers can use to build effective instructional routines.

Simple Explanations

From any given word list, it is important for teachers to identify for students the key features that they want students to focus on in their study. If a list of words includes a pair of rimes, then teachers need to draw students' attention to those rimes. If the list contains high-frequency words, teachers need to help students identify why those words are important to learn to spell and decode. Simple explanations and reinforcements of those explanations can help students develop the foundational knowledge key to their understanding of the words and their spellings.

Display and Practice

Practice does lead to perfection in spelling and decoding. Students should read the words they are learning to spell often and in various contexts—in the context of authentic texts, in isolation, in phrases and sentences, in school, at home, on their own, with a partner, and in a small group. The words to be learned should be easily accessible visually to students so that they can remind themselves of the spelling of the words simply by visually inspecting the word on display. Word walls are wonderful ways to celebrate words and at the same time provide students with immediate visual access to the spelling of the words (Walker, 2001).

Cloze Activities

Cloze activities require students to focus on the meaning of words within the context of a real text. In cloze activities, key words are deleted from a passage (in spelling instruction, the words deleted should be the ones under study). Students use their knowledge of the words and the author's intended meaning to identify and spell the correct word in context. An example of a cloze text activity is provided in Figure 11.8. For more on cloze activities, see Chapter 7.

Word Sorting

Word sorting requires students to examine a list of words for targeted characteristics and then sort the words accordingly. For example, a list of words could be sorted for the presence or absence of a particular rime, the presence of a suffix or inflected endings, the presence of two or more syllables, the presence of a silent letter, the presence of a consonant blend or vowel digraph, the presence of words that are nouns, or words that may describe "how a person could feel."

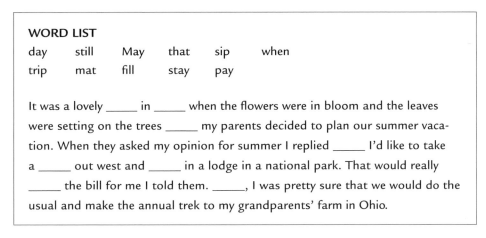

FIGURE 11.8

Example of a cloze activity

2

America's Finest

Jennifer Dyer

Multicultural Literature

Our classrooms are filled with learners from many different cultures. Yet, the books they read usually feature characters and events from the mainstream. Total literacy teachers change that equation by featuring books from many different cultures. They know that when children read stories from their own cultures, their interest in reading is increased, but more important, so is their self-esteem. They also develop pride in their cultures and better understand how important their cultural groups are. Multicultural literature also models for the majority group in the classroom the need to learn more about our neighbors.

At the risk of oversimplifying diversity, we shall discuss four major categories of multicultural literature that total literacy teachers feature in their classrooms. These include African Americans, Asian Americans, Hispanic Americans, and Native Americans. We'll caution you that the categories—for example, Native Americans—are an umbrella of many different subgroups. Tremendous differences exist between Eskimos, Apaches, Comanche, and other Native American tribes.

African Americans

Once a scarcity, children's books featuring African Americans are now plentiful. They include books by African American author/illustrators such as Floyd Cooper, Ashley Bryan, Donald Crews, and Angela Medearis and often deal with key periods of American history. David A. Adler has written several fine, easy-to-read biographies of key figures

in the struggle for civil rights such as Harriett Tubman, Martin Luther King, and Rosa Parks. Publishers have been careful to include African American characters in their books, not just in historical stories but in everyday settings as well. For example, Brian Pinkney's books feature African American protagonists in entertaining, everyday stories that help define the human experience for all of us. Here are a few of our favorite books featuring African American characters:

Adler, D. (1995). *A Picture Book of Rosa Parks*. New York: Holiday House.

Bryan, A. (1998). *Ashley Bryan's African Tales. Uh-Huh*. New York: Atheneum.

Cooper, F. (1998). *Coming Home: From the Life of Langston Hughes*. New York: Paper Star.

Crews, D. (1996). *Shortcut*. New York: Mulberry Books.

Curtis, C. P. (2002). *Bud, Not Buddy*. New York: Yearling Books.

Pinkney, B. (1997). *Max Found Two Sticks*. New York: Alladin.

Hispanic Americans

The United States has more than 31 million Hispanics. However, it's important to remember that Hispanics are not from one country and they do not all share the same customs and language preferences. They may be from one or more racial groups, and not all Latin Americans speak Spanish. In fact, the majority of Hispanic children in the United States were born to U.S. citizens of Hispanic origin. Books

---

In a sense, word sorts, often done with the words to be sorted on cards that students sort into various piles depending on the sort categories, are a form of word practice. However, rather than having students look at a word repeatedly from the same point of view, as is done with typical word list or flashcard reading (where students can learn to identify a word simply from its first letter or two), stu-

are a good link to their Hispanic heritage, and more and more Hispanic authors are sharing their cultural stories. Here are a few of our favorite books featuring Hispanic characters:

Ancona, G. (1999). *Carnaval.* Orlando: Harcourt Brace.

Chavarría-Cháirez, B. (2000). *Magda's Tortillas.* Dallas: Chameleon Creek Press.

Delacre, L. (1992). *Arroz Con Leche.* New York: Scholastic.

Griego, M. (1986). *Tortillitas Para Mama.* New York: Henry Holt.

Soto, G. (1996). *Too Many Tortillas.* Glenview, IL: Scott Foresman.

Asian Americans

Although many books about Asian cultures have been written by non-Asian writers, more and more stories are being written by Asian Americans. These books do an excellent job of sharing remembrances of their family's assimilation into American culture. Other books, such as *Si Won's Victory*, tell the story of newly arrived children in the United States and the friendships they form. Here are a few of our favorite books featuring Asian American characters:

Garland, B. (1993). *The Lotus Seed.* Orlando: Harcourt Brace.

Lewis, B. (2000). *I Love You Like Crazy Cakes.* Boston: Little Brown.

Martin, B. & Sampson, M. (1996) *Si Won's Victory.* Glenview, IL: Celebration Press.

Mochizuki, K. (1995). *Heroes.* New York: Lee & Low.

Say, A. (1993). *Grandfather's Journey.* Boston: Houghton Mifflin.

Tompert, A. (1990). *Grandfather Tang's Story.* New York: Crown.

Young, E. (1996). *Lon Po Po.* New York: Paper Star.

Native Americans

The majority of books about Native Americans focus on retelling legends, myths, and folktales. Yes, many of these books are written by non–Native Americans; and we are fortunate that leading writers and illustrators such as Tomie dePaolo have featured stories about Native American life before the eighteenth century. Here are a few of our favorite books featuring Native American characters:

Bruchac, J. (1997). *Thirteen Moons on Turtle's Back.* New York: Paper Star.

dePaola, T. (1986). *The Legend of the Bluebonnet.* New York: Penguin Putnam.

dePaola, T. (1996). *The Legend of the Indian Paintbrush.* New York: Penguin Putnam.

Goble, P. (1993). *The Lost Children.* New York: Macmillan.

Martin, R. (1998). *Rough-Face Girl.* New York: Paper Star.

McDermott, G. (1977). *Arrow to the Sun.* New York: Viking.

Sneve, V. (1989). *Dancing Teepees.* New York: Holiday House.

dents examine the same set of words several times, but each time from a different perspective. Thus, although students are getting practice at identifying the words, each exposure to the same word requires students to examine the word from a different perspective. As a result, with several word sorts over a period of days, students learn to examine the targeted words deeply and intensively.

Word Making

Word building involves students writing a set of words. However, rather than using the entire list of letters from the alphabet, in word making students are given a limited set of letters. By limiting the number and type of letters to be used, nearly all students can be successful in learning to spell and write words.

Cunningham and Cunningham's (1998) *Making Words* and Rasinski's (1999) *Making and Writing Words* provide fifteen-to-twenty-minute lessons in which students are guided by the teacher through the process of making a series of words from a limited set of letters. The teacher also draws students' attention to structural and semantic patterns, meaning, word length, and other features of the words. Figure 11.9 shows a completed making and writing words activity along with the clues the teacher used to help students figure out the words. After having made the initial set of words, the transfer words (in the T boxes) are made using some of the patterns and other features in the initial set of words but now using the full range of letters and sounds available in English. The lesson is completed by having students, usually on a following day, cut the words they wrote into individual word cards and sort them into a variety of categories identified by the teacher (two or more syllables, presence of a silent letter, presence of a consonant digraph, and so forth).

Word Searching

As the name suggests, in word search activities students look for particular words in their contextual reading and other reading activities. They may be asked to look for words that are part of a given spelling list. As they find the targeted words, they examine the context for how the words were used by the author. Did authors use the same words in different ways? Did the words provide a particular nuance of meaning different from other words of similar meaning? What words were the most commonly found? What words were the rarest?

In a variation of word searching, students are asked to search for interesting words in their reading, and the words that they find become words for spelling and word study. Through this activity, students develop an understanding of words they want to learn and an appreciation for how those words are used in real contexts to convey just the right meaning that the author intends.

Word Discovery

America's Finest

Geoff Ward

Word discovery refers to learning about the origin, history, and background for particular words. Some words have interesting stories behind their development, and learning about those histories may help students develop a greater understanding of the words under study as well as a deeper fascination for words and their histories in general. Many dictionaries as well as books on word origins

Box 1: Two-letter word that means the opposite of "off."

Box 2: Add one letter to word in Box 1 to answer this question: "35 divided by 7 minus 4."

Box 3: Three-letter word that means the opposite of "cold."

Box 4: Add one letter to word in Box 2 to make the word "shot."

Box 5: Three-letter word, pronounced "how."

Box 6: Add one letter to word in Box 5 to make the word "show."

Box 7: Change one letter to word in Box 6 to make an icy precipitation.

Box 8: Four-letter word, two consonants, another name for a brogan.

Box 9: Four-letter word, one letter is silent, pronounced "tore."

Box 10: Add one letter to word in Box 9 to make a place where people shop.

Box 11: Change one letter to word in Box 10 to make a large pebble.

Box 12: Subtract a letter in Box 11 to make a word that describes a sound.

Box 13: Add a letter to word in Box 10 to make the word "toner"—A black powder used in copy machines.

Box 14: Add two letters to word in Box 11 to make a word that describes a spring rain.

Box 15: No clue. Word uses all the letters in the vowel and consonant box.

Box T-1: Add two letters to word in Box 5 to make an informal greeting.

Box T-2: Change one letter to word in Box 10 to make a word that is the name of the bird associated with the birth of babies.

Box T-3: Add three letters to word in Box 7 to make something that can be made from snow, sticks, rocks, a carrot, and a hat.

Vowels			Vowels		
e, o	h, n, r, s, t, w				

1 on	6 show	11 stone	1	6	11
2 one	7 snow	12 tone	2	7	12
3 hot	8 shoe	13 toner	3	8	13
4 shot	9 tore	14 shower	4	9	14
5 how	10 store	15 northwest	5	10	15
T-1 howdy	T-2 stork	T-3 snowman	T-1	T-2	T-3

FIGURE 11.9

Clues used in making and writing words lesson

Source: Rasinski, T. (1999). Making and writing words. *Reading Online,* an electronic journal of the International Reading Association. Available at www.readingonline.org/articles/art_index.asp?HREF=rasinski/index.html (2002, August 12). Reprinted with permission of the author and the International Reading Association

provide teachers and students with fascinating histories behind the words they may be studying. A list of some of our favorite word study books is provided in Figure 11.10.

Mnemonics

Most people have particular words that give them difficulty in spelling. For these unusually challenging words, people often develop special personal rules or memory devices to remember the spelling of the words. These are called pneumonic devices and should be a part of the instructional process and discussion in spelling. Students should be encouraged to come up with special hints for word spellings and share them with their fellow students. Here are a couple pneumonic spelling devices that we have found helpful:

- ◆ The word *together* can be broken into the simple phrase "to get her" for spelling purposes.
- ◆ The homophones *their*, *there*, and *they're* can be a challenge to spell for some students and it may help to know that there is always a *the* in *their*, *there*, and *they're*.

Routines in Direct Spelling Instruction

Now that you have some guidance for how spelling might be taught, the next question often is, "How can I fit all these instructional activities into a twenty-minute daily period?" This is not an easy question to answer. Much of the answer lies in the teaching style of the teacher and the instructional needs and interests of students.

Almond, J. (1985). *Dictionary of Word Origins.* Secaucus, NJ: Citadel Press. ISBN: 0-8065-1713-1

Ayto, J. (1990). *Dictionary of Word Origins: The Histories of More Than 8,000 English-language Words.* New York: Arcade Publishing. ISBN: 1-55970-214-1

Hoad, T. F. (Editor). (1996). *The Concise Oxford Dictionary of English Etymology.* Oxford, England: Oxford University Press. ISBN: 0-19-861182-X

Muschell, D. (1996). *What in the Word? Origins of Words Dealing with People and Places.* Bradenton, FL: McGuinn & McGuire. ISBN: 1-881117-14-6

Random House *Webster's Unabridged Dictionary* (2nd ed.). (1998). New York: Random House. ISBN: 0-375-40383-3

Terban, M. (1988). *Guppies in Tuxedos: Funny Eponyms.* New York: Clarion Books. ISBN: 0-89919-770-1

FIGURE 11.10
Resources for word origins and histories

One model of a weekly instructional routine at the elementary level is offered by Mary Jo Fresch and Aileen Wheaton (1997). In the spelling routine they developed called Sort, Search, and Discover, the week begins with a letter pattern or patterns and words conforming to the patterns that are chosen by the teacher for focused study (as well as other words chosen by the students under the guidance of the teacher). On the first day of the weekly routine, students take a pretest on the selected words, choose words they intend to study and learn over the course of the week, and then copy the list of words three times for home proofreading.

On the second day of the routine, students transfer their words to word cards and proceed to sort words according to patterns or categories, that they and the teacher determine. Students examine their sorts for generalizations and put these generalizations in writing into a spelling journal. Later the students talk about their discoveries in a whole class discussion. Students also engage in a word hunt in which they look for words that conform to the patterns or rules under study in other books and materials. Student findings are put on a chart and become part of the class discussion.

Day three involves students using the words from their personal word list to create a meaningful written text. Spelling and word usage are checked by the students. The sentences that are created will be used on day five when students administer the spelling posttest to a classmate.

Day four is a more open-ended day for word study. The class engages in games with their words and the word patterns/rules under study. Students look up words in dictionaries, thesauri, and other resources to learn more about the words. The teacher shares information and stories about the words' origins with the students. The week's routine ends on day five with buddy testing. Students work in pairs and administer a test on the personal spelling list to their partner. The tester uses the sentences that were made up by the student on day three to add context to the presentation of the words.

Although this routine may not work for all teachers and students, it is a clear model of how informed teachers can put together instructional routines or packages that are balanced with a variety of activities that are focused and intensive. This kind of program empowers students because it gives them some control over the words they choose to study as well as encouraging them to discover the underlying and shared patterns and connections in the words with which they are working. Combined with many opportunities to read and write for real purposes and to draw students' attention to words and spellings during these episodes, a classroom environment is created where words become fascinating objects of study and students develop mastery over the written word.

Bobbi Taylor has taught second grade for five years, and she has come to a crossroads with her spelling program. She has taught a weekly spelling list from her first days of teaching, but she isn't completely satisfied with the results. "I do find that the spelling list does seem to help children's decoding and reading, but the words the kids learn to spell are always the ones they want to use in their writing." Should she give up her more traditional spelling approach in favor of teaching spelling through children's writing process instruction?

After much thought, discussion with colleagues, professional reading and reflection, Bobbi reaches a decision as she muses, "I do see value in having students explore and spell a set of words each week—they learn the letter patterns that are important for reading as well as writing. I'll have to make sure that we don't overdo this part of spelling instruction though. A few minutes per day should be sufficient to explore the weekly word list with my students." In addition to working with a weekly list of words, Bobbi decides to use her writing workshop as an opportunity to teach spelling to students. She conducts an occasional mini-lesson on some aspect of spelling that is important at the time, based on her observations of what the children seem to be struggling with in their writing and spelling. Bobbi wants to provide the very best instruction that she can to her students. She sees value in both a word study approach and a process approach, so she decides to include the best of both approaches in her instructional efforts.

Word Study and Spelling Summary

Words are important in a successful literacy instruction program. The key question is how do we teach words? Is it mainly repeated drills of skills that may end up crushing any potential interest in words or spelling that students may have? Or is spelling and word study based on the notion that spelling and words are important because they make reading easier and make our writing come to life? Put in the context of real reading and writing, and balanced with daily opportunities to explore words and word patterns, students are more likely to put into use the skills and strategies that they do discover through the supportive spelling and word study provided by the teacher.

Our job as teachers is to model, encourage, and inspire as well as to teach and inform. When it comes to word study and spelling, it is easy to fall into a teaching mode that focuses on teaching and informing at the expense of inspiration. The task is not easy, but the most successful teachers are those who rise to the challenge and provide students with word and spelling instruction that is informative, inspirational, and ultimately useful.

Grammar

Grammar and other mechanics of composition and writing also are important, but they must not become goals in and of themselves. The reason we teach grammar, handwriting, punctuation, and capitalization is to help students communicate effectively. Thus, these skills need to be taught within the overall context of reading and writing for real reasons—to communicate with others, to share a story, to express our thoughts and feelings. When students see that correctness and precision in the use of grammar, handwriting, punctuation, and capitalization lead to better writing and better understanding, they will be more motivated to engage themselves in learning and mastering these important literacy skills.

Remember the linguistic guidelines we shared with you in Chapter 1? Those guidelines are important as we ponder ways that children can expand their personal language. Language change is a choice—we can't make children change the way they speak—and the literacy transaction model is the key for language change. Children learn new ways of saying things through Strand 2, Impression. Therefore, we want our classrooms to be rich sources of new language. What comes in the students' ears and eyes will soon come out of their mouths if the language touches their hearts.

Traditional language and literacy education has been rule based. Rules have been taught to children with the expectation that function would follow form. It doesn't. We share this language story with you to illustrate what we mean. In 1980 the Sampsons moved from their Tucson, Arizona, home to Commerce, Texas. In Tucson, they had a rock-covered yard. In East Texas, they inherited a grass yard. Here's how Michael tells the story:

> Our yard looked so beautiful and green. After three days, however, it needed mowing. We had no use for a lawnmower in Arizona, so I had to buy one. I spent two hours mowing that Saturday afternoon. Afterward, I felt so proud of myself, and our yard looked so nice. However, two mornings later I got a big surprise. As I walked out to pick up the morning paper, I felt something brushing against my blue jeans legs. I reached down, touched my leg, and found my hand covered with brown, sticky juice! Weeds had sprung up, and the juice was coming from the seeds that covered the ends of the weeds. Later that morning I mowed again—it wasn't fun this time! And for the next three months I mowed that yard twice every week. I prayed for an early frost; in November my prayers were answered. The frost came and the yard turned brown.

Books that explore the intricacies of language.

Young Readers

***A Mink, a Fink, a Skating Rink: What Is a Noun? (Words Are Categorical),* by Brian P. Cleary.**
A rhyming exploration of nouns. The author has also written books examining adjectives and verbs.
Minneapolis, MN: Lerner, 2000.

***Eight Ate: A Feast of Homonym Riddles,* by Marvin Terban.**
A delightful and educational collection of riddles using homonyms.
New York: Houghton Mifflin, 1982.

***Once There Was a Bull . . . (Frog),* by Rick Walton.**
The clever splitting on compound words on two pages keeps the reader turning the page—and finding surprises!
New York: Penguin Putnam, 1995.

***Word Wizard,* by Cathryn Falwell.**
One morning Anna discovers the letters in her alphabet cereal can be rearranged to make different words and begins to apply that principle to other words and situations!
New York: Houghton Mifflin, 1998.

***There's an Ant in Anthony,* by Bernard Most.**
Anthony discovers an "ant" in his name and begins an exploration of other words.
New York: William Morrow, 1992.

I dreaded the coming of spring. But come it did, and I found myself pushing the lawnmower again. But then I noticed something. My next door neighbor, Jay, only mowed once a week. I asked Jay what the difference between our yards was. Jay replied, "Dalis grass." "Dalis grass," I cried. "What's that?" Jay pointed at the weeds in my yard and said that I needed to get rid of the Dalis grass, so the Bermuda grass could take over. He recommended that I use Round Up, which I soon discovered was an expensive but highly effective week killer. I sprayed the spots where the Dalis grass was, which was about everywhere, and the Dalis grass died. Soon I had a lovely, green Bermuda grass lawn that only needed mowing every week or so.

Why do we share with you this story? Because there is a connection between the Dalis grass and children's language. In cutting the grass twice a week, Michael made no real progress in his battle with the grass. It was only when he went beneath the surface and dealt with the roots that he made progress. No, we aren't going to tell you to spray your students with Round Up! But we are going to tell you that, like grass, language has a surface structure and a deep structure.

The language that flows from children's mouths represents their language surface structure. Surface structure language is composed from the roots, or deep structure of the child's language. You can correct a child when he or she makes a grammatical error, but when you do you are actually only cutting off the surface structure of the child's language. If you really want to change the child's language, you have to change the deep structure. And the deep structure will only change as children, through Strand 2 transactions, acquire different ways of saying things.

We must allow students the freedom of self-expression through Strand 1 activities while trusting that language refinement will occur as students come under the influence of the communications of others through Strand 2 experiences or activities. We must understand that criticizing an individual's dialect is understood by students as an attack on themselves, their family, their language community, and their cultural heritage.

In total literacy classrooms, students are free to express their ideas without fear of rejection. The home-rooted speech and dialects of the students serve as the foundation for their literacy instruction. Students in language-based programs do not need to acquire a new dialect or a new set of noun and verb endings before they engage in writing and language refinement. Contrary to popular assumptions, language users are able to read the sounds of their own speech from standard, printed English regardless of dialect (Goodman, Smith, Meredith, & Goodman, 1988; Lefevre, 1970). Therefore, language instruction must be centered on communication, with refinement as a secondary goal.

As students write, they acquire a desire to share their work with others outside the classroom. This desire can be used by total literacy teachers to encourage students to come in contact with certain conventions of print and communication. Each student will discover basic structural elements in his or her personal language and then will contrast them with those of other dialects, especially those that are required for writing.

The teacher's goal is for students to refine their communication so they can understand, enjoy, and interact with the ideas and language of other dialect communities. Consequently, total literacy teachers structure the classroom environment so students can choose to expand and refine their oral and written discourse by the influence of the communication of others.

Refining Grammar

By the time they start school, most children use all the basic language patterns common to good English speech *without having had any formal instruction.* Their speech approximates fairly accurately the adult language of their families and others in their environment. Adults usually do not realize how phenomenal this is. They are aware that their children are growing and developing, but they do not recognize the complexity of the learning that is taking place as they supply models of speech for their children in the course of everyday living. They often notice "cute" mistakes their children make in the use of language much more than they do the many correct and often sophisticated usages that occur.

Beginning schoolchildren have vocabularies ranging from 8,000 to 20,000 words and are actively using simple, complex, and compound sentences and modifiers of all descriptions. Their sentences may contain occasional errors, but essentially they conform to the grammatical usage standard in the child's environment.

The mistakes the child does make are usually overgeneralizations of the rules of grammar. For example, a child, knowing that in many cases one expresses the past tense by adding "ed" to the end of the verb, may come in and announce, "Mom! Dad! I hitted the ball." The parents think this is a cute error, not realizing it actually demonstrates the child's growing awareness of the "time" context of verbs and how time is expressed.

Four of the most important reasons children make such amazing strides in learning language follow:

- They are free to imitate what they hear.
- They are encouraged to try to say new things, to experiment.

Older Readers

Who Ordered the Jumbo Shrimp?: And Other Oxymorons, by Jon Agee.
A collection of more than fifty expressions we often use that are made up of two contradicting terms with delightful cartoon illustrations.
New York: HarperCollins, 1998.

Miss Alaineus: A Vocabulary Disaster, by Debra Frasier.
A fifth-grader, Sage, misunderstands one of the vocabulary words in her homework assignment with hilarious results.
New York: Harcourt, 2000.

Merry Go Round: A Book About Nouns, by Ruth Heller.
A delightful look at nouns through rhyme and vivid illustrations. This is one of a series by Heller that includes books exploring adjectives, verbs, pronouns, adverbs, prepositions, collective nouns, and interjections/conjunctions.
New York: Grosset & Dunlap, 1990.

Too Hot to Hoot: Funny Palindrome Riddles, by Marvin Terban.
Enjoyable word play as readers try to answer riddles with palindromes (words/phrases that read the same forward and backward).
New York: Houghton Mifflin, 1985.

The Word Eater, by Mary Amato.
Havoc occurs in this novel as Lerner, a lonely sixth-grade girl, discovers that when a hungry baby worm eats a word—the object disappears.
New York: Holiday House, 2000.

**CLASSROOM
LITERATURE
CONNECTIONS**
CONTINUED

The Year of Miss Agnes,
by Kirpatrick Hill.
The joy of exploring art, literature, and individual potentials
is explored in this novel that
shares the impact of one
teacher on the lives of the
children in the one-room
school of an isolated Alaskan
village.
*New York: Simon & Schuster,
2000.*

- They receive real feedback, praise, and approval from adults for what they have said.
- They learn that they can secure many of the things they want by using language correctly.

Because these factors have been highly effective in teaching language grammar to children, it makes no sense to suddenly shift the methods and motivations of learning language. Grammar does not need to be taught in the same way as history, for example. The teacher of history must, of necessity, present students new facts and details, which they are asked to remember. Language grammar, however, has already been internalized in amazing complexity and should not be taught as new material. Children should receive help with specific problems in their use of language grammar as they use it to work on other areas of study. In addition, they should be helped to learn to write their thoughts and use language in its written form to communicate with others.

By taking part in these activities, children can continue to learn about the structures of language usage through the same natural learning processes that enabled them to learn so much in their first five or six years of life.

Three Views of Grammar

Before a teacher can decide how to teach grammar, he or she must first decide *which* grammar or combination of grammars to teach. There are many types or models of grammar, but the three best known are traditional, structural, and transformational-generative. Roughly speaking, *traditional grammar* is prescriptive; it tells you what you should do when you speak and write. *Structural grammar* is descriptive; it describes what is done in actual language usage by describing the surface structure of language. And *transformational-generative grammar* describes how the meaning structure we wish to communicate can be expressed in spoken or written words that are heard or read.

Once the teacher has decided which grammar to teach, he or she must decide how to go about teaching it. The matter of how to teach grammar in the elementary grades has concerned teachers for a long time. Three major differing points of view exist:

1. Those who are convinced from teaching experience and research findings that teaching grammar as a systematized body of information does little or nothing to improve the actual grammar usage of young people.

2. Those who insist on grammar as an organized body of knowledge children must learn in a logical sequence. They continue to measure children's knowledge of grammar in terms of what they know about

grammar rules rather than in terms of how well they observe those rules in speech and writing.

3. Those who have devised means of teaching grammar in situations in which grammar really means something to the students.

Our view of grammar and grammar instruction corresponds to the third category. In this approach, grammar is taught—but not as a separate subject matter. Rather, specific grammatical rules are explored as the occasion arises. Editing and publishing student-produced writing and using some of that production in the school curriculum assure real situations for learning basic grammar. Thus this approach combines the best characteristics of the first two approaches.

In this process the child learns correct grammar without feeling criticized for using the "incorrect" grammar learned in the home environment or for making the mistakes that are inevitable in the complex process of learning to speak and write English. The child is not constantly criticized for making mistakes in ordinary speech or even casual writing. Instead, teachers help students find errors as they prepare their written work for in-class publication or as they prepare for formal oral presentations. Then, in the process of explaining and helping the student correct those errors, the teacher gradually introduces the rules and guidelines of correct formal grammar.

Exploring Grammar

Several guidelines should be observed by teachers in the process of guiding students' exploration of grammar:

◆ The study of grammar is functional when it is derived from the editing of a student's own work

◆ In the process of reading and building sentences and paragraphs that express ideas clearly, students notice change of meaning with change of form and position of words. They learn how meaning is affected by changes in position of various parts of a sentence, and they discover classes of words.

◆ The definitions and principles to be developed are those related to clear thinking and clear expression. They include use of a simple sentence in the expression of a complete thought; the relations involved in the expression of a series of closely related ideas in a compound sentence; and recognition and understanding of the classes of words, for example, how adverbs and adjectives add vividness and color to expression.

◆ Grammar work is neither concentrated in any grade nor presented in isolated lessons. It represents the building of a body of concepts that begin to take form in preschool years and develop gradually through the grades.

Ruth Heller

1. *Which book of yours has given you the greatest pleasure?*

Color, Color, Color, Color. It's my all-time favorite because I love sharing how the printer puts the colors in books.

2. *Which book has surprised you most in terms of its public reception?*

I guess I was most surprised in a negative way by *Plants That Never Ever Bloom,* my fourth book. I liked it so much and was surprised by its slow sales. It could be because the color on the cover was brown.

3. *What would you like people to remember about your work?*

I want people to remember my sincerity in trying to give as much information in my books as possible. It pleases me to know

how much people feed on the information I present in the books.

4. *What impact do you hope your work will have on children?*

I want my work to continue to educate children. I also want children to realize, through my books, that learning can be both enjoyable and exciting.

Ruth Heller tries to make her writing succinct and let the illustrations convey as much information as possible. Her delightfully rhyming, intricately drawn books include *Animals Born Alive and Well, Chickens Aren't the Only Ones, Reason for a Flower, Plants That Never Ever Bloom, Cache of Jewels, Kites Sail High, Fantastic! Wow! and Unreal!, Merry Go-Round, Many Luscious Lollipops,* and *A Sea Within a Sea.*

Reprinted with special permission of Ruth Heller.

♦ Formal grammar is not needed by children or by average adults to carry on their vocational and personal lives. It is the professional tool of the writer, the editor, and the copy editor.

♦ The goal of grammar instruction in the elementary school is to help students communicate more clearly without having to give thought to their use of language.

♦ Writing, more than listening, speaking, or reading, offers meaningful situations in which to discuss and change ways of saying things with reasons that are derived from grammar.

Children's literature is a valuable resource for examples of how the parts of speech are used in meaningful language. A series of books by Ruth Heller use beautiful artwork and language to furnish examples that enhance children's understanding of the parts of speech. Heller's books include *Many Luscious Lollipops: A Book About Adjectives* (1989); *A Cache of Jewels; And Other Collective Nouns* (1989); *Merry-Go-Round: A Book About Nouns* (1990); *Kites Sail High: A Book About Verbs* (1998); and *Up, Up, and Away: A Book About Adverbs* (1991). Marvin Terban's *Your Foot's on My Feet! And Other Tricky Nouns* (1986) and *I Think I Thought: And Other Tricky Verbs* (1984) address the irregularities of many of the nouns and verbs in English in a humorous and memorable manner.

Similarly, when students read real literature, teachers ask them to choose their favorite phrases or sentences and to explain the reasons behind their choices. These sentences and phrases often provide examples of grammatical structures and stylistic features in writing that we want students not just to learn but to emulate. Thus the wonderful language children read in their trade books becomes the very language that models and teaches important grammatical lessons.

We close our discussion of grammar with another language story. Ken Goodman tells the following tale:

> A group of second graders were reading in round-robin fashion. It was Jim's turn. "There was a lot of goats," he read. "There was black goats and white goats."
>
> His teacher smiled encouragingly. "Would you repeat that please, Jim," she said.
>
> Somewhat puzzled, Jim reread: "There was a lot of goats. There was black goats and white goats."
>
> Still smiling, his teacher stepped to the board. In excellent manuscript she wrote two words. "Do you see a difference in these two words?" she asked.
>
> "Yes, they have different endings," said Jim.
>
> "Can you read these words?" the teacher asked.
>
> "**Was, were**," Jim read.
>
> "Good," said his teacher.
>
> "This is **was**, and this is **were**. Now, read again what you just read from the book."
>
> "There **was** a lot . . ." Jim began.
>
> "No, no!" his teacher said with some annoyance. "It's **were**. There **were** a lot of goats.
>
> Now, please reread."
>
> "There **were** a lot of goats. There **was** black goats and . . ." (Goodman et al., 1988 p. 62).

Once again, this story points out that children actually "read" from their deep structure, not the surface structure of the book's print. Jim will only meet his teacher's expectations when his deep structure is modified. And deep structure changes take time and thousands of encounters with language.

Formal grammar is simply a system for analyzing our language and coming up with a set of rules for or consistent descriptions of the way language works. It is merely a tool to help us, not an end in itself. Realizing this, the teacher must introduce grammatical rules gradually as they are needed and present them in enjoyable nonthreatening ways. Teachers should never correct a student's grammar in a way that embarrasses or humiliates the child or implicitly criticizes the dialect spoken in the child's home. Instead, grammar should be presented positively—

how to say something more clearly, not how not to say it. In this way, children will acquire universally intelligible speaking and writing abilities and will come to view grammar as it should be viewed—as a friend, not an enemy.

Refining Punctuation and Capitalization

Punctuation

Punctuation is a matter of courtesy in making meanings clear to the reader. Modern writers take a great deal of liberty with punctuation and capitalization, but there are certain standard forms that everybody should know. These forms should be taught as students become aware of the need for help in making their early writing and dictation meaningful to the reader.

The following list is one that teachers can use as a guide for teaching punctuation. Student editing committees (see Chapter 10) will find these suggestions useful as they help others refine manuscripts. The list is *not* a sequence for teaching skills in punctuation; rather, it suggests the areas of punctuation with which students should be familiar as they mature in creative expression.

1. Use of a period
   - ◆ at the end of declarative sentences
   - ◆ after initials and common abbreviations
   - ◆ after letters and figures prefixed to points in outlines
   - ◆ after numerals in lists of words or sentences

A student develops editing skills.

2. Use a question mark following a question

3. Use of a comma
   - between days of month and year
   - between name of city and state
   - after salutation and complimentary close of a personal letter
   - to replace "and" in a series of words, phrases, and clauses
   - to separate a direct quotation from the rest of the sentence
   - following "yes" and "no"
   - to set off the name of the person addressed

4. Use of an exclamation point after expressions that reflect strong feelings

5. Use of quotation marks
   - around direct quotations
   - around titles of stories and poems

6. Use of a hyphen to separate parts of a word split at the end of a line

7. Use of an apostrophe
   - in common contractions
   - in possessives

8. Use of a colon after the salutation of a business letter

Capitalization

Capitalization, along with punctuation, is a matter of courtesy to help make meanings clear to the reader. Although some options do exist in capitalization, students should become familiar with standard usages. As with punctuation, these should not be directly taught to students; rather, they should be mastered through the actual practices of writing and refinement.

1. Capitalization of the first word of a
   - sentence
   - line of poetry
   - direct quotation

2. Capitalization of the important words in a title

3. Capitalization of names of
   - particular places: schools, streets, cities, nations, and important geographical localities
   - days of week, months, and special days
   - persons and pets
   - initials and abbreviations of proper names
   - organizations

- races, nationalities, and school subjects
- companies and firms
- brands and special products

4. Capitalization of
   - the pronoun "I"
   - the topics of an outline
   - the first, last, and each important word in titles of books, pictures, magazine articles, and so on

Refining Handwriting

Handwriting is an important part of the language arts curriculum. The purpose for writing is communication; therefore, students must strive for legible handwriting that can be read by others. However, like grammar, handwriting must not be an end in itself. Instead, it must be taught within the broader context of communication and not through isolated drills. Graves (1978) complains that handwriting, the proper formation of letters, has become the "main event" in many language arts classrooms, leaving composition as the "side show." When handwriting loses its "toolness," it can interfere with composition or the creative presentation of ideas and thoughts.

When handwriting is divorced from composition and content, significant problems may develop. Graves (1983) has found that "One group of writers feel that their information is good because the handwriting is clear" (p. 180). He also found other writers who "dismissed their experiences and their views about issues because their handwriting had been deemed unacceptable" (p. 180).

Teachers must place emphasis on what is being said, and not on the physical appearance of the manuscript. However, our society does place value on the appearance of handwriting and tends to judge writing by how neat or messy the paper is while sometimes overlooking the underlying quality of the composition. Because of this discrimination, good handwriting is a goal for which students should strive. However, we believe handwriting is best taught within the act of composition without interfering with the process of writing.

Helping Students Refine Their Handwriting

The physical environment is important when students are attempting to produce handwriting that has a pleasing style. The students must be comfortable and relaxed. Teachers should be sure desks and chairs are the proper height. This will enable students to place both feet on the floor and rest their arms comfortably on the desk.

Students' handwriting is improved when the paper is positioned correctly. The edge of the paper should be perpendicular to the front edge of the desk when the student is printing. In cursive writing, the paper should be tilted at a 30-degree angle to the left. Left-handed students should tilt their paper the opposite direction with even more of a slant than right-handed students (Fox & Allen, 1983).

The teacher should provide areas for students to explore and practice forming letters. An area of the chalkboard or an easel set up in a corner of the room may be designated for writing practice and will attract students' attention. Guides (see Figure 11.11) that demonstrate the correct form of the letter should be readily available. Many teachers have found it valuable to attach small copies of writing guides to each child's desk for easy reference.

In addition to comfortable and attractive places in which to write, a variety of writing materials should be provided. Writing is traditionally thought of as a pencil-and-lined-paper task; however, students should be given the opportunity to use many different types of media. Whether using a pen, chalk, marking pen, paintbrush, or fingers in finger paint, a child is still internalizing ways to use print to convey a message. Small pieces of cardboard or plywood sprayed with chalkboard paint provide students with personal chalkboards on which to practice and perfect their penmanship. "Lift and erase" tablets and dry erase boards are also useful. Teachers should realize that the way handwriting is "taught" to students will help to determine their views on the entire process of writing. If students form negative views concerning the mechanical aspects of writing, the creative aspect of the process is directly impacted. Fluency and meaning creation are forgotten in the struggle to "draw" the letters to match a model.

Most school districts have adopted a commercially prepared writing program that gives teachers guidelines on teaching handwriting. Letters are usually grouped for presentation by similarities such as *I*, *l*, and *t*, and the program includes workbooks for students. Activities in these workbooks emphasize copying isolated letters, words, and phrases.

A beginning writer needs to experiment with and manipulate print that has personal meaning. Too much emphasis on copying isolated letters can easily disintegrate into an art lesson, and the bridge between meaning and print is destroyed.

One way of assuring that handwriting is linked with meaning is to incorporate the child's language into the process. Using a child's dictation is an effective way of doing this. The Teacher-to-Teacher feature describes this process:

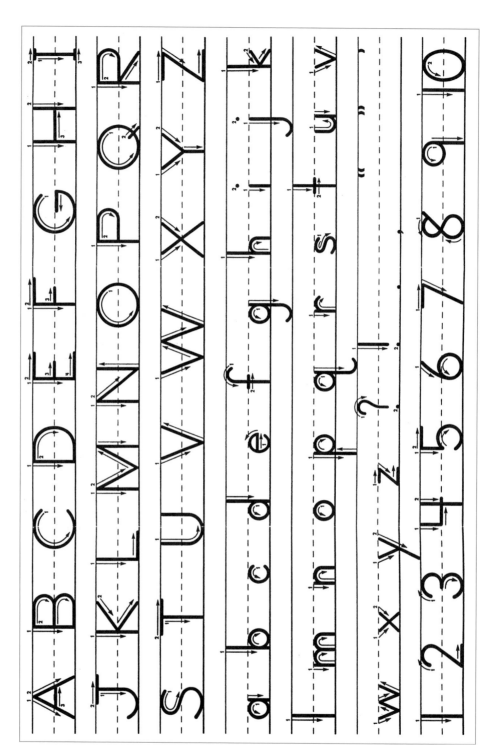

FIGURE 11.11

Manuscript guide

Source: Used with permission from Zaner-Bloser, Inc.

Judy Embry uses group dictation to let her first-graders construct their own daily "writing" lesson. After selection of a topic, students volunteer sentences to form a story or provide information concerning the topic. Judy records these sentences on a large chart tablet in front of the group using a marking pen to write a sentence in the child's favorite color. The child's name is included at the end of the sentence. The chart is left on display in the room, and copies of the sentences are prepared with space left for illustrations. Students decide whether they will trace over the print or recopy it on another line.

As the year progresses, many students decide to use the chart rather than wait for a copy to be made. They copy their own sentences, or others, and sometimes combine them to construct an individual story or to create their own sentences or story. Often students decide to illustrate their work and produce an individual, group, or class book.

Beginning writers generally use a form of manuscript. As students become older, they begin to express an interest in cursive writing, since this is what they see adults using. In past years, controversy has abounded concerning the optimum time to introduce the cursive form of handwriting to students. Currently, flexibility is the key. The practice of moving all second- or third-grade students into cursive at the same time is inappropriate. Just as all literacy processes are developmental and different students acquire them at different ages, students will be ready for cursive writing at different times.

Introducing cursive writing to students involves the same linguistic principles as those discussed in the instruction of manuscript, and many commercially prepared programs for teaching cursive writing are available. These programs include workbooks, charts, and teachers' manuals that delineate the proper way to make the letters and give teachers instructional advice concerning special difficulties that students may encounter with certain letters.

While teaching the forms of cursive, teachers must keep the emphasis on fluency of expression and meaning. If students are asked to focus all their energy on the task of abandoning a familiar writing form in favor of a new one, the emphasis is once again focused on the mechanical aspect of writing rather than the communicative aspect. The transfer from manuscript to cursive must, therefore, be a natural process that stems from the need to communicate.

The teacher can facilitate this transfer by using the cursive form to write meaningful messages to students concerning everyday announcements, schedules, and information necessary for the normal operation of a classroom. In addition, cursive writing may be utilized to share riddles, rhymes, and special events with the students. Soon, many students will begin to experiment with this style and to incorporate it into their writing. This is the time for the teacher to begin to "formalize" instruction by providing students with models of cursive handwriting (Figure 11.12) and sharing the method of making the letters in the most legible and efficient way.

In an effort to bridge the gap between manuscript and cursive writing, Donald Thurber (1987) developed D'Nealian manuscript in the mid-1960s. This writing system consists of characters that are lowercase and simple to write. As illustrated in Figure 11.13, most of the letters contain the same slant as cursive and are made with one continuous stroke.

Evaluating Handwriting

At one time, handwriting was evaluated on the basis of its beauty, and elaborate penmanship was highly valued. However, because the primary everyday purpose of writing is to convey a message and not to be aesthetically pleasing, this emphasis has faded. On the other hand, writing cannot fulfill its purpose if it is not legible. Norms of acceptability exist, and the teacher's understanding of writing as a developmental process that is constantly in the midst of change is crucial. For example, neatness is undoubtedly a consideration because it directly influences legibility; but neatness may suffer as a child struggles to erase and perfect a letter. At times, a lack of neatness may reflect a movement toward legibility.

Change and progress are achievable goals that enhance students' attitudes toward writing as a communicative tool. When perfection becomes the goal, the medium—not the message—becomes the primary concern (Yellin & Blake, 1994). Evaluation must be a process in which teachers help students develop habits that will aid them in writing legibly and efficiently (Fox & Allen, 1983). By demonstrating the most effective way to make a letter and by assisting students who are using inefficient movements in their writing, a teacher can use evaluation as a teaching aid. The teacher must keep in mind that each writing system has certain arbitrary rules. A handwriting system must have a certain number of unique characteristics to be copyrighted. Regardless of what handwriting system is used in a classroom, a teacher must realize that efficiency and legibility are the key factors, not "slavish imitation" (Smith, Goodman, Meredith, 1976, p. 254).

As older students progress in their writing ability, they will begin to develop individuality in their handwriting style. Students may begin to use embellishments as they cross the "t's" and dot the "i's." Slant and size may vary. Although students should be encouraged to develop their own style of writing, they must realize handwriting cannot be stylized to the extent that legibility suffers.

Teachers can emphasize the need for continuous concern about legibility by giving students the opportunity to evaluate handwriting samples. Students can place samples into categories such as "easiest to read" or "most difficult to read"

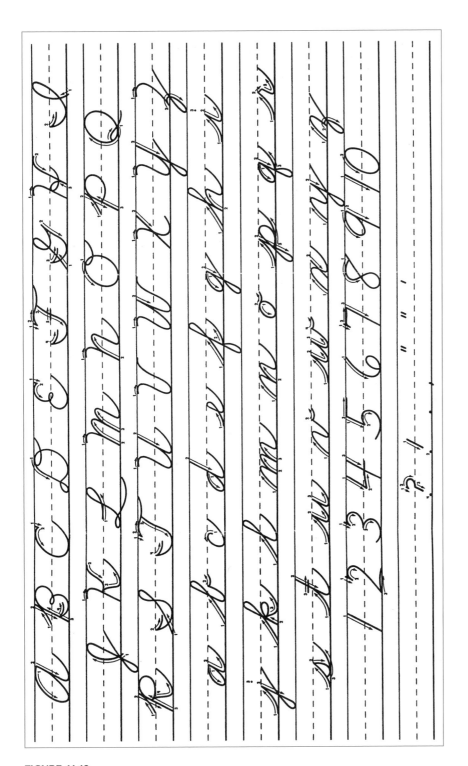

FIGURE 11.12
Cursive handwriting model

Source: Used with permission from Zaner-Bloser, Inc.

FIGURE 11.13

D'Nealian Manuscript

and "neatest" or "messiest." The learning process should be extended as students are given the opportunity to identify the factors that make one paper easier to read than another. The characteristics of size, slant, spacing, and formation of letters will be identified.

Students must apply these same principles of evaluation to their handwriting. By keeping samples of their handwriting, students become aware of changes in its readability. Individual folders are useful for storing samples. Models of cursive handwriting should be available (see Figure 11.12) and time provided for students to compare their handwriting to the models and to identify problem areas (Fox & Allen, 1983).

The acceptability of handwriting depends on its purpose. The legibility and neatness of a paper will vary depending on whether it is a first draft, a scribbled reminder, or a final copy of a paper to be graded. When students learn to adapt their writing style to match their needs, they will view handwriting as a communicative tool rather than as a product in itself.

Linguistic Guidelines for Refining Communication

Language refinement seldom improves without the influence of instruction or interaction with the ways others use language. Teachers should remember these important factors:

1. Improved usage is essentially a problem of enlarging and refining vocabulary so the speaker or writer has alternatives from which to choose.

2. Correctness is not the end of language instruction. Willingness to participate in useful language activities is far more important. Productive language can be refined, but one cannot refine what does not exist.

3. The English language is changing. Some traditionally objectionable forms of expression are now acceptable.

4. Language is a living, growing instrument of communication. It must remain flexible and adaptable to a variety of life situations. Every person needs a "wardrobe of languages" to meet the demands of changing relationships.

5. Standards of acceptable usage vary within communities and with students of different capacities. Efforts of teachers to raise the level of usage far above the standards of the community are usually futile and may be harmful. Teachers must show that they value the community standards and approach instruction as providing alternative ways of expression.

6. The usage program should concentrate on a relatively few serious errors at any given time. Which ones to emphasize should be determined by the standards prevailing in the community and by the basic requirements for success in writing and speaking.

7. Improvement in usage requires much oral work. Correct forms of expression must be repeated to cause the correct forms to "sound right" to the student.

8. Refinement of oral language as a base for written language is accelerated through the use of the dictation process, editing for publication, and the use of student-produced material in the school curriculum.

FURTHER WORDS

 From InfoTrac College Edition

Sharing the Tools of the Writing Trade: New Ways to Teach Children Conventions of Punctuation, Donald Graves, *Instructor (1990)* November–December 1995 v105 n4 p38(4)

Reclaiming the Basics (includes related articles on how to teach spelling and on making a core list of spelling words with colleagues; cover story), Regie Routman, *Instructor (1990)* May–June 1996 v105 n8 p49(7)

Spelling, Oh Spelling! (Poem), Elaine Anderson, *The Reading Teacher* April 2002 v55 i7 p693(1)

A Retrospective on Invented Spelling and a Look Forward, J. Richard Gentry, *The Reading Teacher* November 2000 v54 i3 p318

Invention, Convention, and Intervention: Invented Spelling and the Teacher's Role (highlights the teacher's critical role in spelling instruction and provides examples of how to support spelling development in classrooms; cover story), Lawrence R. Sipe, *The Reading Teacher* November 2001 v55 i3 p264(10)

From Professional Journals and Publications

Bear, D., Invernizzi, M., Templeton, S., & Johnston, F. (1999). *Words Their Way*. Upper Saddle River, NJ: Prentice-Hall.

Blachowicz, C., & Fisher, P. (2002). *Teaching Vocabulary in All Classrooms* (2nd ed.). Upper Saddle River, NJ: Prentice-Hall.

Fresch, M. J., & Wheaton, A. (1997). Sort, Search, and Discover: Spelling in the Child-Centered Classroom. *The Reading Teacher, 51*, 20–23.

Johnston, F. (1998). The Reader, the Text, and the Task: Word Learning in First Grade. *The Reading Teacher, 51*, 666–675.

Rasinski, T. (1999). Making and Writing Words. *Reading Online* (an electronic journal available at www.readingonline.org/articles/words/rasinski.html).

Rasinski, T., & Padak, N. (2001). *From Phonics to Fluency*. New York: Addison, Wesley, Longman.

Templeton, S., & Morris, D. (1999). Questions Teachers Ask About Spelling. *Reading Research Quarterly, 34*, 102–112.

Summary

Are mechanics important? Yes—because they help others understand what we write. Total literacy classrooms structure the classroom environment so students can *choose* change under the influence of other models and patterns. Grammar and handwriting skills can be improved as students strive to communicate in clear and effective ways in classrooms where communication is the instructional goal.

Total Literacy Anchors

SPELLING AND WORD USE IN COMMUNICATION

- The student writes original stories without fear of misspelled words.
- The student writes poetry that uses rhymed and nonrhymed patterns.
- The student reads to find interesting words used by the author.
- The student engages in deep word study through word making, word sorts, and word games.
- The student chooses writing as a recreational activity.
- The student edits his or her own manuscripts for spelling before publishing.
- The student uses spelling resources when writing and editing.
- The student is interested in spelling new words.
- The student is curious about interesting words found while reading.
- The student wants to spell correctly.
- The student accepts responsibility for accuracy.
- The student has no fear of trying to spell new and unusual words in original writing.
- The student studies words spelled in unexpected ways to achieve mastery of those used frequently.
- The student uses word resources when writing and editing.
- The student uses a constantly increasing body of words while writing and speaking.
- The student develops connotative and denotative meanings of words.

GRAMMAR

- The student develops an understanding of grammar as a tool to improve communication through speech and writing.
- The student begins to recognize and write various functions of sentences such as statements, questions, commands, and explanations.
- The student begins to recognize and write various forms of sentences including simple sentences, compound sentences, complex sentences, and clauses.
- The student develops an understanding of the sentence as a language unit.
- The student develops an understanding of the functions of the subject and predicate.
- The student develops an understanding of the functions of words that alter or expand (modify) the meaning of other words in context.
- The student uses regular and irregular verbs correctly.

- ◆ The student develops standards of correct language use and attempts to meet them.
- ◆ The student uses capitalization in appropriate places.
- ◆ The student writes legibly and fluently. Handwriting does not overshadow the need to write for meaning.
- ◆ The student use periods, commas, and other forms of punctuation appropriately.
- ◆ The student avoids double negatives.
- ◆ The student's writing exhibits subject-verb agreement.
- ◆ The student uses appropriate forms of pronouns for subjects and objects. Pronouns agree with their antecedents.
- ◆ The student uses comparative forms of adjectives correctly.

CHAPTER 12

Assessing Literacy Learning

As You Read . . .

◆ How does assessment influence instruction?

◆ What observational techniques can teachers use to gain better understanding of their students' literacy growth?

◆ What is the value of student interaction in terms of assessment data?

◆ How can students' work samplings demonstrate their literacy growth?

◆ How important is it for students to do self-assessment?

◆ What feedback do teachers in total literacy classrooms receive concerning their own teaching and learning?

Author Words

Mary Beth Sampson

The educational system in the United States is driven by testing. With passage of the education bill of 2002, Congress mandated for the first time annual state-designed reading and math tests for students in grades 3 through 8 beginning in 2005–2006. These test results will be used to judge the performance of both schools and teachers. Schools whose students do not make adequate progress toward the goals of proficiency in reading and math could lose funding and have their staff and curriculum changed.

Is such testing a new development? No. Fifteen states already test in those subjects in those grades, but the movement to a national mandate for testing is new. Is this a promising development?

The original purpose for standardized testing was to provide feedback to districts on the effectiveness of instruction and student learning. In practice, however, testing can force school districts and teachers to abandon a broad curriculum in favor of a narrow focus on the components of the test (Koretz & Barron, 1998; Linn, 2000; Stecher, Barron, Kaganoff, & Goodwin, 1998). This may result in higher test scores on the state achievement test but in less true learning by students. For example, Texas (one of the fifteen states that currently has such testing in place) saw scores increase on the Texas Assessment of Academic Skills (TAAS) exam, but scores decreased on the National Assessment of Educational Progress, or NAEP (Klein, Hamilton, McCaffrey, & Stecher, 2000). NAEP scores are a good benchmark because they "reflect national content standards and they are not subject to the same external pressures to boost scores as there are on the TAAS" (p. 2).

Not only does true learning decrease when schools are forced to "teach to the test," but schools also become a very stressful place for students and teachers alike (McNeil & Valenzuela, 2000). The Teacher-to-Teacher feature describes what happened in Jonathan's Texas classroom when it was time to take the TAAS test.

Teacher-to-Teacher

Jonathan, a bright third-grader, became very anxious on a Monday evening during the third week of March. When he was questioned by his mother, the problem surfaced. TAAS tests would begin the next morning and continue for the rest of the week. His teacher's anxiety about the test was clearly comprehended by her students, despite her reassurances of "Just do your best and don't worry. This is our chance to show how good we are." That night Jonathan had a stomachache and couldn't sleep. Jonathan, however, didn't have a *reason* for his worry—he had scored at the 98th percentile on the previous year's standardized test. It was a rough week for Jonathan and his classmates as they answered questions asked by the test writers and struggled with the format of the test. At home the pale little boy worried every night about how he was doing on the tests. On Friday, when the tests were finished, Jonathan sang his teacher this song:

Let's have a celebration,
A big wing ding, a jubilation,
send out the invitations,
we finished all of our tests!
Lets have a celebration,
give our teacher a big ovation
send out the invitations,
we finished all of our tests!

Did Jonathan worry needlessly? No. His test results will determine what programs he can participate in, including the school's gifted and talented program. The results will influence his educational options all the way to which college he can attend (Heubert & Hauser, 1999). In effect, children are being told to put their curiosity away, contain their imagination, and answer other people's questions instead of raising their own. Testing is the culprit.

The teacher actually learned more about Jonathan through the song he wrote than by the test score printout that arrived three months later. Jonathan's song revealed his talent as a writer and his great compassion for his teacher and his classmates.

The January 9, 2002, edition of *Education Week* declared that the Bush education bill "sets in place requirements that will reach into virtually every public school in the nation." It goes on to note that "the mega-measure is accompanied by the largest dollar increase ever in federal education aid. The Department of Education's overall budget will rise by $6.7 billion in fiscal 2002 to nearly $49 billion." As teachers, we must use our collective voices to move assessment toward more formative tests that are designed for instruction—not evaluation of the teacher or school. And we must insist that artifacts like Jonathan's song be included in the assessment of students.

The Culture of Assessment

When you enter the teaching profession, you become a member of a culture with deeply anchored beliefs, philosophies, values, organizational frameworks, and established goals (Stewart & O'Brien, 1989). Many of these involve testing, or evaluative practices. As you begin to examine assessment techniques and make decisions concerning what type of evaluative system you will use in your classroom, remember that many fallacies surround assessment.

Is testing fair? Not really. Research has documented the cultural bias of many standardized tests (Costa, 1989; Eisner, 1990; Haney, 2000) and the view that they do not measure cognitive skills (Marzano & Costa, 1988) or higher level literacy abilities (Hiebert, Valencia, & Afflerbach, 1994).

Some believe tests that require one right answer are objective. This is a false notion. By the selection of the items and the correct answer, the test maker has subjectively decided what the important information is concerning that subject and how the information should be reported. Have you ever been ready to take a test, yet done poorly? Perhaps after taking the multiple-choice exam you realized you had not been able to convey your understanding in that particular mode of evaluation. In essence, the test did not ask what you knew or considered and therefore

FIGURE 12.1

First Grade Takes a Test excerpt

Source: From M. Cohen (1980), *First Grade Takes a Test.* New York: Greenwillow.

George looked at the test. It said:

Rabbits eat

☐ lettuce ☐ dog food ☐ sandwiches

He raised his hand.

remembered as important! Such testing ignores the context of the student, or what the student is thinking, and often fails to tap into the knowledge base of the child (Messick, 1989; Wiggins, 1993). The excerpt in Figure 12.1 from *First Grade Takes a Test* (Cohen, 1980) demonstrates how the format of a standardized test prevents a child from communicating the depth and breadth of his understanding.

Let's consider Jonathan again. When he was in kindergarten, he was given a standardized test to determine his readiness for first grade. When the teacher

"Rabbits have to eat carrots,
or their teeth will get too long
and stick into them," he said.
The teacher nodded and smiled,
but she put her finger to her lips.
George carefully drew in a carrot
so the test people would know.

shared the results with the child's parent, she noted that Jonathan had lost points on the section of the test that required a self-portrait. He had neglected to put fingers and thumbs on the hands and, in accordance with the scoring mandated by the test, was penalized. In conversation with the child, the parent asked the child about his day. He responded by saying, "Well, they said we were going to play games today, but it was really a test." When asked to describe the test, he did so in detail. After discussing the figure he had drawn, the parent asked him why he did not put fingers and thumbs on the two hands of his drawing. "Mother!" Jonathan said with some exasperation, "he (referring to drawing) was taking a test—so his hands were like this!" The child then clenched both of his hands and obviously no fingers or thumbs were in evidence. The context of the testing situation had determined Jonathan's response, yet the evaluative process did not include any input from the child, only a marking system that allowed for one right answer. The cognitive processes that generated Jonathan's answers were ignored.

In reality, very few problem situations in the real world have only one correct solution; therefore, we do students an injustice if our evaluative system relies heavily on tests that require convergent answers for success. Perhaps Grant Wiggins (1993) says it best when he states, "Understanding is not cued knowledge; performance is never the sum of drill; problems are not exercises; mastery is not achieved by the unthinking application of algorithms. In other words, we cannot be said to understand something unless we can employ our knowledge wisely, fluently, flexibly, and aptly in particular and diverse contexts" (p. 200).

Therefore, it is crucial that we use assessment techniques in our classrooms that are an integral part of the ongoing instructional environment. Children must participate in the evaluative process by engaging in self-evaluation, determining what goals should be set, and planning how to reach these goals. By involving children in this active process of self-evaluation, goal setting, and planning action, we are exposing them to a process that will increase their productivity as literate adults.

Yet even though we know testing can have a negative impact on learning, testing seems to demand more instructional time each year. For many students, one week is spent on standardized tests at the beginning and end of each school year. Another week is spent on the locally developed skills test and still another week on state or nationally mandated exams.

In addition, children are confronted with end-of-unit basal tests, weekly spelling tests, end-of-story skill and comprehension tests, tests of isolated writing and grammar skills—the list goes on and on. These tests are then evaluated to determine if children have mastered isolated skill areas such as "initial consonant c" or "the use of plurals."

In this chapter, we briefly examine and comment on standardized tests. Then we provide alternatives to such testing—authentic assessment that is compatible with total literacy classrooms and will complement, not hinder, the literacy learning of students.

What Are Standardized Tests?

The format and content of standardized tests have remained uniform for the past fifty years and do not reflect the current research and practices in language development and instruction. Standardized tests depict views formed by behavioral researchers more than four decades ago, which assumed that literacy is acquired by teaching isolated skills one at a time and testing for mastery of the individual skills (Farr & Carey, 1986; Pearson & Johnson, 1985; Tierney, Johnston, Moore, & Valencia, 2000; Valencia & Pearson, 1987).

In most scenarios, standardized tests consist of questions involving isolated skills in decontextualized settings rather than situations that give children the opportunity to function as real readers and writers. What do such tests communicate to children about reading and writing? Morrow and Smith (1990) offer a condemning description of the message that is sent to emerging writers and readers:

> First, the examples presented to illustrate skills tested portray a picture of isolated, not integrated, reading skills. Second, recognition, not production or even identification dominates as the primary mode of cognitive processing. One wonders what happened to the theory of reading as a constructive process. Third, when they recognize things, children are usually asked to respond to either a picture or something the teacher says. At the very least, real reading involves identification of words in sentences. Finally, what dominates the whole enterprise when children actually take the test is test-taking behavior—filling in bubbles, moving the marker, making sure everything is in the right place. These activities may be related to test taking, but they have nothing to do with reading. An important final point to consider in regard to these formal measures of early literacy is the message they are sending about what really counts. If you take the tests to be a reflection of the field's priorities in early literacy instruction, then what matters most is the child's ability to recognize pictures, letters, and sounds so they will be ready, someday, for the real thing. (p. 38)

What are schools doing in response to standardized testing? Hoffman, Assaf, Pennington, and Paris (2001) found that teachers in low-performing schools reported greater frequency of test preparation than did teachers in higher-performing schools. In some cases, program content that does not meet the child's social, emo-

tional, and developmental needs is adopted in an attempt to raise scores on standardized tests. In many instances, activities are substituted that do not foster the development of curiosity, critical thinking, or creative expression. Conversely, programs developed on the basis of current research are often abandoned on the basis of results of standardized test scores (Stecher et al., 1998; Valencia & Pearson, 1987). Tests encourage or reward convergent thinking and, in effect, penalize divergent thinking. The loss of an emphasis on divergent thinking is particularly disturbing because divergent thinking is the basis of all higher-order thinking skills (Kasten, 1989).

Perhaps the most subtle yet potentially most dangerous result of test-centered evaluation is that the teacher and students are cast in primarily adversarial roles. When undue emphasis is placed on scores of standardized tests, end-of-unit basal tests, or teacher-constructed tests, teachers assume the role of judge, not advocate. Confusion results for children when they receive mixed messages from teachers' assurances that creativity and risk taking, which often result in "mistakes," are part of the learning process, yet are tested in ways that penalize this type of thinking. The environment is contradictory, and process-oriented instruction is negated (Graves, 1983).

A dilemma, therefore, is present. Common sense indicates that evaluation must be a part of effective instruction because the information evaluation yields may be used to modify instruction to fit the needs of learners. Parents and administrators want information concerning what and how students are achieving, yet traditional formal measures often negate or supersede the learning process.

The International Reading Association (IRA) has long been concerned with the issue of literacy assessment and high-stakes testing. In 1999 the IRA Board of Directors approved this position statement concerning high-stakes assessments in reading:

> The International Reading Association strongly opposes high-stakes testing. Alarmingly, U.S. policy makers and educators are increasingly relying on single test scores to make important decisions about students. For example, if a student receives a high score on one high-stakes test, it could place him in an honors class or a gifted program. On the other hand, if a student receives a low score on one test, she could be rejected by a particular college. These tests can also be used to influence teachers' salaries, or rate a school district in comparison with others.
>
> The Association believes that important conceptual, practical, and ethical issues must be considered by those who are responsible for designing and implementing testing programs. Assessment should be used to improve

Kayla Clark — Name
9 years old — Age
Swimming with my friends. — Interests

What do you like most about school?

I Like playing with my friends because they are teaching me how to do things on the monkeybars.

What's your favorite subject? Why?

Math, because I love to Learn new stuff. I also enjoy reading because it helps me write.

What's your favorite book? Why do you like it?

I do not have a favorite book, but I have taken intrest in Harriet Tubman and black history. I guess I think it is interesting.

What advice do you have for teachers?

To make Learning exciting. Also to give visual pictures of measurment, so the children know what you are talking about when you ask them a question.

instruction and benefit students rather than compare and pigeonhole them. Among the Association's recommendations are the following:

Teachers should

- construct rigorous classroom assessments to help outside observers gain confidence in teacher techniques
- educate parents, community members, and policy makers about classroom-based assessment
- teach students how tests are structured, but not teach to the test

Parents and child-advocacy groups should

- ask questions about what tests are doing to their children and their schools
- lobby for the development of classroom-based forms of assessment that improve instruction and help children become better readers and learners

Policy makers should

- design assessment plans that reflect the complexity of reading, learning to read, and teaching reading
- rely on multiple measures of assessment for decision making
- avoid using incentives, resources, money, or recognition of test scores to reward or punish schools or teachers

The full text of the International Reading Association's position statement is available online at www.reading.org.

But is there an alternative to such high-stakes testing? Yes—fortunately, assessment and learning do not have to be at odds with one another. Instructional planning is enhanced by evaluation of the learning of the children and the success of instructional activities. We now turn to the kinds of assessment that are positive and powerful—types of evaluation that do not disrupt or supplant children's learning but enhance it. We start with authentic factors that teachers should consider in evaluating students. We then share one way of collecting or showcasing student knowledge—creating portfolios.

Assessment through Observation

Evaluation can tell us how comfortable children are in the literacy environment and how successful they are in their literacy endeavors. One of the most effective methods of evaluation is simply observing what students are doing as they engage in literacy activities. As a teacher moves about the classroom, intuitive impressions are formed concerning an individual or class. A teacher can quickly jot concerns and evidence of growth in an impressions journal in which notes are recorded on student development. This record is useful to jog the memory if the teacher decides to transfer some information to a more formal account such as an anecdotal record or a checklist.

Anecdotal Records

Anecdotal records (see Figure 12.2) are one cornerstone of the assessment program in total literacy classrooms. Such records are an ongoing study of classroom happenings that center on student and teacher learnings. Teachers note significant events in the record and react to their own recordings with observations or musings as insights develop (Bird, 1989). The Teacher-to-Teacher feature illustrates this process.

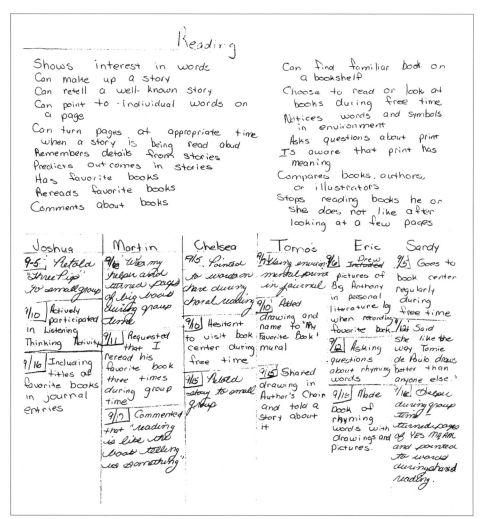

FIGURE 12.2

An anecdotal record

Sylvia Riojas, a first-grade teacher, noted that Carlos seemed tentative in his journal entries. Later, she interpreted her observation:

> At the beginning of the year, I noted that Carlos was tentative in his writing. Now I know that he was insecure because he didn't know what or how to write—he was trying to write for me instead of for himself! Now he knows that what he writes is up to him and that it will not be shared with other kids. Since that realization, Carlos has learned that he can write. His journal entries reflect this as he now processes what's happening in his life and expresses it through writing.

Through Sylvia's notes, she knew that Carlos needed to discover and value the personal nature of writing. She was able to help Carlos, and she helped herself to become a better teacher in the process. As demonstrated in this case, anecdotal records help teachers evaluate their own learning and emerging insights about children and instruction.

Checklists

Checklists can record much of the same information that is found in anecdotal records. Some teachers prefer the checklist format, for after the initial development of the list, less time is required to use this format. Of course, the teacher must be constantly aware of revisions and additions that need to be made as children develop and progress. The comments section of the checklist is perhaps the most crucial aspect. Checklists are convenient and provide at-a-glance information on each child. Figure 12.3 provides a checklist of early reading/writing behaviors that can serve as a basis for teacher designed checklists.

Assessment through Interaction

Observation is a sound assessment procedure, but our greatest understanding of student progress and comprehension comes through direct communications with students. These communications can take many forms: talking with students about their work, conversing during writing conferences, and written conversations with students as teachers respond to their journals.

Unlike observation, this type of assessment goes one step further: Teachers may challenge, encourage, or stimulate children as they interact with them. And such engagements are the key. Goodman (1989) states that interaction may be the most valuable of any process of evaluation because of its "immediate relationship to instruction" (p. 11).

Literacy Observation Guidelines

Children will develop literacy at their own pace and in their own sequence based on the language and experiences they bring to the classroom. These observation guidelines are to help you as you observe and evaluate your children's literacy development—not for purposes of grading, but because observation and evaluation will help you provide appropriate, meaningful experiences as the children form and clarify concepts.

Child's Name _____

Teacher's Name _____   School Year _____

Reading/Writing	Not Yet	In a Structured Situation	Independently
During story time, does the child	Date	Date	Date
1. listen attentively when being read to?			
2. request that you read stories/poems?			
3. recall details from a story/poem?			
4. draw conclusions?			
5. interpret pictures correctly?			
6. identify details in a picture?			
7. make logical predictions?			
8. recite predictable parts of the story/poem?			
9. tell what a story/poem is about or retell the story/poem?			
10. identify characters in a story/poem?			
During free time or library time, does the child			
11. spend time looking at books and other printed material?			
12. attempt to read familiar books?			
During dictation activities, does the child			
13. understand that writing represents speech?			
14. understand that text does not change from day to day?			
15. demonstrate interest in dictating?			
16. dictate words/phrases/sentences/stories?			
17. retell or "read" back things he/she has dictated?			
18. recite predictable text?			
19. follow a line of print?			
When writing, does the child			
20. produce writing-like scribble?			
21. copy or attempt to copy letters/words/sentences?			
22. write using random letters?			
23. write using invented spelling?			
24. write using conventional spellings?			
25. "read" back what he/she has written?			
Does the child			
26. know that a word has a beginning and an end?			
27. understand the directionality of reading and writing?			
28. point out "words" in print?			
29. locate letters within words?			
30. locate a sentence?			
31. identify most letters?			
32. recognize some words on sight?			
33. identify some sound/symbol relationships?			
34. match words?			
35. recognize capitalization and understand its function?			
36. recognize end punctuation and understand its function?			

Comments: _____

_____

_____

FIGURE 12.3

A literacy checklist

Used with permission of the International Institute of Literacy Learning.

Mary Beth Sampson evaluates children's literacy growth through their participation in a story grammar activity.

Teachers may model higher-level thinking strategies during these interactions by asking open-ended questions, or they may choose to have children examine their assumptions by asking "why" they chose a specific answer to a question or "why" they took a specific stance on an issue.

Most interactive assessment is informal and produces a general sentiment in the teacher of how a student is doing. This useful information can be made more formal, however. A student progress diary may be kept by the teacher that records evidence of student growth and provides a written record or discussion of insights concerning students' growth in cognition and literacy.

Conferencing with students about what they've written offers an invaluable opportunity for assessment through interaction. And student growth and development in writing can best be observed by teachers who view themselves not as editors but as coaches (Thomason, 1997, 2002).

An editor is a fixer. Teachers who view themselves as editors see their primary responsibility as working with a student's finished product. Teacher-editors are diligent in fixing grammar, spelling, and punctuation errors. They red-mark writing mechanics, mistakenly believing this will either motivate the writer to do better next time or help the writer to eliminate the errors. It does neither. What it *does* do is discourage the writer and introduce a fear of writing (Thomason, 1997, 2002). A sad example of such editing is seen in 8-year-old Michael. He was saddened by the deaths of two squirrels on his street and was motivated to write a song about squirrels one evening.

He sang the song to his parents and was praised for his creative efforts. The next morning, with great excitement, he took his piece to school to show his teacher. That afternoon he came home dejected. His teacher had immediately assumed the role of editor. Her first thought and action was to "correct" spelling with "a big red marker!" Michael reported, "She didn't even know it was a song." Fortunately, Michael's mother was a teacher too. And she functioned as a coach, not an editor. After much encouragement, she was able to restore Michael's confidence and self-esteem, and he was persuaded to reconstruct the song (Figure 12.4). Michael continues to write, but what about all the children who don't have a parent who functions as a teacher-coach?

Now let's return to the classroom and look more deeply at differences between editors and coaches. If the editor works with the product, the coach works with the writer. In individual conferences, the coach becomes the first "audience" for student writing. Teacher-coaches motivate students by finding positive aspects of their writing and asking questions and encouraging them to expand undeveloped sections. Instead of taking responsibility for marking everything that needs correcting (as the teacher-editor does), the coach helps student writers discover areas that need improvement—anything from a lack of description to a number of misspelled words. Correction is the student's responsibility.

The teacher who functions as a coach finds evaluation much simpler because it is easier to trace the student's development. Coaches encourage rewriting and movement toward publication. The student's writing folder frequently includes many different versions of a piece, allowing the teacher to trace the development of both writing and mechanical skills. This work may be shared with parents and administrators to document children's literacy growth.

Assessment through Analysis of Student Work

Observation and interaction constitute two forms of assessment, but a third type of assessment is used in total literacy classrooms. It involves analysis of the work that children do. Children should be involved in this process—choosing the pieces of writing or other work the teacher will examine, or meeting with the teacher to show the progress the student is achieving (Skillings & Ferell, 2000). We term these collections *work samplings* because they represent but a small part of the activities in which the students are involved.

I'm a little Sqrill
Sitting in a tree.ooo
Whats goingto happan
tome?

I might fall down from
this tree.

cus it has happaned to
a lot of other Squirrels
you see.

Look!! that branch
is breaking Look!! now
mine isto

and now Im falling
down to you.

He

plunk.

FIGURE 12.4
A third-grader's song

Work Samplings

For detailed analysis of an individual's development, it is very beneficial to keep periodic samples of the child's work, which provide examples of growth in a child's sense of story and the use of different genres of writing. In addition, documentation is provided that reveals student progress, which may include the development of mechanical and refinement skills such as spelling, handwriting, punctuation, and grammar conventions. In addition, tape recordings of children's language while dictating, dramatizing, or storytelling show evidence of growth in language development (Heald-Taylor, 1989). Taking samples of writing early in the year provides a base point for determination of individual growth.

A close look at Vincent's work (Figure 12.5) shows his progress as a writer from September through November. Such samples document to the child and the parents the progress the student is making in literacy development. Sometimes children's writings document nationally significant news from the local perspective. Note that Vincent wrote about a San Francisco earthquake—a mammoth earthquake measuring 7.1 that collapsed a section of the Bay Bridge. Was Vincent "shaken"? Notice that he took an opinion poll in his classroom and that he "liked" the earthquake!

Holistic Scoring of Writing

The emphasis on process writing has led to holistic evaluation criteria for student writing. The holistic approach purports that writing is an evolving process and that samples of writing taken under testing situations should be viewed as first drafts. Consequently, the criteria focus on the whole, or the message conveyed by a writer.

Many states evaluate students' writing with holistic tests on an annual basis. Holistic scoring is based on the total piece of writing and evaluates in terms of how organized the essay is and how appropriately the student responds to the purpose and audience of a given writing situation. For example, the Texas Education Agency (1989) reports "since the responses elicited are first-draft compositions, problems with writing mechanics, such as punctuation and spelling, are considered only if they are so serious that they interfere with the communication of the writer's ideas" (p. 16). In a negative vein, the test requires writers to write from an "idea prompt," denying personal choice of a writing topic. The idea prompt may ask for students to write in a persuasive, informative, or expressive mode.

In holistic scoring, each composition is scored independently by two trained readers who assign the paper a score of 1 to 4. If the two scores do not match, the paper is given to a third reader who also evaluates the response independently. If the third score matches one of the previously assigned scores, this matched score becomes the paper's score. If the third score does not match either of the other two, the paper is given to a fourth scorer for resolution.

SEPTEMBER

ARE CLASS LiKES TOO PUBLish
BOOKS! We Go To THE PUBLishing
CENTER. THERe WE PUBLISH
Book's./ AND BiND THE BooKs.
.
we MADE How A BooK is MADE
WRiTE it TAKE TO PeBLiSHing
CENTER Pich out PAPER AND CoveR
Type it ILLiSTATE. AND BiND iT I
LiKE TOO PUBLiSH BOOKS iT'S
FUN TOO WORK WiTH SuSan
SHE HELPS! us wiTH ARE BooKs.
AND HELDS US MAKE. ARE BooKS.
SHE TyPS ARE BOOKS FoR us AND
HELPS US BiND THEM

OCTOBER

ERTHQUAKE! IN OUR CLASS
CLASS ONE BOOK FeLL OFF THE
SHEL iN ARE HOUSE MOST OF
ARE CHiNA BROKE AND ALLOT
GLASS BROKE'S MyMOM ScREAM-
ED BECAUSE THiNGS wrer
FLYiNG EVERY WERE MY HAMSTER
TRIED TO SLEEP THROugh it Its
ScaRy when a earTHQuaKE HAPPens
it is scary. SoME PEOPLE DieD in THiS
one OCTOBER i7 19-89 SeveN PoiNT ONE
THE BAY BRHGE. CIAPEST DiD
You LiKE THE EARTHQUAKE

YES	MAYBe	NO
	PHiliP	C9 HoA
VINCENT		
MAttHeW	ReBeKAh	Phamd veroñica B. DAViD H9H étienne Hunk Otto
MAX		

NOVEMBER

BooKS! JoAN PRoBELY HAS 110
BiLLioN BooKS! SHE PRoBELY BRings
BACK 10 BOOKS! FRom HER TRiPs OR
MAyBE MoRE PRETTY SooN OUR CLASS
is wiLL BE FiLLED wiTH BooKs I LiKE
NON FiceoN THE MoST. SoME OF.
My FAVoRiTE BOOKS ARE BOAConstRi-
CTORS AND SNAKAN JoAN PRoBELY HAS
BOB 205 10000 6000 500 50 60
80 90 100 BooKS OR MAyBE
MORE THAN THAT JoAN PRoBELY
NEVR BUYS HER BOOKS AT HiLiR
BE ES

FIGURE 12.5
Three monthly work samples from Vincent

Measurements of writing on tests reflect a new style of literacy required of to-day's students. Total literacy programs prepare students for this style of writing as well as other more practical, relevant, or creative styles. In states where students' writing is scored with holistic criteria, it is important to provide occasional opportunities for writing in the genre under which they will be tested. Good writers should do well on tests scored holistically, but they do need to know how specific such tests are in the prompts they use. Students should also know that the evaluators are looking for organization and clear communication when they score the test, not just creativity.

Assessment through Student Self-Evaluation

The greatest goal of total literacy classrooms is for students to take charge of their own learning and to become responsible for their own progress (Hansen, 1989; Newman, 1990). When students become responsible for their own learning, they should also become actively involved in the evaluative process. The teacher's role changes from being a judge to being an intellectual agitator. Teachers help students to ask themselves questions: "Do I really understand this?" "How does this relate to what I learned yesterday?" "What can I do to make sure I do better next time?"

Perhaps this interaction is the key difference between evaluation in traditional and total literacy classrooms. In the first, evaluation is viewed as something the

Courtesy of Lisa Bartlett

Chandler tracks her writing.

John Gilbert Fox

Tomie dePaola

1. *Which book of yours has given you the greatest pleasure?*

My greatest pleasure has come from writing those books which are autobiographical, such as, the 26 Fairmount Avenue books. In those types of books, I try to connect with the feelings of what went on in my own life and translate those feelings into art. Then I try to make the text as "bare bones" as possible.

2. *Which book has surprised you most in terms of its public reception?*

I was surprised at first at the public reception to the character of *Strega Nona*, who now appears in eight of my books. I think her popularity can be attributed to the fact that she's the archetypal grandmother.

3. *What would you like people to remember about your work?*

I want people to remember that my books were full of hope.

4. *What impact do you hope your work will have on children?*

As a child, I loved to read. I want my books to invite children to become readers and book lovers. If a child comes to reading and falls in love with books through my work, I'll call myself successful.

Tomie dePaola has brought his distinctive style of illustrating to more than 200 books. He has won numerous awards, including the Caldecott, as well the hearts of children around the world with titles such as *Strega Nona, Now One Foot, Now the Other, Legend of the Bluebonnet, Legend of the Indian Paintbrush, Pancakes for Breakfast, Strega Nona Takes a Vacation,* and *On My Way.*

Reprinted with special permission of Tomie dePaola.

---

teacher "does to the students." In the latter, monitoring of literacy growth is viewed as an interaction in which the growth of the students is being evaluated while the learning environment is being monitored and revised to meet the ever-changing needs of the student.

Glasser (1992) lauded the benefits of self-evaluative behavior by stating there are basically two types of people in the world. One group consists of those who are productive, growing, contributing members of society. The second group consists of nonproductive individuals who are actually a detriment to society. The productive group is actively engaged in self-evaluating, reflecting on their self-evaluation, making decisions such as goals, plans of action, or corrective behavior based on their reflections, and then moving forward in a growth cycle. In contrast, the nonproductive group is constantly evaluating others and assigning blame to others for their own lack of success.

It is critical that we look at our evaluative system and determine if we are providing opportunities for children to participate in the assessment process by engaging in self-evaluative behavior. Children must not feel that evaluation is something "done to them" for the purpose of finding deficits.

This all-too-familiar model of assessment has been termed "teacher as examiner" (Britton, Burgess, Martin, McLeod, & Rosen, 1975) or what Glasser (1992) referred to as the "boss" mentality in which one is dependent on someone else to determine if a job is satisfactorily completed. This is probably the method of assessment that most of us were subjected to during our elementary and secondary school careers. An assignment was given, we completed it, turned it in, and then waited with anxiety for the teacher to "grade" it. If we were successful, we were given a good grade. If unsuccessful, a poor one. If a poor grade was received, there was little or no opportunity for dialogue concerning the strengths and weaknesses of the assignment or opportunity to learn from mistakes and revise and resubmit the work. In essence, that assignment was a "done deal" when it was returned with a grade, and we moved on to the next task, hoping we would improve and "do what the teacher wanted."

This model of assessment has several drawbacks. As mentioned earlier, it places the teacher and students in adversarial roles (Kohn, 1999). When the teacher is the sole evaluator and the job is to find the errors and deduct points, the collaborative relationship is usurped by an adversarial one. Second, it tends to separate subjects for the goal of evaluation. Tests are given in discrete areas such as spelling, science, social studies, math, writing, and reading. In the real world, solving problems requires the integration and concurrent use of all of one's investigative, literate, and content skills and knowledge (Altwerger & Flores, 1994). When subject areas are artificially divided for the purpose of testing, children are not given the opportunity to develop problem-solving strategies that will serve them in later years.

As teachers strive to move their students toward independence in learning, it is important for students to monitor their own growth. One way to do this kind of self-evaluation is through the use of student log books. These are records students keep that document the literacy activities they are involved with and the things they are learning. Most important, they allow students to become actively involved in the evaluative process. It is important that students engage in self-evaluation, but it is also important that they participate in evaluating the literacy program (Betterton & Landis, 1998). When students participate in this documentation of their language development, they are utilizing crucial metacognitive (knowing what and if you know) skills. As active participants in monitoring their own learning, children quickly become aware that learning is a lifelong activity that is not dependent on another person such as a teacher.

Student log books are a valuable way for children to record information concerning their literacy activities, but they are also a valuable format for teacher–student interaction because both can make comments in the log book. As dialogue occurs, progress is seen from the eyes of both teacher and student. In many in-

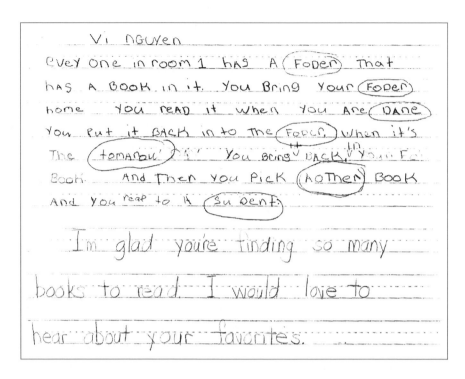

FIGURE 12.6
Student log of a
Vietnamese second-
grader

stances, an interactive log book becomes a method of self-evaluation for the
teacher as well as the student Figure 12.6 shows a portion of one second-grader's
log book. Vi Nguyen has decided to "edit" his own writing by circling words he
wishes to "check the spelling on."

Assessment through Running Records

Teaching Strategies

Reading Recovery

Running records are a varation of miscue analysis, which was discussed in detail in
Chapter 5. Like miscue analysis, running records give teachers insights into the
reader and the process the reader uses as he or she engages with print. They are a
great improvement over the Informal Reading Inventory, the primary assessment
device once commonly used by teachers.

As the student reads, the teacher observes and records what the child says—
marking deviations from text on a record pad. Teachers use the results of running
records to evaluate readers' sophistication as readers, to monitor how they do with
differing levels of text, and to develop an instruction plan.

The best way to learn how to do running records is to talk with a Reading
Recovery teacher. They have been intensively trained not only in the administra-

tion of running records but in how to analyze the results. In addition, you can read the writings of Marie Clay (1989, 2001) to learn "how" and "why" teachers take running records. Once you understand the procedures and concepts that undergird running records and miscue analysis, you will be a better kid watcher and a more informed teacher.

Assessment through Portfolios

In this era of high-stakes testing, there is a call for alternative methods of assessment that allow student input and are part of the ongoing instructional environment (Farr & Tone, 1998; Harp, 1991; Wolf, Bixby, Glenn, & Gardner, 1991). The use of portfolio assessment has been one response to this call. When portfolio assessment is incorporated, children have opportunities to become an integral part of the process of evaluation as they participate in decision making concerning the ongoing documentation of and reflection on their work. Student–teacher dialogue becomes an integral part of the assessment process as both child and instructor collaborate and cooperate to determine the contents of the portfolio and then examine and reflect on those contents (Calfee, 1999–2000).

What Is a Portfolio?

The word *portfolio* traces its origin from the Latin verb *portare,* which means to carry, and the Latin noun *foglio,* which means sheets or leaves or paper. The concept of a portfolio to provide information concerning the strengths and skills of a person is a familiar notion in the business and art worlds. Artists have prepared portfolios that best display their diverse talents and strengths, and executives have compiled portfolios representing their skills and successful projects.

In education, definitions abound for portfolios: collections of children's work for the purpose of demonstrating progress (Farr & Tone, 1998; Sampson, Allen, & Sampson, 1991); a collection of student's work over time that shows development in a particular subject area and is a vehicle for engaging students in the process of self-evaluation and goal setting (Clemmons, Laase, Cooper, Areglado, & Dill, 1993); a collection of all different kinds of things that provide a history of one's learning (Graves & Sunstein, 1992); documentation that paints a portrait of one as a reader, writer, learner, and literate individual (Hansen, 1992); "a systematic, purposeful, and meaningful collection of students' works in one or more subject areas" (DeFina, 1992, p. 13); "a collection of students' writing and other materials, reflecting student reading and thinking as much as writing" (Farr & Tone, 1998, p. 2).

So, exactly what is a portfolio? The good news is that there is no one right answer. One of the strengths of portfolio assessment is that there is not a single predetermined format. The possibilities for portfolios are endless (Calfee, 1999–2000; Graves & Sunstein, 1992). Much of the value of portfolio assessment is derived from the collaborative process in which student and teacher work together to select and reflect on work to be included in the portfolio rather than the display of the final product (Gardner, 1991c; Hansen, 1992; Tierney, Carter, & Desai, 1991; Valencia, 1990; Valencia, McGinley, & Pearson, 1990). Portfolio assessment centers on the evaluative process as a documentation of the strength, growth, and accomplishments of a student rather than emphasizing deficiencies. Therefore, the challenge for teachers and students is to find the format that best "paints a picture" of the literate growth of students in the classroom while involving students in the continual process of self-evaluative reflection on their work and setting goals for growth (Clemmons et al., 1993; Tierney et al., 1991).

The portfolio process must include the opportunity for students to reflect on their work, make self-evaluative judgments, and set goals for future development. Both theory and research have advised that humans function at their optimal levels of performance if they are striving toward goals that they have been involved in determining and that are meaningful to them (Glasser, 1992; McCombs, 1991). This process of goal setting occurs only when students have had the opportunity to self-evaluate and reflect on their strengths and the areas that need growth. Students know more about their own talents and abilities than anyone else; therefore, their judgment should be valued and sought as part of the assessment process (Goodman, 1989; Hansen, 1992; Valencia, Hiebert, & Afflerbach, 1994).

Assessment must not be confined to a review of one's work, however. Students will move toward becoming independent lifelong learners when they have the opportunity to determine goals based on reflective review. As stated by Gardner, reflection means being able to say, "What am I doing? Why am I doing it? What am I trying to achieve? Am I being successful? How can I revise my performance in a desirable way?" (as cited in Brandt, 1988, p. 32). Only when students are involved in this process of reflective self-assessment does assessment become part of the ongoing learning environment. Then students are doing far more than acquiring facts—they are *learning how to learn* (Wiggins, 1993; Wiggins & McTighe, 1998).

What's in a Portfolio?

The vital ingredients to successful portfolio evaluation in classrooms are the components of *voice* and *choice*. Teachers and students must remember that portfolios should first enhance the student's understanding of his or her learning, and the student obtains ownership and optimal benefit from participating in portfolio as-

Students prepare work that will become part of their portfolios.

sessment when she or he assumes the role of active participant in the process. This student participation includes involvement in choosing what makes up the portfolio and reflecting on and responding to the contents. As this process occurs, teachers can survey the individual growth framework of each student through conferences concerning the components of the portfolio and the student's responses, reactions, and goals (Farr & Tone, 1998; Graves & Sunstein, 1992; Murphy & Smith, 1991; Pils, 1991; Tierney et al., 1991).

Therefore, the contents of a portfolio vary. Children should have the opportunity to utilize a variety of sign systems (Harste, 1993) such as music, art, drama, writing, and reading to demonstrate their knowledge and skill as literate individuals. Here are some of the items that might be included in a portfolio:

1. Baseline samples of writing and reading
2. Student's reading log and reactions/responses
3. Student's learning log entries
4. Writing samples such as both edited text with all drafts attached and unedited text of stories (different genres), poems, raps, songs, retellings, letters, essays and reports, story spin-offs, interviews, and posters
5. Attitude surveys
6. Self-reflective notes
7. Records of portfolio conference

All Ages

***Testing Miss Malarkey,*
by Judy Finchler.**
Although the reading level is
appropriate for younger children, adults and older children will be more appreciative
of this sometimes humorous,
sometimes ironic, look at the
upheaval caused by high-
stakes assessment.
*New York: Walker & Company,
2000.*

***Hooray for Diffendoofer Day!*
by Dr. Seuss with
Jack Prelutsky.**
The joyous tale of a school
where "thinking" is taught—
and that leads to overwhelm-
ing success on a standardized
test.
New York: Knopf, 1998.

***First Grade Takes a Test,*
by Miriam Cohen.**
An intriguing view of a wise
teacher, the thought processes
behind first-graders' answers
on a standardized test, and the
impact on the class when one
child scores exceptionally well.
New York: HarperCollins, 1980.

***No Good in Art,* by
Miriam Cohen.**
An exploration of what happens when a first-grader thinks
he is "no good" in a subject
and the influence of a supportive teacher and friends.
New York: HarperCollins, 1980.

8. Student-composed list of goals and progress of accomplishment; teacher input to be added at conference

9. Student-composed list of strengths or what student has learned; teacher input to be added at conference

10. Art projects with attached notes

11. Evidence of literate activity from outside class

12. Audiotape of child reading a favorite text with photocopy of text

13. Audiotape of child reading an unfamiliar text with photocopy of text

14. Audiotape of retelling of a story

15. Projects from thematic units

16. Table of contents

17. Explanation of portfolio contents and organization

18. Comments about portfolio from teacher, peers, parents/guardians, and visitors to the classroom

The teacher may feel that all students should have specific items in their portfolios, such as specific baseline data or a completed writing piece with all of the rough drafts attached. Teacher-determined "external" criteria may be established for this purpose. However, for the portfolio process to be most effective, it is critical that students be given an opportunity to develop "internal criteria" by selecting certain pieces for inclusion in their portfolios and giving their reasons for the selection (Rief, 1990). When students have the opportunity to self-select pieces and reflect on them, they give us a view of who they think they are as readers and writers.

Portfolio Conferences

Portfolio conferences are opportunities for teacher–student dialogue, collaboration, and goal setting concerning the contents and the processes that were involved in producing the contents and selecting them for inclusion in the portfolio. This is in marked contrast to the dominant pattern of interaction between students and teacher that "consists of the following moves: the teacher solicits a student to answer a question; the teacher listens to the student's response; and the teacher evaluates or modifies the student's response" (Alvermann & Moore, 1991, p. 969). As students reflect on and evaluate their learning with their teacher, their role in the instructional environment is valued. Here are some sample questions that facilitate a discussion of this type:

How did you organize your portfolio?

Why did you choose this piece of writing? or What makes this piece of writing best show your strengths? Or growth?

What are its strong points?

What did you struggle with?

What did you learn from this experience?

How have you progressed as a reader?

What shows this?

How have you progressed as a writer?

What goals have you reached?

What supports this?

What does this show about you as a learner/reader/writer?

Tell me more about how you did this.

What makes this your best piece?

How did you go about writing it?

What problems did you experience?

How did you overcome them?

What makes this best piece different from your worst piece?

What are you doing as a reader/writer that you were not doing before?

What evidence supports this?

What are you able to do as a reader/writer that you were not able to do before?

What are some examples of your growth?

In what ways are your reading and writing connected?

How has growth in one affected the other?

How have you met your reading/writing goals?

What documents this?

What are your reading/writing goals for the next semester?

How do you plan to meet them?

Questions of this type might be appropriate for portfolio conferences in your classroom, and obviously you would select only a few questions for each conference. Remember, the conference is a time for *student* reflection on writing and reading progress during the semester and for interactive dialogue that allows the teacher to learn about the student as a reader, writer, and literate individual. Therefore, both student and teacher should review goals and determine the progress that has been made, and then collaboration can occur on the revision and extension of the goals and on a plan for meeting them. During this cooperative experience with the teacher, it is crucial to place the student in the role of articulating the self-evaluative process and making educational decisions based on that self-evaluation. Through this process, the student's learning is anchored and extended. As stated by

***Mr. Tanen's Ties*, by Maryann Cocca-Leffler.** Respecting individuality—and different ways of inspiring students—is humorously explored as Mr. Tanen is told to "get serious" about teaching and replace his "crazy" ties. *Morton Grove, IL: Albert Whitman, 1999.*

For the Teacher

***If You're Riding a Horse and It Dies, Get Off*, by Char Forsten and Jim Grant.** A humorous allegory about the various "fix-its" people devise for education. *Peterborough, NH: Crystal Springs, 1998.*

***The Animal School*, by George Reavis.** A thought-provoking fable addressing what happens when we fail to recognize the unique strengths of each of our students. *Peterborough, NH: Crystal Springs, 1999.*

Glasser (1992), "Without detailed self-evaluation followed by more learning based on that evaluation, little of permanent value will be learned and the purpose of education—to improve the quality of our lives—will be defeated" (p. 202).

The portfolio conference should be documented and included in the portfolio for future reference. A sheet containing the date and highlights of the conference such as student comments or notes, teacher comments or notes, and determination of future goals can be designed to reflect the needs of teacher and student(s). When conferencing, student and teacher can look at the record of the last conference to determine progress toward goals. Figure 12.7 shows a sample portfolio conference record form. Note the signature line for both student and teacher. This signifies that both participated in the conference and are aware of the observations made by each other.

Maintaining the Student Portfolio

As students move from grade to grade and school to school, it's important that their portfolio accompany them. However, work samples can take great amounts of space and deteriorate over time, and some student artifacts are simply too large to fit in a file folder. One solution is electronic storage. Teachers can take digital pictures of student work or scan the artifacts. These images can be added to a CD-RW (rewritable com-

---

PORTFOLIO CONFERENCE RECORD

_____
date

Student's Observations	Teacher's Observations	Goals
Progress toward goals	Progress toward goals	
Strengths	Strengths	
What I learned	Learning demonstrated	
Other observations	Other observations	

_____   _____
        student signature   teacher signature

FIGURE 12.7
Portfolio conference record form

pact disc); each student has his or her own CD, which can hold 700 MB of information, or a DVD-RAM, which holds 4.7 GB. When this technique is used, teachers can add WAV (Windows Audio Video) files to the CD that contain examples of students reading and talking about their work. Technology is an excellent way of sending students from your classroom with accurate representations of their work through portfolios.

Diverse Learners

Prejudice

As told by Dr. Geoff Ward

Are you prejudiced? Most teachers are well aware of the dangers of prejudice—to make a judgment about an individual on the basis of expectations about a group. Often, of course, those expectations are themselves inappropriate and may have been formed by generalizing from a few unfortunate individual examples, or by responding to the way a cultural group is portrayed by elements of a dominant culture.

It is vital that we each realize that we may be unaware of our own prejudices, or we may too easily justify them. Perhaps the most striking and thought-provoking example of dealing with cross-cultural prejudice that I have seen was provided by Dr. Charles Cornell in a seminar for teacher education students.

Dr. Cornell had taught for many years in Central America and had adopted a Mayan girl. She had been an outstanding student in her native country. When the family returned to the United States, the girl worked hard to succeed in the different setting. Dr. Cornell knew that her first English assignment had taken her a great deal of detailed preparation. When it was assessed, it received an "F" with the only comment being, "Obviously copied."

While that in itself is a sad episode of failure to learn about a student before making a judgment, there is more to come. Dr. Cornell went to see the teacher, prepared to argue for his daughter's honesty and ability. However, as soon as he introduced himself as Dr. Cornell

and as the girl's father, the teacher hastily interrupted to say that there had been an unfortunate mix-up. She had inadvertently put the wrong grade on the student's work and would, of course, be happy to regrade the paper.

We observers got a powerful message, but again, there is more to come. Dr. Cornell had presented this story in a polished and confident manner. Then he said, "But imagine if I had presented myself like this." He picked up a straw hat that had been lying on the table. His body language changed as he slumped his shoulders and shuffled forward holding the hat nervously by the brim and rotating it between shaking hands. "I tell you, Missy, my daughter she no cheat. She good girl." It was a powerful and poignant moment. I am sure that, like me, all those present vowed to themselves to avoid making judgments based on race and appearance.

It is easy to decide to do that, but not so easy to follow through. Teachers have to recognize that ability and effort are varied in all groups of people. Our task includes fostering all the abilities of all groups of people. There are many strategies in a total literacy program that will foster that, but the strategies can only work when they are applied, and that means that we have to be prepared to work harder for those who might be disadvantaged by the way they are perceived by people in the mainstream of our diverse multicultural society.

Reprinted with permission of Geoff Ward.

Report Cards

Classroom teachers place a priority on communication with parents. They talk with them by phone, invite them to sessions to explain process-centered instruction, and send letters and notes home. Teachers who use portfolios have clear communication with parents and children concerning the educational progress of the children. However, for many parents, the report card is the major signpost that keeps them informed about how their children are doing in school. Parents may glance at daily work children bring home from school, but report cards are carefully scrutinized.

Unfortunately, the report cards issued by most schools do not reflect the latest research findings and thinking concerning what's important in learning. Most report cards typically identify bits and pieces of the language arts and present a fragmented picture of children's literacy development.

Conflicts arise when teachers and school districts do not agree on the variables that reflect literacy growth. Report cards in such schools may readily accommodate letter or number grades but limit descriptive information or even teacher comments. Teachers become frustrated when their classroom observations of students' literacy growth are overlooked and they are unable to share their knowledge about students (Afflerbach, Norton, & Johnston, 1989).

Many districts simply use traditional report cards because they have not been presented with options. Informed teachers can bring about changes in report card formats by proposing alternate formats to the appropriate decision makers in a district. Some districts require a combination of the traditional and new; other districts are ready to move entirely to report cards that more completely reflect children's academic growth such as the one shown in Figure 12.8. When improvements in report card formats are not possible, teachers may convey similar information through letters to parents and written comments on children's work.

Evaluating the Total Literacy Classroom

Evaluation doesn't end with the students. We must remember that when we point one finger at the students three fingers are pointing back at us! For a total literacy curriculum to evolve, the teacher must be as actively involved in self-evaluation as in student evaluation. Educators should be constantly discovering how children learn and how to be most effective in guiding their learning. Teachers who engage in reflective self-evaluation are in a better position to implement an evaluative system in their classrooms that provides students with opportunities for reflective self-evaluation.

Grade 3 Progress Report

All Students Learning – Whatever It Takes

Explanation of Progress Marks

(+)   The student **consistently** meets and, at times, exceeds expectations.

(✓)   The student **often** meets expectations.

(-)   The student **seldom** meets expectations.

Explanation of Numerical Marks

Each academic subject area is assessed on a six-point scale (rubric). The numbers describe your child's performance over time. The descriptors after each number on the rubric identify what your child has demonstrated he/she knows and is able to do. A score of 4 is considered meeting the standard.

End-of-the-Year Achievement Levels

Exceeds Standards The student consistently meets and at times **exceeds** (more depth/extension with grade level work and/or performing at a higher grade level) **the standard** as it is described by the grade level indicators.   The student, with relative ease and accuracy, grasps, applies, and extends the key concepts, processes, and skills for the grade level.

Meets Standards The student **meets the standard** as it is described by the grade level indicators.   The student demonstrates proficiency in the majority of the grade level indicators.   The student, with limited errors, grasps and applies the key concepts, processes, and skills for the grade level.

Below Standards The student is **beginning to, and occasionally does, meet the standard** as it is described by the grade level indicators.   The student is beginning to grasp and apply the key concepts, processes and skills for the grade level, but produces work that contains errors and misunderstandings.

FIGURE 12.8
A report card that reflects the child's work

Reprinted with permission.

Math – Performance over time provides evidence that the student:	
6-	communicates clear understanding of math concepts through pictures, numbers, symbols, and words; demonstrates highly accurate computation; uses an increasing number of strategies to solve problems across a variety of mathematical concepts.
5-	communicates understanding of math concepts through pictures, numbers, symbols, and words; demonstrates accurate computation with few errors; uses more than one appropriate strategy to solve problems across a variety of mathematical concepts.
4-	*communicates understanding of math concepts through pictures, numbers symbols, or words, but may rely on pictorial models; demonstrates accurate computation with some errors; uses an appropriate strategy to solve problems across a variety of mathematical concepts.*
3-	communicates limited understanding of math concepts through the use of pictures, numbers, symbols, or words; demonstrates inconsistent computation; uses an appropriate strategy inconsistently to solve problems across a variety of mathematical concepts.
2-	communicates minimal understanding of math concepts through beginning use of pictures, numbers, symbols, or words; computes with frequent errors; makes partial attempts to solve problems, but little progress made towards a solution.
1-	communicates little or no understanding of math without prompting; requires assistance to compute; applies a strategy to solve problems with assistance.

History/Social Science – Performance over time provides evidence that the student:	
6-	independently provides examples of connections between the past, present and future; independently uses maps and/or globes to demonstrate and apply thorough understanding of geography; uses and compares many historical sources* to gain information; demonstrates thorough understanding of cultures.
5-	makes relevant connections between the past, present and future; independently uses a map and/or globe to demonstrate understanding of geography; uses and compares historical sources* to gain information; demonstrates understanding of cultures.
4-	*makes connections between the past, present and future; uses a map and/or globe; uses historical sources* to gain information; demonstrates understanding of cultures.*
3-	makes connections between the past, present and future with assistance; is beginning to use a map or globe with occasional assistance; uses historical sources* to gain information with assistance; demonstrates some understanding of cultures.
2-	struggles to make connections between the past, present and future; uses a map or globe with assistance; uses historical sources* to gain information on a limited basis; demonstrates limited understanding of cultures.
1-	is unable to make any connections between the past, present and future; is unable to use maps or globes even with assistance; is unable to use historical sources * to gain information even with assistance; is unable to demonstrate an understanding of cultures.

* **historical sources** may include textbooks, reference books, diaries, photos, artifacts, original documents.

Science – Performance over time provides evidence that the student:	
6-	demonstrates thorough understanding of concepts and makes scientific connections; develops questions and gains information using a wide variety of resources; makes accurate predictions and draws conclusions thoroughly supported by evidence; systematically uses a variety of tools to accurately measure, observe and record results.
5-	demonstrates thorough understanding of concepts; gains information using a variety of resources; makes accurate predictions and draws conclusions using some supporting evidence; independently uses tools to accurately measure, observe and record results with few errors.
4-	*demonstrates understanding of concepts; gains information from available resources; makes logical predictions and draws conclusions; uses tools to measure, observe and records results with some errors.*
3-	demonstrates limited understanding of science concepts; may require assistance to gain information from available resources; requires prompting or re-teaching to make logical predictions and conclusions; may require assistance when using tools to measure, observe and record results.
2-	demonstrates incomplete or inaccurate understanding of concepts; requires assistance to gain information from available resources; requires prompting and re-teaching to make predictions and conclusions; requires assistance when using tools.
1-	is unable to demonstrate an understanding of concepts; is unable to get information from available resources even with assistance; requires re-teaching to make predictions; is unable to use tools even with assistance.

FIGURE 12.8

continued

Teacher(s)_____

Math	1st	2nd	3rd	End of Year
Effort				
Number Sense and Operations				
Computes and understands whole numbers				
Computes and understands fractions and decimals				
Patterns, Functions, and Algebra				
Understands patterns and relationships				
Measurement				
Understands and uses appropriate units of measurement				
Geometry				
Identifies, describes, draws, and classifies geometric figures				
Problem Solving				
Learns, uses, and communicates appropriate strategies to solve problems				

History/Social Science	1st	2nd	3rd	End of Year
Efforts				
Develops and applies historical, geographic and cultural understandings to make connections between the past, present and future.				

Science	1st	2nd	3rd	End of Year
Effort				
Investigates and understands concepts in Life, Physical and Earth Science and applies the processes and skills of scientific inquiry.				

Additional Subjects	1st	2nd	3rd
Visual/Performing Arts			
Physical Education			

Special Services	1st	2nd	3rd
Title 1			
GATE			
*RSP			
*Speech/Language			
*English Language Learner (ELL)			
Reading Specialist			
Intervention			
Other:			

*See IEP or ELL Attachment

Reading – Performance over time provides evidence that the student:

6- uses many strategies to determine the meaning of unfamiliar words in text; demonstrates effortless expression, phrasing, and pacing in oral reading; generalizes themes and summarizes concisely in a variety of advanced materials; makes judgments/opinions using text to strongly support ideas; shows literal and deep inferential understanding in written and oral responses.

5- uses strategies to determine meaning of unfamiliar words in text; demonstrates correct and appropriate expression, phrasing, and pacing in oral reading; summarizes and generalizes themes from materials that are grade level and above; makes judgment/opinions using text to support ideas: shows literal and inferential understanding in written and oral responses.

4- uses some strategies to determine meaning of unfamiliar words in text: demonstrates generally appropriate phrasing and pacing in oral reading: retells text, determining main ideas and supporting details: makes judgments/opinions with some support from the text: shows accurate literal, and some inferential, understanding in written and oral responses.

3- is developing strategies to determine meaning of unfamiliar words in text; demonstrates inconsistent phrasing with some attention to punctuation in oral reading; retells text with limited distinction between main ideas and supporting ideas; makes judgments/opinions with limited support from the text; shows accurate literal understanding and begins to show inferential understanding in written and oral responses.

2- uses limited strategies to determine meaning of unfamiliar words in text; demonstrates choppy phrasing with little attention to punctuation in oral reading; retells details of text without distinguishing between main ideas and supporting ideas; makes judgments/opinions with little or no text support; is limited in oral and written responses.

1- lacks strategies to determine meaning of unfamiliar words from text; demonstrates choppy and word-for-word oral reading; is unable/needs prompting to retell text; needs assistance to make judgments/opinions about text; does not reflect understanding in written and oral responses.

Writing – A collection of work reflects a writer who:

6- demonstrates a purposeful, clear organizational plan; uses a wide range of techniques to engage the reader - effortless writing which shows originality, liveliness, excitement, humor and/or suspense; uses clear sentence sense and variety; uses vocabulary that clearly conveys the author's intent; elaborates ideas through use of multiple sentences and well-chosen details; sustains quality throughout each piece; uses accurate conventions*.

5- demonstrates a solid organizational plan; uses a wide range of techniques to engage reader; uses clear sentence sense and variety; selects vocabulary appropriate for the writing; elaborates ideas through use of multiple sentences and appropriate details; makes minimal errors in conventions*.

4- demonstrates an organizational plan with a clear beginning, middle and end; uses some techniques to engage the reader; uses some variety of sentence structure; makes writing that elaborates ideas through use of multiple sentences; makes few errors in conventions.*

3- demonstrates evidence of an organizational plan but writing may lose focus; uses few, if any, techniques to engage the reader; uses simple or repetitive sentences; uses few descriptive words - little or no elaboration of ideas; makes errors in conventions*.

2- demonstrates an inconsistent organizational plan; makes vague or confusing statements; uses simple sentence structure; uses limited vocabulary; makes frequent errors in conventions*.

1- demonstrates severe problems with sentence structure; uses limited or incorrect word choice; makes severe errors in conventions*.

*conventions=grammar, spelling, and punctuation

Speaking – Over time, oral presentations and contributions to discussion provide evidence that the student:

6- expresses thoroughly-developed and organized ideas; makes relevant comments focused on the topic; uses delivery strategies to engage listeners (eye contact, volume, tone and expression); demonstrates creative command of vocabulary selection and grammar.

5- expresses well-organized ideas with some elaboration; makes relevant comments focused on the topic; usually uses delivery strategies to engage listeners (eye contact, volume, tone and expression); demonstrates strong vocabulary selection and command of grammar.

4- expresses organized ideas with few details; makes comments usually focused on the topic; uses some delivery strategies to engage listeners (eye contact, volume, tone, or expression); demonstrates appropriate vocabulary selection and grammar.

3- expresses ideas with some organization and/or detail; may require prompting to remain on-topic; uses few delivery strategies to engage listeners (eye contact, volume, tone or expression); demonstrates basic, often repetitive vocabulary selection and inconsistent command of grammar.

2- expresses ideas with limited organization and/or detail; makes comments that often stray off-topic; uses minimal delivery strategies to engage listeners (eye contact, volume, tone or expression); demonstrates limited vocabulary selection and grammar.

1- rarely expresses ideas; makes comments that consistently stray off-topic, demonstrates delivery that is difficult to hear and/or understand; requires prompting to demonstrate limited vocabulary selection and grammar.

FIGURE 12.8

continued

Student_____

Reading	1st	2nd	3rd	End of Year
Effort				
Word Analysis				
Decodes and recognizes words				
Learns and uses new words from reading				
Develops fluently				
Comprehension/Literary Response				
Uses strategies to comprehend text				
Identifies and analyzes fiction, nonfiction and poetry				

Writing	1st	2nd	3rd	End of Year
Effort				
Writing Strategies				
Organizes, creates and revises multiple paragraph compositions, both over time and on demand				
Writing Applications & Genres				
Writes narratives				
Writes expository text				
Writes letters				
Language Expressions				
Applies standard English conventions in writing				

Speaking	1st	2nd	3rd	End of Year
Effort				
Delivers a variety of formal and informal presentations				

Social Skills/Work Habits	1st	2nd	3rd
Demonstrates self-control			
Works without disturbing others			
Accepts responsibility for actions and choices			
Respects rights and property of others			
Cooperates with others			
Follows directions			
Listens attentively			
Writes legibly			
Demonstrates organization			
Stays on task			
Completes class assignments on time			
Completes and returns homework on time			

Grade 3 Progress Report

School_____ Year_____

Parents as Partners

In the Poway Unified School District, we believe that a collaborative partnership between parents and teachers is an important key to student success. By working together, we are confident your child will develop the knowledge and skills necessary for continuous growth and achievement of academic standards.

As a parent, you are asked to join us in a partnership agreement:

School Commitment
- ☑ Provide a comprehensive academic program that aligns to rigorous state and District standards
- ☑ Maintain a learning environment that supports your child's academic progress, individual growth, and personal well-being
- ☑ Provide appropriate interventions for any student in need of additional support
- ☑ Maintain open and regular communication with you and your child

Parent Commitment
- ☑ Maintain open and regular communication with my child and his/her teacher(s)
- ☑ Provide time, space, and opportunities that support my child's learning
- ☑ Encourage my child to take responsibility for homework and assigned tasks
- ☑ Ensure my child will attend school regularly, arrive on time, and be ready to learn

_____   _____
Parent Signature   Teacher signature

ATTENDANCE	1st	2nd	3rd
Days Tardy			
Days Absent			

Teacher Comments

FIGURE 12.8

continued

How can you identify a total literacy classroom? Excited students and enthusiastic teachers are two signposts. However, to be more objective, classrooms may be examined and compared with the goals of the literacy transaction model defined in Chapter 1. That curriculum model described three aspects or strands that should be present in the classroom environment and interactions.

STRAND 1 (Self-Expression)   The real language of learners should be valued by the teacher and used in building students' skills for communication. Strive for these results:

- Students participate freely and comfortably in their home-rooted language.
- The real language of students is used as part of the room environment in reading charts, posters, talking murals, and books they have written and published.
- Students are free from the fear of using incorrect language to express themselves.
- Space and time are provided for students to communicate their ideas through many arts-and-crafts media and through dramatization, puppets, rhythmic activities, and discussions.
- Recordings of students' own language are included in the listening activities.
- Edited and unedited stories and poems written by students are part of the oral reading program.

STRAND 2 (Impression)   Students' language is influenced by the language and ideas of other people. Provide an enriched classroom environment with these tools:

- Many books are available for recreational reading, browsing, locating information, and improving reading skills.
- Books written and published by the students are a part of the classroom library.
- Computers and videos bring students who are not necessarily good readers in contact with the language and ideas of others.
- Books with records and/or tapes of the printed text are available to students to provide models of good reading and enjoyment of the ideas of others without their having to be good readers.
- Oral language activities include language patterns of authors that may not be typical of the home-rooted language of the learners.
- Art prints, musical compositions, sculpture, and other creative products are available for individual interpretation.
- Students have opportunities and resources for research on topics of interest.

STRAND 3 (Conventions)   Skills, or conventions of language, are learned in the process of actual reading and writing. Provide these opportunities for students:

- Students fine-tune their writing abilities with repeated opportunities for writing.
- Speech-to-print relations are discussed in informal and friendly ways that permit the natural internalization of a phonetic system for one's own dialect.

- Traditional skills such as sequencing are learned in the context of real literacy activities such as Reader's Theater, not by isolated study.
- The classroom instructional environment reflects an emphasis on the increase in vocabularies of nouns, verbs, adjectives, and adverbs.
- Students participate in editing manuscripts for publication of their stories and poems.

Rating scales such as the checklist shown in Figure 12.9 provide a way to evaluate the implementation of total literacy instruction. Rating scales provide scores that can be interpreted in light of the goals of your total literacy program. The scale may be used by teachers for self-evaluation, by a principal or supervisor for external evaluation, or for cooperative evaluation through conferences that compare and contrast teacher self-evaluation with evaluation by an observer using the rating scale.

Our use of the checklist indicates that students in classrooms where teachers score highest are classrooms where students score highest on reading achievement as judged by standardized tests. The students in a high-scoring environment discover literacy in various places and forms in the classroom. If they fail to comprehend in one setting, another setting or opportunity is available.

CHECKLIST FOR ELEMENTARY LEARNING ENVIRONMENT

This checklist is to be used in rating the extent to which any learning environment has visible evidence that the three strands of a **meaning-centered curriculum** are being implemented. It does not deal with the nonvisible aspects of a program.

Tentative conclusions from the use of this rating scale indicate that children who live and learn in an environment with a rating above 3.0 score higher on reading achievement tests than those in classrooms with lower scores.

THE SCORING SCALE

0—*Does not exist* at the time of the observation
1—*Present* but on a restricted basis—by permission only or after completion of "regular work"
2—*Present during observation period* but little or no evidence as a continuing part of the program
3—*Present during observation* with visible evidence that the condition is a continuing part of the program
4—*Superior performance of part observed* and/or visible evidence that the condition is an essential part of the program

OBSERVATION TIME
Minimum of 30 minutes recommended for external evaluation. No time limit for self-evaluation

SUMMARY	
Mean score Strand One	
Mean score Strand Two	
Mean score Strand Three	
TOTAL Mean scores divided by 3	

INTERPRETATION
The closer the total mean score is to 4.00, the nearer the classroom environment is to satisfying basic requirements for a meaning-centered curriculum.

Scores below 3.00 reflect a need for improvement in communication opportunities that are required of a meaning-centered curriculum.

FIGURE 12.9
Checklist for elementary learning environment

STRAND ONE

SELF-EXPRESSION

MAJOR IDEA
This strand emphasizes the real language of the learners as basic to communication skill development.

	0	1	2	3	4
Superior performance of part observed. Essential part of program					
Present during observation. Continuing part of program					
Present during observation. Not a continuing part					
Present but on a restricted basis					
Does not exist at time of observation					

ITEMS TO BE CHECKED

1. Is there obvious opportunity for each child to participate comfortably with home-rooted language in both talking and writing?
2. Is the real language of the children used as a part of the room environment?
3. Are children free from the fear of using incorrect language?
4. Is space and time provided for children to express their ideas with many media?
5. Do children have opportunity to listen to their own language on tapes and/or through oral reading of their own stories and poems?
6. Is space and time provided for children to participate in puppetry, pantomime, and dramatization?
7. Is there opportunity for children to respond rhythmically to music?
8. Do children produce original manuscripts of poems and stories that are useful in the reading program of the classroom?

Raw score totals
TOTAL RAW SCORE
Mean score (raw score divided by 8)

STRAND TWO

IMPRESSION

MAJOR IDEA
This strand emphasizes the influence of the language and ideas of many people on the personal language of children.

	0	1	2	3	4
Superior performance of part observed. Essential part of program					
Present during observation. Continuing part of program					
Present during observation. Not a continuing part					
Present but on a restricted basis					
Does not exist at time of observation					

ITEMS TO BE CHECKED

1. Are many types of books available for browsing and reading—recreation, information, reading skill development, own publications?
2. Are films and filmstrips used to bring children in contact with the language and ideas of others?
3. Do children have access to records and tapes that accompany books?
4. Do children have opportunities to repeat words, phrases, and sentences of other authors as they listen to reading of stories and poems that are different from home-rooted language?
5. Do children have opportunities to add to the ideas of others as they listen to and read stories and poems?
6. Are art prints, musical compositions, photographs, and other creative materials available for personal interpretation?
7. Is choral reading a part of the reading program that brings children in contact with language and ideas of others without requiring excellent reading skills?
8. Do children have the opportunity to research on topics of interest and relate findings to their personal questions and observations?

Raw score totals
TOTAL RAW SCORE
Mean score (raw score divided by 8)

<table>
<tr><td colspan="2">

STRAND THREE
CONVENTIONS

MAJOR IDEA
This strand emphasizes an understanding of how language works for individuals.

</td></tr>
</table>

	0	1	2	3	4
Superior performance of part observed. Essential part of program					
Present during observation. Continuing part of program					
Present during observation. Not a continuing part					
Present but on a restricted basis					
Does not exist at time of observation					

ITEMS TO BE CHECKED

1. Are children given opportunities to write using natural or invented spellings?
2. Do students have the opportunity to share knowledge of conventions by collaborating on work?
3. Do children have conversational abilities to discuss topics such as names of letters, words, sentences, and spelling?
4. Is there evidence that children are using vocabularies of the form-class words (nouns, verbs, adjectives, and adverbs) as a part to the planned program for extending language?
5. Is there opportunity for the development of a high imagery, descriptive vocabulary?
6. Are skills explored within the context of meaningful activities?
7. Do children participate in editing manuscripts for publication?
8. Do children have opportunities to respond to meanings in their environment not represented by symbol systems—weather, color, shape, emotions, motion, sound, size, texture, etc?

Raw score totals
TOTAL RAW SCORE
Mean score (raw score divided by 8)

FIGURE 12.9

continued

FURTHER WORDS

 From InfoTrac College Edition

Student Generated Rubrics: An Assessment Model to Help All Students Succeed, Kathryn Au, *The Reading Teacher* December 2000 v54 i4 p395

International Assessments of Reading Literacy (international perspectives on literacy), Gerry Shiel and Judith Cosgrove, *The Reading Teacher* April 2002 v55 i7 p690(3)

Red Light, Green Light, 1-2-3: Tasks to Prepare for Standardized Tests (teaching ideas), Kathleen M. Lawrence, *The Reading Teacher* March 2002

Three Paradigms of Assessment: Measurement, Procedure, and Inquiry, Frank Serafini, *The Reading Teacher* December 2000 v54 i4 p384

Assessment Is Instruction: Reading, Writing, Spelling, and Phonics for ALL Learners, Kathryn Au, *The Reading Teacher* December 2000 v54 i4 p394

Testing Pitfalls (guiding students through the taking of standardized tests), Kathe Taylor and Sherry Walton, *Instructor (1990)* October 2001 v111 i3 p26

From Professional Journals and Publications

Barksdale-Ladd , M. A., & Thomas , K. (2000). What's at Stake in High-Stakes Testing? *Journal of Teacher Education, 51*(5), 384.

Bussert-Webb, K. (2000). Did My Holistic Teaching Help Student's Standardized Test Scores? *Journal of Adolescent & Adult Literacy, 43*(6), 572–573.

Cairney, T. H. (2000). The Construction of Literacy and Literacy Learners. *Language Arts, 77*, 496–505.

Cambourne, B. (1995). Toward an Educationally Relevant Theory of Literacy Learning: Twenty Years of Inquiry. *The Reading Teacher, 49*, 182–190.

Eisner , E. W. (1999). The Uses and Limits of Performance Assessment. *Phi Delta Kappan, 80*(9), 658.

Moses, L. (2001) Rethinking Standardized High-Stakes Testing. *Childhood Education, 78*, 58.

Rosengarten, D. (2000). Standing Up to Standardized Tests. *Dollars & Sense,* November 6.

Smith, F. (2001). Just a Matter of Time. *Phi Delta Kappan, 82*(8), 572–576.

Summary

Traditional evaluation has been external—mandated outside the classroom, administered with instruments that may not reflect the instructional program's philosophy, and yielded results that are meaningless for the day-to-day instruction of students.

Assessment in total literacy classrooms is practical and relevant. Responsibility is shared between student and teacher; the teacher documents student literacy growth with checklists, anecdotal records, interaction, and analysis. Students share in their own assessment by keeping a portfolio of their work and choosing pieces of work they wish to have evaluated. Teachers are constantly involved in self-evaluation in total literacy classrooms, constantly seeking better ways of leading their students to literacy. The evaluation includes the entire learning environment as teachers step back and examine their classrooms to see if they indeed are havens for developing authors, artists, and learners.

Total Literacy Anchors

- The teacher recognizes the limitations of standardized tests.
- The teacher observes students as they interact with literacy tasks.
- The teacher records student progress with anecdotal records and checklists.
- The teacher helps children present their learning through portfolios.
- The teacher functions as a coach, not a "fixer."
- The teacher understands the nature of holistic scoring of essays.
- The teacher uses portfolios as a means of showcasing student accomplishments.
- The teacher evaluates teacher learning as well as student learning.
- The teacher evaluates classroom atmosphere and organization on a regular basis.
- The teacher reports student progress to parents in a relevant manner.

CHAPTER 13

Children's Literature

As You Read . . .

◆ What can teachers do to help children develop a love of books?

◆ What are your favorite books? Why?

◆ Why are books the cornerstone of the classroom environment?

◆ Why is it important for children to become their own teachers?

◆ What is the value in sharing books through literature circles?

◆ What is the value of acting out stories?

◆ How can you keep abreast of new children's books?

AUTHORS´ NOTE: We invited Bill Martin Jr to write this chapter on Children's Literature.

Bill Martin Jr is a member of the Reading Hall of Fame and was selected by the International Reading Association as one of the Greats of the 20th Century. He has written more than 300 books for children, including the classics Brown Bear, Brown Bear, What Do You See? *(1983) and* Chicka Chicka Boom Boom *(1991).*

Bill Martin began his career as a teacher in Kansas. His teaching was interrupted by World War II and his subsequent service in the army as a journalist.

After the war, Bill wrote children's books with his brother, Bernard. His quest to learn more about children and how they learn led him to Northwestern University, where he received a doctorate in elementary education. He then returned to the public schools and served as an elementary school principal.

In 1961 he moved to New York to work for Holt, Rinehart and Winston; he developed the literature-based reading programs Sounds of Language *and* The Instant Readers. *Seven years later, he left Holt and launched his career as a writer of children's books.*

Through the years he has given children some of their favorite books, including Polar Bear, Polar Bear, What Do You Hear? *(1991),* The Ghost-Eye Tree *(1985),* Barn Dance *(1986),* Rock It, Sock It, Number Line *(2001), and many more. He now makes his home in Commerce, Texas.*

David Canzoneri, a kindergarten teacher, also contributed to this chapter.

Bill Martin Jr

Kenny Comerford

■ ■ ■

What's the difference between children who like to read and those who don't? Surprisingly, it's not ability. Rather, the answer is that some children have discovered the joys of reading and others have not.

Author Words
Bill Martin Jr

Encouraging Children's Interest in Books

Children are born into a world that swirls with print. Even before a child can talk, that child has favorite books and favorite reading companions. Children fall in love with the sweep of the sentence and the music of the poetic line. They nestle in the arms of a loved one, mesmerized by the cadence of endearing words falling into comfortable patterns. Soon, books become children's best friends. Children get hooked on stories—the spinning of dreams and imaginative releases into a world that beckons them to enter.

These early experiences with stories form the foundation for a lifelong love of reading. But a transition must occur. Children must move from being a hearer of language to the role of being an independent reader and recreator of language and stories.

And there's good news. The secret of keeping children's love for story alive does not reside in a reading method or in the intellect of the child; rather, it resides in children's continuing encounters with stories that bring them to the brink of the best things life has to offer—adventure, intrigue, suspense, love, and excitement. That's what books have to offer.

This chapter examines ways we can help children become lifelong readers. As teachers, we have the opportunity to introduce children to literature—from the classics to this year's bestseller. We must choose with care; each book a child engages with becomes a part of that child—its language, its visions, its excitement. So join me as I share with you my love for books. I'll lead you down a path rich with literature. Along the way I'll introduce you to classroom teachers who are successful in maintaining children's love for books through their daily teaching. And I'll share with you my favorite books and my ideas for how these books can entice children into a lifelong love of reading.

Making Connections with Books

I will always remember Miss Alice Davis, my fifth-grade teacher in Hiawatha, Kansas. She is the first teacher I remember as a reading teacher. All prior reading instruction had left no imprint, either positive or negative. Miss Davis loved books, and she loved sharing this love with us. She enriched us, enabled us, and expanded us by reading aloud twice a day. She read to us in the morning to neutralize the worldly rush we brought to school. And she read to us at day's end to depressurize us from the day's accumulation of scholastic anxieties.

It was under her spell that I came to know and love Rudyard Kipling, Charles Dickens, Jack London, and Robert Louis Stevenson. Their dreams became my dreams, their loves became my loves. Miss Davis convinced me that books are essential to human enrichment and fulfillment. Like a good total literacy teacher of today, she knew precisely what she was doing. Her love for books was contagious, and her reading of

April Neal _____ Name
9 Years old _____ Age
BasketBall _____
Swinging With Friends Interests
Writing and reading

What do you like most about school?

The thing I like most aBout School is
my friends and Learning because friends
Cheer You up and Learning makes You Smarter

What's your favorite subject? Why?

MY favorite SubJect is Writing because
When I get older I am going to
Write lots and lots Of Stories for kids
and adults

What's your favorite book? Why do you like it?

MY favorite book is Aliens Don't Wear Braces
because it is a Very Very CooL book and
and its funny

What advice do you have for teachers?

I Would give this advice to teachers,
let the kids have a Chioce to Work
From text Books or do it the fun way
By hands on.

Eric Carle is one of the world's most-loved picture book illustrators.

2

America's Finest

Candice Ware

favorite books inculcated a view of life that gave us ways of passage. I became a reader that year. Oh, I didn't have the skills of reading that present-day tests measure. But I became a reader because I was filled with a thirst for the excitement and adventures that beckoned to me from books. I developed the skills of reading through encounters with books in the years that were to follow. Books have indeed been for me a way of passage. I hope you can carry on the tradition of Miss Davis by introducing your students to books that will launch them in a lifelong adventure through literacy. Now let's look at a modern-day Miss Davis in the Teacher-to-Teacher feature.

Teacher-to-Teacher

The children in Randy Methven's first grade at Moriches (Long Island, New York) Elementary School are brought to reading by two powerful forces: (1) the teacher has complete confidence that each of them will learn to read easily, and (2) the students themselves are their own teachers. "Children like to be in on the planning," Randy said as he gathered a group of children around a poem hand printed on a large poster board. "The final de-

cision whether this poem, which is a favorite of mine, will become part of our reading and language fare depends on their reaction." Then he suggested, "Children, let's read through this poem to see if you like it." They read from the A. A. Milne poem "The End":

When I was one, I was just begun,
When I was two, I was nearly new,
When I was three, . . .

The young readers reacted with excitement. Yes, yes, they liked the poem. "That's neat! Let's read it again!" And they did. And again. And again. With each chorusing of the poem, the children's reading became more secure, and the structural play of the poem became more cerebral. Every child in this typical class was deeply invested in the act of reading. Every child was mesmerized with reading success.

This was only the beginning of making the Milne poem and all its components (sentences, words, punctuation, rhythmic words, meanings, humor, inferences, nuances) available to each child for the mental and verbal interaction that leads to reading and other language skill acquisitions.

Each day for about two weeks the children read the poem in chorus, along with ten or fifteen other poems they had previously given their "thumbs up." Each poem demanded a different mind-set, a different window on the world. They were not apprehensive about it. They were excited about it! In just a couple of days, they had learned each poem and its game plan and had them imprinted in long-term memory for a lifetime of repetitions and transpositions. Regardless of its thematic and verbal and structural intricacies, any poem the children like can become part of their reading program.

The class poems are stored hanging on the wall, hanging from the ceiling, hanging in clusters like large flip-page books. Any poem the children want to read can be lifted from its storage place and hung in the open for all to see.

In the course of the school year, 183 days, Randy's first-graders select and learn to read eighty to ninety poems. The poems range from this ever-popular childhood Mother Goose lilt:

1, 2, buckle my shoe,
3, 4 shut the door,
5, 6 pick up sticks,
7, 8 lay them straight,
9, 10 a big fat hen.

to this lyrical meditation called "Trees" by Harry Behn:

Trees are the kindest thing I know.
They do no harm, they simply grow.
They make a shade for sleepy cows.
They shelter birds among their boughs.
They give us fruit in leaves above,
And wood to make our houses of.
And leaves to burn at Halloween,
And in the spring new buds of green.
They are the first when day's begun
To catch the glimpse of morning sun.
They are the last to hold the light
When evening changes into night.
And when the moon floats on the sky,
They hum a drowsy lullaby
Of sleepy children long ago.
Trees are the kindest things I know.

The range, breadth, and impact of all the language models the children have impressed in their long-term memory through their association with the poems are the fastest and best way they can possibly come to language usage.

Besides the emphasis on poetry in his classroom reading program, Randy Methven has a second daily reading focus—on children's books, at school, and at home. Randy and his twenty-four pupils and all of their parents are involved. The program works like this: First, on each Monday morning Randy introduces the four children's books of the week. He reads each one aloud and remarks about it in a way that helps the children anticipate the book and the pleasure of the reading.

The chosen titles have a significant relationship—all are written by the same author, all are illustrated by the same artist, or all four books are thematically related. The reading fare for one week is four Ezra Jack Keats titles: *Snowy Day* (1962), *Whistle for Willie* (1964), *Goggles* (1969), and *Pet Show* (1972).

➤ ➤ ➤

Each day each child chooses a title to take home that evening for a family read-aloud. The act of choosing divides the class into four reading groups, there being six copies of each title.

"It is not enough that we ask parents to read aloud to their children," Randy said. "Not all parents have books and the wherewithal to buy books. I send home a book each night to read aloud. This is a book the child has already heard and can discuss, perhaps even read, with parents and siblings. Every day of the school year, 183 days, I send a book home to be read aloud and enjoyed."

The second step of the children's literature/reading program occurs the next morning, Tuesday, when the children return to school bringing the chosen book back to the classroom. Randy invites each group of six children having the same book to meet around the reading table, where the book is again read aloud and discussed. Children's literature is a critical component of a classroom where the insights and opinions of each child are valued and encouraged, as are the sharing of writing, singing, storytelling, drawing, painting, and other talents that were activated by the book experience (Broad, 2001).

The third step of the literature/reading program is selecting another title from the week's chosen four to take home for the family evening read-aloud—and the whole process begins again. On Friday nights each child takes home any book he or she wants for a parent-child-family weekend read-aloud.

"There is an increasing difficulty in the books chosen for the children to read," Randy said. "At the beginning of first grade I use Douglas Florian's *Beach Day* (1990), and Mira Ginsberg's *The Chick and the Duckling* (1972). By year end, it's Leo Lionni's *Swimmy* (1991) and *Frederic* (1990) and Arnold Lobel's *Frog and Toad* (1994)."

Randy never doubts the skill development of the children. "They learn by involvement," he said. "Children who can read eighty or ninety wide-ranging poems and more than 175 books obviously are developing the skills of literacy."

Books I've Come to Love

By category, I'll now share the books that I have come to love, and the books that seem to have tremendous impact on readers. I'll apologize for including some of my own books—the authors of this text insisted that I do so.

Books to Start With

Brown Bear, Brown Bear, What Do You See? by Bill Martin Jr (1967)

Tomie dePaola's Mother Goose by Tomie dePaola (1985)

The Tale of Peter Rabbit by Beatrix Potter (1987)

Where the Wild Things Are by Maurice Sendak (1963)

Charlotte's Web by E. B. White (1952)

Sarah, Plain and Tall by Patricia MacLachlan (1985)

Indian in the Cupboard by Lynne Reid Banks (1980)

The Cat in the Hat by Dr. Seuss (1957)

Goodnight Moon by Margaret Wise Brown (1975)

Important Book by Margaret Wise Brown (1949)

Fortunately by Remy Charlip (1964)

The Very Hungry Caterpillar by Eric Carle (1969, 1987)

Chicka Chicka Boom Boom by Bill Martin Jr and John Archambault (1991)

The Napping House by Audrey Wood (1984)

Humorous Books

Miss Nelson Is Missing! by Harry Allard (1997)

The Stinky Cheese Man and Other Fairly Stupid Tales by Jon Scieszka (1992)

Martha Speaks by Susan Meddaugh (1992)

Kat Kong by Dav Pilkey (1993)

Dogzilla by Dav Pilkey (1993)

I know an Old Lady Who Swallowed a Pie by Alison Jackson (1997)

Poetry

Where the Sidewalk Ends by Shel Silverstein (1974)

Poem Stew by William Cole (1981)

The Random House Book of Poetry for Children by Jack Prelutsky (1983)

And the Green Grass Grew All Around by Alvin Schwartz (1992)

A Child's Garden of Verses by Robert Louis Stevenson (1999)

All The Small Poems & Fourteen More by Valerie Worth (1994)

New Kid on the Block by Jack Prelutsky (1984)

Bill Martin's Big Book of Poetry by Bill Martin Jr and Michael Sampson (in press)

Wordless Picture Books

The Snowman by Raymond Briggs (1978)

Deep in the Forest by Brinton Turkle (1976)

Tuesday by David Wiesner (1991)

Pancakes for Breakfast by Tomie dePaola (1978)

Zoom by Istvan Banyai (1995)

ReZoom by Istvan Banyai (1995)

Rem by Istvan Banyai (1997)

A Boy, A Dog and A Frog by Mercer Mayer (1967)

Meet the Author

Patricia MacLachlan

Patricia MacLachlan

1. *Which book of yours has given you the greatest pleasure?*

Sarah, Plain and Tall. In a way, it captures the lives of my mother and my father. It is accessible to young children and adults. What I hope to do is write books that work on many levels so there's something there for all ages, and that book does that very well.

2. *Are you sometimes surprised by the way a book evolves?*

Yes. Sometimes I think I have it under control, but I don't. I am very surprised, for instance, how *Sarah, Plain and Tall* evolved into many other books. The characters became very important to me, and I became caught up in the lives of these people. Their lives grow and evolve, so I have created a monster, of sorts, that I rather enjoy.

3. *What would you like people to remember about your work?*

Books and characters reflect our lives. Children are under a lot of pressure to be like their peers, but I think it is nice to know that it is okay to be different. Maybe we will find as we are allowed to be different that we are actually more alike than we ever thought.

4. *What impact do you hope your work will have on your readers?*

I would hope that children can see themselves in my work or that they see me reaching out and saying, "I feel this way. How do you feel?" I want it to be a two-way communication.

Drawing on her rich family history, Patricia MacLachlan writes stories that are captivating to a wide variety of ages and, though fiction, have a poignant ring of truth. Her books include the Newbery Award-winning novel *Sarah Plain and Tall* and *All the Places to Love, Journey, Baby, Skylark, Through Grandpa's Eyes,* and *What You Know First.*

Reprinted with special permission of Patricia MacLachlan.

Sector 7 by David Wiesner (1999)

Free Fall by David Wisener (1988)

Do You Want to Be My Friend? by Eric Carle (1976)

Good Dog Carl by Alexandra Day (1985)

Folktales

Three Little Pigs by Steven Kellogg (1997)

The Three Sillies by Steven Kellogg (1999)

Rumpelstiltskin by Paul O. Zelinsky (1986)

Paul Bunyan by Steven Kellogg (1984)

Pecos Bill by Steven Kellogg (1986)

Johnny Appleseed by Steven Kellogg (1988)

John Henry by Julius Lester, pictures by Jerry Pinkney (1994)

There Was an Old Lady Who Swallowed a Fly by Pam Adams (1973)

Donald Crews and Ann Jonas autographing their books.

Books of Artistic Merit

Grandfather's Journey by Allen Say (1993)

A Log's Life by Wendy Pfeffer (1997)

Lon Po Po: A Red Riding Hood Story from China by Ed Young (1989)

Hans Christian Anderson: The Ugly Duckling adapted by Andersen/ Jerry Pinkney (1999)

Jumanji by Chris Van Allsburg (1981)

Round Trip by Ann Jonas (1983)

Informational Books

The Way Things Work by David Macaulay (1998)

Lives of Writers by Kathleen Krull (1994)

Freight Train by Donald Crews (1978)

Bugs by Nancy Winslow Parker (1987)

Underwater Counting Even Numbers by Jerry Pallotta (2001)

Our Natural Homes by Sneed Collard (1996)

Wildflower ABC by Diana Pomeroy (1997)

Realistic Fiction

Hatchet by Gary Paulsen (1987)

The Pinballs by Betsy Byars (1977)

Maniac Magee by Jerry Spinelli (1990)

Dear Mr. Henshaw by Beverly Cleary (1983)

Shiloh by Phyllis Reynolds Naylor (1991)

Because of Winn Dixie by Kate DiCamillo (2000)

Bud Not Buddy by Christopher Paul Curtis (1999)

A Year Down Yonder by Richard Peck (2000)

Where the Red Fern Grows by Wilson Rawls (1961, 1992, 1996)

Historical Fiction and Biography

Johnny Tremain by Esther Forbes (1943)

Across Five Aprils by Irene Hunt (1981)

The Devil's Arithmetic by Jane Yolen (1988)

Lincoln: A Photobiography by Russell Freedman (1987)

John Brown: One Man Against Slavery by Gwen Evert (1993)

Roll of Thunder, Hear My Cry by Mildred D. Taylor (1976)

26 Fairmount Avenue by Tomie dePaola (1999)

Books Focusing on Social Issues

Eggbert the Slightly Cracked Egg by Tom Ross (1994) (self-esteem)

I Love You Like Crazy Cakes by Rose Lewis (2000) (adoption)

I'll Always Love You by Hans Wilhelm (1985) (death of a pet)

Wilfrid Gordon McDonald Partridge by Mem Fox (1985) (memory, aging)

The Great Kapok Tree by Lynne Cherry (1990) (environment)

Be Good to Eddie Lee by Virginia Fleming (1993) (Down's syndrome)

Heroes by Ken Mochizuki (1995) (racial bias)

Storybooks

When I Was Young in the Mountains by Cynthia Rylant (1982)

The Talking Eggs by Robert D. San Souci (1989)

The Little Squeegy Bug by Bill Martin Jr and Michael Sampson (2001)

Harvey Potter's: Balloon Farm by Jerdine Nolen (1989,1994)

Picture Books

Adam, Adam, What Do You See? by Bill Martin Jr and Michael Sampson (2000)

Ira Sleeps Over by Bernard Waber (1972)

Chrysanthemum by Kevin Henkes (1991)

My Great-Aunt Arizona by Gloria Houston (1992)

The Very Busy Spider by Eric Carle (1995)

The Mitten by Jan Brett (1996)

Amber on the Mountain by Tony Johnston (1994)

If You Give a Mouse a Cookie by Laura Joffe Numeroff (1985)

Just the Two of Us by Will Smith (2001)

Little Granny Quarterback by Bill Martin Jr and Michael Sampson (2001)

Rock It, Sock It, Number Line by Bill Martin Jr and Michael Sampson (2001)

Cinderella Folktale Variants

Cinderella by Diane Goode (1988)

Yeh Shen: A Cinderella Story from China by Ai-Ling Louie (1982)

The Rough-Face Girl by Rafe Martin (1998)

Mufaro's Beautiful Daughters by John Steptoe (1987)

The Talking Eggs by Robert D. San Souci (1989)

Cinder Edna by Ellen Jackson (1994)

Cinder Elly by Frances Minters (1997)

Fantasy

The Lion, the Witch and the Wardrobe by C. S. Lewis (1950)

Harry Potter and the Chamber of Secrets by J. K. Rowling (1998)

Tuck Everlasting by Natalie Babbitt (1999)

The Remarkable Journey of Prince Jen by Lloyd Alexander (1991)

Redwall by Brian Jacques (1998)

Holes by Louis Sachar (1998)

The Giver by Lois Lowry (1993)

Read-Alouds

Where the Red Fern Grows by Wilson Rawls (1981)

Casey at the Bat by Ernest Lawrence Thayer (2000)

Leo the Late Bloomer by Robert Kraus (1971)

Whose Mouse Are You? by Robert Kraus (1970)

Little House in the Big Woods by Laura Ingalls Wilder (1971)

In the Year of the Boar and Jackie Robinson by Bette Bao Lord (1984)

Sideways Stories from Wayside School by Louis Sachar (1985)

Mouse & the Motorcycle by Beverly Cleary (1990)

Mr. Popper's Penguins by Richard and Florence Atwater (1976)

King Bidgood's in the Bathtub by Audrey Wood (1985)

Where the Wild Things Are by Marice Sendak (1963)

Mortimer by Robert Munsch (1983)

Barn Dance by Bill Martin Jr and John Archaumbault (1986)

Hatchet by Gary Paulsen (1996)

Knots on a Counting Rope by Bill Martin Jr and John Archaumbault (1987)

The Castle in the Attic by Elizabeth Winthrop (1985)

Ghost Eye Tree by Bill Martin Jr. and John Archaumbault (1985)

Hubert's Hair-Raising Adventure by Bill Peet (1979)

Alexander and the Terrible, Horrible, No Good, Very Bad Day
by Judith Viorst (1972)

Now One Foot, Now the Other by Tomie dePaola (1981)

Sylvester and the Magic Pebble by William Steig (1973)

The Very Quiet Cricket by Eric Carle (1990)

The Jolly Postman by Janet Ahlberg and Allan Ahlberg (2001)

Cloudy with a Chance of Meatballs by Judi Barrett (1978)

American Tall Tales by Mary Pope Osborne (1991)

Frog and Toad Are Friends by Arnold Lobel (1970)

A Rose for Pinkerton by Steven Kellogg (1984)

The Borrowers by Mary Norton (1976)

Facilitating Children's Interactions with Books

So far we've talked about the importance of introducing children to books, and we've looked at titles that should intrigue them. Now let's take a look at the marriage between literature and teaching, and how books can be the cornerstone of the classroom environment.

We'll discuss ways we can help children enjoy and explore books—while acquiring skill in reading at the same time. But first, a word of caution.

We must be very careful to only lightly touch literature through literature strategies. We are experiencing the rebirth of the basal reader—and hour after hour of subjecting readers to drill after drill. Such procedures may result in millions of readers who choose not to read. It doesn't pay to tear literature apart, because children will lose their love for reading when we make readers toil over books. So literacy strategies must be practiced only under the watchful eye of the teacher. Be prepared to move on when children show signs of growing weary of the activities.

Literature Circles

As adults, we love to talk about an exciting book that we are reading. Children deserve the same privilege. An effective way of facilitating this "book talk" is through Literature Circles (Kasten, 1994). Literature Circles provide a stimulating opportunity for students to discuss chapter books or novels they are reading. They are excellent for grouping children of mixed abilities and are rapidly replacing the traditional grouping procedures of basal-oriented classrooms (Kasten, 1993).

Literature Circles make reading a family affair. The excitement of reading a book together binds the group and improves the reading/thinking/ predicting abilities of all. And you'll notice another miracle during the sharing time—a miracle of courtesy as kids are attentive to one another. But the greatest thing you'll notice is growth: growth in confidence, growth in writing ability, growth in knowledge about how writers put stories together, and most of all growth in appreciation for books and reading.

Teaching Strategies
Literature Circles

Teacher~to~Teacher

Gary Bowman is a sixth-grade teacher in Covelo, California. Gary follows Kasten's (1993, p. 380) recommendations for Literature Circles, as his students Read, Write, Discuss, and Share. First, Gary selects, with input from his students, ten books. Next, he shares something about each book with the class. He shares from his own knowledge of having read the book, or from the reviews of the books. He randomly breaks his class into six groups, and allows each group to sign up for a book the group would like to read, indicating a first and second choice. He's now ready for the first step.

STEP 1: Read   Students are given twenty minutes each day to participate in Literature Circles. Gary has volunteers from each book circle read aloud to the group. At the end of the reading period, the students move to Step 2.

STEP 2: Write   Students write whatever they are thinking as a result of what they've heard or read that day. Each student keeps a personal Literature Circle journal (see Figure 13.1). Then the groups move to Step 3.

STEP 3: Discuss   Using their journal entries, students share their reactions and discuss the different ideas and reactions. Students continue the Read, Write, Discuss cycle until the book is completed. This leads them to the most important step in the process, Step 4.

STEP 4: Share   The literature discussion group meets to decide how they can share their book with the entire class without revealing the conclusion of the story. Sometimes groups design an advertisement, act out a skit, or create a video. These presentations serve to make the book memorable to the group and lead others to want to read the book.

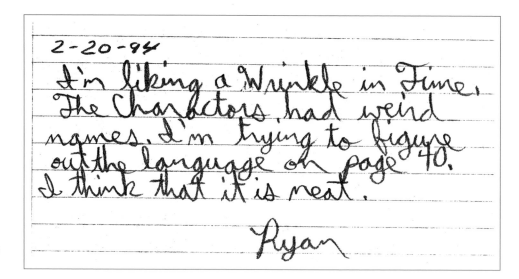

FIGURE 13.1
A student's Literature Circle journal entry

> 2-20-94
>
> I'm liking a Wrinkle in Time. The Characters had weird names. I'm trying to figure out the language on page 40. I think that it is neat.
>
> Ryan

Acting Out Stories

To love a story is to live it. And to live a story is to act it out—to become the characters and to take on their characteristics, their nuances, their view of life.

In the process of becoming actors, children become writers. They study the structure of stories to discover how to modify structure to fit the constraints of moving from print to action on the stage. In short, they ask themselves, "How is it put together and how can we act it out?" And "What will act out and what will not?" They may discover they want more speaking parts so they add new characters. In the process, they discover the need to be flexible—what looks good on paper may not work as well on stage. The Teacher-to-Teacher feature describes how one third-grade teacher incorporates drama in the classroom.

Teacher-to-Teacher

Rick Kilcup, a third-grade teacher from Renton, Washington, is a firm believer in the value of drama in the classroom. Every week his children adapt books into scripts. He calls his classroom productions Story Theater, and he believes four major benefits are achieved when children make books come alive: (1) it brings a story right off the pages and into the kids' lives, (2) it gives kids a chance to perform for an audience, without having to memorize a lot of lines!, (3) Story Theater is a wonderful way to get nonreaders involved, and (4) it brings art into reading through the use of masks and simple costumes.

Latino/Hispanic Children's Books

As shared by Becky Chavarría-Cháirez

The American melting pot remains on simmer, but the flavors from the pot are infinite. Because of the geographic location of the United States and the growing kinship to *las Américas* in this hemisphere, Latino/Hispanic-themed as well as bilingual children's books are on their way to becoming a permanent part of American children's literature.

In recent years, the publishing industry and the children's literary community have taken notice. You may have witnessed how nearly everything Latino/Hispanic is having some influence or impact on pop culture and current events—and the children's book market is no exception. And for those of us who write children's books, this means our writing opportunities are many and the assignment is multidimensional, to write for/to and about an infinite rainbow of young readers on our planet.

Consider that our mainstream is undergoing a dramatic ethnic shift, the mainstream *is* diverse, and the majority is the product of a former minority: Hispanic Americans.

Currently, the United States has more than 31 million Hispanics, making it (us) the fifth-largest Spanish-speaking country in the world. *¿Qué?* You may be asking.

This is not only happening in the southwest region of the United States. The 2000 Census found that North Carolina's Hispanic population registered a 394 percent increase, making it one of the fastest-growing states with a booming Hispanic population. Similar growth has been recorded in Arkansas, Georgia, and in the Northeast.

By 2010, it is projected that *only* Mexico will have more Spanish speakers. (Yes, stop and read that sentence again.) And by 2050, Hispanics will number 96 million, approximately 24 percent of the overall U.S. population. Before you fully fathom that estimate, consider the possibility that this government projection may be somewhat conservative.

The majority of Hispanic children in the United States were born here to U.S. citizens of Hispanic origin. They are predominantly English speakers; yet the continuous arrival of immigrants from Latin American countries, coupled with the growing need for and use of Spanish in the workplace, and the desire of many Latinos to preserve their culture through language, ensures there is and will continue to be a need for children's books and educational materials in Spanish.

Publishers no longer ask if they *should* venture into the Hispanic market. Some regret not entering the market sooner, but they can console themselves in knowing that the genre will remain in demand. The signs are everywhere.

Have you noticed that large chain discount stores have broadened their book inventories to include Spanish and bilingual titles? Spanish is creeping into the workplace and the marketplace. Notice how often you now see signage and advertising in Spanish, Have you read the label on your bottles of hair shampoo or over-the-counter medications lately? Scan the radio dial and you will hear Latin music.

Did you know that bilingual children's books are not just for kids nor just for Hispanic kids? Adults use them too. English as a second language students and Latinos who are learning to read in their first language, Spanish, and then bridging from their native language to English are using children's books to learn a new language.

Bilingual education programs for children are not what they used to be. They, too, are diversifying. Dual-language programs in schools now instruct children on all school

➤ ➤ ➤

subjects in English and Spanish, putting both languages to simultaneous use.

Bilingual books are more user-friendly, not only serving a greater number of readers but also reaching across generations with different levels of language proficiency. In some homes one parent or an older generation may speak Spanish and the other parent and youngest generation may prefer English.

Teachers and librarians affirm the bilingual children's book genre with Hispanic-themed stories is on target, and by adding these books to their classrooms and libraries they are making Hispanic children's books instant classics.

And the genre is expanding. Diversity begets more diversity. Looking within the Latino demographic, there is infinite diversity within this "ethnic" group. Beyond language, there are many other nuances of the culture to capture.

For example, since Hispanics are not from one country, they do not all share the same customs and language preferences. They may be from one or more racial groups, and not all Latin Americans speak Spanish. In South America, Brazilians speak Portuguese. In one Central American country, the official language is English. Which one? Belize.

Foods also vary greatly. In my first book, *Magda's Tortillas* (2000), which tells the story of a young girl's first tortilla-making lesson, is not about an experience all Latino children have. Tortillas are considered Hispanic, but they are not traditionally served in every Latin American country. The same goes for tamales, tacos, chips and salsa—the spicy condiment that has been outselling catsup for some time now. And, to add to the comparison here, salsa is more than just something you eat. Salsa is also a style of music and dance, even an attitude.

Several Latino writers including me have decided to write children's books to meet our personal desire for stories that mirror our real-life cultures and traditions. Some of the best-selling Spanish children's books are not written by Hispanics: they aren't even about Hispanic children. H. A. Rey's *Curious George* series, Ludwig Bemelman's *Madeleine* books, Marc Brown's *Arthur* collection, and others have universal appeal in many languages.

If you are interested in writing for the Latino market, keep in mind these criteria that most publishers want to see in their titles:

- Authentic characters, setting; even in fiction, situations are and should be true to life, easy for Hispanic as well as all young readers to relate to.

- Positive portrayal of Hispanics as leaders, teachers, and role models. Biographical books about Hispanic leaders are much needed as schools seek Latino heroes, writers, sports stars, artists, politicians, educators, and others to focus on the contributions of Latino society in the United States and to celebrate Hispanic Heritage Month.

- Correct use of language, spelling, and grammar. The bilingual text should be impeccably translated. Children's books are not just for entertainment, they reinforce good usage of Spanish. Bilingual books should be easily understood in either language. Translation is a fine art of utmost importance.

- The absence of stereotypical images. Not all Hispanics are poor, short, and dark-skinned, with black hair and use burros for transportation. These images were common in the earliest portrayals of Hispanics. Stereotypes are to be avoided in books by incorporating realistic economic, cultural, religious, and lifestyle diversity to further illustrate who Latinos are today.

◆ Realistic portrayal of cultural issues and traditions to instill ethnic pride and cross-cultural awareness. As Latinos assimilate, they wish to retain their culture and have others understand and respect who they are.

Just as each child is individual and unique, the same is true of the Hispanic/Latino child. Many are part of what I call the Latino melting pot—Latinos among Latinos. Although the majority of Latinos in the Southwestern United States are from Mexico, there are Latinos from dozens of Latin American countries. It is important to remember that each Latino child is part of a distinct family. A growing number of these children are being born into multiethnic homes to Hispanic and non-Hispanic parents.

Given the multitude of Hispanic groups and the number of blended Latino and non-Latino cultures, publishers will expand their titles to reflect these Latino stories. Stories about how a Latino/Hispanic family must familiarize itself with other Latino customs, foods, and ethnic/cultural traditions because mommy is Puerto Rican and daddy is Mexican are needed. These stories will help families build understanding, mutual respect, find common ground, and build family ties.

I want non-Hispanic children who read Hispanic-themed books to discover the universal themes and emotions of Hispanic children—stories about their first day at school, losing a pet, moving to a new house, or welcoming a new baby brother or sister to the family. Multicultural stories underscore the universal connections we all share: family, home, love, compassion, problem-solving, and always, with a generous helping of adventure!

This is not just all in fun; it is a serious endeavor. My visits to schools, libraries, and book fairs affirm that Hispanic youngsters derive a greater sense of belonging and gain a higher self-esteem when they read stories about children like themselves. When Hispanic children are not just viewed as "an other" but as *another* in the American family, this has a visceral and visible impact. Students' body language reveals that they are entranced by Magda making tortillas or creating piñata magic for her little brother's birthday and hearing the characters speak in two languages—as many of them do. The kids' pupils dilate, and they hang on to every word. For Hispanic children, these stories validate who they are, build their cultural self-awareness, and boost their personal self-esteem. Who knows, this new genre in children's books could be the supplemental link that educators seek to help keep Hispanic students in school and celebrate who they are. We won't know right away, but it will be interesting to see the future benefits of this genre in our American melting pot. *Vamos a ver.* We shall see.

Hispanic-themed children's books are an indispensable part of this Latino melting pot. It is not a genre created as an act of political correctness; it is the right thing to do. I consider it just another dimension to what we call the all-American experience.

Children's book author, Becky Chavarría-Cháirez is owner of Chameleon Creek Press, a literary arts communications group based in New Mexico. The veteran award-winning broadcast journalist, freelance writer, bilingual speaker, and multiculturalist can be reached at www.chameleoncreekpress.com or email to: chameleoncreek@aol.com.

Becky Chavarría-Cháirez is the author of *Magda's Tortillas~Las tortillas de Magda* (2000) and *Magda's Piñata Magic~Magda y la piñata mágica* (2001), fully bilingual children's picture books published by Arte Público Press/Piñata Books (1-800-633-ARTE).

Reprinted with special permission of Becky Chavarría-Cháirez.

Keeping Abreast of Children's Books

America's Finest

Jerry Jarrell

More than 5,000 new children's books are published each year. How do busy teachers keep abreast of these new titles? Here are six suggestions.

1. Form a literature share group with other teachers in your district. Schedule one evening per month to get together over snacks at someone's home, with the discussion dedicated to children's books. You might ask one person to moderate the evening, but the important thing is that every teacher who comes brings his or her favorite new book to share. It's fine to ask a special guest to share, such as the manager of the children's section of the local bookstore, but the emphasis should be on teacher-to-teacher sharing.

2. Examine resources that publishers use to alert bookstores about new titles. Baker & Taylor book wholesalers publishes the *Book Alert.* Ingram book wholesalers publishes a similar resource titled *The Advance.* You can also write to publishers of children's books and ask to be placed on their mailing lists.

3. Subscribe to magazines that review books. The University of Illinois publishes *The Bulletin of the Center for Children's Books,* in which they review more than 900 new books each year. *The Horn Book* also has outstanding and extensive reviews, as well as informative articles about children's literature. *The New Advocate* likewise has articles about children's literature and reviews fifty recommended books in each issue. *Booklist* is a biweekly journal that not only reviews children's books but also other media and computer programs. *Book Links,* another publication from the American Library Association, provides teachers with comprehensive lists of books centered around themes and current issues.

4. Take advantage of the National Council of Teachers of English and the International Reading Association (www.reading.org), professional organizations that promote literacy acquisition through a number of publications. The International Reading Association publishes *The Reading Teacher* and *The Journal of Adolescent and Adult Literacy,* which review new books. In addition, *The Reading Teacher* publishes a list in the October issue of new books that children consider their favorites. The National Council of Teachers of English publishes *Language Arts* and *English Education,* which feature book review columns.

5. Make friends with the manager of your local children's bookstore. Bookstores often receive information about author visits to your area; don't let your children miss their visits and storytelling sessions.

6. Consult a comprehensive source, such as textbooks designed for college-level children's literature courses. Bernice Cullinan's *Literature and the Child*

(1994) is an outstanding resource, as are *Children's Literature in the Elementary School* (2000) by Charlotte Huck and *Children and Books* (1996) by Zena Sutherland. Lively interest is also buoyed by the annual announcement (in February) of the best illustrated children's book and the best written children's book of the preceding year. These awards are known as the Caldecott Award and the John Newbery Award, respectively. Past winners are listed in the back of this text; view the current year's selections at the American Library Association Web site (*www.ala.org*).

Author Studies

As a writer of books for children, one of my great joys is in the mail I receive from children who have read my books. Many share that I have been their "Author of the Week!" I once asked Ms. Thomason, a kindergarten teacher, how she chooses the

Courtesy of Michael Sampson

Bill Martin Jr's books provide strong, dependable lines for young writers.

author the children study, and she replied: "I don't—the children do." (That made me feel even better about being the "Author of the Week!") The Teacher-to-Teacher feature describes the process her students use to choose the Author of the Week.

Teacher-to-Teacher

Debby Thomason is a kindergarten teacher who loves books and shares that love with her students. During the first eight weeks of school, she reads her favorite books to the students. Then she moves into an author study—an in-depth analysis of a single author and his or her books. She takes dictation from the children as they share their choices of the author to study. Authors such as Tomie dePaola, Eric Carle, Steven Kellogg, and other emerge. Next, she has students vote on the first author to study. She knows that student choice will ensure a great start for the first author focus. She claps with the children when the vote is revealed and Eric Carle is their choice.

The next Monday Ms. Thomason joins the children in their circle. In her lap she holds a tall stack of Eric Carle books. She shows each one, saying, "Raise your hand if you've read this one!" Hands shoot up for many of the books, including *The Very Hungry Caterpillar* (1987) and *Dream Snow* (2000). She shares that even though she has read these two books she is looking forward to reading them again. She also shares that her very favorite Eric Carle book is in the stack—

but refuses to reveal the title. She tells the students that she'll be asking them their favorite title when the study is completed.

The class spends fifteen school days reading Eric's books. Ms. Thomason engages the children in varied literacy strategies as the books are read—Reader's Theater, art extensions, sharing of personal memories about the books, biographical study of Eric Carle via his Web page and author video, and more.

The class concludes their author study with a grand finale—they make a three-minute video to send to Mr. Carle that expresses their love for his books and their appreciation to him for writing and illustrating them. They burn the video to a DVD using the classroom computer and mail it to Eric Carle.

They are thrilled when Mr. Carle writes them back with literature about himself and a brochure about the Eric Carle Museum of Picture Book Art, located in Northampton, Massachusetts. They love the picture of the panda bear he sends that come from his latest book. And they have a new appreciation for Eric Carle and his work—as one kindergarten child expresses it: "I really like Eric Carle. He writes the kinds of books I just love to read!"

America's Finest
Kay Williams

Author studies are a great way to bring children to the act of reading. As students find and develop an interest in a favorite author, they will want to read more and more things that author has written—just like the adult reader who can't wait for the latest John Grisham novel to come out.

Here are some resources that will help you learn more about authors—Figure 13.2 shows where to find the fifteen authors interviewed for this book. Figure 13.3 gives Web addresses for authors; Figure 13.4 lists author videos.

Chapter 1   Bill Martin Jr   (page 20)
Chapter 2   Eric Carle   (page 42)
Chapter 3   Gloria Houston   (page 78)
Chapter 4   Lynne Cherry   (page 98)
Chapter 5   Brian Pinkney   (page 138)
Chapter 6   Steven Kellogg   (page 168)
Chapter 7   Ted Rand   (page 180)
Chapter 8   Becky Chavarría-Cháirez   (page 236)
Chapter 9   Donald Crews   (page 268)
Chapter 10   Floyd Cooper   (page 316)
Chapter 11   Ruth Heller   (page 356)
Chapter 12   Tomie dePaola   (page 390)
Chapter 13   Patricia MacLachlan   (page 420)
Chapter 14   Jose Aruego   (page 458)
Chapter 15   Jerry Pallotta   (page 472)

FIGURE 13.2

Authors and illustrators featured in this book and where to find them

Karen Ackerman	T.C. Bartlett	Alden R. Carter	Diane deGroat
Carole S. Adler	Stephanie Baudet	David A. Carter	Tomie dePaola
Stephen Alcorn	Barbara Helen Berger	Paul Casale	Ariane Dewey
Sue Alexander	Jody Bergsma	Mary Casanova	Tony DiTerlizzi
Catherine and Laurence Anholt	Raymond Bial	Judith Caseley	Dr. Seuss
Kathi Appelt	Judy Blume	Robert Casilla	Michael Dooling
Caroline Arnold	Louise Borden	Yong Chen	William Durbin
Tedd Arnold	Fred Bortz	Argus Childers	Marianne Dyson
Jim Arnosky	David Bouchard	Yangsook Choi	Sylvia Engdahl
Mike Artell	Linda Crotta Brennan	Eileen Christelow	Douglas Evans
Sandy Asher	Jan Brett	John Clapp	Bill Farnsworth
Jeannine Atkins	Larry Dane Brimner	Brian P. Cleary	Norman H. Finkelstein
Avi	Linda Bronson	Vicki Cobb	Mary Peace Finley
Jim Aylesworth	Joseph Bruchac	Nancy Coffelt	Ralph Fletcher
Sheila Bailey	Jon Buller and Susan Schade	Sneed B. Collard III	Robert Florczak
Ken Baker	Stephanie Calmenson	Shutta Crum	Mem Fox
Bruce Balan	Ann Cameron	Chris Crutcher	David Frampton
Haemi Balgassi	Eric Carle	Doug Cushman	Sherry Garland
Nancy Barnet		Jane Cutler	Jean Craighead George
Ysaye M. Barnwell		Teri Daniels	Kristine O'Connell George
		Katie Davis	
		Terry Davis	

FIGURE 13.3

Authors with Web pages; go to www.cbcbooks.org/html/links.html for links to these sites

Charles Ghigna
Jamie Gilson
Bette Greene
Sheila Greenwald
Kristiana Gregory
Bruce Hale
Wendy Anderson
    Halperin
Virginia Hamilton
David Harrison
Susan Kathleen
    Hartung
Ann Herrick
Will Hillenbrand
Anna Grossnickle
    Hines
Bruce Hiscock
Will Hobbs
Patricia Hubbell
Joan Holub
Henry Horenstein
Gloria Houston
Woodleigh Marx
    Hubbard
Arden Johnson
Layne Johnson
Rebecca Jones
Charles Jordan
Roberta Karim
Kathleen Karr
Susan Katz
Verla Kay
Mona Kerby
Liza Ketchum
Elisa Kleven
Jackie French
    Koller
Robin Michal
    Koontz
Stephen Krensky
Stephen Kroninger
Jarrett J. Krosoczka

Kathleen Krull
Jane Kurtz
Elaine Landau
Francess Lantz
Kathryn Lasky
Marie Lee
Bijou Le Tord
Shar Levine
Sonia Levitin
Betsy Lewin
Ted Lewin
E. B. Lewis
Brian Lies
Grace Lin
Susan Hart
    Lindquist
Janet Taylor Lisle
David Lubar
Suse MacDonald
Gregory Maguire
Jahnna N.
    Malcolm
Leonard Marcus
Michelle Markel
Bill Martin Jr
Jacqueline Briggs
    Martin
Susan Rowan
    Masters
Carol Matas
Nancy Matson
Alice McLerran
Michael McCurdy
Matthew
    McElligott
Bruce McMillan
Janet McNaughton
Laura Krauss
    Melmed
Carolyn Meyer
David Milgrim
Wendell Minor

Cyd Moore
Pat Mora
Bernard Most
William Munoz
Scott Nash
John Nez
Josephine Nobisso
Barbara O'Connor
Sheldon Oberman
Dianne Ochiltree
Susan Heyboer
    O'Keefe
Kevin O'Malley
Bel Mooney
Margie Palatini
Linda Sue Park
Pamela Patrick
Katherine Paterson
Darcy Pattison
Gary Paulsen
Mary E. Pearson
Julie Anne Peters
Margaret Phinney
Dav Pilkey
Daniel Pinkwater
Mark J. Plotkin
Patricia Polacco
Nancy Polette
Diana Pomeroy
Carol Purdy
Robert
    Quackenbush
Marsha Qualey
Peggy Rathmann
Deborah
    Kogan Ray
Omar Rayyan
Laura Regan
James Rice
Bethany Roberts
Joanne Rocklin
Kathy Ross

Michael E. Ross
Jill Rubalcaba
Nicole Rubel
Pam Munoz Ryan
Robert Sabuda
Synthia
    Saint James
Graham Salisbury
Michael Sampson
John Sandford
Vivian Sathre
Linda Dalal
    Sawaya
Judith Byron
    Schachner
Dona Schenker
Stacey Lynn
    Schuett
Elaine Scott
Mark Shasha
Aaron Shepard
Linda Joy Singleton
Janni Lee Simner
Marilyn Singer
Steve Smallwood
Cynthia Leitich
    Smith
Jon Scieszka &
    Lane Smith
Roland Smith
Margo Sorenson
Elsie Lee Splear
Bob Staake
Diane Stanley
Ken Stark
Maggie Stern
Janet Stevens
Dawn Lesley
    Stewart
Martha Bennett
    Stiles
Catherine Stock

FIGURE 13.3
continued

Phoebe Stone

Michael Strickland

Maggie Swanson

Joan Sweeney

Stephen
   Swinburne

Lois Szymanski

Edith Tarbescu

Eleanora E. Tate

Jennifer Thermes

Colin Thompson

Theresa Tomlinson

Maxine Trottier

Terry Trueman

Leslie Tryon

Matthew Van Fleet

Ginger Wadsworth

Rick Walton

April Halprin
   Wayland

Carole B.
   Weatherford

Rosemary Wells

Martha Weston

Lisa Wheeler

David Wiesner

Hans Wilhelm

Suzanne Williams

Linda S. Wingerter

Kay Winters

Elizabeth
   Winthrop

Mike Wohnoutka

Susan
   Wojciechowski

Diane Wolkenstein

Janet Wong

Audrey Wood

Douglas Wood

Thomas F. Yezerski

Jane Yolen

Mary O'Keefe
   Young

Karen Romano
   Young

Jane Breskin
   Zalben

Alexander, Lloyd
A Visit with Lloyd Alexander. New York:
   Penguin.

Avi
Avi. Nashua, NH:Delta Education.

Babbitt, Natalie
Natalie Babbitt. Nashua, NH: Delta
   Education.
*Good Conversations! A Talk with Natalie
   Babbitt.* Tim Podell Productions.

Brown, Marc
Meet Marc Brown. Hightstown, NJ:
   American School Publishers.

Bunting, Eve
A Visit with Eve Bunting. Boston:
   Houghton Mifflin.

Carle, Eric
Eric Carle: Picture Writer. New York:
   Philomel.

Cherry, Lynne
Get to Know Lynne Cherry. New York:
   Harcourt Brace.

Cooney, Barbara
A Visit with Barbara Cooney. New York:
   Penguin.

dePaola, Tomie
A Visit with Tomie dePaola, New York:
   Putnam.

Ehlert, Lois
Hands. New York: Harcourt Brace.
Get to Know Lois Ehlert. New York:
   Harcourt Brace.

Fox, Mem
Trumpet Video Visits Mem Fox. Weston,
   CT: Weston Woods.

Fox, Paula
Paula Fox. Nashua, NH: Delta
   Education.

George, Jean Craighead
A Visit with Jean Craighead George. New
   York: Penguin.

Keats, Ezra Jack
Ezra Jack Keats. Weston, CT: Weston
   Woods.

Kellogg, Steven
How a Picture Book Is Made. Weston,
   CT: Weston Woods.
Trumpet Video Visits Steven Kellogg.
   Weston, CT: Weston Woods.

L'Engle, Madeleine
Madeleine L'Engle. Nashua, NH: Delta
   Education.

Lowry, Lois
A Visit with Lois Lowry. Boston:
   Houghton, Mifflin.

FIGURE 13.4

Some videos that feature children's authors

Macaulay, David
David Macaulay in His Studio. Boston: Houghton Mifflin.

Marshall, James
James Marshall in His Studio. Boston, Houghton Mifflin.

Martin, Bill
A Visit with Bill Martin. New York: Holt.

McCloskey, Robert
Robert McCloskey. Weston, CT: Weston Woods.

McDermott, Gerald
Get to Know Gerald McDermott. New York: Harcourt Brace.

McKissack, Patricia
Good Conversation: A Talk with the McKissacks. Weston, CT: Weston Woods.

McPhail, David
In Flight with David McPhail: A Creative Autobiography. Portsmouth, NH: Heinemann.

Milne, A. A.
Meet the Author: A. A. Milne (and Pooh). Hightstown, NJ: American School Publishers.

Most, Bernard
Getting to Know Bernard Most. New York: Harcourt Brace.

O'Dell, Scott
A Visit with Scott O'Dell. Boston: Houghton Mifflin.

Paterson, Katherine
The Author's Eye: Katherine Paterson. Hightstown, NJ: American School Publishers.
Meet the Newbery Author: Katherine Paterson. Hightstown, NJ: American School Publishers.

Peet, Bill
Bill Peet in His Studio. Boston: Houghton Mifflin.

Pinkney, Jerry
A Visit with Jerry Pinkney. New York: Penguin.
Meet the Caldecott Illustrator: Jerry Pinkney. Hightstown, NJ: American School Publishers.

Polacco, Patricia
Patricia Polacco: Dream Keeper. Weston, CT: Weston Woods.

Potter, Beatrix
Beatrix Potter: Artist, Storyteller and Countrywoman. Weston, CT: Weston Woods.

Rylant, Cynthia
Meet the Newbery Author: Cynthia Rylant. Hightstown, NJ: American School Publishers.
Meet the Picture Book Author: Cynthia Rylant. Hightstown, NJ: American School Publishers.

Sendak, Maurice
Sendak. Weston, CT: Weston Woods.

Speare, Elizabeth George
A Visit with Elizabeth George Speare. Boston: Houghton Mifflin.

Steig, William
Getting to Know William Steig. Weston, CT: Weston Woods.

Tudor, Tasha
Take Joy! The Magical World of Tasha Tudor. Weston, CT: Weston Woods.
Take peace! A Corgi Cottage Christmas with Tasha Tudor. Weston, CT: Weston Woods.

Waber, Bernard
Bernard Waber in His Studio. New York: Harcourt.

Wells, Rosemary
A Visit with Rosemary Wells. Weston, CT: Weston Woods.

Yolen, Jane
Good Conversation: A Talk with Jane Yolen. Weston, CT: Weston Woods.

FIGURE 13.4
continued

From InfoTrac College Edition

A Hero in Brief (TIME bonus section/families) (interview) (brief article), Dav Pilkey, *Time* August 27, 2001 v158 i8 pF18 (The zany author of the Captain Underpants books has written a new one, and tries to explain his appeal.)

A Writer Who's 13 at Heart (author and winner of Newbery Award Sharon Creech) (TIME bonus section/families) (brief article) (interview), Andrea Sachs, *Time* August 27, 2001 v158 i8 pF17+ (Sharon Creech deals with serious themes in a way that delights her young readers.)

A Good Scare: The Wizard of Harry Potter Explains What Kids Need to Know of the Dark Side (interview), J. K. Rowling, *Time* October 30, 2000 v156 i18 p108

Homer on George Street (children's author Jerry Spinelli) (interview), Jennifer M. Brown. *Publishers Weekly* July 17, 2000 v247 i29 p168

PW Talks with Bill Martin Jr (interview), Elizabeth Devereaux, *Publishers Weekly* September 25, 2000 v247 i39 p114

A Poetics of Perfectionism (children's book writer Karen Hesse) (interview), Elizabeth Devereaux. *Publishers Weekly* February 8, 1999 v246 i6 p190(1) also see: Karen Hesse (children's author), Brenda Bowen. *The Horn Book Magazine* July–August 1998 v74 n4 p428(5)

A Quiet and Reflective Craft (PW interview with Cynthia Rylant)(interview), Heather Vogel Frederick, *Publishers Weekly* July 21, 1997 v244 n29 p178(2)

Kevin Henkes (children's book author and illustrator)(interview), Ilene Cooper, *Booklist* January 1, 1997 v93 n9-10 p868(1)

Back from IBBY (children's book author Katherine Paterson travels to India to receive the Hans Christian Andersen Author Award) (abstract), Katherine Paterson. *The Horn Book Magazine* January 1999 v75 i1 p26(1)

Summary

Children's literature and the ways teachers use children's books in the classroom have been explored as productive methods of helping children develop the habits of lifetime readers. As certain books become young children's best friends, they lure the children into an ever-enlarging world of reading and writing, with adventure, intrigue, suspense, love, and excitement. Books become times of temporary escape. They become "treasure islands" to search and explore for guidance, information, and "new worlds to conquer."

For teachers who are just beginning their association with children's books, my carefully chosen list of titles, old and new, will open doorways to continued reading. The publications mentioned that chronicle children's literature will help you keep abreast of what's new in children's books.

For teachers who have already followed Alice "down the rabbit hole," the Teacher-to-Teacher features in this chapter show how master teachers have created dynamic language skill-building programs with poetry readings, family read-alouds, Literature Circles, and creative dramatics, which are but a few of the many uses of books in total literacy classrooms.

Children's literature and active use of themes, aesthetics, knowledge, and humanity conveyed by those books were envisioned as a lively curriculum involving all subject areas and the whole spectrum of children, young and old. The children's librarian is a facilitator of curriculum and a friend of both children and teachers. Children themselves are seen as their own teachers, buoyed by the continued impact of great literature.

Chapter 15 continues the discussion of books for young readers as the authors look at wonderful books that can bring life to each curriculum area.

Total Literacy Anchors

♦ Students inherit their teachers' love of books.

♦ Students develop appreciation of different genres of books.

♦ Students discuss favorite books and authors.

♦ Students bring stories to life through Reader's Theater.

♦ Teachers read aloud to children every day.

♦ Teachers introduce children to different categories, or genres, of books.

♦ Teachers allow time for silent reading of books every day.

♦ Teachers involve children in interactive strategies with books and other readers.

♦ Teachers keep abreast of new children's books.

CHAPTER 14

Using Theme Cycles

As You Read . . .

- ◆ What are the advantages in seeing knowledge from different fields or disciplines as related?

- ◆ How do thematic approaches make learning skills more accessible?

- ◆ What roles does the teacher have in making theme cycles effective?

- ◆ What different styles are possible for thematic approaches?

AUTHOR'S NOTE: We invited Geoff Ward and Cherry Ward to write this chapter because of their expertise in theme cycles and thematic instruction.

Geoff Ward *teaches at James Cook University in Queensland, Australia, and is the past secretary of the Australian Reading Association. He is the author of three books, including* Something to Crow About, *and many articles for professional journals. He is known internationally for his work, which bridges from theory to practice. He is the senior international consultant to the International Institute of Literacy Learning and directs the institute's trainer of trainers program. Geoff began his teaching career in New Zealand, where he taught in the elementary grades.*

Cherry Ward *is an authority on natural literacy acquisition, art, thematic teaching, and the writing process. She has taught grades K–8 in New Zealand and Australia and has served as both a classroom teacher and principal. She currently leads a multiage classroom in Townsville, Queensland, Australia.*

Ashton Ward

Geoff Ward and
Cherry Ward

■ ■ ■

In classrooms around the world, we find students engaged with thematic studies. Students usually enjoy the kind of learning that takes place in these ways of working, and total literacy teachers believe thematic studies are extremely effective for both integrating the curriculum and teaching skills in context. In this chapter we examine the concept of thematic teaching and its artifacts.

The Value of Thematic Approaches for Real Learning

Author Words
Geoff Ward

To begin with, let us clarify our terminology. In our work in Australia and New Zealand, we have happily used the label *thematic units* to refer to any approach that integrates learning across the curriculum with some organizing connection that gives a sense of unity to the study. American writers have tended in recent times to distinguish between *literature-based units,* where one or more books is the integrating device, and *theme cycles,* where the teacher uses many different approaches to thematic learning. Whatever label you prefer, all forms of the thematic approach emphasize making connections in knowledge. When we learn, we connect new information with what we already know, tying it in with our existing knowledge structures or attaching it to concepts we control.

If we focus on very narrow aspects of knowledge, it is difficult to do more than make our own particular connections. But when we look at wider and more complex representations of meaning, we can see more of the variety of ways in which people make sense of the world. Wurman (2000) has demonstrated how easily people become anxious about the overload of having too much information to deal with. He shows that if we understand the ways in which things are connected to our uses, it is easier for us to organize and to understand what they are and what they do. Teachers may choose to use thematic approaches because they facilitate learning. Dalton and Boyd (1992) explore some ways teachers can make choices about leadership in the classroom:

> Instead of choosing to feel overwhelmed by the knowledge explosion, the pressure of external forces and "more and more to teach," they are choosing to move to an economy of learning—learning and teaching that is more economical because it is centered on principles that underpin the way they operate as teaching professionals. Unlike packaged programs, models and activity books, such principles offer guidelines against which to measure the worth of external resources. They provide a holistic or "big" picture for us all to work towards in terms of leadership, learning and human growth, relationship with self and others, individuality, interdependence and harmony. (p. 3)

One of the ways of putting those principles into effect is by using theme cycles. Theme cycles begin with the recognition that many aspects of knowledge are strongly related to each other. In practice, they often involve making some specific connections amongst various aspects of the world we live in, such as these:

◆ Connect different books by the same author

◆ Connect books by different authors on similar topics

◆ Connect different animals by looking at their shared common environment

◆ Connect a range of different kinds of information about a particular topic

◆ Connect different ways of looking at the same kinds of information

◆ Compare different parts of the world

◆ Explore different stages or the sequence of processes.

Whatever the nature of a theme cycle, it will enable students to make significant connections amongst things, people, or events, which will enhance their real knowledge about the world and themselves. Much of what takes place in education at all levels, and particularly in schools, has been—with good intentions—cut up into what seem like manageable pieces to be presented to students. Unfortunately, in the process some of the connections with the real world have been lost. Subject boundaries are often imposed artificially to make information easier to handle; the pieces may seem to be more easily sorted out and identified. But the result can be like a jigsaw puzzle where the little pieces may actually be harder to place because they are not seen in relation to other pieces and they go nowhere until they can be connected to other pieces. Students may identify the pieces, but not get the big picture. Thematic approaches start by making connections, and they provide experiences that are broad and rich enough in detail to enable students to connect their learning with real life.

In real life, what is learned in one situation will apply to other situations, and knowledge gained in a particular discipline is relevant to other disciplines. It often makes more sense to see relationships among different aspects of the real world than to regard them as discrete entities, even though it may be convenient to treat them separately at times. A simple example is isolating the sounds of letters, an artificial notion that gives an unrealistic message to students. Letter–sound relationships are important for reading, but they are learned more effectively when they are looked at in the context of known words and in continuous text (Clay, 1991). Similarly, many forms of graphs are useful in depicting information, but they should be learned as students have a need to display data. To take a more complex example, a logbook is a kind of journal, which systematically records required observations. It would be possible, but rather pointless, to teach students what a logbook is without putting them in the position of needing to use one. They could be taught the differences between the self-selected thoughts and observations of a journal or diary, and the structured, consistent observations of a logbook. They could even undergo simulated experiences where they pretended to be a ship's captain, for example. But if the genre of logbooks is to make practical sense to students, it should be learned, supported by whatever specific teaching is necessary, in the context of a real need—an instance of how logbooks are actually used in our culture. An illustration of this is given in the sample planning unit on "Chickens Aren't the Only Ones" later in this chapter. Observations of chicks in the classroom should be recorded in systematic ways. Then students would readily learn how logbooks work because compiling them would have a real purpose, providing an opportunity to compare the data gathered by the students with that displayed in resource books, and opening up explorations of ways of depicting the records of observations. This indicates something of the advantage that thematic approaches have in associating interesting information across the curriculum and in providing a means to learn both subject matter and language skills.

Name P.J. Winston

Age 13

Interests In sports and a Education

What do you like most about school?

What I like most about school is sports and friend around me. But I like my class another thing I to take time out like recess tim

What's your favorite subject? Why?

My favorite subject is Soc St. Because like to learn about Texas History. The other one is Science because I like to dissect all kinds of animal and insects

What's your favorite book? Why do you like it?

My book is Martin Luther King Jr. I like it because I like to learn about the great power and the way he wasn't scared of anything.

What advice do you have for teachers?

Is Teach and help kids get a education. Next you could let them have a little free time. That's what I think.

Different Styles of Theme Cycles

The word *theme* has several related meanings. At least three of them are significant in understanding the idea of theme cycles. A theme can be a repeated visual or auditory effect in art and music, an element that is common to several parts of a

2

America's Finest

Paula Witt, B

painting or a piece of music around which other elements are arranged. Themes are also organizing or orienting principles that shape ideas, or discourses, in a culture. And this meaning of theme can be extended to denote the topic of discourse—what we talk or write about. In the past, the term *theme* has been used to name a topic assigned by the teacher for students to write about, but this usage is not what we mean when we discuss theme cycles. Our focus is on those meanings that help teachers and students bring together a variety of experiences around a common organizing principle.

Theme cycles always make connections among experiences, but their scope varies greatly. At one extreme, a theme cycle might simply be a single class session that ties together students' experiences with two different books, such as a traditional and a contemporary version of a fairy tale. At the other extreme, a theme cycle might provide a vast range of options centered around an organizing idea such as "Change," which could keep a class occupied gainfully for a whole year.

Theme cycles can be whole class activities in which the teacher leads activities that all the students undertake together or in which more than one class—even a whole school—participates. Units can be conducted as group activities and later combined so that the rest of the class learns from the group that has done each study. Another way of developing theme cycles is to initiate individual projects with related topics so that the class builds up a great deal of information that can be shared (Ward, 1988). This approach benefits from teacher modeling. For example, the teacher could model how to do a biographical miniproject about a notable inventor, gathering information with the students, identifying the key elements of a report, and demonstrating ways of presenting the information. Students could then independently construct projects on other famous inventors, either closely following the structure of the model project or diverging from it, depending on their own stage of development in such work. As will be obvious from these few examples, there is not a single right way to conduct theme cycles.

One of the challenges for teachers in adopting a thematic approach is that such ways of working often are better suited to student-centered learning than to direct instruction, or skill and drill approaches. When teachers move to using student inquiry as a means of learning, however, they often seem to act as if students were meant to learn on their own. Teaching in theme cycles still has a strong role for teachers. They need to create appropriate contexts for learning to take place, make the activities as relevant to the real world as possible, and interact supportively with students. Theme cycles provide learning challenges to students with teachers working on enabling strategies that provide the right kind of instruction to facilitate students' engagement with worthwhile learning tasks. It should be clear that undertaking a theme cycle is not just a matter of doing a set of worksheets on the same topic. Instead, theme cycles should be developing students as "experts" in a field of real learning, developing ways of thinking about subject matter or content in the way professionals in that field would think. Teachers may find that they develop new skills themselves when engaged in such explorations, because often the most effective way for them to work is to take on the mantle of a professional in the relevant field themselves.

Sources for Planning Theme Cycles

Where do ideas for units come from? Planning for theme cycles may begin in a number of ways. Here are a few starting points to consider:

♦ *Curriculum requirements.* The starting point for a plan may be skills or content that the teacher is required to teach by the education authority. The teacher may begin by identifying a skill that must be taught and practiced and then look for content that provides opportunities to work on the skill.

Courtesy of Mary Beth Sampson

These hamsters came to the class during a theme study of animals. They remained as the class pets.

Books for theme cycles. Almost any good children's book might be a starter for an effective theme cycle, but here are some that offer particular opportunities.

Chickens Aren't the Only Ones, by Ruth Heller.
Ruth Heller introduces many animals that lay eggs with interesting information about them. One of several of her books that lead into fascinating topics—in this case, oviparous creatures.
New York: Putnam, 1981.

One Less Fish, by Kim Michelle Toft and Allan Sheather.
This rhyming counting book gives an introduction to the beauty of the Great Barrier Reef and to issues of conservation and preservation. Connect it with one or more of Jerry Pallotta's (1991) alphabet books for the underwater theme, or to Lynne Cherry's *A River Ran Wild* (1992) or others of her books, or to François Place's *The Last Giants* (1993) for the conservation theme cycle.
St Lucia: Qld (Australia) University of Queensland Press, 1997.

That Kookoory! by Margaret Walden Froelich.
Kookoory the rooster can't wait to get to Edgerton Fair, and Weasel can't wait to catch him. Kookoory's long-suffering friends come to his rescue.
San Diego, CA: Browndeer, 1995.

Alternatively, coverage of the content may be required, and the teacher may then focus on identifying the language abilities that will be taught and practiced within the unit.

◆ *The interests of the teacher or students that may emerge from other learning for individuals, a group, or the class.* Often an interesting aspect of some other study may trigger a fascination in the teacher or one or more of the students that leads to a thematic study for the class or for a group or individual project.

◆ *The stimulus of a direct experience.* A particular experience, individual or shared, planned by the teacher or occurring incidentally, may trigger a desire to continue study of related topics. Excursions often provide an organizing focus for a theme cycle.

◆ *The stimulus of a book or other vicarious experience.* Perhaps the teacher reads a book to the class and the story, or the information, or some idea in it arouses such interest that the class or one or more individuals extend their engagement with the ideas into a theme cycle. Web investigations often start from a snippet of information that someone in the class finds on the Internet.

◆ *Seeing a unit that another teacher has found to be successful.* Theme cycles can be versatile so that an effective unit at another grade level or in another school can be adapted to a new situation.

◆ *Events of local or national importance.* These may provide excellent opportunities to explore ideas across the curriculum. However, teachers should avoid overemphasis on theme cycles on holidays or festivals. These can be stimulating and interesting, but they often assume an unrealistic importance in the curriculum and take up a great deal of time without contributing much to students' knowledge.

A Framework for Planning Theme Cycles

The most important idea in planning theme cycles is the realization that the unit should advance students' knowledge of both subject matter content and language and work skills. Each theme cycle undertaken in the classroom automatically fits in some way into a sequence of activities or units. Teachers may plan with an emphasis on the content they want the class to work with or emphasize the skills they want students to develop. In an integrated theme cycle, both strands will always be involved. If it is the first unit of the school year, then it will set the tone for much of what will happen in the class for some time to come. The initial theme cycle provides an orientation to a productive mode of learning. This is a time to establish work habits, to identify the strengths of the class that the teacher will build on in later units, and to begin identifying areas of student performance that may need specific attention. This attention to ways of working is not confined to the opening unit but will be maintained throughout the year. However, it is only one side of the value of theme cycles for learning. The other side is the information students learn to handle. Notice that this is not just a matter of learning information itself but becoming adept at gathering, selecting, transforming, recording, and reporting information.

Teachers using thematic approaches have objectives that address the processes of *how* students learn, and other objectives that address the content of *what* students learn. Both kinds of outcomes are important and should be planned for. Theme cycles allow students to explore so many ideas in such a variety of ways that it must be expected that there will be important and useful outcomes different from and beyond those that were actually intended and planned. This open-endedness of outcomes means that the planning itself must be open-ended. Teachers who use theme cycles effectively *do* plan carefully, but they know that they must adjust their plans as the unit progresses. Some planned activities may no longer fit within the available time and will need to be deleted from the plan. When students and teachers become jointly engaged in developing ideas in theme cycles, the teachers' expectations of what students can do, or what they are ready to learn, tend to be overtaken by the reality of students' accomplishments. An information base for learning provides a launching pad that enables learning to travel far beyond what students are likely to achieve when they are not engaged with real ideas but are simply focusing on language skills. But this learning progress is not just learning content. When students have real purposes for reading, listening, talking, and writing, they develop their language skills to fulfill their need to understand and to communicate. And when they need more information about how to accomplish some task that they really want to complete, they are more easily taught the necessary skills in focused learning episodes or minilessons.

As students learn subject matter and language skills to accomplish language tasks, they need to be provided with opportunities to demonstrate their mastery and control. These opportunities to perform have traditionally been overpowered by the notion of testing. A more productive view would be to see them as a time to display learning by pulling together what the students have learned and transforming it in some way that involves more than just repeating what has been covered in the program.

Several aspects of learning discussed in the preceding paragraphs can be identified as stages when sequencing activities within theme cycles. These three stages are initiating, enhancing, and synthesizing.

Something to Crow About, by Geoff Ward.
There are a multitude of teaching possibilities for using this book in literacy lessons and theme cycles at many different levels.
Dallas, TX: Bridge Press, 2000.

Cook-a-Doodle-Doo! by Janet Stevens and Susan Stevens Crummel.
Big Brown Rooster, the great-grandson of the Little Red Hen, with the "help" of his friends, makes a strawberry shortcake and shows the reader much about cooking in the process. This multilayered text will launch students into cooking, measuring, and a whole lot more.
San Diego, CA: Harcourt Brace, 1999.

How Much Is a Million? by David Schwartz.
A wonderful exploration of relative size and just what big numbers might mean in real-life situations. Steven Kellogg's illustrations will help to launch students into their own explorations.
New York: Lothrop, Lee and Shepard, 1995.

Our Natural Homes, by Sneed Collard III.
A description of the world's different biomes that will encourage students to examine a variety of aspects of how they and the rest of nature fit into the different kinds of places to live.
Watertown, MA: Charlesbridge, 1996.

Initiating Activities

The first stage of a unit is made up of *initiating activities,* which provide an introduction connected to earlier units or experiences but have as their main purpose orienting students to the new theme or topic. This stage focuses on one or more significant ideas and experiences that will frame the unit of study. Stimulus events give the teacher and students an opportunity to shape the unit and to negotiate the kinds of activities that will take place within the theme. Teachers vary in their willingness and readiness to allow students to play a major role in developing the curriculum. For many teachers, it is appropriate that they take the major role in planning themselves, allowing limited scope for students to design or select activities. But a growing number of teachers, especially those who work with middle and upper grades, feel comfortable giving students a considerable say in how they will engage in the study of a topic and in choosing the actual topic to study. Wherever you fit on this continuum, recognize that students learn more effectively when they are able to assume a degree of responsibility for their own learning. The initiating activity should give students an enthusiasm for the thematic topic and a belief that it has many interesting possibilities for learning.

The beginning of a unit is the "WOW stage." Teachers should encourage students to be amazed and excited about the things they are finding out. Well-made video programs or other resources may capture students' imaginations and enthusiasm. Gather a lot of resources that students can start to survey so they develop a sense of how much interesting information is available. Many students enjoy browsing the Web, seeking relevant sites and accessing material that will be helpful for more in-depth study later on. Given that many students are not easily fired up about learning, a lot depends on the teacher's own enthusiasm in getting started. Needless to say, if you are about to start doing the same unit in the same way you have done it for many years, you would be well advised to find a different topic, new resources, and new ways of looking at learning.

Evaluation of the program and assessment of students' learning begins in this stage. Teachers should make observations of student attitudes, for example, and gather samples of work that can be compared with later efforts. Students should be helped to understand how assessment that demonstrates that they do not know something is helpful to both themselves and the teacher because it identifies what needs to be learned during the unit.

Enhancing Activities

The second stage of the unit constitutes the major portion of the study. Planning for this stage involves identifying worthwhile activities that will extend students' knowledge of the content and their control over language functions. This stage consists of *enhancing activities*. Most of the learning within the unit will take place in this stage. Enhancing activities support two functions that might be viewed as parallel or intertwined: (1) learning language skills, and (2) learning subject matter or content. The modes of language—listening, speaking, reading, and writing—are the vehicles for most learning. Enhancing the ability of students to use language for a wide range of purposes in a wide range of situations is one objective of language arts teaching. But these language abilities are learned most effectively when we use language for real purposes in real situations. Teaching language skills is done in the context of using language to get things done. Teachers can vary the focus of their attention from the message in a written or spoken communication to the form or structure of the language used or to some particular element of the language. Changing the focus may be necessary to enhance students' performance of language tasks, to improve students' ability to apply what they learn to new language settings, and to improve students' ability to use the same function with other subject matter.

Thus, at some times during the enhancing activities of a theme cycle, the teacher's focus is on language skills. Nevertheless, the major importance will be attached to the subject matter, content, or message of the material being studied. If students are going to enjoy thematic approaches and benefit from them, it must be clear that the unit is not just a thinly disguised excuse to teach them skills. Students can and often do get excited about learning skills, particularly those that give them access to new information, such as Web searching skills. But they want "to know stuff," and that has to be a central concern of theme cycles.

Evaluation is essential to ensure that students are developing understanding and skills. If this is not happening, the program needs to be adjusted. Part of the evaluation process may involve assessing students' performance, but the emphasis should be on evaluation that is formative rather than summative. Assessing how well students have learned what has been negotiated and what else they have achieved is an ongoing process and depends on careful observation at all stages of the unit.

Synthesizing Activities

The third and final stage of the theme cycle consists of *synthesizing activities*. In many ways this is the most significant part of the evaluation and assessment. It should provide opportunities for students to bring together what they have learned and to display aspects of their learning outcomes. In many instances, this stage should encourage transformation of the material learned so that it is clear that the student has internalized it and is not just reproducing it. Synthesizing activities constitute more than a test situation and more than a single culminating activity, although both of these may be part of their nature. Where possible, synthesizing activities should provide students with opportunities to talk, write, and use other forms of display for an audience that go beyond the teacher and the rest of the class. Parents need to have some involvement in all stages of theme cycles, and synthesizing activities give them a chance to celebrate learning with their children.

A theme cycle may not separate clearly into three stages, but planning within this framework makes it easier for the teacher to visualize progress. The terms used in this framework are similar to those used by the Queensland (Australia) English Syllabus (Queensland Department of Education, 1994), which calls the first phase "orientating activities." Other formats for planning units use different terms. For example, Allen, Sampson, and Teale (1989) use the terms *focusing, developing,* and *continuing* to indicate three stages in each activity within a unit. Whether dealing with activities within units, or the whole of a theme cycle, it is important to be responsive to the students' interest and to extend, adjust, or cut off the activity to get maximum benefit from it. When feasible, let students make decisions for themselves about their progress through a unit. Teachers who want students to develop independence will provide them with options for decision making within the overall plan of the unit.

Principles for Planning Units

Don't Force Coverage of the Curriculum

Teachers planning theme cycles should avoid artificially forcing the unit to cover every area of the curriculum. Some units may naturally have a strong science emphasis, whereas others may not. If useful applications of mathematics activities can be found for the unit, these activities should be included. However, if the math concepts are not being used for genuine math purposes, they should be left out and dealt with separately during the unit. There are many other ways to integrate math as shown in Griffiths and Clyne (1993). If you cannot find good quality poetry that fits the theme, don't use any. Good poetry can be used for other purposes alongside rather than within the theme.

Theme cycles will vary in the emphasis they place on different aspects of the curriculum. One may emphasize social studies/art/health, for example, while another may emphasize science/math/music, but all will be undergirded by language arts.

Provide Balance within or between Units

Among the elements that should be balanced in the curriculum are input and self-expression, fact and fiction, imagination and information, use of computer-based data sources and book or other print sources, simple and complex ideas, historical and contemporary settings, and distant and local issues. Balance does not require an equal amount of each of these. Be sensitive to what has already been covered and to how the students are coping with particular activities. The program should not overemphasize input, for example, without giving students a chance to express their own thoughts. Neither should it expect students to express opinions without being exposed to ideas that will help them form opinions. Balance is also achieved from one unit to another and not necessarily within a unit. Thus, a particular theme cycle may heavily emphasize fictional material, but subsequent units may balance this by a stronger emphasis on factual material. Some units may place a heavy emphasis on developing students' writing of expository text; other units may explore a variety of ways of presenting reports.

Use the Plan as a Guide Only

It is common for theme cycle plans to contain more activities than are required in the program or than can be fitted in to the time available, even when it is the teacher's own plan based on first-hand knowledge of the students. Students' abilities are not static and their interests change; implementing a plan must take account of this. The plan should be used as a guide—almost like a menu to choose from. It is an approximation. If a teacher follows a plan to the last letter of detail, it suggests that the plan has been implemented without an appropriate level of careful observation of the students' learning and development over the duration of the unit.

Identify the Crucial Aspects of the Unit

During the planning phases, identify key elements among the activities. These may be activities that practice requirements of your education system, such as essential elements or common curriculum elements. Identifying these in advance will help you select aspects of the plan must be retained as the plan is adapted. Other aspects of the plan may be optional—activities that are worthwhile but that may be replaced by others that emerge from students' interests, additional information, or resources students bring from home.

Do What Comes Naturally

There is no one right way to plan and implement a theme cycle. Teachers think and work differently, so their units will take different shapes. But individual teachers will also take different pathways to planning their own units depending on such factors as the initiating idea, their familiarity with the topic and resources, and the students' knowledge and perceived learning needs. All of these factors interplay with the personality and creativity of the teacher. Plans should appeal to the students and the teacher. If a topic does not seem worth spending a good deal of quality time with, it would be better to plan a few quick activities to teach the main points or provide resources for a different approach. Theme cycles should be joyful and interesting ex-

Courtesy of Mary Beth Sampson

Children become "authors" during thematic unit research.

periences. Assess how much students are learning and how much they are enjoying following the scent of ideas they encounter in open-ended explorations.

Vary Time for Working on Theme Cycles

As has already been indicated, the length of theme cycles is variable. It is also advisable to vary the amount of time allocated within the timetable on different days within the conduct of a particular unit. Because this kind of work brings so many aspects of language and learning together, it benefits from having blocks of time rather than single short sessions in the daily program. School situations vary so much that it is not possible to recommend a particular way of working. If too much time is allowed, students who do not prioritize their own use of time well may encounter difficulties. If too little time is allowed, students' interests may not develop fully. Once again, a balance must be provided and, if possible, allowance made for some students to continue their individual studies while others have switched to working with the teacher. Some units start from a single event, such as reading a book, and gradually develop as students' interests are extended. In other cases, a whole day might be devoted to a high-impact set of experiences that launch the unit with a bang.

Some theme cycles seem so rich in worthwhile activities that they could continue for a whole year. Extended thematic studies have exciting possibilities, but they put a very heavy demand on the teacher's ability to monitor and support such a complexity of learning. Most teachers employing a thematic approach to teaching and learning find it more effective and more convenient to run a range of themes in a school year.

Teachers need to be careful observers of children's learning behaviors, the outcomes of their work, the level of engagement with tasks within the theme, and the quality of interaction within groups. Ensure that what are intended as worthwhile activities keep being worthwhile. Some types of units can keep students happy and busy yet not really contribute significantly to their learning. Students may become very successful at giving teachers what they want but not be learning new things. Some students get lost on the Internet, finding vast quantities of relevant, or slightly relevant, material but do not really process and understand it. At times, such students can go on and on without any valuable learning. Theme cycles are opportunities to expand students' world and their knowledge and skills. To affect their attitudes in positive ways, teachers need to guard against letting themes drag on too long. The level of interaction and challenge and the quality of outcomes must be considered in deciding how long to continue. Even when these are all satisfactory, it may be better to curtail a study so new challenges and new ideas are faced. Theme cycles that capture the students' interest and enthusiasm can provide the stimulus for further "at home work," which can continue for some students on their own initiative after the unit at school has moved on to another theme.

Teacher-to-Teacher

Melbourne Grade 6 teacher Judy Menotti stimulated her class's interest in varied aspects of their environment and how it affects their lives. Students began a range of individual and group explorations of the relationship of people to their environment. These studies kept branching and extending throughout the curriculum for a whole year's program. The students identified and defined many needs and problems and undertook research on issues, wrote letters, listened to guest speakers they had invited, went on field trips, and reported in depth in a variety of ways to each other on their own studies. They developed sophisticated skills in planning their activities, coordinating their work with others, and in communication. The classroom was always filled with interesting displays mounted by the students themselves, and the students passed on much of what they were learning to students in other classes.

Theme Cycle Teaching as Action Research

Action research is taking place when a researcher *identifies* a problem or issue to investigate, *plans* an action that may overcome the problem, *puts* the plan into effect, *observes* the effects of the action, *modifies* the action plan to improve it based on what is observed about its effects, and *continues* the cycle.

Action research is ideally suited to teachers as researchers in their own classrooms. In an important sense, all teachers should be action researchers all the time, because effective teaching requires a sense of direction, good planning, monitoring of learning and of how the planned activities are working out in practice, and an ability to improve teaching and learning by studying the effects of activities on students' learning. Teaching needs to be accompanied by sensitive observation to be evaluative—so that it determines the value to students' learning of the activities and tasks undertaken. Teachers who see themselves as action researchers will bring an open-minded attitude to their use of theme cycles, which will be productive in improving both planning and monitoring learning.

Commercially produced theme cycles may provide a useful starting point for some teachers, particularly those who are not experienced in integrating different activities across the curriculum. But whether the unit is prepared by the teacher who uses it or by someone else, there is a danger of teachers developing expectations of how a theme cycle should proceed and how the students should progress with it. These expectations may appear to be "set in concrete," with all aspects of scope, sequence, and implementation following already established pathways. Some teachers might implement the same theme cycles in the same way year after year, especially if the previous class enjoyed them. Almost inevitably, this leads to students' learning outcomes being limited. Those who teach evaluatively, who observe students carefully and "kid watch" (Goodman, 1985) and who reflect on students' responses, contributions to discussions, control of written and spoken genres, and their level of interest, will adjust activities and expectations accordingly. The same thematic topic implemented in successive years by such a teacher would most likely vary considerably in development and outcomes because of the nature of the students themselves. In addition, a learning teacher is likely to have new ideas and new resources to try whether the unit is the same or different.

Theme Cycles and Parent Participation

Parent participation in their students' learning programs can be a significant factor, not just in the success of the learning but also in the relationship of home and school. Support from home can provide useful resources of information and experience. When teachers use project work as an important part of their program, especially when the projects are individual and carried out at home as well as at school, there are real difficulties in establishing just what should be the role of parents in supporting their children's learning (Ward, 1988). Theme cycles can use parental support in a variety of ways, if teachers help parents to understand what they are trying to do and why they would value parent participation.

This requires more than just keeping parents informed about what the theme cycle topics will be. Most parents have experienced the following scenario, or one much like it.

"Hi, dear. How was school today?"

"Okay."

"What did you do today?" (Or, "What did you learn today?")

"Oh, not much."

End of conversation. The child and parent may not share anything else about what is happening at school because neither has any real enthusiasm for it and neither has any deeper knowledge of how to share their concerns or interests. Teachers need to find ways of building the interest of students and parents for what is happening in the program (Kelly et al., 1998). Theme cycles make it more possible for parents to be partners in their children's learning.

Teacher~to~Teacher

Cherry Ward, K–2 teacher in Townsville, Australia, seeks to build strong communication links with parents of her class. She uses frequent letters and notes in students' homework folders to keep parents informed about what is happening in the program. She makes copies of her planning available to parents, including a list of the major resources she will use, so they can support their children's learning at home and, where appropriate, send additional resources to school. At times, parents have particular expertise that they can share with the class. At the end of many theme cycles, Cherry and her class hold a celebration concert. On this early evening occasion, the class or individual books written during the unit are officially launched. The children perform songs and instrumental music from their program, display artwork, and read pieces of their informational writing to the parents. The announcements are jointly written in the class and are all made by the children. One of the features of the celebration is that they give all students opportunities to share their work rather than being confined to a few of the more advanced students. Although attendance at ordinary school meetings is not high, these occasions draw great crowds of supportive parents, relatives, and friends.

One of her theme cycles focused on wheat. It included a trip to a bakery, but it also involved a talk from a parent who had grown up on a wheat farm and a demonstration of cooking chappatis by a mother who originated from India. The celebration concluded with a bread party; parents brought a great variety of breads that they had made or bought. There was considerable interest in the children's work and a lot of communication among parents, which added to the enthusiasm for what their children were achieving.

The Teacher's Role in Theme Cycles

Teachers have three important roles in theme cycles. These are (1) choosing language activities that exploit content, (2) monitoring and supporting students' learning, and (3) providing focused learning episodes.

Choosing Language Activities That Exploit Content

Especially during the enhancing activities of a unit, the teacher combines attention to developing students' knowledge with activities that develop particular language abilities. Semantic webs open up vocabulary development; cloze passages constructed on the unit theme by the teacher focus attention on specific aspects of language that can be talked about in a post-cloze discussion and extend comprehension; and note-taking and reconstruction of texts develop the ability to select and retain information. These and many other activities are examples of how the teacher can use what the students are learning to enhance their language skills. Most of the language activities within a unit should be chosen for their relevance to real-life learning. For example, in a unit on spiders, teaching the genres of report writing and description is going to be more productive than activities that list the menu for a spider's lunch, or the spider's invitation to a party sent to a fly. That is not to say that such activities would not provide pleasure and variety for students, but it would make more impact on those students who transfer knowledge less readily if they learned to write menus in the course of preparing a meal and invitations when inviting the principal and their parents to a display of their work.

Monitoring and Supporting Students' Learning

One of the major reasons for using a thematic approach is that it makes independent learning more possible. Teachers need to be realistic in catering to the range of abilities within the class and in considering what their students are capable of doing. If the teacher's expectations are too low, students will be restricted in their learning outcomes because they do not get the chance to think for themselves. If expectations are too high, students may not obtain all the benefit that they should from the unit. Teachers need to monitor carefully the work of individual students, keeping anecdotal records, checklists, and samples of work for portfolios to ensure that they are providing the optimal amount of support. Students who have difficulty completing work may need closer supervision than others. One danger to guard against is the self-fulfilling prophecy that limits students' growth in independence because they already appear to lack independence.

Courtesy of Michael Sampson

Children may work on thematic units in every corner of the classroom.

Focused Learning Episodes

As the teacher monitors the learning experiences of students, particular learning needs will emerge. Sometimes these will be for a solitary student, but very often it will be clear that the class, or at least a significant proportion of the students, would benefit from specific teaching of a skill. These teaching sessions focus on the particular need and give students a chance to practice the new learning. An example would be teaching different text structures or graphic displays for showing comparisons and contrasts. Although students may know how to represent comparisons, some of them need to be taught how to take notes in a way that ensures that all the criteria for comparison can be discussed. For example, if you are comparing frogs and toads, you cannot proceed from having information about the habitat of the frog and the feeding habits of the toad: you need matching details about each of them. A minilesson on such a topic could be fitted easily and effectively into the ongoing work of the class.

Planning a Unit:
A General Sequence

Planning a theme cycle can begin in several different ways. The teacher may begin with an idea for one or more worthwhile activities, with an idea of the content to be explored, with a particular book or other experience as a starting point, or with

Jose Aruego

1. *What book of yours has given you the greatest pleasure?*

Leo the Late Bloomer. It was twenty-four years ago and I was just starting out as an illustrator, and I didn't know a lot of what I do now. I just did it by instinct. I guess I was more of a free spirit then.

2. *Which book has surprised you most in terms of its public reception?*

Gregory the Terrible Eater. I had no idea how popular it would become because of its emphasis on junk food versus healthy food.

3. *What would you like people to remember about your work?*

The books I write and the books I choose to illustrate are humorous. The drawings are fun, and I want people to get a good feeling when they read them.

4. *What impact do you hope your work will have on children?*

Children tend to copy my drawings. Teachers tell me that kids find a favorite character in a favorite book and copy that character. My characters are simple to draw, and the children enjoy getting into the artwork themselves by drawing.

Jose Aruego has delighted readers for years with his lively characterizations of animals. His work includes *Leo the Late Bloomer, Whose Mouse Are You?, Star of the Circus, Mouse in Love, Little Louie the Baby Bloomer,* and *How Chipmunk Got His Stripes.*

Reprinted with special permission of Jose Aruego.

a particular language function or ability that the students need to develop. Planning will not follow an invariable sequence, but the following sections will first describe a general planning procedure and then show how that can be applied to a particular theme cycle.

The first stage of planning can be simply a listing of books, experiences, and worthwhile activities that come to mind immediately. With experience, teachers build up a repertoire of activities and ways of using resources. Usually, it is easier to plan possible activities in separate subject areas. Although this conflicts in some ways with the idea of integrating across the curriculum, it provides a framework for recording the brainstorming process, directs and stimulates thinking, and ensures that all areas of the curriculum will be considered, even though some may not be included in the final plan. Look for connections among the different areas and overlapping activities. For example, an activity may be listed as part of the science curriculum but may involve brainstorming, listing, and classifying, which promote oral language and thinking skills.

The beginning stage of a plan, perhaps with the exception of some of the books listed, is likely to be open enough to suit several different grade levels. This has a side effect of being very beneficial to team planning in situations where teachers work together. The initiating experiences may be shared but lead to different enhancing activities. (Of course, the early stages of planning will not necessarily identify what is actually used as the initiating activity of the unit.) Teachers working in a team can brainstorm possible resources and activities together and then start to sort them into levels of application for different groupings of students. For example, a Grade 1 teacher and a Grade 5 teacher could go through this stage together and then refine the plans for their own classes. They might still benefit from teaming for at least some of the implementation of the plan. Because of the wide range of abilities evident in any class, whether it is multiage or a single grade, the planned experiences and the difficulty level of the tasks must be kept broad. This breadth is also needed to cater to the differences in students' strengths and interests, which vary from one curriculum area to another. In general, older students will start a theme cycle with more background knowledge than will younger ones, but their progress will not necessarily follow the same pathways.

An alternative way of starting the planning process is to ask students to brainstorm possibilities or for the teacher and students to do this together. Many teachers using thematic approaches report that they were surprised at how effective it was to incorporate student input in their planning at different stages in the process (Atwell, 1990; Farnsworth, 1990). Many theme cycles have been initiated by the students' own interests and ideas. The teacher, of course, must always consider whether the idea students come up with has enough potential learning opportunities and available resources to be worthy of extended study.

The teacher then researches the topic, gathers resources, and considers possible visiting experts, excursions, and artifacts to bring into the classroom. As the plan takes shape, the teacher modifies the initial outline, adding or deleting activities after obtaining further information and ideas from the resources consulted. The modifying process will take into account the relevance of different curriculum needs and perceptions about the students' learning needs. Figure 14.1 shows an outline plan for a unit for the primary grades on egg-laying or oviparous creatures that originated from Ruth Heller's book, *Chickens Aren't the Only Ones* (1981). The planning outline is then operationalized by sequencing the activities from the initiating activities through the enhancing activities to the synthesizing activities, and by the teacher considering what language and other skills will be emphasized as the class engages in learning content or subject matter.

The plan is put into effect, but it remains flexible and adaptable throughout the unit. A theme cycle should always be a learning experience and not simply a matter of working through a prepared set of activities.

Two simple forms of project work—SUCCESS and PRISE—may enable teachers who are new to this way of working to get started. Both of them emphasize outcomes of the learning rather than how the learning takes place, but they provide opportunities for both process and content objectives to be achieved in a short time.

OVERVIEW PLAN for Younger Children

Resources
Chickens Aren't the Only Ones - Heller
The Chick and the Duckling - Ginsburg
Good Morning, Chick - Ginsburg
The Ugly Duckling - Mayer / Locker
Childcraft - Animals
Mysteries and Marvels of Bird Life
Mysteries and Marvels of Animal World - Cosman
The Happy Egg - Krauss
Are You My Mother? - Eastman
Pancakes and Painted Eggs - Chapman / Niland
Five Little Chickens - an old jingle in Sounds of Numbers - Martin
Brown Bear, Brown Bear, What do you see? - Martin
Polar Bear, Polar Bear, What do you hear? - Martin
Mysteries and Marvels of Ocean Life - Morris
What's Inside? - Garelick

WRITING
* Innovation on "Good Morning, Chick" - class or personal recount(s) e.g., We (I) did— ; like this, etc.
* Innovation on "Five Little Chickens" e.g., "Three Fat Lizards."
* Innovation - class/group/individual on "Brown Bear..."
* Recipe writing - ways to cook eggs. Compile class recipe book.
* Log writing - noting changes in creatures in classroom.
* Letters - arranging for, thanking for, animals for classroom observation.
* Report writing and description - joint (teacher and children), pairs or individual.

READING
* Teacher-readings of available fiction books.
* Teacher-readings of extracts from informational books; modelling of use of reference books, e.g., table of contents, index.
* Research reading for information.
* Text reconstruction e.g. sentence strips of passages from "The Happy Egg" and "The Chick and the Duckling."
* Sentence-halves cards - texts of familiar books.
* Picture/text matching and sequencing of "The Chick and the Duckling" episodes.
* Story theatre of "Are You My Mother?"
* Reading and following recipes using eggs.

SPEAKING AND LISTENING
* Brainstorming and classifying oviparous creatures - small group activity.

POETRY
* Baby Chick - Aileen Fisher

Chickens Aren't the Only Ones

SCIENCE
* List, research, list and classify oviparous creatures. (word cards or picture cards or both).
* Observation/caring for/researching needs of oviparous creatures in classroom.

ART
* Mural - paint and collage of "The Ugly Duckling".
* Illustrations - crayon and paint for enlarged text of "The Chick and the Duckling", "The Happy Egg" and "Five Little Chickens". Make into class books for shared reading.
* Painting on hollow eggs. Dot designs. Hang as class mobile. Examine painted egg designs from various cultures.
* Crushed egg - shell mosaic designs. Shells dyed, then crushed and glued on small cards. Individual.

MUSIC / MOVEMENT
* Listening - "Ballet of the Unhatched Chicks: Moussongsky". Acting out chicks hatching from eggs to above music.
* Acting out different oviparous creatures hatching. Discuss differences in movements. e.g., compare chicks and tadpoles.
* Singing "There Once was an Ugly Duckling".

MATHEMATICS
Number: * Gathering and comparing numbers of eggs laid, from species to species, or kind to kind. Specific instances or generalised.
* Graphical representation - survey favorite ways to eat eggs, e.g., boiled, poached, fried, not at all ...
* Oral or written word problems using numbers found in research. Solving own and others' problems.
Measurement: * Relative measurements of eggs - length, circumference, weight. Measured with standard and non-standard measures.
* Time - compare incubation and hatching durations. - time to boil an egg.
Space: * Study shapes of eggs, e.g., spherical, ellipsoid. Make out of play dough.

FIGURE 14.1

An outline for a unit on egg-laying or oviparous animals

SUCCESS Stories

SUCCESS stories, adapted from a business idea by Wurman (2000), can be presented orally, but may also be written. They highlight something interesting the student has learned on the thematic topic (or on self-chosen topics). In the earliest grades, they might be presented as an "Interesting Facts" wall display with each student writing one fascinating finding. Note that the success might be in learning a skill and is not limited to learning facts. This activity gives a boost to the initiating activities phase of a unit, being part of that "WOW! experience." SUCCESS stories are very clearly focused. Students should be taught to make them:

Short: perhaps only about three sentences long. Young students might start from, "I learned that . . . ," but at later levels more variety adds impact for both the presenter and the audience.

Unique: this criterion helps students learn to express what they have learned rather than to copy the original wording.

Clear: avoid complex language and jargon. Again, this prevents learners from hiding behind the original language, which may conceal lack of understanding.

Concrete: give specific details. For example in "What I learned in math today" a concrete response would be "I learned that scalene triangles have three sides of different lengths," not "I learned about scalene triangles."

Exciting: encourage students to be enthusiastic about this learning as a genuine achievement. Students have to know that they know interesting stuff.

Sharing-oriented: the purpose is not just to show what a student has learned but to make that learning available to others. That may mean that some time has to be allocated for questions from other learners to be answered.

Strategic: what do you want the listeners/readers to know? Writing with that in mind helps to build communication skills. Teachers also need to be strategic. A conversation with a student may lead to the teacher saying, "That would make a great SUCCESS story."

PRISE Stories

The second "miniproject" approach is adapted from a classroom practice of Alan and Patty Engle that they call PROBE. The acronym PRISE is designed to convey the idea of exploring a topic of study in a short focused period of research. It represents Projects Reporting Interesting Stuff Expertly. A key issue in information reports is that the writer should be an *expert*. Students of all ages often appear to lack skills in writing in this genre when the real problem is that they do not know enough about the topic to be able to select and present information effectively. PRISE reports are

Indigenous Children

Teachers usually recognize that schools may cater better to children who come from backgrounds that seem to suit what school is like. Children who come from different backgrounds may be disadvantaged when teachers do not make adjustments for those differences. In Australia, as in the United States, we have many learners who have been born overseas, who may have little background in the English language, and who have many cultural differences to adjust to in their new country. That creates a problem for schools, but we must not lose sight of the important fact that, like the United States, Australia has indigenous people—Aboriginal and Torres Strait Islander peoples—who tend to do less well in our schools than do mainstream children.

With varying success we are working to overcome the difficulties that indigenous children face in adjusting to school in Australia, just as American teachers are. Much can be done by teachers who recognize that their teaching strategies and content need to be adapted to meet the diverse needs of learners. A starting point is to see that children who are different are just that—different. To start with the alternative view, that these children are "deficient," makes it much harder to work in positive and supportive ways. Such a view implies that you are trying to fill in gaps all the time instead of teaching other ways of doing things for new situations.

Another starting point is to understand some of the ways in which a child's home experiences may provide for ways of behaving that are culturally appropriate for the child but not for the culture of the school. Teachers need to develop understanding of these cultural issues for the children that they teach. Some of them will be quite different from some of those that we need to consider, but these few will give you something to think about.

Many indigenous children in Australia suffer from the effects of middle-ear infections that may have impaired their hearing. Other health issues may also affect attendance. There are a number of cultural reasons indigenous children may have high rates of absenteeism, and it is easy for teachers to fall into a pattern of blaming the child. Indigenous parents may use quite different styles of child-rearing, often giving fewer directions and reprimands. Compliance may, in effect, be optional. Children may be more independent and self-reliant. A teacher might

---

brief—just one or two pages of text in a book or on a wall display—and backed up by an illustration, which could be a drawing or a graphic display such as a flow chart.

As well as providing the title, the acronym PRISE denotes the steps or features of the project.

Plan: the student identifies in advance what the topic will be and how it will be undertaken. A brief plan for the project helps to prevent copying or mere paraphrasing of information.

Research: in the first efforts, this might be from a single source, but PRISE studies should expand to use more than one source, though not too many.

think a child is being deliberately disobedient when the child has not realized that conformity is being insisted upon. At the same time, these children may be used to letting things happen around them rather than actively engaging in making things happen.

Indigenous children in Australia often fit into a cultural expectation of not directly seeking information from others, so classroom patterns of questioning may be quite uncomfortable for them. It may be culturally appropriate for indigenous children to observe and copy others, or to seek help from peers. They may complete only part of an answer, leaving space for others to contribute, and thus interrupting another child's answer might seem quite appropriate to them. Whereas mainstream Australians may expect a child to "look them in the eye," this would generally be regarded as rude behavior by an indigenous child.

It is always important to avoid stereotyping people, so we cannot assume that each of these behaviors will be present in any indigenous child, but catering for diverse learners means that teachers must be aware that there may be differences that should be taken into account in providing for a total literacy and learning program.

Indigenous leaders recognize that their children need the knowledge of mainstream Australian culture to succeed in this largely nonindigenous society. But they provide diversity and richness in their own culture, and indigenous students come to school with a lot of knowledge that should be recognized, valued, and built upon. Teachers need to be open to learn about and understand the beliefs children bring with them. Unless students feel that they and what they know are accepted, it is very hard for them to bridge the chasm between their knowledge and what school seems to be like to them.

We cannot help all our citizens to have equal opportunity by treating them equally at the beginning and at later stages of schooling. Those with special needs will require more and different help to reach the same outcomes. We need to gain greater participation from those students who face barriers of any kind by creating a more inclusive curriculum that identifies what those barriers are and seeks to overcome them. Learning has to be engaging, joyful, and successful for all. Schools with a total literacy program can lead the way.

Illustrate: students are learning to present information in more than one form. Selecting an effective way to convey information graphically as well as verbally is a valuable skill and requires teachers to model a range of possibilities over time.

Summarize: the wording of the report is the student's own wording. It should report "interesting stuff" that the student has understood and plans to remember.

Elaborate: the PRISE project should have some feature that personalizes the learning to demonstrate that the author is an expert in this topic. For example, in a PRISE on clouds, the student might include a titled sketch or photograph made of a cloud in the sky on the day of the study. It is helpful if students get the opportunity to share their reports, perhaps in small groups, as this also aids retention of the information as real learning, not just a written product.

Most thematic units will be much more complex than SUCCESS stories or PRISE projects, but these are ways of getting started on wider studies and are useful activities that provide opportunities for consolidating and sharing learning within thematic units.

FURTHER WORDS

 From InfoTrac College Edition

Leading into Literature Circles Through the Sketch-to-Stretch Strategy: Sketching Can Help Students Deepen Their Understanding of Story Elements and Nurture a Collaborative Classroom Atmosphere, Phyllis Whitin, *The Reading Teacher* February 2002 v55 i5 p444(7)

Guided Reading: Who Is in the Driver's Seat? (questions and answers), Susan Kidd Villaume and Edna Greene Brabham, *The Reading Teacher* November 2001 v55 i3 p260(4)

Interacting with the Curriculum (children's books), Nancy J. Johnson and Cyndi Giorgis, *The Reading Teacher* October 2001 v55 i2 p204(10)

"I Just Need to Draw": Responding to Literature Across Multiple Sign Systems, Kathy G. Short, Gloria Kauffman, and Leslie H. Kahn, *The Reading Teacher* October 2000 v54 i2 p160

From Professional Journals and Publications

Altwerger, B., and Flores, B. (1994). Theme Cycles: Creating Communities of Learners. *Primary Voices K-6, 2,* 2–6.

Barton, K. C., and Smith, L. A. (2000). Themes or Motifs? Aiming for Coherence Through Interdisciplinary Outlines. *The Reading Teacher, 54,* 54–63.

Bergeron, B. S., and Rudenga, E. A. (1996). Seeking Authenticity: What Is "Real" About Thematic Literacy Instruction? *The Reading Teacher, 49,* 544–550.

Five, C. L., and Dionisio, M. (1995). *Bridging the Gap: Integrating Curriculum in Upper Elementary and Middle Schools.* Portsmouth, NH: Heinemann.

Galda, L., Rayburn, S., and Stanzi, L. C. (2000). *Looking Through the Faraway End: Creating a Literature-Based Reading Curriculum with Second Graders.* Newark, DE: International Reading Association.

Hausfather, S. (1998). Changing Students' Relationships to Knowledge in a Theme-Study Classroom. *Journal of Research in Childhood Education, 13,* 33–47.

Lehr, S., and Thompson, D. L. (2000). The Dynamic Nature of Response: Children Reading and Responding to *Maniac Magee* and *The Friendship.* *The Reading Teacher, 53,* 480–493.

Lipson, M. Y., Valencia, S. W., Wixson, K. K., and Peters, C. W. (1993). Integrations and Thematic Teaching: Integrations to Improve Teaching and Learning. *Language Arts, 70,* 252–263.

Manning, G., Manning, M., and Long, R. (1994). *Theme Immersion: Inquiry-Based Curriculum in Elementary and Middle Schools.* Portsmouth, NH: Heinemann.

Metropolitan Toronto School Board. (1995). *Getting It All Together: Curriculum Integration in the Transition Years.* Portland, ME: Stenhouse.

Noddings, N. (1995). Teaching Themes of Care. *Phi Delta Kappan, 76,* 675–685.

Wood, K. D., Roser, N. L., and Martinez, M. (2001). Collaborative Literacy: Lessons Learned from Literature. *The Reading Teacher, 55,* 102–111.

Summary

The variety of thematic approaches to learning adds interest to the program for both the teacher and the students, but they also facilitate learning by making connections easier. Teachers can plan integrated activities that give scope for a wide range of explorations of ideas, learning interesting content, and development of language and other skills. When students participate in the planning process, they are more likely to understand and appreciate what they are learning. Thematic approaches can be more difficult to implement for the teacher because of the adaptability required, but the advantages in interest and learning gains will repay the effort.

Total Literacy Anchors

- The student connects information from many different sources.
- The student recognizes the relationships among different ideas.
- The student experiences a variety of working styles.
- The student uses language for real purposes in many curriculum areas.
- The student develops independence and interdependence in undertaking studies.
- The student demonstrates learning in a wide variety of ways.

- The teacher realizes the advantages of teaching language and other skills while students are engaged in learning content matter.
- The teacher becomes more adaptable in planning activities that cater to students' needs and interests, and in modifying plans as units progress.
- The teacher makes realistic connections among different areas of the curriculum.
- The teacher involves colleagues and parents in building a community of learners.

CHAPTER 15

Content Area Literacy

As You Read . . .

- Why do readers have problems comprehending expository text?

- What are the various text structures, and how do they impact comprehension?

- How does literacy in the total curriculum involve more than reading and writing?

- How can basic research skills be developed in content areas?

- How are art and literacy related?

- How is mathematics language?

- What is the relationship between music and literacy?

- How can literature make social studies more attractive to students?

- How can teachers integrate science and literacy?

Author Words

Mary Beth Sampson

When do children develop literacy skills? During instruction focusing on reading and writing? Yes, to a certain extent. But children actually develop literacy skills throughout the curriculum in science, in math, in social studies, and through art and music activities. In this chapter we examine how literacy learning occurs, not just in language arts and reading classes but throughout the school day, and show the power children's literature has for content learning. We conclude that literacy learning and content learning should go hand in hand, and we show you ways to integrate your curriculum.

Children's Literature and Content Area Instruction

Why do good readers often become poor readers when asked to read their social studies or science books? It's because that material, which has numerous names including expository, nonfiction, informational, and content text, is written in a different style than the stories students encounter in most children's books.

This problem occurs about the time of the "fourth-grade slump" (Chall, 1983; Chall, Jacobs, & Baldwin, 1990) when students are confronted with the responsibility of gleaning much of their academic information from content textbooks. There is often a decrease in the number of children who are categorized at reading "on grade level" or in students' rate of reading growth as they advance from grade to grade in school (Snow, Burns, & Griffin, 1998). This is a frustrating situation for both students and teachers. Why doesn't the skill in reading children's literature transfer to reading content material?

The reasons for problems in reading expository text are numerous. In many primary classrooms, most of the reading materials children encounter consist of stories, poems, and plays; many children lack extended exposure to informational text (Anderson, Hiebert, Scott, & Wilkinson, 1985; Flood & Lapp, 1990; Moss, Leone, & Dipillo, 1997). Although the use of trade books (books written for children that are not textbooks and are available for purchase by the public) for literacy instruction has increased over the last decade, the focus remains on the use of stories rather than nonfiction texts in the classroom (Moss, Leone, & Dipillo, 1997). Consequently, some students may lack essential background knowledge necessary to glean critical information from technical vocabulary, graphs, charts, and labeled illustrations (Moss, Leone, & Dipillo, 1997; Pappas, 1991). In many content classrooms, teachers attempt to overcome students' lack of expertise with informational text by orally presenting the content material (Alvermann & Moore, 1991; Armbruster et al., 1991; Vacca & Vacca, 2002). However, this does not solve the problem, for even if children are exposed to the necessary information, they have not had the opportunity to become proficient readers of content texts.

Due to these challenges, teachers often assume students do not find nonfiction text as engaging as stories. However, research has shown that when children have multiple experiences with informational books they develop equal expertise with—and appreciation of—content material as they have for stories (Pappas, 1991, 1993).

Students' enjoyment is influenced by the *stance* they take when reading the text. In Chapter 5, we discussed Rosenblatt's (1978, 1983, 1991) concepts of *efferent reading* (focusing on meaning, conclusions to be drawn, and propositions to be tested) and *aesthetic reading* (focusing on what is being 'lived" through *during* the reading). Students *may* take an efferent stance when reading informational text— but that is not always the case. Children are fascinated with the world in general— and specific topics in particular. When reading a quality text about a topic that intrigues them, students will often find the images "playing in their mind" just as when they are engaged in reading a story.

To achieve success in school, students must acquire the skills necessary to comprehend expository text. Content texts are used in 75 to 90 percent of U.S. classrooms (Palmer & Stewart, 1997; Tyson & Woodward, 1989). These skills are referred to as "content literacy," and definitions include "the level of reading and writing skill necessary to read, comprehend, and react to appropriate instructional materials in a given subject area" (Readence, Bean & Baldwin, 1998, p. 4) and "the ability to use reading and writing to learn subject matter in a given discipline" (Vacca & Vacca, 1999, p. 8). Even more important, if students are to become productive individuals in our society, they must be able to glean information from numerous nonfiction texts outside of the classroom, such as travel guides, magazine articles, instruction manuals, newspapers, and business forms and memos.

In truth, facts change. We have all experienced learning facts—information about endangered species, names of dinosaurs, or information about countries— and then picked up a current edition of a periodical to find that those "facts" are now "fiction." Students must become proficient consumers of expository text to keep abreast of our rapidly changing world.

Comparing Story/Narrative and Content/Expository Text

Let's consider the basic differences between the structure of story or narrative text and that of content or expository text. Whether it is a mystery, adventure, romance, or comedy, stories contain these key components:

◆ Characters

◆ Setting—may include location, weather, time period, and time

◆ Plot—includes (1) a problem and/or dilemma, (2) a series of events that occur involving the problem/dilemma—typically including events that cause conflict or hinder the solving of the problem/dilemma, (3) high point—when the problem/dilemma is about to be solved, and (4) the solution—problem/dilemma is resolved.

Proficient readers know these important items of "story grammar" contain the crucial information in the story. As a result of being familiar with the text structure, it is easier for students to activate their schemata and monitor their comprehension. Successful readers are able to interact with the text at both a cognitive and affective level and become part of the story. The story "plays in the mind," and understanding occurs.

In contrast, expository text does not possess these familiar elements. There is no "story," and students often are unable to interact with the text in a way that activates their schemata. An expository text might include descriptive text, a sequence of events or instructions, a cause and effect passage, a comparison and contrast session, or a problem and solution section (Armbruster & Anderson, 1981; Meyer, 1975, 1979; Piccolo, 1987). In addition, expository text often deals with information that is new to students. They may not have the prior knowledge essential to understand this factual material. Students are often unsure of what is important and try to remember everything. They may find themselves overwhelmed by the amount of material, fail to understand it, and as a result remember few, if any, of the key concepts. As a result, students who are successful readers of stories may find it difficult to interact with expository text and find themselves merely "calling the words" to finish the assignment. One 10-year-old boy summed it up this way: "The social studies book doesn't give you a lot of detail. You don't imagine yourself there because they're not doing it as if it were a person" (Levstik, 1989, p. 116). For this child, nothing "played in the mind" when he read the social studies text.

Therefore, it is important to provide instructional supports that ensure success for your students. Effective lessons contain experiences involving students in *before* or *prereading, during reading,* and *after* or *postreading* interactions with text. *Before reading* or *prereading* experiences help students activate their schemata, determine a purpose for reading, and provide vocabulary and concept support for new information. Effective *during reading* support involves students in active interaction with the text, and *after reading* or *postreading* experiences aid students in synthesizing, evaluating, revising, extending, and elaborating on the material they have read—and making connections to their prior knowledge. These experiences should enhance their comprehension and "anchor" the new learning. Many strategies discussed in previous chapters do this. For example, Confirming a K-W-L (Sampson, 2002), discussed in Chapter 7, activates students' schemata and sets a purpose for reading as they brainstorm what they think they know and the questions they have about a topic *before reading*. In addition, it provides an opportunity for the teacher to determine the knowledge base of the students and provide support with essential concepts or vocabulary needed for the reading. *During reading* students actively make decisions about the text as they identify facts that confirm or answer the items generated during brainstorming. *After reading,* students share and evaluate information as they collaboratively revise and extend their chart.

In addition, research has shown that familiarity with various types of text and text structures aids students in comprehending expository materials (Caswell & Duke, 1998; Horowitz, 1985; Slater, 1985). In the following section, we explore many children's books that "tell stories" yet still contain text or concepts that expose children to the various expository text structures. Traditional wisdom has often categorized "picture" books as appropriate for primary grades and "chapter" books as the literature of choice for intermediate and middle grades, but we do not abide by those categorizations. Nor do we limit the discussion to books that fall neatly into one genre. Some of the books contain informational material, some tell stories, some are written in a pattern or framework that helps children organize and synthesize content material. Some blend fiction and nonfiction and could be classified as multigenre. As an educator, it is important to share a wide range of books and instructional applications with your students—regardless of their age— to aid them in "bridging the gap" between story/narrative and content/expository text. As you read this chapter, think about how you might use trade books and the suggestions presented here to help your students master expository text material.

Descriptive Text

Books containing descriptive text require students to answer one or more of the following questions:

- ◆ What is it?
- ◆ What is its purpose?

A student discusses his report with his teacher.

◆ What does it look like?

◆ What is it used for?

Key words/phrases may include *for example, characteristics include, in fact, for instance,* or adjectives describing how the subject sounds, looks, feels, or smells.

Many books provide opportunities for children to focus on these questions. For instance, in A *House for Hermit Crab* (Carle, 1987), children have an opportunity to verbalize physical descriptions of the animals by describing the art. Students may use the format of *The Magic School Bus Inside the Earth* (Cole, 1987) and *The Magic School Bus Lost in the Solar System* (Cole, 1986) to categorize and describe items they are studying. As children explore Florian's *Mammalabilia* (2000), they may want to engage in research to extend the descriptions and determine if they consider all of Florian's descriptive terms factual, or if some are his opinion.

Many alphabet books use descriptive language. James Rice (1988) writes vivid descriptions for Texas places, things, and people in the *Texas Alphabet*. Jerry Pallotta provides extensive descriptions of numerous content topics through his alphabet books. His work is explored in the Author Study in this chapter. David Schwartz uses engaging, humorous, and understandable language to describe scientific concepts in *Q Is for Quark: A Science Alphabet Book* (2001) and math terms in *G Is for Googol: A Math Alphabet Book* (1998).

Jerry Pallotta

1. *Which book of yours has given you the greatest pleasure?*

Probably the *Extinct Alphabet Book*. I am always looking for book ideas that are new. I have seen hundreds of dinosaur books, but I have never seen a book of extinct creatures that were not dinosaurs.

2. *Which book has surprised you most in terms of its public reception?*

Probably the *Hershey's Fractions Book*. I thought it would do well, but I had no idea it would do so well. More than 500,000 books were sold in the first eighteen months.

3. *What would you like people to remember about your work?*

I think it is very simple. I want to appeal to the reluctant readers. Kids that would never pick up a book would probably love the *Jet Alphabet, Dory Story,* or *The Skull Alphabet*. Hopefully these books will turn them on to other

books. Reluctant readers, that's where it's at!

4. *What impact do you hope your work will have on children?*

When someone picks up one of my books, I want them to feel that a lot of research, hard work, and fun went into making these books. I always try to have unusual creatures, things adults have never heard of. I try to have colorful illustrations. As best I can, I try to make them fun to read. Science and humor are a rare mix.

Jerry Pallotta is the "King" of the alphabet pattern book. These nonfiction books contain a wealth of information about things readers want to know more about. His more than fifty ABC books also include our personal favorites, *The Icky Bug Alphabet* and *The Dinosaur Alphabet Book.*

Reprinted with special permission of Jerry Pallotta.

Use these books to assist children in recognizing descriptive text and identifying what information is important. Alphabet books provide a framework for students to identify and write descriptively about a subject they are studying. Here are some samples for a "Solar System Alphabet":

A is for Asteroid. An Asteroid is made of rocks and metals and orbits the sun but is way too small to be a planet. They can be as small as pebbles and not have names up to one called Ceres that has a diameter of 1000 kilometers (but still too small to be a planet!)

B is for Blue planet. The Earth is called the Blue Planet because it is mostly water and looks mostly blue when you are looking at it from a spaceship.

C is for Comet. A Comet is mostly made of ice and dust. It is not on fire even though it looks like it is. When it comes near our sun some of the ice melts and the dust looks like a tail.

Additional activities that cause students to focus on the descriptive attributes include writing a personality sketch or wanted poster of a historical or generic character (such as a polluter or an environmentalist). Writing or dramatizing an advertisement for a factual place, procedure, or thing requires students to use highly descriptive language. Students become proficient in descriptive language when they have the opportunity to take a content concept and expand it with descriptive words and phrases that "paint a picture in the mind." For example, descriptive words and phrases could be added to the word *dinosaur* until a specific dinosaur is identifiable by the stated characteristics. Children become aware of the power of descriptive language when they write or verbalize a description of a content concept (place, thing, person, or procedure) in order for another student to draw it. The strength of the description is assessed by the artist's rendering. Often, revision and collaboration result.

Sequential Text

Sequential passages in text require students to ask these questions:

◆ How do you do this?

◆ What are the steps in this?

◆ What happened first, second, third . . . ?

◆ What do I do first?

Key words/ phrases may include *on (date), after, then, now, as, before, to begin with, first, second, finally, in conclusion.*

Books such as *How a Crayon Is Made* (Oz, 1988), *How Does Soda Get into the Bottle?* (Oz, 1988), and *How a Book Is Made* (Aliki, 1986) expose children to the series of steps in making a product. Joanne Cole takes children on sequential tours of the solar system and the water cycle in *The Magic School Bus Lost in the Solar System* (1986) and *The Magic School Bus at the Waterworks* (1986). The *Magic School Bus and the Electric Field Trip* (Cole, 1999) follows the sequence of how electricity is generated and travels via high-voltage wires from a power plant to destinations such as a library, a diner, and a student's house. In *Time Train* (Fleischman, 1991), children take a trip back through time to visit the dinosaurs. *Pepper's Journal: A Kitten's First Year* (Murphy, 2000) uses a journal format and the sequence of dates as a young girl chronicles the important events in her kitten's first year of life.

Biographies and autobiographies expose children to the sequence of significant events in a person's life and often aid children in realizing what it was like to live through a specific time period. Jean Fritz brings historical characters alive by weaving their unique human characteristics into her intriguing presentation of biographical information in books such as *And Then What Happened, Paul Revere?* (1973), *Why Don't You Get a Horse, Sam Adams?* (1974), *Where Was Patrick Henry on the 29th of May?* (1975), *What's the Big Idea, Ben Franklin?* (1982), *Will You Sign Here, John Hancock?* (1987), *The Great Little Madison* (1989), *Traitor: The Case of Benedict Arnold* (1991), and *Leonardo's Horse* (2001). Robert Burleigh's (1991)

Flight: The Journey of Charles Lindbergh shows readers the sequence of events leading to an important historical event in a person's life. *Girls Who Rocked The World: Heroines from Sacajawea to Sheryl Swoopes* (Welden, 1999) contains short biographical sketches discussing the remarkable achievements of women in a variety of fields before they reached the age of twenty. *Bill Peet: An Autobiography* (Peet, 1989) and *I Am Rosa Parks* (Parks, 1997) expose children to the concept that someone can tell about his or her own life through both text and drawings. As children

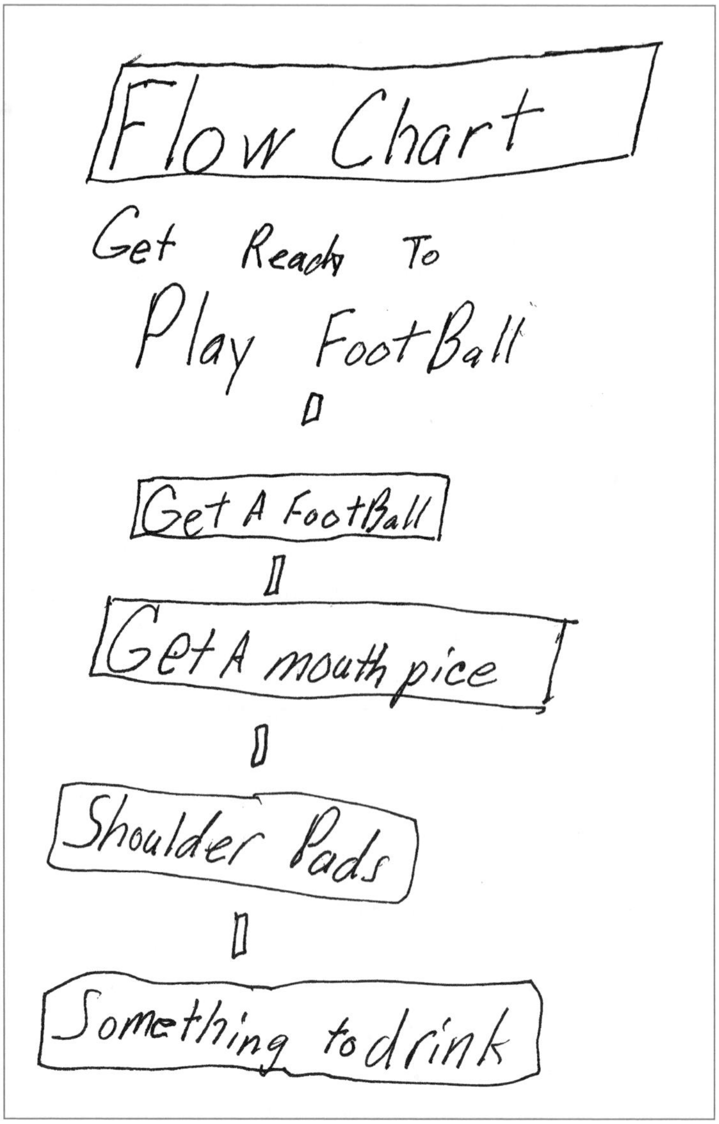

FIGURE 15.1

Flow chart for "How to Get Ready to Play Football"

are exposed to the sequence of events in the lives of real people, they are confronted with what Jean Fritz (1981) refers to as "the very stuff of life."

Students have the opportunity to sequence information by constructing flow charts of the information presented in the children's books. Familiar sequences of events can be charted first, such as two third-graders did in "How to Get Ready to Play Football" (Figure15.1) and "How to Catch a Girl" (Figure 15.2) Children can then move to charting new material, such as "How to Plant Beans" (Figure 15.3).

FIGURE 15.2
Flow chart for "How to Catch a Girl"

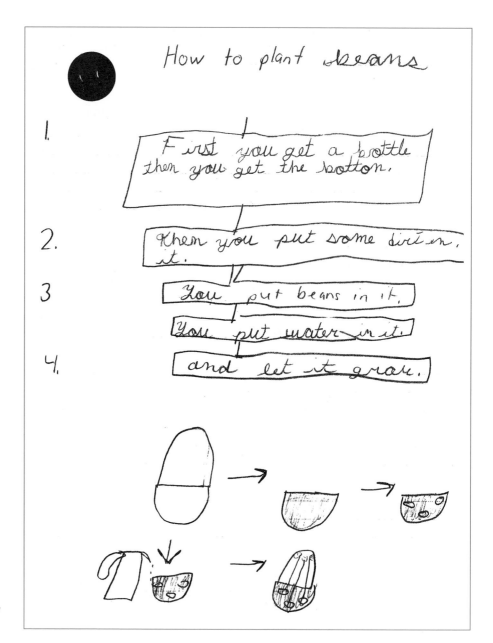

FIGURE 15.3
Flow chart for "How to Plant Beans"

Comic strips are also an excellent format for illustrating the sequence of a procedure or an event. *The Magic School Bus at the Waterworks* (Cole, 1986) contains a wall story of the sequence of the characters' trip through the water cycle. Any sequenced information can be put in this format. In lieu of this, students could construct a flip chart of the information. To provide opportunities for discussion and revision, give children the opportunity to practice the sequence by having each child hold one of the written descriptions and illustrations and placing themselves in the correct order.

Any of these formats can also be used if students are presenting biographical or autobiographical information. If children are attempting to identify the important steps in a procedure, they could write a help wanted ad for someone to do the procedure. The ad must contain the ordered "steps" the person would be responsible for.

Comparison and Contrast Text

Text that has the structure of comparison and contrast focuses on these issues:

◆ How were these things or ideas alike? To what extent?

◆ How were these things or ideas different? To what extent?

◆ How were these things or ideas the same? To what extent?

Key words/phrases may include *however, but, as well as, on the other hand, unless, while, although, not only . . . but also,* and *either . . . or.*

Henry Hikes to Fitchburg (Johnson, 2000) shares the story of two friends who choose very different modes of travel to Fitchburg, which essentially reflects their different approaches to life. The book was inspired by a passage from Henry David Thoreau's *Walden* (1854), which compared and contrasted earning money for a train ticket or walking as two ways of traveling thirty miles in one day.

Karen Hesse uses free verse to present a powerful and often disturbing portrayal of eleven different perceptions of the arrival of the Ku Klux Klan in a small Vermont town in 1924 in *Witness* (2001). As the story progresses, the contrasting views and the unfolding mystery provide a catalyst for older children to explore race and identity from varying viewpoints. Karen Ackerman's *The Tin Heart* (1990) is the story of two friends at the beginning of the Civil War. Their fathers' differing viewpoints on the issues become a dividing point, because one family lives on the Ohio side of the Ohio River and the other lives on the Kentucky side.

Children have the opportunity to compare and contrast changes caused by the passage of time when they read *In Two Worlds: A Yup'ik Eskimo Family* by Aylett Jenness and Alice Rivers (1989) in which a picture of both present and past village life is presented. Patricia Lauber contrasts old beliefs about dinosaurs with updated information in *The News About Dinosaurs* (1989). As children are exposed to the commonly held beliefs about the validity of the existence of the brontosaurus, they are given the update that the brontosaurus was an incorrect classification resulting from the erroneous joining of the head and body of two different dinosaurs. In Paul Goble's *Death of the Iron Horse* (1987), the viewpoints and perceptions of

Native Americans are portrayed and contrasted with those who were instigating the westward expansion of the railroad.

The traditional European viewpoint of Christopher Columbus's "discovery" of America is portrayed in Joan Anderson's *Christopher Columbus: From Vision to Voyage* (1991) and Peter Sis's *Follow the Dream: The Story of Christopher Columbus* (1991), but students are exposed to the reaction and concern of a young Native American boy in *Encounter* (1992) by Jane Yolen. Figure 15.4 shows the contrasting views of Christopher Columbus and a Native American child as portrayed in *Christopher Columbus: From Vision to Voyage* and *Encounter.*

As students are exposed to the varied viewpoints and ideas in the trade books, they can construct Venn diagrams depicting the views that are alike and different. Figure 15.5 demonstrates the differing views of the two fathers in *The Tin Heart* (Ackerman, 1990). Exploration and research of the issues could result in a panel discussion comparing objects, ideas, or viewpoints. During this process, children become aware that different sources often present conflicting information. Therefore, copyright dates, credentials of the author, and reliability of the publication must be examined. Children can write editorials depicting the differing views or write interviews depicting the contrasting opinions. For example, editorials or interviews could be written and conducted depicting Christopher Columbus's and a Native American's views of Columbus's exploration.

Cause/Effect Text

To glean important information from cause/effect text, students must determine these things:

- Why did this happen?
- What action(s) instigated this (these) event(s)?
- What caused this?

Key words/phrases may include *because, since, therefore, consequently, as a result, this led to, nevertheless,* and *if . . . then.* Understanding these relationships is key to comprehension.

When a little boy falls asleep and dreams he is on a train ride, animals explain why they must board the train to escape extinction in *Hey! Get Off Our Train* (1989) by John Burningham. Margery Facklam explores the diverse events that have caused animals to become extinct in *And Then There Was One* (1990). *Tomorrow's Alphabet* (Shannon, 1999) explores the concept of changes in items within an alphabet book format with text such as "A is for seed—tomorrow's APPLE. B is for egg—tomorrow's BIRD" (pp. 1–4). In *The Great Kapok Tree* (1990), Lynne Cherry details how a logger in the Amazon rain forest is made

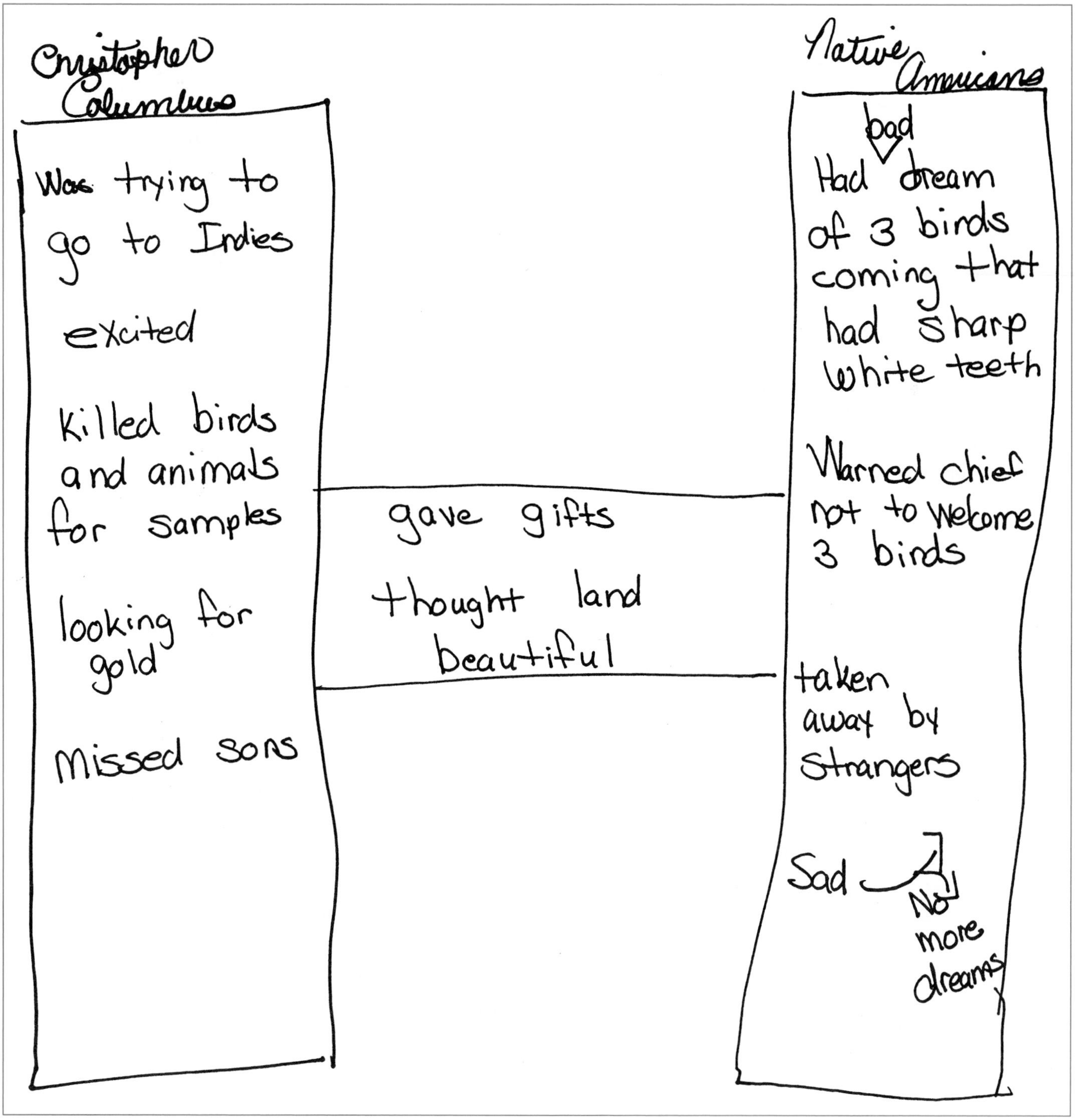

Christopher Columbus

Was trying to go to Indies

excited

Killed birds and animals for samples

looking for gold

Missed sons

Native Americans

bad

Had dream of 3 birds coming that had sharp white teeth

Warned chief not to welcome 3 birds

taken away by strangers

Sad → No more dreams

gave gifts

thought land beautiful

FIGURE 15.4

H chart of contrasting points of view regarding Columbus's discovery

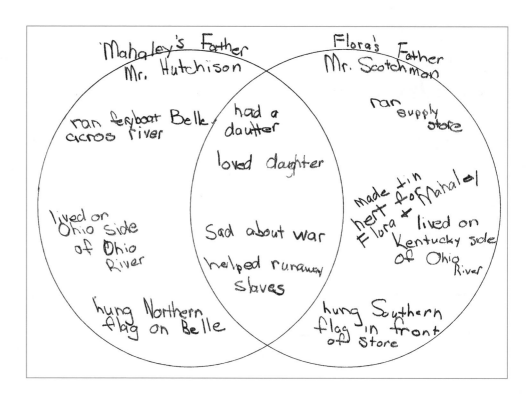

FIGURE 15.5

Venn diagram of two fathers from *The Tin Heart*

The following text appears within the Venn diagram:

Mahaley's Father Mr. Hutchison

Flora's Father Mr. Scotchman

ran ferboat Belle across river

lived on Ohio Side of Ohio River

hung Northern flag on Belle

had a daufter

loved daughter

Sad about war

helped runaway slaves

ran supply store

made tin hert for Mahale & Flora

lived on Kentucky side of Ohio River

hung Southern flag in front of Store

aware of the effect of his actions on the various animals and people who live there. Remy Charlip uses the delightful pattern of *Fortunately, Unfortunately* (1987) to trace the logical effect of each action as a young boy attempts to reach his destination of a birthday party in New York City.

Exploration of *Tomorrow's Alphabet* (Shannon, 1999) provides opportunities for children to verbalize and/or write the cause/effect scenario that must take place for "tomorrow's" situation to occur. Here is one written after reading from "B is for egg—tomorrow's BIRD": "The egg must be kept warm by the mommy bird gently sitting on it to cause a bird to hatch."

Figure 15.6 shows the use of a graphic organizer to depict the plight of the saddle-back tortoises described in *And Then There Was One* (Facklam, 1990). These animals were originally found in abundance on the Galapagos Islands.

When children incorporate the pattern in *Fortunately, Unfortunately* (Charlip, 1987), they can trace the cause/effect relationship of many content concepts. Elisa, a fifth-grader, wrote about the Pilgrims:

Fortunately, the Pilgrims wanted to be free to have their own church. Unfortunately, they couldn't do that in England. Fortunately, the Pilgrims had a ship called the Mayflower. Unfortunately, the ship was very small. Fortunately, they still decided to leave England in September 1620 to come to

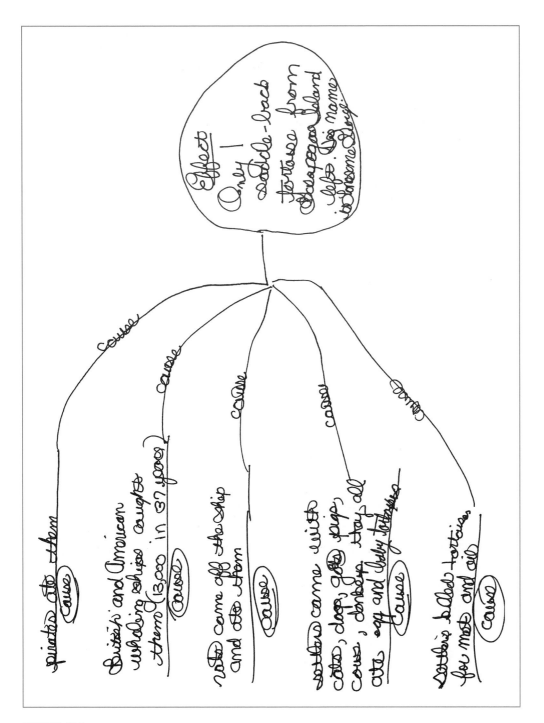

FIGURE 15.6
Graphic organizer for *And Then There Was One*

America. Unfortunately, they did not arrive in America until November 1620. Fortunately, they started Plymouth Colony along Cape Cod Bay. Unfortunately, it was winter and many people died. Fortunately, the Indians showed them how to survive. And, fortunately, some lived so they could have Thanksgiving and fortunately they invited the Indians, and fortunately, they had a big dinner, and fortunately, we still do!!!

The cause/effect relationship can also be explored as children write newspaper stories or editorials depicting the cause of a situation and its effects.

Problem/Solution Text

Text that depicts problems and solutions concentrates on the following issues:

- ◆ What problem occurred and how will it be solved?
- ◆ Can we prevent this problem from occurring again?
- ◆ Was this problem perceived the same way by everyone?

Key words/phrases include *because, since, therefore, consequently, as a result, this led to,* and *the problem is.*

Problems and solutions are examined in *A River Ran Wild* (1991) as Lynne Cherry chronicles the pollution and reclamation of the Nashua River. Ruth Heller depicts the problems animals face in trying to protect themselves in the wild and the solutions provided by protective coloration in her books *How to Hide a Butterfly and Other Insects* (1985), *How to Hide an Octopus and Other Sea Creatures* (1986), *How to Hide a Polar Bear and Other Mammals* (1985), *How to Hide a Crocodile and Other Reptiles* (1986), and *How to Hide a Whip-poor-will and Other Birds* (1986). The life-threatening problem caused by the Alaskan oil spill is examined by Gloria Rand as she chronicles the rescue and treatment of animals in *Prince William* (1992). In *The Secret to Freedom* (Vaughan, 2001), Great Aunt Lucy, a former slave, shares the drama of her involvement in the Underground Railroad and the problem of conveying information to slaves who were seeking freedom. Her great-niece learns how various patchwork quilt patterns were used to give information to escaping slaves as they struggled to find their way to freedom.

Meet the Author

Gloria Rand

Children can examine the problems portrayed in these texts, brainstorm alternative solutions for the problems, and do research to determine if any of their suggestions have been implemented. Panel discussions can also be conducted concerning problems and various solutions. Students enjoy collaboratively constructing a game following the "Jeopardy" format. Groups of students identify problems and solutions and write them on game cards. They play the game by taking turns: one group shares a solution, and the other group tries to decide the problem that is being solved.

Caitlin goakum   Name

9   Age

Basketball   Interests
Baseball friends

What do you like most about school?

Thats hard, my favorite thing about school probably be math and reading because math is a Challenge and I love reading.

What's your favorite subject? Why?

Math and reading are probably my two favorite subjects because in math you have to work for the answer and in reading you just have fun.

What's your favorite book? Why do you like it?

My favorite book would probably be Gentle Annie because it is a story about a civil war nurse and I like patriotic stories.

What advice do you have for teachers?

The advice I have for teachers is that they need to make things more exciting so we can remember things better.

The format of a newspaper provides many models for students to explore problems and solutions. Students could write a story for the front page of a newspaper detailing the problem and how it was solved. Editorials are a valuable format for discussing a problem and the solution—and the writer's reaction.

The "cubing" strategy may be adapted to extend thought and research concerning problems and solutions(Vaughan & Estes, 1986). Cover a cube of foam rubber or a cubical box with contact paper. Using self-stick removable notes, put the following descriptors on the various sides:

◆ Describe the problem.

◆ Describe the solution.

◆ Associate or compare this problem/solution to another situation.

◆ Argue for the solution given in the text.

◆ Argue against the solution given in the text.

◆ Think of an alternative solution.

Students may work in pairs or groups as they "roll" the cube and follow the instruction that comes up.

Becoming Independent Learners

Texts have many structures and convey information in many different formats (Armbruster & Anderson, 1981; Meyer, 1975, 1979; Piccolo, 1987). Vygotsky (1978) refers to the importance of "scaffolding" children to the next level of learning. Fortunately, teachers can aid children as they attempt to "read to learn," for research has shown that familiarity with diverse text structures increases children's proficiency in gleaning information from expository text (Englert & Hiebert, 1983; Horowitz, 1985).

Many teachers have found that compiling collections of children's trade books pertaining to a particular topic or theme enhances both the growth of knowledge and the interest level of students in their study of content material. The Teacher-to-Teacher feature shares sample text sets.

Teacher-to-Teacher

James Gee has found that achievement and interest of his fifth- and sixth-grade science and social studies students improves when he incorporates trade books in his classroom. He constantly searches for both fiction and nonfiction books pertaining to items in his curriculum and is constantly expanding the text sets. In addition, he makes sure his students have access to other sources of information such as magazine and newspaper articles, Internet sources, and reference materials. He includes both narrative and expository texts in the set and is careful to compile text sets that include varied reading levels and both picture and chapter books. Here are the text sets he has compiled for use when his students engage in explorations of the Civil War and the solar system.

Civil War

Collier, J. L. (1999). *With Every Drop of Blood: A Novel of the Civil War.* A docu-novel that tells the story of a young white rebel soldier who is captured by a black Union soldier—and the resulting friendship that occurs.

Fleishman, P. (1993). *Bull Run.* Sixteen different people share their varying perspectives before the battle of Bull Run. Some share after the battle.

Fritz, J. (1993). *Just a Few Words, Mr. Lincoln: The Story of the Gettysburg Address.* Describes the events leading to the Gettysburg Address through historical data and personal anecdotes.

Hakim, J. (1994). *War, Terrible War.* Tells the story of the Civil War through its impact on various people—some well-known, some obscure.

Hansen, J. (1997). *I Thought My Soul Would Rise and Fly: The Diary of Patsy, a Freed Girl.* The tumultous time following the conclusion of the Civil War is detailed in the diary of Patsy, a twelve-year-old.

Marrin, A. (1994). *Unconditional Surrender: U. S. Grant and the Civil War.* Tells of Ulysses S. Grant's life and his actions in the Civil War.

Marrin, A. (1997). *Commander in Chief: Abraham Lincoln and the Civil War.* Chronological, engaging account of facts about and the personality of Abraham Lincoln.

Moore, K. (1994). *If You Lived at the Time of the Civil War.* A question-and-answer format that provides information from Northern and Southern perspectives.

Murphy, J. (1992). *The Long Road to Gettysburg.* A description of the Battle of Gettysburg through the eyes of a nineteen-year-old Confederate lieutenant and a seventeen-year-old Union soldier.

Murphy, J. (1993). *The Boys' War: Confederate and Union Soldiers Talk About the Civil War.* The youngest soldiers of the Civil War tell their stories through diaries, letters, and oral histories.

Polacco, P. (1994). *Pink and Say.* Based on actual events from the author's family history, the story of an interracial friendship between two young Union soldiers. After Say, the white youth, is wounded and nursed back to health by his black friend, Pink, tragedy strikes as they attempt to make their way back to their Northern unit.

Reit, S. (1988). *Behind Rebel Lines: The Incredible Story of Emma Edmonds, Civil War Spy.* The remarkable story of Emma Edmonds who served as a field nurse and a spy for the Union army—disguised as a man.

Rinaldi, A. (2001). *Girl in Blue.* Sixteen-year-old Sarah disguises herself as a male to become an Union soldier—and then assumes the role of a Pinkerton spy.

Robinet, H. G. (1997). *Forty Acres and Maybe a Mule.* Pascal, a twelve-year-old born with a withered leg and hand searches for a farm and freedom with other former slaves.

Taylor, M. D. (2001). *The Land.* The prequel to *Roll of Thunder, Hear My Cry* (1976), tells the story of the Logan family during and after the Civil War in the Deep South and reveals the painful racism they endured.

The Solar System

Branley, F. M. (1998) *The Planets in Our Solar System.* Informative text supplemented with photographs taken from space.

Cole, J. (1990). *The Magic School Bus Lost in the Solar System.* Ms. Frizzle and the Magic School Bus take the class on a tour of the solar system.

➤ ➤ ➤

Davis, K. C. (2001). *Don't Know Much About the Solar System.* Provides mulitple facts through question-and-answers, riddles, and humorous illustrations.

Emberley, B. (1987). *The Moon Seems to Change.* Explains the phases of the moon and provides directions for experiments that children can conduct with a pencil, an orange, and a flashlight to better understand the phenomena.

Fradin, D. B. (1997). *The Planet Hunters: The Search for Other Worlds.* A historical view of the discovery of planets—and failed attempts.

Gibbons, G. (1994) *The Planets.* Provides information and engaging illustrations concerning the planets, the solar system, and astronomy.

Leedy, M. (1996). *Postcards from Pluto: A Tour of the Solar System.* The engaging story of Dr. Quasar who takes a diverse group of children on a holiday trip throughout the solar system. Their postcards provide a wealth of information.

L'Hommedieu, L. (1994). *Children of the Sun.* Important information is shared about each planet, and the illustrator provides a fascinating perspective. Each planet is portrayed from the sun's view.

Morgan, N. (1997). *Louis and the Night Sky.* Louis continually wishes he lived on another planet—one where the lights were on all the time. When he finds himself on a whirlwind tour of the solar system, he finds out that home is best.

Scieszka, J. (2001) *Baloney (Henry P.).* A hilarious trek through space occurs when Henry P. Baloney must come up with a very good excuse for being late. Will not add to students' knowledge about our solar system, but may spark their imagination and interest!

Simon, S. (1992). *Our Solar System.* A comprehensive overview of the solar system with exceptional color photographs, clear comparison charts, and accurate information.

VanCleave, J. (2000). *Janice VanCleave's the Solar System: Mind-Boggling Experiments You Can Turn into Science Fair Projects.* Provides a wealth of information about the solar system and multiple ideas for exciting activities and projects.

It is important to implement strategies as you explore multiple informational texts with your students. Many strategies were discussed in the previous sections. In addition, the majority of the comprehension strategies that were discussed in Chapter 7 are applicable—or easily adapted—for use with content text. Remember when we discussed conceptual mapping? The samples of conceptual maps demonstrated how children represented graphically their understanding of material they have read. Graphic organizers are "maps" that help children understand and remember the important information contained in various expository text structures. Figure 15.7 shows samples of graphic organizers that may be used for various text structures. However, don't limit your students to these frameworks. It is valuable for children to create their own graphic organizers to help them organize and remember content material. Comprehension is enhanced when readers analyze and synthesize material and then create their own graphic representations that demonstrate their understanding.

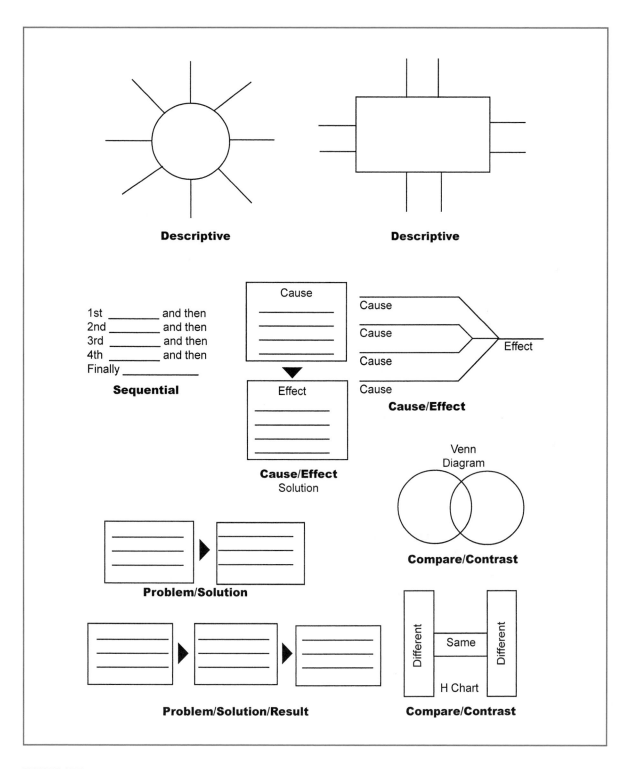

FIGURE 15.7

Graphic organizers for common text structures

Concept squares (Vaughan & Estes, 1986) is a strategy that involves children in making decisions about text *during* and *after* reading. Give students strips of sticky notes to "code" with the following symbols, based on their understandings and place in the text, as they read. A ✓ indicates understanding, a "?" signals they don't understand or have questions about the text , a "!" signifies surprise, and "*" indicates ideas they think are important/worth remembering. *After reading,* the students transfer the information to a chart consisting of four rectangles. During class discussion, students have an opportunity to share their responses. As shown in Figure 15.8, we have modified the strategy and included page numbers as this provides a point of reference that aids in class discussion.

✓ I KNEW THAT (include page numbers)	+ I DIDN'T KNOW THAT (include page numbers)
? I STILL HAVE QUESTIONS ABOUT THIS/WE NEED TO TALK MORE ABOUT THIS (include page numbers)	* THAT'S WORTH REMEMBERING! (include page numbers)

FIGURE 15.8
Modified concept squares strategy chart

Source: Adapted from J. L. Vaughan (1990), *Concept squares: A learning strategy.* Unpublished manuscript.

In addition, we have often asked students to choose their "top 3" items in each category and rank order them by importance. Children then share their "number 1" items, explaining where they found the information and why they chose it, and their response is recorded on a class chart. Or—at other times we have chosen to modify this so it becomes a collaborative experience by providing an opportunity for students meet in small groups after prioritizing their responses to discuss and decide on their group's top three items before sharing with the whole class. For some groups of children, four coding categories may be too many—ask them to mark the text with only two items such as "?"s (things they don't understand or have questions about) and "*"s (ideas they think are important/worth remembering). As you can see, meeting the needs of your students as they interact with expository text requires that you have a knowledge of strategies—but often it is also necessary to modify those strategies.

In addition, as discussed earlier, instructional environments that include quality and quantity exposures to varied text patterns through children's literature provide children with the "scaffold" of the familiar format of a children's book as an introduction to an unfamiliar organizational pattern. When we increase children's ability to comprehend expository text, we are helping them move onto the path of becoming independent lifelong learners.

Developing Research Skills

One technique of teaching literacy in the content areas is to confront students with questions they may not understand—not because answers don't exist, but because they have not found them for themselves. Children are helped to understand that problems are not solved once and for all, but that one problem leads to another. They discover that solving problems is the great adventure of learning.

Literacy in the content areas of the curriculum is enhanced and extended through these six essential strategies and techniques:

- Promoting a searching attitude
- Using a variety of resources
- Using a table of contents and index
- Using alphabetical arrangement
- Using library reference skills

Promoting a Searching Attitude

Children who search for answers to their questions may not always find those answers, but if they continue to seek, they demonstrate an attitude toward solving problems that is far more valuable than finding answers every time. They learn to use a scientific method of thinking that leads to individual, independent searching.

The self-confidence and assurance necessary to launch into the unknown, into creative thinking and creative production, come from repeated opportunities to search for answers to one's own questions. This means that teachers in a total literacy classroom do not emphasize students' ability to fill in blanks of prepared worksheets or select answers on a computer screen. Children may use some such aids as models in preparing their own work to be used with their peers in learning centers, but the *process* is regarded as a more valuable learning experience than the *product*. To be able to ask questions that reflect the intended meaning of an author may be as valuable a skill as the ability to answer questions that already have the major ideas identified.

Students practice numerous oral, writing, and reading skills as they search for answers. In addition, they can gather data from personal interviews, telephone conversations, and observations. They can study pictures, listen to recordings, use computers and online resources, and test possibilities and alternatives.

Teacher~to~Teacher

Lee Davis teaches a fifth-grade class that usually has several students who are labeled "nonreaders." During the early weeks of school, he diminishes the emphasis on reading printed matter and helps every student develop interests around which future reading can be planned. He invites a series of "experts" to visit his class to serve as resource persons for interviews.

Each student is encouraged to formulate questions. Techniques for carrying on interviews are discussed, guides are developed, and students who have special interest in the visitor's area of expertise are invited to lead the interviews. All students can participate, however. Among the people he invites are an automobile mechanic, an architect, a cook, a pilot, and a gardener.

After the series of visiting experts, Lee lets each student choose to become ex-

pert in some field. The student prepares for an interview by the class members. Searching begins. Students use all kinds of resources to prepare. Resources at multiple reading levels are available so all children will be able to find resources they can use. Often, students who are reading below grade level find that they have interests about which they know more than anyone else in the class. Their interest in reading in their specialty mounts as their time for the interview approaches. Vocabularies are extended as students search for words to fit into categories that have been agreed on.

Edna Brown suggests broad topics for word lists that students can extend as they read. She begins with a topic such as "Homes Around the World." Children add to the list any word they find that tells the kinds of homes people live in. She uses other topics too. Some of these topics are "Imaginary Characters," "Roots That Are Used for Food," "Kinds of Weather," "Machines That Have Levers," and "Waste That Pollutes."

Reference books are useful when students search for answers to questions. They should be supplemented with picture sets, books of information that have an index and a table of contents, and technological resources such as training in how to use the various online search engines to locate Web sites and online documents.

Terry Scribner posts questions that have come up in class discussions on a bulletin board. "Do all insects have six legs?" is an example. Children search for scientific information, find pictures, and make displays to answer each question. Terry feels it is much more important to stimulate a positive attitude toward searching than for her to furnish the answers.

People and things in their environment help preschool children find answers to their questions. At school they have additional sources to provide the information needed to satisfy curiosity and widen their scope of thinking.

The oral interchange of young students with classmates, teachers, and other adults is a prime resource for young children. It continues to contribute as they learn to use books and other material that involve reading symbols. In addition, most classrooms have a wealth of nonbook material—computers, toys, plants, animals, machines, maps, pictures, microscopes, charts, study prints, films, videotapes, cassette tapes, and DVDs. At home, most students have access to books, television, computers, tape players, DVDs, and radio. Some schools provide study trips for groups of students to find out firsthand about things they study and discuss. All these can be used to build abilities in using resources and to stimulate interest in listening, speaking, and learning how to write and read.

Teacher-to-Teacher

Patricia Patterson uses textbook sets to teach locational skills. A group of students with identical books race to find answers to questions. They select a question from a stack of cards that Patricia has prepared. She reads the question that is answered somewhere in the book the children are using. The winner—the one who finds the answer first—tells the class what key word or idea in the question was used in conjunction with the index or table of contents to find the answers to the question.

When the class first starts having these races, all the questions have key words that are in the index. As students learn to use this clue, questions are formulated that do not contain a word in the index of the book they

➤ ➤ ➤

are reading. They have to think of synonyms to locate information.

After students learn to find answers to questions by using an index, Patricia inserts cards in the stack that have topics from the table of contents printed on them. When they see or hear one of the topics, students skim the table of contents to locate that topic and then turn to it in the book.

These activities assure students some degree of skill in using other books to find information efficiently and rapidly.

Some books have locational aids, and some do not. In many ways the titles and physical appearance of the books give clues before the books are opened.

Conrad Collins has many books in the classroom, so each time a topic is being studied in depth, he puts an assortment of books on a table and plays a game with the students. He asks them to pick, on the basis of physical appearance and title only, a book they think will contain something on a topic he names. He may take a topic such as "Weather" and work from that to various subtopics.

Students learn rapidly that most books of information have a table of contents and an index where they can verify their prediction. Storybooks may have a table of contents but no index. Books containing stories seldom have either. If needed information is in the book, the reader has to search for it with no locational aids.

Conrad never relies on one source of information on a topic that is studied in depth, so he feels he must help students know how to recognize and use many sources.

Using a Variety of Resources

To give students only one source that contains a satisfying answer is to limit the development of their thinking powers. The goal in a total literacy program is to give students a variety of resources and let them search out the answers that satisfy them and solve their problems.

Even before children learn to read much printed material, they can be introduced to the idea of searching in many places to find answers. Picture books, picture encyclopedias, the Internet, and CD-ROMs and DVDs provide information on many topics. When children think they have located information in a book they cannot read, the teacher or a reading buddy can read to them to verify its usefulness. For example, a kindergartener might locate a picture of a panda in a science encyclopedia and ask the teacher to share the text information.

As reading ability increases, students are encouraged to seek their own answers in reading material. In so doing, they soon discover that different books have different purposes. Some are fiction and are for pleasure reading only. Some are full of facts. Some give most of their information through pictures. Some have an alphabetic arrangement. Some mix fact and fiction.

A student edits a descriptive text.

Social studies and science are examples of subject areas that require students to locate information from numerous sources. The procedure for teaching content subjects should require the student to use the index, the table of contents, topic headings and subheadings, and all the important parts of books, as well as online resources. Students develop the ability to identify unknown words, find their pronunciations in the dictionary, and select appropriate meanings for words in terms of use in context. They use alphabetically arranged material easily, such as dictionaries and encyclopedias and other reference material. Researchers must also learn to skim to locate needed information. Students come to know that no one book, film, collection of objects, or field trip will have all the answers they are seeking. They discover that locating one source of information usually points them to other related information as knowledge builds upon knowledge.

Teacher-to-Teacher

In the first week of school, Lois Lyons begins to take dictation from students in first grade. She displays the stories and reads from them when she is ready to introduce new skills. A bulletin board has several captions on sheets of paper, with room to list words from the stories. The captions may include first-time words, words that begin alike, rhyming words, sentences with commas, first words in quota-tions, first words in sentences, and sentences with question marks. In their own stories, students discover characteristics that they need to recognize in the language of others.

Experimenting with common materials helps young students find answers to ques-

➤ ➤ ➤

tions and ask new ones. Here are some of the questions her students researched through observation:

◆ What colors of paint are mixed to form other colors?

◆ What effect have light and darkness on the growth of plants?

◆ What materials produce electricity when a balloon is rubbed against them?

◆ What kinds of paper absorb water?

◆ What causes evaporation?

Students recorded their discoveries by writing simple statements. Some were able to find information in simple illustrated books on the subject. Others reinforced their information by using a DVD on the topic. Lois's students learned a valuable lesson about asking questions and then using resources to answer those questions.

Teachers initiate research techniques naturally as they provide experiences with items such as these:

◆ A magnifying glass and rocks, leaves, flowers, or wood with different grains. Children discover differences with close examination.

◆ Animal life in an aquarium or terrarium. Children talk about their observations, write or dictate some of them, and extend their information by using books placed in the vicinity.

◆ Simple balances for comparing weights. Children guess weights by size and then put items on a balance to check their predictions. They seek answers to why some small things weigh more than other larger ones.

◆ Simple measuring devices. Children make approximations and then verify them with accurate measurements.

◆ Maps of areas where students live or have traveled. Trips—real and imaginary—can be charted. Children learn to read the grids on maps and other reference techniques for locating places.

Broad experiences of trying things out, of getting into unknown situations, and of being curious about how things work can launch students into research that requires reading and writing. While they are waiting to read and write well enough for mature research activities, students need repeated successes in finding satisfactory solutions to simple personal questions. By using multiple resources that require minimum skills in reading, students become researchers.

Using a Table of Contents and Index

Teachers of content subjects are usually supplied with textbooks that have a table of contents and index. These are of minimal use in teaching locational skills when one book is used day after day as the text. Science and social studies books can be useful, however, in teaching students how to use tables of contents and indexes in other books. Students very quickly learn that researchers do not begin at the first page of a book and read every page to the end to find needed information. Rather, they go as directly as possible to the information they need by using resources that most publishers provide in books.

Teacher-to-Teacher

Students must also come to appreciate the role of headings, subheadings, and bulleted or numbered lists as sources of key information in content area texts. Meredith Barnes, a seventh-grade social studies teacher, achieved this by splitting her class into two groups. She provided one group with a text with headings and bulleted lists. She provided the other group with the same text—but minus the organizational structure. The group with the organization structure cues finished the activity faster and with better comprehension. After the two groups shared, the teacher provided another text, without headings and bullets, to the entire class. As the class worked with the material, adding headings, subheadings, and lists, they came to appreciate their value. Their teacher knows that the students will more likely make use of these organizational aides in their future scanning and reading of content texts.

Using Alphabetical Arrangement

Understanding alphabetical arrangements is an important reading skill for carrying out research. It is a skill that can be introduced early in school programs with assurances that normal activities will require its use over and over.

Some experiences that offer opportunities for teaching alphabetic arrangement are discussed here.

- Use picture dictionaries for browsing and for building an awareness of why and how one word follows another in alphabetical arrangement.
- Make word books that grow from the use of the initial letter to second- and third-letter arrangements. The words can be ones the children collect and write or they can be words cut from magazines.
- Keep word files with dividers for each letter of the alphabet.
- Read and examine a telephone directory to find names of families represented in the classroom.
- List in dictionary order words that have been collected on the Word Wall in the classroom.

◆ List books on a topic by alphabetical arrangement of the authors and titles.

◆ Use encyclopedias to illustrate a major reference source that has alphabetical order. Notice key words for topics and the use of last names of people. Look for cross references that send the researcher to other volumes.

◆ Play games that require students to alphabetize words in order to win.

Share with children that dictionaries are a special kind of alphabetically arranged book for researchers that have these useful features:

◆ Pronunciation keys to aid with new words found during research.

◆ Sources of words that might be useful in research (found in some dictionaries).

◆ Multiple definitions so researchers have a chance to find a meaning that fits the context of their reading material.

Students doing research may find words they recognize on sight but do not understand in a particular setting because the words carry new meanings that need to be looked up in a dictionary.

From the beginning of research activities in primary grades, a collection of dictionaries should be available. Some should be simple enough for good readers to use independently. Others might be difficult to read, but they will probably be the ones the children need when they study topics of interest to them. If they can find in the dictionary words that are new to them in reading material, they can usually find someone to help them with dictionary pronunciation and definitions. It is also valuable for children to use thesauri—both the print versions and ones found on most word processing software.

Using Library Reference Skills

If we want children to become researchers, they need access to a library and assistance in developing library reference skills. They must have opportunities to become secure amid a mass of materials that has nothing to do with the topics being studied.

One way to establish a secure feeling is to teach the use of a *library card catalog*. Most card catalogs are now accessible by computer. With some knowledge of alphabetical order, arrangement, key words, and names of authors and titles, a student can find books, films, picture sets, records, kits of material, and magazines on topics of interest. Everything is coded and arranged in an order; once the code is understood, materials can be located with a minimum of help from librarians.

Skimming is a reading skill that must accompany efficient use of library reference materials. No researcher has time to read everything carefully. Key ideas must be selected and located in materials by skimming to the point at which the needed information is found. Then careful reading for detail may take place.

Art and Literacy

As we've mentioned throughout this text, children need opportunities on a daily basis for self-expression. Art affords such opportunities.

Many art skills are learned naturally as young people progress through developmental levels of expression with art media. Because art is not totally intuitive, direct instruction and modeling of processes and techniques are important. Skills, as well as freedom of expression, are necessary if art is to contribute to language growth. The attributes of creativity are essential in both forms of communication: language arts and visual arts. In school settings, concepts of both language and art must be translated into performance. Speaking, writing, and reading can be natural extensions of the visual arts.

Many books are available that share masterpieces with children. *A Child's Book of Art: Discover Great Paintings* (Micklethwait, 1999) provides a beautiful and engaging framework for children to explore artists' works and lives. *Oxford First Book of Art* (Wolfe, 2002) and *Discovering Great Artists: Hands-On Art for Children in the Styles of the Great Masters* (Kohl & Sogol, 1997) are also valuable resources.

Self-expression in art increases awareness of the elements of composition—line, depth, color, texture, and form. As students have experience in using many media, they use these elements in various combinations. The natural conversation accompanying these experiences requires the use of words of the form classes—nouns, verbs, adjectives, and adverbs. The classifications of descriptive words used most frequently in literary selections are those that are used most often in talking about art—color, size, shape, texture, feelings, contrasts, and comparisons. Talking about the creative process and the finished artwork builds and extends children's language base.

Young children draw, paint, and sculpt forms representing their visual images of real and imaginary subjects. Usually they do not plan the arrangement of forms but place them in the pictures or mold them in accordance with immediate importance. This lack of planning does not detract from the value of their self-expression. To deny children the exploratory phase of art would be like denying speech until they can speak with poetic expressions.

Older students may be aware of creating a design, having a center of interest, developing rhythm in the work through repetition of form and color, and applying all the elements of composition with a selected medium. This development takes place gradually and should always be accompanied with freedom of expression through experimentation.

Teachers who provide time and space for visual portrayal of experiences are guided by some fundamental concepts that help them select activities that contribute to language growth. Let's look more closely at some of them.

100th Day Worries, by Margery Cuyler. Jessica, a first-grader, is worrying about her 100th day project for school and her family rallies round to support her.
New York: Simon and Schuster, 2000.

Older Readers

Light Shining Through the Mist, by Tom L. Matthews. The gripping story of anthropologist Dian Fossey, the gifted scientist whose work with mountain gorillas caused the world to recognize their intelligence—and the necessity of protecting them from hunters.
Washington, DC: National Geographic Society, 1998.

The Story of Clocks and Calendars, by Betsy C. Maestro. Presents a fascinating tour of the history of measuring time.
New York: Lothrop, Lee & Shepard, 1999.

The Journal of Jesse Smoke: A Cherokee Boy, Trail of Tears, by Joseph Bruchac. Sixteen-year-old Jesse Smoke uses a diary format to record both the events leading up to the Trail of Tears and the dramatic journey.
New York: Scholastic, 2001.

Remember the Ladies: 100 Great American Women, by Cheryl Harness. Brief biographies are interwoven with the larger history of women's impact in America.
New York: HarperCollins Juvenile, 2000.

Encourage Creativity

To express themselves in art, students need to be encouraged to invent, to improvise, and to fabricate. Art offers students a chance to arrange common materials such as boxes, buttons, paper rolls, and other objects in pleasing and uncommon ways. *Tissue-paper overlay* with its color and transparency creates not only many hues and values from the variety of colors and shapes of paper torn for the overlay effect, but also a magical effect. *Finger painting* provides opportunities to use fingers, hands, and parts of the arm to apply and distribute paint on a glazed piece of paper.

Evaluate Possible Solutions

To communicate effectively, students must be able to see many possible solutions to a problem and choose one to develop. *Colored chalk* can be used on wet paper to create a color wonderland. Students respond to its ease of application and immediate representation of something bold and bright—a dragon, a field of flowers, a design of flames, the spirit of a circus. Chalk on newspapers yields instant designs suggested by the arrangement of print.

Sand casting with a variety of tools for making impressions in wet sand and with a variety of objects for embedding before pouring plaster offers a chance for expressiveness in a simple but unique way for each student.

Limited palette painting with crayon, watercolor, or tempera interprets a subject in one dominant color and mixes of that color to achieve depth and form. It is a way of varying interpretations of a subject rather than reporting photographic details. Variation can be achieved by cutting colored photographs from magazines, choosing portions of the same basic color, cutting shapes, and arranging them into a design.

Study Design Ideas

To arrange parts into a design with unity is an ability students develop for realistic and abstract representation. *Collage* is a process of forming artistic compositions by placing items such as cloth, buttons, seed, braid, string, and cardboard in an arrangement and gluing them down. Dabs of color and some related lines are usually added to unify the design. Collage techniques can be observed in the work of famous artists such as Braque and Picasso. Collage is a way of doing something unusual with the usual.

Paper-and-paste projects, especially those dealing with abstract designs, provide practice in arranging for unity, variety, contrast, line, rhythm, and form. Students practice arranging and rearranging the cut or torn forms before they paste them together to form the finished work.

Traditions of other cultures, such as the Mexican piñata and Japanese origami, might encourage students to experiment with paper creations of their own. With freedom and encouragement, students naturally apply themselves to the pleasing experiences of tearing, cutting, pasting, building, and shaping constructions.

Harmonize Design Elements

Artists must be able to bring sharply differing elements into harmony through design and color. *Texture painting* with sand, cornmeal, crushed eggshells, and other textured materials can be used to change all or part of the surface of a painting. Students who use textured materials are redefining their use and thinking in new directions about materials for self-expression.

Carving is a subtractive process, the opposite of modeling. As students experiment with cutting, scratching, and gouging with simple tools, they produce works with contrasts in light and shadow, in bright and dull, in smooth and rough.

Incorporate Visual Representations

Students need to be able to translate a word or words into a visual representation. *Tempera painting* is a form of communication that most young students can deal with before they can write for themselves. Later the pictures become illustrations for the written word rather than the story itself. Easels and supplies for tempera painting should be available in every total literacy classroom. Freedom of expression with tempera paint is as significant as the illustration of a word or a story.

As students observe their world in order to paint the things in it, they are able to see variety. A tree is not always green; clouds are not always white; the sky is not always blue.

Crayon is usually the first medium for art that students use. It should be encouraged for expressing ideas and for illustrating.

Clay modeling is a process of working from lumps, slabs, or coils to create three-dimensional objects. Clay can be kneaded, rolled, stretched, cut, joined, pinched, and pulled. Some of the products are fired in a kiln. Much clay work is a series of new beginnings; students decide one thing after another as they create objects with clay.

Accentuate the Feeling Component

To enjoy art, one does not depend on oral statements but on feelings generated by the total effect of the process and product. *Paper sculpture* is the shaping of paper by rolling, folding, pleating, or wadding to achieve structural designs. Paper can be fringed, curled, and punctured to enhance the artistic impact. For a dispensable art form, paper sculpture has no set rules but has many new beginnings as one procedure leads to another.

Paper lamination is a process of applying strips of paper dipped in wet paste to a framework such as newspaper coils, chicken wire, boxes, bottles, and balloons. The student must monitor the changing form to determine the need to build up areas as the form becomes an animal, a totem pole, or a mask.

Drop-dry-draw is a process of dropping thick or dry tempera on very wet paper. The paint "explodes" and runs together. After it dries, the artist decides what is there—real or imaginary—and outlines it with a marker.

Doodling drawn with crayons and pencils can be filled in with color and a few features to represent feelings such as love, happiness, and fear, to create imaginary creatures, or to make pleasing designs.

Interpret Natural Materials

To represent what an artist sees or imagines when handling natural materials requires minimum adjustments. *Natural objects* provide opportunities to apply the maxim "art is in the eye of the beholder." Children see the shapes of animals, machines, and people in rocks, branches, driftwood, seedpods, shells, and clouds. Some natural materials need a little carving, scratching, or painting to bring out features and to highlight areas for a center of interest. The similarities observed require acute visual perception. Collections of look-alike objects foster the use of figurative language in the classroom—similes, metaphors, and personification.

Use Exaggeration for Effect

To exaggerate an idea is permitted and promoted in art activities. *Mosaics* are surface pictures made by inlaying in patterns small pieces of colored glass, stone, seed, cardboard, or other material. Whatever its subjects—animals, birds, people, a landscape, insects—a mosaic should have a strong center of interest around which the remainder of the design is built.

Murals usually exaggerate a few major objects or ideas by making them big and bold. Supporting ideas are small and subdued in comparison with the major ones. Murals can be drawn with tempera, chalk, or crayons. Attached paper sculpture can give depth to major ideas, and cut paper can add boldness to areas of emphasis. A mural is, in effect, an outline of an idea for an essay or other language production.

Show Movement

Artists learn how to show motion with static materials. *Puppets* of all kinds—paper bag, sock, finger, laminated, stick—can transport a student to a land of fantasy and make-believe. Materials are chosen and arranged so motion is possible in the use of puppets in language activities. The personality and voice of

Children Who Find Learning to Read and Write Difficult

Children who struggle to learn, particularly those who struggle when learning to read and write, form another cultural group in our schools. These children are often segregated in separate classrooms or are separated from their classmates for special instruction. They are given different materials and different assignments. Not only do they feel they are different from their classmates but they also often feel inadequate and stupid. These children, too, constitute a culture in the classroom and the school—a culture that teachers need to address.

When working with children who struggle to learn to read and write, perhaps the first thing we need to realize is that good instruction is good instruction. Instruction that works well with normal or excelling learners contains the basic elements that will help children who struggle to learn. Such instruction provides children with what we call "guided immersion"—immersing children in a world of authentic and engaging reading and writing experiences in which a teacher provides appropriate levels of modeling, support, and encouragement.

Richard Allington (2001) has explored the needs of children who struggle in reading, and he provides some insight into their instructional needs across type of difficulty and grade level. According to Allington, children who struggle in learning literacy need to read—and read a lot. Children who struggle with reading often don't get to read very much. They read little in school, and they read little at home. When in school, these children are the most likely to read words out of context—that is, they are given practice using word lists or flash cards.

One of the best predictors of reading achievement is the amount of time spent engaged in real reading. We need to find ways to maximize the amount of real reading done during reading instruction, during other parts of the school day, at home when the school day is over, and at other times when school is not in session (for example, during summer vacation and other holiday periods during the school year).

Not only is it important for students to read a lot, they also need to be reading material that is appropriate in difficulty as well as content. Too often children who struggle are asked to read material that is well beyond their instructional reading level. As a result, these children spend a good deal of their school day and their reading time working and reading in a state of frustration. Constant frustration leads to failure and eventual withdrawal from the learning activity. We need to find ways to match children with a wealth of reading material that is interesting and readable for them and to provide appropriate support for materials that are more challenging.

According to Allington (2001), reading fluency is a neglected area of the literacy curriculum. The report of the National Reading Panel (2000) also indicates that reading fluency is one area that holds great promise for improving children's reading. Children are taught to decode words accurately but lack instruction in reading fluently—that is, with accuracy, appropriate rate, proper phrasing, good expression and, of course, good comprehension.

In many cases, children who struggle in reading can decode words but require so much cognitive effort to do so that little cognitive energy is left over to make sense of what is read. Instructional strategies such as repeated readings and reading while listening to a fluent rendition of the text are simple but powerful ways to improve fluency. More-

➤ ➤ ➤

over, these instructional strategies can easily be adapted into authentic reading experiences. Poetry performances and Reader's Theater festivals offer readers of all levels a chance to practice and become fluent while at the same time becoming a star in real text performance.

Students who struggle also need to develop what Allington (2001) has termed "thoughtful literacy"—literacy that engages students' desire and need to reflect, respond, and inquire about what is read. Too often, according to Allington, children who struggle are placed in an assign-and-assess mode of instruction. A text to be read is assigned, and a set of worksheets is completed at the end of the reading. When students complete the assignment, their work is checked and recorded (assessment) and another set of text and worksheets is assigned. This is not real reading, nor is it the type of instruction that children who struggle in reading need.

Children who struggle need to use reading for the same purposes that normally progressing readers and adults do. These purposes include reading to inform and reading to delight. Similarly, children who struggle need opportunities to respond in creative and thoughtful ways. For example, ask them to try to predict the author's intentions for writing the story, frame a critical moment in the story through artistic representation, write a report that provides new information about some event in history, transform the text that was read into a script for performance or a sequel or a poem, or engage in real discussions about the story that go beyond trying to guess the answer in the teacher's head. These are the kinds of authentic responses to what has been read that require (and inspire) readers to read for deep interpretation and understanding.

Although Allington's work focuses on children who struggle in reading, his recommendations apply equally well to children who struggle in other areas of literacy learning, from writing to spelling. Children who struggle need plenty of opportunities to engage in authentic expressions of what they are supposed to learn. They need appropriate support so that they are not overwhelmed by the challenge of what they are asked to do. They need sufficient and authentic practice at whatever level they may be so that their focus can shift from the mechanics of learning to the real nature and purpose of the activity itself. And children who struggle in learning need opportunities to respond to their instructional experiences in ways that enable them to think through and understand what they are learning.

Instructing children who have difficulty learning to read and write is not an easy task. Just as learning is difficult for these children, it is also challenging for the teachers who provide their instruction. If we can develop an instructional strategy that meets the needs of the most "difficult-to-teach" learners, we will be able to provide effective instruction to all learners.

a puppet can be transmitted by the feelings and voice of a child. Puppets help the manipulator try out new ways of saying things.

Mobiles hang in space and seem to float in the air if their creators have related each part to the whole in such a way that there is balance of the space-line-form concepts. Unity of design permits mobiles to be ever changing as they move. They are just like a well-written story or poem that is ever changing for its readers.

Math and Literacy

Responding to Numerals and Numbers

Numerals (the graphic representation for numbers) are everywhere in the environment of students. Most children have some experience in reading them before entering school programs. They can turn the television dial to a channel they want. They read numbers on houses and streets. They read prices in newspapers and catalogs. Children can identify numerals they know in advertisements, and they can read the numbers that tell team standings in the sports pages.

They watch the digital numerals at gas stations as the pump records the number of gallons and the amount to be paid. Most children play games that use numerals in some way. There is no way an active, involved human being can escape the experience of reading numerals.

Numerals are found in so many places that most students are unaware the numbers they read automatically are important. Many of their activities depend on some use of numbers. The Teacher-to-Teacher feature provides two examples of hownumbers from everyday life can be incorporated in the classroom.

Teacher~to~Teacher

Rita Brown collects enough grocery advertisements for each child to have one page. She names a numeral, and students point to the place where they see it. From there she advances to saying the price of something, and students try to find that number on the advertisement. They find the numbers in both large and small print. With the help of the teacher, they read numbers along with the names of products.

She also provides a blank book for students to use to paste in numbers they can read. When a book is filled, it is placed in the Book Center and used for practice reading.

Michael Martin shares *The Math Curse* (Scieszka, 1995) with his students to initiate an exploration of how math is used in everyday life. After discussion, he places a number diary in the Discovery Center. Students record places where they find numerals they need to read during their studies and other activities. The first pages are easily filled with such items as clock, calendar, page numbers, and room numbers. As the days pass, there are fewer entries, but they are interesting and unusual. Students find serial numerals on school equipment; numerals on graphs, charts, and tickets; and even Social Security numbers.

After filling the number diary for a week, the students are asked to keep a journal of their own activities for one day—from the time they wake until they go to bed. After they have recorded the activities, they cross out all those that have number concepts in them—time, amount, distance, dials, calendars, and so forth. In this way Michael highlights the important part numbers play in everyday life.

Walking in a neighborhood, taking trips to shopping centers, reading newspapers, and viewing films accentuate the variety of ways that numbers are used to make life meaningful. To be independent in everyday life, people must be able to read numerals, and students in school need to gain the assurance they can read number signals accurately. *Fun with Numbers* (Massin, 1995) contains fascinating facts and intriguing illustrations exploring the history of the use of numbers around the world.

Numbers in Stories and Poems

From the earliest nursery rhymes a child hears and says, the concept of number is required for understanding. "Hickory, Dickory, Dock," "Baa, Baa, Black Sheep," "One, Two, Buckle My Shoe," and "Rub-a-Dub-Dub" are examples. Most stories and poems require some understanding of numbers and words that stand for numbers, and the ability to read them is assumed. Many counting books provide support for the development of this understanding by using familiar objects in natural situations. *Anno's Counting Book* (Anno, 1986) shows a changing landscape that portrays many representations of the numbers 1 to 12 in everday living. *Sunrise* (Pittman, 1998) is a counting rhyme that explores the early morning adventures of a large family. Food is counted in many books such as *The M&M's Brand Chocolate Candies Counting Book* (McGrath, 1994), *The Oreo Cookie Counting Book* (Albee, 2000), and *The Cheerios Counting Book: 1, 2, 3* (McGrath, 2000). Children have the opportunity to explore counting crayons by twos with even and then odd numbers in *The Crayon Counting Book* (Ryan & Pallotta, 1996).

Geometric Shapes Surround Us

Geometric shapes are found everywhere. However, often children are given opportunities to identify the various shapes only on a worksheet or in their math book. Children can enhance their understanding of geometric shapes by finding them in their environment. Everyday objects are used to portray geometric shapes in both *Shape Up!* (Adler, 1998) and *When a Line Bends . . . a Shape Begins* (Green, 1997). A triangle continues to change its shape as it adds one side at a time in *The Greedy Triangle* (Burns, 1994). The Teacher-to-Teacher feature shows how one teacher provides her students with opportunities to demonstrate their understanding of geometric shapes.

Teacher~to~Teacher

Janet Anderson believes her fifth-grade students demonstrate their understanding of mathematical concepts when they are able to make real-world applications of the information. After working with geometric shapes, Janet invited her students to write about places where they had seen the shapes in their environment. When Jonathan turned in his book about a summer trip, Janet knew he understood the concept of geometric shapes (Figure 15.9)

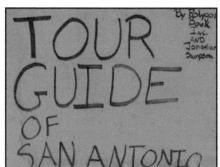

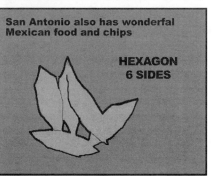

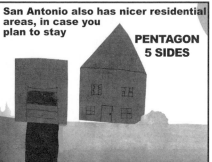

FIGURE 15.9
Jonathan's book about a summer trip

Responding to Graphic Aids

Maps, graphs, charts, signs, and diagrams are in the reading environment of students at home and at school. They usually appear in a combination of symbols that includes lines, shapes, dots, colors, numerals, and words. To be able to read them meaningfully as a life experience may be essential for many students. To be able to read them in school experiences may provide basic meanings in curriculum areas such as social studies, science, and mathematics.

The meanings inherent in graphic aids can be developed best when they are used to record and represent real experiences. Here are a few ideas to try with your students:

◆ Children can make maps of walking trips and field trips.

◆ Those who travel during the school year or during the summer months can be encouraged to collect maps of their travels and bring them to class to share. Children can bring letters postmarked at different places and locate the points of origin on a large map.

◆ Traffic signs that have shape, color, and symbols as a part of the message are available in most communities. Children are usually interested in these and can make miniatures for use in their play in the classroom and on the playground. Some school grounds can be developed with roadways that include the major traffic signs students will encounter.

◆ Graphs showing growth of plants and height and weight of students can be part of an ongoing learning environment. Making and reading these graphs can serve as the basic instruction in how to read other graphs.

◆ Many instructions on how to put things together include diagrams. Children might be willing to bring models to school, such as home appliance manuals, that have diagrams as a major part of the instruction for assembly. School engineers and custodians usually have diagrams showing how machinery works. Parents who work with diagrams may be willing to show students how they read them in their work.

◆ Charts of books read and classroom duties can be initiated in kindergarten through the use of color and shape codes. As students learn to read printed symbols, words can be added to these organizational charts.

Reading that does not depend on motions left to right and top to bottom and on alphabetical symbols is important and needs to be dealt with directly. Experiences in this type of "real-world" reading builds a base for more complex reading of graphic aids as students study technical content. Graphic aids provide ways of communicating specific information and relations that can be expressed effectively without words or with a minimum of words for maximum information.

Ann Lovelace chooses stories appropriate for reading numerals and number words. Children read silently and list all the number words and numerals in a story. For oral reading of the same story, students are asked to skip the words on the lists they have made. They find that many stories lose their meaning when number concepts are omitted.

Juana Garza makes a set of cards with numerals on them for the Writing/Publishing Center. Some are very small numbers, and some are very large. Children draw one, two, or more of the cards and write stories that involve the numbers. They produce scientific stories to include the smallest ones, and often use space travel or astronomy as topics that require the largest numbers.

She also uses sets of cards for storytelling. The cards are placed in a paper bag. She draws a card and begins a story that uses the number written on the card. Then one student after another draws from the bag in turn and includes the numbers drawn in a continuation of the story. An attempt is sometimes made to keep the story realistic; at other times the story is nonsense.

Marcella Valdez uses children's literature to help her students develop concepts about numbers. Her children love the excitement of *Bicycle Race* (1985), a Donald Crews counting book that is bursting with suspense, excitement, and motion. The children chant out the numbers that appear on the riders as the contestants near the finish line.

Children's Books and Mathematical Concepts

Many children's books present mathematical concepts in a familiar and meaningful context. Books such as Eric Carle's *The Grouchy Ladybug* (1986) expose children to the concept of time through the memorable travels and adventures of the cranky ladybug; his *The Very Hungry Caterpillar* (1987) exposes children to counting as the caterpillar tries to appease his ravenous appetite. *Rock It, Sock It, Number Line* (Martin & Sampson, 2001) takes counting into the garden with scarecrows and vegetables. In Judith Viorst's *Alexander, Who Used to Be Rich Last Sunday* (1978), children are exposed to the concept of how quickly money can disappear if you do not count it and remain aware of the balance, and Raffi's *Five Little Ducks* (1999) presents a delightful retelling of a familiar chant as baby ducks leave their mother (subtraction) and return (addition). The concept of remainders is explored as *A Remainder of One* (Pinczes, 1995) recounts the tale of the 25th Army Corps beetle brigade daily marching in rows past the queen. She desires the rows to be even, so "Private Joe" must drop out and be a "remainder of one" until they march in rows of five. *Counting on Frank* (Clement, 1994) creatively explores the concept of measurement as a boy uses his dog, Frank, as a unit of measure. *Twelve Snails to One Lizard* (Hightower, 1997) uses the more traditional measurements of inches, feet, and yards as Milo the Beaver and Bubba Bullfrog repair the local dam. Both the metric and the customary (inch, pound) systems of measurement are explored by David Adler (1999) in *How Tall, How Short, How Far Away*.

2

America's Finest

Ralph Sanders, A

Jim Hicks uses films to focus on reading numerals. Children watch for numerals as they view films. They either call them out or write them down as they see them flash on the screen on highway signs, license numbers, prices of things, street numbers, house numbers, and other common places. Reading numerals for meaning and for the purposes intended is not automatic. Most students need opportunities to try out their skills, check for accuracy, and try again to make meaningful responses to numerals they see in and out of school.

Sue Ward gives her students many opportunities to talk about the numerals they see in their environment and how they are used. She brings in real-world materials such as advertisements, road maps with mileage charts, catalogs, newspapers, cookbooks, and magazines, and students use these materials to write story problems (see Figure15.10). Children discuss the decision-making processes involved in formulating the problem and how it is solved. Writing the story problems and the resulting talk about the process enhance the children's understanding of the structure of story problems and their proficiency in reading and solving story problems.

FIGURE 15.10

Tom Thumb: A math story problem

Tom Thumb

Nora, Susana, and I were going to give a party. We needed to buy bread to make sandwiches. We went to Tom Thumb and saw that all the bread we needed cost $8.89. But we didn't have enough money. We only had $2.57. How much more money do we need to buy the bread?

Music and Literacy

America's Finest

Herb Parker Jr.

Rhythmic responses are basic to every person's communication. As nonverbal forms, they are as significant in many cases as the verbal forms of response that may or may not accompany them.

The printed word can suggest only basic body responses, but most literary works draw on our background of self-expression through rhythmic experiences.

Courtesy of Michael Sampson

Scott Beesley sings with his fifth-grade students.

Movement is so basic to life that every sentence spoken or printed has a verb in it or one implied. As children move freely to music, they understand and engage in a wide variety of rhythmic responses that are basic to creative self-expression.

Many children are shy and inhibited about expressing themselves with their hands, feet, fingers, toes, and body. Further, they have been made to feel that to be still and quiet is a virtue of highest priority. These children, along with all the others, are expected to enter into reconstructing the meanings of cold print not reflective of familiar language or ideas, and to call that process reading. Students who lack the self-confidence and self-concept needed to make personal responses to music are often the same ones who cannot remember words, cannot reply to questions of meaning, and cannot decide which book to read when given a choice. As total literacy teachers open up the self-expression of students through music, these students often soar into literacy success.

The language of movement can be fostered and refined through rhythmic responses. The words of movement and their meaning can be learned in other ways, but efficient instruction links the actual movements to the words. These words of movements, when experienced and verbalized, can be used for writing and will be recognized in reading to an extent not possible without meaningful interpretation. Here are some ways in which children develop language through rhythmic response:

◆ Moving to rhythmic music

◆ Pantomiming with body movements while listening to music

◆ Responding to films without words

◆ Responding by writing

Through instructions and demonstrations, children acquire a repertoire of responses from which they can select some that could become personalized at later times.

Mary Miller, a second-grade teacher, involves her children in rhythms for the following body movements when they are appropriate to a story or song:

Skipping	Galloping
Hopping	Swimming

Mary participates by actually helping students move to the rhythm of music rather than by just moving while music is playing. She shows students how to clap the accents and be a partner while another student claps, marches, or tiptoes. Then the students can improvise, experiment, vary, and create.

Clapping of hands	Slapping of abdomen
Clicking of tongue	Swinging of arms
Rocking of body	Jumping
Marching	Running

Social Studies and Literacy

Social studies has the unfortunate reputation of being the least popular subject among elementary school students. That's probably because social studies, particularly history, is often presented as a long, long series of names, dates, and events (Beesley, 1994). When social studies is reduced to such trivia, its heart and soul—culture—is left out.

Where textbooks have failed in the inclusion of culture, children's books have succeeded. More children's books than ever before focus on their world and its history. In addition to excellent historical fiction, students can now read outstanding biographies written in a style that lures them in. Jean Fritz illuminates the revolutionary war period with *Shh! We're Writing the Constitution* (1987) and *Can't You Make Them Behave, King George?* (1996). Fritz continually makes historical figures more human and understandable to children in books such as *The Double Life of Pocohontas* (1987), *You Want Women to Vote, Lizzie Stanton?* (1995), and *Harriet Beecher Stowe and the Beecher Preachers* (1994).

Readers are given a firsthand look at the experiences of fifteen-year-old Annie Moore, the first Irish immigrant to be processed through Ellis Island, in *Dreaming of America: An Ellis Island Story* (Bunting, 2000). Civil War history comes alive in *The Boy's War* (1993) by Jim Murphy. Likewise, young readers can encounter the horrors of the holocaust in Lois Lowry's *Number the Stars* (1990) and Jane Yolen's *The Devil's Arithmetic* (1990).

Farm life is featured in Nancy Price Graff's *The Strength of the Hills: A Portrait of a Family Farm* (1989). This outstanding book is an in-depth examination of a family farm in Vermont; it provides children with outstanding pictures and text of farm life.

Books such as *A Is for America* (Scillian, 2001) present a potpourri of information on various aspects of a subject that often spurs children to engage in further research, and books such as *The Flag We Love* (Ryan, 1996), *Fireworks, Picnics, and Flags: The Story of the Fourth of July Symbols* (Giblin, 2001), *Give Me Liberty: The Story of the Declaration of Independence* (Freedman, 2000), and *The Pledge of Allegiance* (Martin & Sampson, 2002) provide historical information on specific subjects.

Hundreds of books are now available that look at ethnic life. Bill Martin Jr tells the penetrating story of a young Korean American in *Yo Grocer* (in press).

Thus, as you can see, social studies is best presented in the school curriculum when children's books are an integral part of the curriculum. Textbooks serve best as overviews and reference books; children's books do a better job of telling the stories of the people and their homes.

Science and Literacy

Science should be students' favorite subject. And it would be, if the teaching of science was turned upside down. Instead of memorizing the scientific names of parts of the human body or the chemical properties of a specific substance, children need to be freed to explore the world of science from the perspective of their own interests. Since elementary science textbooks tend to be explanatory and technical (Chall, Bissex, Conard, & Harris-Sharples, 1996), this means that students cannot learn about science just from textbooks. Students need to experience science at an understandable, hands-on level.

The Teacher-to-Teacher feature provide two examples of how teachers have effectively integrated writing and children's literature in their science program.

Teacher-to-Teacher

Gary Bowman, a middle school science teacher in California, believes literacy learning and scientific learning are best learned together. Students in his class are always challenged to apply what they are studying; they must approach all learning with the idea that I must understand this because I have to present this information to someone else.

Gary capped a study of the digestive system with a competition—students were asked to write and illustrate a poem that would express some aspect of what they had learned. Three of his students from Round Valley Middle School wrote "Ode to a Broccoli" (Figure 15.11).

➤ ➤ ➤

Meet the Author

Elaine Scott

There is one constant in all of Gary Bowman's teaching—he always begins a unit of study with a rich stack of children's books like these that capture the students' interest and desire to learn:

Aardvarks, Disembark, by Ann Jonas.

Baby Beluga, by Raffi, illustrated by Ashley Wolgg.

Bartholomew and the Oobleck, by Dr. Seuss.

Close Encounters: Exploring the Universe with the Hubble Telescope, by Elaine Scott.

Color Dance, by Ann Jonas.

Feathers for Lunch, by Lois Ehlert.

Flash, Crash, Rumble, and Roll, by Franklyn Branley, illustrated by Barbara and Ed Emberly.

Hurricane, by David Wiesner.

Is Your Mama a Llama? by Deborah Guarino, illustrated by Steven Kellogg.

Listen to the Rain, by Bill Martin Jr and John Archambault, illustrated by James Endicott.

McElligot's Pool, by Dr. Seuss.

Plants That Never Bloom, by Ruth Heller.

The Very Quiet Cricket, by Eric Carle.

Water's Way, by Lisa Westberg Peters, illustrated by Ted Rand.

Deanne Barker believes writing anchors her second-graders' understanding of information. During a study of dinosaurs, she shared Margaret Wise Brown's *The Important Book* (1949) and provided materials for her students to research and determine what they considered the most important items about the various dinosaurs. Some of the responses from the children are shown in Figure 15.12, as they used the format from *The Important Book* to portray their knowledge.

Note that some of the pages give factual information such as length or number of teeth but others demonstrate children's personal understanding of the information such as "The most important thing about a brontosaurus is he could give another dinosaur a ride, " or "The most important thing about a stegosaurus is that you couldn't hug his tail!" The child is using personal language to demonstrate the understanding that the brontosaurus was one of the largest dinosaur and that the stegosaurus had spikes on his tail.

FIGURE 15.11

"Ode to a Broccoli"

There was a piece of broccoli on my plate.

Stuck it in my mouth, and then it was ate.

Bit it with my teeth. Pushed it with my tongue.

How it was eaten is the big question.

It's just a little thing called "digestion."

Down my esophagus, Boy, that was fun!

Digestive juices from the pancreas and a bladder called the "gall."

Wrung out by my stomach, Nutrients absorbed through the walls.

From there, into the small intestine.

Because that's the place with the most digestion.

There the villi separate.

The nutrients from the broccoli. That was on my plate.

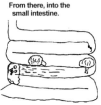

FIGURE 15.12

Student responses about the importance of dinosaurs

From InfoTrac College Edition

Considering Genre, Content, and Visual Features in the Selection of Trade Books for Science Instruction: Analyses of Different Aspects of Stories and Informational Books Can Help Teachers Make Informed Decisions to Enhance Science Instruction, Carol A. Donovan and Laura B. Smolkin, *The Reading Teacher* March 2002 v55 i6 p502(19)

Fostering Thought, Talk, and Inquiry: Linking Literature and Social Studies: Certain Texts and Tasks Seem to Promote Better Discussion and Exchange of Ideas, Nancy L. Roser and Susan Keehn, *The Reading Teacher* Feb 2002 v55 i5 p416(11)

A Strategy for Previewing Textbooks: Teaching Readers to Become THIEVES (teaching ideas), Suzanne Liff Manz. *The Reading Teacher* February 2002 v55 i5 p434(2)

Zooming In and Zooming Out: Enhancing Vocabulary and Conceptual Learning in Social Studies, Janis M. Harmon and Wanda B. Hedrick, *The Reading Teacher* October 2000 v54 i2 p155

From Professional Journals and Publications

Camp, D. (2000). It Takes Two: Teaching with Twin Texts of Fact and Fiction. *The Reading Teacher, 53,* 400–408.

Caswell, L., and Duke, N. (1998). Non-Narrative as Catalyst for Literacy Development. *Language Arts, 75,* 108–117.

Harvey, S. (1998). *Nonfiction Matters.* York, ME: Stenhouse.

Hynes, M. (2000). "I Read for Facts": Reading Nonfiction in a Fictional World. *Language Arts, 77,* 485–494.

Merkley, D. M., and Jefferies, D. (2000/2001). Guidelines for Implementing a Graphic Organizer. *The Reading Teacher, 54,* 350–357.

Moss, B. (1995). Using Children's Nonfiction Tradebooks as Read-Alouds. *Language Arts, 72,* 122–126.

Moyer, P. S. (2000). Communicating Mathematically: Children's Literature as a Natural Connection. *The Reading Teacher, 54,* 246–255.

Piazza, C. L. (1999). *Multiple Forms of Literacy: Teaching Literacy and the Arts.* Columbus, OH: Merrill.

Romano, T. (2000). *Blending Genre, Alternating Style: Writing Multigenre Papers.* Portsmouth, NH: Heinemann/Boynton Cook.

Tierney, R. J., and Readence, J. E. (2000). *Reading Strategies and Practices: A Compendium* (5th ed.). Boston, MA: Allyn & Bacon.

Topping, D. H., and McManus, R. (2002). *Real Reading, Real Writing: Content-Area Strategies.* Portsmouth, NH: Heinemann/Boynton Cook.

Yopp, R. H., and Yopp, H. K. (2000). Sharing Informational Text with Young Children. *The Reading Teacher, 53,* 410–423.

Summary

We began this chapter with a comprehensive look at how children's books can be used across the curriculum. Strategies for interacting with expository text were examined through many Teacher-to-Teacher features. Art and music were highlighted as threads that cut across the curriculum. Mathematics was considered in a holistic manner as we looked at ways for children to connect their world with the world of mathematics. Social studies was examined from a cultural perspective. We concluded with a look at Gary Bowman's California classroom and its emphasis on hands-on science and Deanne Barker's use of patterned text to provide a support for students to synthesize and demonstrate their understanding of content material.

Total Literacy Anchors

- The student is aware of the differences between story/narrative and content/expository/informational text.
- The student appropriately uses a variety of strategies when engaging with content/expository/informational text.
- The student can read and comprehend content/expository/informational text for a variety of purposes.
- The student can use a variety of resources in the classroom and find answers to questions.
- The student is aware of numerous resources outside the classroom and can use them.
- The student uses tables of contents and indexes of books as guides to finding information.
- The student searches through reference books to find out if the books contain material relevant to the problem.
- The student uses dictionaries.
- The student develops skill in using alphabetical arrangements.
- The student skims to locate specific information that needs detailed study and analysis.
- The student summarizes information and ideas.
- The student keeps records of sources used to collect information.
- The student uses a variety of art materials to express ideas.
- The student enjoys artistic products of others.
- The student appreciates and uses the art of other cultures.
- The student reports on visits to galleries, art shows, and art museums.
- The student can tell stories about some of his or her own paintings.
- The student uses descriptive categories of words in talking and writing about art—color, shape, size, texture, feelings, contrast, comparison.
- The student uses names of things in talking about art.
- The student uses art to illustrate his or her own books.
- The student uses art to display poems in the classroom.
- The student uses abstract art for self-expression.
- The student creates imaginary characters and creatures.
- The student responds in meaningful ways to numerals and numbers in the environment.

- The student grows to understand the language and concepts of mathematics.
- The student responds to graphic aids in the environment in ways that help solve problems.
- The student responds to music listening by writing thoughts, interpretations, and feelings.
- The student increases vocabulary of verbs as a response to rhythms.
- The student composes simple rhythms to accompany poetry.
- The student responds rhythmically to words of movement.
- The student pantomimes meanings of common words.
- The student substitutes words to fit basic rhythms of chants and games.
- The student selects movements for hands, head, feet, and body while listening.
- The student knows and responds rhythmically to games and chants that repeat language patterns.
- The student reads the biographies of great people.
- The student looks at the world through the eyes of other people.
- The student takes a more personal look at history by reading historical fiction.

AFTERWORD

The End of Our Voyage

We began this text with a hope for the literacy future of children. We close with great confidence in the abilities of children to build a literacy storehouse for themselves that will sustain them for their lifetime voyage of learning. These are the truths we've arrived at.

America's Finest
Ralph Sanders, B

Teachers who love the language of literature demonstrate that love through the choices they make in their reading *with* students—but they reflect the feeling that the best books are yet to be written.

Teachers share art objects and art prints that are meaningful and that, to them, demonstrate the great art of the past—but they imply in their interaction with students that the greatest paintings are yet to be painted.

Teachers share the inventions of great scientists with enthusiasm and appreciation—but they remind students that the greatest inventions for the benefit of humankind are yet to be made.

Teachers bring students in contact with the great masters of classical and modern music—but they remind children that the greatest music will be composed in the future. Reading in the content fields of the school curriculum is important, and teachers use it as a base for understanding places and people and a few of the reasons they act as they do—but the teacher who is responsive to students and their potential remains convinced that the greatest explorations are in the future, the greatest governments are yet to be formed, the greatest structures are yet to be built, and the most important ideas for the benefit of humanity are ahead of us.

And, perhaps, by some chance, some of those who will bring it all about are in our classrooms today. Can we offer these potential leaders less than an opportunity to respond in personal ways to writing that generates productive thinking, allows freedom of expression, values ingenuity, and satisfies curiosity?

There are many ways for literacy programs to instill in students the complex skills and knowledge that permit literacy to be a significant part of children's lives. We believe the three major ideas presented in our literacy transaction model (discussed in Chapter 1) will assure a measure of success for every student. We encourage you to be guided by these fundamentals as you practice the craft of teaching the children of our future:

> **Idea 1:** *Self-expression.* The natural language a student uses for communication is a basic ingredient in reading and writing. It must remain used and useful throughout the period when refined skills are being developed.

> **Idea 2:** *Impression.* Language development is influenced by many sources and by many people. Each student deserves to try out new forms of communication under the influence of successful practitioners. These influences culminate in personal responses that seek ever-higher levels of quality, fluency, and flexibility in communication.

> **Idea 3:** *Conventions.* Reading and writing development are influenced by the literacy children find in their environments. Children develop as writers when they compare and contrast their writing with the works of others.

We close this book with an appeal for teachers to structure language arts programs in a creative manner and to provide students with opportunities and activities that will enable them to reach their potential as fluent language users. Indeed, learning should be a joyful experience because language truly is as magical as this poem suggests.

> *When instruction becomes*
> *destructive to the joy of*
> *learning—*
> *that instruction should be abolished*
> *or modified*
> *in such a manner*

as to lead potential learners
to experience
the power
the beauty
and the magic of their language.

FROM *MARKINGS*, BY DAG HAMMARSKJÖLD

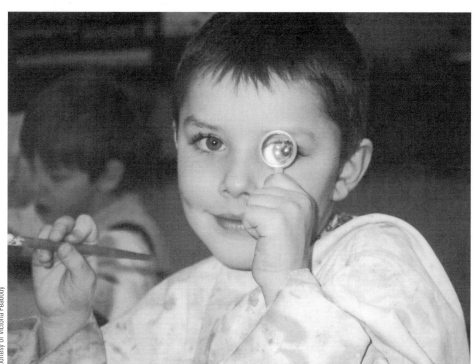

APPENDIX A

Caldecott Medal Winners

2002 *The Three Pigs,* by David Wiesner (Clarion/Houghton Mifflin)

2001 *So You Want to Be President?* by Judith St. George, Illustrated by David Small (Philomel Books)

2000 *Joseph Had a Little Overcoat,* by Simms Taback (Viking)

1999 *Snowflake Bentley,* by Jacqueline Briggs Martin, Illustrated by Mary Azarian (Houghton)

1998 *Rapunzel,* by Paul O. Zelinsky (Dutton)

1997 *Golem,* by David Wisniewski (Clarion)

1996 *Officer Buckle and Gloria,* by Peggy Rathmann (Putnam)

1995 *Smoky Night,* by Eve Bunting, Illustrated by David Diaz (Harcourt)

1994 *Grandfather's Journey,* by Allen Say; Edited by Walter Lorraine (Houghton)

1993 *Mirette on the High Wire,* by Emily Arnold McCully (Putnam)

1992 *Tuesday,* by David Wiesner (Clarion Books)

1991 *Black and White,* by David Macaulay (Houghton)

1990 *Lon Po Po: A Red-Riding Hood Story from China,* by Ed Young (Philomel)

1989 *Song and Dance Man,* by Karen Ackerman, Illustrated by Stephen Gammell (Knopf)

1988 *Owl Moon,* by Jane Yolen, Illustrated by John Schoenherr (Philomel)

1987 *Hey, Al,* by Arthur Yorinks, Illustrated by Richard Egielski (Farrar)

1986 *The Polar Express,* by Chris Van Allsburg (Houghton)

1985 *Saint George and the Dragon,* retold by Margaret Hodges, Illustrated by Trina Schart Hyman (Little, Brown)

1984 *The Glorious Flight Across the Channel with Louis Bleriot,* by Alice & Martin Provensen (Viking)

1983 *Shadow,* translated and illustrated by Marcia Brown; original text in French by Blaise Cendrars (Scribner)

1982 *Jumanji,* by Chris Van Allsburg (Houghton)

1981 *Fables,* by Arnold Lobel (Harper)

1980 *Ox-Cart Man,* by Donald Hall, Illustrated by Barbara Cooney (Viking)

1979 *The Girl Who Loved Wild Horses,* by Paul Goble (Bradbury)

1978 *Noah's Ark,* by Peter Spier (Doubleday)

1977 *Ashanti to Zulu African Traditions,* by Margaret Musgrove, Illustrated by Leo and Diane Dillon (Dial)

1976 *Why Mosquitoes Buzz in People's Ears,* retold by Verna Aardema, Illustrated by Leo and Diane Dillon (Dial)

1975 *Arrow to the Sun,* by Gerald McDermott (Viking)

1974 *Duffy and the Devil,* illustrated by Margot Zemach; retold by Harve Zemach (Farrar)

1973 *The Funny Little Woman,* retold by Arlene Mosel, Illustrated by Blair Lent (Dutton)

1972 *One Fine Day,* retold and illustrated by Nonny Hogrogian (Macmillan)

1971 *A Story A Story,* retold and illustrated by Gail E. Haley (Atheneum)

1970 *Sylvester and the Magic Pebble,* by William Steig (Windmill Books)

1969 *The Fool of the World and the Flying Ship,* retold by Arthur Ransome, Illustrated by Uri Shulevitz (Farrar)

1968 *Drummer Hoff,* adapted by Barbara Emberley, Illustrated by Ed Emberley (Prentice-Hall)

1967 *Sam, Bangs & Moonshine,* by Evaline Ness (Holt)

1966 *Always Room for One More,* by Sorche Nic Leodhas, pseud. [Leclair Alger], Illustrated by Nonny Hogrogian (Holt)

1965 *May I Bring a Friend?* by Beatrice Schenk de Regniers, Illustrated by Beni Montresor (Atheneum)

1964 *Where the Wild Things Are,* by Maurice Sendak (Harper)

1963 *The Snowy Day,* by Ezra Jack Keats (Viking)

1962 *Once a Mouse,* retold and illustrated by Marcia Brown (Scribner)

1961 *Baboushka and the Three Kings,* by Ruth Robbins, Illustrated by Nicolas Sidjakov (Parnassus)

1960 *Nine Days to Christmas,* by Marie Hall Ets and Aurora Labastida, Illustrated by Marie Hall Ets (Viking)

1959 *Chanticleer and the Fox,* adapted from Chaucer's *Canterbury Tales* by Barbara Cooney, Illustrated by Barbara Cooney (Crowell)

1958 *Time of Wonder,* by Robert McCloskey (Viking)

1957 *A Tree Is Nice,* by Janice Udry, Illustrated by Marc Simont (Harper)

1956 *Frog Went A-Courtin',* retold by John Langstaff, Illustrated by Feodor Rojankovsky (Harcourt)

1955 *Cinderella, or the Little Glass Slipper,* translated from Charles Perrault by Marcia Brown, Illustrated by Marcia Brown (Scribner)

1954 *Madeline's Rescue,* by Ludwig Bemelmans (Viking)

1953 *The Biggest Bear,* by Lynd Ward (Houghton)

1952 *Finders Keepers,* Will, pseud. [William Lipkind], Illustrated by Nicolas, pseud. [Nicholas Mordvinoff] (Harcourt)

1951 *The Egg Tree,* by Katherine Milhous (Scribner)

1950 *Song of the Swallows,* by Leo Politi (Scribner)

1949 *The Big Snow,* by Berta and Elmer Hader (Macmillan)

1948 *White Snow, Bright Snow,* by Alvin Tresselt, Illustrated by Roger Duvoisin (Lothrop)

1947 *The Little Island,* by Golden MacDonald, pseud. [Margaret Wise Brown], Illustrated by Leonard Weisgard (Doubleday)

1946 *The Rooster Crows,* by Maude and Miska Petersham (Macmillan)

1945 *Prayer for a Child,* by Rachel Field, Illustrated by Elizabeth Orton Jones (Macmillan)

1944 *Many Moons,* by James Thurber, Illustrated by Louis Slobodkin (Harcourt)

1943 *The Little House,* by Virginia Lee Burton (Houghton)

1942 *Make Way for Ducklings,* by Robert McCloskey (Viking)

1941 *They Were Strong and Good,* by Robert Lawson (Viking)

1940 *Abraham Lincoln,* by Ingri and Edgar Parin d'Aulaire (Doubleday)

1939 *Mei Li,* by Thomas Handforth (Doubleday)

1938 *Animals of the Bible, A Picture Book,* text selected by Helen Dean Fish, Illustrated by Dorothy P. Lathrop (Lippincott)

APPENDIX B

Newbery Medal Winners

2002 *A Single Shard,* by Linda Sue Park (Clarion Books/Houghton Mifflin)

2001 *A Year Down Yonder,* by Richard Peck (Dial)

2000 *Bud, Not Buddy,* by Christopher Paul Curtis (Delacorte)

1999 *Holes,* by Louis Sachar (Frances Foster)

1998 *Out of the Dust,* by Karen Hesse (Scholastic)

1997 *The View from Saturday,* by E. L. Konigsburg (Jean Karl/Atheneum)

1996 *The Midwife's Apprentice,* by Karen Cushman (Clarion)

1995 *Walk Two Moons,* by Sharon Creech (HarperCollins)

1994 *The Giver,* by Lois Lowry (Houghton)

1993 *Missing May,* by Cynthia Rylant (Jackson/Orchard)

1992 *Shiloh,* by Phyllis Reynolds Naylor (Atheneum)

1991 *Maniac Magee,* by Jerry Spinelli (Little, Brown)

1990 *Number the Stars,* by Lois Lowry (Houghton)

1989 *Joyful Noise: Poems for Two Voices,* by Paul Fleischman (Harper)

1988 *Lincoln: A Photobiography,* by Russell Freedman (Clarion)

1987 *The Whipping Boy,* by Sid Fleischman (Greenwillow)

1986 *Sarah, Plain and Tall,* by Patricia MacLachlan (Harper)

1985 *The Hero and the Crown,* by Robin McKinley (Greenwillow)

1984 *Dear Mr. Henshaw,* by Beverly Cleary (Morrow)

1983 *Dicey's Song,* by Cynthia Voigt (Atheneum)

1982 *A Visit to William Blake's Inn: Poems for Innocent and Experienced Travelers,* by Nancy Willard (Harcourt)

1981 *Jacob Have I Loved,* by Katherine Paterson (Crowell)

1980 *A Gathering of Days: A New England Girl's Journal, 1830–1832,* by Joan W. Blos (Scribner)

1979 *The Westing Game,* by Ellen Raskin (Dutton)

1978 *Bridge to Terabithia,* by Katherine Paterson (Crowell)

1977 *Roll of Thunder, Hear My Cry,* by Mildred D. Taylor (Dial)

1976 *The Grey King,* by Susan Cooper (McElderry/Atheneum)

1975 *M. C. Higgins, the Great,* by Virginia Hamilton (Macmillan)

1974 *The Slave Dancer,* by Paula Fox (Bradbury)

1973 *Julie of the Wolves,* by Jean Craighead George (Harper)

1972 *Mrs. Frisby and the Rats of NIMH,* by Robert C. O'Brien (Atheneum)

1971 *Summer of the Swans,* by Betsy Byars (Viking)

1970 *Sounder,* by William H. Armstrong (Harper)

1969 *The High King,* by Lloyd Alexander (Holt)

1968 *From the Mixed-Up Files of Mrs. Basil E. Frankweiler,* by E. L. Konigsburg (Atheneum)

1967 *Up a Road Slowly,* by Irene Hunt (Follett)

1966 *I, Juan de Pareja,* by Elizabeth Borton de Trevino (Farrar)

1965 *Shadow of a Bull,* by Maia Wojciechowska (Atheneum)

1964 *It's Like This, Cat,* by Emily Neville (Harper)

1963 *A Wrinkle in Time,* by Madeleine L'Engle (Farrar)

1962 *The Bronze Bow,* by Elizabeth George Speare (Houghton)

1961 *Island of the Blue Dolphins,* by Scott O'Dell (Houghton)

1960 *Onion John,* by Joseph Krumgold (Crowell)

1959 *The Witch of Blackbird Pond,* by Elizabeth George Speare (Houghton)

1958 *Rifles for Watie,* by Harold Keith (Crowell)

1957 *Miracles on Maple Hill,* by Virginia Sorenson (Harcourt)

1956 *Carry On, Mr. Bowditch,* by Jean Lee Latham (Houghton)

1955 *The Wheel on the School,* by Meindert DeJong (Harper)

1954 *. . . And Now Miguel,* by Joseph Krumgold (Crowell)

1953 *Secret of the Andes,* by Ann Nolan Clark (Viking)

1952 *Ginger Pye,* by Eleanor Estes (Harcourt)

1951 *Amos Fortune, Free Man,* by Elizabeth Yates (Dutton)

1950 *The Door in the Wall* by Marguerite de Angeli (Doubleday)

1949 *King of the Wind,* by Marguerite Henry (Rand McNally)

1948 *The Twenty-One Balloons,* by William Pène du Bois (Viking)

1947 *Miss Hickory,* by Carolyn Sherwin Bailey (Viking)

1946 *Strawberry Girl,* by Lois Lenski (Lippincott)

1945 *Rabbit Hill,* by Robert Lawson (Viking)

1944 *Johnny Tremain,* by Esther Forbes (Houghton)

1943 *Adam of the Road,* by Elizabeth Janet Gray (Viking)

1942 *The Matchlock Gun,* by Walter Edmonds (Dodd)

1941 *Call It Courage,* by Armstrong Sperry (Macmillan)

1940 *Daniel Boone,* by James Daugherty (Viking)

1939 *Thimble Summer,* by Elizabeth Enright (Rinehart)

1938 *The White Stag,* by Kate Seredy (Viking)

1937 *Roller Skates,* by Ruth Sawyer (Viking)

1936 *Caddie Woodlawn,* by Carol Ryrie Brink (Macmillan)

1935 *Dobry,* by Monica Shannon (Viking)

1934 *Invincible Louisa: The Story of the Author of* Little Women, by Cornelia Meigs (Little, Brown)

1933 *Young Fu of the Upper Yangtze,* by Elizabeth Lewis (Winston)

1932 *Waterless Mountain,* by Laura Adams Armer (Longmans)

1931 *The Cat Who Went to Heaven*, by Elizabeth Coatsworth (Macmillan)

1930 *Hitty, Her First Hundred Years*, by Rachel Field (Macmillan)

1929 *The Trumpeter of Krakow*, by Eric P. Kelly (Macmillan)

1928 *Gay Neck, the Story of a Pigeon*, by Dhan Gopal Mukerji (Dutton)

1927 *Smoky, the Cowhorse*, by Will James (Scribner)

1926 *Shen of the Sea*, by Arthur Bowie Chrisman (Dutton)

1925 *Tales from Silver Lands*, by Charles Finger (Doubleday)

1924 *The Dark Frigate*, by Charles Hawes (Little, Brown)

1923 *The Voyages of Doctor Dolittle*, by Hugh Lofting (Lippincott)

1922 *The Story of Mankind*, by Hendrik Willem van Loon (Liveright)

APPENDIX C

Coretta Scott King Award Winners

2002

Author Award Winner
The Land, by Mildred Taylor (Phyllis Fogelman Books/Penguin Putnam)
Honor Books
Money-Hungry, by Sharon G. Flake (Jump at the Sun/Hyperion)
Carver: A Life in Poems, by Marilyn Nelson (Front Street)
Illustrator Award Winner
Goin' Someplace Special, illustrated by Jerry Pinkney; text by Patricia McKissack (Anne Schwartz Book/Atheneum)
Honor Books
Martin's Big Words, illustrated by Bryan Collier; text by Doreen Rappoport (Jump at the Sun/Hyperion)

2001

Author Award Winner
Miracle's Boys, by Jacqueline Woodson (G. P. Putnam's Sons)
Honor Books
Let It Shine! Stories of Black Women Freedom Fighters, by Andrea Davis Pinkney, illustrated by Stephen Alcorn (Gulliver Books, Harcourt)
Illustrator Award Winner
Uptown, by Bryan Collier (Henry Holt)
Honor Books
Freedom River, by Bryan Collier (Jump at the Sun/Hyperion)
Only Passing Through: The Story of Sojourner Truth, illustrated by R. Gregory Christie; text by Anne Rockwell (Random House)
Virgie Goes to School with Us Boys, illustrated by E.B. Lewis; text by Elizabeth Fitzgerald Howard (Simon & Schuster)

2000

Author Award Winner
Bud, Not Buddy, by Christopher Paul Curtis (Delacorte)
Honor Books
Francie, by Karen English (Farrar, Straus and Giroux)

Black Hands, White Sails: The Story of African-American Whalers, by Patricia C. and Frederick L. McKissack (Scholastic Press)
Monster, by Walter Dean Myers (HarperCollins)
Illustrator Award Winner
In the Time of the Drums, illustrated by Brian Pinkney; text by Kim L. Siegelson (Jump at the Sun/Hyperion Books for Children)
Honor Books
My Rows and Piles of Coins, illustrated by E. B. Lewis; text by Tololwa M. Mollel (Clarion Books)
Black Cat, by Christopher Myers (Scholastic)

1999

Author Award Winner
Heaven, by Angela Johnson (Simon & Schuster)
Honor Books
Jazmin's Notebook, by Nikki Grimes (Dial Books)
Breaking Ground, Breaking Silence: The Story of New York's African Burial Ground, by Joyce Hansen and Gary McGowan (Henry Holt and Company)
The Other Side: Shorter Poems, by Angela Johnson (Orchard Books)
Illustrator Award Winner
i see the rhythm, illustrated by Michele Wood; text by Toyomi Igus (Children's Book Press)
Honor Books
I Have Heard of a Land, illustrated by Floyd Cooper; text by Joyce Carol Thomas (Joanna Cotler Books/HarperCollins)
The Bat Boy and His Violin, illustrated by E. B. Lewis; text by Gavin Curtis (Simon & Schuster)
Duke Ellington: The Piano Prince and His Orchestra, illustrated by Brian Pinkney; text by Andrea Davis Pinkney (Hyperion Books for Children)

1998

Author Award Winner
Forged by Fire, by Sharon M. Draper (Atheneum)
Honor Books
Bayard Rustin: Behind the Scenes of the Civil Rights Movement, by James Haskins (Hyperion)
I Thought My Soul Would Rise and Fly: The Diary of Patsy, a Freed Girl, by Joyce Hansen (Scholastic, Inc.)
Illustrator Award Winner
In Daddy's Arms I am Tall: African Americans Celebrating Fathers, illustrated by Javaka Steptoe; text by Alan Schroeder (Lee & Low)
Honor Books
Ashley Bryan's ABC of African American Poetry, by Ashley Bryan (Jean Karl/Atheneum)
Harlem, by Walter Dean Myers; illustrated by Christopher Myers (Scholastic, Inc.)
The Hunterman and the Crocodile, by Baba Wagué Diakité (Scholastic, Inc.)

1997

Author Award Winner
Slam, by Walter Dean Myers (Scholastic, Inc.)
Honor Books
Rebels Against Slavery: American Slave Revolts, by Patricia C. and Frederick L. McKissack (Scholastic, Inc.)
Illustrator Award Winner
Minty: A Story of Young Harriet Tubman, illustrated by Jerry Pinkney; text by Alan Schroeder (Dial Books for Young Readers)
Honor Books
The Palm of My Heart: Poetry by African American Children, illustrated by Gregorie Christie; edited by Davida Adedjouma (Lee & Low Books Inc.)
Running the Road to ABC, illustrated by Reynold Ruffins; text by Denize Lauture (Simon & Schuster, Books for Young Readers)

Neeny Coming, Neeny Going, illustrated by Synthia Saint James; text by Karen English (BridgeWater Books)

1996
Author Award Winner
Her Stories, by Virginia Hamilton (Scholastic/Blue Sky Press)
Honor Books
The Watsons Go to Birmingham—1963, by Christopher Paul Curtis (Delacorte)
Like Sisters on the Homefront, by Rita Williams-Garcia (Delacorte)
From the Notebooks of Melanin Sun, by Jacqueline Woodson (Scholastic/Blue Sky Press)
Illustrator Award Winner
The Middle Passage: White Ships Black Cargo, by Tom Feelings (Dial Books for Young Readers)
Honor Books
Her Stories, illustrated by Leo and Diane Dillon; text by Virginia Hamilton (Scholastic/Blue Sky Press)
The Faithful Friend, illustrated by Brian Pinkney; text by Robert San Souci (Simon & Schuster Books for Young Readers)

1995
Author Award Winner
Christmas in the Big House, Christmas in the Quarters, by Patricia C. & Frederick L. McKissack (Scholastic, Inc.)
Honor Books
The Captive, by Joyce Hansen (Scholastic)
I Hadn't Meant to Tell You This, by Jacqueline Woodson (Delacorte)
Black Diamond: Story of the Negro Baseball League, by Patricia C. and Frederick L. McKissack (Scholastic, Inc.)
Illustrator Award Winner
The Creation, illustrated by James Ransome; text by James Weldon Johnson (Holiday House)
Honor Books
The Singing Man, illustrated by Terea Shaffer; text by Angela Shelf Medearis (Holiday House)
Meet Danitra Brown, illustrated by Floyd Cooper; text by Nikki Grimes (Lothrop, Lee & Shepard)

1994
Author Award Winner
Toning the Sweep, by Angela Johnson (Orchard)
Honor Books
Brown Honey in Broom Wheat Tea, by Joyce Carol Thomas; illustrated by Floyd Cooper (HarperCollins)
Malcolm X: By Any Means Necessary, by Walter Dean Myers (Scholastic, Inc.)
Illustrator Award Winner
Soul Looks Back in Wonder, illustrated by Tom Feelings; text edited by Phyllis Fogelman (Dial Books for Young Readers)
Honor Books
Brown Honey in Broom Wheat Tea, illustrated by Floyd Cooper; text by Joyce Carol Thomas (HarperCollins)
Uncle Jed's Barbershop, illustrated by James Ransome; text by Margaree King Mitchell (Simon & Schuster)

1993
Author Award Winner
Dark Thirty: Southern Tales of the Supernatural, by Patricia A. McKissack (Knopf)
Honor Books
Mississippi Challenge, by Mildred Pitts Walter (Bradbury)
Sojourner Truth: Ain't I a Woman? by Patricia C. and Frederick L. McKissack (Scholastic, Inc.)
Somewhere in the Darkness, by Walter Dean Myers (Scholastic, Inc.)
Illustrator Award Winner
The Origin of Life on Earth: an African Creation Myth, illustrated by Kathleen Atkins Wilson; retold by David A. Anderson/SANKOFA (Sights)
Honor Books
Little Eight John, illustrated by Wil Clay; text by Jan Wahl (Lodestar)
Sukey and the Mermaid, illustrated by Brian Pinkney; text by Robert San Souci (Four Winds)
Working Cotton, illustrated by Carole Byard; text by Sherley Anne Williams (Harcourt)

1992
Author Award Winner
Now is Your Time: the African American Struggle for Freedom, by Walter Dean Myers (HarperCollins)
Honor Books
Night on Neighborhood Street, by Eloise Greenfield, illustrated by Jan Spivey Gilchrist (Dial)
Illustrator Award Winner
Tar Beach, by Faith Ringgold (Crown)
Honor Books
All Night, All Day: A Child's First Book of African American Spirituals, illustrated and selected by Ashley Bryan (Atheneum)
Night on Neighborhood Street, illustrated by Jan Spivey Gilchrist; text by Eloise Greenfield (Dial)

1991
Author Award Winner
The Road to Memphis, by Mildred D. Taylor (Dial)
Honor Books
Black Dance in America, by James Haskins (Crowell)
When I Am Old with You, by Angela Johnson (Orchard)
Illustrator Award Winner
Aida, illustrated by Leo and Diane Dillon; text by Leontyne Price (Harcourt)

1990
Author Award Winner
A Long Hard Journey: The Story of the Pullman Porter, by Patricia C. and Frederick L. McKissack (Walker)
Honor Books
Nathaniel Talking, by Eloise Greenfield, illustrated by Jan Spivey Gilchrist (Black Butterfly)
The Bells of Christmas, by Virginia Hamilton (Harcourt)
Martin Luther King, Jr., and the Freedom Movement, by Lillie Patterson (Facts on File)
Illustrator Award Winner
Nathaniel Talking, illustrated by Jan Spivey Gilchrist; text by Eloise Greenfield (Black Butterfly)
Honor Books
The Talking Eggs, illustrated by Jerry Pinkney; text by Robert San Souci (Dial)

1989

Author Award Winner
Fallen Angels, by Walter Dean Myers (Scholastic, Inc.)
Honor Books
A Thief in the Village and Other Stories, by James Berry (Orchard)
Anthony Burns: The Defeat and Triumph of a Fugitive Slave, by Virginia Hamilton (Knopf)
Illustrator Award Winner
Mirandy and Brother Wind, illustrated by Jerry Pinkney; text by Patricia McKissack (Knopf)
Honor Books
Under the Sunday Tree, illustrated by Amos Ferguson; text by Eloise Greenfield (Harper)
Storm in the Night, illustrated by Pat Cummings; text by Mary Stolz (Harper)

1988

Author Award Winner
The Friendship, by Mildred L. Taylor (Dial)
Honor Books
An Enchanted Hair Tale, by Alexis De Veaux (Harper)
The Tales of Uncle Remus: The Adventures of Brer Rabbit, by Julius Lester (Dial)
Illustrator Award Winner
Mufaro's Beautiful Daughters: An African Tale, by John Steptoe (Lothrop)
Honor Books
What a Morning! The Christmas Story in Black Spirituals, illustrated by Ashley Bryan; selected by John Langstaff (Macmillan)
The Invisible Hunters: A Legend from the Miskito Indians of Nicaragua, illustrated by Joe Sam; compiled by Harriet Rohmer et al. (Children's Press)

1987

Author Award Winner
Justin and the Best Biscuits in the World, by Mildred Pitts Walter (Lothrop)
Honor Books
Lion and the Ostrich Chicks and Other African Folk Tales, by Ashley Bryan (Atheneum)
Which Way Freedom, by Joyce Hansen (Walker)

Illustrator Award Winner
Half a Moon and One Whole Star, illustrated by Jerry Pinkney; text by Crescent Dragonwagon (Macmillan)
Honor Books
Lion and the Ostrich Chicks and Other African Folk Tales, by Ashley Bryan (Atheneum)
C.L.O.U.D.S., by Pat Cummings (Lothrop)

1986

Author Award Winner
The People Could Fly: American Black Folktales, by Virginia Hamilton; illustrated by Leo and Diane Dillon (Knopf)
Honor Books
Junius Over Far, by Virginia Hamilton (Harper)
Trouble's Child, by Mildred Pitts Walter (Lothrop)
Illustrator Award Winner
The Patchwork Quilt, illustrated by Jerry Pinkney; text by Valerie Flournoy (Dial)
Honor Books
The People Could Fly: American Black Folktales, illustrated by Leo and Diane Dillon; text by Virginia Hamilton (Knopf)

1985

Author Award Winner
Motown and Didi, by Walter Dean Myers (Viking)
Honor Books
Circle of Gold, by Candy Dawson Boyd (Apple/Scholastic)
A Little Love, by Virginia Hamilton (Philomel)
Illustrator Award Winner
No award

1984

Author Award Winner
Everett Anderson's Good-bye, by Lucille Clifton (Holt)
Special Citation
The Words of Martin Luther King, Jr., compiled by Coretta Scott King (Newmarket Press)
Honor Books
The Magical Adventures of Pretty Pearl, by Virginia Hamilton (Harper)

Lena Horne, by James Haskins (Coward-McCann)
Bright Shadow, by Joyce Carol Thomas (Avon)
Because We Are, by Mildred Pitts Walter
Illustrator Award Winner
My Mama Needs Me, illustrated by Pat Cummings; text by Mildred Pitts Walter (Lothrop)

1983

Author Award Winner
Sweet Whispers, Brother Rush, by Virginia Hamilton (Philomel)
Honor Books
This Strange New Feeling, by Julius Lester (Dial)
Illustrator Award Winner
Black Child, by Peter Mugabane (Knopf)
Honor Books
All the Colors of the Race, illustrated by John Steptoe; text by Arnold Adoff (Lothrop)
I'm Going to Sing: Black American Spirituals, illustrated by Ashley Bryan (Atheneum)
Just Us Women, illustrated by Pat Cummings; text by Jeanette Caines (Harper)

1982

Author Award Winner
Let the Circle Be Unbroken, by Mildred D. Taylor (Dial)
Honor Books
Rainbow Jordan, by Alice Childress (Coward-McCann)
Lou in the Limelight, by Kristin Hunter (Scribner)
Mary: An Autobiography, by Mary E. Mebane (Viking)
Illustrator Award Winner
Mother Crocodile: Maman-Caiman (An Uncle Amadou Tale from Senegal), illustrated by John Steptoe; text translated and adapted by Rosa Guy (Delacorte)
Honor Books
Daydreamers, illustrated by Tom Feelings; text by Eloise Greenfield (Dial)

1981

Author Award Winner
This Life, by Sidney Poitier (Knopf)

Honor Books
Don't Explain: A Song of Billie Holiday, by Alexis De Veaux (Harper)
Illustrator Award Winner
Beat the Story Drum, Pum-Pum, by Ashley Bryan (Atheneum)
Honor Books
Grandmama's Joy, illustrated by Carole Byard; text by Eloise Greenfield (Collins)
Count on Your Fingers African Style, illustrated by Jerry Pinkney; text by Claudia Zaslavsky (Crowell)

1980
Author Award Winner
The Young Landlords, by Walter Dean Myers (Viking)
Honor Books
Movin' Up, by Berry Gordy (Harper)
Childtimes: A Three-Generation Memoir, by Eloise Greenfield and Lessie Jones Little (Harper)
Andrew Young: Young Man with a Mission, by James Haskins (Lothrop)
James Van Der Zee: The Picture Takin' Man, by James Haskins (Dodd)
Let the Lion Eat Straw, by Ellease Southerland (Scribner)
Illustrator Award Winner
Cornrows, illustrated by Carole Byard; text by Camille Yarborough (Coward-McCann)

1979
Author Award Winner
Escape to Freedom, by Ossie Davis (Viking)
Honor Books
Benjamin Banneker, by Lillie Patterson (Abingdon)

I Have a Sister, My Sister Is Deaf, by Jeanne W. Peterson (Harper)
Justice and Her Brothers, by Virginia Hamilton (Greenwillow)
Skates of Uncle Richard, by Carol Fenner (Random)
Illustrator Award Winner
Something on My Mind, illustrated by Tom Feelings; text by Nikki Grimes (Dial)

1978
Author Award Winner
Africa Dream, by Eloise Greenfield; illustrated by Carole Bayard (Crowell)
Honor Books
The Days When the Animals Talked: Black Folk Tales and How They Came to Be, by William J. Faulkner (Follett)
Marvin and Tige, by Frankcina Glass (St. Martin's)
Mary McCleod Bethune, by Eloise Greenfield (Crowell)
Barbara Jordan, by James Haskins (Dial)
Coretta Scott King, by Lillie Patterson (Garrard)
Portia: The Life of Portia Washington Pittman, the Daughter of Booker T. Washington, by Ruth Ann Stewart (Doubleday)
Illustrator Award Winner
Africa Dream, illustrated by Carole Bayard; text by Eloise Greenfield (Crowell)

1977
Author Award Winner
The Story of Stevie Wonder, by James Haskins (Lothrop)
Illustrator Award Winner
No award

1976
Author Award Winner
Duey's Tale, by Pearl Bailey (Harcourt)
Illustrator Award Winner
No award

1975
Author Award Winner
The Legend of Africana, by Dorothy Robinson (Johnson Publishing)
Illustrator Award Winner
No award

1974
Author Award Winner
Ray Charles, by Sharon Bell Mathis; illustrated by George Ford (Crowell)
Illustrator Award Winner
Ray Charles, illustrated by George Ford; text by Sharon Bell Mathis (Crowell)
(*Note:* Prior to 1974, the CSK Award was given to authors only)

1973 Award Winner
I Never Had It Made: The Autobiography of Jackie Robinson, as told to Alfred Duckett (Putnam)

1972 Award Winner
17 Black Artists, by Elton C. Fax (Dodd)

1971 Award Winner
Black Troubador: Langston Hughes, by Charlemae Rollins (Rand McNally)

1970 Award Winner
Martin Luther King, Jr.: Man of Peace, by Lillie Patterson (Garrard)

APPENDIX D

Reader's Theater Scripts

A Bug's Picnic

Rick Kilcup

Characters: narrator, bugs . . . as many as you want . . . , and humans.

Props: Picnic stuff! Like a basket, paper plates, blanket, etc. Will need a spray can labeled "People Repellent." Might even have some sandwiches.

Costumes: Not really necessary but if the bugs had headband bug masks it would really look great!

Narrator: It's summer and the weather's just right for picnics! How'd you like to come along on one? Well, let's go . . . but I've got to warn you that this isn't your everyday ordinary picnic!

(Bugs enter, crawling, hopping, flying, etc. They are looking around for something and carry picnic basket.)

Bug 1: This looks like a good spot for a picnic!

Bug 2: Yup, it sure does!

Bug 3: Let's just hope that THEY don't find us!

All Bugs: You can say that again! (They settle down, unpack the picnic basket, spread out the table cloth, and get ready to eat.)

Bug 4: Sandwiches anyone? We've got nectar on rye and aphid on whole wheat!

All Bugs: Sounds great, let's pig out! (Sandwiches get passed out.)

Bug 5: This is the life!

Bug 6: Yup and THEY haven't found us yet!

Bug 7: They'd better not! Nothing can spoil a picnic faster than THEY can! (Others nod in agreement, ad lib.)

Human 1: We were right, there was a picnic going on here!

Human 2: Yup, we can smell a good picnic a mile away!

Human 3: Just look at those goodies!! Let's go mess up their picnic and have a feast!

Other Humans: Great idea! (They sneak over and begin pestering and gobbling the food!)

Bug 8: Eeeek! THEY'RE here!

Bug 9: Oh no, humans! Shoo! Go away you pests! (All bugs begin swatting at humans who dodge out of way and continue to pester and eat, the bugs can ad lib yucky comments.)

Bug 10: (Reaches into picnic basket and pulls out can of spray.) I'll put an end to these pesky critters! (Sprays.) Take that you bothersome humans!

All Humans: Oh no! Not That! We'd better split! (They run off, coughing.)

Bug 11: (Bugs settle back to eat in peace, #11 holds up can for audience to see.) People Repellent, never leave home without it!

THE END!

Rip Van Winkle Reader's Theatre Adaptation

David Canzoneri

Narrator: In a small Dutch community in the Catskill Mountains, a crowd gathered at the Union Hotel beneath a brand new flag made up of stars and stripes. They were discussing the new government led by General George Washington when an old man with a long grizzled beard, worn-out clothes and a rusty worm-eaten musket wandered into the meeting. A crowd gathered around the man, stroking their chins and laughing at his worn-out clothes.

Crowdmember 1: On which side did you vote, old timer?

Rip: What?

Crowdmember 2: Are you a federal?

Crowdmember 3: Or are you a Federalist?

Rip: I don't even know what that means!

Narrator: A wise old man elbowed his way through the crowd, planted his hands on his hips and eyed Rip sideways.

Old Man: He wants to know if you believe that power should rest with the people or with the government. I want to know what brings you to the election with a gun on your shoulder. Are you trying to start a riot?

Rip: Alas! Sir! I am a poor, quiet man, a native of the place, and a loyal subject of the king, God bless him!

Crowdmember 1: The king? I thought we got rid of all those filthy redcoats!

Crowdmember 2: He must have missed the ship when we chased those redcoats back home!

Crowdmember 3: Maybe he's a spy. Maybe they're planning to attack again!

Crowdmember 1: Grab him!

Crowdmember 2: Away with him!

Narrator: The crowd advanced angrily toward Rip, who held up his hands pleadingly.

Rip: Please! Please! I mean no harm! I merely come in search of my neighbors who used to keep about the tavern.

Narrator: The wise old man held up his hand, halting the crowd. Then he turned to Rip and demanded . . .

Old Man: Well, who are they? Name them.

Rip: Nicholas Vedder, for one. Where is Nicholas Vedder?

Crowdmember 1: Nicholas Vedder? Why, he is dead and gone these eighteen years! There was a wooden tombstone in the churchyard that used to tell about him, but that's rotten and gone, too.

Rip (puzzled): What's become of Brom Dutcher?

Crowdmember 2: Oh, he went off to the army in the beginning of the war; some say he was killed at the storming of Stony Point—others say he was drowned in a squall at the foot of Anthony's Nose. I don't know—he never came back again.

Rip (even more puzzled): Where's Van Bummel, the schoolmaster?

Crowdmember 3: He went off to the wars too, was a great militia general, and is now in Congress.

Rip (utterly despairing): War? Congress? Eighteen years! What has happened? What has happened to my dear, dear friends? What has happened to my town? What has happened to Rip Van Winkle?

Crowdmember 1: Rip Van Winkle? Oh yes, I remember him. He was a simple, good natured man, a kind neighbor and . . .

Crowdmember 2: . . . a henpecked husband. A real shrew of a wife he had at home!

Crowdmember 1: Yes, but her temper produced his meekness of spirit. Some even say a nagging wife is a blessing in disguise.

Crowdmember 2: If that's the case then he was thrice blessed!

Judith: Rip Van Winkle was my father, sir. But, it's twenty years since he went away from home with his gun, and never has been heard of since—his dog Wolf came home without him, but whether he shot himself or was carried away by the Indians, nobody can tell. I was then but a little girl.

Rip: Judith. This grown up woman, you are Judith?

Judith: Yes, sir, but how do you know me?

Rip: I am your father! Young Rip Van Winkle once—old Rip Van Winkle now! Does nobody know poor Rip Van Winkle?

Judith (in disbelief): Father! This is you?

Old Man: Sure enough! It is Rip Van Winkle. It is himself! Welcome home again, old neighbor.

Rip: Judith, you said Wolf came home, where is he, the little rascal!

Judith (sadly): Dear Father, remember that was twenty years ago. He is long since gone.

Rip: Oh, yes. I haven't yet realized it. Twenty years! And all my friends gone! Where is your mother?

Judith: Oh, she too died a short time later; she broke a blood vessel in a fit of passion at a New England peddler.

Rip (sighs): A drop of comfort, at least, in that!

Old Man: Where have you been these twenty long years?

Rip: It seems but yesterday. I had gone squirrel hunting with Wolf, rest his soul, and we unconsciously scrambed to one of the highest parts of the Catskills. Panting and fatigued, I threw myself on a green knoll overlooking the lordly Hudson River. As evening approached and I began to descend, I heard a voice calling . . .

Narrator: Rip Van Winkle, Rip Van Winkle.

Rip: Through a clearing came a short, square-built old fellow dressed in the antique Dutch fashion. He was bent under the weight of a keg and I hurried to offer him neighborly assistance.

Old Man: That was indeed the Rip Van Winkle I knew: ready to attend anybody's business but his own. He always found tending his own farm and family matters next to impossible.

Rip: The stranger led me through a ravine and into a hallow where his strange companions were playing at ninepins. Whenever they rolled the balls, a sound like rumbling peals of thunder echoed along the mountains. The men looked like the figures in the old Flemish painting hanging in the parlor of Dominie Van Shaik, the village parson. I suppose Dominie is . . .

Crowdmember 1: Yes, long gone, too.

Judith: Please continue, if you can, Father.

Rip (takes a deep breath): Well, the men beckoned me to serve the ale. As I passed the flagons around I felt compelled to sample the liquor. Being a naturally thirsty soul, I was soon tempted to repeat the draft. After several tastes, however, my eyes began to swim, my head reeled, and I fell into a deep sleep, waking only this morning. My musket is no longer blue steel, but rust and wormwood. My dog, my friends and my wife are all gone. My house is in shambles. And I have become an old man. At first, I thought the ale was playing tricks on me, but you have convinced me that everything really has changed by twenty years!

Crowdmember 1: You really expect us to believe this story?

Crowdmember 2: The only part I believe is the sampling of the ale!

Crowdmember 3: He's as crazy as he looks.

Narrator: The crowd laughed and jeered at Rip. Then, a small bespectacled man pushed his way through the crowd and held up his hand for silence. Almost immediately the crowd fell silent. The man adjusted his jacket, cleared his throat and began to speak.

Peter: You have no reason to disbelieve this man. I, Peter Vanderdonk, ancestor of the great historian, can assure you that his story is most certainly true. The Catskills have always been visited with strange happenings. It is well known that Henry Hudson, the first discoverer of the river and surrounding country, keeps a vigil there every twenty years. With his crew of the Half Moon, they keep a guardian eye over the river and the great city called by his name. My own father once saw them playing ninepins in the hollow and I myself heard the sound of the balls like peals of distant thunder one summer afternoon. I say Welcome home, Rip Van Winkle. It is good to have you back.

Old man: Whatever the learned Vanderdonk says is fine by me.

Crowdmember 1: Me, too. Let's welcome our old neighbor back.

Narrator: The crowd gathered around Rip, patting him on the back and shaking his hand. With such an affirmation coming from the famous and respected Peter Vanderdonk, Rip was quickly welcomed back into the village. Having reached the age where he could be idle without criticism, he became a regular fixture and was reverenced as a patriarch of the village, telling his story to every stranger who would give him an audience. To this day, the villagers never hear a thunderstorm without thinking that Henry Hudson and his crew are at a game of ninepins. And it is a common wish of all henpecked husbands to have a taste of Rip Van Winkle's ale to escape the tirades of the shrew. As for Rip, he never tells the tale without tugging thoughtfully at his beard and saying . . .

Rip: Hmm. Maybe now I should change my name to Rip van Wrinkle!

END

Old Bike and New Bike

Bill Martin Jr

Old Bike: Don't wobble, You've got to keep your balance.

New Bike: I'm trying! I'm trying!

Old Bike: You're less than a day old and already you've got a wobbly front wheel.

New Bike: It wasn't my fault. That stupid dog stood right there and refused to move. I hit him. Ker-plunk!

Old Bike: Oh, that was funny!

New Bike: No, it wasn't funny! I was doing my best and what happens! I get sprocket shock and a wobbly wheel. That may be funny to you but not to me.

Old Bike: Calm down, little one, calm down. We all went through it. Use your training wheels!

New Bike: Training wheels? So you know what everybody would say?

Old Bike: What about the new bike next door? He uses training wheels.

New Bike: He's a sissy!

Old Bike: Then take your knocks and forget it.

New Bike: *(after a pause)* Say, Old Bike, did you hear that kid holler when I dumped him last night? *(he chuckles)* He thought he was killed. The sight of a little blood and he powed out of his mind!

Old Bike: Donald is going to take a lot of spills until you get the hang of balancing.

New Bike: He thinks he's so smart! He thinks he has to learn to ride. He can't figure out that it's us bikes that do the learning.

Old Bike: I don't like to bear bad news, but look who's coming!

New Bike: Oh, no! It's Donald's little sister!

Old Bike: Yes, you're going to get a workout. With Donald and his little sister both riding you before you get your balance—you'll be bent and twisted forever.

New Bike: Why don't you take her for a ride? Give me a break.

Old Bike: I'm willing but she likes you. Face up to it! I've had my day. Everybody likes a new bike. She wouldn't ride me.

New Bike: Well, here goes. Wish me luck!

Old Bike: Well, c'est la guerre!

Knots on a Counting Rope

Bill Martin Jr

Boy: Grandfather, tell me the story again. Tell me who I am.

Grandfather: I have told you many times, Boy.

Boy: But tell me again, Grandfather. Tell me about my name.

Grandfather: You know your name, Boy. You know the story by heart.

Boy: But it sounds better when you tell it. Please tell it over and over, Grandfather. I like to hear you say my name.

Grandfather: Then listen carefully, Boy. This may be the last time for telling the story. The counting rope is almost filled with knots.

Boy: This cannot be the last time, Grandfather. Promise that this will not be the last time.

Grandfather: I cannot promise you anything, Boy. I love you. I love you very much. That is better than a promise.

Boy: And I love you, Grandfather. Tell me the story again. Please.

Grandfather: Once there was a boy child. . . .

Boy: I was the boy child, wasn't I, Grandfather?

Grandfather: Yes, you were the boy child in the story.

Boy: And I was very strong, wasn't I, Grandfather?

Grandfather: No, you were not strong, Boy. You were very little and very sick. We thought you were going to die.

Boy: But *you* knew that I wouldn't die, Grandfather. Tell me that part again.

Grandfather: One day when you were very sick and your breath was too weak for crying, two great blue horses came galloping by. Suddenly they turned and looked at you. You reached up your arms to them.

Boy: And that is when you named me!

Grandfather: Yes, we named you Boy Strength-of-Blue-Horses. It is a strong name.

Boy: Did I need a strong name, Grandfather?

Grandfather: All children need strong names to grow strong.

Boy: And what did you say, Grandfather?

Grandfather: I said, 'See how the horses speak to him. They are his brothers from beyond the dark mountain. This boy child will not die. The blue horses have given him strength to live.'

Boy: Did I grow strong, Grandfather?

Grandfather: Yes, Boy, you grew strong and you are becoming stronger every day. Some day you will be strong enough to cross over beyond the dark mountains.

Boy: How strong must I be, Grandfather? Tell me that part again.

Grandfather: You must be so strong, Boy, that you will not speak with anger even when your heart is filled with anger.

Boy: And that is not all, Grandfather. Tell me the next part.

Grandfather: You must be so strong, Boy, that you want to know what other people are thinking even when you are listening to your own thoughts.

Boy: Now tell me the last part, Grandfather.

Grandfather: You must be so strong, Boy, that you will stop to think of what happened yesterday and what will happen tomorrow in knowing what you want to do today.

Boy: Is it hard to be strong like you, Grandfather?

Grandfather: Strong people are not born strong, Boy. They become strong by thinking they are strong. They dream of themselves as being strong enough to cross over the dark mountains.

Boy: Will I ever be strong enough to cross over the dark mountains, Grandfather?

Grandfather: You already have crossed over some of the dark mountains, Boy. The mountains have no beginning and no ending. They are all around us. We only know that we are crossing them when we want to be weak but choose to be strong.

Boy: Maybe I will not be strong enough, Grandfather, to cross over all of the dark mountains.

Grandfather: Oh, yes, you will be, Boy Strength-of-Blue-Horses.

Boy: Then you must keep telling me the story, Grandfather. You must never stop telling me the story.

Grandfather: But I will stop telling the story, Boy, when I have tied the last knot on the counting rope. Now that I have told the story again, I tie another knot, just as I did before. When the rope is filled with knots, you will start telling the story to yourself. That is the way you know you are strong. That is the way you become strong.

Gettysburg and Mr. Lincoln's Speech

Adapted by Timothy Rasinski

Parts: 5 Total

Narrators 1 and 2; Southern Soldier; Northern Soldier, Abraham Lincoln.

Possible Additional Materials: A map, blue and gray caps for the soldiers, stovepipe hat for Mr. Lincoln.

Narrator 1: The Civil War was a tragic time in America. It pitted the Southern states against the Northern states.

Narrator 2: It also pitted brother against brother and friend against friend.

Northern Soldier: I fight to end slavery and to make our country whole again—although we may come from many states, we are one nation and always will be one nation.

Southern Soldier: I fight against the Northerners who try to impose their will on the South, telling us that we have to put an end to slavery, telling us that we cannot live our lives the way that we wish.

Narrator 1: The war was a bloody one. More soldiers died in the Civil War than in any other war that the United States took part in.

Narrator 2: Through the first few years of the Civil War, the Southern or Confederate army, under General Robert E. Lee, won battle after battle against the North.

Southern Soldier: One of us rebels can whip the tar out of ten Yankees!

Northern Soldier: We are good soldiers and we're ready to fight. Our generals, however, are no match for the Confederate generals—Robert E. Lee and Stonewall Jackson.

Narrator 1: By 1863 General Lee felt strong enough to invade Pennsylvania, an important Northern state. By taking the war to the North, Lee thought that he could convince the North to give up its attempt to reunite the states and end slavery.

Narrator 2: The Union Army under General George Meade knew that it had to stop the Confederates. It met up with the Southern army during the first three days of July 1863 in a small Pennsylvania town called . . .

All: GETTYSBURG!

Narrator 1: For three days, under the hot summer sun the two huge armies struggled.

Southern Soldier: Long live the Confederacy!

Northern Soldier: Union forever! Rally round the flag boys!

Narrator 2: The battle swung back and forth over those blistering hot days. It finally ended in a failed attempt by the Confederates to break through the line of Northern soldiers.

Southern Soldier: We called it Pickett's Charge. It was a disaster. Thousands of gray clad soldiers were cut down in the murderous fire coming from the Yankee lines.

Narrator 1: Pickett's Charge failed, and Lee knew he had lost the battle. He knew he had to withdraw his army to Virginia, his home state, . . . friendlier territory.

Narrator 2: And so Lee moved his battered and defeated army from Pennsylvania on the evening of July third. He had to leave so quickly that many of the dead and wounded Southern soldiers were left lying on the battlefield.

Southern Soldier: We didn't want to leave our fallen brothers lying on Northern soil. But we had to retreat South or risk being annihilated by the victorious Northerners.

Narrator 1: Meade's Army of the Potomac followed Lee out of Pennsylvania, hoping to catch up with him and complete the destruction of the Southern army. He too left many of his dead lying on the Gettysburg Battlefield. All told, nearly 40,000 soldiers, Northern and Southern were killed, wounded, or missing at Gettysburg.

Northern Soldier: We tasted victory at last. Now we wanted to finally put an end to this bloody war. We had to chase the enemy wherever he may go.

Narrator 2: But for the people living in Gettysburg, the battle was far from over. When the few thousand residents of Gettysburg returned to their homes, they were greeted by the sight and stench of death.

Narrator 1: Imagine the scene. . . . Thousand of bodies of dead soldiers and animals, lying out in the middle of the battlefields and in shallow graves under the broiling July sun. Something had to be done quickly to prevent the spread of disease from all the dead and decaying bodies.

Narrator 2: In previous battles, bodies of dead soldiers were sent to their hometowns for burial.

Narrator 1: But this was not possible at Gettysburg. There were simply too many dead and not enough workers to prepare the bodies for transport home. It would take too long.

Narrator 2: The governor of Pennsylvania then made an important decision: the dead soldiers would be buried in a new cemetery in Gettysburg. Burying the bodies in Gettysburg could be accomplished quickly. The threat from the spread of disease could be averted. All the Northern states were asked to contribute money for the cemetery for the Gettysburg dead.

Northern Soldier: And so, from July to November, in that year, 1863, workers gathered the bodies of our fallen comrades and buried them in the new cemetery.

Southern Soldier: Even some of our Southern martyrs were buried at Gettysburg.

Narrator 1: By November, the cemetery was finished. By November, the country understood just how important the battle of Gettysburg was. No more would the Confederate army threaten the Northern states. The Confederacy had reached its high mark and was now in decline.

Narrator 2: Thus it was decided that a dedication for the cemetery should take place to honor those Northern soldiers who made the ultimate sacrifice at Gettysburg.

Narrator 1: Dignitaries from around the country were invited. President Lincoln came. The greatest orator, or speechmaker, of the day, Edward Everett, was also asked to give a grand speech. He spoke for over two hours.

Narrator 2: Those who came to the dedication were tired and wanted to go home by the time Everett had finished his long speech.

Narrator 1: But then President Lincoln was asked to make a few brief remarks.

Narrator 2: Slowly, and so very deliberately, President Lincoln stood up and made his way to the podium. Quietly, he faced the crowd of public dignitaries and ordinary citizens standing in front of him. Somberly, he looked over the countless rows of dead soldiers behind him. And, in just 272 words, Mr. Lincoln helped all of us, those living in 1863 and those of us alive today, understand what is special about our country and why it could not be broken up into free and slave, Union and Confederate, North and South.

Lincoln:

Four score and seven years ago,
our fathers brought forth on this continent,
a new nation,
conceived in liberty,
and dedicated to the proposition that *all men are created equal.*

Narrator 1: Lincoln uses words from the Declaration of Independence to remind us why the United States was founded in the first place.

Lincoln:

Now we are engaged in a great civil war,
testing whether that nation, or any nation so conceived and so dedicated, can long endure.
We are met on a great battlefield of that war.
We have come to dedicate a portion of that field,
as a final resting place for those who here gave their lives that
the nation might live.
It is altogether fitting and proper that we should do this.
But in a larger sense,
we cannot dedicate, we cannot consecrate, we cannot hallow this ground.
The brave men, living and dead, who struggled here,
have consecrated it, far beyond our poor power to add or detract.

Narrator 2: Although the dedication that Lincoln was speaking at was meant to make this land special, Lincoln knew, and he told the audience, that the brave soldiers who fought here that summer had made it much more special through their actions than by anything Lincoln could say or do.

Lincoln:

The world will little note nor long remember what we say here.
But it can never forget what they did here.
It is for us the living, rather, to be dedicated here to the unfinished
work which they who fought here have thus far so nobly advanced.
It is rather for us to be here dedicated to the great task
remaining before us.
That from these honored dead we take increased devotion to that
cause for which they gave the last full measure of devotion.

Narrator 1: Although the soldiers who died here saved the Union, much fighting, and much hard work still needs to be done before the nation is made whole again.

Narrator 2: Lincoln realized that the United States was a grand and never-tried-before experiment for all the world to see—can a government created by its citizens and run by its citizens truly work? The world was watching and waiting to find out.

Lincoln:

That we here highly resolve that these dead
shall not have died in vain.
That this nation, under God, shall have a new birth of freedom.
And that . . .
Government of the people, by the people, for the people, shall
not perish from the earth.

REFERENCES

Adams, M. J. (1990). *Beginning to read: Thinking and learning about print.* Cambridge, MA: MIT Press.

Afflerbach, P., Norton, J. L., & Johnston, P. (1989). *The composition of the report card: Making the grade in the language arts.* Paper presented at the National Reading Conference, Austin, TX.

Allen, R.V. (1976). *Language experience activities* (2nd ed.). Boston: Houghton Mifflin.

Allen, R. V. (1985). Let students have their say. *Forty-ninth yearbook, Claremont Reading Conference.* Claremont, CA: Claremont Graduate School Center for Developmental Studies.

Allen, R.V. (1999). Using language experience in beginning reading: How a language experience program works. In O. Nelson & W. Linek (Eds.), *Practical classroom applications of Language Experience.* Boston: Allyn & Bacon.

Allen, R.V., Sampson, M. R., & Teale, W. (1989). *Experiences for literacy.* Worthington, OH: SRA.

Allington, R. L. (2001). *What really matters for struggling readers: Designing research-based programs.* New York: Longman.

Altwerger, B., & Flores, B. (1994). Theme cycles: Creating communities of learners. *Primary Voices K–6, 2*(l), 2–6.

Alvermann, D. E., & Moore, D. W. (1991). Secondary school reading. In P. D. Pearson, R. Barr, M. L. Kamil, & P. Mosenthal (Eds.), *Handbook of reading research* (2nd ed., pp. 951–983). New York: Longman.

Anderson, R. A., & Pearson, P. D. (1984). A schema-theoretic view of basis processes in reading comprehension. In P. D. Pearson (Ed.), *Handbook of reading research* (pp. 255–292). New York: Longman.

Anderson, R. C., Hiebert, E. H., Scott, J. A., & Wilkinson, I. A. G. (1985). *Becoming a nation of readers. The report of the Commission on Reading.* Urbana: University of Illinois, Center for the Study of Reading.

Armbruster, B., & Anderson, T. (1981). *Content area textbooks.* (Reading Education Report No. 23). Urbana-Champaign: University of Illinois at Urbana-Champaign, Center for the Study of Reading.

Armbruster, B. B., Anderson, T. H., Armstrong, J. O., Wise, M. A., Janisch, C., & Meyer, L. A. (1991). Reading and questioning in content area lessons. *Journal of Reading Behavior, 23,* 35–59.

Aronson, E. (1978). *The jigsaw classroom.* Beverly Hills, CA: Sage.

Atwell, N. (1987). *In the middle.* Portsmouth, NH: Heinemann.

Atwell, N. (1990). *Coming to know: Writing to learn in the intermediate grades.* Portsmouth, NH: Heinemann.

Atwell, N. (1998). *In the middle: Writing, reading, and learning with adolescents* (2nd ed.). Portsmouth, NH: Heinemann-Boynton/Cook.

Baghban, M. J. M. (1984). *Our daughter learns to read and write: A case study from birth to three.* Newark, DE: International Reading Association.

Barbieri, M., & Reif, L. (Eds.). (1994). *Workshop: The teacher as writer.* Portsmouth, NH: Heinemann.

Beck, I.L., & McKeown, M.G. (2001). Text talk: Capturing the benefits of read-aloud experiences for young children. *The Reading Teacher, 55,* 10–20.

Beesley, S. (1994). *The social studies connection.* Paper presented at the conference of the International Institute of Literacy Learning, Memphis, TN.

Bettelheim, B., & Zelan, K. (1982). *On learning to read.* New York: Knopf.

Betterton, M., & Landis, D. (1998). Seeking students' perspectives about reading instruction. *Wisconsin State Reading Journal 41*(3), 15–21.

Betts, E. A. (1946*). Foundations of reading instruction.* New York: American Book Company.

Biemiller, A. (1999). *Language and reading success: From reading research to practice* (vol. 5). Cambridge, MA: Brookline.

Bingham, A. A., Dorta, P., McClaskey, M., & O'Keefe, J. (1995). *Exploring the multiage classroom.* Portland, ME: Stenhouse.

Bird, L. B. (1989). The art of teaching: Evaluation and revision. In Y. M. Goodman & W. J. Hood (Eds.), *The whole language evaluation book.* Portsmouth, NH: Heinemann.

Bissex, G. L. (1980). *GNYS AT WRK: A child learns to write and read.* Cambridge, MA: Harvard University Press.

Bissex, G. L. (1985). Watching young writers. In A. Jaggar & M. Smith-Burke (Eds.), *Observing the language learner.* Urbana, IL: National Council of Teachers of English.

Blachowicz, C. L., & Fisher, P. (2000). Vocabulary instruction. In M. Kamil, P. Mosenthal, P. D. Pearson, & R. Barr (Eds.), *Handbook of reading research* (vol. 3, pp. 503–523). New York: Longman.

Bloome, D., & King Dail, A. (1997). Toward (re)defining miscue analysis: Reading as a social and cultural process. *Language Arts, 74,* 610–617.

Bloome, D., Landis, D., & Villemare, J. (1998). Reading reading miscue research. In Carole Edesky & Ann Marek (Eds.), *Reflections and connections: Essays on the influence of Kenneth S. Goodman.* Cresskill, NJ: Hampton Press.

Bloomfield, L. (1933). *Language.* New York: Holt, Rinehart and Winston.

Boomer, G. (1984). Literacy, power, and the community. *Language Arts, 61,* 575–584.

Bortnick, R., & Lopardo, G. S. (1976). The cloze procedure: A multipurpose classroom tool. *Reading Improvement, 13,* 113–117.

Brandt, R. (1988). On assessment in the arts: A conversation with Howard Gardner. *Educational Leadership, 45*(4), 30–34.

Bransford, J. D., & McCarrell, N. S. (1974). A sketch of a cognitive approach to comprehension: Some thoughts about understanding what it means to comprehend. In W. B. Wiemer & D. S. Palermo (Eds.), *Cognition and the symbolic processes.* Hillsdale, NJ: Erlbaum.

Brent, R., & Anderson, P. (1993). Developing children's classroom listening strategies. *The Reading Teacher, 47,* 122–126.

Bridge, C. (1979). Predictable materials for beginning readers. *Language Arts, 56,* 503–507.

Bridge, C. (1986). Predictable books for beginning readers and writers. In M. Sampson (Ed.), *The pursuit of literacy: Early reading and writing.* Dubuque, IA: Kendall Hunt.

Brimer, R. W. (1990). *Students with severe disabilities: Current perspectives and practices.* Mountain View, CA: Mayfield.

Britton, J. N., Burgess, T., Martin, N., McLeod, A., & Rosen, H. (1975). *The development of writing abilities (11–18).* London: Macmillan Education Ltd.

Broad, K. (1999). *When computer is a four letter word: Overcoming the fears of implementing technology outcomes in division one and two classrooms.* A workshop presented at the Canadian Rockies School Division professional development day, Canmore Collegiate School, Canmore, Alberta, Canada, October 8.

Broad, K. (2001). *Creating a classroom context for guided/strategic reading instruction.* A paper presented at the Arizona Reading Association Fall Conference, Tucson, AZ, November 2–3.

Broad, K. (2001). *Using children's literature as a catalyst for stepping into reading and writing.* Northern Arizona University Celebrations of Beginnings Conference, Flagstaff, AZ, March 17.

Broad, K. (2002). Nurturing young readers' lives through experiences with text: Reader response instruction for emergent readers. In M. Hunsberger and G. Labercane (Eds.), *Making meaning in the response-based classroom* (pp. 13–29). Boston: Allyn & Bacon.

Button, K., Johnson, M. J., & Furgerson, P. (1996). Interactive writing in a primary classroom. *The Reading Teacher, 49,* 446–454.

Buzzeo, T. (1998). The finely tuned author visit. *Book Links, 7*(4), 10–15.

Cairney, T. H. (1995). Developing parent partnerships in secondary literacy learning. *Journal of Reading, 38,* 520–526.

Cairney, T. H. (1997). Acknowledging diversity in home literacy practices. Moving towards partnership with parents. *Early Childhood Development and Care, 127–128,* 191–199.

Cairney, T. H. (2000). The construction of literacy and literacy learners. *Language Arts, 77,* 496–505.

Calfee, R. C. (1999–2000). A decade of assessment. *Educational Assessment, 6*(4), 217–219.

Calfee, R. C., & Patrick, C. L. (1995). *Teach our children well.* Stanford, CA: Stanford Alumni Association.

Calkins, L. M. (1983). *Lessons from a child: On the teaching and learning of writing.* Portsmouth, NH: Heinemann.

Calkins, L. M. (1986). *The art of teaching writing.* Portsmouth, NH: Heinemann.

Calkins, L. M. (1994). *The art of teaching writing.* Portsmouth, NH: Heinemann.

Calkins, L. M., & Harwayne, S. (1987). *The writing workshop: A world of difference.* Portsmouth, NH: Heinemann.

Cambourne, B. (1995). Toward an educationally relevant theory of literacy learning: Twenty years of inquiry. *The Reading Teacher, 49*(3), 182–190.

Cambourne, B., & Turbill, J. (1988). *Coping with chaos.* Portsmouth, NH: Heinemann.

Canady, R. J. (1977). *Consistency of teachers' methods of teaching reading to specific learning theories.* Unpublished doctoral dissertation, University of Arizona, Tucson.

Carlton, L., & Moore R. H. (1971). *Reading, self-directive dramatization and self-concept.* Columbus, OH: Merrill, 1971.

Caswell, L. & Duke, N. (1998). Nonnarrative as catalyst for literacy development. *Language Arts, 75,* 108–117.

Chall, J. (1983). *Stages of reading development.* New York: McGraw-Hill.

Chall, J. S., Bissex, G. L., Conard, S. S., & Harris-Sharples, S. H. (1996). *Qualitative assessment of text difficulty: A practical guide for teachers and writers.* Cambridge, MA: Brookline.

Chall, J., Jacobs, V., & Baldwin, L. (1990). *The reading crisis: Why poor children fall behind.* Cambridge, MA: Harvard University Press.

Chamot, A. U. (1998). *Promoting learning for culturally and linguistically diverse students.* Belmont, CA: Wadsworth.

Chaney, A. L., & Burk, T. L. (1998). *Teaching oral communication in grades K–8.* Boston: Allyn & Bacon.

Chase, P., & Doan, J. (1999). *Choosing to learn.* Portsmouth, NH: Heinemann.

Chatton, B., & Collins, L. D. (1999). *Blurring the edges: Integrated curriculum through writing and children's literatures.* Portsmouth, NH: Heinemann.

Chihak, J. (1999). Success is in the details: Publishing to validate elementary authors. *Language Arts, 76*(6), 491–498.

Chomsky, C. (1969). *The acquisition of syntax in children 5 to 10.* Cambridge, MA: MIT Press.

Chomsky, C. (1971). Write first, read later. *Childhood Education, 47,* 296–299.

Chomsky, C. (1980). Stages in language development and reading exposure:

Thought and language. In M. Wolf, M. McQuillan, & E. Radwin (Eds.), *Harvard Educational Review, 14,* 201–229.

Chomsky, N. (1965). *Aspects of a theory of syntax.* Cambridge, MA: MIT Press.

Clark, L., DeWolf, S., & Clark, C. (1992). Teaching teachers to avoid having culturally assaultive classrooms. *Young Children, 47*(5), 4–9.

Clark, R. P. (1989). *Free to write.* Portsmouth, NH: Heinemann.

Clay, M. (1975). *What did I write?* Auckland, New Zealand: Heinemann.

Clay, M. (1991). *Becoming literate: The construction of inner control.* Auckland, New Zealand: Heinemann Educational.

Clay, M. (1998). *By different paths to common outcomes.* York, ME: Stenhouse.

Clay, M. (2001). *The Magic of language.* Keynote address presented at the Reading Recovery/ Early Literacy Conference, Dallas, TX.

Clem, C., & Feathers, K. (1986). I lic spiders: What one child teaches us about constant learning. *Language Arts, 63,* 143–147.

Clemmons, J., Laase, L., Cooper, D., Areglado, N., & Dill, M. (1993). *Portfolios in the classroom: A teacher's sourcebook.* New York: Scholastic.

Cohen, D. (1968). The effect of literature on vocabulary and reading achievement. *Elementary English, 45,* 209–213, 217.

Condon, M., & McGuffee, M. (2001). *Real ePublishing, really publishing!: How to create digital books by and for all ages.* Portsmouth, NH: Heinemann.

Costa, A. L. (1989). Re-assessing assessment. *Educational Leadership, 46*(9), 35–57.

Covey, S. (1990). *The 7 habits of highly effective people.* New York: Simon & Schuster.

Cramer, R. L. (2001). *Creative power: The nature and nurture of children's writing.* New York: Longman.

Cullinan, B. (1994). *Literature and the child.* Toronto, Ontario: International Thomson.

Cullinan, B. E., Scala, M. C., & Schroder, V. C. (1995). *Three voices: An invita-tion to poetry across the curriculum.* Portland, ME: Stenhouse.

Cunningham, P. M., & Cunningham, J. W. (1992). Making words: Enhancing the invented spelling-decoding connection. *The Reading Teacher, 46,* 106–115.

Cunningham, P. M., Moore, S. A., Cunningham, J. W., & Moore, D. W. (1983). *Reading in elementary classrooms.* New York: Longman.

Dahl, K. L., Scharer, P. L., Lawson, L. L., & Grogran, P. R. (2001). *Rethinking phonics: Making the best teaching decisions.* Portsmouth, NH: Heinemann.

Dalton, J., & Boyd, J. (1992). *I teach: A guide to inspiring classroom leadership.* Melbourne: Eleanor Curtain.

Daniels, H. (1994). *Literature circles: Voice and choice in the student-centered classroom.* York, ME: Stenhouse.

Davey, B. (1983). Think aloud: Modeling the cognitive processes of reading comprehension. *Journal of Reading, 17*(1), 44–47.

DeFina, A. (1992). *Portfolio assessment. Getting started.* New York: Scholastic.

DeFord, D. E. (1981). Literacy: Reading, writing and other essentials. *Language Arts, 58,* 652–658.

DeFord, D. E. (1985). Validating the construct of theoretical orientation in reading instruction. *Reading Research Quarterly, 20,* 351–357.

Delpit, L. (1995). *Other people's children: Cultural conflict in the classroom.* New York: New Press.

Denman, G. A. (1988). *When you've made it your own . . . : Teaching poetry to young people.* Portsmouth, NH: Heinemann.

Dewey, J., & Bentley, A. E. (1949). *Knowing and the known.* Boston: Beacon Press.

Dickinson, D. K., & Smith, M. W. (1994). Long-term effect of preschool teachers' book readings on low-income children's vocabulary and story comprehension. *Reading Research Quarterly, 29,* 104–122.

Doake, D. (1988). *Reading begins at birth.* Toronto: Scholastic Tab.

Donaldson, M. (1978). *Children's minds.* Glasgow, Scotland: Fontana/Collins.

Dorn, L. J., & Soffos, C. (2001). *Shaping literate minds.* Portland, ME: Stenhouse.

Downes, T., & Fatouros, C. (1995). *Learning in an electronic world: Computers in the classroom, 1,* 3–10, Australia: Primary Education Teacher's Association.

Dudley-Marling, C. (1985). Microcomputers, reading, and writing: Alternatives to drill and practice. *The Reading Teacher, 38,* 388–391.

Dudley-Marling, C., & Dippo, D. (1991). The language of whole language. *Language Arts, 68,* 548–554.

Dunn, S. (1999). *All together now.* Markham, ON: Pembroke.

Durham, J. (1997). On time and poetry. *The Reading Teacher, 51,* 76–79.

Durkin, D. (1978–1979). What classroom observations reveal about reading comprehension instruction. *Reading Research Quarterly, 14,* 481–533.

Durkin, D. (1981). What is the value of the new interest in reading comprehension? *Language Arts, 58,* 23–43.

Durkin, D. (1983). *Teaching them to read* (4th ed.). Boston: Allyn & Bacon.

Durkin, D. (1993). *Teaching them to read.* (6th ed.). Boston: Allyn & Bacon.

Durkin, D. (1996). *Children who read early.* New York: Teachers College Press.

Duthie, C. (1994). Nonfiction: A genre study for the primary classroom. *Language Arts, 71,* 588–595.

Dyson, A. (1987). The value of "time-off task": Young children's spontaneous talk and deliberate text. *Harvard Educational Review, 57,* 396–420.

Eanet, M. (1978). An investigation of the REAP reading/study procedure: Its rationale and efficacy. In P. D. Pearson & J. Hanson (Eds.), *Reading: Discipline inquiry in process and practice.* Urbana, IL: National Council of Teachers of English.

Eanet, M. G., & Manzo, A. V. (1976). REAP—A strategy for improving reading/writing/study skills. *Journal of Reading, 19,* 647–652.

Eisner, E. (1990). Winning race not a valid goal, ASCD told. *ASCD Update, 32*(4), 1–3.

Elley, W. (1989). Vocabulary acquisition from listening to stories. *Reading Research Quarterly, 24,* 174–187.

Englert, C., & Hiebert, E. (1983). Children's developing awareness of text structures in expository materials. *Journal of Educational Psychology, 76,* 65–74.

Erickson, F. (1989). Literacy risks for students, parents, and teachers. In J. B. Allen & J. M. Mason (Eds.), *Risk makers, risk takers, risk breakers: Reducing the risks for young literacy learners.* Portsmouth, NH: Heinemann.

Evans, J. (Ed) (2001). *Writing in the elementary classroom.* Portsmouth, NH: Heinemann.

Farnsworth, L. (1990). In the schema of things. In N. Atwell (Ed) *Coming to know: Writing to learn in the intermediate grades.* Portsmouth, NH: Heinemann Educational.

Farr, R., & Carey, R. F. (1986). *Reading: What can be measured?* (2nd ed.). Newark, DE: International Reading Association.

Farr, R., & Tone, B. (1998). *Portfolio and performance assessment. Helping students evaluate their progress as readers and writers* (2nd ed.). Fort Worth, TX: Harcourt Brace.

Farris, P. J. (1993). *Language arts: A process approach.* Madison, WI: Brown & Benchmark.

Feitelson, D., Goldstein, Z, Iraqi, J., & Share, D. (1993). Effects of listening to story reading on aspects of literacy acquisition in a diglossic situation. *Reading Research Quarterly, 28,* 70–79.

Ferreiro, E., & Teberosky, A. (1982). *Literacy before schooling.* Portsmouth, NH: Heinemann.

Flesch, R. (1955). *Why Johnny can't read—and what you can do about it.* New York: Harper.

Fletcher, R., (1993). *What a writer needs.* Portsmouth, NH: Heinemann.

Fletcher, R., (1996). *Keeping a writer's notebook,* Portsmouth, NH: Heinemann.

Flood, J., & Lapp, D. (1990). Types of writing included in basal reading programs, kindergarten through second grade: An investigation of changes from 1983 to 1989. In J. Zutell & S. McCormick (Eds.), *Theory and research: Analyses from multiple paradigms. Thirty-ninth yearbook of the National Reading Conference.* Chicago, IL: National Reading Conference.

Forsten, C., & Grant, J. (1998). *If you're riding a horse and it dies, get off.* Peterborough, NH: Crystal Springs.

Fountas, I. C., & Pinnell, G. S. (2001). *Guiding readers and writers (grades 3–6): Teaching comprehension, genre, and content literacy.* Portsmouth, NH: Heinemann.

Fox, S. E., & Allen, V. G. (1983). *The language arts: An integrated approach.* New York: Holt, Rinehart and Winston.

Fresch, M. J., & Wheaton, A. (1997). Sort, search, and discover: Spelling in the child-centered classroom. *The Reading Teacher, 51,* 20–31.

Fritz, J. (1981). The very truth. In B. Hearne & M. Kaye (Eds.), *Celebrating children's books.* New York: Lothrop, Lee & Shepard.

Fuhler, C. (1994). Response journals: Just one more time with feeling. *The Journal of Reading, 37,* 400–405.

Furth, H. G. (1970). *Piaget for teachers.* Englewood Cliffs, NJ: Prentice-Hall.

Galda, L., Cullinan, B. E., & Strickland, D. S. (1993). *Language, literacy and the child.* Fort Worth, TX: Harcourt Brace.

Gardner, H. (1991a). *Intelligence reframed: Multiple intelligences for the 21st century.* New York: Basic Books.

Gardner, H. (1991b). *To open minds.* New York: Basic Books.

Gardner, H. (1991c). *The unschooled mind: How children think and how schools should teach.* New York: Basic Books.

Gardner, H. (1993). *Multiple intelligences: The theory in practice.* New York: Basic Books.

Gardner, H. (1999). *Intelligence reframed.* New York: Basic Books.

Giacobbe, M. E. (1991). The politics of process. In N. Atwell (Ed.), *Workshop 3.* Portsmouth, NH: Heinemann.

Glasser, W. (1992). *The quality school: Managing students without coercion.* New York: HarperCollins.

Gollnick, D., & Chinn, P. (1990). *Multicultural education is a pluralistic society* (3rd ed.). New York: Macmillan.

Goodman, K. S. (1976). *What's universal about the reading process?* Paper presented at the First Japan International Reading Conference, Tokyo.

Goodman, K. S., & Goodman, Y. A. (1978). *Reading of American children whose language is a stable rural dialect of English or a language other than English.* Final Report, Project NIE-C-00-3-0087. Washington, DC: HEW, National Institute of Education.

Goodman, K. S., Smith, E. B., Meredith, R., & Goodman, Y. (1988). *Language and thinking in school: A whole language curriculum.* Katonah, NY: Richard C. Owen.

Goodman, Y. M. (1980). The roots of literacy. In M. P. Douglass (Ed.), *Forty-fourth yearbook, Claremont Reading Conference.* Claremont, CA: Claremont Graduate School.

Goodman, Y. M. (1985). Kidwatching: Observing children in the classroom. In A. Jaggar & M. T. Smith-Burke (Eds.), *Observing the language learner.* Newark, DE: International Reading Association.

Goodman, Y. M. (1989). Evaluation of students: Evaluation of teachers. In K. S. Goodman, Y. M. Goodman, & W. J. Hood (Eds.), *The whole language evaluation book.* Portsmouth, NH: Heinemann.

Goodman, Y. M., & Anders, P. L. (1999). Listening to Erica read: Perceptions and analysis from six perspectives. In T. Shannahan & F. V. Rodriguez-Brown, (Eds.), *Forty-eighth yearbook of the National Reading Conference.* Chicago, IL: National Reading Conference.

Goodman, Y. M., & Burke, C. L. (1972). *Reading miscue inventory: Procedure for diagnosis and evaluation.* New York: Macmillan.

Gordon, C. J., & Pearson, P. D. (1983). *The effects of instruction in metacomprehension and inferencing in children's comprehension abilities* (Tech. Rep. No. 277). Urbana, IL: University of Illinois, Center for the Study of Reading.

Graves, D. (1978). *Balance the basics: Let them write.* New York: Ford Foundation.

Graves, D. (1994). *A fresh look at writing.* Portsmouth, NH: Heinemann.

Graves, D. (1999). *Bring life into learning: Create a lasting literacy.* Portsmouth, NH: Heinemann.

Graves, D. H. (1975). An examination of the writing processes of seven-year-old children. *Research in the Teaching of English, 9,* 227–241. Urbana, IL: National Council of Teachers of English.

Graves, D. H. (1981). Patterns of child control of the writing process. In R. D. Walshe (Ed.), *Donald Graves in Australia "Children want to write . . ."* Portsmouth, NH: Heinemann.

Graves, D. H. (1983). *Writing: Teachers and children at work.* Portsmouth, NH: Heinemann.

Graves, D. H. (1986). *The Mast Way Project.* Paper presented during the New Hampshire Writing Project seminar, Durham, NH.

Graves, D. H. (1989a). *Experiment with fiction.* Portsmouth, NH: Heinemann.

Graves, D. H. (1989b). *Experiment with nonfiction.* Portsmouth, NH: Heinemann.

Graves, D. H. (1992). *The reading/writing teacher's companion: Explore poetry.* Portsmouth, NH: Heinemann.

Graves, D. H., & Hansen, J. (1983). The author's chair. *Language Arts, 60,* 176–183.

Graves, D. H., & Stuart, V. (1985). *Write from the start. Tapping your child's natural writing ability.* New York: New American Library.

Graves, D., & Sunstein, B. (Eds.). (1992). *Portfolio portraits.* Portsmouth, NH: Heinemann.

Graves, M. F., Juel, C., & Graves, B. B. (2001). *Teaching reading in the 21st century* (2nd ed.), Boston: Allyn & Bacon.

Griffiths, R., & Clyne, M. (1993). Real books and real mathematics. In M. Stephens, A. Waywood, D. Clarke, & J. Izard (Eds), *Communicating mathematics: Perspectives from classroom practice and current research.* Melbourne: Australian Council for Educational Research.

Haney, W. (2000). The myth of the Texas miracle in education. *Education Policy Analysis Archives, 8* (41). Retrieved May 6, 2002, at http://epaa.asu.edu/epaa/v8n41/

Hansen, J. (1989). Anna evaluates herself. In J. B. Allen & J. M. Mason (Eds.), *Risk makers, risk takers, risk breakers: Reducing the risks for young literacy learners.* Portsmouth, NH: Heinemann.

Hansen, J. (1992). Literacy portfolios emerge. *The Reading Teacher, 45*(8), 604–707.

Hansen, J. (2001). *When writers read.* Portsmouth, NH: Heinemann.

Harp, B. (Ed.). (1991). *Assessment and evaluation in whole language programs.* Norwood, MA: Christopher Gordon.

Harris, T. H., & Hodges, R. E. (1995). *The literacy dictionary: The vocabulary of reading and writing.* Newark, DE: International Reading Association.

Harste, J. C. (1993). Inquiry-based instruction. *Primary Voices K–6.* Premier issue, pp. 2–5.

Harste, J. C., Burke, C. L., & Woodward, V. A. (1982). Children's language and world: Initial encounters with print. In J. A. Langer & M. T. Smith-Burke (Eds.), *Reader meets author: Bridging the gap* (pp. 105–131). Newark, DE: International Reading Association.

Harste, J. C., Burke, C. L., & Woodward, V. A. (1983). *The young child as writer-reader, and informant.* Final Report, NIE Grant 80-0121. Bloomington: Indiana University Press.

Harste, J. C., & Carey, R. F. (1979). Comprehension as setting. In J. C. Harste & R. F. Carey (Eds.), *Monograph in language and reading studies: New perspectives on comprehension* (pp. 4–22). Bloomington: Indiana University School of Education.

Harste, J. C., Short, K., & Burke, C. (1988). *Creating classrooms for authors.* Portsmouth, NH: Heinemann.

Harste, J. C., Woodward, V. A., & Burke, C. L. (1984a). Examining our assumptions: A transactional view of literacy and learning. *Research in the Teaching of English, 18,* 84–108. Urbana, IL: National Council of Teachers of English.

Harste, J. C., Woodward, V. A., & Burke, C. L. (1984b). *Language stories and literacy lessons.* Portsmouth, NH: Heinemann.

Head, M. H., & Readence, J. E. (1986). Anticipation guides: Meaning through prediction. In E. K. Dishner, T. W. Bean, J. E. Readence, & D. W. Moore (Eds.), *Reading in the content areas* (2nd ed., pp. 229–234). Dubuque, IA: Kendall/Hunt.

Heald-Taylor, G. (1989). *The administrator's guide to whole language.* Katonah, NY: Richard C. Owen.

Heard, G. (1989). *For the good of the earth and sun: Teaching poetry.* Portsmouth, NH: Heinemann.

Heath, S. B. (1983a). *Ways with words: Ethnography of communication, communities, and classrooms.* Cambridge, England: Cambridge University Press.

Heath, S. B. (1983b). *Ways with words: Language, life and work in communities and classrooms.* Cambridge, England: Cambridge University Press.

Heimlich, J. E., & Pittelman, S. D. (1986). *Semantic mapping: Classroom applications.* Newark, DE: International Reading Association.

Henderson, E. H. (1986). Understanding children's knowledge of written language. In D. B. Yaden Jr. & S. Templeton (Eds.), *Metalinguistic awareness and beginning literacy. Conceptualizing what it means to read and write* (pp. 65–77). Portsmouth, NH: Heinemann.

Henderson, E. H., & Beers, J. W. (1980). *Development and cognitive aspects of learning to spell: A reflection of word knowledge.* Newark, DE: International Reading Association.

Hendricks, T. (2002). Taming tension. *San Francisco Chronicle,* April 29, 2002, B1–B2.

Heubert, J. P., & Hauser, R. M. (Eds.). (1999). *High stakes: Testing for tracking, promotion, and graduation.* A Report of the National Research Council, Washington, DC: National Academy Press.

Hiebert, E. H., Valencia, S. W., & Afflerbach, P. P. (1994). Definitions and perspectives. In S. W. Valencia, E. H. Hiebert, & P. P. Afflerbach (Eds.), *Authentic reading assessment. Practices and possibilities* (pp. 6–21). Newark, DE: International Reading Association.

Hittleman, D. R. (1988). *Developmental reading, K–8: Teaching from a whole-language perspective* (3rd ed.). Columbus, OH: Merrill.

Hoffman, J. V., Assaf, L., Pennington, J., & Paris, S. G. (2001). High stakes testing in reading: Today in Texas, tomorrow? *The Reading Teacher, 54,* 482–492.

Holdaway, D. (1979). *The foundations of literacy.* Portsmouth, NH: Heinemann.

Holdaway, D. (1986). The structure of natural learning as a basis for literacy instruction. In M. R. Sampson (Ed.), *The pursuit of literacy.* Dubuque, IA: Kendall/Hunt.

Horowitz, R. (1985). Text patterns: Part 2. *Journal of Reading, 28,* 534–541.

Hotchkiss, P. (1990). Cooperative learning models: Improving student achievement using small groups. In M. A. Gunter, T. H. Estes, & J. H. Schwab (Eds.), *Instruction: A models approach* (pp. 167–184). Boston: Allyn & Bacon.

Hubbard, R. (1985). Drawing parallels: Real writing, real reading. In J. Hansen, T. Newkirk, & D. Graves (Eds.), *Breaking ground: Teachers relate reading and writing in the elementary school.* Portsmouth, NH: Heinemann.

Huck, C., Hepler, S., Hickman, J., & Ziefer, B. (2000). *Children's literature in the elementary school.* Columbus, OH: McGraw Hill.

Hunsaker, R. A. (1989). What listening skills should be taught to teachers and students? In P. Cooper & K. Galvin (Eds.) *The future of speech communication education* (pp. 27–30). Annandale, VA: Speech Communication Association.

Hunsaker, R. A. (1990). *Understanding and developing the skills of oral communication: Speaking and listening* (2nd ed.). Englewood, CO: Morton.

Idol-Maestas, L., & Croll, V. J. (1985). *The effects of training in story mapping procedures on the reading comprehension of poor readers* (Tech. Rep. No. 352). Urbana: University of Illinois, Center for the Study of Reading.

Individuals with Disabilities Education Act. (1991). Washington, DC: U.S. Government Printing Office.

Jaggar, A., & Smith-Burke, T. (Ed.). (1985). *Observing the language learner.* Newark, DE: International Reading Association.

Jenkins, C. B. (1999). *The allure of authors.* Portsmouth, NH: Heinemann.

Jenkins, L. (2001). *American schools in crisis: Problems and solutions.* Paper presented at the International Institute of Literacy Learning Conference, Tampa, FL.

Johnson, D. W., & Johnson, F. P. (1998). *Learning together and alone: Cooperative, competitive, and individualistic learning.* New York: Allyn & Bacon.

Johnson, D. W., Johnson, R. T., & Bartlett, J. K. (1990). *Cooperative learning lesson structures.* Edina, MN: Interaction.

Johnson, D.W., Johnson, R.T., & Holubec, E. J. (1993). *Circles of learning. Cooperation in the classroom.* Edina, MN: Interaction.

Johnston, F.R. (2001). Spelling exceptions: Problems or possibilities? *The Reading Teacher, 54,* 372–389.

Kagan, S. (1990). *Cooperative learning resources for teachers.* San Juan Capistrano, CA: Resources for Teachers.

Kamil, C., & Randazzo, M. (1985). Social interacting and invented spelling. *Language Arts, 62,* 124–133.

Kamler, B. (1984). Ponch writes again: A child at play. *Australian Journal of Reading, 7,* 61–70.

Karchmer, R. A. (2001). The journey ahead: Thirteen teachers report how the Internet influences literacy and literacy instruction in their K–12 classrooms. *Reading Research Quarterly, 36,* 442–466.

Kasten, W. (1989). *Celebrating the writing of children.* Paper presented at the International Institute of Literacy Learning Conference, Boston, MA.

Kasten, W. (1993). The meaning-centered classroom. In M. Sampson & T. Thomason (Eds.), *Reading, writing and literacy learning* (2nd ed.). Dallas, TX: International Institute of Literacy Learning.

Kasten, W. (1994). Literature circles for the teaching of literature-based reading. In L. G. McKay (Ed.), *Flexible grouping in the elementary grades.* Boston: Allyn & Bacon.

Kasten, W. C., & Clark, B. K. (1993). *The multi-age classroom: A family of learners.* Katonah, NY. Richard C. Owen.

Kasten, W. C., & Lolli, E. M. (1998). *Implementing multiage education: A practical guide.* Norwood, MA: Christopher-Gordon.

Kelly, P.A., Brown, K., Butler, A., Taylor, C., & Zeller, P. (1998). A place to hang our hats. *Educational Leadership, 56,* 62–64.

Klein, S. P, Hamilton, L. S., McCaffrey, D. F., & Stecher, B. M. (2000). What do test scores in Texas tell us? *Education Policy Analysis Archives, 8*(49), 1–12. Retrieved May 6, 2002, at http://epaa.asu.edu/epaa/v8n49/

Kohn, A. (1999). *Punished by rewards: The trouble with gold stars, incentive plans, A's, praise, and other bribes.* Boston: Houghton Mifflin.

Koretz, D., & Barron, S. I. (1998). *The validity of gains on the Kentucky Instructional Results Information System (KIRIS).* Santa Monica, CA: RAND.

Retrieved May 6, 2002, at www.rand.org/publications/MR/MR1014/

LaBerge D., & Samuels, S. J. (1974). Toward a theory of automatic processing in reading. *Cognitive Psychology, 6,* 293–323.

Labov, W. (1982). *The study of nonstandard English.* Urbana, IL: National Council of Teachers of English.

Larrick, N. (1991). *Let's do a poem: Introducing children to poetry.* New York: Delacorte.

Lefevre, C. A. (1970). *Linguistics, English, and the language arts.* Boston: Allyn & Bacon.

Leu, D. J. (2000). Literacy and technology: Deictic consequences for literacy education in an information age. In M. L. Kamil, P. B. Mosenthal, P. D. Pearson, & R. Barr (Eds.), *Handbook of reading research* (vol. 3, pp. 843–870). Mahwah, NJ: Erlbaum.

Levstik, L. S. (1989). Coming to terms with history: Historical narrativity and the young reader. *Theory into Practice, 29,* 114–119.

Lindfors, J. W. (1987). *Children's language and learning* (2nd ed.). Englewood Cliffs, NJ: Prentice-Hall.

Lindgren, H. C. (1986). *Educational psychology in the classroom.* New York: John Wales & Sons.

Linn, R. L. (2000). Assessments and accountability. *Educational Researcher, 29*(2), 4–16.

Lukens, R. J. (1999). *A critical handbook of children's literature* (5th ed.). New York: HarperCollins.

Lundsteen, S.W. (1976). *Language arts: A problem-solving approach.* New York: Harper & Row.

Lundsteen, S. W. (1989). *Language arts: A problem-solving approach.* New York: Harper & Row.

Manzo, A. V. (1969). The ReQuest procedure. *Journal of Reading, 13,* 123–126.

Martin, B., Jr. (2001). *And now the storyteller.* Keynote address presented at the Dallas Area Texas Association for the Improvement of Reading Conference, Dallas, TX.

Martin, B., Jr., & Sampson, M. R. (1994). *Touching tomorrow with language.* Pa-

per presented at the annual conference of the International Reading Association. Toronto, Canada.

Martin, B., Jr., & Sampson, M. R. (2002). *The sound of poetry.* Speech presented at the annual convention of the International Reading Association, San Francisco, CA.

Marzano, R. J., & A. L. Costa. (1988). Question: Do standardized tests measure general cognitive skills? Answer: No. *Educational Leadership 45*(8), 66–71.

McCarrier, A., Pinnell, G. S., & Fountas, I. C. (2000*). Interactive writing: How language & literacy come together, K–2.* Portsmouth, NH: Heinemann.

McCombs, B. L. (1991). Motivation and lifelong learning. *Educational Psychologist, 26(2),* 117–128.

McDanial, T. R. (1984). A primer on motivation: Principles old and new. *Phi Delta Kappan, 66*(2), 119–121.

McGee, L. E., & Richgels, D. J. (1996). *Literacy beginnings.* Boston: Allyn & Bacon.

McGuffee, M. (2001). *Web books for everyone.* Speech given at the International Institute of Literacy Learning Conference, Tampa, FL.

McIntyre, E., & Pressley, M. (Eds). (1996). *Balanced instruction: Strategies and skills in whole language.* Norwood, MA: Christopher-Gordon.

McNeil, L., & Valenzuela, A. (2000). *The harmful impact of the TAAS system of testing in Texas: Beneath the accountability rhetoric.* Cambridge, MA: Harvard University Civil Rights Project.

Messick, S. (1989). *Validity in educational measurement.* In R. Linn (Ed.), *Educational measurement* (3rd ed.). New York: Macmillan.

Meyer, B. J. (1975). *The organization of prose and its effects on memory.* Amsterdam: North Holland.

Meyer, B. J. (1979). Organizational patterns in prose and their use in reading. In M. L. Kamil & A. J. More (Eds.), *Reading research: Studies and applications. Twenty-eighth yearbook of the National Reading Conference* (pp.109–117).

Meyer, B. J., & Freedle, R. O. (1984). Effects of discourse type on recall. *American Educational Research Journal, 21,* 121–143.

Miyata, C. (2001). *Speaking rules!* Markham, ON: Pembroke.

Moffett, J. (1981). *Active voice.* Portsmouth, NH: Heinemann.

Moffett, J., & Wagner, B. J. (1983). *Student-centered language arts and reading, K–13: A handbook for teachers* (3rd ed.). Boston: Houghton Mifflin.

Morrow, L. M. (1992). *Literacy development in the early years: Helping children read and write* (2nd ed.). Boston: Allyn & Bacon.

Morrow, L. M., & Ashbury, E. (1999). Best practices for a balanced early literacy program. In L. Gambrell, L. Morrow, S. Neuman, & M. Pressley (Eds.), *Best practices in literacy instruction* (pp. 49–67). New York: Guilford.

Morrow, L. M., & Smith, J. K. (1990). *Assessment for instruction in early literacy.* Englewood Cliffs, NJ: Prentice-Hall.

Moss, B., Leone, S., & Dipillo, M. (1997). Exploring the literature of fact: Linking reading and writing through information trade books. *Language Arts, 74,* 418–429.

Murphy, S., & Smith, M. A. (1991). *Writing portfolios: A bridge from teaching to assessment.* Markham, Ontario: Pippin.

Murray, D. (1984). *Write to learn.* New York: Holt, Rinehart and Winston.

Murray, D. (1989). *Expecting the unexpected.* Portsmouth, NH: Heinemann.

Musser, B. (2002). *Books and activities to develop family literacy.* Paper presented at the Read Aloud West Virginia Conference, Charleston, WV.

Nason, J. (1983). *An investigation of the transition from oral language to written language of selected elementary students.* Unpublished doctoral dissertation, East Texas State University, Commerce, TX.

National Reading Panel. (2000). *Report of the National Reading Panel: An evidence-based assessment of the scientific research literature on reading and its implications for reading instruction.* Washington, DC: National Institute of Child Health and Human Development.

Neuman, S. B., & Roskos, K. (1997). Literacy knowledge in practice: Contexts of participation for young writers and readers. *Reading Research Quarterly, 32,* 10–32.

Newman, J. (1984). *The craft of children's writing.* New York: Scholastic.

Newman, J. (1989). *Finding our own way. Teachers exploring their assumptions.* Portsmouth, NH: Heinemann.

Nielsen, D. C., & Monson, D. L. (1996). Effects of literacy environment on literacy development of kindergarten children. *Journal of Educational Research, 89,* 259–271.

Nistler, R. J., & Maiers, A. (2000). Stopping the silence: Hearing parents' voices in an urban first-grade family literacy program. *Reading Teacher, 53*(8), 670–680.

Novick, R. (1999). Supporting early literacy development. *Childhood Education, 76,* 70.

Ogle, D. M. (1989). The know, want to know, learn strategy. In K. D. Muth (Ed.), *Children's comprehension of text* (pp. 205–223). Newark, DE: International Reading Association.

Opitz, M., & Rasinski, T. (1999). *Goodbye ROUND ROBIN: Twenty-five effective oral reading strategies.* Portsmouth, NH: Heinemann.

Orellana, M. F., & Hernandez, A. (1999). Talking the walk: Children reading urban environmental print. *The Reading Teacher, 52*(6), 612–619.

Osborne, J. (1997). *The Texas reading initiative.* Paper presented at the Southwest Regional Meeting of the International Reading Association, Fort Worth, TX.

Page, W. D., & Pinnell, G. S. (1979). *Teaching reading comprehension.* Urbana, IL: National Council of Teachers of English.

Palmer, R. G., & Stewart, R. (1997). Nonfiction trade books in content area instruction: Realities and potential. *Journal of Adolescent & Adult Literacy, 40*(8), 630–641.

Pappas, C. C. (1991), Fostering full access to literacy by including information books. *Language Arts, 68,* 449–462.

Pappas, C. C. (1993). Is narrative "primary"? Some insights from kindergartners' pretend reading of stories and information books. *Journal of Reading Behavior, 25,* 97–129.

Pearson, P. D., & Johnson, D. D. (1985). *Teaching reading comprehension.* New York: Holt, Rinehart and Winston.

Perfect, K. A. (1999). Rhyme and reason: Poetry for the heart and head. *The Reading Teacher, 52,* 728–737.

Perl, S. (1994). Composing tests, composing lives. *Harvard Educational Review 64*(4), 427–449.

Petre, R. M. (1969). *Quantity, quality and variety of pupil responses during an open-communication structured group Directed Reading-Thinking Activity and a closed-communication structured group Directed Reading-Thinking Activity.* Unpublished doctoral dissertation, University of Delaware.

Pflaum, S. W. (1986). *The development of language and literacy in young children* (3rd ed.). Columbus, OH: Merrill.

Phinney, M. (1989). *Reading with the troubled reader.* Portsmouth, NH: Heinemann.

Piaget, J. (1959). *The language and thought of the child* (rev. ed.). New York: Humanities Press.

Piccolo, J. (1987). Expository text structure: Teaching and learning strategies. *The Reading Teacher, 40,* 838–847.

Pils, L. J. (1991). Soon anofe you tout me: Evaluation in a first-grade whole language classroom. *The Reading Teacher, 45,* 46–50.

Pittelman, S. D., Heimlich, J. E., Berglund, R. L., & French, M. P. (1991). *Semantic feature analysis: Classroom applications.* Newark, DE: International Reading Association.

Queensland (Australia) Department of Education. (1994). *English in years 1 to 10, Queensland syllabus materials.* Brisbane, QLD: Queensland Education Department.

Raine, I. L. (1994). *Spelling is a developmental process.* Paper presented at the Center for Professional Development and Technology Conference, Commerce, TX.

Rankin, E. F. (1977). Sequence strategies for teaching reading comprehension with the cloze procedure. In P. D. Pearson & J. Hanson (Eds.), *Reading theory, research, and practice. Twenty-sixth yearbook of the National Reading Conference.* Washington, DC: National Reading Conference.

Rankin, P. T. (1928). The importance of listening. *English Journal, 19,* 623–630.

Rasinski, T., & Padak, N. (2000). *Effective reading strategies: Teaching children who find reading difficult.* Englewood Cliffs, NJ: Prentice-Hall.

Rasinski, T. V. (1999). Making and writing words. *Reading Online.* (an electronic journal available at www.readingonline.org/articles/words/rasinski.html)

Ratekin, N., Simpson, M., Alvermann, D., & Dishner, E. (1985). Why teachers resist content reading instruction. *Journal of Reading, 28,* 432–437.

Read, C. (1980). What children know about language: Three examples. *Language Arts, 57,* 144–148.

Readence, J. E., Bean, T. W., & Baldwin, S. R. (1998). *Content area literacy: An integrated approach* (6th ed.). Dubuque, IA: Kendall/Hunt.

Rhodes, L. K. (1979, May). *Visible language acquisition: A case study.* Paper presented at Twenty-fourth Annual Reading Association Convention, Atlanta, GA.

Rhodes, L. K. (1981). I can read! Predictable books as resources for reading and writing instruction. *Reading Teacher, 34,* 511–518. Newark, DE: International Reading Association.

Rief, L. (1990). Finding the value in evaluation; Self-assessment in a middle school classroom. *Educational Leadership, 47,* 24–29.

Robbins, C., & Ehri, L. C. (1994). Reading storybooks to kindergartners helps them learn new vocabulary words. *Journal of Educational Psychology, 86,* 54–64.

Rosenblatt, L. M. (1978). *The reader, the text, the poem.* Carbondale, IL: Southern Illinois University.

Rosenblatt, L. M. (1983). The reading transaction: What for? In R. P. Parker & F. A. Davis (Eds.), *Developing literacy. Young children's use of language* (pp. 118–136). Newark, DE: International Reading Association.

Rosenblatt, L. M. (1991). Literature—S.O.S. *Language Arts, 68*(6), 444–448.

Rosenblatt, M. (1993). *Reading as transaction.* Paper presented at the Federation of Northeast Texas Universities, Denton, TX.

Routman, R. (1988). *Transitions.* Portsmouth, NH: Heinemann.

Routman, R. (1991). *Invitations: Changing as teachers and learners.* Portsmouth, NH: Heinemann.

Routman, R. (1995). *Invitations: Changing as teachers and learners* (updated ed.). Portsmouth, NH: Heinemann.

Rumelhart, D. E. (1980). Schemata: The building blocks of cognition. In R. Spiro, B. Bruce, & W. Brewer (Eds.), *Theoretical issues in reading comprehension.* Hillsdale, NJ: Erlbaum.

Rumelhart, D. E. (1984). Understanding understanding. In J. Flood (Ed.), *Understanding reading comprehension* (pp. 1–20). Newark, DE: International Reading Association.

Sampson, M. R. (1997). Panel discussion. Retrieved May 6, 2002, at www.readingonline.org/critical/houston/panintro.htm#weaone.

Sampson, M. B. (2002). Confirming a K-W-L: Considering the source. *The Reading Teacher, 55,* 528–532.

Sampson, M. B., Sampson, M. R., & Linek, W. (1994). Circle of questions: Engaging students in interaction with text. *Reading Teacher, 47,* 543–545.

Sampson, M. R. (1982). A comparison of the complexity of children's dictation and instructional reading materials. In J. A. Niles & L. A. Harris (Eds.), *New inquiries in reading research and instruction. Thirty-first yearbook of the National Reading Conference* (pp. 177–179). Washington, DC: National Reading Conference.

Sampson, M. R. (Ed.). (1986). *The pursuit of literacy: Early reading and writing.* Dubuque, IA: Kendall/Hunt.

Sampson, M. R. (1997). Critical issues, critical connections. *Reading Online,* www.readingonline.org

Sampson, M. R. (2002). *Comprehending language.* Paper presented at the annual conference of the International Reading Association, San Francisco, CA.

Sampson, M. R., Allen, R. V., & Sampson, M. B. (1991). *Pathways to literacy: A meaning-centered perspective.* Fort Worth, TX: Holt, Rinehart and Winston.

Sampson, M. R., & Briggs, L. D. (1983). A new technique for cloze scoring: A semantically consistent method. *Clearing House, 57,* 177–179.

Sampson, M. R., Briggs, L. D., & Coker, D. R. (1984). Assessing the listening comprehension of children. *Reading Improvement, 21,* 59–63.

Sampson, M. R., Briggs, L. D., & Sampson, M. B. (1986). Language, children and text: Match or mismatch? In M. Sampson (Ed.), *The pursuit of literacy: Early reading and writing.* Dubuque, IA: Kendall/Hunt.

Sampson, M. R., & Sampson, M. B. (1980). Components of a language experience approach: Catalyst for change. *Journal of the National School Development Council, 9,* 10–14.

Sampson, M. R., & Sampson, M. B. (2001). *The language experience approach.* Paper presented at the conference of the International Institute of Literacy Learning, Louisville, KY.

Sampson, M. R., & Sampson, M. B. (2002). *Comprehension connections: 3 new strategies.* Paper presented at the conference of the International Institute of Literacy Learning, Tampa, FL.

Sampson, M. R., Sampson, M. B., & Allen, R.V. (1995). *Pathways to literacy: Process transactions.* Fort Worth, TX: Harcourt.

Sampson, M. R., Valmont, W. J., & Allen, R. V. (1982). The effects of instructional cloze on the comprehension, vocabulary, and divergent production of third-grade students. *Reading Research Quarterly, 17*(3), 89–99.

Sampson, M. R., & White, J. A. (1983). *The effect of student-authored, patterned language, and basal reader materials on the performance of beginning readers.* Final Report. Grant #1501-9309. Commerce, TX: Graduate School, East Texas State University.

Samuels, S. J. (1994). Toward a theory of automatic information processing in reading, revisited. In R. B. Ruddell, M. R. Ruddell, & H. Singer (Eds.), *Theoretical models and processes of reading* (4th ed., pp. 816–837). Newark, DE: International Reading Association.

Seaborg, M. B. (1994). Making the parent connection. In M. Sampson & T. Thomason (Eds.) *Reading, writing and literacy learning* (pp. 334–337). Dallas: Bridge Publishing.

Searfoss, L. W., & Readence, J. E. (1985). *Helping children learn to read.* Englewood Cliffs, NJ: Prentice-Hall.

Senechal, M., Cornell, E. H. (1993). Vocabulary acquisition through shared reading experiences. *Reading Research Quarterly, 28,* 360–374.

Senechal, M., LeFevre, J., Thomas, E., & Daley, K. (1998). Differential effects of home literacy experiences on the development of oral and written language. *Reading Research Quarterly, 33,* 96–116.

Senechal, M., Thomas, E., & Monker, J. (1995). Individual differences in 4-year-old children's acquisition of vocabulary during storybook reading. *Journal of Educational Psychology, 87,* 218–229.

Sharan, S. (1999). *Handbook of cooperative learning methods.* Westport, CT: Praeger.

Sharan, Y., & Sharan, S. (1990). Group investigation expands cooperative learning. *Educational Leadership, 47*(4), 17–21.

Short, E., & Ryan, E. (1984). Metacognitive differences between skilled and less skilled readers: Remediating deficits through story grammar and attributional training. *Journal of Educational Psychology, 76,* 225–235.

Sims Bishop, R. (1992). Multicultural literature for children: Making informed choices. In V. Harris (Ed.), *Teaching multicultural literature in grades K–8* (pp. 37–54). Norwood, MA: Christopher-Gordon.

Singer, H., & Donlan, D. (1983). Active comprehension: Problem-solving schema with question generation for comprehension of complex short stories. *Reading Research Quarterly, 17,* 166–185.

Skillings, M. J., & Ferrell, R. (2000). Student-generated rubrics: Bringing students into the assessment process. *Reading Teacher, 53*(6), 452–455.

Skinner, B. F. (1957). *Verbal behavior.* Boston: Appleton-Century-Crofts.

Slater, W. (1985). Teaching expository text structure with structural organizers. *Journal of Reading, 28,* 712–718.

Smith, E. B., Goodman, K. S., & Meredith, R. (1976). *Language and thinking in school* (2nd ed.). New York: Holt, Rinehart and Winston.

Smith, F. (1973). *Psycholinguistics and reading.* New York: Holt, Rinehart and Winston.

Smith, F. (1982). *Writing and the writer.* New York: Holt, Rinehart and Winston.

Smith, F. (1985). Demonstrations, engagements, and sensitivity: A revised approach to language learning. In M. R. Sampson, J. H. White, K. M. Feathers, & I. L. Rorie (Eds.), *Literacy and language instruction.* Lexington, MA: Ginn Press.

Smith, F. (1993). *Whose language? What power?* New York: Teachers College Press.

Smith, F. (2001). Just a matter of time. *Phi Delta Kappan, 82*(8), 572–576.

Snow, C. E., Burns, M. S., & Griffin, P. (1998). *Preventing reading difficulties in young children.* Washington, DC: National Academy Press.

Sommers, N. (1994). Revision strategies of student writers and experiences adult writers. In S. Perl (Ed.), *Landmark essays on writing process* (pp. 75–84). Davis, CA: Heragoras Press.

Spencer, P. L. (1970). *Reading reading.* Claremont, CA: Claremont College Press.

Spiegel, D. L. (1992). Blending whole language and systematic direct instruction. *The Reading Teacher, 46,* 38–44.

Stahl, S. A., & Murray, B. (1998). Issues involved in defining phonological awareness and its relation to early reading. In J. L. Metsala & L. C. Ehri (Eds.), *Word recognition in beginning literacy.* Mahwah, NJ: Lawrence Erlbaum.

Standards. (2002). Joint position statement of the IRA and NCTE. Retrieved May 6, 2002, from www.ira.org

Stauffer, R. G. (1969). *Directing reading maturity as a cognitive process.* New York: Harper & Row.

Stauffer, R. G. (1976). *Teaching reading as a thinking process.* New York: Harper & Row.

Stauffer, R. G. (1980). *The language-experience approach to the teaching of reading* (2nd ed.). New York: Harper & Row.

Stecher, B. M., Barron, S., Kaganoff, T., & Goodwin, J. (1998). *The effects of standards-based assessment on classroom practices: Results of the 1996–97 RAND Survey of Kentucky Teachers of Mathematics and Writing (CSE Technical Report 482).* Los Angeles: Center for Research on Evaluation, Standards, and Student Testing.

Steele, B. (1998). *Draw me a story: An illustrated exploration of drawing-as-language.* Winnipeg, Canada: Peguis Publishers.

Stetson, E., Seda, M., & Newman, C. (1988). *Spelling instruction: What research supports as effective.* Paper presented at the 78th Annual Conference of the National Council of Teachers of English, Boston, MA.

Stewart, R., & O'Brien, D. (1989). Resistance to content area reading: A focus on preservice teachers. *Journal of Reading 32*(5), 396–401.

Sulzby, E., Teale, W. H., & Kamberelis, G. (1989). Emergent writing in the classroom: Home and school connections. In D. S. Strickland & L. M. Morrow (Eds.), *Emergent literacy: Young children learn to read and write.* Newark, DE: International Reading Association.

Sutherland, Z. (1996). *Children and books.* Boston, MA: Addison-Wesley.

Taylor, D. (1983). *Family literacy: Young children learning to read and write.* Portsmouth, NH: Heinemann.

Taylor, D. (1986). *Family literacy.* Portsmouth, NH: Heinemann.

Taylor, W. L. (1953). Cloze procedure: A new tool for measuring readability. *Journalism Quarterly, 30,* 415–433.

Teale, W. H. (1982). Toward a theory of how children learn to read and write naturally. *Language Arts, 59,* 555–570.

Teale, W. H. (1984). Reading to young children: Its significance for literacy development. In H. Goelman, A. A. Oberg, & F. Smith (Eds.), *Awakening to literacy* (pp. 110–121). London: Heinemann.

Teale, W. H. (1986a). The beginnings of reading and writing: Written language development during the preschool and kindergarten years. In M. Sampson (Ed.), *The pursuit of literacy.* Dubuque, IA: Kendall/Hunt.

Teale, W. H. (1986b). Home background and young children's literacy development. In W. H. Teale & E. Sulzby (Eds.), *Emergent literacy: Writing and reading.* Norwood, NJ: Ablex.

Texas Education Agency. (1989). *TEAMS instructional strategies guide.* Austin, TX: Texas Education Agency.

Thomason, T. (1993). *More than a writing teacher.* Commerce, TX: Bridge Press.

Thomason, T. (1997). *Writer to writer: How to conference young authors.* Norwood, MA: Christopher-Gordon.

Thomason, T. (2002). Writer to writer: How to conference young authors. In M. Sampson & M. B. Sampson

(Eds.), *Total literacy for all learners* (p. 79). Dallas, TX: Bridge Press.

Thomason, T., & York, C. (2000). *Write on target: How to prepare young writers for success on state writing achievement tests.* Norwood, MA: Christopher-Gordon.

Thomason, T., & York, C. (2002). *Absolutely write!* Norwood, MA: Christopher-Gordon.

Thurber, D. N. (1987). *D'Nealian handwriting (Grades K–8).* Glenview, IL: Scott, Foresman.

Tiedt, I. M. (1983). *The language arts handbook.* Englewood Cliffs, NJ: Prentice-Hall.

Tierney, R. J., Carter, M., & Desai, L. (1991). *Portfolio assessment in the reading-writing classroom.* Norwood, MA: Christopher-Gordon.

Tierney, R .J., Johnston, P., Moore, D. W., & Valencia, S. W. (2000). Snippets: How will literacy be assessed in the next millennium? *Reading Research Quarterly, 35*(2), 244–250.

Tierney, R. J., Readence, J. E., & Dishner, E. K. (1995). *Reading strategies and practices: A compendium* (4th ed.). Boston: Allyn & Bacon.

Tierney, R. J., & Readence, J. E. (2000). *Reading strategies and practices: A compendium.* Boston, MA: Allyn & Bacon.

Toffler, A. (1980). *The third wave.* New York: Bantam.

Tompkins, G. E. (2003). *Literacy for the 21st century* (3rd ed.). Upper Saddle River, NJ: Prentice-Hall.

Trelease, J. (1989). *The new read-aloud handbook* (3rd ed.). New York: Penguin.

Trelease, J. (1995). *The new read-aloud handbook* (4th ed.). New York: Penguin.

Tuinman, J. J. (1979). Reading is recognition—When reading is not reasoning. In J. C. Harste & R. F. Carey (Eds.), *New perspectives on comprehension* (pp. 38–48). Bloomington: Indiana University School of Education.

Tyson, H., & Woodward, A. (1989). Why students aren't learning very much from textbooks. *Educational Leadership, 47,* 14–17.

Unia, S. (1985). From sunny days to green onions: On journal writing. In J. Newman (Ed.), *Whole language: Theory in use.* Portsmouth, NH: Heinemann.

Vacca, R. T., & Vacca, J. A. L. (1993). *Content area reading* (4th ed.). New York: HarperCollins.

Vacca, R. T., & Vacca, J. A. L. (1999). *Content area reading: Literacy and learning across the curriculum.* New York: Longman.

Vacca, R. T., & Vacca J. A. L. (2002). *Content area reading: Literacy and learning across the curriculum* (7th ed.). Boston, MA: Allyn & Bacon.

Valencia, S. (1990). A portfolio approach to classroom reading assessment: The why, whats, and hows. *Reading Teacher, 43,* 338–340.

Valencia, S. W., Hiebert, E. H., & Afflerbach, P. P. (Eds.). (1994). *Authentic reading assessment. Practices and possibilities.* Newark, DE: International Reading Association.

Valencia, S., McGinley, W., & Pearson, P. D. (1990). Assessing reading and writing. In G. Duffy (Ed.), *Reading in the middle school* (2nd ed., pp. 124–153). Newark, DE: International Reading Association.

Valencia, S., & Pearson, P. D. (1987). Reading assessment: Time for a change. *The Reading Teacher, 40,* 726–732.

Van Metre, P. (1972). *Syntactic characteristics of selected bilingual children.* Unpublished doctoral dissertation, University of Arizona, Tucson.

Vaughan, J. L. (1982). Instructional strategies and adolescents' reading: Research revelations. In A. Berger & H. A. Robinson (Eds.), *Secondary school reading: What research reveals for classroom practice.* Urbana, IL: National Council of Teachers of English.

Vaughan, J., & Estes, T. (1986). *Reading and reasoning beyond the primary grades.* Newton, MA: Allyn & Bacon.

Vaughn, S., Bos, C. S., & Schumm, J. S. (2000). *Teaching exceptional, diverse and at-risk students in the general education classroom.* Boston, MA: Allyn & Bacon.

Vopat, J. (1998). *More than bake sales: The resource guide to family involvement in education.* Portland, ME: Stenhouse.

Vygotsky, L. S. (1962). *Thought and language.* Cambridge, MA: The MIT Press.

Vygotsky, L. S. (1978). *Mind in society.* Cambridge, MA: Harvard University Press.

Vygotsky, L. S. (1981). The genesis of higher mental functions. In J. V. Wertsch (Ed.), *The concept of activity in psychology* (pp. 144–188). Armonk, NY: M. E. Sharpe.

Vygotsky, L. S. (1986). *Thought and language.* Cambridge, MA: Harvard University Press.

Walker, L. (2002). *Wonderful Word Walls.* Paper presented at the International Institute of Literacy Learning Conference, Tampa, FL.

Walker, V., & Brokaw, L. (1998). *Becoming aware* (7th ed.). Dubuque, IA: Kendal/Hunt.

Ward, G. (2001a). *Language for literacy.* Keynote address presented at the International Institute of Literacy Learning Conference, Louisville, KY.

Ward, G. (2001b). Will the real shared book experience please stand up? In M. Sampson & M. B. Sampson (Eds.), *Total literacy.* Dallas, TX: International Institute of Literacy Learning.

Ward, G. E. (1988). *I've Got a Project On . . .* Melbourne: Australian Reading Association.

Wardhaugh, R. (1971). Theories of language acquisition in relation to beginning reading instruction. In F. B. Davis (Ed.), *The literature of research in reading, with emphasis on models.* New Brunswick, NJ: Graduate School of Education, Rutgers University.

Webb, N., & Palinscar, A. (1996.). Group processes in the classroom. In D. C. Berliner & R. C. Calfee (Eds.), *Handbook of educational psychology* (pp. 841–873). New York: Simon & Schuster.

Weber, R. M. (1970). First graders' use of grammatical context in reading. In H. Levin & J. P. Williams (Eds.), *Basic studies in reading*. New York: Basic Books.

Wells, G. (1986). *The meaning makers*. Portsmouth, NH: Heinemann.

Whitin, P. (1996). *Sketching stories, sketching minds*. Portsmouth, NH: Heinemann.

Whitman, W. (1900). *Leaves of grass*. Philadelphia: David McKay.

Whitmore, K., & Goodman, K. (1996). Practicing what we teach: The principles that guide us. In K. Whitmore and Y. Goodman (Eds.), *Whole language voices in teacher education*. Urbana, IL: National Council Teachers of English.

Wickwire, M. (1990). Why teachers must be writers. In J. Newman (Ed.), *Finding our own way: Teachers exploring their assumptions*. Portsmouth, NH: Heinemann.

Wiggins, G. (1993). Assessment: Authenticity, context, and validity. *Phi Delta Kappan, 75*(3), 200–214.

Wiggins, G., & McTighe, J. (1998). *Understanding by design*. Alexandria, VA: ASCD.

Wiggins, R. A. (1994). Large group lesson/small group follow-up: Flexible grouping in a basal reading program. *The Reading Teacher, 47,* 450–460.

Witt, P. (2002). *Transitions for literacy: Finger plays, stories & songs*. Paper presented at the conference of the International Institute of Literacy Learning, Tampa, FL.

Wolf, D. Bixby, J., Glenn, J. III, & Gardner, H. (1991). To use their minds well: Investigating new forms of student assessment. In G. Grant (Ed.), *Review of research in education* (vol. 17). Washington, DC: American Educational Research Association.

Wuertenberg, J. (1990). *Writing is for celebration*. Paper presented at meeting of the International Institute of Literacy Learning, Seattle, WA.

Wurman, R. S. (1990). *Information anxiety*. London: Pan Books.

Wurman, R. S. (2000). *Information anxiety 2*. New York: QUE.

Yellin, D., & Blake, M. E. (1994). *Integrating language arts: A holistic approach*. New York: HarperCollins.

Yopp, H. K. (1995). A test for assessing phonemic awareness in young children. *The Reading Teacher, 49,* 20–29.

Yopp, H. K., & Yopp, R. H. (2000). Supporting phonemic awareness development in the classroom. *The Reading Teacher, 54,* 130–143.

Zaharias, J. A. (1983). Microcomputers in the language arts classroom: Promises and pitfalls. *Language Arts, 60,* 990–995.

Zebroski, J. T. (1994). *Thinking through theory: Vygotskian perspectives on the teaching of writing*. Portsmouth, NH: Boyton Cook.

CHILDREN'S BOOK REFERENCES

Ackerman, K. (1990). *The tin heart.* New York: Atheneum.

Adams, P. (1973). *There was an old lady who swallowed a fly.* New York: Child's Play International Ltd.

Adler, D. (1995). *A picture book of Rosa Parks.* New York: Holiday House.

Adler, D. (1998). *Shape up!* New York: Holiday House.

Adler, D. (1999). *How tall, how short, how far away?* New York: Holiday House.

Agee, J. (1998). *Who ordered the jumbo shrimp? And other oxymorons.* New York: HarperCollins.

Ahlberg, J., & Ahlberg, A. (2001). *The jolly postman.* New York: Little Brown Children's Books.

Albee, S. (2000). *The Oreo cookie counting book.* New York: Little Simon.

Alexander, L. (1991). *The remarkable journey of Prince Jen.* New York: E. P. Dutton.

Aliki. (1986). *How a book is made.* New York: Harper & Row.

Aliki. (1991). *How a book is made.* New York: HarperCollins.

Aliki. (2000). *William Shakespeare & the globe.* New York: HarperCollins.

Aliki, Bentley, N., & Guthrie, D. (2000). *The young journalist's book: How to write and produce your own newspaper.* Brookfield, CT: Millbrook.

Allard, H. (1977). *Miss Nelson is missing!* Boston: Houghton Mifflin.

Amato, M. (2000). *The word eater.* New York: Holiday House.

Ancona, G. (1999). *Carnaval.* Orlando: Harcourt Brace.

Anderson, J. (1991). *Christopher Columbus: From vision to voyage.* New York: Dial.

Angelou, M. (1998). *Life doesn't frighten me.* New York: Stewart Tabori & Chang.

Anno, M. (1986). *Anno's counting book.* New York: HarperCollins.

Atwater, R., & Atwater, F. (1976). *Mr. Popper's penguins.* New York: Little Brown.

Babbitt, N. (1999). *Tuck everlasting.* New York: Scholastic Trade.

Banks, L. (1980). *Indian in the cupboard.* New York: Avon Books.

Banyai, I. (1995). *Rezoom.* New York: Viking Children's Books.

Banyai, I. (1995). *Zoom.* New York: Viking Children's Books.

Banyai, I. (1997). *Rem.* New York: Viking Children's Books.

Barchers, S. (1993). *Reader's Theater for beginning readers.* Englewood, CO: Teachers Idea Press.

Barrett, J. (1978). *Cloudy with a chance of meatballs.* New York: Alladin.

Bauer, C. F. (2002). *Presenting Reader's Theater: Plays and poems to read aloud.* New York: H. W. Wilson.

Baur, J. (2000). *Hope was here.* New York: Putnam.

Baylor, B. (1978). *The other way to listen.* New York: Scribner's.

Behn, H. (1992). *Trees.* New York: Henry Holt.

Bentley, N., & Guthrie, D. (2000). *The young journalist's book: How to write and produce your own newspaper.* Brookfield, CT: Millbrook.

Bloom, B. (2001). *Wolf!* New York: Orchard Books.

Branley, F. M. (1998). *The planets in our solar system.* New York: Harper Trophy.

Branley, F. M. (1999). *Flash, crash, rumble, and roll.* New York: HarperCollins.

Brett, J. (1996). *The mitten.* New York: Putnam.

Briggs, R. (1978). *The snowman.* New York: Random House.

Brown, A. (1998). *Voices in the park.* New York: DK Publishing.

Brown, C. (1999). *Polkabats and octopus slacks: 14 stories.* New York: Houghton Mifflin.

Brown, M. W. (1947). *Goodnight moon.* New York: Harper & Row.

Brown, M. W. (1949). *The important book.* New York: Harper & Row.

Brown, M. W. (1975). *Goodnight, moon* (reissue edition). New York: HarperCollins.

Bruchac, J. (1997). *Thirteen moons on turtle's back.* New York: Paper Star.

Bruchac, J. (2001). *The journal of Jesse Smoke: A Cherokee boy, trail of tears.* New York: Scholastic.

Bryan, A. (1998). *Ashley Bryan's African tales, uh-huh.* New York: Atheneum.

Bunting, E. (2000). *Dreaming of America: An Ellis Island story.* Glen Ellyn, IL: Bridgewater.

Burleigh, R. (1991). *Flight. The journey of Charles Lindbergh.* New York: Philomel.

Burleigh, R. (2001). *I love going through this book.* New York: HarperCollins.

Burningham, J. (1989). *Hey! Get off our train.* New York: Crown.

Burns, M. (1994). *The greedy triangle.* New York: Scholastic.

Byars, B. (1977). *The pinballs.* New York: HarperCollins.

Calmenson, S. (2001). *The frog principal.* New York: Scholastic.

Carle, E. (1969 & 1987). *The very hungry caterpillar.* New York: Penguin Putnam.

Carle, E. (1976). *Do you want to be my friend.* New York: HarperTrophy.

Carle, E. (1986). *The grouchy ladybug.* New York: HarperCollins.

Carle, E. (1987). *A house for hermit crab.* Saxonville, MA: Picture Book Studio.

Carle, E. (1987). *The very hungry caterpillar.* New York: Philomel.

Carle, E. (1990). *The very quiet cricket.* New York: Philomel.

Carle, E. (1995). *The very busy spider.* New York: Putnam.

Carle, E. (2000). *Dream snow.* New York: Philomel.

Charlip, R. (1964). *Fortunately.* New York: Simon & Schuster.

Charlip, R. (1987). *Fortunately, unfortunately.* New York: Macmillan.

Chavarría-Cháirez, B. (2000). *Magda's tortillas ~ Las tortillas de Magda.* Houston, TX: Arte Publico Press.

Chavarría-Cháirez, B. (2001). *Magda's piñata magic ~ Magda y la piñata magico.* Houston, TX: Arte Publico Press.

Cherry, L. (1990). *The great kapok tree— A tale of the Amazon rain forest.* New York: Harcourt Brace.

Cherry, L. (1991). *A river ran wild.* San Diego: Harcourt Brace.

Christelow, E. (1995). *What do authors do?* New York: Clarion.

Christelow, E. (1999). *What do illustrators do?* New York: Houghton Mifflin.

Cleary, B. (1983). *Dear Mr. Henshaw.* New York: William Morrow.

Cleary, B. (1990). *Mouse & the motorcycle.* New York: Avon.

Cleary, B. P. (2000). *A mink, a fink, a skating rink: What is a noun? (Words are categorical).* Minneapolis, MN: Lerner.

Clement, R. (1994). *Counting on Frank.* New York: Houghton Mifflin.

Clifton, L. (1988). *Everett Anderson's goodbye.* New York: Henry Holt.

Cocca-Leffler, M. (1999). *Mr. Tanen's ties.* Morton Grove, IL: Albert Whitman.

Cohen, M. (1980). *First grade takes a test.* New York: HarperCollins.

Cohen, M. (1980). *No good in art.* New York: HarperCollins.

Cole, J. (1986). *The magic school bus at the waterworks.* New York: Scholastic.

Cole, J. (1986). *The magic school bus lost in the solar system.* New York: Scholastic.

Cole, J. (1987). *The magic school bus inside the earth.* New York: Scholastic.

Cole, J. (1990). *The magic school bus lost in the solar system.* New York: Scholastic.

Cole, J. (1999). *The magic school bus and the electric field trip.* New York: Scholastic.

Cole, W. (1981). *Poem stew.* New York: HarperCollins.

Collard, S. (1996). *Our natural homes.* Watertown, MA: Charlesbridge.

Collier, J. L. (1999). *With every drop of blood: A novel of the Civil War.* New York: Delacorte.

Cooper, F. (1998). *Coming home: From the life of Langston Hughes.* New York: Paper Star.

Cox, J. (2001). *Weird stories from the Lonesome Café.* New York: Harcourt Brace.

Crapsey, A. (1914). *Verse.* Rochester, NY: Manas Press.

Crews, D. (1978). *Freight train.* New York: Greenwillow.

Crews, D. (1985). *Bicycle race.* New York: William Morrow.

Crews, D. (1996). *Shortcut.* New York: Mulberry Books.

Cronin, D. (2000). *Click, clack, moo: Cows that type.* New York: Simon & Schuster.

Curtis, P. (1999). *Bud, not Buddy.* New York: Delacorte.

Cuyler, M. (2000). *100th day worries.* New York: Simon & Schuster.

Davis, K. C. (2001). *Don't know much about the solar system.* New York: HarperCollins.

Day, A. (1985). *Good dog, Carl.* New York: Simon & Schuster.

de Vos, G. (1996). *Tales, rumors, and gossip: Exploring contemporary folk literature with young adults.* Englewood, CO: Teachers Idea Press.

de Vos, G., & Altmann, A. E. (2001). *Tales, then and now: More folktales as literary fictions for young adults.* Englewood, CO: Teachers Idea Press.

Delacre, L. (1992). *Arroz con leche.* New York: Scholastic.

dePaola, T. (1978). *Pancakes for breakfast.* Orlando, FL: Harcourt Brace.

dePaola, T. (1981). *Now one foot, now the other.* New York: Sandcastle.

dePaola, T. (1985). *Tomie dePaola's Mother Goose.* New York: Putnam.

dePaola, T. (1986). *The legend of the bluebonnet.* New York: Penguin Putnam.

dePaola, T. (1996). *The legend of the Indian paintbrush.* New York: Penguin Putnam.

dePaola, T. (1999). *26 Fairmount Avenue.* New York: Penguin Putnam.

Dewey, A., & Aruego, J. (1998). *Five little ducks.* New York: Random House.

DiCamillo, K. (2000). *Because of Winn Dixie.* Cambridge, MA: Candlewick.

Dragonwagon, C. (1999). *This is the bread I baked for Ned.* New York: Simon & Schuster.

Duke, K. (1992). *Aunt Isabel tells a good one.* New York: E. P. Dutton.

Duke, K. (1996). *Aunt Isabel makes trouble.* New York: E. P. Dutton.

Ehlert, L. (1990). *Feathers for lunch.* New York: Harcourt.

Emberley, B. (1987). *The moon seems to change.* New York: HarperTrophy.

Essley, R. (1999). *Angels in the dust.* Seattle, WA: Bridgewater Books.

Evert, G. (1993). *John Brown: One man against slavery.* New York: Rizzoli International.

Facklam, M. (1990). *And then there was one.* Boston: Little, Brown.

Falwell, C. (1998). *Word wizard.* New York: Houghton Mifflin.

Feiffer, J. (1999). *Bark, George.* New York: HarperCollins.

Finchler, J. (2000). *Testing Miss Malarkey.* New York: Walker & Company.

Fleischman, P. (1991). *Time train.* New York: HarperCollins.

Fleischman, P. (1993). *Bull Run.* New York: HarperTrophy.

Fleischman, P. (1999). *Weslandia.* New York: Candlewick.

Fleming, V. (1993). *Be good to Eddie Lee.* New York: Putnam.

Florian, D. (1990). *Beach day.* New York: Greenwillow.

Florian, D. (1998). *Insectlopedia: Poems and paintings.* New York: Harcourt Brace.

Florian, D. (2000). *Mammalabilia: Poems and paintings.* New York: Harcourt.

Florian, D. (1990). *Beach day.* New York: Greenwillow.

Forbes, E. (1943). *Johnny Tremain.* New York: Bantam Doubleday Dell.

Fox, M. (1985). *Wilfrid Gordon McDonald Partridge.* New York: Kane/Miller.

Fradin, D. B. (1997). *The planet hunters: The search for other worlds.* New York: Margaret McElderry.

Frasier, D. (2000). *Miss Alaineus: A vocabulary disaster.* New York: Harcourt.

Freedman, R. (1987). *Lincoln: A photobiography.* New York: Houghton Mifflin.

Freedman, R. (2000). *Give me liberty: The story of the Declaration of Independence.* New York: Holiday House.

Fritz, J. (1973). *And then what happened, Paul Revere?* New York: Coward, McCann & Geogegan.

Fritz, J. (1974). *Why don't you get a horse, Sam Adams?* New York: Scholastic.

Fritz, J. (1975). *Where was Patrick Henry on the 29th of May?* New York: Putnam.

Fritz, J. (1982). *What's the big idea, Ben Franklin?* New York: Putnam.

Fritz, J. (1987). *Shh!! We're writing the Constitution.* New York: Putnam

Fritz, J. (1987). *The double life of Pocohontas.* New York: Viking.

Fritz, J. (1987). *Will you sign here, John Hancock?* New York: Scholastic.

Fritz, J. (1989). *The great little Madison.* New York: Scholastic.

Fritz, J. (1991). *Traitor: The case of Benedict Arnold.* New York: Penguin.

Fritz, J. (1993). *Just a few words, Mr. Lincoln: The story of the Gettysburg Address.* Los Angeles: Price, Stern, Sloan.

Fritz, J. (1994). *Harriet Beecher Stowe and the Beecher preachers.* New York: Putnam.

Fritz, J. (1995). *You want women to vote, Lizzie Stanton?* New York: Putnam.

Fritz, J. (1996). *Can't you make them behave, King George?* New York: Coward McCann.

Fritz, J. (2001). *Leonardo's horse.* New York: Putnam.

Froelich, M. W. (1995). *That Kookoory!* San Diego, CA: Browndeer.

Gardiner, J. R. (1980). *Stone Fox.* New York: Harper & Row.

Garland, B. (1993). *The lotus seed.* Orlando: Harcourt Brace.

Geis, D. (1982). *Dinosaurs & other pre-historic animals.* New York: Grossett & Dunlap.

George, K. O. (1997). *The great frog race and other poems.* New York: Clarion.

Gibbons, G. (1994). *The planets.* New York: Holiday House.

Giblin, J. (2001). *Fireworks, picnics, and flags: The story of the fourth of July symbols.* Boston: Clarion.

Giles, J. (1995). *Oh, how I wish I could read!* New York: United Publishers.

Ginsberg, M. (1972). *The chick and the duckling.* New York: Simon & Schuster.

Goble, P. (1987). *Death of the iron horse.* New York: Bradbury.

Goble, P. (1993). *The lost children.* New York: Macmillan.

Gollub, M. (2000). *The jazz fly.* Santa Rosa, CA: Tortuga.

Goode, D. (1988). *Cinderella.* New York: Knopf.

Graff, N. (1989). *Strength of the hills: A portrait of a family farm.* New York: Little Brown.

Green, R. G. (1997). *When a line bends . . . a shape begins.* New York: Houghton Mifflin.

Greenfield, E. (1995). *Honey, I love (let's read aloud).* New York: HarperFestival.

Griego, M. (1986). *Tortillitas para mama.* New York: Henry Holt.

Grossman, B. (2001). *Timothy Tunny swallowed a bunny.* New York: HarperCollins.

Guarino, D. (1990). *Is your mama a llama?* New York: Scholastic.

Guittier, B. (1999). *The father who had 10 children.* New York: Dial.

Haddix, M. P. (1999). *Just Ella.* New York: Simon & Schuster.

Hakim, J. (1994). *War, terrible war.* New York. Oxford University Press.

Hamilton, V. (1990). *Cousins.* New York: Philomel.

Hamilton, V. (2000). *The girl who spun gold.* New York: Blue Sky.

Hansen, J. (1997). *I thought my soul would rise and fly: The diary of Patsy, a freed girl.* New York: Scholastic.

Harness, C. (2001). *Remember the ladies: 100 great American women.* New York: HarperCollins Juvenile.

Heck, C. J. (2000). *Barking spiders and other such stuff: Poetry for children.* Pittsburgh, PA: Sterling House.

Heller, R. (1981). *Chicken's aren't the only ones.* New York: Putnam.

Heller, R. (1984). *Plants that never ever bloom.* New York: Penguin Putnam.

Heller, R. (1985). *How to hide a butterfly and other insects.* New York: Grosset & Dunlap.

Heller, R. (1985). *How to hide a polar bear and other mammals.* New York: Grosset & Dunlap.

Heller, R. (1986). *How to hide a crocodile and other reptiles.* New York: Grosset & Dunlap.

Heller, R. (1986). *How to hide an octopus and other sea creatures.* New York: Grosset & Dunlap.

Heller, R. (1986). *How to hide a whip-poor-will and other birds.* New York: Grosset & Dunlap.

Heller, R. (1987). *A cache of jewels: And other collective nouns.* New York: Grosset & Dunlap.

Heller, R. (1989). *Many luscious lollipops: A book about adjectives.* New York: Grosset & Dunlap.

Heller, R. (1990). *Merry-go-round: A book about nouns.* New York: Grosset & Dunlap.

Heller, R. (1991). *Up, up, and away: A book about adverbs.* New York: Grosset & Dunlap.

Heller, R. (1998). *Kites sail high: A book about verbs.* New York: Grosset & Dunlap.

Henkes, K. (1991). *Chrysanthemum.* New York: Greenwillow.

Hesse, K. (2001). *Witness.* New York: Scholastic.

Hest, A. (1998). *The great green notebook of Katie Roberts—Who just turned 12 on Monday.* Boston: Candlewick.

Hightower, S. (1997). *Twelve snails to one lizard: A tale of mischief and measurement.* New York: Simon & Schuster.

Hill, K. (2000). *The year of Miss Agnes.* New York: Simon & Schuster.

Hoberman, M. A. (2001). *It's simple, said Simon.* New York: Knopf.

Holt, K. W. (1999). *When Zachary Beaver came to town.* New York: Henry Holt.

Holt, K.W. (2001). *Dancing in Cadillac light.* New York: Putnam.

Holzer, H. (Ed.). (2000). *Abraham Lincoln the writer: A treasure of his greatest speeches and letters.* Honesdale, PA: Boyds Mills.

Houston, G. (1992). *My great-aunt Arizona.* New York: HarperCollins.

Hunt, I. (1981). *Across five Aprils.* New York: Berkley.

Isadora, R. (2000). *Listen to the city.* New York: Putnam.

Jackson, A. (1997). *I know an old lady who swallowed a pie.* New York: Penguin.

Jackson, E. (1994). *Cinder Edna.* New York: Lothrop, Lee & Shepard.

Jacques, B. (1998). *Redwall.* Boston: The Horn Book.

Jenkins, M. (1999). *The emperor's egg.* Boston: Candlewick.

Jenness, A., & Rivers, A. (1989). *In two worlds: A Yup'ik Eskimo family.* Boston: Houghton Mifflin.

Johnson, D. B. (2000). *Henry hikes to Fitchburg.* Boston: Houghton Mifflin.

Johnston, T. (1994). *Amber on the mountain.* New York: Puffin.

Jonas, A. (1983). *Round trip.* New York: Greenwillow.

Jonas, A. (1990). *Aardvarks, disembark.* New York: Greenwillow.

Jonas, A. (1990). *Color dance.* New York: HarperCollins.

Keats, E. J. (1962). *The snowy day.* New York: Viking.

Keats, E. J. (1964). *Whistle for Willie.* New York: Viking.

Keats, E. J. (1969). *Goggles.* New York: MacMillan.

Keats, E. J. (1972). *Pet show.* New York: MacMillan.

Kellogg, S. (1984). *A rose for Pinkerton.* New York: Dial Books for Young Readers.

Kellogg, S. (1984). *Paul Bunyan.* New York: William Morrow.

Kellogg, S. (1986). *Pecos Bill.* New York: William Morrow.

Kellogg, S. (1988). *Johnny Appleseed.* New York: William Morrow.

Kellogg, S. (1997). *The three little pigs.* New York: William Morrow.

Kellogg, S. (1999). *The three sillies.* Cambridge, MA: Candlewick.

Ketteman, H. (1998). *I remember papa.* New York: Dial.

King, M. R. (1997). *A good day for listening.* Ridgefield, CT: Morehouse.

Kohl, M. F., & Sogol, K. (1997). *Discovering great artists: Hands-on art for children in the style of the great masters.* Bellingham, WA: Bright Ring.

Kraus, R. (1970). *Whose mouse are you?* New York: Simon & Schuster.

Kraus, R. (1971). *Leo the late bloomer.* New York: Windmill Books.

Kraus, R. (1989). *Where are you going little mouse?* New York: William Morrow.

Kraus, R. (1994). *Leo the late bloomer* (reissue edition). New York: Harper-Collins.

Krull, K. (1994). *Lives of writers.* New York: Harcourt Brace.

L'Hommedieu, L. (1994). *Children of the sun.* Ojai, CA: Nivaria Press.

Lauber, P. (1989). *The news about dinosaurs.* New York: Bradbury.

Leedy, M. (1996). *Postcards from Pluto: A tour of the solar system.* New York: Holiday House.

Lester, H. (1997). *Author: A true story.* New York: Houghton Mifflin.

Lester, H. (1997). *Listen Buddy.* New York: Scott Foresman.

Lester, J. (1994). *John Henry.* New York: Dial.

Lewis, B. (2000). *I love you like crazy cakes.* Boston: Little Brown.

Lewis, C. (1950). *The lion, the witch and the wardrobe.* New York: Harper-Collins.

Lewis, J. P. (Ed.). (1999). *The bookworm's feast: A potluck of poems.* New York: Dial.

Lionni, L. (1990). *Frederick.* New York: Knopf.

Lionni, L. (1991). *Swimmy.* New York: Knopf.

Lobel, A. (1970). *Frog and toad are friends.* New York: HarperCollins.

Lobel, A. (1994). *Frog and toad.* New York: Harcourt.

Lord, B. (1984). *In the year of the boar and Jackie Robinson.* New York: HarperCollins Children's Books.

Louie, A. (1982). *Yen Shen: A Cinderella story from China.* New York: Putnam.

Lowry, L. (1990). *Number the stars.* New York: Houghton Mifflin.

Lowry, L. (1993). *The giver.* New York: Bantam Doubleday Dell.

Lowry, L. (2000). *Gathering blue.* Boston: Houghton Mifflin.

Lyon, G. E. (1999). *Book.* New York: DK Publishing.

Macaulay, D. (1988). *The way things work.* Boston: Houghton Mifflin.

MacLachlan, P. (1985). *Sarah, plain and tall.* New York: Harper & Row.

Maestro, B. C. (1999). *The story of clocks and calendars.* New York: Lothrop, Lee & Shepard.

Marrin, A. (1994). *Unconditional surrender: U. S. Grant and the Civil War.* New York: Atheneum.

Marrin, A. (1997). *Commander in chief: Abraham Lincoln and the Civil War.* New York: Dutton.

Martin, B., Jr (1967). *Brown bear, brown bear, what do you see?* New York: Henry Holt.

Martin, B., Jr (1991). *Polar bear, polar bear, what do you see?* New York: Henry Holt.

Martin, B., Jr (1996). *Fire! Fire! Said Mrs. McGuire.* New York: Harcourt.

Martin, B., Jr (1996). *Old devil wind.* New York: Voyager Books.

Martin, B., Jr (2003). *Panda bear, panda bear, what do you see?* New York: Henry Holt.

Martin, B., Jr (in press). *Yo Grocer.* New York: Henry Holt.

Martin, B., Jr, & Archaumbault, J. (1985). *Ghost eye tree.* New York: Henry Holt.

Martin, B., Jr, & Archaumbault, J. (1986). *Barn dance.* New York: Henry Holt.

Martin, B., Jr, & Archaumbault, J. (1987). *Knots on a counting rope.* New York: Henry Holt.

Martin, B., Jr, & Archambault, J. (1989). *Chicka chicka boom boom.* New York: Simon & Schuster.

Martin, B., Jr, & Archambault, J. (1991). *Chicka chicka boom boom* (paperback edition). New York: Simon & Schuster.

Martin, B., Jr, & Archambault, J. (1991). *Listen to the rain.* New York: Henry Holt.

Martin, B., Jr, & Archambault, J. (1997). *Knots on a counting rope* (paperback edition). New York: Henry Holt.

Martin, B., Jr, & Kellogg, S. (1999). *A beasty story.* New York: Harcourt.

Martin, B., Jr, & Sampson, M. (1996). *Si Won's victory.* Glenview, IL: Celebration Press.

Martin, B., Jr, & Sampson, M. (1997). *Swish!* New York: Henry Holt.

Martin, B., Jr, & Sampson, M. (2000). *Adam, Adam, what do you see?* Nashville, TN: Tommy Nelson.

Martin, B., Jr, & Sampson, M. (2001). *Little granny quarterback.* Honesdale, PA: Boyds Mills Press.

Martin, B., Jr, & Sampson, M. (2001). *The little squeegy bug.* New York: Winslow Press.

Martin, B., Jr, & Sampson, M. (2001). *Rock it, sock it, number line.* New York: Henry Holt.

Martin, B., Jr, & Sampson, M. (2002). *I pledge of allegiance.* Boston: Candlewick.

Martin, B., Jr, & Sampson, M. (2002). *Trick or treat.* New York: Simon & Schuster.

Martin, B., Jr, & Sampson, M. (in press). *All kinds of kids.* New York: Henry Holt.

Martin, B., Jr, & Sampson, M. (in press). *Bill Martin's big book of poetry.* New York: Simon & Schuster.

Martin, R. (1998). *Rough-face girl.* New York: Paper Star.

Massin, L. (1995). *Fun with numbers.* San Diego, CA: Creative Publications.

Matthews, T. L. (1998). *Light shining through the mist.* Washington, DC: National Geographic Society.

Mayer, M. (1967). *A boy, a dog and a frog.* New York: Puffin Pied Piper.

McDermott, G. (1977). *Arrow to the sun.* New York: Viking.

McGrath, B. (1994). *The M & M's brand chocolate candies counting book.* Watertown, MA: Charlesbridge.

McGrath, B. (2000). *The Cheerios counting book: 1, 2, 3.* New York: Scholastic.

Meddaugh, S. (1992). *Martha speaks.* Boston: Houghton Mifflin.

Micklethwait, L. (1999). *A child's book of art: Discover great paintings.* New York: Dorling Kindersley.

Milgrim, D. (1998). *Cows can't fly.* New York: Viking.

Minters, F. (1997). *Cinder Elly.* New York: Puffin.

Mochizuki, K. (1995). *Heroes.* New York: Lee & Low.

Moore, K. (1994). *If you lived at the time of the Civil War.* Boston: Houghton Mifflin.

Mora, P. (1997). *Tomas and the library lady.* New York: Random House.

Morgan, N. (1997). *Louis and the night sky.* New York: Random House.

Moss, Marissa. (2002). *Amelia lends a hand.* New York: Pleasant Company.

Most, B. (1992). *There's an ant in Anthony.* New York: Morrow, William & Co.

Munsch, R. (1983). *Mortimer.* Willowdale, Ontario, Canada: Annick Press.

Murphy, J. (1992). *The long road to Gettysburg.* Boston: Houghton Mifflin.

Murphy, J. (1993). *The boys' war: Confederate and Union soldiers talk about the Civil War.* Boston: Houghton Mifflin.

Murphy, S. J. (2000). *Pepper's journal: A kitten's first year.* New York: HarperCollins.

Nagda, A. W., & Bickel, C. (2000). *Tiger math: Learning to graph from a baby tiger.* New York: Henry Holt.

Naylor, P. (1991). *Shiloh.* New York: Bantam Doubleday Dell.

Nixon, J. L. (1995). *If you were a writer.* New York: Simon & Schuster.

Nolen, J. (1989, 1994). *Harvey Potter's balloon farm.* New York: Lothrop, Lee & Shepard.

Norton, M. (1976). *The borrowers.* New York: Harcourt Brace.

Numeroff, L. (1985). *If you give a mouse a cookie.* New York: HarperCollins.

Opie, I. A. (Ed.). (1999). *Here comes Mother Goose.* New York: Candlewick.

Osborne, M. (1991). *American tall tales.* New York: Knopf.

Oz, Charles. (1988). *How a crayon is made.* New York: Simon & Schuster.

Oz, Charles. (1988). *How does soda get into the bottle?* New York: Simon & Schuster.

Pallotta, J. (1991). *The underwater alphabet book.* Watertown, MA: Charlesbridge.

Pallotta, J. (2001). *Underwater counting even numbers.* Watertown, MA: Charlesbridge.

Parker, N. W., & Wright, J. R. (1987). *Bugs.* New York: Greenwillow.

Parks, R. (1997). *I am Rosa Parks.* New York: Dial.

Paulsen, G. (1987). *Hatchet.* New York: Aladdin.

Paulsen, G. (1996). *Hatchet.* New York: Simon & Schuster.

Peck, R. (1998). *A long way from Chicago.* New York: Dial.

Peck, R. (2000). *A year down yonder.* New York: Dial.

Peck, R. (2001). *A year down yonder.* New York: Dial.

Peet, B. (1959). *Hubert's hair-raising adventure.* Boston: Houghton Mifflin.

Peet, B. (1979). *Hubert's hair-raising adventure.* Boston: Houghton Mifflin.

Peet, B. (1989). *Bill Peet: An autobiography.* New York: Houghton.

Perrault, C. (1988). *Cinderella.* New York: Knopf.

Perrault, C. (1991). *Puss in Boots.* New York: Farrar, Straus, & Giroux.

Peters, L. W. (1991). *Water's way.* Boston: Arcade.

Pfeffer, W. (1997). *A log's life.* New York: Simon & Schuster.

Pfeffer, W. (1999). *Sounds all around (paperback edition).* New York: HarperCollins.

Pilkey, D. (1993). *Dogzilla.* Orlando, FL: Harcourt Brace.

Pilkey, D. (1993). *Kat Kong.* Orlando, FL: Harcourt Brace.

Pinczes, E. (1995). *A remainder of one.* Boston: Houghton Mifflin.

Pinkney, B. (1997). *Max found two sticks.* New York: Alladin.

Pinkney, J. (1999). *Hans Christian Anderson: The ugly duckling.* New York: William Morrow.

Pittman, H. (1998). *Sunrise.* San Diego, CA: Harcourt Brace.

Place, F. (1993). *The last giants.* Boston, MA: Godine.

Polacco, P. (1994). *Pink and Say.* Boston: Houghton Mifflin.

Pomeroy, D. (1997). *Wildflower abc.* New York: Harcourt Brace.

Potter, B. (1902). *The tale of Peter Rabbit.* New York: Penguin.

Potter, B. (1987). *The tale of Peter Rabbit.* New York: Penguin.

Prager, E. J. (2000). *Sand.* Washington, DC: National Geographic Society.

Prelutsky, J. (1983). *Random House book of poetry for children.* New York: Random House.

Prelutsky, J. (1984). *New kid on the block*. New York: Greenwillow.

Prelutsky, J. (2000). *It's raining pigs & noodles*. New York: Greenwillow.

Raffi. (1986). *Baby Beluga*. New York: Crown.

Raffi. (1999). *Five little ducks*. New York: Crown.

Rahaman, V. (1997). *Read for me, Mama*. Hinsdale, PA: Boyd Mills Press.

Rand, G. (1992). *Prince William*. New York: Henry Holt.

Rawls, W. (1961, 1992, 1996). *Where the red fern grows*. New York: Delacorte.

Rawls, W. (1981). *Where the red fern grows*. New York: Bantam.

Reavis, G. (1999). *The animal school*. Peterborough, NH: Crystal Springs.

Reit, S. (1988). *Behind rebel lines: The incredible story of Emma Edmonds, Civil War spy*. Boston: Houghton Mifflin.

Rice, J. (1988). *Texas alphabet*. New Orleans, LA: Pelican.

Rinaldi, A. (2001). *Girl in blue*. Boston: Houghton Mifflin.

Robinet, H. G. (1997). *Forty acres and maybe a mule*. Boston: Houghton Mifflin.

Rosenthal, P. (1998). *Yo Aesop! Get a load of these fables*. New York: Simon & Schuster.

Ross, R. (1994). *Eggbert the slightly cracked egg*. New York: G. P. Putnam's Sons.

Rowling, J. K. (1999). *Harry Potter and the chamber of secrets*. New York: Scholastic.

Ryan, P. (1996). *The flag we love*. Watertown, MA: Charlesbridge.

Ryan, P., & Pallotta, J. (1996). *The crayon counting book*. Watertown, MA: Charlesbridge.

Ryder, J. (1997). *Shark in the sea*. New York: William Morrow.

Rylant, C. (1982). *When I was young in the mountains*. New York: Dutton Children's Books.

Sachar, L. (1985). *Sideways stories from Wayside school*. New York: Avon.

Sachar, L. (1998). *Holes*. New York: Dell Yearling.

Sampson, M. (1999). *The football that won . . .* (First Owlet paperback edition). New York: Henry Holt.

Sampson, M., & Sampson, M. B. (1997). *Star of the circus*. New York: Henry Holt.

San Souci, R. (1989). *The talking eggs*. New York: Dial.

Say, A. (1993). *Grandfather's journey*. New York: Houghton Mifflin.

Schanzer, R. (1997). *How we crossed the west: The adventures of Lewis & Clark*. Washington, DC: National Geographic Society.

Schotter, R., & Brooker, K. (1999). *Nothing ever happens on 90th Street*. New York: Scholastic.

Schwartz, A. (1992). *And the green grass grew all around*. New York: HarperCollins.

Schwarz, D. (1995). *How much is a million?* New York: Lothrop, Lee, & Shepard.

Schwartz, D. (1998). *G is for googol: A math alphabet*. Berkeley, CA: Tricycle Press.

Schwartz, D. (1999). *If you hopped like a frog*. New York: Scholastic.

Schwartz, D. (2001). *Q is for quark: A science alphabet book*. Berkeley, CA: Tricycle Press.

Scieszka, J. (1992). *The stinky cheese man and other fairly stupid tales*. New York: Viking.

Scieszka, J. (1995). *Math curse*. New York: Viking.

Scieszka, J. (1998). *Summer reading is killing me*. New York: Viking.

Scieszka, J. (2001). *Baloney (Henry P.)*. New York: Viking.

Scillian, D. (2001). *A is for America*. Chelsea, MI: Sleeping Bear Press.

Sendak, M. (1963). *Where the wild things are*. New York: Harper & Row.

Seuss, Dr. (Theodor S. Geisel). (1957). *The cat in the hat*. New York: Random House.

Seuss, Dr. (Theodor S. Geisel). (1966). *McElligot's pool*. New York: Random House.

Seuss, Dr. (Theodor S. Geisel). (1970). *Bartholomew and the oobleck*. New York: Random House.

Seuss, Dr. (Theodor S. Geisel), with Prelutsky, J. (1998). *Hooray for Diffendoofer Day!* New York: Knopf.

Shannon, G. (1999). *Tomorrow's alphabet*. New York: Mulberry.

Showers, P. (1991). *The listening walk*. New York: HarperCollins.

Shulman, J. (Ed.). (2001). *You read to me & I'll read to you: Stories to share from the 20th century*. New York: Knopf.

Sierra, J. (2000). *The gift of the crocodile: A Cinderella story*. New York: Simon & Schuster.

Silverstein, S. (1974). *Where the sidewalk ends: Poems and drawings*. New York: Harper.

Simon, S. (1992). *Our solar system*. New York: Viking.

Sis, P. (1991). *Follow the dream: The story of Christopher Columbus*. New York: Knopf.

Smith, W. (2001). *Just the two of us*. New York: Scholastic.

Sneve, V. (1989). *Dancing teepees*. New York: Holiday House.

Sobel, S. (2000). *Presidential elections and other cool facts*. New York: Barrons Juveniles.

Soto, G. (1996). *Too many tortillas*. Glenview, IL: Scott Foresman.

Spinelli, J. (1990). *Maniac Magee*. Boston: The Horn Books.

Spinelli, J. (1998). *The library card*. New York: Scholastic.

Spinelli, J. (2000). *Stargirl*. New York: Knopf.

Spinelli, J. (2000). *Who put that hair in my toothbrush?* New York: Little Brown.

Steig, W. (1973). *Sylvester and the magic pebble*. New York: Simon & Schuster.

Steptoe, J. (1987). *Mufaro's beautiful daughters*. New York: Lothrop, Lee & Shepard.

Stevens, J. (1995). *From pictures to words: A book about making a book*. New York: Holiday House.

Stevens, J., & Crummel, S. S. (1999). *Cook-a-doodle-doo!* San Diego, CA: Harcourt Brace.

Stevenson, R. (1999). *A child's garden of verses* (revised edition). New York: Simon & Schuster.

Stewart, S. (1999). *The library*. New York: Farrar, Straus & Giroux.

Tang, G. (2001). *The grapes of math: Mind-stretching math riddles*. New York: Scholastic.

Taylor, M. (1976). *Roll of thunder, hear my cry*. New York: Puffin.

Taylor, M. D. (2001). *The Land*. New York: Puffin.

Terban, M. (1982). *Eight ate a feast of homonym riddle*. New York: Houghton Mifflin.

Terban, M. (1984). *I think I thought: And other tricky verbs*. New York: Clarion.

Terban, M. (1985). *Too hot to hoot: Funny palindrome riddles*. New York: Houghton Mifflin.

Terban, M. (1986). *Your foot's on my feet! and other tricky nouns*. New York: Clarion.

Thayer, E. (2000). *Casey at the bat*. Brooklyn, NY: Handprint.

Thoreau, H. D. (1854). *Walden, or life in the woods*. Boston, MA: Ticknor & Fields.

Toft, K. M., & Sheather, A. (1997). *One less fish*. St Lucia, Qld (Australia) University of Queensland Press.

Tompert, A. (1990). *Grandfather Tang's story*. New York: Crown.

Turkle, B. (1976). *Deep in the forest*. New York: Dutton.

Twain, M. (1987). *The adventures of Tom Sawyer*. New York: Viking.

Van Allsburg, C. (1982). *Jumanji*. Boston: Houghton Mifflin.

VanCleave, J. (2000). *Janice VanCleave's the solar system: Mind-boggling experiments you can turn into science fair projects*. New York: Puffin.

Vaughan, M. (2001). *The secret to freedom*. New York: Lee & Low.

Viorst, J. (1972). *Alexander and the terrible, horrible, no good, very bad day*. New York: Simon & Schuster.

Viorst, J. (1978). *Alexander, who used to be rich last Sunday*. New York: Macmillan.

Waber, B. (1972). *Ira sleeps over*. Boston: Houghton Mifflin.

Walton, R. (1995). *Once there was a bull . . . (frog)*. New York: Penguin Putnam.

Welden, A. (1999). *Girls who rocked the world: Heroines from Sacajawea to Sheryl Swoopes*. Hillsboro, OR: Beyond Words.

Wells, R. (2000). *Max cleans up*. New York: Viking.

Whatley, B. (2001). *Wait! No paint!* New York: HarperCollins.

White, E. B. (1952). *Charlotte's web*. New York: Harper.

Wiesner, D. (1988). *Free fall*. New York: Lothrop, Lee & Shepard.

Wiesner, D. (1990). *Hurricane*. Boston: Houghton Mifflin.

Wiesner, D. (1992). *Tuesday*. New York: Clarion.

Wiesner, D. (1999). *Sector 7*. New York: Clarion.

Wilbur, R. (2000). *The pig in the spigot: Poems*. New York: Harcourt Brace.

Wilder, L. (1971). *Little house in the big woods*. New York: HarperCollins.

Wilhelm, H. (1985). *I'll always love you*. New York: Crown.

Winthrop, E. (1985). *The castle in the attic*. New York: Holiday House.

Wolfe, G. (2002). *Oxford first book of art*. New York: Oxford University Press.

Wood, A. (1984). *The napping house*. San Diego, CA: Harcourt Brace.

Wood, A. (1985*). King Bidgood's in the bathtub*. San Diego, CA: Harcourt Brace.

Worth, V. (1994). *All the small poems & fourteen more*. Canada: HarperCollins.

Yolen, J. (1981). *Sleeping ugly*. New York: Coward.

Yolen, J. (1988). *The devil's arithmetic*. New York: Puffin.

Yolen, J. (1992). *Encounter*. San Diego, CA: Harcourt Brace.

Yolen, J. (1998). *The devil's arithmetic*. New York: Viking.

Young, E. (1989). *Lon Po Po: A Red Riding Hood story from China*. New York: Penguin Putnam.

Young, E. (1996). *Lon Po Po: A Red Riding Hood story from China*. New York: Paper Star.

Zelinsky, P. (1986). *Rumpelstiltskin*. New York: Dutton.

NAME INDEX

Ackerman, Karen, 477, 478, 479
Adams, Marilyn Jager, 123, 234
Adler, David, 504, 507
Afflerbach, P. P., 373, 394, 400
Agee, Jon, 353
Albee, S., 504
Aliki, 84, 312, 473
Allen, Claryce, 275
Allen, R. V., 203, 228, 277, 329, 393, 450
Allen, V. G., 361, 364, 367
Allington, Richard, 501, 502
Altmann, Anna E., 85
Altwerger, B., 391
Alvermann, D. E., 396, 468
Amato, Mary, 353
Anders, P. L., 132
Anderson, Janet, 504
Anderson, Joan, 478, 479
Anderson, P., 92
Anderson, R. A., 133
Anderson, R. C., 467
Anderson, T., 469, 484
Angelou, Maya, 223
Anno, M., 504
Archambault, John, 40, 84, 296
Areglado, N., 393
Armbruster, B. B., 468, 469, 484
Aronson, E., 28
Artiz, Juan, 101–102
Aruego, Jose, 458
Ashbury, E., 6
Ashley, Caroline, 302–303
Assaf, L., 377
Atwell, Nancy, 225, 228, 298, 459

Baghban, M. J. M., 48
Baldwin, L., 467
Baldwin, S. R., 468
Barbieri, M., 257
Barchers, Suzanne, 84
Barker, Deeanne, 271–272, 274, 512
Barnes, Carson, 252, 253
Barnes, Meredith, 495
Barron, S. I., 372
Bartlett, J. K., 28
Bauer, Caroline Feller, 85
Baur, Joan, 7
Baylor, Byrd, 94, 105
Bean, T. W., 468

Beck, I. L., 104
Beers, J. W., 324
Beesley, Scott, 314–315, 509, 510
Behn, Harry, 417
Bentley, A. E., 127
Bentley, Nancy, 312
Berglund, R. L., 192
Bettelheim, B., 131
Betterton, M., 391
Betts, E. A., 153
Bickel, Cindy, 496
Biemiller, A., 104
Bingham, A. A., 33
Bird, L. B., 381
Bishop, Rudine Sims, 151
Bissex, G. L., 48, 298, 324, 325, 511
Bixby, J., 393
Blachowicz, C. L., 186, 330
Blake, M. E., 263, 324, 364
Blankenship, Margaret, 313
Bloom, Becky, 132
Bloome, D., 130, 132
Bloomfield, L., 4
Boomer, Garth, 7
Bortnick, R., 203
Bos, C. S., 55
Bowman, Gary, 425, 511–512
Boyd, J., 441
Brandt, R., 394
Bransford, J. D., 134–135
Brent, R., 92
Bridge, Connie, 263
Briggs, L. D., 104, 116, 204
Brimer, R. W., 210
Britton, J. N., 391
Broad, K., 43, 155, 312, 418
Brokaw, L., 97
Brooker, Krysten, 310
Brown, Calef, 223
Brown, Edna, 490–491
Brown, Margaret Wise, 59, 512
Brown, Rita, 503
Browne, Anthony, 94
Bruchac, Joseph, 497
Bunting, Eve, 510
Burgess, T., 391
Burk, T. L., 92
Burke, Carolyn L., 7, 40, 43, 47, 48, 131,
    200, 213, 325

Burleigh, Robert, 6, 473–474
Burningham, John, 478
Burns, M. S., 145, 467, 504
Burton, Lila, 276
Button, K., 232
Buzzeo, T., 315, 317

Cairney, T. H., 3, 34
Calfee, R. C., 193, 393, 394
Calkins, Lucy M., 226, 227, 228, 243,
    294, 298, 300–301, 308
Calmenson, Stephanie, 265
Cambourne, B., 38, 120, 324
Canady, R. J., 7
Canzoneri, David, 105–106, 528–530
Carey, R. F., 44, 138, 377
Carle, Eric, 42, 268, 270, 416, 432, 471,
    507
Carlton, L., 81
Carter, M., 394
Caswell, L., 470
Chall, J. S., 467, 511
Chamot, A. U., 55
Chaney, A. L., 92
Chapin, Evan, 107
Charlip, Remy, 480, 482
Chase, P., 33
Chatton, B., 220
Chavarría-Cháirez, Becky, 236–237,
    427–429
Cheatham, Pam, 177–178
Cherry, Lynne, 98, 478, 480, 482
Chihak, J., 301
Chinn, P., 68
Chomsky, Carol, 6, 48, 94, 324
Chomsky, Noam, 6
Christelow, Eileen, 311
Clark, C., 150
Clark, Kayla, 379
Clark, L., 150
Clark, Roy Peter, 322, 330
Clarke, B. K., 33
Clay, Marie, 7, 40, 130, 393, 442
Cleary, Brian P., 352
Clem, C., 324
Clement, R., 507
Clemmons, J., 393, 394
Clifton, L., 151
Clyne, M., 450

Cocca-Leffler, Maryann, 397
Cohen, D., 105
Cohen, Miriam, 374, 396
Coker, D. R., 104
Cole, Joanna, 471, 473, 476
Collard, Sneed, III, 447
Collins, Conrad, 492
Collins, L. D., 220
Conard, S. S., 511
Condon, M., 313
Connell, Megan, 136
Cooper, D., 393
Cooper, Floyd, 316
Cornell, Charles, 399
Costa, A. L., 373
Covey, S., 97
Cox, Judy, 7
Cramer, R. L., 229, 256
Crane, Linda, 279
Crapsey, Adelaide, 280
Crews, Donald, 268, 507
Croll, V. J., 193
Cronin, Doreen, 6
Crosby, Lakeya, 327
Crummel, Susan Stevens, 447
Crump, Myra, 280
Cullinan, Bernice E., 70, 92, 430–431
Cunningham, J. W., 184, 346
Cunningham, P. M., 184, 346
Cuyler, Margery, 497

Dahl, K. L., 232
Daley, K., 46, 49
Dalton, J., 441
Daniels, H., 166
Davey, Beth, 179
Davis, Alice, 414, 416
Davis, Becky, 252
Davis, Lee, 490
DeFina, A., 393
DeFord, D. E., 119, 120
Delpit, Lisa, 298, 299
Denman, G. A., 70
dePaola, Tomie, 84, 390
Desai, L., 394
Dewey, J., 127
DeWolf, S., 150
Dicamillo, Kate, 7
Dickinson, D. K., 105
Dill, M., 393
Dipillo, M., 467, 468
Dippo, D., 232
Dishner, E. K., 212

Dixon, Reggie, 80
Doake, D., 40
Doan, J., 33
Donaldson, M., 132
Donlan, D., 193
Dorn, L. J., 6
Downes, T., 312
Dragonwagon, Crescent, 267
Drennan, Devalin, 111
Dudley-Marling, C., 312
Duke, Kate, 310
Duke, N., 470
Dunn, S., 70
Durham, J., 70
Durkin, D., 104, 141, 171, 245, 273
Duthie, C., 245
Dyson, A., 298

Eanet, M. G., 207, 212
Edgar, Judith, 99
Egielski, Richard, 265
Ehri, L. C., 105
Eisner, E., 373
Elley, W., 105
Embry, Judy, 363
Engle, Alan, 25–27, 73, 461
Engle, Arielle, 17
Engle, Patty, 25–27, 206, 461
Englert, C., 484
Erickson, F., 34
Essley, Roger, 496
Estes, Thomas, 190, 204, 484, 488
Evans, J., 242

Facklam, Margery, 478, 480
Falwell, Cathryn, 352
Farnsworth, L., 459
Farr, R., 377, 393, 395
Farris, P. J., 324
Fatouros, C., 312
Faulkner, William, 227
Feathers, K., 324
Feiffer, Jules, 264
Feitelson, D., 105
Ferell, R., 385
Ferreiro, E., 6, 49
Fielder, Dorothy, 106
Finchler, Judy, 396
Finley, Dee, 194–195
Fisher, P., 186, 330
Fleischman, Paul, 6, 473
Fleming, V., 151
Flesch, Rudolph, 161

Fletcher, Ralph, 226
Flood, J., 467
Flores, B., 391
Flores, Maria, 44
Flores, Rosalinda, 269–270
Florian, Douglas, 224, 471
Forsten, Char, 397
Fountas, Irene C., 231, 254
Fountoukidis, D. L., 332–334
Fox, S. E., 361, 364, 367
Frasier, Debra, 353
Freedman, R., 511
French, M. P., 192
Fresch, Mary Jo, 349
Fritz, Jean, 473, 475, 510
Froelich, Margaret Walden, 446
Fry, Edward, 331, 332–334, 335
Fuhler, C., 236
Furgerson, P., 232
Furth, Hans G., 54

Galda, L., 92
Gallegos, George, 282
Gantos, Jack, 95, 237
Gardiner, John Reynolds, 7, 295
Gardner, H., 178, 393, 394
Garza, Juana, 507
Gee, James, 484
Geis, Darlene, 192
George, Kristin O'Connell, 224
Giacobbe, Mary Ellen, 295
Giblin, J., 511
Giles, John, 132
Glasser, W., 90, 391, 394, 398
Glenn, J., III, 393
Goakum, Caitlin, 483
Goble, Paul, 477–478
Goldstein, Z., 105
Gollnick, D., 68
Gollub, Matthew, 95
Gonzales, Johnny, 249–252
Good, Jane, 230–231
Goodman, K. S., 119, 120, 130, 133, 352, 357, 364
Goodman, Y. A., 119, 120, 352
Goodman, Yetta M., 40, 42, 43, 129, 131, 132, 141, 382, 394, 454
Goodwin, J., 372
Gordon, C. J., 193
Gore, Julia, 242–243
Graff, Nancy Price, 510
Grant, Jim, 397
Graves, B. B., 161

Graves, D., 393, 394, 395
Graves, Donald H., 69, 220, 222–223, 224, 225, 229, 245, 256, 257, 297, 310, 360, 378
Graves, M. F., 161
Green, R. G., 504
Greenfield, Eloise, 222
Griffin, P., 145, 467
Griffiths, R., 450
Grossman, Bill, 222
Guccini, Gina, 61
Guettier, Benedicte, 264
Guthrie, Donna, 312

Haddix, Margaret Peterson, 265
Hamilton, L. S., 372
Hamilton, Virginia, 7, 265
Hammarskjöld, Dag, 518–519
Haney, W., 373
Hansen, J., 222–223, 224, 389, 393, 394
Harness, Cheryl, 497
Harp, B., 393
Harris, T. H., 160
Harris-Sharples, S. H., 511
Harste, Jerry C., 7, 40, 43, 44, 47, 48, 117, 138, 139, 200, 212, 213, 325, 395
Hart, Katie, 241–242
Harwayne, Shelley, 294
Hauser, R. M., 373
Head, M. H., 199
Heald-Taylor, G., 387
Heard, G., 69
Heath, S. B., 46, 49
Heather, Gail, 315
Heck, C. J., 222
Heimlich, J. E., 192
Heller, Ruth, 353, 356, 446, 459
Henderson, E. H., 324
Henderson, Kim, 118
Hendricks, T., 278
Hernandez, A., 40
Hernandez, Maria, 60
Hesse, Karen, 477
Hest, Amy, 311
Heubert, J. P., 373
Hicks, Jim, 508
Hiebert, E. H., 373, 394, 467, 484
Hightower, S., 507
Hill, Kirpatrick, 354
Hittleman, D. R., 192
Hoberman, Mary Ann, 200
Hodges, R. E., 160
Hoffman, J. V., 377

Holdaway, D., 43, 52, 53, 130, 181
Holt, Kimberly Willis, 85, 201
Holubec, E. J., 27
Holzer, Harold, 310
Hopkins, Lee Bennett, 277
Horowitz, R., 470, 484
Hotchkiss, P., 28
Houser, Sally, 158
Howard, Laura, 86–87
Hubbard, R., 304
Huck, Charlotte, 431
Hunsaker, R. A., 92

Idol-Maestas, L., 193
Iraqi, J., 105
Isadora, Rachel, 94

Jacobs, V., 467
Jenkins, C. B., 315
Jenkins, L., 203
Jenkins, Martin, 58
Jenness, Aylett, 477
Johnson, D. B., 477
Johnson, D. D., 126, 377
Johnson, Debby, 295–296
Johnson, D. W., 27, 28
Johnson, F. P., 27, 28
Johnson, M. J., 232
Johnson, R. T., 27, 28
Johnston, Francine, 335
Johnston, P., 377, 400
Jones, Charles, 31
Juel, C., 161

Kagan, S., 28
Kaganoff, T., 372
Kamberelis, G., 228
Kamil, C., 324, 325, 329
Kamler, B., 48
Karchmer, R. A., 312
Kasten, W. C., 33, 378, 425
Keats, Ezra Jack, 59
Kellogg, Steven, 168, 262, 264, 270
Kelly, P. A., 455
Ketteman, Helen, 200
Kilcup, Rick, 77, 426, 528
King, Mary Ellen, 95
King Dail, A., 130
Klein, S. P., 372
Kohl, M. F., 497
Kohn, A., 391
Koretz, D., 372
Kraus, Robert, 59, 271
Kress, J., 332, 332–334

Laase, L., 393
LaBerge, D., 132
Labov, W., 5
Landis, D., 132, 391
Lapp, D., 467
Larrick, Nancy, 256
Lauber, Patricia, 477
Lefevre, C. A., 352
LeFevre, J., 46, 49
Leone, S., 467, 468
Lester, Helen, 94, 311
Leu, D. J., 312
Levingston, Ceretha, 176
Levstik, L. S., 469
Lewis, J. Patrick, 223
Lewis-White, Linda, 239–240
Lindfors, J. W., 84
Lindgren, H. C., 28
Linek, W., 191
Linn, R. L., 372
Lolli, E. M., 33
Lopardo, G. S., 203
Lovelace, Ann, 507
Lowry, Lois, 26, 147, 201, 295, 510
Lundsteen, S. W., 92, 97
Lyon, George Ella, 132
Lyons, Lois, 493–494

MacLachlan, Patricia, 420
Maestro, Betsy C., 497
Mahy, Margaret, 168
Maiers, A., 33
Manzo, A. V., 201, 202, 207, 212
Martin, Bill, Jr, 5, 20, 40, 58, 59, 70, 76, 84, 92, 125, 140, 146, 163, 168, 200, 220, 241, 262, 264, 265, 266, 268, 296, 328, 413, 431, 507, 511, 530–532
Martin, Michael, 503
Martin, N., 391
Marzano, R. J., 373
Massin, L., 504
Matthews, Tom L., 497
Mattox, Laurie, 187–189, 190
McCaffrey, D. F., 372
McCarrell, N. S., 134–135
McCarrier, A., 231, 232
McCombs, B. L., 394
McDanial, T. R., 27
McGee, L. E., 38, 43
McGinley, W., 394
McGrath, B., 504
McGuffee, Michael, 313

McIntyre, E., 232
McKeown, M. G., 104
McLeod, A., 391
McNeil, L., 372
McTighe, J., 394
Menotti, Judy, 453
Meredith, R., 119, 352, 364
Merillen, Heather, 60
Merrill, Jean, 147
Messick, S., 375
Methven, Randy, 23, 24, 25, 416–418
Meyer, B. J., 469, 484
Micklethwait, L., 497
Milgrim, David, 200
Miller, Mary, 510
Milne, A. A., 416–417
Miyata, C., 84
Moffett, J., 92, 221
Monker, J., 105
Monson, D. L., 43
Moore, D. W., 184, 377, 396, 468
Moore, Jane, 108
Moore, R. H., 81
Moore, S. A., 184
Mora, Pat, 133
Morehouse, Ian, 233
Morrow, L. M., 6, 46, 49, 377
Moss, B., 467, 468
Moss, Marissa, 96
Most, Bernard, 352
Murphy, Jim, 510
Murphy, S., 395
Murphy, S. J., 473
Murray, B., 44
Murray, Donald, 221, 229, 257

Nagda, Ann Whitehead, 496
Naizet, Michael, 285
Nason, J., 104
National Reading Panel, 120, 122, 170, 501
Neal, April, 415
Neuman, S. B., 43
Newman, Judith, 257, 389
Newman, J., 239
Nguyen, Vi, 392
Nielsen, D. C., 43
Nistler, R. J., 33
Nixon, Joan Lowery, 311
Noland, Stephanie, 292–293
Norton, J. L., 400
Nottingham, Bob, 294
Novick, R., 49
Numeroff, Laura, 270–271

O'Brien, D., 373
Ogle, Donna M., 196
Opie, Iona Archibald, 222
Opitz, M., 97, 133
Orellana, M. F., 40
Osborne, J., 163
Oz, Charles, 473

Padak, N., 85
Page, W. D., 7
Palinscar, A., 94
Pallotta, Jerry, 471, 472, 504
Palmer, R. G., 468
Palmer, Shan, 282
Pappas, C. C., 468
Paris, S. G., 377
Park, Linda Sue, 96
Parks, Rosa, 474
Parnall, Peter, 105
Patrick, C. L., 193
Patterson, Patricia, 491–492
Patterson, Rachel, 111
Paulsen, Gary, 213, 214
Pearce, Kim, 277
Pearson, P. D., 126, 133, 193, 377, 378, 394
Peck, Richard, 201, 295
Peet, Bill, 474
Pennington, J., 377
Perez, Angel, 317–318
Perfect, K. A., 71
Perl, S., 225
Petre, R. M., 184
Pfeffer, Wendy, 94
Pflaum, S. W., 6, 38
Phinney, M., 130
Piaget, Jean, 54, 116
Piccolo, J., 469, 484
Pils, L. J., 395
Pinczes, E., 507
Pinnell, Gay Su, 7, 231, 254
Pittelman, S. D., 192
Pittman, H., 504
Polacco, Patricia, 146
Prager, Ellen J., 496
Prelutsky, Jack, 223, 396
Pressely, M., 232

Queensland Department of Education, 450

Rabb, Eli W., 185
Raffi, 507
Rahaman, Vashanti, 132

Raine, I. L., 326
Rand, Gloria, 482
Rand, Ted, 180
Randazzo, M., 324, 325, 329
Rankin, E. F., 203
Rankin, Paul, 92
Rasinski, Timothy V., 85, 97, 133, 346, 347, 532–534
Read, C., 38, 324
Read, Jennifer, 336
Readence, J. E., 83, 184, 199, 201, 202, 203, 212, 468
Reavis, George, 397
Reeves, Lisa, 140
Reif, L., 257
Rhodes, L. K., 48, 263
Rice, James, 471
Richgels, D. J., 38, 43
Rief, L., 396
Riojas, Sylvia, 382
Rivers, Alice, 477
Robbins, C., 105
Rosen, H., 391
Rosenblatt, L. M., 127–128, 132, 138, 139, 140, 468
Rosenblatt, M., 132
Rosenthal, Paul, 266
Roskos, K., 43
Routman, Regie, 34, 238
Rumelhart, D. E., 127, 134
Ryan, E., 193
Ryan, P., 504, 511
Rylant, Cynthia, 95

Sampson, Mary Beth, 58, 116, 136, 176, 178, 191, 197, 229, 271, 329, 393, 470
Sampson, Michael R., 40, 58, 65, 70, 85, 104, 116, 120, 125, 128, 136, 138, 139, 140, 163, 176, 178, 191, 200, 203, 204, 208–209, 220, 229, 264, 267, 271, 329, 351–352, 393, 450, 507, 511
Samuels, S. J., 132, 133
Sanders, Ralph, 225
Santana, Hugo, 87
Santana, Josh, 249, 250
Scala, M. C., 70
Schanzer, Rosalyn, 496
Schmidt, Jonathan, 245–246
Schotter, Roni, 310
Schroder, V. C., 70
Schumm, J. S., 55
Schwartz, David, 447, 471, 496

Scieszka, Jon, 133, 503
Scillian, D., 510–511
Scott, J. A., 467
Scribner, Terry, 491
Seaborg, M. B., 34
Searfoss, L. W., 203
Self, Daniel, 159
Sendak, Maurice, 262
Senechal, M., 46, 49, 105
Seuss, Dr., 396
Shannon, G., 478, 480
Sharan, S., 27, 29
Sharan, Y., 29
Share, D., 105
Sheather, Allan, 446
Short, E., 193
Short, K., 200, 213
Showers, Paul, 94
Shulman, Janet, 6
Shumway, JenAnne, 121
Sierra, Judy, 264
Singer, H., 193
Sis, Peter, 478
Skillings, M. J., 385
Skinner, B. F., 3–5
Slater, W., 470
Slavin, R.S., 27
Smith, E. B., 119, 352, 364
Smith, Frank, 6, 116, 119, 127, 131,
    221–222, 262, 329
Smith, Jeannie, 60
Smith, J. K., 377
Smith, M. A., 395
Smith, M. W., 105
Smith, Robert K., 95
Smith, Sue, 182–183
Snow, C. E., 145, 467
Sobel, Syl, 498
Soffos, C., 6
Sogol, K., 497
Sommers, N., 227
Sonata, Josh, 313–314
Spencer, Peter, 21, 54, 56, 116
Spiegel, D. L., 171
Spinelli, Jerry, 133, 199, 201
Stahl, S. A., 44
Standards, 18, 19
Stauffer, R. G., 84, 182
Stecher, B. M., 372, 378
Steele, B., 21
Stevens, Janet, 311, 447
Stewart, R., 373, 468
Stewart, Sarah, 133

Strickland, D. S., 92
Stuart, Virginia, 297
Sulzby, E., 228
Sunstein, B., 393, 394, 395
Sutherland, Zena, 431

Tang, Gregg, 498
Taylor, Bobbi, 350
Taylor, D., 47, 49
Taylor, W. L., 203
Teale, W. H., 40, 46–47, 104, 228, 450
Teberosky, A., 6, 49
Terban, Marvin, 352, 353, 356
Texas Education Agency, 387
Thomas, E., 46, 49, 105
Thomason, Debby, 432
Thomason, Tommy, 228, 257, 295, 296,
    299, 300, 308, 384
Thurber, Donald, 364, 366
Tiedt, Iris M., 284
Tierney, R. J., 83, 184, 201, 202, 203, 212,
    377, 394, 395
Toffler, A., 312
Toft, Kim Michelle, 446
Tollison, Susan, 328
Tompkins, G. E., 119
Tone, B., 393, 395
Trelease, J., 104
Tuinman, J. J., 141
Turbill, J., 324
Turner, Jarred, 293
Twain, Mark, 296
Tyson, H., 468

Unia, S., 235

Vacca, J. A. L., 28, 468
Vacca, R. T., 468
Valdez, Marcella, 507
Valencia, S. W., 373, 377, 378, 394
Valenzuela, A., 372
Valmont, W. J., 203
Van Allen, Roach, 19, 88, 117
Van Allsburg, Chris, 147
Van Metre, Patricia, 94
Vaughan, Joseph L., 190, 204, 207, 484,
    488
Vaughan, M., 482
Vaughan, S., 55
Villemare, J., 132
Viorst, Judith, 507
Vopat, J., 35
Vos, Gail de, 85

Vygotsky, L. S., 27, 47, 94, 220–221,
    484

Wagner, B. J., 92
Walker, L., 343
Walker, V., 97
Walton, Rick, 352
Ward, Cherry, 455
Ward, Geoff E., 181, 203, 227, 399, 444,
    447, 454
Ward, Sue, 508
Wardhaugh, R., 4
Webb, N., 94
Weber, R. M., 131
Welch, Kimberly, 125–126
Welden, A., 474
Wells, G., 40, 49, 104
Wells, Rosemary, 58, 222
Welsh, Christopher, 41
Whatley, Bruce, 265
Wheaton, Aileen, 349
White, J. A., 128, 139
Whitin, P., 21
Whitman, Walt, 54
Whitmore, K., 133
Wickwire, M., 257
Wiggins, Grant, 375, 376, 394
Wiggins, R. A., 165
Wilbur, Richard, 223
Wilkinson, I. A. G., 467
Winston, P. J., 443
Witt, Paula, 31, 48, 95, 100–101
Wolf, D., 393
Wolfe, G., 497
Wood, Audrey, 146, 268
Wood–Brady, Esther, 147
Woodward, A., 468
Woodward, V. A., 7, 40, 43, 47, 48, 325
Wrightman, Tom, 22–23
Wuertenberg, Jacque, 229
Wurman, R. S., 441, 461

Yellin, D., 263, 324, 364
Yolen, Jane, 265, 478, 479, 510
Yopp, Hallie K., 45
Yopp, R. H., 45
York, C., 295, 308
Young, Ed, 146

Zaharias, J. A., 312
Zebroski, J. T., 94
Zelan, K., 131
Zimmerman, Belinda, 169

SUBJECT INDEX

Abraham Lincoln the Writer: A Treasury of His Greatest Speeches and Letters (Holzer), 310

Absolutely Write! (Thomason & York), 295

accountability, 168, 170

acquisition activities, 14–15

action research, 453–454

Advance, The, 430

The Adventures of Tom Sawyer (Twain), 296

aesthetic reading, 140–41, 468

aesthetic sensibility, 10

African Americans
 literature, 344
 vernacular English, 68

A Is for America (Scillian), 510–511

Alexander, Who Used to Be Rich Last Sunday (Viorst), 507

Allen word list, 309

alliteration, 45, 122–123

All Kinds of Kids (Martin & Sampson), 264

alphabet, 38–40, 234

alphabetical arrangement, 495–496

Amelia Lends a Hand (Moss), 96

analytical phonics, 159–160

And Then There Was One (Facklam), 478, 480, 481

anecdotal records, 381–382

Angels in the Dust (Essley), 496

The Animal School, (Reavis), 397

Anno's Counting Book (Anno), 504

annotations, 207–212

anticipation–reaction guides, 199

appreciation of others' writing, 10

approximal stage of spelling, 326

The Armadillo from Amarillo, (Cherry), 98

art
 and content area literacy, 497–500, 502
 and early literacy, 50
 as element of language arts, 21
 illustrations, 215, 304–306, 421
 RISE procedure, 178–179
 sketch to stretch strategy, 212–213

Asian Americans
 diversity among, 278
 literature, 345

assessment, 372–410
 and basal reading programs, 152
 holistic evaluation criteria, 387–389
 interactive, 382, 384–385
 observation, 141, 380–382, 383
 portfolios, 393–399
 program evaluation, 400, 407–410
 reading comprehension, 141
 report cards, 400, 401–406

running records, 392–393

self-evaluation, 389–392

standardized testing, 372–378, 380

theme cycles, 449–450, 456

work samplings, 385, 387–388

at-home activities. *See* homework

attention, 132–133

Aunt Isabel Makes Trouble (Duke), 310

Aunt Isabel Tells a Good One (Duke), 310

Australia, 462–463

Author: A True Story (Lester), 311

author/illustrator studies, 431–436
 Jose Aruego, 458
 Eric Carle, 42
 Becky Chavarría-Cháirez, 236–237
 Lynne Cherry, 98
 Floyd Cooper, 316
 Donald Crews, 268
 Tomie dePaola, 390
 Ruth Heller, 356
 Gloria Houston, 78
 Steven Kellogg, 168
 Patricia MacLachlan, 420
 Bill Martin Jr, 20
 Jerry Pallotta, 472
 Brian Pinkney, 138
 Ted Rand, 180
 videos, 435–436
 Web sites, 433–435

Author's Chair, 222

automaticity, 132–133

Bark, George (Feiffer), 264

Barking Spiders and Other Such Stuff: Poetry for Children (Heck), 222

Barn Dance (Martin), 20

basal reading programs, 145–172
 appropriate roles for, 166, 168–172
 and children's literature, 424–425
 current versions, 164
 and diversity issues, 161, 164
 and inconsiderate text, 137–138
 linguistic basals, 161–162
 "look-say" method, 158–161
 program elements, 146–153
 and readability, 147, 162, 167
 teaching methods, 153–158
 and whole language approach, 162–164

A Beasty Story (Martin), 168, 262

Because of Winn-Dixie (Dicamillo), 7

Be Good to Eddie Lee (Fleming), 151

behaviorism, 3–6

Bicycle Race (Crews), 507

big books
 and basal reading programs, 147–148
 shared book experience, 181, 182–183

Bigmama's (Crews), 268

Bilingual Education Act (1968), 55

bilingual students, 236–237
 and children's literature, 427–428
 dialogue journals, 239
 See also English Language Learners

Bill Peet: An Autobiography (Peet), 474

biographies, 422, 473

A Blue-Eyed Daisy (Rylant), 95

Book (Lyon), 132

Book Alert, 430

book binding, 306, 307

book clubs. *See* literature discussion groups

book jacket activity, 216

Book Links, 430

Booklist, 430

book reviews, 216

The Bookworm's Feast: A Potluck of Poems (Lewis), 223

boredom, 97

The Boy's War (Murphy), 510

The Boy Who Was Followed Home (Mahy), 168

brainstorming, 187–190

Brown Bear, Brown Bear, What Do You See? (Martin), 20, 42, 59, 163, 262, 266

A Bug's Picnic (Kilcup), 528

The Bulletin of the Center for Children's Books, 430

Cabin Key (Rand), 180

Caldecott Medal, 431, 520–521

Can't You Make Them Behave, King George? (Fritz), 510

capitalization, 359–360

card catalogs, 496

carving, 499

case studies. *See* Teacher-to-Teacher

cassette tapes. *See* multimedia

cause/effect text, 478, 480–482

CD-ROMs. *See* multimedia

chants, 15

chapter books, 243, 244

checklists, 382, 383

The Cheerios Counting Book: 1, 2, 3 (McGrath), 504

Chicka Chicka Boom Boom (Martin & Archambault), 40

Chickens Aren't the Only Ones (Heller), 446, 459, 460

Children and Books (Sutherland), 431

children's literature, 413–436
  current publishing, 430–431
  dramatization, 426
  encouraging interest, 413–414, 416–418
  Literature Circles, 166, 425–426
  quality, 162, 163, 164
  recommended books, 418–424
  See also content area literacy; literature
    selection; reading; reading
    comprehension
Children's Literature in the Elementary School
  (Huck), 431
A Child's Book of Art: Discover Great Paintings
  (Micklethwait), 497
Chocolate Fever (Smith), 95
choral reading
  and basal reading programs, 155–156
  and English Language Learners, 56
  and listening, 110
  and prediction activities, 15
Christopher Columbus: From Vision to Voyage
  (Anderson), 478, 479
chronological patterns, 268
cinquains, 279–281
circle of questions strategy, 191–192
circle patterns, 270–272
Civil Rights Act (1964), 55
civil rights movement, 161
class discrimination, 298
class newsletters, 34
classroom environment, 21–27
  and early literacy, 50–54
  and handwriting, 360–361
  instructional schedules, 22–23, 348–350
  and listening, 94–95
  and reading aloud, 106
  Teacher-to-Teacher, 22, 23, 24, 25–27
  See also writing environment
classroom examples. *See* Teacher-to-Teacher
clay modeling, 499
Click, Clack, Moo: Cows That Type
  (Cronin), 6
cloze procedure
  and reading comprehension, 203–204
  and spelling, 343
  and theme cycles, 456
cognitive field theory, 3, 4, 7–8
collaborative committees, 302–306
collaborative writing, 228–235
  and computers, 315
  and conventions, 232–235
  dictation, 228–231, 242–243, 315, 329,
    361, 363
  interactive writing, 231–232
  Teacher-to-Teacher, 230–231, 242–243
collage, 498
Color, Color, Color, Color (Heller), 356
colored chalk, 498
comic strips, 476

communicative speech, 221
community, sense of, 94. *See also* classroom
    environment
comparison/contrast text, 477–478, 479
computers, 312–315
concept squares, 488–489
conceptual mapping
  and content area literacy, 486
  and reading comprehension, 187,
    192–193
  and theme cycles, 456
conferencing
  and assessment, 384–385, 396–398
  and reading comprehension, 200–201
  and revision, 227
  and writing environment, 297–301
Confirming a K-W-L, 197–198, 470
content area literacy, 467–512
  and art, 497–500, 502
  cause/effect text, 478, 480–482
  comparison/contrast text, 477–478, 479
  descriptive text, 470–473
  difficulty of, 467–468
  expository vs. narrative text, 469–470
  math, 503–508
  and music, 508–510
  problem/solution text, 482–484
  and reading comprehension, 486–489
  recommended books, 485–486
  science, 511–513
  sequential text, 473–477
  and SMART strategy, 207
  social studies, 510–511
  See also research; theme cycles
context, 138–139
contrast, 81
conventions, 12, 322–368, 518
  capitalization, 359–360
  and collaborative writing, 232–235
  guidelines for, 367–368
  handwriting, 360–367
  and poor children, 298
  program evaluation, 407–408, 410
  punctuation, 358–359
  See also grammar; spelling
conversation. *See* discussion
Cook-a-Doodle-Doo! (Stevens & Crummel),
  447
cooperative learning, 27–31, 56. *See also*
    grouping
Coretta Scott King Award, 524–527
counting books, 504, 507
Counting on Frank (Clement), 507
couplets, 279
courtesies, 86–87
Cousins (Hamilton), 7
Cows Can't Fly (Milgrim), 200
The Crayon Counting Book (Ryan & Pallotta),
  504

crayons, 499
creative language experiences. *See* self-
    expression
creative listening, 99
critical annotation, 212
critical listening, 99
cubing strategy, 484
cultural differences, 43–44, 48. *See also*
    diversity issues
culturally familiar patterns, 270
culturally generic literature, 151
culturally neutral literature, 151
culturally specific literature, 151
cumulative patterns, 267–268
curiosity, 54
current interest writing, 253, 255
curriculum
  and basal reading programs, 170
  and theme cycles, 445–446, 450
  See also content area literacy
cursive writing, 363–364, 365. *See also*
    handwriting

Dancing in Cadillac Light (Holt), 85
daydreaming, 95
The Death of the Iron Horse (Goble),
  477–478
decodable texts, 164
descriptive text, 470–473
descriptive writing, 252, 254
The Devil's Arithmetic (Yolen), 510
dialects, 68, 80, 352. *See also* natural
    language, acceptance of
dialogue journals, 236, 239–240
diamantes, 281–282
dictation, 228–231, 242–243
  and computers, 315
  and handwriting, 361, 363
  and spelling, 229–230, 329
dictionaries, 123, 495, 496
Dinosaurs and Other Prehistoric Animals
  (Geis), 192
Directed Listening–Thinking Activity
  (DL–TA), 105, 184, 186
Directed Reading–Thinking Activity
  (DR–TA), 182–184
*Discovering Great Artists: Hands-On Art for
  Children in the Styles of the Great Masters*
  (Kohl & Sogol), 497
discriminative listening, 97–98
discussion, 83–88
  circle of questions strategy, 191–192
  and listening, 109
  literature discussion groups, 156, 166
  and reading aloud, 106
  reading response activities, 156, 166
  ReQuesT, 201–203
  think-alouds, 180
  See also prediction

divergent thinking
    and anticipation–reaction guides, 199
    and DL–TA, 182
    and English Language Learners, 56
    and listening, 95
    and miscues, 130
    and self-expression, 10
diversity issues
    African Americans, 68, 344
    Asian Americans, 278, 345
    and basal reading programs, 161, 164
    courtesies, 86–87
    dialects, 68, 80, 352
    diversity within cultural groups, 278, 429
    health impairments, 210–211
    Hispanic Americans, 236–237, 278,
        344–345, 427–429, 429
    indigenous people, 86–87, 345, 462–463
    learning difficulties, 501–502
    legal requirements, 55–56
    and literature selection, 150–151,
        344–345
    melting pot view, 5
    multicultural awareness, 225
    multicultural literature, 236–237,
        344–345, 427–429
    poverty, 298
    prejudice, 399
    and self-expression, 9–10
    sign language, 96
    welcoming ESL students, 122–123
DL–TA (Directed Listening–Thinking
    Activity), 105, 184, 186
D'Nealian manuscript writing, 364, 366
doing, 53–54. *See also* experiences
doodling, 500
double entry journals, 237
The Double Life of Pocahantas (Fritz), 510
Do You Want to Be My Friend? (Carle), 42
drafting, 226–227
dramatization, 79–82
    and children's literature, 426
    and listening, 109, 110
    and reading comprehension, 179, 215
    RISE procedure, 179
    Story Theater, 76, 77, 426
drawing. *See* art
Dreaming of America: An Ellis Island Story
    (Bunting), 510
drop-dry-draw, 500
DR–TA (Directed Reading–Thinking
    Activity), 182–184
Duke Ellington (Pinkney), 138

early literacy, 38–61
    classroom environments for, 50–54
    and experiences, 54, 56–61
    reading, 38–40, 42–47
    spelling, 324–325

    Teacher-to-Teacher, 44
    writing, 47–50
echo technique, 104
editing, 17, 227–228
efferent reading, 140–141, 468
egocentric speech, 221
Eight Ate: A Feast of Homonym Riddles
    (Terban), 352
ELL. *See* English Language Learners
emotional needs
    and dramatization, 79
    and listening, 95
    and self-expression, 10
The Emperor's Egg (Jenkins), 58
Encounter (Yolen), 478, 479
encyclopedias, 496
"The End" (Milne), 416–417
English as a second language (ESL). *See*
    English Language Learners
English Language Learners (ELL)
    legal issues, 55–56
    and listening, 96
    welcoming, 122–123
enhancing activities, 448–449
environmental print, 40, 42–43
ESL/ESOL students. *See* English Language
    Learners
Everett Anderson's Good-bye (Clifton), 151
experiences
    and discussion, 83–84
    and doing, 53–54
    and early literacy, 54, 56–61
    importance of, 2–3
    and reading process, 116
    and theme cycle planning, 446
    written responses to, 252
extension/enrichment activities, 157–158,
    215–216
Extinct Alphabet Book (Pallotta), 472

family involvement. *See* parent involvement
fantasy books, 423
The Father Who Had 10 Children (Guettier),
    264
favorite books. *See* recommended books
feelings. *See* emotional needs
finger painting, 498
"Fire! Fire!" Said Mrs. McGuire* (Martin), 265
*Fireworks, Picnics, and Flags: The Story of the
    Fourth of July Symbols* (Giblin), 511
First Grade Takes a Test (Cohen), 374, 396
Five Little Ducks (Raffi), 507
The Flag We Love (Ryan), 511
Flight: The Journey of Charles Lindbergh
    (Burleigh), 473–474
flip charts, 216, 476
flow charts, 474, 475, 476
fluency, 501–502
folktales, 420, 423

*Follow the Dream: The Story of Christopher
    Columbus* (Sis), 478
The Football That Won… (Sampson), 267
Formulate-Share-Listen-Create activity, 28
Fortunately, Unfortunately (Charlip), 480, 482
Freight Train (Crews), 268
A Fresh Look at Writing (Graves), 310
The Frog Principal (Calmenson), 265
*From Pictures to Words: A Book about Making
    a Book* (Stevens), 311
Fry word list, 331, 332–334
Fun with Numbers (Massin), 504

games, 109
Gathering Blue (Lowry), 201, 295
genre patterns. *See* patterned language
geometric shapes, 504–505
The Ghost-Eye Tree (Martin & Archambault),
    296
The Gift of the Crocodile: A Cinderella Story
    (Sierra), 264
*Girls Who Rocked the World: Heroines from
    Sacajawea to Sheryl Swoopes* (Welden),
    474
The Girl Who Spun Gold (Hamilton), 265
G Is for Googol: A Math Alphabet Book
    (Schwartz), 471
*Give Me Liberty: The Story of the Declaration
    of Independence* (Freedman), 511
The Giver (Lowry), 26
A Good Day for Listening (King), 95
Goodnight, Moon (Brown), 59
grammar, 351–358
    models of, 354–355
    and natural language, 352–353
    refining, 353–354
grand conversations. *See* literature discussion
    groups
*The Grapes of Math: Mind Stretching Math
    Riddles* (Tang), 498
graphic aids, 506
graphic organizers, 480, 481, 486, 487
graphophonic cueing system
    defined, 119
    and phonics instruction, 120, 122–125
    and redundancy, 126
The Great Frog Race and Other Poems
    (George), 224
*The Great Green Notebook of Katie Roberts—
    Who Just Turned 12 on Monday* (Hest),
    311
The Great Kapok Tree (Cherry), 98, 478, 480
The Greedy Triangle (Burns), 504
Gregory the Terrible Eater (Aruego), 458
The Grouchy Ladybug (Carle), 507
grouping, 32, 95. *See also* cooperative
    learning
group investigations, 29–30
guided reading, 155–156

haiku, 273–274
handwriting, 360–367
    aids for, 361, 362, 365, 366
    and classroom environment, 360–361
    cursive, 363–364, 365
    and dictation, 361, 363
    evaluating, 364, 367
Harriet Beecher Stowe and the Beecher Preachers (Fritz), 510
Hatchet (Paulsen), 213, 214
health impairments, 210–211
hearing loss, 95
Henry Hikes to Fitchburg (Johnson), 477
Here Comes Mother Goose (Opie), 222
Hershey's Fractions Book (Pallotta), 472
heuristic annotation, 209
Hey! Get Off Our Train (Burningham), 478
high-frequency words, 12
    and collaborative writing, 232–234
    and spelling, 324, 331, 332–334
Hispanic Americans
    diversity among, 278, 429
    literature, 236–237, 344–345, 427–429
historical fiction, 422
holistic evaluation criteria, 387–389
home environment, 46–47. *See also* parent
    involvement
home-rooted language. *See* natural language,
    acceptance of
homework, 34, 35
Honey, I Love (Let's Read Aloud) (Greenfield),
    222
Hooray for Diffendoofer Day (Seuss), 396
Hope Was Here (Baur), 7
The Horn Book, 430
A House for Hermit Crab (Carle), 471
"The House That Jack Built," 267
How a Book Is Made (Aliki), 312, 473
How a Crayon Is Made (Oz), 473
How Does Soda Get Into the Bottle? (Oz),
    473
How Much Is a Million? (Schwartz), 447
How Tall, How Short, How Far Away (Adler),
    507
*How We Crossed the West: The Adventures of
    Lewis & Clark* (Schanzer), 496
humorous books, 419

I Am Rosa Parks (Parks), 474
IDEA (Individuals with Disabilities Act),
    210
idea starters, 308, 310
If You Give a Mouse a Cookie (Numeroff),
    270–271
If You Hopped Like a Frog (Schwartz), 496
If You're Riding a Horse and It Dies, Get Off
    (Forsten & Grant), 397
If You Were a Writer (Nixon), 311

illustrations
    and publication, 304–306
    and reading comprehension, 215
    recommended books, 421
I Love Going through This Book (Burleigh), 6
imagination, 10, 249
The Important Book (Brown), 512
impression strand, 11–12, 518
    program evaluation, 407, 409
inconsiderate text, 137–138
indexes, 494–495
indigenous people, 462–463
    courtesies, 86–87
    literature, 345
individual differences. *See* diversity issues
Individuals with Disabilities Act (IDEA),
    210
infancy, 38
informational books, 421
information, listening for, 98
initiating activities, 448
inner-city children, 298
inner speech, 221
innovation activities, 176, 177
Insectlopedia: Poems and Paintings (Florian),
    224
Inspector role, 30
instructional schedules, 22–23
    spelling, 348–350
intelligence, 97
intention annotation, 210–211
interactive assessment, 382, 384–385
Interactive Listener role, 30
interactive writing, 231–232
interlocking patterns, 266
International Reading Association (IRA), 378,
    380, 430
interpretive listening, 98
interviews, 216
In Two Worlds: A Yup'ik Eskimo Family
    (Jenness & Rivers), 477
invented spelling, 229–230, 290–292, 324–325
I Pledge Allegiance… (Martin & Sampson), 58
IRA (International Reading Association), 378,
    380, 430
I Remember Papa (Ketteman), 200
It's Raining Pigs & Noodles (Prelutsky), 223
It's Simple, Said Simon (Hoberman), 200

Jack and the Beanstalk, 270
The Jazz Fly (Gollub), 95
Jigsaw activity, 28
Joey Pigza Loses Control (Gantos), 95, 237
John Newbery Award. *See* Newbery Medal
The Journal of Adolescent and Adult Literacy,
    430
*The Journal of Jesse Smoke: A Cherokee Boy,
    Trail of Tears* (Bruchac), 497

journals, 235–238
Just Ella (Haddix), 265

kid watching, 141
Knots on a Counting Rope (Martin &
    Archambault), 84, 180, 531–532
K-W-L strategy, 196–198
    and brainstorming, 187
    confirming, 197–198, 470

LAD (language acquisition device), 6
language acquisition device (LAD), 6
language acquisition theories, 3–8
    behaviorism, 3–6
    cognitive field theory, 3, 4, 7–8
    and listening, 96
    nativism, 4, 6–7
language arts
    elements of, 19–21
    standards for, 18–19
Language Arts and English Education, 430
language, defined, 2
language experience approach (LEA), 88, 117
    and dictation, 228–230
    and spelling, 329
language-minority children. *See* English
    Language Learners
language setting, 139
Latinos/Latinas. *See* Hispanic Americans
Lau v. Nichols, 55
LEA. *See* language experience approach
learning difficulties, 501–502
learning logs, 236
legal issues, 55–56
The Legend of the Bluebonnet (dePaola), 84
Leo the Late Bloomer (Aruego), 458
Leo the Late Bloomer (Kraus), 59
lesson plans. *See* Teacher-to-Teacher
*Let's Do a Poem: Introducing Children to
    Poetry* (Larrick), 256
letter stage of spelling, 326
leveling, 167. *See also* readability
The Library (Stewart), 133
The Library Card (Spinelli), 133
library skills, 496
Life Doesn't Frighten Me (Angelou), 223
Light Shining Through the Mist (Matthews),
    497
limericks, 283–284
limited palette painting, 498
linguistic basals, 161–162
linguistic diversity. *See* dialects; diversity
    issues; natural language, acceptance of
link strategy, 190
Listen Buddy (Lester), 94
listening, 92–112
    abilities, 102–103
    difficulty of, 92, 94

Directed Listening–Thinking Activity, 105, 184, 186
  as element of language arts, 19
  factors affecting, 94–97
  and propaganda, 101–102
  and reading aloud, 103–106, 110
  and storytelling, 106, 108
  types of, 97–100
The Listening Walk (Showers), 94
Listen to the City (Isadora), 94
Listen to the Rain (Martin), 146
literacy cueing systems, 118–127
  and cloze procedure, 204
  and phonics instruction, 120, 122–125
  and redundancy, 126–127
  and spelling, 335, 339–342
literacy transaction model, 115–116,
  127–128, 181
literary conventions. *See* conventions
Literature and the Child (Cullinan),
  430–431
literature-based units, 440
Literature Circles, 166, 425–426
literature discussion groups, 156, 166
literature selection
  Caldecott Medal Winners, 520–521
  content area literacy, 470
  Coretta Scott King Award Winners,
    524–527
  and diversity issues, 150–151, 344–345
  and learning difficulties, 501
  Newbery Medal Winners, 522–523
  poetry, 70
  and ReQuesT, 201
  for storytelling, 108
  See also recommended books
Littlejim (Houston), 78
Little Red Riding Hood, 270
A Long Way from Chicago (Peck), 201
"look say" method, 158–161

*The M&M's Brand Chocolate Candies
  Counting Book* (McGrath), 504
Magda's Tortillas ~ Las tortillas de Magda
  (Chavarría-Cháirez), 236, 428, 429
*The Magic School Bus and the Electric Field
  Trip* (Cole), 473
The Magic School Bus at the Waterworks
  (Cole), 473, 476
The Magic School Bus Inside the Earth (Cole),
  471
The Magic School Bus Lost in the Solar System
  (Cole), 471, 473
main ideas, 98
Making and Writing Words (Rasinski), 346
Making Words (Cunningham &
  Cunningham), 346
Mammalabilia (Florian), 471

manuscript writing. *See* handwriting
mapping. *See* conceptual mapping; story
  maps
marathon writing, 31
markers, 308
Materials Handler role, 30
math, 503–508
The Math Curse (Martin), 503
Max Cleans Up (Wells), 58
Max Found Two Sticks (Pinkney), 138
meaning, reading for, 130, 131
mechanics, 227–228. *See also* conventions
melting pot view, 5
Merry Go Round: A Book About Nouns
  (Heller), 353
minilessons
  prewriting stage, 226
  and Writer's Workshop, 295–297
*A Mink, a Fink, a Skating Rink: What Is a
  Noun?* (Cleary), 352
miscue analysis, 128–133
  grammar, 357–358
  running records, 392–393
Miss Alaineus: A Vocabulary Disaster
  (Frasier), 353
mnemonics, 348
mobiles, 216, 502
More Than a Writing Teacher (Thomason),
  257
mosaics, 500
motivation annotation, 211
Mountain Valor (Houston), 78
movement
  and art, 500, 502
  and dramatization, 82
  and music, 508–510
  and phonics instruction, 122
Mr. Tanen's Ties (Cocca-Leffler), 397
multiage instruction, 32–33
multicultural literature, 236–237, 344–345,
  427–429
multimedia
  and basal reading programs, 152
  and listening, 99–100
  Teacher-to-Teacher, 100–101
multiple intelligence theory, 178
murals, 500
music
  and content area literacy, 508–510
  and listening, 103, 112
  and prediction activities, 15
My Great Aunt Arizona (Houston), 78
The Mysteries of Harris Burdick (Van
  Allsburg), 147

NAEP (National Assessment of Educational
  Progress), 372
The Napping House (Martin), 268

National Assessment of Educational Progress
  (NAEP), 372
National Council of Teachers of English, 430
Native Americans. *See* indigenous people
nativism, 4, 6–7
natural environment, 57–59
natural language, acceptance of
  and discussion, 84
  and early literacy, 51
  and grammar, 352–353, 355
  oral language, 65, 81
natural objects, art with, 500
"never-ending story review," 216
The New Advocate, 430
Newbery Medal, 431, 522–523
The News About Dinosaurs (Lauber), 477
newspaper activities, 215, 483
The Night Before Christmas, 270
No Good in Art (Cohen), 396
Nothing Ever Happens on 90th Street
  (Schotter & Brooker), 310
number concept, 504
Number the Stars (Lowry), 147, 510
numerals, 503–504, 508
nursery rhymes, 45, 504. *See also* poetry

observation, 141, 380–382, 383
Odyssey of the Mind (OM), 73–76
Oh, How I Wish I Could Read! (Giles), 132
Old Bike and New Bike (Martin), 530–531
Old Devil Wind (Martin), 268
OM (Odyssey of the Mind), 73–76
Once There Was a Bull…(Frog) (Walton), 352
100th Day Worries (Cuyler), 497
One Less Fish (Toft & Sheather), 446
onsets, and spelling, 335, 336
option-awareness phase of author concept
  assimilation, 223
oral language, 65–88
  discussion, 83–88
  dramatization, 79–82
  importance of, 65–67
  language experience approach, 88, 117,
    228–230, 329
  poetry, 69–71, 72
  Reader's Theater, 56, 72–76, 502, 528–534
  reading, 103
  reporting, 76–79
  spontaneous expression, 69
  storytelling, 67–68, 106, 108
  Story Theater, 76, 77, 426
  Vygotsky's theories, 220–221
oral reading
  and basal reading programs, 155
  and listening, 103, 110
  See also miscue analysis; reading aloud
The Oreo Cookie Counting Book (Albee), 504
organization, 11, 98

The Other Way to Listen (Baylor & Parnall), 94, 105–106
Our Natural Homes (Collard), 447
Oxford First Book of Art (Wolfe), 497

panel discussions, 215
paper, 308
paper-and-paste projects, 498
paper lamination, 500
paper sculpture, 499
paragraphs, 282
parent conferences, 34
parent involvement, 33–35
    and assessment, 400, 401
    and basal reading programs, 152
    and children's literature, 417–418
    and theme cycles, 454–455
patterned language, 262–286
    chronological patterns, 268
    circle patterns, 270–272
    culturally familiar patterns, 270
    cumulative patterns, 267–268
    interlocking patterns, 266
    predictable books, 15, 163, 181,
      263–274
    repetitive structure, 264–265
    rhyming words, 265
    and shared book experience, 181
    Teacher-to-Teacher, 266, 269–270,
      271–272
    value of, 262–263
    See also poetry, patterned
peer editing, 301, 302–303, 304
Pepper's Journal: A Kitten's First Year
    (Murphy), 473
perception activities, 15
personal observations, writing about,
    246–247
phonetic stage of spelling, 326
phonics instruction
    current basal reading programs, 164
    and graphophonic cueing system, 120,
      122–125
    linguistic basals, 161–162
    and look–say method, 159–160
phonological awareness, 12, 44–45
physical classroom environment
    and handwriting, 360, 361
    and listening, 94–95
    and reading aloud, 106
    Teacher-to-Teacher, 24, 25
    See also classroom environment
Piaget for Teachers (Furth), 54
Piagetian theory, 54
picture books, 422–423
The Pig in the Spigot: Poems (Wilbur), 223
planning, 103
Plants That Never Ever Bloom (Heller), 356

The Pledge of Allegiance (Martin & Sampson),
    511
poetry
    encouraging interest, 416–417
    and fluency, 502
    oral interpretation, 69–71, 72
    and phonics instruction, 124–125
    Reader's Theater, 72
    recommended books and poets, 70, 71, 419
    and writing process, 253–254, 256–257
    See also poetry, patterned
poetry, patterned, 272–284, 286
    cinquains, 279–281
    couplets, 279
    diamantes, 281–282
    haiku, 273–274
    limericks, 283–284
    and phonological awareness, 45
    and prediction activities, 15
    renga, 283
    senryu, 275
    shape patterns, 284, 286
    sijo, 277–278
    snapshots, 275–276
    tanka, 276–277
    terquains, 281, 282
point of view, 99
Polar Bear, Polar Bear, What Do You Hear?
    (Martin), 266
Polkabats and Octopus Slacks: 14 Stories
    (Brown), 223
portfolio assessment, 393–399
    conferencing, 396–398
    contents, 394–396
    definitions, 393–394
    maintenance, 398–399
poster activity, 216
poverty, 298
PRAISE procedure, 175–178
Praiser role, 30
predictability, 163. *See also* patterned
    language; predictable books
predictable books, 263–264
    and prediction activities, 15
    and shared book experience, 181
    and whole language approach, 163
    See also patterned language
prediction, 15–16
    DL–TA, 105, 184, 186
    DR–TA, 183–184
    PRAISE procedure, 176, 177
    prevoke strategy, 186–187
    ReQuesT, 202–203
    think–alouds, 179
    and whole language, 163
predictogram strategy. *See* prevoke strategy
preformed opinions, 96–97
prejudice, 399

prereading activities
    anticipation–reaction guides, 199
    and basal reading programs, 153–154
    brainstorming, 187–190
    K-W-L strategy, 187, 196–198, 470
    See also prediction
preschool years. *See* early literacy
*Presenting Reader's Theater: Plays and Poems
    to Read Aloud* (Bauer), 85
Presidential Elections and Other Cool Facts
    (Sobel), 498
prevoke strategy, 186–187
prewriting, 226
primary reading, 54, 56–57, 116
Prince William (Rand), 482
print awareness, 40, 42–44, 48
print directionality, 43
PRISE stories, 459, 461–464
PROBE, 461
problem/solution text, 482–484
production activities, 16–17. *See also*
    publication
program evaluation, 400, 407–410
    theme cycles, 449
propaganda, 101–102
psycholinguistic approach. *See* whole
    language approach
psychological environment, 95
publication
    collaborative committees, 302–306
    and computers, 313
    Publishing Center, 311–312
    Teacher-to-Teacher, 301
    value of, 16–17
    and writing process, 228
Publishing Center, 311–312
punctuation, 358–359
puppets, 500, 502
The Pushcart War (Merrill), 147

Q Is for Quark: A Science Alphabet Book
    (Schwartz), 471
quadrangle poems, 284, 286
question annotation, 209–210
questioning, for writing conferences,
    299–301
Quick as a Cricket (Wood), 146

racism, 298
readability, 147, 162, 167
read-along technique, 104
read, encode, annotate, ponder technique. *See*
    REAP technique
Reader role, 30
Reader's Theater, 72–76
    and English Language Learners, 56
    and fluency, 502
    sample scripts, 528–534

Reader's Theater for Beginning Readers (Barchers), 84
Read for Me, Mama (Rahaman), 132
reading
  as element of language arts, 20
  and grammar, 356–357
  See also reading aloud; reading comprehension; reading, early instruction; reading process
reading aloud
  and basal reading programs, 155–156
  Directed Listening–Thinking Activity, 105, 184, 186
  and listening, 103–106, 110
  poetry, 254
  PRAISE procedure, 176, 177
  recommended books, 423–424
  RISE procedure, 178–179
  shared book experience, 181
  think–alouds, 179–180
  and vocabulary, 85
reading comprehension, 133–141, 175–216
  anticipation–reaction guides, 199
  assessment, 141
  brainstorming, 187–190
  circle of questions strategy, 191–192
  cloze procedure, 203–204
  conceptual mapping, 187, 192–193
  conferencing, 200–201
  and content area literacy, 486–489
  and context, 138–139
  Directed Listening–Thinking Activity, 105, 184, 186
  Directed Reading–Thinking Activity, 182–184
  extension/enrichment activities, 215–216
  and inconsiderate text, 137–138
  K-W-L strategy, 187, 196–198, 470
  link strategy, 190
  PRAISE procedure, 175–178
  prevoke strategy, 186–187
  and reading stance, 139–141, 468
  REAP technique, 207–212
  reciprocal questioning technique, 201–203
  RISE procedure, 178–179
  save the last word for me strategy, 213–214
  and schema theory, 133–136, 187
  shared book experience, 181–183
  sketch to stretch strategy, 212–213
  SMART strategy, 204–207
  story maps, 193–195
  and storytelling, 67–68
  think–alouds, 179–180
reading, early instruction, 38–40, 42–47
  alphabet, 38–40
  and home environment, 46–47
  phonological awareness, 44–45

print awareness, 40, 42–44
  and writing, 48–49
reading process, 115–133
  children's views, 116–117
  definitions, 115–116
  and miscues, 128–133
  as transaction, 115–116, 127–128, 181
  See also literacy cueing systems; reading comprehension
"reading readiness" programs, 40, 43
Reading Recovery, 392–393
reading response activities
  and basal reading programs, 156, 166
  PRAISE procedure, 176, 177–178
  See also reading comprehension
reading stance, 139–141, 468
The Reading Teacher, 430
realistic fiction, 421–422
REAP technique, 207–212
Reciprocal Questioning Technique (ReQuesT), 201–203
recommended books
  children's literature, 418–424
  content area literacy, 485–486
  multicultural literature, 344–345
  poetry, 70, 71, 419
  word discovery, 348
  writing, 258–259
Recorder role, 30
redundancy, 126–127
A Remainder of One (Pinczes), 507
Remember the Ladies: 100 Great American Women (Harness), 497
renga, 283
repetitive structure, 264–265
replication phase of author concept assimilation, 223
report cards, 400, 401–406
Reporter role, 30
reporting, oral, 76–79
research, 489–496
  action research, 453–454
  alphabetical arrangement, 495–496
  cooperative activities, 28–30
  group investigations, 29–30
  Jigsaw activity, 28
  library skills, 496
  locational tools, 494–495
  report writing, 243, 245–246
  resource use, 492–494
  and searching attitude, 489–491
response journals, 237
revision, 227
rhyming words
  and listening, 110
  and patterned language, 265
  and phonics instruction, 124–125
  See also poetry, patterned

rhythm, 112, 508–510. *See also* music
rimes, 123–124
  and collaborative writing, 234–235
  and spelling, 335, 336, 337–338
Rip Van Winkle, 528–530
RISE procedure, 178–179
A River Ran Wild (Cherry), 98, 482
Rock It, Sock It, Number Line (Martin & Sampson), 507
role playing, 80
roles in groups, 156, 166
round robin reading, 155
running records, 392–393

Sand (Prager), 496
sand casting, 498
Sarah, Plain and Tall (MacLachlan), 420
save the last word for me strategy, 213–214
schema theory
  and brainstorming, 187, 190
  and content area literacy, 469, 470
  and K-W-L strategy, 196, 470
  and literacy transaction model, 127–128
  and reading comprehension, 133–136, 187
  and think–alouds, 179–180
science, 511–513
Scope and Sequence, 147, 157
scribble–pictorial stage of spelling, 325–326
The Secret to Freedom (Vaughan), 482
self-concept, 249–252
self-confidence, 10
self-esteem, 229, 298–299
self-evaluation, 389–392
self-expression, 9–10, 518
  program evaluation, 407, 409
  and writing, 21, 247–249
  See also production activities
self-monitoring approach to reading and thinking. *See* SMART strategy
semantic cueing system
  and basal reading programs, 162–163
  and cloze procedure, 204
  defined, 120
  and redundancy, 127
  and spelling, 335, 339–342
semantic mapping. *See* conceptual mapping
senryu, 275
sensory impressions, 59–61
sentence difficulty, 167
sequels/prequels, 216
sequence, 147
sequential text, 473–477
Seven Blind Mice (Young), 146
shape poems, 284, 286
Shape Up! (Adler), 504
shared book experience, 181–183
sharing, 52

Shh! We're Writing the Constitution (Fritz), 510

sight, sense of, 59, 60

sight vocabulary, 159, 160

sign language, 96

sijo, 277–278

silent reading, 155

simple listening, 97

singing, 15, 112. *See also* music

A Single Shard (Park), 96

sketch to stretch strategy, 212–213

skimming, 496

Sleeping Ugly (Yolen), 265

SMART strategy, 204–207

smell, sense of, 61

snapshots, 275–276

The Snowy Day (Keats), 59

social issues, 422

social studies, 510–511

sociodrama, 80

Something to Crow About (Ward), 447

sound awareness. *See* phonological awareness

Sounds All Around (Pfeffer), 94

sound, sense of, 59–60, 105–106

speaking, 20. *See also* oral language

spelling, 290–292, 322–350

    developmental stages, 325–327

    and dictation, 229–230, 329

    early development, 324–325

    instructional schedules, 348–350

    instructional strategies, 338, 342–348

    invented, 229–230, 290–292, 324–325

    principles for, 322–324

    process-centered model, 328–330

    word selection, 330–331, 335

    See also spelling aids

spelling aids, 308, 330

    Allen word list, 309

    commonly misspelled words, 331

    high-frequency letter patterns, 336

    high-frequency words, 332–334

    rimes, 337–338

    semantic patterns, 339–342

spontaneous expression, 69

Spring Days Are Made of Blooming Flowers (Martin), 241

Spy/Explorer role, 30

standardized testing, 372–378, 380

    inappropriateness of, 373–378

    responses to, 377–378, 380

    stress resulting from, 372–373

standards, 18–19

Standards (IRA & NCTE), 18, 19

standard stage of spelling, 326

Stargirl (Spinelli), 201

Star of the Circus (Sampson & Sampson), 58, 136, 271

Stone Fox (Gardiner), 7, 295

story charades, 216

story maps, 193–195

The Story of Clocks and Calendars (Maestro), 497

storytelling, 67–68, 106, 108

Story Theater, 76, 77, 426

strands, in basal reading programs, 147

The Strength of the Hills: A Portrait of a Family Farm (Graff), 510

structural grammar, 354

student log books, 391–392

SUCCESS stories, 459, 461

Summarizer role, 30

summarizing activities, 215

summary annotation, 209

Summer Reading Is Killing Me (Scieszka), 133

Sunrise (Pittman), 504

Swish! (Martin & Sampson), 200

syntactic cueing system

    and basal reading programs, 162–163

    defined, 120

    and redundancy, 126–127

synthesizing activities, 449–450

synthetic phonics, 161. *See also* phonics instruction

tables of contents, 494–495

Tales, Rumors, and Gossip: Exploring Contemporary Folk Literature with Young Adults (Vos), 85

Tales, Then and Now: More Folktales as Literary Fictions for Young Adults (Vos & Altmann), 85

tanka, 276–277

taste, sense of, 61

teacher's guide (TG), 152–153, 170–171

teacher-student relationships

    and assessment, 378, 391

    and dramatization, 81, 82

    and listening, 94

    See also conferencing

Teacher-to-Teacher

    assessment, 382

    author/illustrator studies, 432

    basal reading programs, 158

    brainstorming, 187–189

    children's literature, 416–418

    classroom environment, 22, 23, 24, 25–27

    collaborative writing, 230–231, 242–243

    computers, 313–315

    content area literacy, 484–486

    cooperative learning, 31

    courtesies, 86–87

    dialects, 80

    dialogue journals, 239–240

    dramatization, 426

    environmental print, 44

    handwriting, 363

    listening, 99, 111

    Literature Circles, 425

    math, 503, 504–505, 508

    multimedia, 100–101

    patterned language, 266, 269–270, 271–272

    patterned poetry, 274, 276, 277, 279, 282

    peer editing, 302–303

    phonics instruction, 125–126

    PRAISE procedure, 177–178

    propaganda, 101–102

    publication, 301

    Reader's Theater, 73–76

    reading aloud, 105–106

    reading stance, 140

    research, 245–246, 490–492, 493–494, 495

    schema theory, 136

    science, 511–513

    sensory impressions, 60, 61

    shared book experience, 182–183

    spelling, 328, 336, 350

    standardized testing, 372–373

    story maps, 194–195

    storytelling, 108

    Story Theater, 77, 426

    theme cycles, 453, 455

    Writer's Workshop, 294, 295–296

    Young Authors' Conference, 317–318

technology. *See* multimedia

tempera painting, 499

terquains, 281, 282

Testing Miss Malarkey (Finchler), 396

Texas Alphabet (Rice), 471

textbooks, 147

texture painting, 499

TG (teacher's guide), 152–153, 170–171

That Kookoory! (Froelich), 446

theme cycles, 440–464

    action research, 453–454

    parent involvement, 454–455

    planning framework, 446–450

    planning principles, 450–453

    planning sequence, 457–460

    planning sources, 445–446

    PRISE stories, 459, 461–464

    SUCCESS stories, 459, 461

    teacher role, 456–457

    types of, 443–445

    value of, 440–442

There's an Ant in Anthony (Most), 352

"There Was a Child Went Forth . . ." (Whitman), 54

thesauri, 496

thesis annotation, 209

think–alouds, 179–180

Think-Pair-Share activity, 28

This Is the Bread I Baked for Ned (Dragonwagon), 267

The Three Little Pigs, 270

The Three Little Pigs (Kellogg), 264

Thunder Cake (Polacco), 146

Tiger Math: Learning to Graph from a Baby Tiger (Nagda & Bickel), 496
Timekeeper role, 30
time lines, 215
Time Train (Fleischman), 473
Timothy Tunny Swallowed a Bunny (Grossman), 222
The Tin Heart (Ackerman), 477, 478, 479
tissue-paper overlay, 498
Toliver's Secret (Wood–Brady), 147
Tomas and the Library Lady (Mora), 133
Tomorrow's Alphabet (Shannon), 478, 480
Too Hot to Hoot: Funny Palindrome Riddles (Terban), 353
total literacy model, 8–12
    conventions strand, 12, 518
    and future hopes, 517–519
    implementation, 13–17
    impression strand, 11–12, 518
    interactive nature of, 8–9
    self-expression strand, 9–10, 518
touch, sense of, 61
trade books, 467
traditional grammar, 354
transaction model. *See* literacy transaction model
transformational–generative grammar, 354
transition phase of author concept assimilation, 223
"Trees" (Behn), 417
triangle triplet poems, 284
Trick or Treat (Martin & Sampson), 125–126
Twelve Snails to One Lizard (Hightower), 507

Venn diagrams, 478, 479
The Very Hungry Caterpillar (Carle), 42, 268, 270, 507
videos. *See* multimedia
viewing, 21
visual representation. *See* art
vocabulary
    and DR–TA, 184
    enrichment sources, 310
    and ESL students, 123
    and oral language, 84–85
    sight, 159, 160
Voices in the Park (Browne), 94

Wait! No Paint! (Whatley), 265
wall stories, 215
webbes, 313
Weird Stories from the Lonesome Café (Cox), 7
Weslandia (Fleischman), 6
What Do Authors Do? (Christelow), 311
What Do Illustrators Do? (Christelow), 311
When a Line Bends…a Shape Begins (Green), 504
When Zachary Beaver Came to Town (Holt), 201
Where Are You Going Little Mouse? (Kraus), 271
Where the Wild Things Are (Sendak), 262
Whistle, Mary, Whistle, 265
whole language approach, 162–164
Who Ordered the Jumbo Shrimp?: And Other Oxymorons (Agee), 353
Who Put That Hair in My Toothbrush? (Spinelli), 199
Whose Language? Whose Power? (Smith), 221–222
Why Johnny Can't Read (Flesch), 161
William Shakespeare and the Globe (Aliki), 84
Witness (Hesse), 477
Wolf! (Bloom), 132
word classes, 278–282
word difficulty, 167
word discovery, 346, 348
The Word Eater (Amato), 353
wordless picture books, 419–420
word making activities, 346, 347
word processing, 312–313
word search activities, 346
word sorting, 343–345
Word Wizard (Falwell), 352
workbooks, 149
work samplings, 385, 387–388
worksheets, 149
writer's notebook, 226
Writer's Workshop, 294–297
writing
    early instruction, 47–50
    as element of language arts, 21
    and phonological awareness, 12
    and reading comprehension, 215, 216
    See also writing environment; writing process

Writing Center, 306, 308–311
writing environment, 289–318
    and children as authors, 223
    collaborative committees, 302–306
    and computers, 312–315
    conferencing, 297–301
    Publishing Center, 311–312
    Writer's Workshop, 294–297
    Writing Center, 306, 308–311
    Young Authors' Conference, 315–318
writing models, 308
writing process, 220–259
    aspirations, 247–249
    chapter books, 243, 244
    and children as authors, 222–224
    collaborative writing, 228–235
    current interest writing, 253, 255
    descriptive writing, 252, 254
    and imagination, 249
    individual stories, 238, 241–243
    journals, 235–238, 239–240
    language experience approach, 88, 117, 228–230, 329
    personal observations, 246–247
    poetry, 253–254, 256–257
    recommended books, 258–259
    research reports, 243, 245–246
    response to experiences, 252
    and self-concept, 249–252
    stages in, 224–228
    teacher modeling, 257
    Vygotsky's theories, 220–222

A Year Down Yonder (Peck), 295
The Year of Miss Agnes (Hill), 354
Yo Aesop! Get a Load of These Fables (Rosenthal), 266
Yo Grocer (Martin), 511
Young Authors' Conference, 315–318
The Young Journalist's Book: How to Write and Produce Your Own Newspaper (Bentley & Guthrie), 312
You Read to Me & I'll Read to You: Stories to Share from the 20th Century (Shulman), 6
You Want Women to Vote, Lizzie Stanton? (Fritz), 510
"yucky" word list, 330

PHOTOGRAPH CREDITS

Chapter 1. 2: Lisa Bartlett 11: Michael Sampson 25: Michael Sampson 29: Michael Sampson

Chapter 2. 46: Melanie Schauwecker 48: Michael Sampson 53: The International Institute of Literacy Learning 57: Michael Sampson

Chapter 3. 69: Michael Sampson 73: Michael Sampson 83: Michael Sampson

Chapter 4. 93: © 2001 Bill Lisenby 105: Randy Methven 109: Michael Sampson

Chapter 5. 118: Michael Sampson 128: © 2001 Bill Lisenby 137: © 2001 Bill Lisenby

Chapter 6. 145: Michael Sampson 157: © 2001 Bill Lisenby 165: © 2001 Bill Lisenby

Chapter 7. 176: Michael Sampson 191: Michael Sampson 206: Michael Sampson

Chapter 8. 222: Michael Sampson 224: Michael Sampson 238: Michael Sampson 243: Mary Beth Sampson

Chapter 9. 263: Michael Sampson 267: Mary Beth Sampson 271: Melanie Schauwecker 280: Michael Sampson

Chapter 10. 292: Lisa Bartlett 305: Lisa Bartlett 316: Irma Fridge

Chapter 11. 323: Michael Sampson 335: Lisa Bartlett

Chapter 12. 384: Michael Sampson 389: Lisa Bartlett 390: Jon Gilbert Fox 395: © 2001 Bill Lisenby

Chapter 13. 413: Kenny Comerford 416: Laura Godwin 421: David Canzoneri 431: Michael Sampson

Chapter 14. 440: Ashton Ward 445: Mary Beth Sampson 452: Mary Beth Sampson 457: Michael Sampson

Chapter 15. 471: © 2001 Bill Lisenby 493: © 2001 Bill Lisenby 508: Michael Sampson

Afterword. 518: Victoria Peabody